HELEN RAPPAPORT

THE ROMANOV SISTERS

The Lost Lives of the Daughters of Nicholas and Alexandra

ST. MARTIN'S PRESS ❧ NEW YORK

www.stmartins.com

Library of Congress Cataloging-in-Publication Data

Rappaport, Helen.
  The Romanov sisters : the lost lives of the daughters of Nicholas and Alexandra / Helen Rappaport. — First U.S. edition.
    p. cm.
  ISBN 978-1-250-02020-8 (hardcover)
  ISBN 978-1-250-02021-5 (e-book)
  1. Nicholas II, Emperor of Russia, 1868–1918—Assassination. 2. Nicholas II, Emperor of Russia, 1868 1918—Family—Assassination. 3. Romanov, House of—History—20th century—Sources. 4. Princesses—Russia—Biography—Sources. 5. Sisters. I. Title.
  DK258.6.R374 2014
  947.08'30922—dc23

                                                              2014003159

First published in Great Britain under the title *Four Sisters: The Lost Lives of the Romanov Grand Duchesses* by Macmillan, an imprint of Pan Macmillan, a division of Macmillan Publishers Limited

10   9   8   7   6   5

In memory of

Olga, Tatiana, Maria and Anastasia Romanova

four extraordinary young women

Contents

List of Illustrations

Glossary of Names

Listed below are the most frequently occurring names in the text, in the form in which they are generally cited.

OTMA = the sisters' own acronym for Olga, Tatiana, Maria and Anastasia

AKSH: acronym of Alexander Konstantinovich Shvedov, one of Olga's favourite officers in the Tsar's Escort

ALEXANDRA (SHURA) TEGLEVA: OTMA's nurse and later general maid; married *Pierre Gilliard*

ALICE: Princess Alice of Great Britain, later Grand Duchess of Hesse and by Rhine, Alexandra's mother

ALICKY: Queen Victoria's pet name for Alexandra, used to distinguish her from Alix, who in the British royal family was Alexandra, Princess of Wales

ALIX: Nicholas's pet name for his wife Alexandra

ANNA (NYUTA) DEMIDOVA: Alexandra's maid in waiting

ANNA VYRUBOVA: Alexandra's close friend and confidante; later appointed a maid of honour

BIBI: pet name for Varvara Vilchikovskaya, OT's friend and nurse at the annexe

CHEMODUROV: Terenty Chemodurov, Nicholas's valet

COUNT BENKENDORF: Pavel Benkendorf, chief marshal and master of ceremonies at the imperial court

COUNT FREEDERICKSZ: Vladimir Freedericksz, head of the imperial household

COUNT GRABBE: Nikolay Grabbe, commander of the Tsar's Escort

DEREVENKO: Andrey Derevenko, Alexey's sailor *dyadka*

DICKIE: Louis of Battenberg, later Lord Mountbatten, OTMA's cousin

DMITRI PAVLOVICH: Grand Duke Dmitri Pavlovich, OTMA's cousin

DMITRI (MITYA) MALAMA: Tatiana's favourite wounded officer at the hospital

DMITRI (MITYA) SHAKH-BAGOV: Olga's favourite wounded officer at the hospital

DOLGORUKOV: Prince Vasili Dolgorukov, adjutant general, with Nicholas at Stavka

DR BOTKIN: Evgeny Botkin, physician to the Imperial Family

DR DEREVENKO: Vladimir Derevenko, Alexey's personal physician (no relation to *Andrey Derevenko*)

DR GEDROITS: Princess Vera Gedroits, senior surgeon at the Court Hospital

DUCHESS OF SAXE-COBURG: formerly Grand Duchess Maria Alexandrovna of Russia, also Duchess of Edinburgh

DUCKY: pet name for Princess Victoria Melita of Saxe-Coburg, first wife of *Ernie*, Alexandra's brother

ELIZAVETA ERSBERG: Alexandra's maid in waiting

ELIZAVETA NARYSHKINA: Alexandra's mistress of the robes from 1910; the most senior lady at court

ELIZAVETA OBOLENSKAYA: Alexandra's lady in waiting

ERNIE: Grand Duke Ernest of Hesse and by Rhine, Alexandra's brother

GENERAL MOSOLOV: Alexander Mosolov, head of the Court Chancellery

GENERAL SPIRIDOVICH: Alexander Spiridovich, Chief of the Kiev section of the Okhrana; from 1906 head of the tsar's personal security services

GLEB BOTKIN: son of *Dr Botkin*; with him at Tobolsk

GRAND DUCHESS VLADIMIR: Maria Pavlovna the elder, wife of Grand Duke Vladimir Alexandrovich; also known in the family as Miechen

GRAND DUKE GEORGIY: Georgiy Alexandrovich, Nicholas's younger brother and tsarevich till his death in 1899

GRAND DUKE KONSTANTIN: Konstantin Konstantinovich, father of *Ioannchik*

GRAND DUKE MIKHAIL: Mikhail Alexandrovich, Nicholas's youngest brother

GRAND DUKE NIKOLAY: Nikolay Nikolaevich; Nicholas's uncle, and until 1915 C-in-C of the Russian Army. Second husband of *Stana*

GRAND DUKE PAVEL: Pavel Alexandrovich, Nicholas's uncle; father of *Dmitri Pavlovich* and *Maria Pavlovna*

GRAND DUKE PETR: Petr Nikolaevich, husband of *Militza*

GRIGORY/FATHER GRIGORY: Grigory Rasputin, the imperial family's religious guru

IOANNCHIK: Prince Ioann Konstantinovich, OTMA's second cousin

IVAN SEDNEV: OTMA's footman; *Leonid Sednev*'s uncle

IZA BUXHOEVEDEN: Baroness Sophia Buxhoeveden, Alexandra's honorary lady in waiting; the post was made official in 1914

KATYA: Ekaterina Zborovskaya, sister of *Viktor Zborovsky*, Anastasia's most regular correspondent in captivity

KHARITONOV: Ivan Kharitonov, cook; with the family at Tobolsk and Ekaterinburg

KLAVDIYA BITNER: the children's tutor at Tobolsk; later married *Evgeny Kobylinsky*

KOBYLINSKY: Evgeny Kobylinsky, commander of the guard at Tsarskoe Selo. Commandant of the Governor's House at Tobolsk

LEONID SEDNEV: kitchen boy; with the family at Tobolsk and Ekaterinburg. Nephew of *Ivan Sednev*

LILI DEHN: Yuliya Dehn, one of the ladies closest to Alexandra in the final years, but who held no official position at court

LOUISE: Princess Louise of Battenberg; daughter of Alexandra's sister Victoria; later Queen Louise of Sweden; OTMA's second cousin

MADELEINE (MAGDALINA) ZANOTTI: Alexandra's most senior personal maid, who had come with her from Darmstadt

MARGARETTA EAGAR: OTMA's governess; dismissed in 1904

MARIYA BARYATINSKAYA: Princess Mariya Baryatinskaya, Alexandra's maid of honour

MARIA FEODOROVNA: the dowager empress, Nicholas's mother; a sister of the Princess of Wales, later Queen Alexandra. Also known in the family as Minny

MARIYA GERINGER: Alexandra's principal lady in waiting, responsible for her jewellery

MARIA PAVLOVNA: Grand Duchess Maria Pavlovna u. sister of *Dmitri Pavlovich* and OTMA's cousin

MARIYA (TUDELS/TOODLES) TUTELBERG: Alexandra's maid in waiting

MARIYA VASILCHIKOVA: Alexandra's lady in waiting; dismissed 1916

MARIYA VISHNYAKOVA (MARY): OTMA's under nursemaid; later nursemaid to Alexey

MASHKA: Maria's pet name in the family

MERIEL BUCHANAN: daughter of the British ambassador to St Petersburg, Sir George Buchanan

MILITZA: Princess Militza of Montenegro; wife of *Grand Duke Petr*

NAGORNY: Klementy Nagorny, Alexey's sailor *dyadka*

NASTYA/NASTASKA: Anastasia's pet name in the family

NASTENKA (ANASTASIA) HENDRIKOVA: Alexandra's personal maid of honour

NIKOLAY (KOLYA) DEMENKOV: Maria's favourite officer from the Guards Equipage

NIKOLAY RODIONOV: officer on the *Shtandart*, Tatiana's favourite tennis partner

NIKOLAY SABLIN: Nikolay Pavlovich Sablin, officer on the *Shtandart* and a close friend of the imperial family. No relation to *Nikolay Vasilievich Sablin*

NIKOLAY VASILIEVICH SABLIN: a favourite officer on the *Shtandart*. No relation to *Nikolay Pavlovich Sablin*

OLGA ALEXANDROVNA: Grand Duchess Olga Alexandrovna, OTMA's aunt, Nicholas's youngest sister

ONOR: Princess Eleonore of Solms-Hoensolms-Lich, second wife of Alexandra's brother *Ernie*

PANKRATOV: Vasily Pankratov, commissar in charge of the imperial family at Tobolsk; dismissed January 1918

PAVEL VORONOV: officer on the *Shtandart* with whom Olga fell in love in 1913

PHILIPPE: Maitre or Monsieur Philippe; Nizier Anthelme Philippe, French 'healer' and mystic

PIERRE GILLIARD: the girls' Swiss tutor in French

PRINCESS HELENA OF SERBIA: wife of *Ioannchik*

...ariya Golitsyna, Alexandra's mistress of the

PRINCESS _... _ death in 1910

_...tr_ Vasilievich Petrov, the girls' tutor in Russian language
P˙ and literature

RITA KHITROVO: Margarita Khitrovo, Olga's friend and fellow nurse at the annexe hospital

SANDRO: Grand Duke Alexander Mikhailovich, _Xenia_'s husband

SERGEY MELIK-ADAMOV: a favourite of Tatiana's at the hospital

SHURIK: pet name for _Alexander Shvedov_

SHVYBZIG: Anastasia's pet name, given to her by her aunt Olga; also the name of her dog that died in May 1915

SOFYA TYUTCHEVA: OTMA's maid of honour and unofficial governess; dismissed in 1912

STANA: Princess Anastasia of Montenegro; wife of the Duke of Leuchtenberg; remarried 1907 to _Grand Duke Nikolay_

SYDNEY GIBBES (SIG): English tutor to OTMA and later Alexey

TATIANA BOTKINA: _Dr Botkin_'s daughter, with him at Tobolsk

TATISHCHEV: Count Ilya Tatishchev, an adjutant general in the imperial suite; with Nicholas at Stavka

THORA: Helena Victoria, daughter of Princess Helena and Prince Christian of Schleswig-Holstein, OTMA's second cousin

TRINA SCHNEIDER: Ekaterina Schneider, Alexandra's _lectrice_, who often acted as chaperone to OTMA

VALENTINA CHEBOTAREVA: senior nurse at OT's annexe hospital

VIKTOR (VITYA) ZBOROVSKY: Anastasia's favourite officer in the Tsar's Escort

VLADIMIR (VOLODYA) KIKNADZE: a favourite officer of Tatiana's at the annexe hospital

VOLKOV: Alexey Volkov, Alexandra's valet

XENIA: Grand Duchess Xenia Alexandrovna, the girls' aunt, Nicholas's sister

ZINAIDA TOLSTAYA: family friend of OTMA; a correspondent in captivity

Author's Note

Readers familiar with Russian history will know that any author taking on the pre-revolutionary period has to deal with the frustrations of two dating systems – the Julian calendar in use in Russia until February 1918 and the Gregorian calendar, then in use in most of the rest of the world, and which was adopted in Russia on 14 February 1918. For the sake of clarity, all dates relating to events taking place in Russia prior to this date are given in the Julian (Old Style) form (which was 13 days behind the Gregorian system); all events taking place in Europe during that period and reported in the foreign press or letters written outside Russia are given in the Gregorian (New Style). In cases where confusion might occur both dates are given, or qualified as OS or NS.

The transliteration of Russian words and proper names is a minefield of confusion, disagreement, and perceived error – depending on which transliteration system one favours. No single system has been set in stone as the correct one although authors are regularly belaboured for getting their transliteration supposedly wrong. Some systems are decidedly unattractive to the non Russian-speaking lay reader; many are unnecessarily pedantic. For this reason I have made the decision to drop the use of the Russian soft and hard signs, represented by the apostrophe, which in the main serve only to confuse and are a distraction to the eye. I have in the end gone with my own slightly modified version of the Oxford Slavonic Papers transliteration system, opting for example to represent the name Aleksandr as Alexander, in hopes of sparing the reader. I have also avoided using patronymics unless needed to differentiate one person of the same name from another.

When I first began writing *The Romanov Sisters* I had to make a very clear decision about where my story was going to end, having already written about the Romanovs in my 2008 book *Ekaterinburg: The Last Days of the Romanovs*. In that book I undertook a close-up examination of the last fourteen days in the lives of the family at the Ipatiev House in Ekaterinburg and charted in forensic detail the horrific circumstances of their murder and the disposal of their bodies. I shall not repeat that part of the story here. Judging when and where exactly to end my narrative has therefore been difficult and I take full responsibility for the decision I have made about when to stop. I hope that readers will find that the Epilogue ties up the most important loose ends.

Finally, and most importantly, it is not my intention in the narrative that follows to give space to any of the numerous false claimants, a trail of whom, since Berlin in 1920, have variously attempted to persuade the world that they are one or other of the four sisters – somehow miraculously escaped from the bloodbath at the Ipatiev House. This book is not for anyone wanting to read more about the much mythologized Anna Anderson aka Franziska Szankowska, nor does it give the oxygen of publicity to the conspiracy theorists who continue to claim Anastasia's survival – or that of any of her sisters – in the face of extensive and rigorous scientific analysis and DNA testing undertaken since the most recent discoveries in the Koptyaki Forest in 2007.

This is a book about the *real* Romanov sisters.

So now faith, hope, and love abide, these three;
but the greatest of these is love

1 Corinthians 13: 13

Prologue

THE ROOM OF THE FIRST
AND LAST DOOR

※

The day they sent the Romanovs away the Alexander Palace became forlorn and forgotten – a palace of ghosts. The family had spent the previous three days frantically packing for their departure, having been informed at short notice by Kerensky's provisional government of their imminent removal. But when it came to the final moments, although the children took their three dogs with them, the cats – Zubrovka, the stray rescued by Alexey at Army HQ, and her two kittens – had to be left behind, with a plaintive request from the tsarevich asking that someone take care of them.[1]

Later, when Mariya Geringer – the tsaritsa's senior lady-in-waiting, charged with caretaking the palace after their departure – arrived, the hungry creatures emerged like wraiths from the shadows and hurled themselves at her, wailing for attention. But all forty doors of the rooms inside had been sealed; the palace kitchens were closed; everything was locked. Only the cats remained in a deserted Alexander Park, the last remnants of a family now heading hundreds of miles east into Siberia.

*

In the years that followed the Russian Revolution of 1917 anyone curious about where Russia's last imperial family had lived could travel the 15 miles (24 km) from the former capital to take a look. You could get there either on a grubby suburban train, or – avoiding

1

the many potholes – by car, along the old royal road that led, straight as a ribbon, across the plain of low flat fields and woodland to Tsarskoe Selo – The Tsar's Village. Once considered the Russian equivalent of Versailles, in the dying days of the tsarist empire Tsarskoe Selo had acquired an increasingly melancholic air – a kind of *'tristesse impériale'*, as one former resident expressed it.[2] By 1917, almost 300 years since Catherine the Great had first commissioned its construction, this village of the tsars was already anticipating its own imminent demise.

The Soviets were, indeed, quick to strip Tsarskoe Selo of its imperial links, renaming it Detskoe Selo – the Children's Village. Located on higher ground away from the marshy Gulf of Finland, its unpolluted air and orderly grid of wide boulevards surrounded by parkland was considered the perfect place for vigorous exercise. The Alexander Park was transformed into a centre for sport and recreation that would breed healthy young citizens for the new communist order. Communism took a while, however, to make its mark on the town itself, which was still small, neat and mainly wooden. Beyond its modest market square, avenues of grand summer villas, built there by aristocrats who served the court, surrounded the two imperial palaces. Their once legendary occupants – the now vanished great Russian families of the Baryatinskys, Shuvalovs, Yusupovs, Kochubeys – were long gone, their homes requisitioned by the Soviets and already crumbling with neglect and decay.[3]

The focal point of this pleasant and peaceful little town had until the revolution been the elegant, golden-yellow Alexander Palace with its white Corinthian columns, but in previous centuries the even grander Catherine Palace next door, in all its gilded baroque splendour, had held centre stage. But in 1918 both were nationalized, transformed into object lessons in 'the aesthetic decay of the last of the Romanovs'.[4] In June the state rooms located on the ground floor of the Alexander Palace were opened to the public after a careful inventory had been made of all their contents. People paid their 15 kopeks to enter and gawp – not at what they had anticipated would be the lavish style in which their former tsar had lived, but rather in disbelief that such a homespun environment could have been the residence of the last Tsar of All the Russias.[5]

The interiors were unexpectedly modest by former imperial standards – no grander perhaps than those of a public library or museum in the capital, or the country house of a moderately well-off gentleman. But for the Romanov family the Alexander Palace had been a much loved home.

Dutiful members of the newly liberated proletariat, 'munching apples and caviar sandwiches', sometimes joined by a few intrepid foreign tourists, were encouraged to visit on Sundays, Wednesdays and Fridays, making sure first to don the ugly but obligatory felt overshoes to protect the beautiful waxed parquet floors from damage.[6] After doing so, they would be ushered through the imperial apartments to an accompanying – and frequently contemptuous – account of their former occupants. The well-drilled official guides did their best to decry the decidedly bourgeois tastes of Russia's last tsar and his wife. The old-fashioned, art-nouveau-style furniture, the cheap, outmoded oleographs and sentimental pictures, the English wallpaper, the profusion of knick-knacks scattered around on every available surface (predominantly factory-made goods of the most ordinary kind), reminded visitors of the 'typical parlour of an English or American boarding house' or a 'second-class Berlin restaurant'.[7] The family themselves were dismissed in the glib phrases of Soviet-speak as an historical irrelevance.

As visitors were conducted from room to room, their doorways guarded by waxwork models of the scarlet and gold liveried real-life footmen who had once stood there, they could not avoid an increasing sense of Nicholas II, not as the despotic ruler painted to them but rather as a dull family man, who had crammed his study and library – where he received his ministers on matters of important state business – with photographs of his children at every stage of their development from babyhood to adulthood: children with dogs, on ponies, in the snow, by the seaside, a happy family smiling to the camera for home-made photographs taken on the Box Brownies that they took with them everywhere. Even in his private study the tsar had a table and chair where his invalid son could sit with him when he was working. This, the hub of now defunct tsarist power, could not have appeared more unremarkable, more domestic and child-friendly. Was it really the last home of 'Nicholas the Bloody'?

The tsar and tsaritsa's suite of interconnecting private rooms further testified to their three consuming passions: each other, their children and their devout religious faith. Their overcrowded bedroom with its English chintz wallpaper and curtains was more Russian Orthodox shrine than boudoir. Two modest single iron bedsteads – of the kind found in 'second-rate hotels', as one American visitor observed in 1934 – stood pushed together in a heavily curtained alcove, every inch of wall space behind which was crammed from floor to ceiling with religious images, crucifixes and 'pathetic, cheap little tin ikons'.[8] On every shelf and table top in her private sitting room the tsaritsa had set out yet more knick-knacks and photographs of her children and her darling Nicky. Personal possessions were few and surprisingly trivial – useful domestic items such as a gold thimble, sewing materials and embroidery scissors, as well as cheap toys and trinkets – 'a china bird and a pincushion made like a shoe. The kind of things that one of the children might have given her.'[9]

At the far end of the corridor toward the gardens, the cupboards in Nicholas's dressing room still held his neatly pressed uniforms and, nearby, the Great Library of glass-fronted bookcases was full of carefully ordered French, English and German books bound in fine Moroccan leather of the kind that he often sat and read aloud to his family in the evenings. Visitors were often taken aback by what greeted them in the Mountain Hall beyond. This, one of the palace's formal parade rooms, had instead served as a downstairs playroom for the tsarevich Alexey. In the centre of this elegant hall of coloured marbles, caryatids and mirrors, a large wooden slide or 'American glide'[10] – on which the children of previous tsars had happily played – still took pride of place, along with Alexey's three favourite toy motor cars. Near a door leading out to the garden stood a poignant reminder of the tragedy that had dominated the lives of the last imperial family of Russia – Alexey's 'small wheelchair, upholstered in red velvet', an evocative reminder of the merciless attacks of haemophilia that frequently disabled him, the contours of his body still visible on it.[11]

Two flights of stone steps led up to the now deserted children's apartments – where once again the adored Alexey's large playroom dominated – full of wooden and mechanical toys: a music box that played the Marseillaise, picture books, boxes of bricks, board games, and his favourite ranks of toy lead soldiers. Languishing among them a large teddy bear – one of the last gifts from the Kaiser before war changed everything – stood sentinel by the door.[12] The tsarevich's adjacent personal bathroom often made visitors gasp in sympathy; it was 'full of beastly surgical instruments' – the calipers and other 'encasements for the legs, arms and body made of canvas and leather' that had been used to support him when his attacks of bleeding had left him temporarily disabled.[13]

Beyond, and modestly subsidiary to the tsarevich's larger apartments – just as its occupants had been secondary to him in the eyes of the nation – were the bedrooms, classroom, dining and reception rooms of his four older sisters: Olga, Tatiana, Maria and Anastasia. Their light and spacious bedrooms were furnished with simple ivory-painted and polished lemonwood furniture and English chintz fabric curtains.[14] A stencilled frieze of pink roses and bronze butterflies above pink coloured wallpaper had been chosen by the younger sisters Maria and Anastasia. For Olga and Tatiana, the frieze was of convolvulus flowers and brown dragonflies. On the girls' matching dressing tables there was still a scattering of boxes, jewellery cases, manicure sets, combs and brushes – just as they had left them.[15] Elsewhere, on their writing tables, were piles of their exercise books with multicoloured covers, and in profusion on every surface, framed photographs of family and friends. Yet in the midst of so much typical, girlish ephemera, one could not fail to notice the presence everywhere in the sisters' rooms of icons and popular religious prints and pictures. By their bedsides there were gospels and prayer books, crosses and candles – rather than the usual clutter one might expect to find.[16]

In their wardrobes, the girls had left behind many of their clothes, hats, parasols and shoes; the uniforms worn by the elder sisters with such pride when they rode side saddle at the big military parades for the Tercentary of the Romanov dynasty in 1913; even their baby clothes and christening robes. They would have no need in Siberia of their finely made formal court dresses – four of everything: matching sets in pink satin with silver embroidery, with pink brocade *kokoshniki* headdresses; or for that matter of the four sets of large summer hats, all meticulously stored in boxes. Outside in the hallway trunks and hampers still stood, half-packed with many more of the girls' possessions – ready for that last journey, but never taken.

In the children's dining room the table was still laid with monogrammed Romanov china ready for the next meal. 'You feel the children are out playing somewhere in the garden', wrote a visitor in 1929. 'They will be back at any moment.'[17] But outside, in the acres of parkland beyond the high iron railings surrounding the palace, a wilderness had grown up among the neat and orderly avenues of lindens, where in the soft undergrowth on either side the Siberian buttercups, 'large, double, and fragrant as roses', the wood anemone and forget-me-nots had bloomed in such profusion in the spring.[18] The palace itself might have been preserved as a historical monument but its once admired park was now overgrown with weeds, the grass waist-high in places. The long leafy avenue where the Romanov children had once played and ridden their ponies and their bicycles; the neatly ordered canals where they went boating with their father; the little blue-and-white painted playhouse on the Children's Island with its profusion of lily of the valley and nearby the little cemetery where they buried their pets . . . everywhere and everything connected with those vanished lives now had about it a sense of absolute desolation.

*

The Alexander Palace might have once been the residence of now denigrated 'former people' liquidated by the revolution, of whom ordinary Russians were increasingly fearful to speak, but, as the palace's devoted curator recalled, that last lingering indefinable 'aroma of the epoch' was never quite eradicated. The honeyed scent of the beeswax used to polish the floors and the odour of Moroccan leather from the many volumes in the tsar's library lingered – along with the faint smell of rose oil in the icon lamps in the tsaritsa's bedroom – until the onset of the Second World War and the palace's occupation by the German military command consigned it to near destruction.[19]

In the days before the war, the tour of the state apartments culminated in the central, semicircular hall at the rear of the palace, where the tsar had held official receptions and dinners for visiting dignitaries, and where, during the First World War, the family had sat down together on Saturday evenings to enjoy film shows. That last night, 31 July–1 August 1917, the Romanov family had patiently waited out the long tedious hours here, dreading the final order to leave their home for ever.

During the preceding days the four Romanov sisters had had to make painful choices about which of their precious possessions – their many albums of photographs, letters from friends, their clothes, their favourite books – they should take with them. They had to leave their childhood dolls behind, carefully arranged on miniature chairs and sofas, along with other treasured toys and mementoes, in hopes that they might be cherished by those who came after.[20]

Legend has it that it was through the central door in the semicircular hall that Catherine the Great had first entered the palace in 1790, carrying her young grandson, the future Alexander I, when the palace that she had ordered to be built, and later presented as a gift to him, was completed. Just after sunrise on 1 August 1917, 127 years later, with the cars pulled up and waiting for them outside, the last imperial family of Russia passed out of the echoing space of the Italian architect Giacomo Quarenghi's eighteenth-century hall with its great arc of windows, through that same glass door and into an uncertain future – 1,341 miles (2,158 km) away in Tobolsk in western Siberia.

The four Romanov sisters, still thin from the after-effects of the severe attack of measles they had suffered early in the year, wept inconsolably as they left the home where they had spent so many of the happy days of their childhood.[21] After they had gone, a dejected Mariya Geringer spoke of her still lingering hopes for them. Perhaps the girls would be lucky somewhere in exile and find decent, ordinary husbands and be happy, she said. For her, and for other loyal retainers and friends left behind, the memory of those four lovely sisters in happier times, of their many kindnesses, of their shared joys and sorrows – the 'laughing faces under the brims of their big flower-trimmed hats' – would continue to linger during the long, deadening years of communism.[22] As, too, would the memory of their vivacious brother who daily challenged his life-threatening disability and refused to be cowed by it. And always, hovering in the background, a woman whose abiding virtue – and one that, perversely, destroyed them all in the end – was a fatal excess of mother love.

Chapter One

MOTHER LOVE

❧

There once were four sisters – Victoria, Ella, Irene and Alix – who lived in an obscure grand duchy in south-western Germany, a place of winding cobbled streets and dark forests made legendary in the fairy tales of the Brothers Grimm. In their day, these four princesses of the house of Hesse and by Rhine were considered by many to be 'the flowers of Queen Victoria's flock of granddaughters', celebrated for their beauty, intelligence and charm.[1] As they grew up they became the object of intense scrutiny on that most fraught of international stages – the royal marriage market of Europe. Despite their lack of large dowries or vast territories, each sister in turn married well. But it was to the youngest and most beautiful of the four that fate dealt the biggest hand.

The four Hesse sisters were daughters of Princess Alice – second daughter of Queen Victoria – and her husband Prince Louis, heir to the Grand Duke of Hesse. In July 1862, aged only eighteen, Alice had left England heavily veiled and in mourning for her recently deceased father Prince Albert, after marrying Louis at Osborne House. By the dynastic standards of the day it was a modest match for a daughter of Queen Victoria, but one that added another strand to the complex web of royal intermarriage between European first and second cousins. During her long reign Victoria had orchestrated the marriages of all her nine children, and remained meddlesome enough into old age to ensure that, after them, their children and even their grandchildren secured partners befitting their royal status. Princess Alice might well have achieved something better had she not fallen in love with the rather dull Prince Louis. As royal domains went, Hesse was relatively small, perpetually financially overstretched and politically powerless. 'There are English noblemen who could endow their daughter with a richer dower than falls to the lot of the Princess Alice', observed one newspaper at the time. Hesse Darmstadt was a 'simple country, of pastoral and agricultural character', with an unostentatious court. It was pretty but its history till now had remained unremarkable.[2]

The capital, Darmstadt, set in the oak-forested hills of the Odenwald, was deemed 'a place of no importance' in the eyes of the pre-eminent Baedeker tourist guide.[3] Indeed, another contemporary traveller found it 'the dullest town in Germany', a place 'on the way to everywhere' – nothing more.[4] It was built on a uniform plan of long, straight streets and formal houses populated by 'well-fed burghers and contented hausfraus', not far from the River Darmbach, and 'the general absence of life' in the capital gave it 'an air of somber inactivity'.[5] The older, medieval quarter had a degree of bustle and character, but aside from the grand-ducal palace, the opera house and a public museum full of fossils there was little to redeem the city from the insipid stiffness that permeated the Darmstadt court.

Princess Alice had been dismayed upon her own arrival there, for although her upbringing had been authoritarian it had been liberal, thanks to her father Prince Albert. For him, Alice was 'the beauty of the family', and she had grown up happy and full of fun.[6] Her wedding day had, however, been totally overshadowed by her father's premature death and her mother's crippling state of grief. The brightness of an all too brief childhood was soon further dimmed by painful separation from her beloved siblings, particularly her brother Bertie, all of which heightened her deeply felt sense of loss. There was an air of sorrow about the princess that nothing would ever quite assuage.

Her new life at Hesse promised to be undistinguished. The old order that persisted there kept clever, forward-thinking women such as herself down.[7] Virtue and quiet domesticity were all that counted, and Alice found the hidebound protocols at the Hessian court burdensome. From the outset, she suffered the frustrations of not being able to exercise her own considerable progressive and intellectual gifts. An admirer of Florence Nightingale, Alice would have liked to take up nursing, having more than demonstrated her skills during her father's final illness in 1861. If this was not to be then there were other ways in which she was determined to make herself of use in her new home.

With this in mind she embraced a range of philanthropic activities, including regular hospital visiting and the promotion of women's health, fostering the establishment of the Heidenreich Home for Pregnant Women in 1864. During the wars of 1866 against Prussia and 1870–1 against France that stirred Darmstadt from obscurity and took her husband off on campaign, Alice refused any suggestion of taking refuge in England and took on the mothering of her children alone. But this was not enough for her crusading social conscience; during both wars she also organized hospital nursing of the wounded and founded the Frauenverein (Ladies' Union) for the training of women nurses. 'Life', Alice resolutely told her mother in 1866, 'is meant for work, and not for pleasure.'[8] The duty that had ruled her father's life had become the watchword of her own.

Alice produced seven children in rapid succession with the same kind of stoicism with which her mother had given birth to her own nine. But there the similarities ended; unlike Queen Victoria, Princess Alice was a practical, hands-on mother who took an interest in every aspect of her children's daily lives, down to managing the nursery accounts herself. And, like her elder sister Vicky – and much to Queen Victoria's 'insurmountable disgust for the process' – Alice insisted on breastfeeding several of her babies, causing the queen to name one of her prize cows at Windsor after her.[9] Alice also studied human anatomy and childcare, in preparation for the inevitability of nursing her own brood through childhood illnesses. There seemed to be no limits to her devotion as a mother, but she did not spoil her children; she allowed them only a shilling a week pocket money until their confirmation, after which it was doubled. She was an advocate of frugality, much like Queen Victoria, though in Alice's case economizing was often out of brutal necessity. The house of Hesse was far from wealthy and Alice often knew the 'pinch of poverty'.[10] But at the Neues Palais, built during 1864–6 with money from her dowry, she created a warm home-from-home, furnished with chintz fabrics and unremarkable pieces sent from England and cluttered with family portraits and photographs.

Born on 6 June 1872, Princess Alix – the sixth child of the family and future Empress of Russia – was a pretty, smiling, dimpled girl who loved to play. They called her Sunny and from the start her grandmother looked upon her as a golden child. Alicky was 'too beautiful . . . the handsomest child I ever saw', thought Queen Victoria, and she made no attempt to disguise her favouritism.[11] Although Princess Alice was much more closely involved in her children's upbringing than many royal mothers, her various welfare and charity projects consumed a lot of her time, and her children's day-to-day life was organized by their English head nurse Mrs Orchard.

Victorian values reigned in the plainly furnished Darmstadt nursery: duty, goodness, modesty, hygiene and sobriety, accompanied by generous amounts of plain food, fresh air (whatever the weather), long walks and pony rides. When she had time Alice walked with her children, talked with them, taught them to paint, dressed their dolls and sang and played the piano with them – even when little fingers, as she laughingly complained, 'thrust themselves under hers on the keyboard to make music like big people'.[12] She taught her daughters to be self-sufficient and did not believe in spoiling them; their toys were unostentatious and brought from Osborne and Windsor. Moments of idleness for the Hesse girls were always filled by something their mother deemed useful – cake-making, knitting, or some kind of handicraft or needlework. They made their own beds and tidied their rooms and there was of course always regular, obligatory letter-writing to *Liebe Grossmama* and annual visits to her at Balmoral, Windsor or Osborne. Other, more frugal family seaside holidays – of donkey rides, paddling, shrimping and sandcastles – were spent at Blankenberge on the treeless, wind-swept North Sea coast of Belgium; or at Schloss Kranichstein, a seventeenth-century hunting lodge on the edge of the Odenwald.

When it came to her children's religious and moral development Princess Alice took a very personal hand and inspired high ideals in them, her greatest wish being that they 'should take nothing but recollections of love and happiness from their home into the battle of life'.[13] Life's battle included being taught to appreciate the sufferings of the sick and poor, visiting hospitals with armfuls of flowers every Saturday and at Christmas. But Alice's own life was increasingly one of chronic pain – from headaches, rheumatism and neuralgia, as well as overwhelming exhaustion brought on by her commitment to so many worthy causes. The last child of the family, May, was born two years after Alix in 1874, but by then the happy childhood idyll at Darmstadt was over.

Gloom had irrevocably settled over the family, when at the age of two Alice's second son Frittie had, in 1872, shown the first unmistakable signs of haemophilia; his godfather, Queen Victoria's fourth son Leopold, also was blighted by the disease. Barely a year later, in May 1873, the bright and engaging little boy, on whom Alice had absolutely doted, died of internal bleeding after falling 20 feet (6 m) from a window. Alice's consuming morbidity thereafter – a species of *douleur* so clearly in tune with that of her widowed mother – meant that a mournful dwelling on the dead, and on the trials and tribulations rather than the pleasures of life, became part of the fabric of the young lives of the surviving siblings. 'May we all follow in a way as peaceful, and with so little struggle and pain, and leave an image of as much love and brightness behind', Alice told her mother after Frittie died.[14]

The loss of one of her 'pretty pair' of boys opened up a four-year gap between the only other son, Ernie – who also was forever haunted by Frittie's death – and his next sibling Alix.[15] With her three older sisters growing up and inevitably distancing themselves from her, Alix instinctively gravitated to her younger sister May and they became devoted playmates. With time, Princess Alice took solace in her 'two little girlies'. They were 'so sweet, so dear, merry, and nice. I don't know which is dearest,' she told Queen Victoria, 'they are both so captivating.'[16] Alix and May were indeed a consolation, but the light had gone from Alice's eyes with Frittie's death and her health was collapsing. At a time when she and her husband were also becoming sadly estranged, Alice retreated into a state of settled melancholy and physical exhaustion. 'I am good for next to nothing,' she told her mother, 'I live on my sofa and see no one.'[17]

The accession of Prince Louis to the throne of Hesse in 1877 and her own promotion to grand duchess brought only despair at the additional duties that would be placed upon her: 'Too much is demanded of me,' she told her mother, 'and I have to do with so many things. It is more than my strength can stand in the long run.'[18] Only Alice's faith and her devotion to her precious children was keeping her going but her air of fatalistic resignation cast a shadow over her impressionable daughter Alix.

In November 1878 an epidemic of diphtheria descended upon the Hesse children; first Victoria, then Alix fell sick, followed by all the others bar Ella, and then their father too. Alice nursed each of them in turn with absolute devotion; but even her best nursing skills could not save little May, who died on 16 November. By the time she saw May's little coffin taken off for burial Alice was in a state of collapse. For the next two weeks she struggled to keep the news of May's death from the other children, but a kiss of consolation for Ernie on telling him the news may well have been enough for the disease to be transmitted to Alice herself. Just as her children were recovering Alice succumbed and she died on 14 December, at the age of thirty-five, achieving the longed-for *Wiedersehen* with her precious Frittie.

The trauma for the six-year-old Alix of seeing both her mother and her beloved little playmate May taken from her within days of each other was profound. Her treasured childhood tokens were taken from her too – her toys, books and games all destroyed for fear of lingering infection. Ernie was the closest to her in age but now under the separate control of tutors as heir to the throne, and she felt her isolation acutely. Her eldest sister Victoria recalled happier times to their grandmother: 'It sometimes seems as if it were only yesterday that we were all romping about with May in Mama's room after tea – & now we are big girls & even Alix is serious & sensible & the house is often very quiet.'[19]

It would be Grandmama, the solid and reassuring Mrs Orchard – known to Alix as Orchie – and her governess Madgie (Miss Jackson) who would fill the terrible void of her mother's death, but the little girl's sense of abandonment ran very deep. Her sunny disposition began to fade into an increasing moroseness and introspection, laying the foundations of a mistrust of strangers that became ever more deeply ingrained as the years went by. Queen Victoria was anxious to act as a surrogate mother, for Alix had always been one of her favourite granddaughters. Annual visits to England by Alix and her siblings, especially to Balmoral in the autumn, had consoled Victoria in her own lonely widowhood, and such regular proximity allowed her to supervise Alix's education, her tutors in Hesse sending her monthly reports on her progress. Alix herself seemed content to play the role of the 'very loving, dutiful and grateful Child', as she so often signed her letters to the queen, and she never forgot a birthday or an anniversary, sending numerous gifts of her own exquisite embroidery and handiwork.[20] After her mother's death England became a second home to her.

*

During her lifetime, Princess Alice had had strong feelings about the future for her daughters; she wanted to do more than educate them to be wives. 'Life is also meaningful without being married', she had once told her mother, and marrying merely for the sake of it was, in her view, 'one of the greatest mistakes a woman can make'.[21] As she grew into a teenager, the best that the beautiful but poor Princess Alix of Hesse could have hoped for to relieve her from the unchallenging tedium of Darmstadt provincialism was marriage to a minor European princeling. But everything changed when on her first visit to Russia in 1884 (for the marriage of her sister Ella to Grand Duke Sergey Alexandrovich), Alix's third cousin, Nicholas Alexandrovich, heir to the Russian throne, had taken a shine to her. He was sixteen and she was only twelve, but thereafter Nicky, as she would always call him, remained besotted. Five years later, when Grand Duke Louis took Alix back to Russia on a six-week visit, Nicky was still stubbornly determined to win her as his wife. The shy schoolgirl had become a slender, ethereally beautiful young woman and Nicky was deeply in love. But by now – 1889 – Alix had been confirmed in the Lutheran faith prior to coming out, and she made clear to Nicky that despite her deep feelings for him, marriage was out of the question. Virtue prevailed. She could not and would not change her religion, but she did agree to write to him in secret, their letters being sent via Ella as intermediary.

The royal marriage stakes at that time were unforgiving to girls who did not grasp a golden opportunity when it presented itself; as one contemporary newspaper observed, 'Love in royal circles is not an epidemic affection'.[22] It seemed that Alix's inflexibility was going to deprive her of the one thing so many of her young royal contemporaries craved – a marriage based on love and not expediency. To a forlorn Nicky there seemed an insurmountable gulf between them and he allowed himself to be temporarily distracted by other pretty faces. For her own part, Alix was enjoying a degree of status back home, as a big fish in the very small Hesse pond. Her widowed father, whom she adored, increasingly depended upon her, as the only unmarried daughter, to take on formal duties for him at the Hesse court. Alix became his constant companion; the little time she did not spend in her father's company was devoted to study, to painting and drawing, making and mending her own modest dresses, playing the piano (at which she was most accomplished) and a great deal of quiet, religious contemplation. And so, when Louis suddenly collapsed and died aged only fifty-four in March 1892 'dear Alicky's grief' was 'terrible', as Orchie confided to Queen Victoria. Worse, it was 'a silent grief, which she locked up within her', as she did most things.[23] Alix's concerned grandmama gathered her orphaned granddaughter to her bosom, vowing that 'while I live Alicky, till she is married, will be *more* than *ever my own child*'.[24] Alix joined her, in deep mourning, at Balmoral for several weeks of quiet, womanly commiseration. But by this time the press, paying little deference to royal grief, had other things on its mind.

Princess Alix was twenty and highly marriageable, and gossip began circulating about a possible match between her and the young Prince George, second son of Bertie, Prince of Wales. Three years previously, a surprisingly determined young Alix had vigorously resisted the queen's attempt to marry her off to Bertie's heir, Eddy, Duke of Clarence. Victoria had been extremely put out that Alix, by then in love with Nicky, should turn down the opportunity of being a future queen of the United Kingdom. As the last of the four daughters of the House of Hesse yet to be married, Alix's prospects were hardly the best. Never mind; perhaps she could be persuaded to marry George instead, thought the queen, particularly once the unfortunate Eddy succumbed to pneumonia in January 1892. It

didn't work; Alix was adamant, and when George settled instead for
Eddy's disconsolate fiancée May of Teck, it soon became evident
where Alix's affections were firmly fixed. She only had eyes for the
Russian tsarevich. Queen Victoria's anxiety at the prospect of such
a marriage mounted. She had been highly mistrustful of Russia since
the Crimean War, looking upon Britain's former enemy as 'false'
and 'unfriendly' and much of its population 'half oriental'. Russia
was 'a corrupt country, where you can trust no one'.[25] She fired off
exhortatory letters to Alix's eldest sister Victoria, demanding she
and Ernie intervene to prevent it: 'for the younger Sister to marry
the son of an Emperor – would never answer, and lead to no happiness . . . The state of Russia is so bad, so rotten that any moment
something dreadful might happen.'[26]

In Russia, Alix's other sister Ella was meanwhile quietly working
against the queen's plan to subvert the match. She had seen the
lovelorn Nicholas at first hand and despite the fact that his father
Alexander III and his wife were also, at this time, opposed to the
match, Ella gave it her full support. In the midst of all the behind-
the-scenes discussion of her future, Alix maintained a stony silence,
locked into a personal vow made to her father before his death, that
she would never change her religious faith. Since Louis's death she
had become more devoted than ever to Ernie, for whom she was
now performing a similar central role at the Hesse court. Behind
the impenetrable, dignified *froideur* that she projected, Alix was
proud of the high standards she set for herself; proud of her own
purity of heart and her independence of thought and moral integrity.
'Of course, I am gay sometimes, and sometimes I can be pleasant,
I suppose,' she admitted to a visitor from Romania, 'but I am rather
a contemplative, serious being, one who looks into the depths of all
water, whether it be clear or dark.'[27] But such high-mindedness and
virtue carried with it a fatal flaw: Alix had not learned 'that virtue
must be amiable'.[28] She already took herself and life far too seriously.
There would be more than enough deep, dark waters for her to
negotiate in the years to come.

*

In 1894 another royal wedding drew Alix and Nicky together once
more. Her brother Ernie at last found a suitable bride in his cousin

Victoria Melita (daughter of Queen Victoria's second son Prince Alfred) and the extended royal family of Europe gathered en masse in Coburg in April for the celebrations. It was here, after much earnest and tearful persuasion from Nicky, that Alix finally succumbed, backed up by the reassurances of Ella, who herself had now converted to Russian Orthodoxy. Perhaps also there was another reason: Alix knew that her pre-eminence in the Hesse court was over with Ernie's marriage: 'life will indeed be very different for me, as I shall be feeling myself de trop', she told the queen.[29] In the months that followed it became clear that she did not much like playing second fiddle to her new sister-in-law the grand duchess, but marriage to Nicky was far more than a welcome escape. Alix had at last allowed herself to be happy. She put to the back of her mind 'all those horrid things which were said about cousins marrying' (she and Nicholas were third cousins) and refused to worry about the 'disease which poor Frittie had' which had been 'so frightening'. 'Who else is there to marry?' she asked a friend; she at least had the great good fortune to be marrying for love.[30]

Love also won over Alix's dictatorial grandmother Victoria. She quickly cast aside her disappointment and the considerable personal loss to her of someone she had considered her own child – no doubt remembering that she too had married for love back in 1840. She pushed her instinctive fears for her granddaughter on that 'very unsafe Throne' – and with it the dangers of political unrest and assassination – to the back of her mind and focused on the job in hand.[31] Her beloved Alicky must prepare for the onerous public role to come and Victoria immediately ordained that she enter a period of retreat in England with her. And so the summer passed: quietly sewing, reading, playing the piano and going for drives with Grandmama. Alix also began taking lessons in Russian with Ella's *lectrice*, Ekaterina Schneider, sent specially from Russia, and entered into earnest discussion with Dr Boyd Carpenter, Bishop of Ripon, on how to reconcile her Lutheran faith with conversion to Russian Orthodoxy.

She was, however, far from well, already suffering the sciatic pain that would plague her throughout her life. This was a cause of some concern to her grandmother and other relatives. 'Alix is again lame and cannot walk at all, she had even to drive to church', wrote the Duchess of Saxe-Coburg to her daughter during the visit. 'What a deplorable health she has'.*[32] Rumours had already been circulating that Alix had inherited her mother's sickly physique and nervous constitution, a fact that could not be advertised abroad when the wife of the future heir to the Russian throne should, above all things, be robust enough to produce healthy babies. She suffered also with inflammation of the ear (otitis), frequent nervous headaches that turned to migraines, and poor circulation. But it was the sciatic pain – often so severe that it was impossible for her to walk, ride, or play tennis – that was the real problem. Alix rarely complained about her 'wretched legs', but they frequently consigned her to long hours lying down or reclining on a sofa.[33] The European press had already got wind of her health problems and gossip was – and had been – circulating for some time, to the point where an official statement was issued in the summer of 1894 asserting that reports on the princess's poor health were 'absolutely without foundation'.[34]

But Queen Victoria was taking no chances. Vigilant as she always was about her own health, she was a great believer in bed rest at every opportunity. She regretted that Alix had not been ordered 'a strict regime of life as well as diet' sooner (the fault of the family doctor at Hesse – 'a stupid man'), nor had she been able, the previous autumn, to take her granddaughter for a rest cure to Balmoral 'which is the finest air in the world' – Alix having previously found Scotland a tad too 'bracing'.[35] The queen had no doubt that all the stresses and strains of the young princess's engagement to Nicky had 'tried her *nerves very much*' and so, after Alix arrived from Darmstadt, on 22 May she was despatched to Harrogate to take the waters.

Alix's incognito as the 'Baroness Starkenburg' failed to convince anyone and word was soon out, fuelling further speculation in the press. 'Princess Alix would not have buried herself at a Yorkshire

---

* The former Grand Duchess Maria Alexandrovna, a daughter of Alexander II, who had married Queen Victoria's son Prince Alfred. She took the title Duchess of Edinburgh until Alfred inherited the throne of Saxe-Coburg and Gotha in 1893, his older brother Bertie having relinquished his right of succession to it.

watering-place in the height of the London season if she was in perfect health', commented the *Westminster Budget*:

> The anxiety of the Court to contradict the report that [she] is in delicate health is unquestionably due to an apprehension that it may cause her engagement to be broken off. It is a *sine qua non* that the wife of the heir to the throne of Russia should be of a thoroughly sound constitution, and his marriage to anyone not in good health is positively prohibited by the Romanoff family statutes.[36]

Alix's four-week stay in Harrogate with her lady-in-waiting, Gretchen von Fabrice, was, despite the press attention, a happy one. She made the most of the home comforts of a roomy, terraced villa at Prospect Place in High Harrogate – the fashionable end of town. But every morning she had to run the gauntlet of prying eyes watching her – some even through opera glasses – as she went down the hill by bath chair or carriage to the Victoria Bathing House for sulphur or peat baths and glasses of the evil-smelling sulphurous waters. Every afternoon she would re-emerge, to be taken on excursions in a special Coventry Cycle Chair (a combination of bath chair and pedal cycle), to admire local beauty spots and be further invigorated by the bracing Yorkshire air. A detective followed by bicycle at a discreet distance.[37] Soon, however, Alix had to adopt avoidance tactics, as she told Nicky: 'They stand in a mass to see me drive out and tho' I now get in at the backyard, they watch the door and then stream to see me . . . when I go into a shop to buy flowers, girls stand and stare in at the window.'[38] The crippling embarrassment she felt was made doubly so by the fact that she was in a bath chair and felt vulnerable. For most of her stay it poured with rain and the pain in her legs was little better by the end of it, but she remained at all times cheerful and polite to the attendants and local people whom she encountered, all of whom remembered her as 'affable and unassuming, nothing stiff or formal about her'.[39]

Shortly after her arrival at Prospect Place, Alix had been delighted to discover that her hostess, Mrs Allen, had just given birth to twins, a boy and a girl. She felt this was a lucky sign and asked to see the babies. She was extraordinarily informal around the household, insisting that they treat her like an ordinary person, and 'tripping and singing about the house, like a happy English girl, just home from school',

> now popping into her bedroom, and alarming the servant by helping her to make the bed; then startling Mrs. Allen by tapping at the kitchen door, with a pretty 'May I come in,' dandling the lucky twins, or standing with her back to the fire, like a Yorkshire man, whilst she chatted as to the cooking operations, or held lengthy discussions along with the Baroness Fabrice as to the best way of dressing and training children.[40]

At the Allens' request Alix agreed to stand as godparent for the twins at their christening on 13 June at St Peter's Church, Harrogate, when they were given the names Nicholas Charles Bernard Hesse and Alix Beatrice Emma. Afterwards, she presented the children with generous gifts of gold jewellery, as well as photographs of herself and her fiancé, so that when they grew up the children would see who they were named after.* It was a happy interlude, filled with hopes for her own future life as a wife, surrounded by the children she longed for; a time when Princess Alix was her natural self – open, loving and generous to those who mattered within her own private, domestic world.

In mid-June, Alix was joined in England by Nicky – ecstatic to find himself at last 'in the embrace of my destined one, who seemed to me even more beautiful, even more dear, than before', as he told his mother.[41] For three idyllic days by the River Thames at Walton, staying with Alix's sister Victoria and her husband Louis of Battenberg, the couple spent time walking; sitting on a rug in the shade of a chestnut tree, with Nicholas reading aloud as Alix sat sewing; or going for drives, the latter, for once, unchaperoned. Then they joined the queen at Windsor and travelled on to Osborne

---

* A year later when the twins had their first birthday Alix sent gifts of Russian gold and enamelled cutlery, serviette rings and salt cellars bearing the imperial coat of arms and the babies' initials, as well as two matching pink and blue petticoats that she herself made specially for the occasion. Further presents followed from Russia in 1910 when the twins were confirmed and again in 1915 when they reached twenty-one.

with her, during which time Nicholas's domestic chaplain, Father Yanyshev, arrived from Russia to give Alix instruction in the Russian Orthodox religion. He had a hard time of it; Alix was a rigorous and questioning pupil. Her evangelical upbringing had taught her to dislike dogma and she refused adamantly to make a formal statement renouncing her Lutheranism as heretical. A compromise had to be reached.

With the wedding scheduled for the spring of 1895, Alix anticipated having several quiet months back home in Hesse to prepare, but plans were dramatically changed with news from Russia that Alexander III had fallen dangerously ill and was not expected to live. By now reconciled to the marriage, he wished to see Alix before he died and she left Hesse in great haste, making the long train journey south to Simferopol in the Crimea accompanied by her loyal friend Gretchen. After she had joined Nicky at the Romanov palace at Livadia, the couple was formally betrothed in front of the dying tsar. Alexander's death on 20 October* was followed the day after by Alix's formal acceptance into the Russian Orthodox Church. As Nicholas was now tsar the marriage was brought forward. But it did not take place as the couple would have wished, in private, at Livadia.[42] The Russian grand dukes objected; court protocol demanded a formal ceremony in the capital. And so in a bitterly cold St Petersburg, after three weeks of exhausting and excruciatingly protracted court mourning for the late tsar, Nicholas and Alexandra were married on 14 November in front of hundreds of invited guests at the chapel of the Winter Palace.

Alix could not have looked more beautiful or serene that day – tall and statuesque in her white-and-silver brocade dress, the train heavily trimmed in ermine and the imperial mantle of cloth of gold across her shoulders, her lovely figure complemented by her limpid blue eyes and her wavy reddish gold hair enhanced by the diamond-encrusted wedding crown. British envoy Lord Carrington was deeply impressed: 'She looked the perfection of what one would imagine

---

* All events taking place in Russia prior to February 1918 are given according to the Old Style, Julian calendar then in use there. Where confusion might arise, New Style dates are added in brackets.

an Empress of Russia on her way to the altar would be', he informed Queen Victoria.[43] Other witnesses noted the commanding stature of the princess alongside her shorter and rather delicate-looking consort; to all intents and purposes she appeared to be the one with the physical strength, a woman of considerable presence, 'much above the traditional level of Duchy Princesses'.[44]

There was, however, something about the royal bride's solemn, guarded look and the thin tight mouth that told a different story, of a strong, determined personality fighting a natural, but violent, antipathy to being on public display after having enjoyed the domestic privacy of the Hessian court for so long. Alix endured the ordeal, but at the end of her wedding day, much like her grandmother Victoria before her, she retreated to bed early with a headache. For others who had attended the proceedings that day, such as Princess Radziwill, it had been 'one of the saddest sights I ever remember having seen'. So long as the authoritarian Alexander III had lived the Russian aristocracy had felt safe, but their sense of security had vanished with his untimely death, and had been replaced with 'the feeling of approaching calamity'.[45]

After a few nights spent in the relatively cramped surroundings of Nicholas's bachelor apartments at the Anichkov Palace in St Petersburg (their own at the Winter Palace still being redecorated) the newly married couple travelled to the Alexander Palace at Tsarskoe Selo. They ensconced themselves in the dowager empress's apartments in the east wing, where Nicky himself had been born in 1868, for four blissful days of absolute privacy, 'hand in hand and heart to heart', as Nicky told his brother-in-law Ernie.[46] Alix had also written shortly before her wedding assuring Ernie that 'I am so happy & never can thank God enough for having given me such a treasure as my Nicky'.[47] The obscure and serious-minded Alix of Hesse, whom even her own grandmother had described as 'ein kleines deutsches Prinzesschen with no knowledge of anything beyond small German courts', had won for herself not only one of the greatest royal catches but the richest man in the world.[48]

But in leaving Darmstadt prematurely the new tsaritsa had arrived in Russia ignorant of its customs and profound superstitions, with a limited knowledge of its language and having made the enormous leap of faith from the militant austerity of her devout Lutheranism to the mystical and opulent rituals of Russian Orthodoxy. The cultural divide was enormous. Princess Alix of Hesse encountered the same problems – on a much grander scale – that her mother before her had first met in Darmstadt, and – for that matter – her grandfather Prince Albert, who as a homesick Coburger had arrived in an alien English court fifty-four years before. Alix's adoptive country was as wary of her, as a German and an interloper – the fifth princess of German blood to become a Russian empress in barely a century – as England had been of the obscure Saxe-Coburg princeling Albert.

She might have embraced Orthodoxy with all her heart, but Alix was English through and through, with English habits, English sentiments and a no-nonsense English approach to family life bred in the bone by her mother and grandmother before her. Such a background would have served her well had she remained within the familiar sphere of her Western-European bloodline, but Russia – despite the seductive beauty of its landscape, which she already loved – was unknown territory, a country legendary for its turbulent history and for the overpowering wealth and grandeur of its court. *Fin-de-siècle* imperial St Petersburg was a far cry from the comfortable domesticity of the Neues Palais and the rose gardens of Darmstadt.

Nevertheless, for the sake of love, 'gentle simple Alicky' had summoned up all her courage to leave the shelter of her brother's quiet and peaceful *residenz* in Darmstadt to become 'the great Empress of Russia'.[49] To counter her apprehensions about the unfamiliar court practices she was presented with, she closed the door to the hostile world outside and everything in it that frightened her. Instead, she clung to those few close, familiar things in which she took comfort, and to her role as Nicholas's devoted 'little wifey'. For now, the world – and Russia – could wait.

Except in one respect: shortly after Alexander III's death, Nicholas had issued a proclamation commanding his subjects to swear the oath of allegiance to him as their new tsar. His younger brother Grand Duke Georgiy Alexandrovich, he proclaimed, would bear the title of tsarevich 'until it please God to bless our approaching union with the Princess Alix of Hesse-Darmstadt with the birth of a son'.[50] In the dynastic scheme of things, Alix's primary and most urgent duty was to provide a male heir to the Russian throne.

Chapter Two

LA PETITE DUCHESSE

From her very first days in Russia, Princess Alix of Hesse was determined to counter anything she saw as a threat to the quiet family life that she had envisaged for herself and Nicky. Family had been her only security when death had taken those most dear from her; she was far from home, lonely and apprehensive, and dreaded being exposed as an object of curiosity. But in protecting her own deeply held insecurities by retreating, at every opportunity, from public view, she only succeeded in accentuating her already marked air of chilly reserve. Alexandra Feodorovna, as she was now styled, found herself at the receiving end of hostile looks from a Russian aristocracy that was already critical of her English upbringing and manners – and, to their horror, her poor French, which was still very much the language of their elite circles.[1] Worse, this insignificant German princess had, in the eyes of the court, displaced the much loved and highly sociable former empress, Maria Feodorovna – a still vigorous widow in her forties – from her central position at court.

From the first, Alexandra found the strain of fulfilling her ceremonial duties almost intolerable, such as in January 1895, when she had to face a line of 550 court ladies for the New Year *baise-main* ceremony at which they all processed to kiss her imperial hand. Her visible discomfort and habit of recoiling in horror when anyone tried to get too close were quickly misinterpreted as manifestations of a difficult personality. Her new sister-in-law Grand Duchess Olga Alexandrovna later recalled: 'Even in that first year – I remember so well – if Alicky smiled they called it mockery. If she looked grave they said she was angry.'[2] And so, in response, Alexandra retreated behind the protective wall of domesticity, preoccupied with the one thing primarily expected of her – getting pregnant. Everyone was watching for the telltale signs. Grand Duke Konstantin Konstantinovich pointedly noted in his diary within weeks of the wedding that 'the young Empress again felt faint in church. If this is for the reason the whole of Russia longs for, then praise be to God!'[3] Sure enough, by the end of February Alexandra was confiding to Ernie (whose own wife was about to give birth to her first child in Darmstadt, and to whom Alexandra was sending the imperial *accoucheur* Madame Günst to attend her): 'I *think* now I can have hopes – a certain thing has stopped – and I think . . . Oh I cannot believe it, it would be too good and too great a happiness.' She swore Ernie to secrecy; her sister Ella had 'fidgeted in December already about it' and her other sister Irene too, but she would tell them in her own time.[4] As for her old nurse, whom she had brought with her from Darmstadt, 'Orchie watches me the whole time in a tiresome way'. Within a week of this letter, Alexandra was 'feeling daily so terribly sick' that she could not attend the funeral service for the young Grand Duke Alexey Mikhailovich who had died of tuberculosis, and thereafter she was frequently confined to bed with violent nausea.[5] Orchie coaxed her to have the occasional mutton chop, which more often than not would send her fleeing from the dining table to vomit. Alexandra was fearful that she was being watched for signs of her legendary poor health, and again begged Ernie not to tell anyone about how severe her morning sickness was.[6] From now until her due date tsarist officialdom protected Alexandra's health and welfare behind a wall of censorship; there were no announcements or bulletins in the Russian press and the people at large knew nothing of her condition.

For the time being the couple was still living at the Anichkov Palace in St Petersburg. Alexandra spent her days here resolutely hidden away from view in a 'big armchair in a corner, half-hidden by the screen', reading the *Darmstadter Zeitung*, sewing and painting, while her adored husband dealt with his 'aggravating people'. She resented Nicky's absence on official business for even a couple of hours in the morning (echoes of her grandmother Victoria's solipsism and inability to let her beloved Albert out of her sight). But she did have him to herself in the afternoons: 'whilst he usually reads his heaps of papers from the ministers, I look through the begging letters, of which there are not [a] few & cut out the stamps', the latter act a mark of her ingrained Hessian frugality.[7] The business of state seemed an irritating diversion – 'a horrid bore'.[8] Evenings were spent listening to Nicky reading aloud, after which, while he decamped to his study for more paperwork, Alexandra would spin out the time playing the board game halma with her mother-in-law until Nicky returned for more bedtime reading. What few perfunctory duties Alexandra was obliged to fulfil – meeting foreign deputations or line-ups of ministers – were now made doubly unpleasant, for she was feeling dreadfully sick and suffering constant headaches.

Nevertheless, the tsaritsa had every reason to be confident that she would produce the expected son before the year was out. The statistics certainly favoured it, there having been plenty of boys born to the previous three Romanov tsars. Male children were crucial in a country where the succession laws, changed in 1797 by Tsar Paul I, were based on male primogeniture.[9] The Russian throne could pass to a woman only if all legal male lines of descent were extinct. But in Russia at the time, beyond Nicholas's two younger brothers Georgiy and Mikhail – who would be next in line – there were several more grand dukes with sons aplenty.

While eagerly awaiting the birth of her child, Alexandra set about creating something no Russian empress before her had ever attempted: an intimate family home for herself, Nicky and the children to come. They both loved the Alexander Palace out at Tsarksoe Selo, preferring its location well away from inquisitive St Petersburg society. 'The quiet here is so delightful,' she told Ernie, 'one feels quite another creature, than when in town.'[10] She and Nicholas chose not to take over Alexander III's family apartments in the east wing, but instead the somewhat neglected and sparsely furnished west wing closer to the palace gates. The interior was to be neither imperial in style nor in any way grandiose but renovated to Alexandra's own simple provincial tastes, the perfect environment in which she anticipated living the life of a devoted *hausfrau* and mother. Simple modern furniture like that familiar from her childhood in Darmstadt was ordered from Maples, the London-based furniture manufacturer and retailer, which sent out orders from its Tottenham Court Road store. The ambience of this intentionally family-oriented home, in which Nicholas and Alexandra would spend the majority of their time – aside from the obligatory winter season in St Petersburg from Christmas to Lent – was to be cosily Victorian, as Grandmama would have liked it. St Petersburg society was of course duly horrified at the new tsaritsa's bourgeoise tastes, for she had commissioned the Russian interior designer, Roman Meltzer, to refurbish the rooms in the *Jugendstil* or art nouveau style then popular in Germany, rather than in ways that would match the palace's Russian location and its classical exterior.

The heat was intolerable that summer of 1895 and as her pregnancy progressed and with it her discomfort, Alexandra was glad to escape to the sea breezes of the Lower Dacha at Peterhof, located in the Alexandria Park, one of six English-style landscaped parks on the Peterhof estate. The Lower Dacha inhabited a world entirely its own, located well out of sight of the golden cupolas of Peter the Great's grand palace and its cascading fountains and ornamental gardens, a charming, unobtrusive building of red and cream brickwork laid in alternating, horizontal stripes. Between 1883 and 1885 Alexander III had had it enlarged from a two-storey turreted structure into a four-storey Italianate pavilion with balconies and glazed verandas. But it was still rather high and narrow with smallish rooms and low ceilings, giving it more the feel of a seaside villa than an imperial residence. The location, however, was idyllic – tucked away at the far north-east corner of the park behind a grove of shady pine and deciduous trees and in sight of the boulder-strewn shoreline of the Gulf of Finland. The park itself, where the wild flowers grew in profusion and which was full of rabbits and hares, was surrounded by railings 7 feet (2 m) high, with a soldier with fixed bayonet posted every 100 yards (90 m) and Cossacks of the Tsar's Escort – Nicholas's personal bodyguard, who went with him everywhere – patrolling on horseback inside the grounds.[11] The Lower Dacha itself was encircled by a lawn and a flower garden of lilies, hollyhocks, poppies and sweet peas. It reminded Alexandra of the lovely gardens at Wolfsgarten, Ernie's hunting lodge in the heart of the Hessian forest, and she felt safe and at home here. Anticipating the need for more rooms, Nicholas ordered an additional wing to be constructed. The interior would remain much as the couple's new apartments at Tsarskoe Selo, only more modest in scale, with plain and mainly white furniture and the familiar chintz draperies, and everywhere, as always, Alexandra's trademark: 'tables, brackets, and furniture . . . laden with jars, vases, and bowls filled with fresh-cut, sweet-smelling flowers'.[12]

She spent the months of June to September in absolute seclusion at Peterhof. Her pregnancy was exhausting and the baby was very active. As she told Ernie in July, 'My tiny one hops like mad some-times, and makes me feel quite giddy, and gives me stiches [sic] (downstairs) when I walk.'[13] She spent much of her time resting on a couch in sight of the sea, or taking gentle daily walks and drives with Nicky, in between drawing, painting and making quilts and baby clothes. 'What a joy it must be to have a sweet little wee child of one's own', she wrote in July to Ernie, who now had a baby daughter, Elisabeth. 'I am longing for the moment when God will give us ours – it will be such a happiness for my darling Nicky too . . . he has so many sorrows and worries that the appearance of a tiny Baby of his very own will cheer him up. . . . So young, and in such a responsible position and so many things to fight against.'[14]

At the end of August the apartments at Tsarskoe Selo were ready for use. Despite its modest size, the palace and its 14 miles (22.5 km) of parkland would need a 1,000-strong staff of servants and court officials to run it and a much larger military garrison to guard it.[15] Alexandra loved her new rooms and was busy organizing her layette, although suffering a lot of discomfort. 'I do hope I shall not have to wait much longer – the weight and movements get so strong', she told Ernie.[16] At the end of September she experienced a bout of acute pain in her abdomen. Madame Günst was sent for and immediately called in Dr Dmitri Ott – director of the St Petersburg Institute of Midwifery and the most influential gynaecologist in

---

* Alexandra's spelling was extremely idiosyncratic and her erratic grammar simply the result of writing in haste. All instances of misspelling and bad grammar in quotations from her letters and diaries are therefore *sic*.

Russia at the time – and with whom Günst had recently attended the birth of Nicholas's sister Xenia's first child.[17] Meanwhile Alexandra was thinking about a nurse for the baby. Like Xenia, she wanted her to be English: 'If I can only find a good one – they mostly dread going so far away, and have extraordinary ideas about the wild Russians and I don't know what other nonsense – the nursery maid will of course be a Russian.'[18]

Nicholas and Alexandra were both convinced their baby would arrive around the middle of October but it still had not been born when Ella arrived from Moscow at the end of the month. She found Alix looking 'remarkably well thank God so much plumper in the face such a healthy complexion better than I had seen for years', she reported to Queen Victoria. She was concerned that the baby was 'probably immense', but Alix was transformed – 'full of fun quite like as a child & that dreadfully sad look which Papa's death had printed on her disappears in her constant smiles'.[19]

Nicholas was keeping careful watch over his wife: 'the "babe" has sunk lower and makes her very uncomfortable, the poor dear!' he told his mother.[20] So preoccupied was he with its imminent arrival, that he hoped his ministers would not 'swamp' him with work when the time came. Anticipating a son, he and Alexandra had already decided on the name Paul. Maria Feodorovna, however, was not at all keen on it, because of its associations with Paul I, who had been murdered, but she was anxious to be there when labour began. 'It is understood, isn't it, that you will let me know as soon as the first symptoms appear? I shall fly to you, my dear children, and shall not be a nuisance, except perhaps by acting as *policeman*, to keep everybody else well away.'[21]

The baby's size and position were causing Alexandra such terrible pain in her back and legs that she was now forced to lie in bed or on the sofa for much of the time. 'Baby won't come – it is at the door but has not yet wished to appear & I do *so terribly* long for it', she told Ernie.[22] Dr Ott was now staying overnight and Madame Günst had been there for the past two weeks. With no news emanating from official sources about the progress of the Empress of Russia's pregnancy, rumour abroad was rife, just as it had been in the run-up to her marriage. The gossip prompted a firm rebuttal in the British press, based on 'well-informed quarters in Darmstadt and Berlin':

> With reference to certain disquieting rumours which have been circulated respecting the health of the Empress of Russia, and the statement that some other physicians will be called in, a St Petersburg correspondent says that Her Imperial Majesty, according to the declaration of her medical adviser, is going on as well as possible, and that she neither needs nor desires any extraneous assistance.[23]

At around 1 o'clock in the morning of 3 November, Alexandra finally went into labour. Ella was joined by Maria Feodorovna, and together, as Ella reported to Queen Victoria, they 'gently rubbed her back & legs which relieved her'.[24] Alexandra was grateful for their presence and that of her husband too, for her labour lasted twenty hours, during which Nicholas was frequently in tears and his mother often on her knees in prayer.[25] Finally, at 9 p.m. 'we heard a child's squeal, and all heaved a sigh of relief', as Nicholas recalled.[26]

It was not, however, the longed-for boy, but a girl, and Ella's apprehensions had been correct: 'The Baby was colossal but she was so brave & patient & Minny [Maria Feodorovna] a great comfort encouraging her.'[27] The baby girl weighed 10 pounds (4.5 kg); it had required the combined skill of Ott and Günst to deliver her, an episiotomy and forceps having been necessary, with the help of chloroform.[28] It was, Nicholas wrote in his diary, 'A day I will remember for ever', but he had 'suffered a very great deal' at the sight of his wife in the agonies of labour. His baby daughter, whom he and Alexandra named Olga, seemed so robust that he remarked that she didn't look like a newborn at all.[29]

Queen Victoria was enormously relieved to hear the news: 'At Carlisle got a telegram from Nicky saying: "Darling Alix has just given birth to a lovely enormous little daughter, Olga. My joy is beyond words. Mother & child doing well." Am so thankful.'[30] She was even more relieved to hear from Ella that 'The joy of having their baby has never one moment let them regret little Olga being a girl'.[31] Indeed Nicholas was quick to emphasize his and Alexandra's joy, in a story later widely circulated in the press. Upon being congratulated by the court chamberlain he is said to have remarked, 'I am glad that our child is a girl. Had it been a boy he would have belonged to the people, being a girl she belongs to us.'[32] They were, quite simply, besotted. 'They are so proud of themselves & each other & the baby that they think nothing could be more perfect', wrote the wife of a British diplomat.[33] 'For us there is no question of sex,' Alexandra asserted, 'our child is simply a gift from God.'[34] She and Nicholas were quick to reward the skills of Dr Ott and Madame Günst in the safe delivery of their daughter: Ott was appointed *leib-akusher** to the imperial court and presented with a jewelled snuffbox of gold and diamonds and an honorarium of 10,000 roubles (as he would be for delivering all the Romanov children); Evgeniya Günst received around 3,000 roubles each time.[35]

There was, inevitably, a sense of disappointment in the wider Romanov family, expressed by Grand Duchess Xenia, who thought Olga's birth 'a great joy, although it's a pity it's not a son!'[36] Such disquiet was not of course expressed in any of the heavily censored Russian press. The whole of St Petersburg had been eagerly anticipating the event, to be announced by the boom of cannons across the Neva. When the moment came, 'people opened their windows, others rushed out into the street to hear and count the volleys'. But alas the number of rounds fired was only 101; for a first son and heir it would have been 301.[37] The news reached many of the theatres in St Petersburg just as people were leaving at the end of the evening performance. It 'duly called forth patriotic demonstrations from the audiences, in response to whose wish the Russian national anthem had to be played several times'.[38] In Paris's Little Russia, a *Te Deum* was sung at the St Alexander Nevsky Orthodox Church on rue Daru in celebration of the tsaritsa's safe delivery. But the British press was quick to note an element of dismay in Russian political and diplomatic circles: 'A son would have been more welcome than a daughter, but a daughter is better than nothing', observed the *Pall Mall Gazette*.[39] At a time when Russia and England were still to some extent political rivals, the *Daily*

---

* The Russian equivalent of Obstetrician-in-Ordinary.

Chronicle wondered whether baby Olga 'might be made a peg to hang an Anglo-Russian understanding on' at some future date. The seed was sown for a rapprochement between the Russian and British royal families, and what better way than through a future dynastic marriage?

On 5 November 1895 an Imperial Manifesto was issued in St Petersburg greeting Grand Duchess Olga's birth: 'Inasmuch as we regard this accession to the Imperial House as a token of the blessings vouchsafed to our House and Empire, we notify the joyful event to all our faithful subjects, and join with them in offering fervent prayers to the Almighty that the newly born Princess may grow up in happiness and strength.'[40] In a magnanimous gesture to celebrate his daughter's birth, Nicholas announced an amnesty for political and religious prisoners, who were given a free pardon, as well as ordering remittances in sentence for common criminals.

But not everyone shared the optimistic view of little Olga's future; early in the new year of 1896 a curious story appeared in the French press. Prince Charles of Denmark (soon to be married to Princess Maud of Wales, daughter of Alexandra's cousin Bertie) had, it appeared, been 'exercising his ingenuity in drawing the horoscope of the Czar's infant daughter'. In it the prince predicted critical periods in Olga's health at 'her third, fourth, sixth, seventh, and eighth years'. In so doing, he felt unable to 'guarantee that she will even reach the last-named age, but if she does she will assuredly reach twenty'. This, the prince concluded, would grant 'twelve years of peace to be thankful for'. For 'it is certain . . . that she will never live to be thirty'.[41]

*

The moment her new great-granddaughter was born, Queen Victoria, as godmother, took it upon herself to ensure that the baby had a good English nanny and promptly set about recruiting one. But she was horrified when Alexandra announced her intention to breastfeed, just as her mother Alice had done. The British press quickly got wind of what, for the times, was sensational news. It was unheard-of for sovereigns – particularly imperial Russian ones – to breastfeed their children. The news had 'astonished all the Russians' although a wet-nurse was also to be appointed as essential back-up. 'A large number of peasant women . . . were gathered from various parts' for the selection process. 'None of them was to be the mother of fewer than two or more than four children, and those of dark complexion were to be preferred.'[42] Alexandra's first attempts at breastfeeding did not, however, go to plan, for baby Olga rejected her, and, as Nicholas recalled, it 'ended up with Alix very successfully feeding the son of the wet-nurse, while the latter gave milk to Olga! Very funny!' 'For my part I consider it the most natural thing a mother can do and I think the example an excellent one!' he told Queen Victoria soon after.[43]

Alexandra, as one might expect, bloomed as a nursing mother; her whole world, and Nicholas's, revolved around their adored newborn daughter. The tsar delighted in recording every detail of her life in his diary: the first time she slept through the night, how he helped feed and bathe her, the emergence of her baby teeth, the clothes she wore, the first photographs he took of her. Neither he nor Alexandra of course noted that little Olga was in fact not the prettiest of babies – her large moon-shaped head with its awkward quiff of blonde hair that replaced the long dark hair she was born with, was too large for her body, and made her seem almost ugly to some members of the imperial family. But she was, from the outset a good, chubby and happy baby and her doting parents rarely let her out of their sight.

On the morning of 14 November 1895 – her parents' wedding anniversary and the Dowager Empress's forty-eighth birthday – Olga Nikolaevna Romanova was christened (with just the one given name, according to Russian Orthodox practice). It was a particularly joyful occasion for the imperial court as it marked the end of official mourning for Tsar Alexander III. The baby was dressed in Nicholas's own christening robes and conveyed in a gold state coach drawn by six white horses, accompanied by Cossacks of the Tsar's Escort, to the Church of the Resurrection, the imperial chapel at Tsarskoe Selo. From here, Princess Mariya Golitsyna, the mistress of the robes, carried Olga to the font on a golden cushion. In line with Russian Orthodox practice, Nicholas and Alexandra did not attend the actual ceremony, at which members of the Orthodox synod, illustrious royal relatives, diplomats and foreign VIPs, all in full court dress, were gathered. The baby had seven sponsors including Queen Victoria and the dowager empress. But most of these could not attend in person, so Maria Feodorovna presided, resplendent in Russian national dress and jewelled *kokoshnik*, surrounded by most of the Russian grand dukes and duchesses. During the service, the baby 'was dipped three times into the water in the orthodox way and then was straight laid into a pink satin quilted bag, dried and undressed, & returned to the gamp [nurse], who was very important in corded silk'.[44] Olga was then anointed with holy oil on her face, eyes, ears, hands and feet and carried round the church three times by Maria Feodorovna, with one of the godfathers on either side of her. When the ceremony was over, Nicholas invested his daughter with the Order of St Catherine.

Olga's difficult birth had, inevitably, left Alexandra considerably weakened and she was not allowed out of bed until 18 November. Thereafter, she went for quiet drives in the park with Nicky but despite the presence of her brother and his wife Ducky (Victoria Melita's pet name in the family), she took little advantage of their company, even though they were only there for a week. Ducky complained in letters to relatives of her boredom, of how Alix was rather distant and that she talked endlessly of Nicky and 'praise[d] him so much all the time', that she came to the conclusion that her sister-in-law preferred being on her own with him.[45] She certainly jealously guarded her time with Nicky; the rest of it was spent mothering Olga. Orchie was still in evidence, as a superannuated family retainer, given the token role of supervising the running of the nursery, but she was not entrusted with the baby's care, even when Madame Günst – who stayed on as maternity nurse for three months – was laid up for a couple of days.[46] The presence of Günst caused considerable disgruntlement. 'Orchie slept in the blue room and scarcely spoke to me, so offended we did not have Baby with her', Alexandra told Ernie.[47]

Professional English nannies were sticklers for routine and did not like being usurped in their roles, and the arrival on 18 December of Queen Victoria's hand-picked recruit, the redoubtable Mrs Inman, was not a happy one. Nicholas remarked that his wife was worried that 'the new English nanny would in some way affect the way of things in our daily family life'. And sure enough she did, for the protocols of royal nannying demanded that 'our little daughter will have to be moved upstairs, which is a real bore and a shame'.[48] The day after Mrs Inman arrived baby Olga was duly removed from Nicholas and Alexandra's ground-floor bedroom to the nursery and Nicholas was already writing to his brother Georgiy, complaining that he and Alexandra '[did] not particularly like the look of Mrs Inman'. 'She has something hard and unpleasant in her face,' he told him, 'and looks like a stubborn woman.' Both he and Alexandra thought she was 'going to be a lot of trouble', for she had immediately started laying down the law: 'she has already decided that our daughter does not have enough rooms, and that, in her opinion, Alix pops up into the nursery too often.'[49]

For the time being, the only sight the Russian people might be likely to get of their tsar and tsaritsa would not be at court in St Petersburg but wheeling their baby in the grounds of the Alexander Park. The world beyond knew even less of them. The British press had hoped that the tsaritsa's informal approach to mothering might have a positive effect politically: 'The right feeling shown in the young wife's decision is likelier to rally the mothers of Russia to her Majesty's side than many more imposing actions on the part of the Czar's Consort. And with their support the Empress may go far.'[50] It was an ambitious hope, but one that would fall on fallow ground; for the fact that the empress had not produced a firstborn son was already a source of disfavour among many Russians.

In the new year of 1896 and much to her dismay, Alexandra was obliged to abandon the intimacy of the Alexander Palace and transfer to her newly renovated apartments at the Winter Palace for the St Petersburg season. Although Ella had taken a hand in their design, the unworldly and inexperienced Alexandra did not take to the grand, ceremonial ambience of the palace. Nor was she warming to Mrs Inman. 'I am *not at all* enchanted with the nurse', she told Ernie:

> she is good & kind with Baby, but as a woman most antipathetic, & that disturbs me sorely. Her manners are neither very nice, & she will mimic people in speaking about them, an odious habit, wh.[ich] would be awful for a Child to learn – most headstrong, (but I am too, thank goodness). I foresee no end of troubles, & only wish I had an other [sic].[51]

By the end of April Alexandra was forced to give up breast-feeding Olga in preparation for travelling to Moscow for the arduous coronation ceremony: 'that is so sad as I enjoyed it so much', she confided to Ernie.[52] By this time the domineering Mrs Inman had been sent packing. Nicholas had found her 'insufferable' and on 29 April noted with glee that 'we were delighted finally to be rid of her'. Motherhood clearly became Alexandra, as her sister Victoria of Battenberg noted when she arrived for the coronation in May 1896. Alix, she told Queen Victoria,

> is looking so well & happy, quite a different person & has developed into a big, handsome woman rosy cheeked & broad shouldered making Ella look small near her – she feels her leg a little from time to time & gets a headache off & on – but there is nothing left of the sad & drooping look she used to have.[53]

As for baby Olga, Victoria thought her 'magnificent & a bright intelligent little soul. She is especially fond of Orchie smiling broadly whenever she catches sight of her.'[54] Although Orchie was still in evidence, in fading hopes of a role, a new English nurse was taken on temporarily while a replacement for Mrs Inman was sought.[55] Miss Coster was the sister of Grand Duchess Xenia's nanny and arrived on 2 May. She had an extraordinarily long nose, and Nicholas didn't much like the look of her.[56] In any event, nanny or no nanny, Alexandra was still doing things determinedly her own way, now insisting that baby Olga 'has a salt bath every morning according to my wish, as I want her to be as strong as possible having to carry such a plump little body'.[57] After the exertions of Moscow another important trip was approaching: a visit to Grandmama at Balmoral, where baby Olga could at last be formally inspected.

*

On the surface the visit to Scotland would be an entirely private family visit,* but the logistics were a security nightmare for the British police, totally inexperienced in dealing with high-risk Russian

---

* Although Nicholas took advantage of the visit to hold several important wide-ranging political conversations with the British prime minister, Lord Salisbury.

tsars legendary as the target of assassins. The Russian royals arrived just as hysterical stories appeared in the British press of a 'dynamite conspiracy' led by Irish-American activists working with Russian nihilists, to kill the queen and the tsar too.[58] Thankfully the 'plotters' were arrested in Glasgow and Rotterdam prior to the visit, and press suggestions of an attack on the tsar were later proved erroneous, but the scare underlined fears for the safety of the imperial couple – two of the most closely guarded monarchs in the world. In the run-up to the visit, the queen's private secretary Sir Arthur Bigge had consulted closely with Lieutenant-General Charles Fraser, superintendent of the Metropolitan Police, who submitted a special report outlining the provision of detectives in addition to Nicholas's own three Okhrana men. Ten police constables were to be on patrol in and around Balmoral Castle throughout the visit; railway employees would patrol the entire route of the tsar's train and all bridges and viaducts be supervised by local police. Assistant Commissioner Robert Anderson admitted to Bigge that he was glad that the tsar was 'at Balmoral and not in London. I should be very anxious indeed if he were *here*.'[59]

On 22 September (NS) Nicholas and Alexandra arrived at the port of Leith on their yacht the *Shtandart* in the midst of a chilly Scottish downpour. 'The sight of the Imperial baby moved every female heart in the crowd, and there was an animated display of pocket handkerchiefs', reported the *Leeds Mercury*.[60] Bonfires burning from hill to hill greeted every stage of the journey by train from Leith to Ballater, where a guard of honour made up of Highland pipers and men of the Royal Scots Greys (of whom Nicholas had been made an honorary colonel on his marriage to Alexandra) met the couple. But the bunting decorating the station was sadly bedraggled by the heavy rain by the time they arrived. The rain, although 'repellent' as Nicholas recorded in his diary, did not, however, dampen the spirits of the crowds who gathered to watch the five carriages of the Russian entourage – one exclusively for the use of Grand Duchess Olga and her two attendants – pass by.[61] As they approached Balmoral the bells of nearby Crathie Church rang out and bagpipes played, as a line of estate workers and kilted Highlanders stood holding burning torches along the roadside in the rain. And there on the doorstep was Grandmama waiting to greet them, surrounded by many of her extended family.

Everyone at Balmoral was charmed by the chubby and happy ten-month-old Olga, including her admiring great-grandmother. 'The baby is magnificent', she told her eldest daughter Vicky in Berlin; all in all she was 'a lovely, lively grandchild'.[62] 'Oh, you never saw such a darling as she is,' wrote the queen's lady-in-waiting Lady Lytton, 'a very broad face, very fat, in a lovely high Sir Joshua baby bonnet – but with bright intelligent eyes, a wee mouth and so happy – contented the whole day.' Lady Lytton thought Olga 'quite an old person already – bursting with life and happiness and a perfect knowledge how to behave'.[63] The British press remarked on Alexandra's 'pride and joy at having a little daughter to bring with her' as being 'almost pathetic to witness'.[64] 'The tiny Grand Duchess takes very kindly to her new surroundings,' reported the *Yorkshire Herald*, 'and it is said that the moment she saw her great-grandmother she delighted that august lady by adopting her as her first and most willing slave.'[65] Queen Victoria was so smitten that she even went to see Olga taking her bath, as did other members of the royal household, all of whom admired a happy and informal Russian empress enjoying the pleasure of her child – so totally in contrast to her normal stiff and haughty manner.

Nicholas meanwhile was having rather a miserable time of it, suffering from neuralgia and a swollen face – caused by the decayed stump of a tooth (he was fearful of the dentist). He complained during the visit that he saw even less of Alix than at home, because his uncle Bertie insisted on dragging him out grouse-shooting and deer-stalking all day in the cold, wind and rain. 'I am totally exhausted from clambering up hills and standing for ages . . . inside mounds of earth', he wrote in his diary.[66]

During their stay baby Olga had been trying to take her first steps and her two-year-old cousin David – son of the Duke of York and the future Edward VIII – had taken a shine to her, going to see her daily and offering an encouraging hand, so that by the time the family left, Olga was able to toddle across the drawing room holding his hand. Queen Victoria noted the children together with marked interest. It was a pretty pairing; 'La Belle Alliance', she is said to have approvingly remarked to Nicholas. The imagination of the British press quickly ran riot, with claims even of an informal betrothal.[67]

On one of the finer days of their visit the first and only cinematograph film of Nicholas and Alexandra with Queen Victoria was made in the courtyard at Balmoral, filmed by William Downey, the royal photographer. Before leaving, the couple planted a tree to commemorate their visit. Alexandra had enjoyed being back in Scotland and was sad to go: 'It has been such a very short stay and I leave dear kind Grandmama with a heavy heart', she told her old governess Madge Jackson. 'Who knows when we may meet again and where?'[68]

*

On 3 October (NS) the imperial family took the train south to Portsmouth where they boarded the *Polyarnaya zvezda* for a five-day state visit to France. From Cherbourg to Paris, they were greeted by huge crowds lining the streets, and arrived in the capital to a grand reception at the Elysée Palace hosted by President Faure. The French were fascinated that such distinguished monarchs should have their baby on tour with them rather than leave her behind in the nursery. Olga was so adaptable and had such a placid temperament that she travelled well, sitting on her nurse's lap in an open landau. Her smiling presence, with her nurse helping her wave her hand to the crowd and blow them kisses, endeared her to everyone. 'Our daughter made a great impression everywhere', Nicholas told his mother. The first thing President Faure asked Alexandra each day was the health of *la petite duchesse*. Everywhere they went little Olga was greeted by shouts of *'Vive la bébé'*; some even called her *La tsarinette*.[69] A polka was specially composed 'Pour la Grande Duchesse Olga' and all kinds of souvenirs and commemorative china were on sale, featuring her picture as well as that of her parents. By the end of Nicholas and Alexandra's foreign tour, the little Russian grand duchess was one of the most discussed royal children in the world. She was certainly the richest, with it being alleged that £1 million (something like £59 million today) had been invested in her name in British, French and other securities when she was born.[70] Nicholas had certainly settled money on his daughter, as he would for all his children, but it would be far less than the outlandish amounts suggested and was, effectively, money left them in Alexander III's will.[71] Nevertheless rumours of Croesus-like riches being heaped on the child led to fanciful ideas put about in the American press that little Olga was rocked in a mother-of-pearl cradle, her nappies fixed with gold safety pins set with pearls.[72]

After a private nineteen-day visit to Ernie and his family in Darmstadt in October, Nicholas and Alexandra returned to Russia overland on the imperial train and promptly retreated to their quiet life at Tsarskoe Selo, where they celebrated Olga's first birthday in November. Alexandra was by now pregnant again and her second pregnancy proved a difficult one. By December she was suffering severe pain in her side and back and there were fears of a miscarriage.[73] Ott and Günst were summoned and confined Alexandra to bed; there was a total clampdown on news and it was early the following year, 1897, before even members of the imperial family were told.

After a long and wearying seven weeks of bed rest, Alexandra was finally allowed outside in a wheelchair. She was not sorry to have to miss the winter season in Petersburg, but in PR terms this was a disaster. Her absence from view and the rumours of her continuing poor health had done their work in further eroding what little goodwill she enjoyed in Russia. Superstition and rumour began to gain a foothold and persisted ever after, focusing on the tsaritsa's desperate hopes for a boy. One story in circulation was that 'four blind nuns from Kiev' had been brought to Tsarskoe Selo at the suggestion of the Montenegrin princess, Militza (wife of Grand Duke Petr Nikolaevich), who herself was a fan of faith healing and the occult. These women, it was said, had brought with them 'four specially blessed candles and four flasks of water from a well in Bethlehem'. Having lit the candles at each corner of Alexandra's bed and sprinkled her with the Bethlehem water, they assured her she would have a boy.[74] Another tale suggested that a deformed and half-blind cripple called Mitya Kolyaba, who had supposed powers of prophecy that only became apparent during violent epileptic fits, was also brought in to work a miracle on the empress. On being taken to see her he had said nothing, but had later prophesied the birth of a male child and was sent gifts by the grateful imperial couple.[75] But nothing could allay either Alexandra's rising anxiety or the pressure she was under, made worse when her sister Irene, Princess Henry of Prussia, gave birth to a second boy in November and her sister-in-law Xenia produced her second baby – a son – in January.

Although she was up and about again, Alexandra could not face a return to public duties, even in a wheelchair – her sciatica being aggravated by the discomforts of the pregnancy. 'I am beginning to look a pretty sight already, & I dread appearing half high for the Emperor of Austria after Easter,' she told Ernie, 'I can only walk half an hour, more tires me too much, & stand I can't at all.'[76] She endured the pain with characteristic fortitude, for 'what happiness can be greater than living for a little being one is going to give one's treasured husband'. As for Olga, 'Baby is growing & tries to chatter, the beautiful air gives her nice pink cheeks. She is such a bright little Sunbeam, always merry & smiling.'[77]

At the end of May Nicholas and Alexandra decamped to Peterhof to await the arrival of their second child, which came on 29 May 1897, with Ott and Günst once more in attendance. The labour was less protracted this time, and the baby was smaller too, at 8¾ lb (3.9 kg) although forceps were once more needed.[78] But it was another girl. They called her Tatiana. She was exceptionally pretty, with dark curly hair and large eyes, and she was the image of her mother.

It is said that when Alexandra came round from the chloroform administered during delivery, and saw the looks on the 'anxious and troubled faces' around her, she 'burst into loud hysterics'. 'My God, it is again a daughter,' she was heard to cry. 'What will the nation say, what will the nation say?'[79]

Chapter Three

MY GOD! WHAT A DISAPPOINTMENT!
. . . A FOURTH GIRL!

On 10 June 1897 (NS) Queen Victoria sent a trenchant note to her daughter, Princess Beatrice: 'Alicky has got a 2nd daughter which I fully expected.'[1] While the queen may have been gifted with the art of prophecy, Nicholas accepted the arrival of a second daughter with quiet equanimity. It was, he wrote, 'the second bright, happy day in our family life . . . God blessed us with a little daughter – Tatiana'. His sister Xenia visited soon after: 'I went in to see Alix, who was nursing the baby girl. She looks wonderful. The little one is so dear, and she and her mother are like as two peas in a pod! She has a tiny mouth, so pretty.'[2]

But elsewhere in the Russian imperial family a sense of gloom prevailed; 'everyone was very disappointed as they had been hoping for a son', admitted Grand Duke Konstantin. From the Caucasus, where he was taking the cure for his tuberculosis, Nicholas's brother Georgiy telegraphed to say that he was disappointed not to have a nephew to relieve him of his duties as tsarevich: 'I was already preparing to go into retirement, but it was not to be.'[3]

'The joys of the Czar have been increased, but scarcely with satisfaction', observed one British paper in response to the news. 'The Czarina has yesterday presented his Imperial Majesty with a second daughter, which, to a monarch praying for a son and heir, is not comforting. Little wonder if the Court party is shaking its head, and the hopes of the Grand Dukes are rising.'[4] While Nicholas showed no public signs of disappointment, a few days later the *Boston Daily Globe* reported that the tsar was 'taking it very hard that he had yet again been denied a male heir', and stated – totally erroneously – that he was 'sunk in melancholia'. Meanwhile, it was claimed that the ambitious Maria Pavlovna, wife of Grand Duke Vladimir – and herself the mother of three boys – 'had consulted a gypsy fortune teller, who had predicted that one of her sons would sit on the throne of Russia'.[5]

It is little wonder that Nicholas and Alexandra detached themselves from such insidious gossip and kept well out of sight at Tsarskoe Selo. Alexandra was exhausted, though she recovered from this pregnancy rather quicker than the first. Now that she had two children to mother, the focal point of family life at the Alexander Palace increasingly became her Meltzer-designed mauve boudoir, the room where she spent most of her day. In it, as her family grew, Alexandra accumulated an eclectic mix of sentimental objects, and aside from occasional redecoration, nothing in the room would be altered in the twenty-one years that followed.

Two high windows looked east, out onto the Alexander Park and the lakes beyond. Within and close to the windows was a large wooden plant holder full of vases of freshly cut, heavily scented flowers – in particular the lilac Alexandra adored. In addition there were roses, orchids, freesias and lilies of the valley – many specially grown for Alexandra in the palace hothouses – and ferns, palms and aspidistras, and other flowers in abundance filling vases of Sèvres and other china placed around the room. Simple white-painted lemonwood furniture, cream wood panelling and opalescent grey and mauve silk wall coverings and draped curtains were all carefully chosen to match the lilac hues of Alexandra's upholstered chaise-longue-cum-daybed with its lace cushions. This bed was concealed behind a wooden screen to keep away draughts. Further into the room were a white upright piano and a writing desk, and the tsaritsa's personal library of favourite books. But always, too, a basket of toys and children's games were at hand, for this is where the family would usually gravitate in the evenings.[6]

In August of 1897, on a reciprocal visit to Russia in furtherance of the Franco-Russian alliance, President Faure was eager to see 'La Grande Duchesse Olga' once more. He took great delight in dandling her on his knee – far longer, it was said, than 'arranged for by the Protocol' – and he held baby Tatiana in his arms as well.[7] The president brought with him an expensive gift of a Morocco leather trunk emblazoned with Olga's initials and coat of arms, containing three exquisite French dolls.[8] One of them had a 'complete trousseau: dresses, lingerie, hats, slippers, the entire equipment of a dressing-table, all reproduced with remarkable art and fidelity'.[9] She was dressed in blue surah silk trimmed with the finest Valenciennes lace and when a spring was pressed on her chest her waxen lips would open and say *'Bonjour ma chère, petite mama! As-tu bien dormi cette nuit?'*[10]

President Faure was not the only person to be smitten with the two little sisters: everyone found them the most sweet and winning children. 'Our little daughters are growing, and turning into delightful happy little girls', Nicholas told his mother that November. 'Olga talks the same in Russian and in English and adores her little sister. Tatiana seems to us, understandably, a very beautiful child, her eyes have become dark and large. She is *always* happy and only cries once a day without fail, after her bath when they feed her.'[11] Many were already beginning to note Olga's precocious and friendly manner, among them Princess Mariya Baryatinskaya who was invited to Tsarskoe Selo to meet the tsaritsa by her niece and namesake, who was a lady-in-waiting:

> She had her little Olga by her side, who, when she saw me, said, 'What are you?' in English, and I said, 'I am Princess Baryatinsky!' 'Oh but you can't be,' she replied, 'we've got one already!' The little lady regarded me with an air of great astonishment, then, pressing close to her mother's side, she adjusted her shoes, which I could see were new ones. 'New shoes,' she said. 'You like them?' – this in English.[12]

Everyone remarked on Alexandra's relaxed manner in the privacy of their home with her children, but by November she was feeling very sick again, could not eat and was losing weight. Maria Feodorovna was swift to offer her own homespun medical advice:

She ought to try eating raw ham in bed in the morning before breakfast. It really does help against nausea . . . She must eat something so as not to lose strength, and eat in small quantities but often, say every other hour, until her appetite comes back. It is your duty, my dear Nicky, to watch over her and to look after her in every possible way, to see she keeps her feet warm and above all that she doesn't go out in the garden in shoes. That is very bad for her.[13]

If another baby was on the way, nothing was said and the pregnancy did not progress. Alexandra's English cousin Thora (daughter of her aunt Princess Helena) was making a four-month visit to Russia at the time and made no mention of it.[14] Thora described Olga's second birthday that November in a letter to Queen Victoria: 'there was a short service in the morning . . . Alix took little Olga with us as it only last[ed] ten minutes or a quarter of an hour & she behaved beautifully & enjoyed the singing & tried to join in which nearly made us laugh.'[15] Later that day they went to open an orphanage for 180 6–15-year-old girls and boys established to commemorate Olga's birth, its upkeep personally funded by Alexandra.[16] Life at Tsarskoe Selo was, as Thora told Grandmama, modest and familial:

> We lead a very quiet life here and one can scarcely realize that they are an Emperor & Empress as there is, here in the country, an entire absence of state. None of the gentlemen live in the house & the one lady on duty takes her meals in her own room, so one never sees any of the suite unless people come or there is some function.[17]

The self-imposed isolation of her granddaughter clearly concerned Queen Victoria (who had been through her own troubled period of retreat from public view in the 1860s). Victoria demanded further elaboration from Thora, who responded: 'As to what you say about Alix & Nicky seeing so few people . . . I think she quite knows how important it is she should get to know more of the society but the truth is she & Nicky are so absolutely happy together that they do not like to have to give up their evenings to receiving people.'[18]

No one caught a glimpse of Alexandra that winter – even in St Petersburg, and nothing was imparted to newspaper readers eager to know something of the domestic life of their monarchs. 'It was almost a minor state secret to know if they took sugar with their tea, or had mustard with their beef', observed Anglo-Russian writer Edith Almedingen.[19] In any event, Alexandra seemed to be perpetually ill or pregnant – or both. In February 1898 she went down with a severe bout of measles – caught on a visit to one of the charity schools she supported – and suffered severe bronchial complications.[20] The St Petersburg season was over by the time she recovered and many of her royal relatives were beginning to worry. When the Duchess of Saxe-Coburg visited Russia in August that year she opted to stay in St Petersburg rather than endure the domestic boredom of the Alexander Palace. 'It seems that Nicky and Alix shut themselves up more than ever and never see a soul', she told her daughter, adding that 'Alix is not a bit popular'.[21] Alexandra for her part cared little. On 21 September, when Nicholas unexpectedly had to go to Copenhagen with his mother for the Queen of Denmark's funeral, she was distraught: 'I cannot bear to think what will become of me without you – you who are my one and all, who make up all my life', the words eerily like those of her grandmother whenever she was separated from Prince Albert. All Alexandra wanted was that she and Nicky should 'live a quiet life of love'; besides, she thought she might be pregnant again. 'If I only knew whether something is beginning with me or not', she wrote to Nicky as he left. 'God grant it may be so, I long for it and so does my Huzy too, I think.'[22]

Alexandra spent Nicholas's absence at Livadia in the Crimea, where he rejoined her on 9 October, but it was the end of the month before his mother heard the news: 'I am now in a position to tell you, dear Mama, that with God's help – we expect a new happy event next May.' But, he added:

> She begs you not to talk about it yet, although I think this is an unnecessary precaution, because such news always spreads very quickly. Surely everyone here is guessing it already, for we have both stopped lunching and dining in the common dining room and Alix does not go driving any more, twice she fainted during Mass – everybody notices all this, of course.[23]

Privately, Alexandra was apprehensive not just about the sex of her unborn child, but the physical suffering to come: 'I never like making plans', she told Grandmama in England. 'God knows how it will all end.'[24] Fits of giddiness and severe nausea forced her to spend much of her third pregnancy lying down, or sitting on the balcony of the palace at Livadia. Her husband's devotion to her was exemplary; he pushed his wife around in her bath chair and read to her daily and at length: first *War and Peace* and then a history of Alexander I. They remained in Livadia until 16 December. Till now managing only with a temporary nanny, Alexandra had set about finding a permanent one. Her cousin Thora's lady-in-waiting Emily Loch had good contacts in England and knew whom to ask, and in December wrote to Alexandra recommending a Miss Margaretta Eagar. The thirty-six-year-old Irish Protestant came with good domestic skills as cook, housekeeper and needlewoman, as well as considerable experience in looking after children. She had trained as a medical nurse in Belfast and had worked as matron of a girls' orphanage in Ireland, and was the older sister of one of Emily Loch's friends. Emily sent a personal report on Miss Eagar to Alexandra, emphasizing that she was straightforward and unsophisticated, with no interest in court intrigues. When approached about the position, Margaretta had hesitated at first, fearful of the responsibility of looking after a newborn baby in addition to two small children. But as one of ten herself – seven of them girls – she had had plenty of experience looking after younger female siblings and took some additional training with babies before travelling to Russia.[25] Her life there would, however, be extremely sheltered. She would have no opportunity of sharing her experiences with other British nannies and governesses, of whom there were many in St Petersburg. Any excursions with the children, and even on her own, would be strictly monitored by the tsar's security police, allowing her little or no opportunity to see anything of 'the land of the Czar' beyond the confines of the imperial residences.[26]

On 2 February 1899, Margaretta Eagar arrived at the Winter Palace by train from Berlin. After resting, she was taken by Alexandra to see her new charges. It was the feast of the Purification of the Virgin and Olga and Tatiana were exquisitely dressed 'in transparent white muslin dresses trimmed with Brussels lace, and worn over pale-blue satin slips. Pale-blue sashes and shoulder ribbons completed their costumes.' 'Innumerable Russian nurses and chambermaids' would of course assist Margaretta in her duties, including trained children's nurse Mariya Vishnyakova who had been hired in May 1897. Grand Duchess Maria Pavlovna* recalled how the nursery staff at Tsarskoe Selo wore uniforms, 'all in white, with small nurse-caps of white tulle. With this exception: two of their Russian nurses were peasants and wore the magnificent native peasant costumes.'[27] Maria and her brother Dmitri (the children of Grand Duke Pavel Alexandrovich), who were a few years older than Olga and Tatiana, were among the first playmates the girls had within the Romanov family. Maria remembered how pleasant the ambience of the girls' apartments was: 'The rooms, light and spacious, were hung with flowered cretonne and furnished throughout with polished lemon-wood', which she found 'luxurious, yet peaceful and comfortable'. After playing upstairs, the children would have an early supper in the nursery and then be taken down to see Nicholas and Alexandra, where they would be greeted and kissed 'and the Empress would take from the nurse's arms her youngest daughter, keeping the baby beside her on the chaise-longue'. The older children would sit and look at photograph albums 'of which there was at least one on every table'. Everything was extremely relaxed; Nicholas sitting opening and reading his sealed dispatches, as Alexandra passed round the glasses of tea.[28]

Although Alexandra's attitude to family life was unusually informal for an empress, she was certainly glad of Miss Eagar's presence; for by March 1899 her pregnancy was proving extremely uncomfortable. The baby was lying in an awkward position that aggravated her sciatica; yet again she was spending most of her pregnancy in a bath chair.[29] On 9 May the family left Tsarskoe Selo for Peterhof to await the arrival of the new member of the family, which was mercifully quick and straightforward. At 12.10 p.m. on 14 June 1899 another robust girl was born, weighing 10 lb (4.5 kg). They called her Maria,

---

* Maria (or Marie) Pavlovna was often referred to as 'the younger' in order to differentiate her from Maria Pavlovna 'the elder', the wife of Grand Duke Vladimir. In order to avoid confusion, the older Maria Pavlovna will be referred to throughout as Grand Duchess Vladimir.

in honour of her grandmother, and Alexandra was soon happily breastfeeding her.

Nicholas registered no obvious air of dismay, his religious fatalism no doubt playing a part in his phlegmatic response. Nevertheless, it was noticed that soon after the baby was born 'he set off on a long solitary walk'. He returned, 'as outwardly unruffled as ever', and noted in his diary that this had been another 'happy day'. 'The Lord sent us a third daughter.' God's will be done; he was reconciled.[30] Grand Duke Konstantin, however, once again expressed what Nicholas was probably feeling deep inside: 'And so there's no Heir. The whole of Russia will be disappointed by this news.'[31]

'I am so thankful that dear Alicky has recovered so well', wrote Queen Victoria on receiving the telegram, but she could not conceal the serious dynastic issue it raised: 'I regret the 3rd girl for the country. I know that an Heir would be more welcome than a daughter.'[32] 'Poor Alix . . . had another daughter, and it seems she was so ill the whole time with it poor thing', wrote Crown Princess Marie of Romania to her mother the Duchess of Saxe-Coburg. 'Now I suppose she will have to begin over again and then once more she will shut herself up and it discontents everyone.'[33]

When the European press got news of the arrival of yet another daughter they had a field day. The talk in St Petersburg, alleged *Lloyds Weekly Newspaper*, is

> that the birth of a third daughter to the Czar is regarded as an event of great political importance. Absurd as it may sound, there is a strong party there which waited only for this event to resume their mischievous intrigues against the Czarina, in whom they hate the Princess of Anglo-German blood. The influence of the Empress-Dowager, whose relations with her daughter-in-law are, as is known, anything but cordial, is expected to increase.[34]

Another paper came up with a more chilling claim: 'it is reported that the Dowager-Empress, who is evidently superstitious, on her arrival at Peterhof, met the Czar with the accusatory words: "Six daughters have been foretold unto me: to-day the half of the prophecy has been fulfilled."'[35] At home in Russia the birth of a third daughter certainly fuelled the widespread superstitious belief that Alexandra's arrival in Russia – in the dying days of Alexander III – had been a bad omen for the marriage: 'The birth of three daughters in succession with the empire still lacking an heir was seen as proof that their forebodings had been well founded.'[36] A manifestation of how close rampant superstition lay beneath the surface of official Orthodoxy was brought home to Margaretta Eagar at Maria's christening a fortnight later. After the baby was dipped in the font three times, 'the hair was cut in four places, in the form of a cross. What was cut off was rolled in wax and thrown into the font.' Eagar was told that 'according to Russian superstition the good or evil future of the child's life depends on whether the hair sinks or swims'. She was happy to note: 'Little Marie's hair behaved in an orthodox fashion and all sank at once, so there is no need for alarm concerning her future.'[37]

Nicholas put a brave face on it and sent his wife a note: 'I dare complain the least, having *such happiness* on earth, having a treasure like you my beloved Alix, and already the three little cherubs. From the depth of my heart do I thank God for all His blessings, in giving me you. He gave me paradise and has made my life an easy and happy one.'[38] Such depth of feeling did not square with the confident claim of the Paris correspondent of *The Times* that the tsar was 'weary of rule'. Apparently so dejected was Nicholas at the birth of another daughter that he had declared himself 'disappointed and tired of the throne' and was about to abdicate. 'The absence of an heir excites his superstitious feelings,' it went on to explain, 'and he connects himself with a Russian legend according to which an heirless czar is to be succeeded by a Czar Michael, predestined to occupy Constantinople.'[39]

*

As things turned out Margaretta Eagar coped happily with the arrival of the new baby. She found her charges most endearing, particularly the precociously bright and quizzical Olga. The two older girls were fine-looking children and Tatiana had a particular delicate beauty. But it was the new baby who stole Margaretta's heart: Maria 'was born good, I often think, with the very smallest trace of original sin possible'.[40] And who could resist her? She was 'a real beauty, very big with enormous blue eyes', according to the Duchess of Saxe-Coburg; a gentleman at court went one better, remarking that little Maria 'had the face of one of Botticelli's angels'.[41]

By 1900 the three little Romanov sisters were attracting considerable attention abroad, with much discussion of which was the prettiest, cleverest, or most endearing. 'The flower of the flock, as far as looks are concerned . . . is Grand Duchess Tatiana', was the opinion of the British magazine, *Woman at Home*. 'She is a real beauty, with dark pathetic eyes, and wistful little mouth. But the Grand Duchess Olga, the eldest, is such a hearty, merry child, everybody loves her.' The author of the article wondered, as others had done since the Balmoral visit, 'whether she is destined to be our future Queen Consort!'[42]

Although Alexandra had plenty of staff at her disposal, she continued to spend so much time in the nursery that 'they began to say at court that the empress was not a tsaritsa but only a mother'. Even when dealing with day-to-day official business in the mauve boudoir, she would often be dandling one child on her knee or rocking another in her cradle, 'while with the other hand she signed official papers'. She and Nicholas were hardly seen, even by members of their own entourage. When her ladies did have a moment's conversation with the empress alone, she only ever had two topics of conversation – Nicky and her children. As Princess Baryatinskaya recalled, it was only when talking of how 'deeply interesting' she found it to 'watch the gradual development of a child step by step' that Alexandra's mournful shyness was 'for once subsumed in a moment's true pleasure'.[43]

Maria Feodorovna strongly disapproved of so much mothering by her daughter-in-law. An empress should be visible, performing her ceremonial duties, but Alexandra stubbornly refused to put herself or her children on show, although she genuinely wished to play an active role in philanthropic work, as her mother Alice had done. Her social projects included establishing workhouses for the poor, crèches for working mothers, a school for training nurses at Tsarskoe Selo and another for housemaids. Having a particular concern about the high infant mortality rate and the welfare of women during pregnancy, she also set about organizing midwives for rural areas.[44] The illustrated magazines, however, were left to create their own fantasy figure of the 'womanly woman, who lives in a secluded mansion and nurses her own children'. The tsaritsa was to be commended, readers of the *Young Woman* were told, for she was 'something more than a figurehead. Even if she had done nothing else, she has nursed her own baby, and an Empress nursing a baby is a sight worth living to see.'[45]

*

The first intimations of a possible crisis in the Russian succession came in August 1899 when Nicholas's brother the tsarevich, Grand Duke Georgiy, died suddenly at Abbas Tuman in the Caucasus. A manifesto was issued soon after, declaring that the next in line to the throne was now Nicholas's youngest brother Grand Duke Mikhail, but he was only named as heir and not given the formal title of tsarevich, in anticipation that Nicholas would soon have a son. Gossip in Russia had it that this was a superstitious act on the part of the couple, out of a fear that to make Michael tsarevich would in some way jinx them and 'prevent the appearance in the world of [their own] boy'.[46]

It is certainly clear that after Grand Duke Georgiy's death, the level of concern escalated, for the first time arousing real fears that the tsaritsa might never have a boy. After Maria was born letters of advice began arriving – from England, France, Belgium, and as far afield as the USA, Latin America and Japan – offering the secret of begetting a son. Many correspondents solicited thousands of dollars from the imperial couple in return for divulging their miracle panaceas. Most of the theories on offer were in fact variants of those much talked about since publication in 1896 of *The Determination of Sex* by the Austrian embryologist, Dr Leopold Schenk. Himself the father of eight sons, of whom six had survived, Schenk considered this proof that his method worked. In October 1898 when Alexandra had been trying to fall pregnant for a third time she had apparently instructed one of her doctors in Yalta 'to study Dr Schenk's theory thoroughly and to communicate with him'; she had subsequently 'lived exactly according to Dr Schenk's precepts', supervised at St Petersburg and Perhof by that Yalta doctor. The story first broke in an article on Dr Schenk in the American press in December 1898, which reported that he was 'at present, with an assistant, working in the court of Russia, where the Czar of all the Russias longs for an heir'. The article claimed that it was 'an open secret in Russia that the Czarina . . . has placed herself under Dr Schenk's treatment and is willing to await the result'.[47]

At a time when the genetics of conception were still not understood, Schenk's theories had been pooh-poohed by many of his medical contemporaries but he stuck to his guns, arguing that the sex of the child depended upon which ovary had ovulated: an unripe ovum, released soon after menstruation, would produce female children and a ripe one males. Schenk also believed that nutrition played a key role in the development of sexual characteristics, and his advice focused on the nutrition of the mother up to and during pregnancy. A woman wanting a son, he argued, should eat more meat in order to raise the level of blood corpuscles (perhaps Maria Feodorovna had also read Dr Schenk's book?), there being more in the male than the female. Other unsolicited advice was offered from within Russia, based on more superstitious practice.* 'Ask your wife, the empress, to lie on the left hand side of the bed' wrote one correspondent, instructing that he, Nicholas, lie on the right – a euphemistic allusion to the popular belief that 'if the husband mounts his wife from the left a girl will be born, if from the right a boy' (the 'missionary position' in Russian being *na kone* 'on a horse').[†48]

Whatever the efficacy of the remedies offered them, in October 1900, while they were staying in Livadia, Nicholas was pleased to inform his mother that Alexandra was once again pregnant. As with her previous pregnancies, she was receiving no one, he said, 'and is in the open air all day'.[49] The happy couple's quiet retreat was, however, suddenly disrupted at the end of that month when Nicholas

---

* Over 260 such letters survive in RGIA, the State Historic Archive in St Petersburg.

† Such fanciful suggestions continued to be taken seriously in Russia well into the twentieth century; in his autobiography of 1990 the former Russian president Boris Yeltsin described how he was advised to 'place an axe and a man's peaked cap under the pillow to ensure that his wife had a boy'.

fell seriously ill with what was at first put down to a severe case of influenza and then diagnosed as 'an abdominal typhus peculiar to the Crimea', although the foreign press widely referred to it as typhoid fever.[50] Its onset provoked widespread concern for Nicholas, at a time when Russia was viewed as an important international power during the hostilities of the Boer War in Africa and the Boxer Rebellion in China.

Many papers referred to the tsar's supposed delicate health and that he appeared to have suffered from attacks of vertigo and severe headaches in the previous three years.[51] The reality was that despite being a heavy smoker, Nicholas in general enjoyed very good health and was extremely physically active. The attack of typhoid while serious was not ultimately life-threatening, but in all he was confined to bed for five weeks, suffering at times from agonizing pain in his back and legs and becoming very thin and weak. Despite her pregnancy, Alexandra had from the first taken exclusive control of his nursing and proved an exceptionally capable sickbed nurse. Aside from the loyal help of Mariya Baryatinskaya, she allowed virtually nobody near her precious husband and demonstrated 'a very strong will'. She also 'made the most of the fact that she found herself alone with the Czar in such an emergency', vetting any urgent documents regarding affairs of state and 'with exquisite tact . . . know[ing] how to keep from the Czar all that might have caused him excitement or worry'.[52]

Nicholas was flattered by his wife's excessive care: 'My darling Alix nursed and looked after me like the best of sisters of mercy. I can't describe what she was for me during my illness. May God bless her.'[53] The girls meanwhile were sent away from the palace, for fear of infection, and lodged at the house of one of the imperial entourage who had daughters of his own. Alexandra insisted on having them brought to the palace every day, 'to a place where she could see them through a window, and looked at them for some time to convince herself that they were in perfect health'. Beyond the sickroom, however, the spectre of a Russian throne without a male heir once more rose, provoking considerable concern about what would happen should Nicholas die.

Back in 1797, Emperor Paul I had regularized the transfer of power in Russia by abandoning the old law of primogeniture and setting down clear rules on a male-only line of succession. This had been done in an attempt to avoid palace coups of the kind that had brought the mother he hated, Catherine the Great, to power.[54] Until now, with previous tsars having plenty of sons, there had been no reason to seek changes to the Fundamental Laws on the succession. Even though Olga was not yet five years old, neither Nicholas nor Alexandra wished his brother, twenty-one-year-old Grand Duke Mikhail, to accede to the throne in preference to their own daughter or the child Alexandra was carrying. She certainly was distraught at the prospect; her baby might well be a boy, and she insisted that she be nominated regent in anticipation of that and until her son came of age. Although desperately ill, Nicholas was consulted and sided with his wife. His minister of finance, Count Witte, held a meeting with other ministers in Yalta; they all agreed that there was no precedent in Russian law that allowed a pregnant tsaritsa to rule in hopes of eventually producing a son, and it was decided that if the tsar died, they would swear an oath of allegiance to Mikhail as tsar.[55] Should Alexandra's baby turn out to be a boy, Witte was confident that Mikhail would renounce the throne in his nephew's favour.

In the aftermath of his illness, Nicholas remained mindful of protecting his eldest daughter's dynastic interests, and instructed government ministers to draft a decree to the effect that Olga would succeed to the throne if he should die without a son and heir.[56] The impact on Alexandra of this debate over the succession was profound; psychologically, it marked the onset of a creeping paranoia that the throne might be wrested from her yet-to-be-born son by plotters in court circles and it further alienated her from the rest of the Romanov family, whom she mistrusted. In one thing she was fiercely resolute: she would defend the Russian throne for her future son, at *absolutely any* cost.

While their parents had both been hidden from view for weeks, the three Romanov sisters had been seen a great deal in and around Yalta that autumn. 'Nothing can be prettier', wrote a local correspondent, 'than the three little girls in the carriage, chattering and asking questions, and bowing when passers-by take their hats off to them', adding somewhat mischievously that 'the smallest Princess is living proof of the inefficiency of Professor Schenk's theories'.[57] For some time the girls continued to be the only public face of the Russian imperial family and according to press reports were extraordinarily unspoilt, thanks to the tsaritsa's principle that her children should be 'brought up without any extreme or special consideration on account of their high position and imperial birth'. They were always modestly dressed in 'cheap, white dresses, short English stockings and plain, light shoes'; the temperature in their rooms was 'always kept moderate' and they went out into the fresh air even in the coldest of weather. 'All useless, heavy etiquette and luxury are forbidden.' The tsar and tsaritsa often went to see their children in the nursery; but even stranger and contrary to normal royal protocol, the correspondent reported with incredulity that 'the august parents play with their daughters as mortal parents usually do'.[58]

The two older girls were already developing very clear and different personalities. Olga was 'very kind hearted and of noble character'. She spoke Russian and English fluently, was talented at music and already a good pianist. Although she and Tatiana had a little English donkey, the tsar had recently indulged Olga's request to ride side saddle 'as grown up people do', after she had admired the Cossack members of the Tsar's Escort. 'Charming Tatiana', meanwhile, was 'of a gay and lively temperament, and always quick and playful in her movements'. Both were very attached to their baby sister.[59] No doubt they were, but Nicholas had already noted that Maria, who was now toddling, 'falls often, because her elder sisters push her about and when one does not watch them they are altogether inclined to treat her very roughly'. He was pleased to report to his mother that Miss Eagar was doing an excellent job: 'In the nursery all runs smoothly between nurse and the other girls, – it is real paradise in comparison with the dismal past.'[60]

With Nicholas's doctors insisting he take a long convalescence in the Crimea, it was 9 January 1901 before the family left a beautiful, balmy Yalta in the *Shtandart*. At Sevastopol where they disembarked for the imperial train to St Petersburg, Nicholas and Alexandra received the news that Queen Victoria, whose health had been failing for some time, had died at Osborne on 22 January (NS).

When they arrived back to a grey and gloomy St Petersburg, the Russian court season was immediately cancelled and the entire imperial household went into mourning. As Alexandra was now four months pregnant, the doctors would not allow her to travel to England for the funeral. Instead she attended a memorial service for her grandmother at the English Church in the capital, supported by Nicholas, where, much to everyone's surprise, she openly wept. It was the first and only time many saw the tsaritsa give public display to her feelings.[61]

The loss of her beloved grandmama was profound but fortunately Alexandra remained well during this fourth pregnancy. Grand Duke Konstantin thought she was looking 'very beautiful' when he saw her in February and what is more she was feeling 'wonderful, unlike the other occasions'. For this reason, the grand duke noted in his diary, 'everyone is anxiously hoping that this time it will be a son'. But such preoccupations were forgotten in May when five-year-old Olga contracted typhoid at Peterhof.[62] 'She is separated from her sibling upstairs in the only empty room . . . but under the roof it is pretty hot', Alexandra told a friend. 'I spend most of the day with her; the stairs are tiring in my present condition.' Olga was ill for five weeks and became very pale and thin; her long blonde hair had to be cut short because the illness had started to make it fall out. 'She loves to have me with her, and for as long as I am on my feet, it is a delight to sit with her', Alexandra added, for 'to see a sick child really hurts and my heart weeps – God watch over her'.[63] So changed was Olga by the illness that when Tatiana was taken in to see her sister she did not recognize her and wept.

When Madame Günst arrived at Peterhof in preparation for the fourth baby, she became concerned that the tsaritsa's exertions looking after Olga might trigger a premature birth and she called in the doctors.[64] But all was well. At 3 a.m. on 5 June, Alexandra went into labour at the Lower Dacha. It was very quick this time; three hours later, and without complications, she gave birth to a large, 11½ lb (5.2 kg) baby girl. Nicholas had little time to register any disappointment. It all happened so quickly, before the household were up and about, giving himself and Alexandra 'a feeling of peace and seclusion'.[65] They gave their new daughter the name Anastasia, from the Greek *anastasis*, meaning 'resurrection'; in Russian Orthodox usage the name was linked to the fourth-century martyr St Anastasia, who had succoured Christians imprisoned for their faith and was known as the 'breaker of chains'. In honour of this Nicholas ordered an amnesty for students imprisoned in St Petersburg and Moscow for rioting the previous winter.[66] Anastasia was not a traditional Russian imperial name but in naming her thus the tsar and tsaritsa were perhaps expressing a profoundly held belief that God would answer their prayers and that the Russian monarchy might yet be resurrected – by the birth of a son.

The Russian people and the imperial family were, however, extremely despondent; as US diplomat's wife Rebecca Insley Casper observed, the arrival of Anastasia had 'created such indescribable agitation in a nation clamouring for a boy'.[67] 'My God! What a disappointment! . . . a fourth girl!' exclaimed Grand Duchess Xenia. 'Forgive us Lord, if we all felt disappointment instead of joy; we were so hoping for a boy, and it's a fourth daughter', echoed Grand Duke Konstantin.[68] 'Illuminations, but Disappointment' ran the headlines of the *Daily Mail* in London on 19 June (NS). 'There is much rejoicing, although there is a popular undercurrent of disappointment, for a son had been most keenly hoped for.' The newspaper could not but offer commiserations: 'the legitimate hopes of the Czar and Czarina have so far been cruelly frustrated, whatever may be their private parental feelings towards their four little daughters . . . [who] had been born into an expectant world with distressing regularity'.[69] In Russia the response was once again heavy with superstitious resentment, as the French diplomat Maurice Paléologue reported: 'We said so, didn't we! The German, the *nemka*, has the evil eye. Thanks to her nefarious influence our Emperor is doomed to catastrophe.'[70]

In the face of so much negativity, and determined to show how proud he was of his fourth daughter, Nicholas ordered the fullest possible pageantry at her christening in August, which followed the same format as those for her sisters, and after which 'the cannon boomed all the way from Peterhof back to the capital'. Later Nicholas entertained his illustrious guests to lunch, during which they 'went up to the supposedly happy father to present their felicitations'.

Rebecca Insley Casper reported that for once the tsar seemed unable to conceal his dismay, for, when he turned to one of the ambassadors, he was heard to say with a sad smile – 'We must try again!'[71]

Three months later, Nicholas and Alexandra visited the new French president, Emile Loubet, at Compiègne, leaving the girls at Kiel in the care of Alexandra's sister Irene. The security surrounding them was intense: the town swarmed with French police who were even sent to 'beat the forest and search every copse and thicket' for undesirables. The chateau where Nicholas and Alexandra stayed was searched 'from garret to basement' and plain clothes detectives mingled with the staff.[72]

The imperial couple seemed clearly devoted, but there was an air of unmistakable melancholy about Alexandra. At a public reception Margaret Cassini, daughter of the Russian ambassador to Washington, thought her withdrawn air very marked. She looked luminous, as usual, dressed in white and wearing exquisite jewels 'mostly pearls and diamonds, from ears to waist'. But, as Cassini could not help noticing, 'she wears them without joy'. The French found the sombre Russian empress hard to fathom: 'Oh, la la! *Elle a une figure d'enterrement*,'* they complained. Her sadness, thought Cassini, was a reflection of her being 'a mother only of girls'. 'Have you children?' Alexandra would ask of ladies presented to her at court, only for sadness to descend whenever the lady in question replied as she curtsied, 'A son, Your Majesty.'[73]

'Nicholas would part with half his Empire in exchange for one Imperial boy', remarked the travel writer Burton Holmes that year, wondering 'Will one of the dear little duchesses some day ascend the throne of Catherine the Great?'[74]

But privately the imperial couple had not given up hope. Barely a month after Anastasia's birth a new person was in evidence within their inner circle at Peterhof and was being referred to by them as 'our friend'. A certain 'Maître Philippe' – a fashionable French faith-healer-cum-mystic – had arrived in Russia at the invitation of Grand Duke Petr and his wife Militza, and was staying with them at their home, Znamenka, not far from the Lower Dacha.[75] It was

---

* 'She looks like someone at a funeral.'

there that Nicholas and Alexandra – who had met Philippe briefly in March – soon became locked into long evenings of earnest conversation with this mysterious French visitor. In their desperation for a son they were now turning to faith healing and the occult.

Chapter Four

THE HOPE OF RUSSIA

In the Russian imperial family there was a custom, whereby all brides on the night before their wedding would go to St Petersburg's Kazan Cathedral to pray before the wonder-working icon of the Mother of God. According to Russian superstition, failure to perform this ritual would lead to infertility or the birth of only girls. When the tsaritsa had been told this before her wedding in 1894 – so the gossip in St Petersburg went – she had refused to go, saying that she had no intention of kowtowing to obsolete practices.[1] For the highly superstitious Russian peasantry it seemed clear, by 1901, that 'the Empress was not beloved in heaven or she would have borne a son'.[2] God was angry.

Under such intense pressure, Alexandra was naturally susceptible to the insidious influence of men such as Nizier Anthelme Philippe.[3] His background was shadowy and medically dubious. The son of peasant farmers from Savoy, he had been working in his uncle's butcher's shop in Lyons, when at the age of thirteen he began claiming extra-sensory powers. Aged twenty-three, and without completing any formal medical training, he set himself up in practice without a licence, offering treatment with mysterious 'psychic fluids and astral forces'.[4] In 1884 Philippe had presented a paper, 'Principles of Hygiene Applicable in Pregnancy, Childbirth and Infancy', in which he had claimed he could predict the sex of a child and, even more outlandishly, that he could use his magnetic powers to change its sex inside the womb.[5] Philippe's occult medicine was geared to hypnosis sessions with patients and business prospered, despite his being fined several times for practising illegally; by the late 1890s his consulting rooms in Paris were besieged by fashionable French society. The Russian aristocracy too was becoming interested in mysticism and the occult at this time; in the south of France the Montenegrin princess, Militza, had solicited Philippe's help in treating her sick son Roman.[6] So convinced were she and her husband Grand Duke Petr of Philippe's supposed miraculous powers of healing, that they invited him to St Petersburg. On 26 March 1901 they introduced him to Nicholas and Alexandra. 'This evening we met the amazing Frenchman Mr Philippe', Nicholas recorded in his diary. 'We talked with him for a long time.'[7]

Militza soon began badgering Nicholas to arrange for Philippe to be allowed to practise in Russia, despite objections from the medical establishment. A medical diploma was contrived for him, under duress, from the Petersburg Military Medical Academy and Philippe was given the rank of State Councillor and the uniform of an imperial military doctor, complete with gold epaulettes. Close relatives – including Xenia, Maria Feodorovna and Ella – were alarmed and warned Nicholas and Alexandra to stay well away from Philippe, but all attempts to discredit him in their eyes failed. Even a report on his dubious practices, sent to Nicholas by the Okhrana in Paris with the connivance of Maria Feodorovna, had no effect; Nicholas promptly dismissed the agent who had prepared it.[8]

Convinced that at last they had found a sympathetic ear, the couple hung on Maître Philippe's words of pseudo-mystical wisdom at every opportunity. When he returned on a twelve-day visit in July they went to see him daily, making the short drive from the Lower Dacha to Znamenka, and often staying late into the night. 'We were deeply moved listening to him', wrote Nicholas; 'what wonderful hours' they spent with their friend.[9] They even cut short a visit to the theatre on the 14th to go straight to Znamenka and sit talking to Philippe until 2.30 in the morning. The evening before Philippe left they all sat and prayed together and said goodbye with heavy hearts. During their brief visit to Compiègne Nicholas and Alexandra contrived to see Philippe again, and snatched another meeting with him when he returned to Znamenka in November.

Beyond this inner sanctum, Nicholas and Alexandra's association with Philippe was a closely guarded secret, though rumour at the time was rife. It was alleged that Philippe 'carried out experiments in hypnotism, prophecy, incarnation and necromancy' in the imperial couple's presence and that utilizing his own particular combination of 'hermetic medicine, astronomy and psychurgy' he had claimed to direct 'the evolution of the embryonic phenomena'.[10] Psychobabble or not, during his visit in July Philippe had won the confidence of the empress and penetrated her intensely private world; after his departure he continued to offer advice to the imperial couple on achieving the birth of an heir, as well as passing on overtly political prognostications, advising that Nicholas should never grant a constitution, 'as that would be the ruin of Russia'.[11]

By the end of 1901, and within five months of giving birth to Anastasia, the tsaritsa had once more fallen pregnant. It seemed a total vindication of Philippe's prayers and powers of autosuggestion. They kept the news of the pregnancy from their family as long as they could, but by the spring of 1902, it was clear that the tsaritsa was getting fatter and had stopped wearing a corset. Xenia, who by now was also pregnant – for a sixth time – did not find out for certain until April, when Alexandra wrote to her, admitting that 'now it begins to be difficult to hide. Don't write to Motherdear [the dowager empress], as I want to tell it to her when she returns next week. I feel so well, thank God; in August! – My broad waist all winter must have struck you.'[12]

Philippe spent four days in St Petersburg in March of 1902, staying with Militza's sister Stana – another devoted acolyte – and her husband the Duke of Leuchtenburg, where once again Nicholas and Alexandra visited. 'We listened to him over supper and for the rest of that evening until one a.m. We could have gone on listening to him for ever', Nicholas recalled.[13] Philippe's hold over Alexandra was such that he advised her not to allow any doctors to examine her, even as her due date approached. But by the summer she was showing worryingly little physical sign of what should have been an advanced state of pregnancy. Nevertheless, in August manifestos announcing the imminent birth were made ready. When Dr Ott took up residence at Peterhof for the delivery, he immediately realized something was wrong. It took considerable persuasion before

Alexandra would agree to his examining her, upon which Ott immediately announced that she was not pregnant.

Alexandra's 'phantom pregnancy' provoked considerable consternation in the imperial family: 'From 8 August we have been waiting every day for confirmation of the Empress's pregnancy,' wrote Grand Duke Konstantin. 'Now we have suddenly learned that she is not pregnant, indeed that there never was any pregnancy, and that the symptoms that led to suppose it were in fact only anaemia! What a disappointment for the Tsar and Tsarina! Poor things!' A deeply distressed Alexandra wrote to Elizaveta Naryshkina, who had been anxiously awaiting news at her estate in the country: 'Dear Friend, do not come. There will be no christening – there is no child – there is nothing! It is a catastrophe!'[14]

Such had been the level of rumour that an official, face-saving bulletin on the tsaritsa's health was published by the court physicians Ott and Gustav Girsh on 21 August: 'Several months ago there were changes in the state of health of Her Imperial Highness the Empress Alexandra Feodorovna, indicating a pregnancy. At the present time, owing to a departure from the normal course of things, the pregnancy has resulted in a straightforward miscarriage, without any complications.'[15]

Alexandra's true condition had, however, been an unusual one that was never made public. In a secret report submitted to Nicholas, Dr Girsh gave the precise details. Alexandra had last menstruated on 1 November 1901 and had genuinely believed she was pregnant, anticipating a birth at the beginning of the following August, even though, approaching her due date, she had not significantly increased in size. Then on 16 August she had had a bleed. Ott and Günst had been called in but Alexandra had refused to let them examine her; on the evening of the 19th she experienced what seemed like early labour pains and had another show of blood that continued till the following morning. But when she got up to wash, she suffered a discharge – of a spherical, fleshy mass the size of a walnut, which when examined under the microscope by Ott was confirmed as a dead fertilized egg in the fourth week of gestation. In his opinion the tsaritsa had been suffering from a condition known as 'Mole Carnosum' (hydatidiform mole) – and the loss of blood had flushed the egg out.[16]

The news that the tsaritsa had 'miscarried', far from winning sympathy for her among the Russian people, sadly had the reverse effect. It sparked a wave of merciless vilification and all kinds of outlandish rumour that she had given birth to some kind of deformed child – a monster, 'a freak with horns'. Such was official paranoia about this that part of the libretto of Rimsky-Korsakov's opera *The Tale of Tsar Saltan*, referring to how 'the tsaritsa gave birth in the night not to a son, nor a daughter, nor a dog, nor a frog but – some kind of unknown wild creature', was censored.[17] As far as the suspicious Russian people were concerned, the hand of God lay heavy on their ill-fated sovereigns. The absence of a son was the tsar's punishment, many said, for the Khodynka tragedy of 1896, when thousands had been trampled to death during a stampede at the coronation festivities in Moscow.[18]

In England, the *Anglo-Russian* responded, albeit with a jaundiced eye, to the growing criticism being heaped on the unfortunate tsaritsa for failing to produce an heir, by striking a blow for a female Russian monarch:

> Once again the Tsaritsa has disregarded the Salic law and disappointed the sex-biased Russian populace, who even show dislike amounting to hatred toward the gifted mother . . . yet a little knowledge of natural law and of history would demonstrate that 'a perfect woman nobly planned' is 'Nature's Crown', and a female sovereign has often been the salvation of a people, denoting their era of greatest material and social progress.[19]

Word was by now leaking into the foreign press that Philippe's influence over the imperial couple went well beyond 'psychical methods of healing' in the conception of a son and that Nicholas had even subjected himself to 'hypnotic experiments', during which Philippe 'calls forth the spirit of Alexander III, foretells the future, and inspires the Czar with one or another decision concerning not only his domestic, but also State affairs'.[20] Philippe's reputation took a dip and accusatory voices that he was a charlatan bent on meddling in affairs of state mounted, making his position at the Russian court untenable. Nicholas and Alexandra were loath to part with him but at the end of 1902 Philippe returned to France with gifts from his grateful imperial patrons including a Serpollet motor car.[21] In return Philippe presented Alexandra with an icon with a small bell, which, he told her, would ring to alert her should anyone meaning her harm enter the room. She also kept a frame with dried flowers that he gave her, which he claimed had been touched by the hand of the saviour. And then he departed, leaving one final, tantalizing prediction: 'Someday you will have another friend like me who will speak to you of God.'[22]

In the persisting climate of recrimination at the absence of an heir to the throne, rumours began circulating after the 'miscarriage' of 1902 that Nicholas would be prevailed upon to divorce Alexandra – much as Napoleon Bonaparte had divorced Empress Josephine in 1810, after fourteen years of marriage, for failing to provide him with a son. There was even talk that the tsar would abdicate if his next child was another daughter. Within Russia, the tsaritsa's position was growing 'extremely precarious'. Rumour abounded that she had become the victim of 'profound and growing melancholy since her hope of becoming a mother again was dashed', so much so that her desire to produce an heir had become 'almost a mania with her'.[23] Meanwhile sympathy abroad grew for the four imperial daughters so systematically marginalized in the Russian public's imagination, such as in this quip published in the Pittsburgh press in November 1901:

Mrs Gaswell: The Czar of Russia has now four little daughters.
Mr Gaswell: Oh, the dear little Czardines.[24]

*

The year 1903 was an important one for the Romanov family, beginning with the celebrations for the bicentenary of the foundation of St Petersburg. In a rare court appearance – as it turned out, their last for several years to come – Nicholas and Alexandra took centre stage at what would be the last great costume ball held before the revolution. Alexandra looked magnificent, if rather uncomfortable, ornately dressed as the Tsaritsa Maria Miloslavskaya in a heavy gold brocade costume and unwieldy crown, with her husband at her side and rather eclipsed by her, dressed as their favourite tsar, Alexey I. Alexandra seemed a beautiful vision, a 'Byzantine Madonna come down from among the jewelled *ikons* of a cathedral'.[25] But it was an image of autocratic remoteness that, seen at the centre of this splendid gathering of St Petersburg's wealthy aristocratic elite, served only to accentuate both her and Nicholas's total isolation from the ordinary Russian people. Later that summer, however, the Russian people would be rewarded with a very rare glimpse of the royal couple, in their continuing quest for a son.

Before Philippe had left for France he had recommended that the imperial couple pray for the intercession of St Seraphim of Sarov, and they would have a son. There was, however, a problem: there was no official saint of that name in the Russian Orthodox calendar. After a frantic search, it was eventually ascertained that a monk at the Diveevo Monastery at Sarov in the Tambov region, 250 miles (403 km) east of Moscow, had been revered locally for performing miracles. But none of these had been officially verified and Seraphim had been dead for seventy years. Nor had his body, when his coffin was opened for inspection, passed the acid test of sanctity by appearing miraculously uncorrupted. It was in an advanced state of decay. As emperor, Nicholas nevertheless had the power to order that this unknown miracle-worker be canonized, whatever the state of his corpse. The Metropolitan of Moscow found himself obliged to find a way of upholding Seraphim's sanctity, as being 'fully established by the many miracles performed in connexion with his remains, including the soil in which he lies buried, the stone on which he prayed, and the water from the well which he bored – by all of which many believers have been restored to health'.[26] As Elizaveta Naryshkina noted, the contrivance of Seraphim's saint-hood was seen as a direct result of Alexandra's involvement with her new 'friend': 'It would be difficult to know where Philippe ends and Seraphim begins.'[27] In February 1903 the Metropolitan finally sanc-tioned the canonization.

Leaving their daughters behind in the care of Margaretta Eagar, Nicholas and Alexandra travelled in intense heat to Sarov for the formal ceremony, in the company of Nicholas's sister Olga, Maria Feodorovna, Ella and Sergey, and Militza and Stana. Nicholas was well aware that the canonization ceremony would serve an important purpose, as an act of collective religious faith underpinning his autocratic rule, for the imperial guests were joined by something approaching 300,000 devout pilgrims, who descended on Sarov, raising a huge cloud of dust in the process. Hordes of the blind, the sick and the crippled, all seeking a miracle, tried to mob their little father and kiss his hand. In an atmosphere saturated with mystical religious fervour and the incessant ringing of bells, the family attended three days of protracted church services, often of over three hours' duration, in the boiling heat.[28] Despite the pain in her legs, Alexandra endured the devotions on her feet, with deep piety and without complaint. The intense faith manifested at Sarov by the many pilgrims fuelled her own unshakeable belief in the sacred, inviolable communion between tsar and people. Nicholas helped carry the coffin containing Seraphim's sacred relics on a litter during the ceremonies, culminating in its interment on 19 August in a specially created shrine built in St Seraphim's honour. That evening, as an important, symbolic act of religious faith, Alexandra and Nicholas went in private down to the nearby Sarova River, where Seraphim himself had once bathed and – as Philippe had instructed them – submerged themselves in its sacred waters in the hope that they might be blessed with a son.

*

In the autumn of 1903 the Romanov family made a visit to Darmstadt for the wedding of Princess Alice of Battenberg and Prince Andrew of Greece.* Ernie and Ducky – a mismatched couple from the first – had by now sadly separated and divorced, but Ernie was devoted to their eight-year-old daughter Elisabeth, who spent six months of the year with him. After the wedding, the two families travelled to Wolfsgarten for a private holiday, where Olga and Tatiana played happily with their cousin, riding bicycles and ponies and going out mushroom-picking. Elisabeth was a strange, ethereal child with eyes full of pathos and a halo of dark curly hair that contradicted her warm and lively personality. She was greatly taken with her 'tiny cousin' Anastasia, took to mothering her and wanted to take her back home with her to Darmstadt.[29]

---

* The future parents of the Duke of Edinburgh.

When the imperial family left Hesse, Ernie and Elisabeth travelled on with them to the tsar's hunting lodge on the imperial estate at Skierniewice near the Białowieża Forest in today's Poland, where Nicholas went for regular hunting trips. But on the morning of 15 November, and without warning, Elisabeth suddenly fell sick. It seemed at first to be a bad sore throat, but her temperature continued to rise and, lying dangerously ill, she begged Margaretta Eagar to send for her mother. The illness, however, overwhelmed her and there was nothing the doctors could do. Within forty-eight hours Elisabeth was dead, carried off by a particularly virulent form of typhoid that had caused heart failure.[30] The sisters were greatly distressed by their cousin's sudden death and immediately afterwards Margaretta took all four of them back to Tsarskoe Selo, so that their rooms at Skierniewice could be fumigated. Olga was bewildered: 'What a pity that the dear God has taken away from me such a good friend!' she told Margaretta plaintively. Later, at Christmas, she remembered Elisabeth again, wondering to Margaretta whether God had purposely 'sent for her to keep with him' in Heaven.[31]

Almost immediately after Ernie took Elisabeth's sad little coffin back to Darmstadt, Alexandra fell ill with a severe ear infection and instead of travelling on to Elisabeth's funeral, remained confined to bed at Skierniewice for six long weeks. The pain was so bad that an ear specialist was called in from Warsaw. Desperate to be with her children for Christmas and arrange the tree and presents for them and the staff, Alexandra travelled back to Russia before she was fully recovered.[32] No sooner had she arrived at Tsarskoe Selo than she went down with influenza and on Christmas Eve, as Margaretta Eagar recalled, she was 'very ill and could not see the children'.[33] Instead Nicholas supervised the tree and the distribution of presents. This was no mean task, for the family had eight large trees brought in at Christmas – for themselves, the staff and even the Tsar's Escort. Alexandra liked to decorate them all herself, in addition to laying out the huge array of presents for the household on long tables covered with crisp white tablecloths – very much in the German style adopted by her grandmother at Windsor. The girls as usual took pride in making their own little gifts, but Christmas that year was a sad and subdued one, haunted by the death of their cousin and with their mother confined to bed. 'Wanting her, we wanted more than half of our usual gaiety', Margaretta remembered.

The tsaritsa remained bedridden until mid-January and the family did not transfer to St Petersburg for the winter season until the following month.[34] It was a difficult time to be laid so low by illness for Alexandra was pregnant again – her child probably conceived at Skierniewice – and her illness only exacerbated her anxieties. Xenia was sympathetic when she was finally told the news by Maria Feodorovna on 13 March: 'It's become noticeable now, but she, poor thing, had been concealing it as no doubt she was afraid that people would find out about it too soon.'[35]

Alexandra was saved from further criticism when the St Petersburg season was cut short with the outbreak in January 1904 of the Russo-Japanese War, triggered by Nicholas's expansionist policies in southern Manchuria, a territory long contested by the Japanese. Many at court believed it to be a direct result of the insidious influence of Philippe, who had assured the couple that a short, sharp war would be a triumphant demonstration of Russian imperial might that would underline the inviolability of their autocracy. But it was an ill-judged conflict for which Russia was not prepared, her troops even less so, and the initial burst of patriotic fervour rapidly faded.

During the war, the little grand duchesses were inevitably susceptible to the racist and xenophobic talk prevalent at court; Margaretta Eagar recalled that it was 'very sad to witness the wrathful, vindictive spirit that the war raised in my little charges'. Maria and Anastasia were perplexed by images of the 'queer little children' of the Crown Prince of Japan that they saw in magazines. 'Horrid little people,' exclaimed Maria, 'they came and destroyed our poor little ships and drowned our sailors.' Mama had told them 'the Japs were all only little people'. 'I hope the Russian soldiers will kill all of the Japanese', exclaimed Olga one day, upon which Margaretta explained that the Japanese women and children were not to blame. The bright and opinionated Olga seemed satisfied after several of her questions had been answered: 'I did not know that the Japs were people like ourselves. I thought they were only like monkeys.'[36]

The war, meanwhile, had galvanized Alexandra's talent for philanthropic work and despite her pregnancy, she had engaged in war relief, sending portable field chapels to the troops and organizing supplies and hospital trains. For the first time in years she was once again conspicuous in St Petersburg, overseeing groups of women gathered to make clothing and sort linen and bandages for the hospital trains in the ballrooms of the Winter Palace. Just as Queen Victoria and her daughters had sat knitting and sewing during the Crimean War of 1854–6, so Alexandra and her four daughters crocheted caps and knitted scarves for the troops; and young though she was, Anastasia proved herself extraordinarily adept at frame knitting.[37] The girls also helped Margaretta Eagar fold and stamp piles of letter-forms for wounded troops to write home to their families on.

As the months passed and the birth of the tsaritsa's fifth baby approached, the foreign press inevitably was awash with speculation. 'That great events may hinge on small ones is, unfortunately, a truism', observed an editorial in the *Bystander*:

> A few days will decide whether the Czarina is to be the most popular woman in Russia, or regarded by the great bulk of the people as a castaway – under the special wrath of God. It is said that she prays night and day that the coming child may prove a son in order that she may win the hearts of her husband's people by giving an heir to the sovereignty of All the Russias. Just at this minute the Czarina – waiting for the mysterious decision of God and Nature – is one of the most pitiful figures in Europe, all the more so that her position allows her no shelter from the sympathy or curiosity of the world.[38]

'Royal and imperial families make themselves very unhappy over matters American families never think of', observed another editorial commenting on the simple, unspoilt lives of the consistently overlooked imperial daughters. 'There are four of these little girls. They are bright, intelligent children, but nobody in Russia wants them, unless it be their parents.' In the midst of so much speculation, there was no doubt how much Nicholas and Alexandra loved their daughters – their 'little four leaved clover' as Alexandra described them. 'Our girlies are our joy and happiness, each so different in face and Character.' She and Nicholas firmly believed that 'Children are the apostles of God, which day after day He sends us, to speak of love, peace and hope'.[39] But, as Edith Almedingen observed: 'However beloved by their parents, the four little girls were just four prefaces to an exciting book which would not begin until their brother was born.'[40]

*

The onset of Alexandra's fifth labour came very quickly indeed, at Peterhof on 30 July 1904. Ella and Sergey had been visiting from Moscow when, over lunch, Alexandra suddenly experienced strong labour pains and quickly retreated upstairs. Barely half an hour later, at 1.15 p.m., she gave birth to a large boy weighing 11½ lb (5.2 kg). She felt extremely well and looked radiant and soon after was happily breastfeeding.[41]

At long last the cannon of the Peter and Paul Fortress in St Petersburg were able to boom out the 301-gun salute across the River Neva announcing the birth of a *naslednik* – an heir – the first to be born to a reigning monarch (rather than a tsarevich) since the seventeenth century. People stopped in their tracks to count the number of salutes, which came every six seconds. 'The aspect of the streets' suddenly changed, as the St Petersburg correspondent of the *Daily Express* reported on the paper's front page: 'National flags seemed to spring from every quarter, and in five minutes after the 102nd gun had boomed out its glad tidings the whole city was ablaze with flags. Work automatically stopped for the day and the people gave themselves over to public rejoicing.' That evening the streets were bright with electric illuminations of the imperial twin-headed eagle and Romanov crowns; orchestras played in the parks, constantly repeating the National Anthem. Later, in many of the capital's best restaurants the champagne flowed freely 'at the expense of the proprietors'.[42]

'We were nearly deafened by the church bells ringing all day', remembered Baroness Sophia Buxhoeveden, a visitor to court.[43] Nicholas and Alexandra's prayers had been answered; it was 'an unforgettable, great day for us', the tsar recorded in his diary. 'I am sure it was Seraphim who brought it about', remarked his sister Olga.[44] The happy parents blessed the day they had met Maître Philippe: 'Please, somehow or other, pass on our gratitude and joy . . . to Him', Nicholas wrote to Militza.[45]

The general feeling elsewhere was that 'the birth of an heir after all these anxious years of disappointed hopes changes the destinies of Russia'; for Nicholas it was certainly a dramatically charged moment that brought renewed optimism in time of war. 'I am more happy at the birth of a son and heir than at a victory of my troops, for now I face the future calmly and without alarm; knowing by this sign that the war will be brought to a happy conclusion.'[46] With this in mind, and as a morale-booster, Nicholas named the entire Russian army fighting in Manchuria as Alexey's godfathers. An imperial manifesto followed, granting numerous political concessions, abolishing corporal punishment for the peasantry and armed forces and remitting fines for a wide range of offences. A political amnesty was issued to prisoners (excepting those convicted of murder) and a fund set up for military and naval scholarships.[47]

*

With his large blue eyes and head of golden curls the little tsarevich was the most beautiful of babies. They named him Alexey after the second Romanov tsar, Alexey I (who ruled 1645–76), and father of Peter the Great, the name coming from the Greek meaning 'helper' or 'defender'. Russia had had enough Alexanders and Nicholases, said the tsar. Unlike his charismatic son, who had looked to the West for inspiration, Alexey I had been a pious tsar in the tradition of old Muscovite Russia – the kind of traditional monarch that Nicholas and Alexandra wished their son to be. An official announcement was soon published revoking the nomination of Grand Duke Mikhail as successor: 'From now on, in accordance with the Fundamental Laws of the Empire, the Imperial title of Heir Tsarevich, and all the rights pertaining to it, belong to Our Son Alexei.'[48] In celebration Nicholas took his three eldest daughters to a *Te Deum* at the chapel of the Lower Dacha, as hundreds of telegrams and letters of congratulation flooded into Peterhof. Dr Ott and Madame Günst were once more handsomely rewarded for their services; the doctor this time receiving a blue-enamel box by Fabergé set with rose-cut diamonds in addition to his handsome fee.[49]

Like his sisters Alexey had a Russian wet-nurse and it was Mariya Geringer's special duty to ensure that she was given plenty of good food. On one occasion she asked the nurse how her appetite was. 'What sort of appetite can I have,' she complained, 'when there is nothing salted or pickled?' The wet-nurse may have grumbled about the plain food on offer but 'this did not prevent her from doubling her weight, as she would eat everything on the table and leave not a scrap'. After Alexey was weaned, the nurse received a pension and numerous gifts; her child back in the village received presents too and at Christmas and Easter and her name day a grateful Alexandra would continue to remember her boy's wet-nurse with money and other gifts.[50]

On the occasion of Alexey's christening twelve days later, an enlarged cortège of carriages wound its way a fifth time to the imperial chapel at Peterhof. Mistress of the robes Mariya Golitsyna was once more entrusted with carrying the Romanov baby to the font on a golden cushion, but by now elderly, she feared she might drop the precious boy. As a precaution an improvised gold sling attached the cushion to her shoulder and she wore non-slip rubber-soled shoes. The baby's older sisters, nine-year-old Olga and seven-year-old Tatiana, were there in the procession – Olga as one of his godmothers – and clearly enjoying their first taste of formal public ceremonial. They looked especially beautiful, dressed in child-size versions of full Russian court dresses of blue satin with silver-thread embroidery and buttons and silver shoes. They also wore miniature versions of the order of St Catherine and blue velvet *kokoshniki* decorated with pearls and silver bows. The two proud sisters rose to the importance of the occasion: 'Olga blushed with pride when, holding a corner of Alexey's cushion, she walked with Maria Feodorovna to the font' and she and Tatiana 'allowed themselves to relax into a smile only when they passed a group of still smaller children, their two tiny sisters, and several little cousins, standing near a doorway and gazing open-mouthed as the procession passed'.[51]

Although still very young, Olga created a deep impression on one of her Romanov cousins that day. Sixteen-year-old Prince Ioann Konstantinovich – or Ioannchik as everyone called him – was besotted with her, as he told his mother:

I was so enraptured by her I can't even describe it. It was like a wildfire fanned by the wind. Her hair was waving, her eyes were sparkling, well, I can't even begin to describe it!! The problem is that I am too young for such thoughts and, moreover, that she is the Tsar's daughter and, God forbid, they might think that I am doing it for some ulterior motive.

Ioannchik would continue to nurse a deep attachment to Olga and the hope of marrying her (which had first entered his head, he said, in 1900) for several years to come.[52]

Baroness Buxhoeveden was impressed with the two older girls that day; they remained as 'solemn as judges', throughout the four-hour ceremony, during which several noticed that, as he was being anointed with holy oil, the little baby 'raised his hand and extended his fingers as though pronouncing a blessing'. Such inadvertent religious symbolism did not pass unnoticed by the Orthodox faithful: 'Everyone said that it was a very good omen, and that he would prove to be a father to his people.'[53] The birth of this one precious little boy provided a field day for soothsayers and omen seekers, although some were deeply malevolent. For even now, the worst kind of superstitious nonsense was being put about that the little tsarevich was in a fact a changeling – substituted by Nicholas and Alexandra for an unwanted fifth daughter who had been spirited away.[54]

A rather more balanced line was taken outside Russia, where Alexey's was the most talked-about royal birth in a century. Many were relieved for Alexandra's sake as much as for the tsar's; 'the Empress will acquire a prestige that will exalt her influence above that of the Dowager Empress. She is the mother of a man-child!' wrote one tongue-in-cheek American commentator, pointing up the increasingly difficult position Alexandra had been in – as a grand-daughter of Queen Victoria living in a 'semi-savage', Asiatic country where rampant superstition prevented any compassion being shown for her misfortune in repeatedly producing girls.[55] A former American ambassador to Russia was not alone in repeating the view that such was the bad feeling towards Alexandra up till that point that 'if the last had been a girl . . . there would possibly have been demand for the Tsar to take another wife in order to obtain an heir'.[56]

Some observers abroad objected to the sexual discrimination being exercised against the four Romanov daughters, denigrating the fact that they had merited only 101-gun salutes each, as opposed to 301 for a boy. The US journal *Broad Views* thought the tsar's four young daughters more than capable of 'guarantee[ing] the security of the succession':

> If the present Czar had reverted to the idea of Peter the Great, and had declared the Grand Duchess Olga heiress to the throne irrespective even of any future little brothers . . . the Russian people might have reflected that in a few years more, for Olga has now attained the advanced age of nine, the Czar would be supported by an heiress old enough to wield the scepter, if he himself should lose his life to the Nihilists. As it is, the birth of the infant who has already, regardless of humour, been made a Colonel of Hussars, will merely guarantee the evils of a long regency in that far from impossible event.[57]

Within the larger Romanov family not everyone was delighted by the new arrival. The American military attaché Thomas Bentley Mott remembered dining with Grand Duke Vladimir – Nicholas's eldest uncle – who would be next in line to the throne after the childless Mikhail, and after him, his sons Kirill, Boris and Andrey. On 30 July Mott had joined the grand duke for lunch after attending army manoeuvres. Upon arriving, Vladimir was handed a telegram and immediately disappeared. His guest was left waiting for an hour before the grand duke returned:

> We sat down in silence; and as our host did not speak, the rest of us could not do so. The changing of the plates and the constant presenting of a fresh cigarette to the Grand Duke by the tall Cossack who stood at other times immovable behind his chair, alone relieved the stillness.[58]

After lunch the grand duke once more absented himself. It was only later that Mott learned that the telegram that had cast such a gloom over their lunch had contained the news of the birth of Alexey.

Had he known then what Nicholas and Alexandra already knew, the grand duke might well have been less gloomy. It has generally been accepted that it was not until 8 September, nearly six weeks after Alexey was born, that the baby first experienced ominous bleeding from the navel. But bleeding had in fact occurred almost as soon as the umbilical cord was cut, and it had taken two days for the doctors to bring it under control. On 1 August, Nicholas wrote at length to Militza, on behalf of Alexandra, telling her that:

> Thank God the day has passed calmly. After the dressing was applied from 12 o'clock until 9.30 that evening there wasn't a drop of blood. The doctors hope it will stay that way. Korovin is staying overnight. Feodorov is going into town and coming back tomorrow . . . The little treasure is amazingly placid, and when they change the dressing he either sleeps or lies there and smiles. His parents are now feeling a little easier in their minds. Feodorov says that the approximate amount of blood loss in 48 hours was from 1/8th to 1/9th of the total quantity of blood.[59]

The bleeding was frightening. Little Alexey had seemed so robust – he had 'the air of a warrior knight' as Grand Duchess Xenia remarked when she had first seen him.[60] Militza had no doubt from the start. With their exclusive access to Nicholas and Alexandra at the time, she and Grand Duke Petr had driven over to the Lower Dacha the day Alexey was born to congratulate his parents, as their son Roman later recalled:

> When they returned in the evening to Znamenka, my father remembered that when he had bidden farewell, the Tsar had told him that even though Alexey was a big and healthy child, the doctors were somewhat troubled about the frequent splatters of blood in his swaddling clothes. When my mother heard this, she was shocked and insisted on the doctors being told about the cases of haemophilia that were occasionally passed down in the female line from the English Queen Victoria, who was the Tsaritsa's maternal grandmother. My father tried to calm her and assured her that the Tsar had been in the best of spirits when he had left. All the same, my father did indeed phone the palace to ask the Tsar what the doctors had to say about the blood splatters. When the Tsar answered that they hoped that the bleeding would soon stop, my mother took the receiver and asked if the doctors could explain the cause of the bleeding. When the Tsar could not give her a clear answer, she asked him with the calmest of voices she could manage: 'I beg you, ask

them if there is any sign of haemophilia', and she added that should that be the case, then the doctors of today would be able to take certain measures. The Tsar fell silent on the phone for a long time and then started to question my mother and ended by quietly repeating the word that had staggered him: haemophilia.[61]

Mariya Geringer later recalled how Alexandra had sent for her soon after Alexey was born. The bleeding, she told Mariya, had been triggered by the midwife Günst swaddling the baby too tightly. This was traditional Russian practice but the pressure of the tight binding over Alexey's navel had provoked a haemorrhage and had caused him to scream out in a 'frenzy' of pain. Weeping bitter tears, Alexandra had taken Mariya's hand: 'If only you knew how fervently I have prayed for God to protect my son from our inherited curse', she had told her, already only too aware that the blight of haemophilia had indeed descended on them.[62] Nicholas's first cousin, Maria Pavlovna, had no doubt that he and Alexandra had known almost immediately that Alexey 'carried in him the seeds of an incurable illness'. They hid their feelings from even their closest relatives, but from that moment, she recalled, 'the Empress's character underwent a change, and her health, physical as well as moral, altered'.[63]

For the remainder of that first month the couple were in a state of denial, hoping against hope, once the bleeding had stopped, that all would be well. And then almost six weeks later it had started again, confirming their very worst fears.[64] Dr Feodorov, whom Nicholas and Alexandra liked and trusted, had been on hand at all times and had drawn on the best possible medical advice in St Petersburg. But it was already clear that the medical men could do little. Nicholas and Alexandra's son's fate rested on a miracle: only God could protect him. But nobody in Russia must know the truth. The life-threatening condition of the little tsarevich – 'the hope of Russia' – would remain a closely guarded secret, even from their nearest relatives.[65] Nothing must undermine the security of the throne that Nicholas and Alexandra were absolutely determined to pass on, intact, to their son.

Alexandra Feodorovna, Empress of Russia, was only thirty-two but was already a physical wreck after ten physically and mentally draining years of pregnancy and childbirth. Her always precarious mental state was severely undermined by the discovery of Alexey's condition and she tormented herself that she of all people had unwittingly transmitted haemophilia to her much-loved and longed-for son.* Her already melancholic air henceforth became an inexplicably tragic one to those not privy to the truth. The whole focus of the family now dramatically shifted, to protecting Alexey against accident and injury – to literally keeping him alive within their own closely controlled domestic world. Nicholas and Alexandra therefore abandoned their newly refurbished apartments in the Winter Palace and ceased staying in town for the court season. Tsarskoe Selo and Peterhof would from now on be their refuge.

Alexey's four still very young but highly sensitive sisters – Olga, Tatiana, Maria and Anastasia – would bond ever more closely in response to the family's retreat and in support of their physically vulnerable mother. In the late summer of 1904, the world of the four Romanov grand duchesses began to shrink, at the very point when they were eager to rush out and explore it. What no one then, of course, knew was that as female children of the tsaritsa, one or all of the sisters might be carriers of that terrible defective gene – a hidden time bomb that had already begun to reverberate across the royal families of Europe. Alexandra's elder sister Irene – who like her was a carrier and who had married her first cousin, Prince Henry of Prussia – had already given birth to two haemophiliac sons. The youngest, four-year-old Heinrich, had died – 'of the terrible illness of the English family', as Xenia described it – just five months before Alexey was born. In Russia they called it the *bolezn gessenskikh* – 'the Hesse disease'; others called it 'the Curse of the Coburgs'.[66] But one thing was certain; in the early 1900s, the life expectancy of a haemophiliac child was only about thirteen years.[67]

---

* Even in the early twentieth century haemophilia was little understood and was thought to be caused by a weakness in the blood vessels. It was not until the 1930s that scientists concluded that the fatal defect lay in the lack of proteins in the blood platelets which prevented the blood clotting in those with the condition.

Chapter Five

THE BIG PAIR AND
THE LITTLE PAIR

By the beginning of 1905, and despite the arrival of the long-awaited tsarevich, Russia was in crisis, as war continued to rage with Japan. The Russian Imperial Army had not proved invincible in the East, as Maître Philippe had predicted, and was demoralized, weary and undersupplied. Press censorship had become even more rigorous as a result. All comments in foreign newspapers and magazines arriving in Russia that were in any way critical of the war – and, by association, the tsarist system – were heavily blacked out. A notable casualty was an article on the Russian succession in the *Illustrated London News* by journalist Charles Lowe. Published shortly after Alexey's birth it had been accompanied by a portrait of Alexandra, captioned 'The Mother of a Czar to Be', congratulating the Russians on 'this ray of sunshine amidst the heavy clouds of national misfortune', but adding provocatively that 'the advent of the Czarevitch has probably averted a revolution'. The Russian censor had been much exercised in how to deal with this inflammatory statement. It would have been considered sacrilegious to obliterate the tsaritsa's portrait on the page, so in the end the entire article surrounding it was blacked out when the magazine reached Russian readers.[1] Such draconian censorship was a futile gesture: on the discontented streets of St Petersburg industrial and political unrest continued to build. It seemed to Grand Duke Konstantin 'as if the dam has been broken'. Russia, he said, 'has been seized with a thirst for change . . . Revolution is banging on the door'.[2]

In a rare performance of public ceremonial Nicholas attended the ritual of the Blessing of the Waters, traditionally marking the end of the Christmas festival, held on 6 January in the Orthodox calendar. The key moment came when he descended the Jordan Staircase of the Winter Palace to the edge of the frozen River Neva, to witness the Metropolitan of St Petersburg dip the gold cross into the water three times through a hole in the ice in commemoration of the baptism of Christ. After this a flagon of the sacred water was presented to the tsar to cross himself with. However, during the traditional gun salute that followed, three of the charges fired from the battery on the opposite bank of the Neva – whether by accident or design – proved to be lives not blanks. One of them smashed into the windows of the Winter Palace's Nicholas Hall which was crowded with guests, including the dowager, Maria Feodorovna, and showered grapeshot and glass over them as well as the temporary wooden chapel on the ice in which Nicholas and other dignataries were gathered. Nicholas was unhurt, and 'never moved a muscle except to make the Sign of the Cross', as one eyewitness recalled, although his 'quiet, resigned smile' seemed 'almost unearthly'.[3] A later investigation suggested it had been a genuine error – shotted cartridges having been left in the breech of the cannon after target practice. The fatalistic Nicholas was, however, convinced that the live shells had been intended for him.[4] For a nation reading catastrophe into every unfortunate incident in this ill-fated reign it was further proof that the autocracy was doomed.

Three days later, tragedy on a grand scale unfolded across St Petersburg, which had been gripped for weeks by bitter industrial unrest, exacerbated by mounting discontent with the war with Japan. Hundreds were left dead and wounded when Cossack troops fired on a rally of unarmed workers and their families who had marched to the Winter Palace to present a petition to Nicholas begging for political and industrial reform. The advent of Bloody Sunday, as it became known, brought about a radical shift in the traditional popular perception of the tsar as the protective 'little father' and a volatile nation descended into extreme violence as the year went on. In February the Russian army was routed at Mukden in Manchuria, and in mid-May the Baltic Fleet was decimated at

Tsushima Strait. By the time peace was negotiated with Japan in August, Nicholas's Minister of the Interior, Petr Stolypin, had instigated a round of courts martial and summary executions to counter the escalating violence.

Widespread unrest went hand in hand with a dramatic escalation in the assassination of prominent government figures. Two of Stolypin's predecessors in succession had been assassinated: Dmitri Sipyagin in 1902, and Vyacheslav von Plehve – the victim of a bomb attack on the streets of St Petersburg – two weeks before Alexey was born. The Romanov family had long been living in the shadow of political terrorism and in February 1905 the revolutionaries scored their most chilling success yet, when Ella's husband, the much-hated Grand Duke Sergey, was blown to pieces in a bomb attack in Moscow. Such was the perceived danger to the imperial family that Nicholas and Alexandra were not allowed to attend his funeral. Other attacks followed thick and fast: in May the head of the Kiev section of the Okhrana, Alexander Spiridovich, was shot and seriously wounded. In August 1906 General Vonlyarlyarsky, the Russian military governor of Warsaw, was assassinated, as too was General Min, commander of the Life Guards regiment, who was gunned down by a female revolutionary at Peterhof Railway Station in front of his wife.[5]

Such were the dangers now threatening Nicholas that it 'led to the organization of a curiously complicated system of spying and tattling; spies were set to watch spies; the air was filled with whisperings, cross-currents of fear and mistrust', as the overstretched tsarist police struggled to cope.[6] Although the imperial family never walked out informally in crowded places in St Petersburg, every eventuality had to be covered – such as those occasions when they went out for drives in a landau or troika, or attended church services or public ceremonies where they might be surrounded by crowds. This elaborate security network was bolstered by a ban on any press announcements about their day-to-day appointments or any journeys they might be making.[7] Nothing escaped the rigorous inspection of the Press Censor's Department. As a result, the Russian people, as one London paper observed, had absolutely no sense of the 'sweet family life' of their tsar and tsaritsa; 'the papers dare not print it

– it is spoken about rarely, if at all, and always with bated breath.'
A few anodyne bulletins were released for public consumption, along
with official photographs and postcards available for sale, but that
was the sum of it. The Russian imperial family was becoming famous
for its 'dazzling inaccessibility'.[8]

Four different security networks now guarded the Romanovs'
every move: the Tsar's Escort was backed up by a special police force
at Tsarskoe Selo that watched the surrounding streets and vetted all
visitors to the palace. A specially designated railway battalion monitored the line from St Petersburg out to Tsarskoe Selo and Peterhof.
All other railway lines were closely guarded by cordons of troops
positioned along both embankments of any route taken by the imperial train and guards on board gave added protection to the family.[9]
Even here, though, Alexandra would insist that the blinds be drawn
and she refused to allow the children – or even Nicky – to go to
the windows to wave at passers-by. On one such journey, Alexander
Mosolov, head of the Court Chancellery, recalled how 'the children
pressed their faces against the slits on either side between curtain
and window frame', hungry for sight of the world beyond.[10]

The assassination of General Min so close to home – for the
imperial family had been in residence at the Lower Dacha at Peterhof
at the time – was unnerving for Nicholas, but far more so for
Alexandra, who lived in constant fear for his life and the safety of
her children.[11] The growing isolation of the imperial family was
even felt abroad; a major article in the *Washington Post* at the end
of May, headed 'Children Without a Smile', featured the latest set
of official photographs, the paper remarking on the sweetness of
the Romanov sisters' expressions, but concluding that 'melancholy
has marked them for her own', living as the family now did as 'almost
prisoners in their palaces, surrounded by servants and guards whose
fidelity, in the light of past events, must always be distrusted'.[12]

Under threat of further political upheaval, in the autumn of 1905
Nicholas reluctantly agreed to the creation of a legislative assembly
– the State Duma – that was inaugurated in April 1906. Alexandra
abhorred his decision, for she resented any political concessions that
might endanger the safe transition of the throne to their heir Alexey,
and predictably, the Duma was short-lived. Deeply conservative and

fearful of change, Nicholas lost his nerve and prorogued it two months later, having come to the conclusion that it was a hotbed of political conflict. Violence inevitably escalated in response. On the afternoon of 12 August 1906 Prime Minister Stolypin narrowly escaped death when a massive bomb attack on his wooden summer dacha in St Petersburg, which was full of visitors at the time, practically demolished the building and killed thirty people, leaving another thirty-two wounded. Stolypin himself was miraculously unharmed, but as they dug him out of the wreckage he was heard to repeat over and over again, 'My poor children, my poor children.'[13] Two of them, his son Arkady and one of his daughters, Natalya, who had both been on the balcony at the time, had been hurled onto the road below by the explosion. Arkady, who was three years old, broke his hip, and fifteen-year-old Natalya was very seriously injured. She lay in hospital in a critical state for weeks. The doctors had expected her to die or face the amputation of both of her badly broken legs, when, on 16 October, a note came from Nicholas telling Stolypin and his wife that a man of God – 'a peasant from the government of Tobolsk' – wished to come and bless Natalya with an icon and pray for her. Nicholas and Alexandra had met the man recently and he had made 'such a distinctly powerful impression' on them that Nicholas urged Stolypin to let him visit the children in hospital.[14] 'When he came, the man did not touch the child, just stood at the foot of the bed holding up an icon of the miracle worker, St Simeon of Verkhotur'e, and prayed. On leaving, he said "Don't worry, everything will be all right".' Natalya's condition improved soon after and she eventually recovered, though she was left with a permanent limp as the result of having one heel blown off.[15]

The mysterious healer was a *strannik* – a semi-literate, thirty-seven-year-old lay pilgrim – named Grigory Rasputin, who had been gaining a reputation in St Petersburg as a mystic and healer since his arrival there during Lent 1903.[16] Nicholas and Alexandra had already met him, briefly, in November 1905, at Stana's home, Sergievka, near Peterhof and saw him there again in July 1906. With Philippe now dead, the Montenegrin sisters had recently adopted this new mystic and healer and, being privy to the truth of Alexey's incurable condition, they were concertedly steering Rasputin in the highly vulnerable couple's direction. On the evening of 13 October 1906 Rasputin had come to see the imperial family at the Lower Dacha, at his own request, to give them a wooden painted icon of St Simeon, one of the most celebrated Russian saints from Siberia, whom he particularly revered. While he was there he was allowed the privilege of meeting the children and 'gave them blessed bread and holy images, and spoke a few words to them'.[17] But this is as far as it went and Rasputin was not invited back. For now, Nicholas and Alexandra remained impressed, and curious – but cautious.

The shock of the injuries to Stolypin's children was, however, profound for both of them; particularly as Stolypin and his wife had finally had a son after five daughters in succession. Alexandra was, at all times, inordinately protective of Alexey; she seemed to 'press the little boy to her with the convulsive movement of a mother who always seems in fear of her child's life'.[18] The harrowing events of 1905–6 coupled with the strain of Alexey's haemophilia had already taken a heavy toll on her. When her sisters Irene and Victoria visited that summer they thought she had aged and were alarmed by how frequently incapacitated she was by her sciatica. She was complaining too of shortness of breath and pain in her heart, convinced that it was 'enlarged'. Victoria went back home greatly saddened by what she had seen; it was 'only in the faces of the four winsome little girls' that she had seen any real happiness at Tsarskoe Selo.[19]

The total clampdown on news about the Russian imperial family was in stark contrast to the daily court circulars issued in Britain on every royal carriage ride, ribbon-cutting and unveiling, however trivial. In an attempt to lift the veil of secrecy surrounding the imperial family, St Petersburg was awash with foreign correspondents chasing stories about the 'home life' of the tsar. The 'Four Little Russian Princesses' were the object of endless curiosity across the women's and girls' magazines of Europe and America.[20] Occasionally – before Nicholas and Alexandra quit the Winter Palace in 1905 – the girls had sometimes been seen out in the streets of St Petersburg in a landau with their nannies, often behaving in an unruly fashion, climbing on the seats, standing up and bowing to passers-by and eagerly taking in everything around them. An odd glimpse could still also be caught of them, from beyond the perimeter fence of the Alexander Palace, riding their ponies or bicycles in the park, or running around picking flowers. They seemed full of energy and vivacity and the newspapers hungered for more.[21]

One of the first to provide an inside view was Margaretta Eagar, who had, quite suddenly, been 'let go' from her post on 29 September 1904 not long after the birth of Alexey. No explanation was given, either by Eagar in her later memoir and articles, or in Nicholas's brief diary entry alluding to her departure. But it is possible that the forthright Margaretta had become too combative for Nicholas and Alexandra's tastes – much like Mrs Inman before her – when she had insisted on her right, as nanny, to discipline the children. Having spoken to Alexandra out of turn once on this matter, insisting that she was 'charged by Your Majesty with the education of the little princesses', the tsaritsa had been obliged to remind Margaretta that she was talking to the Empress of Russia.[22] Margaretta had always been highly opinionated and talkative; perhaps the imperial couple had come to see her as a loose cannon at a time when they were anxious to keep Alexey's condition secret.

Nevertheless, it had clearly been difficult for Alexandra to let Margaretta Eagar go, for the nanny had performed her role with considerable skill and dedication and the girls all adored her, but she decided from now on to take charge of the girls' upbringing herself and not hire any more English nannies. This ran entirely counter to Russian tradition, or for that matter the normal way of things among most aristocratic parents at that time, who handed over the everyday care of their children to a retinue of servants. Alexandra did of course have the service of Russian nursemaids to help with the girls' day-to-day care, two of the most loyal and long-serving being Mariya Vishnyakova, who would increasingly take care of Alexey, and Alexandra – 'Shura' – Tegleva.

As for the girls' education, Alexandra had already started tutoring them herself in English and French and basic spelling, having taught them needlework the moment they were able to hold a needle. She enlisted her own *lectrice* Trina Schneider to teach the older two in other general subjects. Trina also acted as a chaperone, much as Margaretta Eagar had done, when the girls went out for walks or drives. Meanwhile male tutors for other subjects were sought out.[23]

One of the first to be recruited was Petr Vasilevich Petrov – a teacher and former army officer who had been a senior government administrator responsible for military schools and who began teaching Olga and Tatiana Russian language and literature in 1903. Although approaching retirement Petrov was devoted to his charges, and they responded to his genial manner with great affection, referring to him by his initials, PVP.[24] But he found them a handful; the girls at times could be wild and out of control. 'They used to play with him, shouting, laughing, pushing him, and generally hauling him about without mercy', recalled Baroness Buxhoeveden. Olga and Tatiana could be 'meek as mice' when studying but once their teacher had departed the schoolroom, 'a wild scramble' often followed during which Olga would jump on the sofa and race along the row of neatly positioned chairs against the wall, only for the younger two to come rushing in from the nursery to join in until the next teacher saw them once more demurely seated in their places.

The most important new arrival in the schoolroom was undoubtedly the twenty-six-year-old Swiss tutor Pierre Gilliard, so dapper with his stiff wing collars, twirled moustache and goatee beard. He began teaching Olga and Tatiana French at Peterhof in September 1905 while still in the employ of Stana, Duchess of Leuchtenberg, and her husband. Gilliard travelled over from their nearby dacha at Sergievka several days a week, running the gauntlet of endless security checks in the process. He was unnerved to have the tsaritsa sit in on his lessons until she was satisfied with their quality; thereafter a lady-in-waiting would attend as an informal chaperone. Gilliard's first impression of his charges was that Olga was 'spirited like a runaway horse and very intelligent' and Tatiana, in comparison, 'calm and fairly lazy'.[25] He liked their frankness and the fact that they 'didn't try to hide their faults', and better still he found the simplicity of the tsar's family a refreshing contrast to his stultifying, 'desiccated' life with the Leuchtenbergs, with all its tensions and intrigues (the couple was in the throes of a scandalous separation and divorce).[26]

*

After the summer sojourn at Peterhof, life at Tsarskoe Selo in the autumn returned to its set routine. Nicholas was up long before his wife in the mornings, her ill health often preventing her from getting up till after 9. The children meanwhile ate breakfast in the upstairs nursery and had the plain food so beloved of English families – porridge, bread and butter, milk and honey. Nicholas occasionally joined them before heading off to his study for meetings with ministers. Once they reached 8–10 years old the girls were considered well behaved enough to join their parents at the adult table downstairs. Lunch, when guests or members of the entourage often joined them, was always simple. With the children back at their lessons Alexandra would spend the afternoons at her needlework, or painting and writing letters till afternoon tea at around five in the mauve boudoir, where she liked to have Nicky to herself if she could and the children only came by invitation, in their best frocks – though they could always come to her at any time if there was a particular reason. Family supper, when the children were older, was usually very modest, after which the evenings were spent with more sewing, board and card games till bedtime, with Nicholas often reading aloud to them all.[27] No one ever saw the girls idle or bored for Alexandra ensured that they were never at a loss for something to do. When she had to be apart from them on official duties with Nicholas, she sent them little admonitory notes: 'Be sure to be very good and remember, elbows off the table, sit straight and eat your meat nicely.'[28] She expected notes back from them – however brief. A typical response to 'Maman' from Tatiana in 1905 in her best and neatest handwriting went as follows:

> J'aime maman, qui promet et qui donne
> Tant de baisers à son enfant,
> E si doucement lui pardonne
> Toutes les fois qu'il est méchant.*[29]

The most notable aspect of the tsar's home life when details of it made their way into the western press was how simple and

---

* 'I love mama, who promises and gives so many kisses to her child, and so gently forgives her every time she is naughty.' Tatiana has clearly copied this from somewhere else as, grammatically if referring to herself, it should be 'qu'elle est méchante'.

uneventful it was. People seemed surprised that the four sisters enjoyed 'only the healthy pleasures of ordinary children'.[30] Reporters were impressed by the Englishness of their upbringing, with lessons interspersed with lots of fresh air and exercise, all planned in advance to a fixed schedule. During the morning break between lessons at around eleven, Alexandra would often walk or drive out in the park with the children and one of her ladies – usually her now honorary lady-in-waiting Baroness Buxhoeveden, whom they all called Iza, or Trina Schneider. In winter she and the children would often go out in a large four-seater sledge. At such times little Anastasia, already an irrepressible clown, would 'slip down under the thick bear-rug . . . and sit, clucking like a hen or barking like a dog', imitating Aera, Alexandra's nasty little dog that was noted for biting people's ankles. Sometimes the girls would sing as the sledge rolled along, 'the Empress giving the key-note' to which from under the bear rug Anastasia would offer up an accompanying 'boom, boom, boom', asserting 'I'm a piano.'[31]

The Romanov girls were seldom ostentatiously dressed and even on the coldest days they were never 'muffled up in the prevailing fashion', so the *Daily Mirror* told its readers, 'as the Tsarina has quite British ideas on the subject of hygiene'.[32] With Anastasia now four, Alexandra began dressing the girls in their own informal 'uniform' of matching colours, as two identifiable couples – the 'Big Pair' and the 'Little Pair' as she called them – a shorthand which, however affectionate the intention, marked the beginning of a family habit of referring to the girls collectively rather than as individuals. The big pair and the little pair each shared a room, where they slept on simple, narrow nickel campbeds (of the portable kind used by the army; a vestige of Nicholas's own Spartan childhood). They took cold baths in the morning and were allowed warm ones in the evening. The older girls dressed themselves and Alexandra expected them to make their own beds and tidy their rooms. The streak of Lutheran puritanism in her ensured that their clothes and shoes were handed down from one to the next. 'The toy cupboards of the imperial nurseries do not contain the host of expensive playthings deemed indispensable in so many middle-class households', observed the *Daily Mail*, indeed 'the splendid dolls sent by Queen Victoria to her great-great-grandchildren are only brought out on high days and holidays.'[33]

Most notable to foreign observers was the degree of access that the children had to their mother and father. Despite his heavy workload Nicholas, from the first, had tried to be back from his study in the evening to see the latest baby having its bath and he always found time to play with or read to them in the evenings. Both parents set their children high moral standards; Alexandra was inspired by the popular American Presbyterian minister, James Russell Miller, whose homiletic pamphlets such as *Secrets of Happy Home Life* (1894) and *The Wedded Life* (1886) sold in their millions. She noted down many quotations from Miller on the joys of married life, on children as 'God's ideal of completeness', and on parental responsibility for the formation of their characters within a Christian and loving home. 'May God help us to give them a good and sound education and make them above all brave little Christian soldiers fighting for our saviour', she told her old friend Bishop Boyd Carpenter in 1902.[34]

In 1905, approaching her tenth birthday, Olga already had an inherent awareness of her position as the eldest and loved giving a military salute to soldiers standing on guard as she passed by. Until Alexey was born people had often greeted her as their 'little empress' and Alexandra underlined this by demanding that her ladies kiss Olga's hand rather than offer more impulsive expressions of affection. Although she could be boisterous with her sisters, Olga already had a serious side. There was an earnestness and integrity about her that would have served her well, had it come to it, as a future tsaritsa. From the start Alexandra invested a level of responsibility in Olga, constantly reminding her of this in little notes: 'Mama kisses her girly tenderly and prays that God may help her to be *always* a good loving Christian child. Show kindness to all, be gentle and loving, then all will love you', she wrote in 1905.[35]

It was clear to Margaretta Eagar that from a very young age Olga had inherited her mother's and her grandmother Alice's altruistic spirit. She was highly sensitive to the plight of others less fortunate than herself; driving in St Petersburg one day she had seen a policeman arrest a woman for being drunk and disorderly and had begged Margaretta that she be let off; the sight of poor peasants falling on their knees by the roadside in Poland as they passed in their carriage also unsettled her and she wanted Margaretta to 'tell them not to do it'.[36] Not long after Christmas one year when they were out driving, she had seen a little girl crying in the road. '"Look," she exclaimed, in great excitement; "Santa Claus could not have known where she lived"; and she had immediately thrown the doll she had with her out of the carriage, shouting "Don't cry, little girl; here's a doll for you."'[37]

Olga was curious and full of questions. Once when a nursemaid reprimanded her for her grumpiness, saying that she had 'got out of bed on the wrong foot', the following morning Olga had pertly asked which was 'the right foot to get out with' so that the 'bad foot won't be able to make me naughty to-day'.[38] Cranky, scornful and difficult she certainly could be, especially during puberty, and her flashes of anger revealed a dark side that she sometimes found difficult to control, but Olga also was a dreamer. During a game of I-spy with the children Alexandra had noticed that 'Olga always thinks of the sun, clouds, sky, rain or something belonging to the heavens, explaining to me that it makes her so happy to think of that'.[39] In 1903 at the age of eight she made her first confession, and soon after her cousin's tragic death that same year developed a fascination with heaven and the afterlife. 'Cousin Ella knows, she is in heaven sitting down and talking to God, and He is telling her how He did it and why', she insisted to Margaretta Eagar when once discussing the plight of a blind woman.[40]

Tatiana at eight years old was pale-skinned, slender and with darker, auburn hair, and eyes rather greyer than the sea-blue of her sisters. She was already arrestingly beautiful, 'the living replica of her beautiful mother', with a naturally imperious look enhanced by her fine bones and tilted-up eyes.[41] On the surface she seemed an extraordinarily self-possessed young girl, but she was in fact emotionally cautious and reserved, like her mother. She was never hostage to her temperament as Olga sometimes could be and unlike Olga – who had a volatile relationship with their mother as she grew older – Tatiana was unquestioningly devoted; it was she in whom Alexandra always confided. She was the most polite and deferential at table with adults and proved to be a natural-born organizer with a methodical mind and a down-to-earth manner that her sisters could not match. No wonder her sisters called her 'the governess'. Whereas Olga was musical and played the piano beautifully, Tatiana was a gifted needlewoman like her mother. She too was deeply altruistic and sensitive to what others did for her. On once discovering that her nursemaid and Miss Eagar were paid for their services because they had no money of their own and needed to earn a living, she came to Eagar's bed the next morning and got in and cuddled her, saying 'Anyway, you are not paid for this.'[42]

The third sister, Maria, was a shy child who suffered later from being piggy in the middle between her two older sisters and her younger siblings. Her mother may have coupled her with Anastasia as the 'little pair' but as time went on Maria occasionally found herself adrift from Anastasia and Alexey – the more natural little pair – and she sometimes felt that she did not get the love and attention she craved. Her strong physique made her seem rather ungainly and she had a reputation for clumsiness and boisterousness. Yet for many who knew the family, Maria was by far the prettiest, with her peaches-and-cream complexion, her rich brown hair and an earthy Russian quality not possessed by any of the other children; everyone remarked on her eyes that shone 'like lanterns' and her warm smile.[43] She was not especially bright but had a real gift for painting and drawing. Mashka, as her sisters often called her, was the least affected by any sense of her station. She 'would shake hands with any palace attendant or servant, or exchange kisses with chambermaids or peasant women whom she happened to meet. If a servant dropped something, she would hurry to help her pick it up.'[44] Once when watching a regiment march past below her window at the Winter Palace she exclaimed, 'Oh! I love these dear soldiers; I should like to kiss them all!' Of all the sisters she was the most open-hearted and sincere and she was always extremely deferential towards her parents. Margaretta Eagar felt that she was Nicholas's favourite and that he was touched by her natural affection. When she once sheepishly admitted to stealing a forbidden biscuit from a plate at teatime he was relieved for he had been 'always afraid of the wings growing'. It had made him 'glad to see she is only a human child'.[45]

Having such a compliant personality, it was perhaps inevitable that Maria would be completely in thrall to the dominating personality of her younger sister Anastasia, for the youngest Romanov daughter was a force of nature to whose presence it was impossible to remain indifferent. Even at four years old she was 'a very sturdy little monkey, and afraid of nothing'.[46] Of all the children, Nastasya or Nastya as they called her, was the least Russian in looks. She had dark blonde hair like Olga and her father's blue eyes but her features were very much like those of her mother's Hesse family. She was not shy like her sisters either, in fact was extremely forthright, even with adults. She may have been the youngest of the four but was always the one who commanded the most attention. She had the great gift of humour and 'knew how to straighten out wrinkles on anybody's brow'.[47] One day, shortly after Alexey was born, Margaretta caught Anastasia eating peas with her fingers: 'I reproved her, saying seriously, "Even the new baby does not eat peas with his fingers." She looked up and said, "'es him does – him eats them with him's foots too!"'[48] Anastasia balked at doing anything she was told; if ordered not to climb on things she did precisely that. When told not to eat apples gathered in the orchard to be baked for nursery supper she deliberately gorged herself and when reprimanded was unrepentant: 'You don't know how good that apple was that I had in the garden', she told Margaretta teasingly. It took a total ban from the orchard for a week before Anastasia finally promised she would not eat any more.[49]

Everything with Anastasia was a battle of wills. She was an impossible pupil; distracted, inattentive, always eager to be doing anything other than sit still, yet despite not being academically bright she had an instinctive gift for dealing with people. When punished for bad behaviour she always took it on the chin: 'she could sit down and count the cost of any action she wished to perform, and take the punishment "like a soldier"', as Margaretta recalled.[50] But this never stopped her from being the major instigator of naughtiness, and she got away with far more than her sisters. At times, as she got bigger, she could be rough and even spiteful when playing with other children, scratching and pulling hair, leading to complaints from cousins when they visited that she was 'nasty to the point of being evil' when things didn't go her own way.[51]

The anodyne public image of four sweet little girls in white embroidered cambric with blue bows in their hair thus gave little or no indication of the four very different personalities developing behind the closed doors of the Alexander Palace. By 1906 public perception of the Romanov sisters was being set in stone by the many official photographs of them that were circulated for mass consumption. But it remained one that conveyed a superficial, saccharine image of them right up to the war years.[52]

Chapter Six

THE *SHTANDART*

❧

Throughout the disturbances of 1905 the Romanov family had had no choice but to remain at Peterhof, shut away as virtual prisoners. The head of the tsar's secret personal bodyguard, General Spiridovich (having recovered from the recent terrorist attack on him), was one of the few people in the imperial entourage with close access to the family.[1] He took particular charge of security arrangements in the summer of 1906 when, with even Peterhof considered by him to be unsafe, the family boarded their yacht the *Shtandart* and headed off on holiday. For three weeks, they cruised the granite skerries in the Virolahti region off the coast of southern Finland between Kronstadt and Helsinki, stopping off at favourite spots such as Björkö, Langinkoski, Pitkäpaasi and the Pukkio islands. The security police made a thorough search for undesirables in the area ahead of the *Shtandart*'s arrival and the yacht's moorings were constantly changed as an additional security measure. But such was official neurosis about the threat of attack that the yacht was escorted by a squadron of eight ships of the imperial fleet – including torpedo boats and courier vessels – which stopped any other boats from coming too close.[2] On board the yacht there were no security guards, the imperial family trusting to the intense loyalty of the officers and crew; 'we form a united family', Alexandra remarked.[3]

The children loved the *Shtandart* and came to know many of the 275 sailors and cabin staff who crewed it, remembering all their names; they felt safe on board and she soon became a home from home. At 420 feet (128 m) long she was the biggest and fastest of all the imperial yachts and enjoyed the best modern amenities of electric lighting, steam heating and hot and cold running water. Her luxurious formal staterooms featured chandeliers and mahogany wall panelling; the private chapel was complete with its own iconostasis and the dining room could seat seventy-two at dinner. The family rooms were comfortable but quite modest, echoing the ubiquitous homely English style of the Lower Dacha and the Alexander Palace, although boxes of fresh-cut flowers from Tsarskoe Selo were sent out regularly by tender, along with Nicholas's dispatch boxes, to feed Alexandra's one abiding indulgence.

At first the girls shared small cramped cabins on the lower deck with their maids. Their parents considered this arrangement more than adequate while the girls were young, but after 1912, they were given their own bigger cabins up on the imperial deck, though even these did not compare with the spacious suite set aside for Alexey.[4] Small or not the girls loved their little cabins but it was up on the sundeck that they felt liberated and where, kitted out in their navy blue sailor suits (white when the weather was warm), straw boaters and button boots, they could talk to the officers, play deck games and rollerskate on the smooth wooden surface. Alexandra would be near, sitting sewing in a comfortable wicker chair or resting on a couch under a canvas awning, always watching over them. Whenever the family sailed, each of the Romanov children was appointed its own personal bodyguard or *dyadka* ('uncle') from among the crew to take care of the child's safety at sea. That summer of 1906 the children had been rather shy of the *Shtandart* crew at first sight, but they soon warmed to their *dyadki*, who would sit for hours regaling them with seafaring stories and telling them about their homes and their families. Andrey Derevenko was assigned to the special care of Alexey, who now he was walking had to be extremely closely watched at all times, for fear that he would fall or knock himself and cause haemorrhaging. The girls meanwhile attached themselves to certain of the officers; they held their hands when they went ashore and would sit alongside them in the rowing boats helping with the oars. Most mornings they would be up and on the deck at 8 a.m. to see the crew gather for the formal raising of the flag to the sound of the ship's band playing the Nikolaevsky March.

For their part the crew, who relished the prestige of serving in the *Shtandart*, loved the four sisters, and found them enchanting, as Nikolay Vasilievich Sablin recalled later in his memoirs. Such was the informality on board that the sailors addressed the sisters by name and patronymic rather than by title, and could not do enough for them. From out of these first innocent, tentative acquaintances developed deep friendships; on that first trip in 1906 Olga attached herself to Nikolay Sablin and Tatiana to his namesake (no relation) Nikolay Vasilievich Sablin. Nikolay Vadbolsky was Maria's favourite, while little Anastasia took a shine, surprisingly, to a rather taciturn navigator called Alexey Saltanov. She gave him and everyone else the run-around, including her sailor *dyadka* Babushkin, rushing around the yacht from dawn to dusk, climbing up to the bridge when no one was looking, always dishevelled and difficult to control, only to be finally carried off kicking and screaming to bed at the end of the day. Her phlegmatic sister Maria had a rather more relaxed approach to life on board. As Sablin remembered, she 'liked to sit a little, have a read and eat sweet biscuits', getting ever plumper in the process, no doubt explaining her sisters' choice of nickname – 'fat little bow-wow'.[5]

Alexandra was a quite different woman in the *Shtandart* – happier and more relaxed than anywhere else. She now had the companionship of a new-found friend, Anna Vyrubova, who had arrived at court in February 1905. Although she was never formally made a lady-in-waiting, Anna quickly filled the gap left by Alexandra's favourite, Princess Sonya Orbeliani, who had been with her since 1898 but who was now suffering from a chronic wasting disease and was no longer able to serve.[6] Soon Anna was the tsaritsa's indispensable confidante and an almost permanent fixture in her daily life. God had sent her a friend, Alexandra said, and friends as trustworthy as Anna were hard to find in the closed-off world that she inhabited.

Small, dumpy and unprepossessing, with a short neck and an ample bosom, Anna Vyrubova had a credulous manner and was 'so childish-looking in fact that she seemed only fit for boarding school'.[7] It was precisely this unworldliness and her malleability that appealed to Alexandra: Anna was too simple-minded for intrigues and was thus no threat, indeed Alexandra took pity on her. Her uncharacteristic intimacy with the twenty-year-old ingénue provoked considerable resentment and jealousy among the other long-serving ladies of the imperial household – notably the displaced Orbeliani and Madeleine Zanotti. But on board the *Shtandart* Alexandra and Anna were inseparable. They would often sing duets and sit playing four-handed pieces at the piano together. The docile and adoring Anna hung on Alexandra's every word and within a year the tsaritsa had, in motherly fashion, helpfully orchestrated her marriage.

The simple but idyllic Finnish sailing holidays that became a regular feature of Romanov family life until the outbreak of war in 1914 were for the four sisters the best and happiest of times; for unlike any on dry land, these voyages provided a degree of special intimacy with their parents, and in particular more time in the company of the father they all worshipped. 'To be at sea with their father – that was what constituted their happiness', recalled the tsar's aide-de-camp Count Grabbe.[8] There was nothing of the usual stultifying Victorian condescension in Nicholas's attitude to his children, and they in turn were content just to be in his company, enjoying the simplest of pleasures. On board the *Shtandart* the Romanovs could act out the kind of idealized, untrammelled family life that they craved but which they could never enjoy on shore.

Sailing leisurely in the still golden autumn sunshine along the Finnish coast, out past the chain of small, wooded islands thick with fir, spruce and birch trees, and uninhabited bar a few fishermen's huts, the family could stop off at will. The children delighted in going onshore in the launch with their nurses and *dyadki* to play ball games or tag, have picnics or go mushroom- and berry-picking. They often went out rowing with their father and many of their expeditions were captured in numerous photographs taken by General Spiridovich, who was always at hand, casting an eagle eye over their safety. Nicholas was never much of a huntsman and didn't like fishing. But he did love long, vigorous walks and few in the entourage could keep up with him. Even on holiday he still had to give a great deal of time to his dispatch boxes, but when he did have time to himself he sometimes went ashore to play tennis on some local landowner's court, or went off alone in his *baidarka* – a type of kayak – in the still waters as dusk fell, with an escort of officers following in a rowing boat at a discreet distance. At other times he would go on deck to check the weather, discuss navigation with the flag captain and inspect the ship's company, or simply sit with Alexandra, cigarette in hand, reading a book or playing dominoes with his officers.

Day after tranquil day passed, the air clean and clear and the September sun low in the sky, but soon the nights were gathering in and the first frosts descending. On 21 September 1906 the family enjoyed their last day of 'wonderful free-and-easy life', as Nicholas ruefully described it.[9] He loved Virolahti more than anywhere and would have liked to build a summer retreat there or buy one of the small islands. After the yacht docked at Kronstadt and the time came to leave and go ashore the girls clung to each other weeping at having to say goodbye to their special 'family' on board. Before they left, as on every trip they made in the *Shtandart*, the family gave generous gifts to all the crew.

*

By November 1906 the family was once more ensconced at the Alexander Palace and, as always, the girls loved being out in the park. They liked to skate on the frozen ponds and cross over the ice to the little house built in 1830 for the children of Nicholas I in the middle of the Children's Island, where they could enter their own fantasy play world.[10] But their favourite winter pursuit, enjoyed from the moment they were big enough to sit on their father's knee, was sledging down ice hills specially made for them. That particular winter, they had the pleasure of a newly constructed 'American hill' – a 200-foot-long (61-m-long) artificial toboggan run. A journalist from the *Washington Post* was fortunate to catch sight of them on it when reporting on security arrangements at Tsarskoe Selo. A group of red-coated officials 'covered with so many medals they overlapped' solemnly inspected the construction, followed by the girls' nannies who tested the run, after which the three older girls, wearing thick bearskin coats, 'appeared in such a tremendous hurry that they nearly upset the officials . . . and screamed so loudly in Russian that their governesses reprimanded them'. They then took their seats 'without regard to precedence', and 'while the officials' attention was momentarily distracted, they gave the toboggan a push and whizzed down the hill without any attendants. The governess screamed with horror, the little grand duchesses with delight. They had evidently played the trick before.' Thereafter the officials insisted on keeping hold of the toboggan much to the disgust of the girls, who kept trying to slide down unguarded. 'The tenth journey was signalized by the Grand Duchess Marya flopping down on the ice brink of the chute and attempting the feat known to Coney Islanders as "bumps".'[11]

The long dark days were further enlivened that winter by regular visits from their Aunt Olga, Nicholas's younger sister. Every Saturday she would take the train out to Tsarskoe Selo from her home in St Petersburg. 'I think I can say that they were awfully pleased when I visited them and brought some change into their daily lives', she later remarked. 'The first thing I did was to run upstairs to the nursery where I generally found Olga and Tatiana finishing their last lesson before lunch . . . If I arrived before the professors had finished the morning's work, they would be just as delighted to be interrupted as I had once been.'[12] At 1 o'clock they would 'rush down the staircase leading from the nursery to their mother's room', after which they would all have lunch, and then sit and chat and sew in the mauve boudoir. A walk in the Alexander Park would follow; after changing out of their coats and boots Olga and the girls would often indulge in a spate of high jinks on the stairs. The light would be turned off as they descended and 'someone would lie down on one of the steps and when I trod on her she would grab me by the ankle and tickle me or think of other tricks. There was much laughter and screaming as we all rolled down to the bottom of the stairs in a heap – knocking our heads against the bannister on the way.'[13]

Over the years the girls would become closer to Aunt Olga than any of their other female relatives; she was like an older sister and frequently filled the breach when their mother was ill, accompanying them to public functions. 'Someone had to be there to ensure that the children behaved properly, stood up when necessary and greeted people as they should – and anything else there was to look out for', she later recalled. 'In the end, it was taken for granted that I always had to come along wherever they went.'[14] Olga was closest to her eldest niece and namesake, who was only thirteen years younger than she. 'She resembled me in character, and that was perhaps why we understood each other so well.' But as time went on she could not disguise her special affection for the seductively engaging Anastasia, whom she nicknamed Shvybzik (a German colloquialism meaning 'little mischief') in recognition of her incorrigible behaviour. The child had such courage, such a fierce love of life, and embraced everything as a great adventure; Olga had no doubt that of the four she was the most intelligent.[15]

Those Saturday games with their aunt were a time to be treasured: 'this was how we appeared at the tea table every Saturday afternoon, happy, laughing and squabbling about all the dreadful things "the others" had thought of.'[16] As dusk fell the family attended evensong together and Aunt Olga would stay till bedtime, after which she travelled back to St Petersburg. At the end of that year, she persuaded Nicholas and Alexandra to allow her to stay the night and take the girls back with her the following morning for the day.[17] Here after lunch with Grandmama, Maria Feodorovna, at the Anichkov Palace – where even Anastasia would be on her best behaviour – they would then go to Aunt Olga's to meet their favourite officers from the entourage, have tea, play games, enjoy music – and dance – before one of the ladies-in-waiting would come from Tsarskoe Selo to take them back home.

In later life Olga Alexandrovna reflected on those happy 'red-letter Sundays' with her nieces before the war. The extraordinary closeness and self-sufficiency that was the mark of the four Romanov sisters persisted, as too their touchingly childlike innocence about the world. But it was a strange hothouse atmosphere in which to grow up. 'My nieces did not have any playmates,' Grand Duchess Olga wistfully observed, 'but they had each other, and probably did not miss them.'[18]

*

Over in England, although it was four years since she had left her post, Margaretta Eagar had not forgotten her former charges. Now living in straitened circumstances, running a boarding house in Holland Park, she still wrote to the girls from time to time and sent gifts on their birthdays. But sitting in her drawing room, as she often did, gazing at the many treasured photographs in silver frames that she had of them, she was pining for news. Margaretta hated the London fogs; her life, she told Mariya Geringer, was '*horrible* . . . I wish I were returning to Russia. I do not think I shall ever be happy in this country.' Sending Tatiana birthday wishes in June 1908, she wistfully commented: 'I suppose you still have cakes and almond Toffee. How good they used to be!'[19]

No doubt the girls were missing her too, for since Margaretta's departure at the end of 1904, the absence of a governess's discipline had begun to have a detrimental effect. With so much natural energy and a huge curiosity about the world, the girls were increasingly boisterous. Alexandra was often too busy or indisposed to supervise her daughters herself, leaving them under the supervision of Trina Schneider. Modest and devoted Trina might be but she was clearly feeling the strain, as too was the girls' exasperated general nursemaid, Mariya Vishnyakova, to whom they gave the constant run-around.[20]

In March 1907, therefore, Alexandra made the decision to appoint Sofya Tyutcheva – who had served as a lady-in-waiting at Peterhof the previous summer – as maid of honour-cum-governess to the girls, with responsibility for helping them prepare their lessons and chaperoning them on walks and other excursions. Sofya came on the recommendation of Grand Duchess Ella, and had an old-school pedigree, as granddaughter of the famous Russian poet Feodor Tyutchev. She also had a strong conservative streak. She was a stickler for good behaviour and took her role very seriously, but it was a challenge: the girls 'wouldn't listen and tried every which way to test my patience', she recalled. She appealed to Olga: 'You have an influence over your sisters, you're the eldest and can persuade them to listen to me and not play up so much.' 'Oh no,' Olga had replied, 'then I would always have to behave myself, and that's impossible!' Sofya could not help thinking Olga was right, that it was hard for one so young to have to be forever setting an example to her siblings, though she later overheard her reprimanding Anastasia for her mischievous behaviour by saying 'Stop it, or Savanna [Tyutcheva's pet name] will leave, and then it will be even worse for us!'[21]

That same year another new female friend entered the girls' lives in the shape of Lili Dehn, whose husband, a lieutenant in the Guards Equipage, was already a favourite with the family. The girls took to Lili immediately, for just like Aunt Olga she was willing to join in their often silly and very physical games, and would even race down the slide in Alexey's downstairs playroom with them. While others outside the close family circle had already suggested that the four sisters were 'Cinderellas who were entirely subservient in family life owing to the attention paid the Tsarevitch', Lili found this was far from the truth.[22] Alexandra loved her daughters; 'they were her inseparable companions'. But there was no denying that the lives of the four sisters were very sheltered: 'They had no idea of the ugly side of life', as Lili recalled. The general assumption of the world's press certainly was that the Romanov children lived stunted lives, hidden away for their own safety 'in a land which resembles a great powder-magazine'; that they had to be 'guarded by regiments of soldiers and thousands of highly paid spies'. Yet sufficient information was emerging by 1908 for the world to have a sense that Olga was 'a very interesting girl, highly imaginative, and fond of reading'.[23] More than that, she had a natural aptitude at arithmetic and read better in English than in Russian.[24]

The four sisters in fact all spoke good English, and had received additional tuition since 1905 from a Scotsman, John Epps.[25] His legacy, however, was a strange Scottish twang acquired by Olga and Tatiana that their uncle Edward VII remarked on when the families met briefly in 1908 (it has also been suggested they had an Irish accent picked up from Margaretta Eagar).[26] To replace Epps, Sofya Tyutcheva suggested an Englishman named Charles Sydney Gibbes, a Cambridge graduate who had been teaching in St Petersburg for several years. She sent a note to Alexandra's secretary, enclosing a testimonial from the director of the Imperial School of Law where Gibbes had lately been running courses in modern languages, and which praised him as being 'extremely talented'.[27]

When Gibbes took up his post with the imperial family in November 1908, Sofya Tyutcheva introduced him to thirteen-year-old Olga and eleven-year-old Tatiana. He thought them 'good-looking, high-spirited girls, simple in their tastes and very pleasant to deal with'. Although they could be inattentive at times, 'they were quite clever, and quick when they gave their minds to it', but the atmosphere induced by the presence of Tyutcheva as chaperone made those first lessons somewhat tense.[28] Gibbes also gave occasional, separate, tuition to Maria, who struck him as sweet and compliant and he was impressed by her gift for painting and drawing. The arrival in his classroom in 1909 of the whirlwind that was eight-year-old Anastasia changed everything. Gibbes later tactfully remarked that she was not always an easy child to teach but like everyone else, he was won over by her effervescent charm and her quirky intelligence. Gibbes thought her 'fragile and dainty . . . a little lady of great self-possession, always bright, always happy'. He also found her endlessly inventive – always coming up with 'some new oddity of speech or manner; her perfect command of her features was remarkable' – he had never come across anything to equal it in any other child.[29] As for Alexey, at this point Gibbes, like the other tutors, had little contact with him apart from the occasional encounter in the classroom at break time when the little boy, who could be painfully shy with strangers, would come in and 'gravely shake hands'.[30]

For now, Gibbes's lessons with the girls took the form of English grammar, spelling and usage in the mornings and dictation in the afternoons. With all four sisters now in the classroom and Gibbes settled in, Pierre Gilliard – in addition to his duties as French teacher – was officially appointed to take overall charge of the girls' curriculum. Like Gilliard, Gibbes chose to maintain his independence by living in St Petersburg and travelling out to Tsarskoe Selo for lessons five days a week. Both, like Tyutcheva (aka Savanna), were accorded pet names by the girls: Zhilik and Sig, the latter based on Gibbes's initials. Other tutors also came and went from town: PVP continued to teach Russian; Konstantin Ivanov taught history and geography; M. Sobolev mathematics; a Herr Kleikenberg gave German lessons to Olga and Tatiana – a language they never took to, or him either; Dmitry Kardovsky, a professor from the Russian Academy of Arts, was their drawing master; and Father Alexander Vasiliev drilled them in their catechism.[31]

In March 1907 a major assassination plot against Nicholas, his uncle Grand Duke Nikolay and Prime Minister Stolypin had been uncovered in St Petersburg, leading to the pre-emptive arrest of twenty-six 'very prominent anarchists' and the confiscation of an arsenal of bombs and arms.[32] The story inevitably prompted sensationalist reports in the western press that the tsar was 'cowering in terror, and dreading to visit his own capital' and that the Alexander Palace was 'a huge bastioned fortress, with barred windows suggesting the gloom of a prison-house'.[33] Yet, in fact the only sop to security within the palace at this time of heightened alert was the habit – actually adopted after an attempt on Alexander II many years before – for Nicholas and Alexandra to have their meals served in different rooms in alternation. A Russian general recently invited to lunch with the tsar had been surprised to find the table set in the tsaritsa's mauve boudoir. Noticing his surprise, young Tatiana had pertly remarked, 'Next time . . . I suppose we shall lunch in the bathroom!'[34]

Security nevertheless remained extremely tight when the family took their annual Finnish holiday in the *Shtandart* in 1907. All was following its normal uneventful pattern until 29 August when, with the yacht travelling at 15 knots towards Riilakhti with an experienced Finnish pilot on board, there was a terrible accident not far from the port of Hanko. As Anna Vyrubova recalled:

> We were seated on deck at tea, the band playing, a perfectly calm sea running, when we felt a terrific shock which shook the yacht from stem to stern and sent the tea service crashing to the deck. In great alarm we sprang to our feet only to feel the yacht listing sharply to starboard. In an instant the decks were alive with sailors obeying the harsh commands of the captain, and helping the suite to look to the safety of the women and children.[35]

Although the *Shtandart* was not in immediate danger, the captain ordered a speedy evacuation. This prompted a sudden panic for Alexey could not be found on deck, where he had last been seen playing with the ship's cat and her kittens. Alexandra went into paroxysms of terror as a frantic search began, only for the boy to appear with his *dyadka* Derevenko who, when the impact had happened and fearful that the boilers might blow, had gathered Alexey up in his arms and carried him to the prow of the yacht where it was safer.[36] Nicholas remained his usual uncannily impassive self, calmly calculating the yacht's degree of list and how long they might have before she sank, as the outlying escort of some 15–20 vessels hurried to the crippled *Shtandart*'s assistance.[37] With Nikolay Sablin escorting the children to safety, Alexandra regained her composure enough to dash down to her cabin with Anna Vyrubova and gather up all her valuables into sheets, as did Nicholas with his important state papers; the yacht was leaning at a 19-degree angle by the time they disembarked.

When Sablin and other officers later went down into the ship to examine the damage, they found a huge dent in the bottom of the hull, which if it had been breached would have caused the yacht to sink very fast. As it was, only one compartment had let in any water and this was sealed.[38] The official inquiry into the accident revealed that the rock that had caused it was uncharted; on subsequent maps it was named after Blomkvist, the unfortunate Finnish pilot who had failed to spot it. Members of the crew involved in the swift and speedy evacuation of the family and in the yacht's preservation were rewarded with money, gold and silver watches, and medals. Meanwhile, the accident had attracted widespread coverage in the world's press, with newspaper correspondents flocking to Hanko. Considerable shock was registered in the Russian papers, with the finger of blame being pointed first at the Finns, then the revolutionaries and then the whole tsarist system. Many were convinced it had been a terrorist attack and that the yacht had hit a mine or that a bomb had been planted in her prow.

The children, though, had found the adventure of a real-life shipwreck hugely exciting, even down to being crammed together overnight in one small and rather grubby cabin in an escort cruiser, before being transferred to the *Aleksandriya*. The family eventually continued their holiday in the dowager Empress's yacht, the *Polyarnaya zvezda*. Once more the children contented themselves with happy days of picnicking, mushroom-gathering and roasting potatoes on bonfires on the island of Kavo and walking with Nicholas in the woods on Paationmaa, gathering flowers.[39]

Chapter Seven

OUR FRIEND

By the autumn of 1907 Alexey was out of his baby skirts and into long trousers; his girlish curls were turning smooth and brown, but he still was an engagingly beautiful child, similar in looks to his sister Tatiana. His outward robustness, however, belied the fact that he was already a 'Child of many Prayers', as Lili Dehn described him.[1] With little to go on about the heir to the Russian throne, the foreign press was full of fanciful stories about plots to kidnap or murder him, or to poison his bread and butter or his porridge. It was also, already, discussing rumours about his 'ill health', which for now was 'ascribed to the misfortune that so many residences of the Czars leave much to be desired from the point of view of sanitary science'.[2]

The first stories about the tsarevich to emerge tended to focus on his rather spoilt behaviour. Little Alexey had a mind of his own and a strength of personality to equal Anastasia's. He loved attending army inspections and manoeuvres with his father, strutting around in his miniature uniform, complete with toy wooden rifle, and playing the despot – even at the tender age of three. He was already a stickler for the due respect that should be accorded him as heir and at times showed a marked air of impertinence – a trait he also shared with his nearest sibling.[3] He rather liked the outmoded ritual of being kissed on the hand by the officers on board ship and 'didn't miss his chance to boast about it and give himself airs in front of his sisters', as Spiridovich recalled. On the recent *Shtandart* cruise off Finland Alexey had taken it into his head to have the ship's band got out of their beds to play for him in the middle of the night. 'That's the way to bring up an Autocrat!' Nicholas had remarked, with paternal pride.[4] There were times, however, when Nicholas took his son's peremptory behaviour in hand, such as when he discovered that Alexey took particular delight in suddenly creeping up on the guards posted at the front of the Alexander Palace, 'watching them out of the corner of his eye as they sprang to attention and stood like statues while he strolled nonchalantly past'. Nicholas forbade the guards to salute unless another member of the family accompanied Alexey; the boy's humiliation 'when the salute failed him' had, it was said, 'marked his first taste of discipline'.[5]

For a while everyone had had to contend with the reign of 'Alexey the Terrible', as Nicholas called his son, but mercifully he soon began to grow out of the worst of his bad behaviour.[6] Some of it no doubt was a response to the limitations placed upon him by his condition. For here was a little boy who had everything:

> the most costly and expensive playthings, great railways, with dolls in the carriages as passengers, with barriers, stations, buildings, and signal boxes, flashing engines and marvelous signalling apparatus, whole battalions of tin soldiers, models of towns with church towers and domes, floating models of ships, perfectly equipped factories with doll-workers, and mines in exact imitation of the real thing, with miners ascending and descending,[7]

– all of which were mechanical and could be made to work at the press of a button. But Alexey did not have his health. As time went on and the restrictions on what he could and could not do increased he rebelled at constantly hearing the word 'no'. 'Why can other boys have everything and I nothing?' he kept on asking angrily.[8] Alexey proved difficult at times for his *dyadka* Derevenko to control, for he was naturally adventurous and constantly challenged all his carers. He liked nothing better than hurtling down his indoor slide at the Alexander Palace or riding round in his pedal car, but every knock and bang was potentially dangerous.

In the early 1900s there was nothing any doctor could do to control the bleeding into the joints that followed the tsarevich's numerous accidents other than to apply ice and confine the little boy to bed. At the time, acetylsalicylic acid – an early form of aspirin available from the 1890s – was considered a useful painkiller (Alexandra had taken salicylic acid for her sciatica). But in Alexey's case it was counterproductive – thinning the blood and thus intensifying the bleeding. Nicholas and Alexandra were fiercely resistant to the use of morphine because of its powerful addictive effect and so the best and only way to protect Alexey was to have him constantly watched, but this did not prevent him having his worst accident yet, in the autumn of 1907, when, out playing in the Alexander Park, he fell and hurt his leg. There was hardly any visible bruising but the internal haemorrhage triggered by the fall caused him excruciating pain. As Olga Alexandrovna – who had rushed over on hearing the news – recalled: 'The poor child lay in such pain, dark patches under his eyes and his little body all distorted, and the leg terribly swollen.'[9] The doctors could do nothing, nor could Professor Albert Hoffa, an eminent orthopaedic surgeon who was called in haste from Berlin. 'They looked more frightened than any of us and they kept whispering among themselves', Olga Alexandrovna recalled. 'There seemed just nothing they could do, and hours went by until they had given up all hope.'[10]

In desperation, and remembering how Grigory Rasputin had helped Stolypin's daughter, Alexandra telephoned Stana, whom she knew was in regular contact with him. Stana sent her servants out to find Rasputin, who hastened to Tsarskoe Selo. Arriving late, he entered by a side entrance and up the back stairs where he could not be seen. Nicholas, Alexandra and the four girls were anxiously awaiting him in the tsarevich's bedroom, along with Anna Vyrubova, the imperial physician Dr Evgeny Botkin and Archimandrite Feofan (the tsar's and tsaritsa's personal confessor). Rasputin's daughter Maria later described the scene as her father had told it to her:

Papa raised his hand, and making the sign of the cross, blessed the room and its occupants . . . Then he turned to the sickly boy, and observing the pallid features wracked with pain, he knelt beside the bed and began to pray. As he did this . . . each knelt as if overcome by a spiritual presence, and joined in the silent prayer. For a space of ten minutes, nothing was to be heard but the sound of breathing.[11]

Finally, Rasputin stood up and told Alexey to open his eyes. Bewildered, the boy looked around him and finally focused on Rasputin's face. 'Your pain is going away; you will soon be well. You must thank God for healing you. And now, go to sleep', he told him gently. As he left, Rasputin assured Nicholas and Alexandra: 'The tsarevich will live.' Soon after he had left, the swelling in Alexey's leg began to subside. When his aunt Olga saw him the next morning he 'was not just alive – but well. He was sitting up in bed, the fever gone, the eyes clear and bright, not a sign of any swelling on his leg.'[12]

Alexey had cheated death, but no one could explain his miraculous recovery. Rasputin clearly had great powers of intuition and auto-suggestion that had had some kind of calming effect, causing his haemorrhaging blood vessels to contract, (much as adrenalin has the reverse effect and dilates them).[13] Many of his followers saw Rasputin's gift of healing as being in the Vedic tradition of the Siberian shamans who believed in the connectivity between the natural and spiritual worlds. Like all the imperial doctors, Alexey's paediatrician Dr Sergey Feodorov – who had been called in on several occasions when there had been a crisis – had an instinctive dislike of the man, but he could not explain why what Rasputin did worked, while conventional medicine failed him.[14] In treating the tsarevich, Rasputin insisted that the use of aspirin and all drugs should be abandoned in favour of a reliance solely on prayer and spiritual healing – and this, ironically, may also have been of some benefit. But the ability to stop the flow of blood was not exclusive to him; it was a gift he shared with other folk healers. As Iza Buxhoeveden observed, it was not uncommon for Russian peasants to control bleeding in their injured livestock by 'exercising pressure on the smaller blood-vessels and thus stopping bleeding', but it was a secret gift that they 'jealously guarded'.[15] Princess Barbara Dolgorouky also recalled:

> Among the peasants in Russia there were most remarkable healers. Some healed burns, some stopped blood and some cured toothaches – I know of some exceptional cases of toothaches which were stopped not only for these particular minutes of pain, but for ever. And from a distance . . . I knew and later was

a great friend of a Russian lady, Madame de Daehn, who cured burns by touching the burned places and murmuring something.[16]

One thing is certain: the unquestioning trust Nicholas and Alexandra invested in Grigory, as they called him, was based on a profound and genuine belief that he was – pure and simple – not just a healer but a man of God, sent to help them when no one else could. If Alexey were to survive with Grigory's help, then it was God's will.[17]

During those first occasional visits Rasputin made to Tsarskoe Selo (and sources vary on how often he came), Olga and Tatiana were sometimes allowed to sit in on his discussions about religion with their parents, but the younger girls, especially Anastasia, were for a while excluded. Mariya Geringer remembered hurrying over to see the empress on an urgent matter one evening, when Anastasia 'rushed to meet her in a corridor, threw out her arms and blocked her way, saying "You and I can't go there, the New One (the name given to Rasputin by Alexey) is there."' Anastasia 'was not allowed to enter' when Rasputin was visiting, as she 'always laughed when he spoke or read about religious matters', unable to take such discussions seriously.[18]

It was not long, however, before even she had begun to relate to him. On one occasion Aunt Olga arrived on a visit and was taken upstairs by Nicholas and Alexandra, where she found Rasputin with the children 'all in white pyjamas . . . being put to bed by their nurses':

> When I saw him I felt that gentleness and warmth radiated from him. All the children seemed to like him. They were completely at their ease with him. I still remember their laughter as little Alexis, deciding he was a rabbit, jumped up and down the room. And then, quite suddenly, Rasputin caught the child's hand and led him to his bedroom, and we three followed. There was something like a hush as though we had found ourselves in church. In Alexis's bedroom no lamps were lit; the only light came from the candles burning in front of some beautiful icons. The child stood very still by the side of that giant, whose head was bowed. I knew he was praying. It was all most impressive. I also knew that my little nephew had joined him in prayer.[19]

Olga Alexandrovna always freely admitted that she had never liked Rasputin – he was 'primitive' and 'uncouth' and paid no lip-service to court etiquette, addressing the imperial family by the informal *ty* rather than the formal *vy* and often calling Nicholas and Alexandra 'papa and mama'. She was discomfited by Rasputin's unbridled familiarity, which she saw as intrusive and impertinent – as well as, probably, sexually intimidating. It was a common response, for wherever he went Grigory Rasputin sparked controversy. He remains one of the most written-about personalities in late imperial Russian history, and one who has attracted some of the most sensationalist and contradictory claims. As the English novelist and travel writer Carl Eric Bechhofer, who met him, recalled: 'Before I went to Russia and all the time I was there, I never could make any two accounts of Rasputin tally'; in Bechhofer's view, the levels of his perceived wickedness were always 'in large proportion to the political liberalism of the reporter'.[20] Part of this stems no doubt from Rasputin's inherently contradictory personality. Depending on whether one was with him or against him Rasputin was either pious, mild and benevolent or the polar opposite – promiscuous, bestial and repellent. But who was he in reality – 'sensual hypocrite' or 'wonder-working mystic'?[21] History has struggled for the last 100 years to make up its mind.

It is certainly clear that despite being a man of religion, Rasputin was also a shrewd opportunist, nor did he ever make any attempt to hide his physical appetites. On arriving in the capital, he did the rounds of the salons of a *fin-de-siècle* St Petersburg noted for its decadence, pandering to rich society ladies who dabbled in the then-fashionable cults of faith healing, table turning and eastern mysticism, and built a following among them. He was, for his detractors, an easy personality to caricature in his loose peasant blouse and long boots, with his heavy frame, his long oily black hair and beard, and his coarse bulging lips. But there is no denying the astonishing force of his personality: his sonorous voice was hypnotic and those legendary blue eyes, which he apparently could dilate at will, gave him the look of an Old Testament prophet. Rasputin consciously and cleverly exploited the innate theatricality of these two gifts, the unfamiliar, archaic church Russian that he spoke adding to his strange other-worldliness. The salacious gossip circulating about him seemed to have no adverse effect on his devoted followers, who remained drawn to Rasputin's inexplicable powers of healing, for there was absolutely no doubt about the deep and affecting influence he had over the sick. By 1907 the impressionable Anna Vyrubova had become an ardent follower and was regularly inviting him to visit her at her little house close by the Alexander Palace.

Having witnessed her son's recovery at first hand the tsaritsa wanted desperately to believe in this holy man's unexplained gifts, for here at last was a lifeline when all conventional medicine had failed. Rasputin made no inflated claims to her about his healing powers and why they were effective; nor was he paid for his services (he once complained to Lili Dehn that he 'was never even given his cab-fares'; though often lavish gifts from Nicholas and Alexandra, including tunics hand-embroidered by her, were from time to time sent to him).[22] For Rasputin, healing was a simple matter of unquestioning faith and the power of prayer. And those two great weapons in the Christian armoury – faith and prayer – were fundamental to Alexandra's credo. She called him Grigory – 'Our Friend' – seeing in him not just the saviour of her son, but something bigger – a holy man and seer. She responded warmly to his Christian wisdom and the simplicity of his message: 'Man must live to praise God . . . asking for nothing, giving all.'[23] Here was an ordinary man of the people, a true *muzhik*, a valuable conduit between herself and Nicholas – as *batyushka* and *matyushka* (little father and little mother) – and the Russian people.[24] At a time when they saw danger all around, Nicholas and Alexandra at last felt they had met someone they could truly trust.

They had no illusions, however, about Rasputin's libidinous personality. Unbridled gossip about him was raging in the city and investing their hopes in him might provoke scandal. With this in mind Alexandra enlisted Nikolay Sablin, one of her and Nicholas's most trusted friends, and one who was particularly close to the children, to visit Rasputin in St Petersburg to find out more. Sablin knew nothing of Rasputin but went to see him, having been told by the empress that he was 'very pious and wise, a true Russian peasant'.[25] He was repelled by Rasputin's appearance and found his manner unnerving. But he spoke very animatedly to Sablin about the imperial family, religion and God and like everyone else Sablin admitted there was something compelling about Rasputin's pale, deep-set eyes. He sensed that Rasputin was eager to ingratiate himself with the imperial family – for he had certainly already been bragging about his illustrious connections. Sablin suggested that he should never request audiences with the tsar, in response to which Rasputin had grumbled: 'When they need me to pray for the tsarevich they call me, and when they don't – they don't!'[26]

After several meetings with him Sablin had no option but to admit to the tsaritsa that he had come away with a negative impression. Alexandra refused to accept his view: 'You cannot understand him because you are so far removed from such people,' she had replied stubbornly, 'but even if your opinion was correct, then it is God's will that it is such.'[27] As far as she was concerned, God had willed that they should meet Grigory, just as God had willed it that everyone else should despise and revile him. This was the cross that Grigory had to bear; just as Alexey's affliction was her own for having transmitted haemophilia to him. In befriending Grigory the outcast she truly believed that in his godliness he would rise above the slander; and, more importantly, he would keep her precious boy alive.

Sydney Gibbes later recorded his impressions of Rasputin. Not long after taking up his post with the imperial family, he had been invited to go and meet Rasputin in St Petersburg. The children heard of this and the next day came bursting into the schoolroom. 'What did you think of our friend?' they asked. 'Isn't he wonderful?' Gibbes noticed Rasputin was always on his best behaviour with the tsar and tsaritsa and that 'his table-manners, which were much complained of by his critics, were those of a decent peasant'. He was never aware of Rasputin exerting any influence at court, though conceded that he had an instinctive 'naïve cunning'. But there was no doubting Rasputin's 'extraordinary powers over the little boy's bleeding attacks'; Rasputin could always cure them, he recalled, and once did so 'by speaking to the boy over the telephone'.[28]

In March 1908 Alexey had another fall, this time hitting his forehead. The swelling was so bad that he could hardly open his eyes.

But on this occasion Rasputin was not called in, for he was back at his home in Pokrovskoe in western Siberia (where he had a wife, Praskovya, and three children), under investigation by the Church. His enemies had accused him of spreading false doctrine as the leader of a dissident and disreputable sect known as the *Khlysty*, notorious for the use of self-flagellation in religious rites.[29]

It was three weeks before Nicholas was relieved to write and tell his mother that Alexey was recovering and that 'the swelling and bruising have disappeared without trace. He is well and happy, just like his sisters.'[30] Whether this was in any way the result of intervention, by telegram or over the telephone, by Rasputin is unknown. Two months later Alexey was still unwell when members of the wider imperial family gathered at Tsarskoe Selo for the wedding of the girls' childhood playmate, Grand Duchess Maria Pavlovna, to Prince Wilhelm of Sweden. After the day's ceremonials, which she steeled herself to sit through despite her anxieties for her son, and looking beautiful but extremely strained, Alexandra went up to Alexey's bedroom. The nurse told her his temperature had finally fallen at 8 p.m. There was a telegram waiting for her – from Grigory in Pokrovskoe – which, when she opened it, assured her that all would be well and that 'he would say a special prayer at eight that very evening'.[31] Coincidence or not, such manifestations of the power of Grigory's prayers for her boy were for the tsaritsa incontrovertible proof that he alone could save him from death – even at a distance. How could she not but invest all her desperate hopes in him? Wouldn't any other mother have done the same?

Many of Nicholas and Alexandra's European relatives who came to Russia for the wedding, and knew nothing of Alexey's haemophilia, commented on how isolated the family had become by 1908 – 'shut away from the rest of the world', as Crown Princess Marie of Romania observed. The 'happy family life' that Nicholas and Alexandra clearly fostered was all very laudable in her view, but 'their exclusiveness was little conducive towards that fine, loyal unity which had always been traditional in the Russian Imperial Family during the two former reigns and which had constituted its great power'.[32] Marie felt the two of them were 'too self-centered, too exclusively interested in their own children'; in so doing they neglected their European relatives, and this had led to their alienation from them. Brief state visits with the children in the *Shtandart* in the summers of 1907 and 1908 to Reval* in the Baltic – for a meeting between Nicholas, Edward VII and Kaiser Wilhelm – and to the King and Queen of Sweden at Stockholm had done nothing to change the general consensus. In the meantime, rumours continued to circulate about the tsarevich's ill health, with whisperings that he suffered from 'convulsions', and from a 'certain form of infantile tuberculosis which gives rise to acute alarm'; another source suggested 'one of the layers of his skin was missing', which predisposed him to constant haemorrhage.[33] But nobody as yet had publicly uttered the dreaded word – haemophilia.

Because of the intense secrecy surrounding Alexey's condition little record survives of the various attacks he suffered over the next four years or how often Rasputin visited Tsarskoe Selo or treated him from a distance, but just before Christmas 1908, in Rasputin's continuing absence at Pokrovskoe, Dr Feodorov was summoned urgently from Moscow to attend the child.[34] Anxiety within the family was further compounded that winter when Alexandra's own health took a turn for the worst and she was laid up for eight weeks. 'It is too sad and painful to see [Alix] always ailing and incapable of taking part in anything', Maria Feodorovna wrote to Nicholas. 'You have enough worries in life as it is – without having the ordeal added to it of seeing the person you love most in the world suffer.'[35]

Alexandra's daughters too were increasingly feeling the separation from their mother through her constant illness and had taken to sending her plaintive little notes. 'So sorry that never see you alone Mama dear', wrote Olga on 4 December,

> can not talk so should trie to write to you what could course better say, but what is to be done if there is no time, and neighter can I hear the dear words which sweet Mama could tell me. Good-bye. God bless you. Kisses from your very own devoted daughter.†[36]

---

* The capital of Estonia, now known as Tallinn.
† The idiosyncratic spelling and grammatical errors of the Romanov sisters when writing in English, as here, are reproduced as given throughout.

Tatiana took it particularly hard: 'I hope you wont be today very tied', she wrote on 17 January 1909,

and that you can get up to dinner. I am always so awfuy sorry when you are tied and when you cant get up. . . . Perhaps I have lots of folts but please forgive me . . . I try to listen what Mary [Mariya Vishnyakova] says now as much as I kan. . . . Sleep well and I hope that you wont be tied. Your loving daughter Tatiana. I will pray for you in church.[37]

Alexandra responded from her sickroom with motherly exhortations: 'Try to be as good as you can and not cause me worries, then I will be content,' she told Tatiana, 'I really can't come upstairs and check how things are with lessons, how you are behaving and speaking.'[38]

In most cases, though, the onus was on Olga to set an example. 'Remember above all to always be a good example to the little ones,' Alexandra told her in the new year, 'then our Friend will be contented with you.'[39] Alexandra's advice that Olga be kind and considerate extended to the servants as well, especially Mariya Vishnyakova, who of late had been getting cross with her: 'Listen to her, be obedient and always kind . . . you must always be good with her and also S. I. [Sofya Ivanovna Tyutcheva]. You are big enough to understand what I mean.'[40] It was advice that Olga responded to gratefully: 'Mama dear it helps me very much when you write to me what to do, and then I try to do it is better as I can.' The motherly exhortations followed thick and fast: 'Try to have a serious word with Tatiana and Maria about how they should conduct themselves towards God.' 'Did you read my letter of the 1st? It will help when you speak to them. You must have a positive influence over them.'[41] It is clear that Olga felt frustrated that she and her mother never had 'time to talk things over properly'. 'We will soon,' Alexandra reassured her, 'but right now I'm just too tired.'[42] She was, however, concerned that Olga found it hard to contain her patience with her younger siblings: 'I know that this is especially difficult for you because you feel things very deeply and you have a hot temper,' Alexandra told her, 'but you must learn to control your tongue.'[43]

By now, the children had come to enjoy visits from their 'friend' Grigory as a welcome diversion from their mother's sickbed. He played with them and let them ride round the room on his back; he told them Russian folk tales and talked to them about God in a way that seemed entirely natural. He was clearly playing a key role as the girls' moral guardian and kept in regular touch with them, sending telegrams such as one received in February in which he thanked them for remembering him, 'for your sweet words, for your pure heart and your love for the people of God. Love the whole of God's nature, the whole of His creation in particular this earth.'[44] On 29 March 1909 he arrived unexpectedly on a visit, which delighted all the children. 'I'm glad you had him so long to yourselves', Alexandra told Olga from her sickbed.[45] In June, at Peterhof, young Olga sent a note to her father, who was away on a visit to the King of Sweden: 'My dear kind Papa. Today the weather is lovely, it's very warm. The little ones [Anastasia and Alexey] are running around barefoot. Grigoriy is coming to see us this evening. We are all so very happy that we will see him again.'[46]

Despite her misgivings about the man himself, Olga Alexandrovna always refuted any suggestion of impropriety by Rasputin towards her nieces: 'I know what their upbringing was down to the tiniest detail. The least sign of what is known as "freshness" on Rasputin's part would have dumbfounded them! None of it ever happened. The girls were always glad to see him because they knew how greatly he helped their little brother.'[47] Nevertheless, Alexandra continued to worry about the derogatory gossip in circulation about Rasputin. Although the charge of heresy had been abandoned as unproven, other accusations had followed and Stolypin (unmoved by Rasputin's bedside manner in 1906) now had him under police investigation.[48] St Petersburg was rife with talk of Rasputin's disreputable drunken behaviour, his sexual exploits and the dubious company he kept. Even the faith of his erstwhile supporters Militza and Stana had waned, particularly now that Anna Vyrubova – whom they despised – had gained privileged access to him, supplanting them as the link between Rasputin and the throne. The Montenegrin sisters began actively trying to dissuade Nicholas and Alexandra from having any further dealings with Rasputin, whom they now looked upon as a 'devil'. As a result, the close relationship they had until now enjoyed with the imperial family disintegrated. The imperial couple refused to be influenced by the gossip and doggedly clung to their own perception of Grigory as a true friend, despite his obvious faults – to which they were far from oblivious. The true reason for their friendship and their increasing dependency – Alexey's haemophilia – 'was kept a strict secret and it bound the participants still closer to one another, separating them still further from the rest of the world'.[49]

By the end of 1909 Alexandra was seeking regular spiritual advice from Grigory and meeting him at Anna Vyrubova's house. Such was her trust in him that she was making unguarded and potentially compromising remarks in letters to him such as 'I wish only one thing: to fall asleep, fall asleep for ages on your shoulders, in your embrace', a comment which would later be seized on by her enemies and used against her.[50] The girls too were writing regular notes, thanking Grigory for his help, eager to see him again and asking his advice. Now at a highly impressionable age, Olga, in her isolation from other more suitable mentors, looked upon her friend almost as a father confessor. She wrote in November 1909 saying how much she had missed seeing him, for she had been confiding in him about a teenage crush and was finding it hard to control her feelings as Grigory had advised her. She wrote again in December once more asking what she should do:

> My precious friend! We often remember you, how you visited us and talked to us about God. It's hard without you: I have no one to turn to about my worries, and there are so very many of them. Here is my torment. Nikolay is driving me crazy. I only have to go to the Sophia Cathedral* and I see him and could climb the wall, my whole body shakes . . . I love him . . . I want to fling myself at him. You advised me to be cautious. But how can I be when I cannot control myself . . . We often go to Anna's. Every time I wonder whether I might meet you there, my precious friend; oh if only I could see you there again soon and ask your advice about Nikolay. Pray for me and bless me. I kiss your hands. Your loving Olga.[51]

---

* Olga is referring to the Ascension Cathedral at Sophia – a suburb of Tsarskoe Selo, where the imperial entourage often worshipped before their own private church, the Feodorovsky Sobor, near the Alexander Palace was built.

Olga's three sisters were all writing to Grigory in an equally trusting manner. Tatiana had sent a letter in March that year, asking him how long it would be before he returned from Pokrovskoe and wishing that they could all visit him there. 'When will that time come?' she asked impatiently. 'Without you it is boring, so boring.' Tatiana's words were echoed by Maria, who told him she was pining in his absence and finding life so dull without his visits and his kind words: 'As soon as I wake up in the morning I take the Gospel you gave me from under my pillow and kiss it . . . then I feel as though I am kissing you.' Even the normally subversive Anastasia was demanding when she would see Grigory again:

> I love it when you talk to us about God . . . I often dream about you. Do you dream about me? When are you coming? . . . Come soon, and then I will try to be good, like you have told me. If you were always around us then I would be good all the time.[52]

Such was the solitary existence of the four Romanov sisters that, by 1909, apart from each other's company and occasional contact with other royal cousins, they were largely reliant on the friendship of adults: their Aunt Olga, a few close officers, servants and ladies-in-waiting – and a forty-year-old reprobate and religious maverick whose continuing influence over their family life was already sowing the seeds of their ultimate destruction.

Chapter Eight

ROYAL COUSINS

In the late summer of 1909 the Romanov sisters at last found themselves with something exciting to look forward to – a visit to their royal cousins in England. It would be their first proper official trip abroad, apart from private family visits to Uncle Ernie at Darmstadt and Wolfsgarten. Crossing the North Sea, the *Shtandart* encountered strong winds from the south and the water was very choppy. All the children were seasick, and many of the entourage too.[1] The crew made up an area of plaids and pillows for the children to sleep on where the rocking of the ship was less intense. But Tatiana still suffered terribly; she had never been a good sailor and had sometimes been seasick even when the yacht was at anchor. 'A whole trunkful of special remedies from America' had been sent for but nothing worked.[2] En route to England, the family had stopped briefly at Kiel to visit Alexandra's sister Irene and her family, and then they had made a three-day visit to President Fallières of France at Cherbourg, where they were greeted with the usual pageantry of gun salutes, crowds, bunting and massed bands playing the *Marseillaise*. After three days of diplomatic meetings, formal dinners and a review of the French fleet – at which the girls had been thrilled to be allowed to take photos of French submarines with their Box Brownies – the *Shtandart* finally set sail for England.[3]

Having met at Reval for three days the previous year, both Nicholas and his uncle Edward VII had been keen to rehabilitate Russia in the eyes of the world after the terrible events of 1905, at a time when talk of war with Germany was increasing. But it was also an opportunity for a much-wanted family reunion. There was, however, a problem: the impending visit of the tsar caused considerable disquiet in Parliament and the British press, far more so than the 1896 visit. After the events of 1905 British radical groups had damned Nicholas as a brutal despot, the architect of Russian imperial oppression. In the run-up to the visit he was further vilified in socialist rallies at Trafalgar Square and elsewhere, with the evidence of Stolypin's repressive measures against political activists stacked up against him. In short, Nicholas II was seen as the repository of all evil: 'The Czar of the "Bloody Sunday", the Czar of Stolypins and the Czar of Pogroms and Black Hundreds'.[4] The impending visit divided public opinion in Britain, although Lord Hardinge, permanent under-secretary at the Foreign Office, put much of the protest down to scaremongering and dismissed the Trafalgar Square 'demonstrators' as a motley collection of 'five hundred Frenchmen, six hundred German waiters, a few Russian Jews and Italian ice-vendors'.[5] One of the most strident opponents of Nicholas's visit was the Labour leader Keir Hardie, who inspired 130 resolutions from socialist groups, schools, evangelical societies, trade unions, pacifist groups and branches of the Labour Party and the Women's Labour League that were sent to the Home Secretary condemning the visit.[6] At some radical meetings there were open calls for Nicholas's assassination, should he step onto English soil.

Mindful of the huge security problem for the police on the Isle of Wight, it was soon made clear that the tsar and his family would not stay on land but on board the *Shtandart* off Cowes, where it was much easier to protect them, surrounded as the yacht would be by two Russian cruisers and three destroyers as well as ships of the British fleet. Nevertheless, the most elaborate security arrangements were put into effect, with 'every possible means of entrance, not only to Cowes, but to the Isle of Wight' – landing stages, roads and railways, and 'even the peaceful rural villages of the interior' – being watched by hundreds of plain clothes detectives, backed up by a special 'bicycle corps' of thirty men. Many of the detectives adopted the token disguise of double-breasted yachtsmen's jackets and white sailing caps, but as one newspaper observed, 'this was really more of an advertisement of constabulary duty than a disguise. Instead of avoiding attention they invited it . . . As yachtsmen who wandered about in couples without visible means of support afloat they were marked men.'[7] Cowes itself, as the Liberal peer Lord Suffield recalled, 'was crowded with detectives on the watch for possible assassins, and everyone seemed to be in fear for the poor hunted Czar'. The detectives were not just British either; Spiridovich had brought his own Okhrana men. Suffield had found it all rather unnerving: 'I do not know how any man can submit to such thralldom; it is too big a price to pay for being a potentate.'[8]

On the evening of 2 August (NS) the *Shtandart* and its escort sailed towards Spithead in the Solent for a rendezvous with the British royal family on board their yacht the *Victoria and Albert*. The event was filmed and photographed too, as an impressive naval review and regatta of 152 ships was watched by both families, following which the royal yachts sailed into Cowes harbour to be greeted by an armada of gaily pennanted steam and sail boats and yachts of every description.[9] Four days of intensive receptions and meetings followed, during which the only meal not shared with the British royals was breakfast. The strain of it all on the empress's face was evident to Alice Keppel, Edward VII's long-standing mistress. Up on deck in the *Shtandart* surrounded by a dense crowd of people the tsaritsa had 'presented a frigid calm', yet, strangely, Alexandra's moral probity did not prevent her from inviting Mrs Keppel to join her below in her suite. As soon as the cabin door was closed behind them 'there was a sudden lightening of the atmosphere', recalled Alice. 'Dropping her regal mask, the Empress had at once become a friendly housewife, "Tell me, my dear, where do *you* get your knitting wool?" she had urgently demanded.'[10]

For the Romanov children, spared the strains of officialdom, the visit was an all too brief glimpse of an entirely new landscape, though for those protecting them it was yet another security nightmare. They had till now seen little or nothing beyond their homes at St Petersburg, Tsarskoe Selo and Peterhof. On the morning of 3 August all five of them made their first trip ashore, to East Cowes and a visit by open landau to Osborne Bay, just down from Osborne House (the large part of which had now become a naval officers' training college). Here they played with their cousins on the private beach, paddling in the sea, collecting shells and digging sandcastles, much as their mother and their grandmother Alice had done before them. Olga and Tatiana made a second impromptu trip ashore that afternoon with their chaperones and a posse of detectives, and were delighted to be allowed to walk rather than take the carriage into West Cowes to do some shopping in the main street. It was such a rare thing for them to be able to move freely in this way; the cobbled high street of West Cowes might not be the glamorous Nevsky Prospekt, but *Shtandart* officer Nikolay Vasilievich Sablin noted that many of the shops were subsidiaries of the big London stores, open specially for the yachting season and the Cowes Regatta, and had plenty of luxury goods and souvenirs with which to tempt the girls' pocket money. Olga and Tatiana were extremely animated throughout their visit. They talked in English to the shopkeepers and took great pleasure in spending their money in a newsagent's shop on pennants of the various nations, commemorative picture postcards of their royal relatives and even of their own parents. After that they moved on to a jeweller's where they snapped up gifts for members of the crew. They also treated themselves to some perfume from Beken & Son's pharmacy.[11]

West Cowes meanwhile had come to a complete standstill, for word had quickly spread about these charming young Russian visitors in their smart matching grey suits and straw hats. Soon the sisters were being followed round the town by a large crowd of curious holiday-makers and across the floating bridge into East Cowes, where they visited Whippingham Church and saw the chair Great-grandmama had sat in when attending services. Throughout their visit, as *The Times* reported on 7 August, Olga and Tatiana 'behaved with complete self-possession, smiling when one or two enthusiasts raised a cheer for them'. They were still laughing and talking excitedly at the end of their three-hour visit.[12]

The whole family came ashore the following day, the girls and Alexey bowing and waving at the crowd, on their way to see the private wing of Osborne House and the Swiss Cottage – a playhouse for learning practical skills, created in the garden for his children by Prince Albert – in which Alexey took particular delight. After enjoying five o'clock tea at Barton Manor with their cousin George,

Prince of Wales, and his family, everyone sat for their photographs. The Princess of Wales thought the Romanov children 'delicious' and everyone commented on how unaffected and delightful they were.[13] The two cousins, George and Nicholas, who had not seen each other for twelve years, seemed remarkably alike with their blue eyes, neatly trimmed beards and similar stature, particularly when they posed for photos with their two sons – David in his naval uniform (the future King Edward VIII was then at the Royal Naval College at Dartmouth) and Alexey in his own trademark white sailor suit.[14] David had been delegated to escort his cousins at Osborne, that task having originally been earmarked for his younger brother Bertie (the future King George VI). But Bertie had gone down with whooping cough shortly before the visit and such had been the imperial doctors' paranoia of exposing the tsarevich to any possible infection that he was bundled off to Balmoral and his role given to his brother. During the visit David took rather a shine to Tatiana (despite his grandmother having seen Olga as a possible future bride for him). He could see how protective she was of her timid little brother and could not help noticing a 'frightened' look in Alexey's large, watchful eyes.[15] But as for the 'elaborate police guard' thrown around the tsar's every movement, he later recalled that it 'made me glad I was not a Russian prince'.[16]

During those four idyllic, sunny days in August 1909, when 'all the world was on the water' and the Solent was 'like a sea of glass, the sun going down like a red ball leaving the evenings still and warm', one stately ceremony had followed another. As General Spiridovich later recalled, 'the colossal fleet' that had gathered at Cowes 'motionless and as if asleep, seemed a vision from a fairytale' – the effect enhanced by the night sky illuminated by the lights from all the ships anchored off shore. The night before the Romanovs' departure the bands played and there were fireworks and dancing, with the Admiral of the Fleet, Lord Fisher, partnering each of the girls in turn. Then everyone sat down to a final grand dinner – the ladies with Alexandra in the *Shtandart* – the men with King Edward in the *Victoria and Albert*. After a final lunch party on the 5th – the hottest, and most windless, day of the year so far – the *Shtandart* weighed anchor at 3.30 p.m. and, with Nicholas, Alexandra and their five children up on deck waving goodbye to their relatives in the *Victoria and Albert*, the imperial yacht headed off into the English Channel. As it disappeared from view, Superintendent Quinn of the Cowes police force was seen 'offering a cigarette out of a gorgeous gold cigarette case, shining with newness, and bearing the intimation that it was "a present from the Czar"'. One of his colleagues was wearing 'a scarf pin with the Imperial crown in diamonds, and still another sported a gold watch' – all of them 'gifts for their care' from a grateful Russian emperor and empress. But the British police were, nevertheless, intensely relieved that 'the strain was over'.[17]

All in all the Russian imperial visit to England was a triumph – an unforgettable coming together of two great royal families that would retrospectively become an indelible emblem of the dying days of the old world order. 'The four Russian Grand Duchesses had enchanted everybody, and the poignant little Tsarevich melted all hearts.'[18] But many shared the sobering thoughts of Sir Henry William Lucy:

> Thus it came to pass that the great autocrat, master of the lives of millions, was deprived of the privilege enjoyed by the humblest tourist from the Continent. He visited England, and left its shores without setting foot upon them, save in the way of a hasty, furtive visit to Osborne House.[19]

The British and Russian royal families would never meet again.

*

By the time the Romanovs arrived home, Alexandra was once again prostrated. 'How I am paying for the fatigues of my visits,' she wrote to Ernie on 26 August, 'a week already in bed.'[20] Her health was causing serious concern for it had been in rapid decline since the winter of 1907 when Alexandra had called in her physician Dr Fischer forty-two times in the space of two months.[21] Spiridovich had privately sought the opinion of an eminent Russian medical professor at around this same time. He had concluded that the tsaritsa had inherited something of the 'vulnerability' to nervous illness and 'great impressionability' of the house of Hesse and that there was a distinct 'hysterical nature' to her 'nervous manifestations'. These took the physical form of general weakness, pain around the heart, oedema of the legs caused by poor circulation, and problems with her neuro-vascular system which manifested itself in red blotches on her skin – all of which were getting worse as she approached middle age. 'As for the psychic troubles,' the professor concluded, 'these are principally expressed by a state of great depression, by great indifference to that which surrounds her, and by a tendency to religious revery.'[22]

Dr Fischer had been called in again in 1908 to treat Alexandra for a bout of painful neuralgia that had been affecting her sleep.[23] As a specialist in nervous disorders he had prescribed absolute rest. He had also felt very strongly that the presence of Anna Vyrubova – who now spent almost every day with the tsaritsa – was detrimental, if not harmful.[24] He advised Nicholas in writing that he could not treat the tsaritsa properly all the time Anna was in such close proximity. But Alexandra would not countenance Anna's removal and Fischer soon after requested leave to resign from his post. He was replaced in April 1908 by Dr Evgeny Botkin, who immediately suggested that an upcoming trip to the Crimea – where Nicholas was to review the Black Sea Fleet – would be beneficial to the empress's health.

From now on Alexandra would be loath to consult anyone but Botkin. His appointment as court physician was, however, something of a poisoned chalice: Alexandra was the kind of patient who only tolerated doctors who agreed with her own self-diagnosis. He played up to her view of herself as a chronic invalid who must bear her affliction, as Father Grigory had taught her, 'in the nature of an offering'.[25] Her confirmed invalidism became a useful tool when dealing with the misbehaviour of her daughters, who were clearly affected by her constant absences from family life. 'When God thinks the time comes to make me better, He will, and not before', she told them, and they had better behave themselves to ensure this happened.[26]

In September 1909 the family headed for the Crimea by rail – the longest train ride any of the children had ever made and their first visit to the region, for Nicholas and Alexandra had not spent any real time there since Alexander III's death in 1894. At the port of Sevastopol they joined the *Shtandart* and sailed round the Crimean coast to welcoming fireworks and illuminations at Yalta and a warm, holiday atmosphere, before travelling on to the old summer palace at Livadia, 53 miles (85 km) further south. During the holiday the children rode, played tennis and swam from their private beach, often with their favourite cousin, eighteen-year-old Grand Duke Dmitri Pavlovich, who was now spending a great deal of time with the family. Nicholas was glad of Dmitri's company as he had always had a soft spot for him, and they spent much time going off on walks and rides together.[27] Alexandra kept to her bed for most of the time or sat on the veranda, receiving no one and often not even joining the family for lunch. Her recovery was very slow and affected everyone's spirits. But she refused to see any specialists, trusting to Botkin and her own self-medication with carrot juice, 'saying that this substance liquefied the blood, which was too thick'.[28] Perhaps her rigorous vegetarian diet was beneficial; by the end of October she had recovered sufficiently to take gentle walks and drives with her daughters and go shopping with them in Yalta.

That autumn at Livadia Alexey suffered another attack of bleeding when he once again hurt his leg. A French medical professor was called in and visited three times in secret. But he was a specialist in tuberculosis and 'declared himself incompetent to diagnose what it was', clearly not being told the child was suffering from haemophilia. Nor could another medical expert summoned from St Petersburg offer any palliatives.[29] By this time, as Spiridovich noted, it was becoming increasingly difficult to disguise the fact that there was something profoundly wrong with the tsarevich, 'which, like the Sword of Damocles, hung menacingly over the Imperial Family'. It was clear that in Alexey's case, as well as her own, Alexandra had given up on conventional medicine and, under the influence of her spiritual adviser Grigory, 'only counted upon the help of the Most High'.[30] Alexey's condition coupled with his mother's poor state of health meant that the family remained in Livadia almost until Christmas. But as the brilliant, sunny Crimean autumn turned to a cold and wet winter, there were only endless games of dominoes, halma and lotto and occasional film shows to divert the members of the household from the stultifying boredom that consumed them.

Their mother's chronic ill health was an emotional burden that her daughters struggled to cope with. 'God help that dearest mama will not be sick any more this winter,' Olga wrote to Grigory in November, 'or it will be so awful, sad and difficult.' Tatiana was anxious too, telling him that 'we feel bad seeing her so sick. Oh, if only you knew how hard it was for us to endure Mama's sickness. But yes, you *do* know, because you know everything.'[31] For the best part of six months that year of 1909 the imperial family had been almost totally absent from view in Russia. The four sisters were beginning to show the signs of their isolation from the real world and the natural interchange they needed with young people of their own age. Yet even now, Nicholas and Alexandra were planning the family's continued retreat – for the sake of Alexandra's and Alexey's poor health. Before leaving Livadia that Christmas they commissioned the building of a new palace to replace the dark and damp existing main palace (although the nearby brick-built Maly Palace where Alexander III had died was left standing). In this new home they intended to spend the whole of every spring and summer. For ordinary Russians it would continue to be, as the peasant saying went, 'a great height to God and a long way to the tsar'.[32]

*

New Year 1910 was a gloomy one in imperial Russia. For the first two months the court was in mourning for Grand Duke Mikhail Nikolaevich, the tsar's great-uncle, who had died in Cannes on 18 December (NS) the previous year. In April Alexandra lost her mistress of the robes, Princess Mariya Golitsyna, a woman whom she had counted as one of her closest ladies at court and a personal friend; barely a month later she was plunged into black again on the death of her uncle King Edward VII.[33]

In normal circumstances Nicholas and Alexandra would have led the public mourning in St Petersburg for Grand Duke Mikhail, but Alexandra was ill yet again. Everywhere that year 'the conversation wore the topic of the Imperial Family's seclusion threadbare', with mounting concern being voiced about 'the effect on public opinion and the nation of the long-continued absence from the capital of the Tsar and the imperial family'.[34] As the US diplomat in St Petersburg, Post Wheeler, recalled:

> They spent the spring and fall at Livadia in the Crimea. In the summer, when they were not at Peterhof, they were yachting on the imperial yacht, the *Standart*. The coast of Finland saw more of them than their own capital. In between they were at Tsarskoe Selo, the 'Tsar's City' only a handful of miles away, but so far as St. Petersburg was concerned it might have been a hundred . . . Society was at a loose end. It was not a wholesome situation either for them or for the nation. So the talk ran.[35]

St Petersburg had become 'a city with a frown', a sombre place oppressed by its history, concluded British journalist John Foster Fraser.[36] The social life of the capital was moribund and increasingly corrupt, its aristocracy deeply resistant to political change or social reform and fixated on rank. An outmoded, Gogolian bureaucracy still divided the population into two main camps – officials and non-officials – with the mass of the population looking upon the members of the inflated tsarist bureaucracy as 'vampires'. 'The hatred is covered, smothered, but it is there all the time', Foster Fraser argued.[37] At the heart of this polarized system stood an elusive tsar – 'timorous and brave, hesitant and resourceful, secretive and open-minded, suspicious and trusting' – a man who, far from the blood-thirsty image projected, was kindly, sincere and modest, a devoted husband and loving father but who, as tsar, was utterly ill equipped emotionally or morally for the task with which an accident of birth had charged him. The burden of responsibility was ageing Nicholas fast; and so was the emotional strain of having an invalid wife and son. 'Nature had framed him for a placid country gentleman, walking amid his flower beds in a linen blouse, with a stick instead of a sword. Never for a Tsar', concluded Post Wheeler.[38]

Stagnating in the absence of the tsar and tsaritsa, and with it their moral example, St Petersburg society was increasingly dominated by the reactionary grand dukes and their wives who saw themselves – in the face of Nicholas's incorrigible weakness as monarch – as the 'true champions of Imperial power', intent as they were on protecting their own wealth and power by propping up a tottering autocracy implacably opposed to democratic reform.[39] St

Petersburg society, as the French ambassador's wife put it, consisted of 'two or three hundred cliques, all of them social cut-throats', backed up by a Camorra of court officials, many of them also highly antipathetic to the imperial couple.[40] Holding centre stage was Nicholas's aunt, Maria Pavlovna, whose husband Vladimir (a man of expensive vices who had dissipated thousands of roubles on gambling and women) had died the previous February. Grand Duchess Vladimir, as she was often referred to, was German by birth. Like the tsaritsa she had converted to Russian Orthodoxy, albeit shortly before her husband's death and with a very determined eye on the dynastic future of her sons. But she had married almost as well as her monarch, coming, like Alexandra, from a fairly minor German dukedom – of Mecklenburg-Schwerin.

At her luxurious Florentine-style mansion on the Palace Embankment by the River Neva, a residence which more than rivalled the Alexander Palace, Grand Duchess Vladimir held court in the absence of Russia's real monarchs, her fabulous wealth enabling her to throw the most lavish receptions, charity bazaars and costume balls. Her four-day bazaar traditionally opened the Christmas-to-Lent season in St Petersburg and in the weeks that followed, hers were the most sought-after invitations in the capital. The grand duchess's lofty and forceful manner might be intimidating but her brilliant social connections and her natural energy ensured that she had a finger on the pulse of Russian high society. It also meant that she was at the centre of much intrigue in the capital focused against the increasingly unpopular tsaritsa.

As a result of her wide-reaching literary interests, Grand Duchess Vladimir had, at the end of 1909, invited a distinguished foreign visitor to come and stay. The best-selling British novelist Elinor Glyn had recently scored a big success in Russia with her romantic novel *Three Weeks*, and the grand duchess suggested Glyn might like to come to Russia to gather material for a Russian-based story.[41] 'Everyone always writes books about our peasants,' she had told her, 'come and write one about how the real people live.' Few remarks could be more symptomatic of the staggering indifference of her class to the plight of the ordinary Russian population.[42] Unfortunately for Glyn, having set off for Russia on the promise that the tsar and tsaritsa were about to emerge from Tsarskoe Selo and take a greater part in St Petersburg social life, she arrived to find the city in mourning for Grand Duke Mikhail. Far worse from a social point of view, she had come with an entirely new wardrobe of clothes from the couturier Lucile, as well as hats from Reboux of Paris, but she had no mourning clothes. The British ambassador's wife had had to go to her rescue and buy her 'the regulation headgear . . . a mourning bonnet of black crepe with a long and flowing veil'.[43]

From a window of the British Embassy on the Palace Embankment, on a cold grey day of receding snow and slush, Glyn watched the funeral cortège heading for the Peter and Paul Cathedral across the Neva on Zayachy Island, with the empress 'crouching back in her carriage' and Nicholas and the grand dukes walking behind, he pale-faced and like his cousins patently aware of their vulnerability to assassins. Advance warnings of bomb outrages had prompted the authorities to ban all spectators from watching at windows (bar the British Embassy) and soldiers and policemen had been set 'shoulder to shoulder, and back to back, in a double row facing both ways' along the entire 3-mile (4.8-km) route.[44] As the procession passed, Glyn noticed that the huge crowds stood there 'mute but unmoved'; there was none of the genuine mourning she had witnessed at Queen Victoria's funeral in 1901. 'The atmosphere was filled, not with grief but with apprehension, not with sorrow but with doom.'[45] For Glyn 'the blind, silent houses, the massed guards, and the hostile people proclaimed to all the world the inevitable passing of this tragic regime'. As she wrote in her journal that evening: 'Oh! How we should thank God for dear, free, safe, happy England.'[46]

The following day Glyn was deeply impressed by the ritual of the magnificent funeral service, the candles and incense and the beautiful but strangely alien singing of the priests. Only Nicholas was present, 'unnaturally composed, as though he wore a mask'; Alexandra, she was told, had 'refused' to come.[47] That, no doubt, is how her absence was perceived by the gossips; the reality was that the empress would have been incapable of standing through the four-hour-long ceremony. But inexorably, the drip-drip of negative gossip about her was doing its work, as Glyn noted: 'I was shocked to find that her unpopularity amounted to hatred, even as early as

1910.'[48] She had the distinct impression that St Petersburg society looked upon Grand Duchess Vladimir as the real Empress of Russia, for Alexandra now hardly ever emerged from her retirement at Tsarskoe Selo.[49] Indeed, Glyn professed herself to be 'shocked to witness the atmosphere of unhappiness and dread' that Alexandra's morbid personality shed over the Russian court – even in her absence.[50] It was the strained but dignified figure of Nicholas leading the mourning that had impressed her. But his presence at the grand duke's funeral had been considered reckless by those charged with his security, particularly his insistence on walking in the street procession behind the bier, and it had been 'an anxious day for everybody concerned'.

'Would the tsar and tsaritsa come to the Winter Palace when the court mourning was lifted?' everyone was asking two months later. 'That would mean one court ball, at least, which was better than nothing.'[51] In diplomatic circles a posting to St Petersburg was considered 'poisonous' and one that few enjoyed. Post Wheeler, who was there for six years, encountered a considerable amount of criticism of the restrictions placed on the Romanov daughters, as one society hostess complained to him:

> Poor things! . . . What a way to bring up imperial children! They might as well be in Peter-Paul [the fortress prison]. It is all right for the little Anastasia and for Marie . . . But for Tatiana and especially for Olga, who is fifteen, it is ridiculous.[52]

The isolation imposed on the girls by their mother was seen by many as cruel and narrow-minded: 'She wants them to grow up in ignorance of what she calls "the tragedy of the Russian court"', asserted one lady, alluding to Alexandra's horror of its immorality.[53] All of which makes it all the more extraordinary that the four Romanov sisters seemed so natural and well-rounded. Everyone who met them concurred that they were fine young women, who demonstrated affection, loyalty and a dignified sense of their role: 'They never let you forget that they are grand duchesses; but they are not forgetful of the feelings of others', as one lady-in-waiting commented.[54] But sightings of the imperial children in the city, especially Alexey, were incredibly rare. One had far more chance of seeing them out at Tsarskoe Selo. Post Wheeler recalled having the good fortune of encountering the tsarevich out with a Cossack minder, when he visited Tsarskoe with Countess Tolstoy one day. The boy was 'bundled in a long overcoat with a white astrakhan collar and a fur cap at a jaunty tilt', and 'talking eagerly, with many gestures, pausing now and then to kick up a cloud of snow'. 'I was all eyes', Wheeler admitted. 'The child was almost a legend, I knew no one who had ever seen him.' The countess, who knew the imperial family well, felt intensely sorry for Alexey: 'Poor child! With only his sisters, no boys of his own age to play with! The Empress is doing a great wrong to him, and to the girls too, but no one can make her see it!'[55] This widely held view of the imperial children could not of course be countered, although one English visitor granted an audience at Tsarskoe Selo was given the rare privilege of meeting Alexey and the girls.

> He seemed somewhat shy, and stood at one end of the room surrounded by his sisters, handsome young ladies, simply but neatly dressed. They seemed quite at their ease, and their manners were the frank unaffected manners of ordinary well brought up children. The moment they entered, a smile of motherly pride spread over the features of the Empress, and she advanced towards them placing her arm lovingly round her son's neck.[56]

Alexey was clearly the centre of their mother's universe, as a result of which the Romanov girls seemed doomed to a bland interchangeability, forever in the shadows of their charismatic brother. Yet behind the scenes shifts in the relationship between the five siblings were beginning to appear. Olga had increasingly been tasked by Alexandra with trying to make the wilful Alexey behave in public during her own frequent periods of indisposition. Once, attending a Boy Scout parade, he had tried to get out of the carriage to join in and when Olga had restrained him had 'slapped her face as hard as he could'. In response Olga hadn't so much as winced but had taken his hand and stroked it till Alexey had recovered his equilibrium. It was only when they were safely back at home that she had run to her room and burst into tears. Alexey was duly contrite; for two days he 'was repentance itself and made Olga accept his portion of dessert at table'. He loved Olga perhaps more than the others, for whenever he was reprimanded by his parents, he would 'declare that he was Olga's boy, pick up his toys, and go to her apartment'.[57]

By now Olga and Tatiana were becoming noticeably detached from the 'little pair', and Maria, the most self-effacing of the four, was beginning to suffer. Jealousy had also crept in for she sensed that perhaps her mother favoured Anastasia more. 'I have no secrets with Anastasia, I do not like secrets', Alexandra reassured her in one of her notes, only to send another within days: 'Sweet child you must promise me never again to think that nobody loves you. *How* did such an extraordinary idea get into your little head? Get it quickly out again.' Feeling unwanted by her older sisters, Maria had of late been seeking consolation in the friendship of her cousin Irina, Xenia's only daughter. But Alexandra told her this would only make things worse: her sisters would 'imagine then that you do not want to be with them; now that you are getting a big girl it is good that you should be more with them'.[58]

Maria clearly was anxious to win the approval and attention of her older siblings, hence perhaps the motive behind a letter on their behalf that she wrote to Alexandra in May 1910:

> My dear Mama! How are you feeling? I wanted to tell you that Olga would very much like to have her own room in Peterhof, because she and Tatiana have too many things and too little room. Mama at what age did you have your own room? Please tell me if it's possible to arrange. Mama at what age did you start wearing long dresses? Don't you think Olga would also like to let down her dresses. Mama why don't you move them both or just Olga. I think they would be comfortable where you slept when Anastasia had diphtheria. I kiss you. Maria. P.S. It was my idea to write to you.[59]

In the meantime, Maria's egocentric younger sibling Anastasia, who inhabited her own little world, was busy thinking along entirely different, idiosyncratic lines, scribbling in her notebook a list of birthday wants that year:

> For my birthday I would like to receive toy hair-combs [for her dolls], a machine on which I can write, an icon of Nikolay the Wonderworker, some kind of outfit, an album for sticking in

pictures, then a big bed, like Maria has, for the Crimea, I want a real-life dog, a basket for spoiled paper when I write some book or other . . . then a book in which to write little plays for children that can be performed.[60]

The need for someone to watch over four such different and rapidly developing personalities during the crucial years of puberty was increasing in the absence of their mother, but throughout 1910 problems had been developing with the person on whom most of this had devolved – Sofya Tyutcheva. She hadn't made many friends and several of the staff disliked her authoritarian manner; according to one diarist she was referred to as a 'man in skirts' for her domineering manner and the way in which she still treated the growing sisters like naughty little children.[61] Fond as she was of the girls, the highly moral Tyutcheva was worried about the increasing attention – or rather distraction – in their lives of the young officers in the *Shtandart* and troubled by the propriety of their deepening relationships with them during their Finnish holidays.[62]

Although her devotion to the family was undeniable and her intentions well-meant, Sofya's judgemental manner and her constant laying-down of the law meant she was in danger of crossing the line between her own duties as carer and those of Alexandra as the girls' mother, with the ultimate responsibility – rather than she – for their moral welfare. Tyutcheva had never got on with the empress and she did not approve of the more relaxed 'English' style of the girls' upbringing. According to Anna Vyrubova, 'She wished to change the whole system, make it entirely Slav and free from any imported ideas', and was now openly criticizing the tsaritsa even in front of her charges.[63] She had hated Rasputin from the first and was highly critical of the relationship the girls and their mother had with him, which she considered demeaning and inappropriate. The sisters were clearly anxious about the gathering hostility towards Grigory, as Tatiana intimated in a note to her mother in March 1910: 'I am so afread that S. I. [Sofya Ivanovna] can speak to Maria [Vishnyakova] about our friend some thing bad. I hope our nurse will be nice to our friend now.'[64]

That January and February of 1910, Alexey had been plagued with pains in his arm and leg and Rasputin had visited the family on ten occasions at Tsarskoe Selo, often staying late and talking at length with them. Having been asked by Alexandra to say no more to the children on the matter of Rasputin's visits Sofya Tyutcheva pulled back for a while, but then once more began gossiping with Grand Duchess Xenia about his free access to the family, and the children in particular. 'He's always there, goes into the nursery, visits Olga and Tatiana while they are getting ready for bed, sits there talking to them and *caressing* them', she had told her.* Under instruction from their mother, the children were becoming increasingly secretive; even Elizaveta Naryshkina (who had taken over from the recently deceased Princess Golitsyna as mistress of the robes), felt that such was their mother's fear of scandal, that the children were being drilled to 'hide their thoughts and feelings about Rasputin from others'.[65] 'It can hardly be beneficial to accustom the children to such dissimulation', thought Grand Duke Konstantin.[66] Certainly Tyutcheva's renewed assault in the summer of 1910 was a criticism too far; it further undermined the view of Alexandra within the imperial family, with even her sister Ella and Xenia questioning the wisdom of her continuing patronage of Rasputin.

Those such as Lili Dehn, who loved Alexandra and respected her trust in Rasputin, put Tyutcheva's behaviour down to 'spite and jealousy'; Anna Vyrubova and Iza Buxhoeveden both were convinced that she was the source of much of the unfavourable gossip about the empress and Rasputin circulating in St Petersburg. But the damage had already been done; the rumours were becoming ever more lurid by the day. Dehn herself soon had good reason to be grateful for Rasputin's help, when her two-year-old son Alexander (known to everyone as Titi) contracted diphtheria. Seeing how desperately ill Titi was, Alexandra and Anna Vyrubova had persuaded her to ask for Grigory's help. When he arrived, he had sat for a long time on the boy's bed, looking intently at him. Suddenly Titi woke up, 'stretched out his little hand, laughed and mouthed the

---

* In her book *My Father*, p. 56, Maria Rasputin denied this allegation vehemently: 'My father was never received in Their Majesties' bedchamber, nor in those of the Grand Duchesses, but only in that of Alexis Nicolaievitch [*sic*], or in one of the drawing rooms, and once or twice in the schoolroom.'

words "uncle, uncle"'. Titi told him that his head ached 'ever so badly' but all Rasputin did was 'take the boy's hand, ran his finger down the side of his nose, stroked his head and kissed him'. As he left he told Lili that the fever was going; her son would live.[67] By the following morning Titi's symptoms had indeed abated; he recovered a few days later. Lili remained convinced that this was entirely coincidental with Rasputin's visit, but she was aware that Alexandra's faith in him was based on her absolute conviction that he was the only person who could help her son. In this regard, any power Rasputin had over the empress was, as far as Lili was concerned, entirely mystical – and never mercenary or political.[68]

But on the pages of the influential daily newspaper *Moskovskie vedomosti* and elsewhere, the campaign of vilification against the empress and her 'friend' was mounting. The satirical magazine *Ogonek* was publishing interviews with his followers – giving lurid details of their 'Egyptian nights of initiation' into Rasputin's circle.[69] With Prime Minister Stolypin renewing his investigation of him, Rasputin once more felt it best to beat a retreat to the safety of Siberia.

Chapter Nine

IN ST PETERSBURG WE WORK,
BUT AT LIVADIA WE LIVE

❦

In the summer of 1910, in the face of the continuing dramatic decline in the tsaritsa's health, Dr Botkin persuaded her to go for a rest cure at Bad Nauheim in Hesse, combining it with a visit to Ernie and other European relatives. 'It is very important for her to get better, for her own sake and the children's and mine', Nicholas told his mother before they left. 'I am completely run down mentally by worrying over her health.' His words to Anna Vyrubova were even more candid: '"I would do anything," he said in quiet desperation, "even going to prison, if she could only be well again."'[1]

The Romanov family arrived at Schloss Friedberg near Nauheim at the end of August. Most of their 140-strong entourage (inflated by the presence of so many security officers) was farmed out to guest houses in town. Welcome though it was to Ernie and his family, the visit was a logistical nightmare, not to mention an enormous expense. During the four weeks of their stay, which was an entirely private visit, Nicholas for once adopted civvies, and made occasional excursions incognito into town. Nevertheless, the security was as tight as at Cowes in 1909, with marksmen and dogs patrolling the grounds of the castle, and Nicholas's Cossack Escort supplemented by Okhrana agents under the supervision of Spiridovich shadowing the family's every move.[2]

An English visitor, the writer and literary hostess Violet Hunt, recalled the hoo-ha attendant on the Romanovs' arrival. One evening a notice was posted up in her *pension*, begging the guests not to pursue, persecute, or mob the Tzar of Russia, who was staying at Friedberg, three miles off, and who came in every day with the Tzaritza and her children . . . He went in danger of his life so obvious and so imminent that the craven and business-like municipality of Friedberg had insisted on his insuring the public monuments of that place at his own expense!

Determined efforts were made by Spiridovich to 'disseminate fallacious announcements' of the tsar's movements, in order to deflect the curious from pursuit of the imperial couple. 'When [Nicholas] was supposed to be going to the baths it was at the Kursaal [public rooms] you would find him; when it was the riding school it was much more likely to be the lake.'[3] Violet Hunt caught sight of him there, 'a disconsolate figure, encouraging his boy to sail his tiny boat or being rowed about in one'. She often saw Alexandra on her way to the baths, 'in black with pearls . . . her face a tragic mask . . . haughty, dejected. She looked a lovely fool; nay hardly lovely now – the morbid shadow of a queen.'[4] At a shop in town full of Venetian glass she again encountered Nicholas with Alexey, intently examining some *objets d'art*:

> I saw his face through the beautiful clear glass; it did not exhibit mere terror, for he was a brave man, but all at once it seemed implicit with a summing up, a résumé of the composite agony of all this race of kings consciously marked down for destruction. His grandfather before him – his uncle – and only the little son with his head below the counter to carry on the monstrous imposthume of Russian Royalty![5]

Well might Nicholas have been worried, for during his stay at Friedberg came news of the *coup d'état* in Portugal on 5 October against the constitutional monarch Manuel II; it was yet another warning, for Manuel's father, like Nicholas's grandfather, had been assassinated (in 1908). A lady witnessed Nicholas's reaction when the newsboy came to the Kurhaus (the spa house) where they were taking tea. 'The Czar seemed to turn white and apparently was greatly shocked.' Pulling out a coin to pay the boy he read the news story from end to end: 'I could read from his face how it had affected him. In his eyes was fright and occasionally they seemed almost desperate. With some effort he shook off his feelings and realized he was the object of curious persons' gaze. Assuming an air as if nothing had happened he walked to his waiting automobile.'[6]

At Friedberg the two families were joined by several more relatives: Prince Andrew of Greece, his wife Alice and their two daughters Margarita and Theodora; Alexandra's sister Victoria of Battenberg and her husband Louis and their children Louise, George and Louis. Alexandra's two other sisters also briefly joined them: Irene, with her husband Prince Henry and their two boys Sigismund and the haemophiliac Waldemar, and the widowed Grand Duchess Ella – who had recently taken the veil and founded a convent in Moscow – wearing the most stylish of grey nun's habits and wimple, looking like Elizabeth, the pious heroine of Wagner's opera *Tannhäuser*.

The four Romanov sisters adored the company of their second cousins Louise and Louis, better known to them as Dickie. Although only ten at the time, in later life, and by then Lord Mountbatten, Dickie vividly remembered the girls: 'Oh, they were lovely, and terribly sweet, far more beautiful than their photographs.' He was totally smitten with the third sister: 'I was crackers about Marie, and was determined to marry her. She was absolutely lovely.'* Indeed, to his eyes all four girls were blossoming: 'They seemed to get more and more beautiful every time we saw them.'[7]

Cousin Thora had also come over from England with Emily Loch. The morning after their arrival, Olga and Tatiana were eager to go out shopping with Thora in Nauheim, where the jewellers' shops entranced them, just as had happened in Cowes. They returned the next day and 'chose heaps to be inspected by the Empress which we took back with us', recalled Emily, but the crowds that gathered round them had been considerable, and the girls had little opportunity to spend their pocket money, which had been regulated at 15 roubles a month by Alexandra in January of that year.[8] At

---

* In Hough's 1985 biography, Mountbatten misremembers this meeting as being at Heiligenberg in 1913, but the family did not travel out of Russia that year. The last time they visited Germany *en famille* was this particular summer of 1910. Dickie did not see Maria again but he never forgot her. In later life, he kept her photograph on the mantelpiece in his bedroom until his death.

Friedberg and among their cousins, the four sisters seemed happy to play childish games of diablo (a juggling toy) and 'bumble puppy' (a game for two with a ball on a string tied to a post). There were plenty of carriage and bicycle rides in the park too, while Alexey had fun playing with Ernie's two sons Georg Donatus and Louis and was taken out on bike rides by Derevenko, sitting in a specially adapted bicycle seat. They also enjoyed several motor car expeditions with the tsar (who enjoyed driving rather too fast), travelling into the densely wooded countryside for picnics. It was such a rare opportunity for the girls to mix and play with cousins of their own age, with even Nicholas for once letting go. 'He seemed as happy as a schoolboy in holiday-time.'[9] Everyone found the girls polite and solicitous, impressed by how conscientiously 'they took the greatest pains at table to make conversation for the Gentleman-in Waiting'.[10]

After more than a month at Bad Nauheim the family moved on to Wolfsgarten for an additional three weeks with Ernie and his second wife, Onor. Alexandra's health had improved; Dr Georg Grote, who had attended her at Nauheim, had found no sign of organic heart trouble but confirmed that the state of the empress's health was so serious that 'had she not occupied such an exalted position, she should have been sent to a sanatorium with two sisters of mercy to take care of her, not letting her see anyone'. She 'takes too much on herself', said Grote, 'and hides her sufferings from everyone'.[11] Nevertheless, Alexandra was transformed by being among close family that summer, as Dickie Mountbatten recalled. 'Even that crazy lunatic my aunt the Empress was absolutely sweet and charming.' However, many of her relatives were seriously worried about her mental stability. Dickie overheard his father say to his mother at Nauheim: 'Alicky is absolutely mad – she's going to cause a revolution. Can't you *do* anything?'[12]

The tsaritsa's constant ill health was often being put down to hypochondria. But Alexandra was adamant that her ailments were not imagined. 'If people speak to you about my "nerves",' she wrote to Mariya Baryatinskaya, 'please strongly contradict it. They are as strong as ever, it's the "overtired heart".'[13] She was aware of how her ill health was affecting the children; 'having a mama who is always ill does not make life bright for you', she told Maria that December, but it had its positives: 'I know it's dull . . . but it teaches you all to be loving and gentle.'[14] She was now having to deal with one of eleven-year-old Maria's first adolescent crushes, which she had confided in her. Grigory had clearly once more been acting as agony aunt, and had told Maria not to 'dwell too much on him', and not to give anything away in the presence of others. 'Now that you are a big girl, you must always be more careful and not show those feelings', Alexandra reiterated. 'One must not let others see what one feels inside.'[15] Such studied reticence had encouraged the view people on the outside now held of Alexandra as aloof and unfeeling. 'It was the usual policy of hush-hush', recalled Iza Buxhoeveden; Alexandra told her that it was 'not *comme il faut* for our family to be known to be ill' – and that included Alexey. The only time the public were to be told something was wrong was 'when someone is dying'.[16]

It was therefore left to the foreign press to speculate. 'The Czarina Slowly Dying of Terror' ran one headline, relaying a story from the Rome *Tribuna* claiming that Alexandra had 'long been the unhappiest royal personage in Europe' as a result of the high security isolating her and the family from the outside world, for it had made her 'a victim of melancholia and morbid fears'.[17] It was almost impossible, the papers claimed, to recognize in 'this sad-faced sombre-eyed woman the merry girl who once delighted the hearts of the cottagers at Balmoral'. 'Her fear of attack by revolutionaries was now all-consuming.' There was, said one Australian paper, 'no more pitiful tragedy in the history of any royal house'.[18]

*

By November 1910 and back at Tsarskoe, Nicholas was determined that his daughters should enjoy something of the winter season in the capital. In January he and Olga attended a performance of *Boris Godunov* starring the famous bass Feodor Chaliapin, a great favourite with the family. In February Olga and Tatiana were his companions at Tchaikovsky's opera *Eugene Onegin* and later Nicholas took all four girls to see the ballet *The Sleeping Beauty*. Such trips were small consolation for the absence of their mother, but all five children thoroughly enjoyed a concert that winter featuring their favourite army balalaika orchestra.

Post Wheeler and his wife Hallie were there, surrounded by members of the diplomatic community and the ubiquitous Okhrana men. The imperial party arrived: Maria Feodorovna, Maria Pavlovna, and 'trooping after her, not only the two older daughters, Olga and Tatiana, but the younger pair, Marie and Anastasia' – an event remarkable because it was the first time that the Wheelers had seen all four sisters together. 'The two older ones were in simple white, each with a string of small pearls, and with their heavy dark hair hanging over their shoulders looked very girlish and sweet.' Olga carried 'a little bunch of violets' and Maria and Anastasia had boxes of 'silver-wrapped chocolates'. Anastasia sat down in the box immediately next to Hallie 'and gave me a demure little smile as she set her box of chocolates on the railing between us'.[19] Then, as Hallie recalled, 'there was a stir, the whole audience was rising and facing the back', as the tsar in marshal's uniform entered with the tsarevich 'dressed all in white cloth braided with gold'.[20]

'The house was very still, for it was witnessing what Russia had never seen before. People were completely taken aback', recalled Hallie. The tsarevich was so little seen in public, that for most Russians 'he had been only a fable'.[21] During the balalaika concert that followed Alexey thrilled to the performance, for he loved the instrument and was learning to play it himself. At the end the entire audience rose to its feet roaring its approval, Alexey by his father's side, sweet and childishly solemn, 'stealing cautious glances now and then to right and left'. '*Mon dieu! Comme il est adorable*', Hallie heard a woman near her remark:

> There was on every face the adoration that through the centuries had been lavished on the person of the 'Great White Tsar', and it was more than that, for this little lad, with his boyish beauty, typified the future to which Russia looked . . . The Tsar stood for the reign that Russia knew and was now coming to distrust, but in the hands of the little future autocrat were the lambent possibilities of which it dreamed.[22]

Such adoration of the little heir to the throne served to underline the feelings expressed by Maria Feodorovna back in 1906 that the 'unfortunate little girls are moved into secondary importance' with Alexey's arrival.[23] They certainly were in the public's estimation, for everyone's eyes were on the tsarevich. Returning to her box after the interval, Hallie noticed that Anastasia and Maria had already taken up their places near her side of the railing. 'She was not a beautiful child, but there was something frank and winning about her', she recalled of Anastasia. 'On the flat railing sat the now depleted box of chocolates and her white gloves were sadly smudged. She shyly held out the box to me, and I took one.' As the music struck up Anastasia began softly humming the folk tune they were playing. Hallie asked her what it was. 'Oh,' she replied, 'it is an old song about a little girl who had lost her doll.' The lingering notes of that lovely song hummed by the young grand duchess, and the sight of her chocolate-soiled gloves that evening, would stay with Hallie for many years.[24]

*

In the spring of 1911 Alexandra admitted to her sister-in-law Onor that the 'cure' at Nauheim had done her no good: 'Personally I have felt no benefit . . . and have been so bad again.'[25] Olga was despairing of ever seeing her mother well again. 'Don't get downhearted, my darling, if she is not getting as strong as you would like her to be,' her aunt Ella consoled her, 'it won't happen quickly, the real effect of the treatment won't be felt for a month or two, if not after a second course of it.' Meanwhile Ella advised that Olga invest her best efforts in patient prayer on her mother's behalf.[26] In the spring at least Olga had the excitement of reviewing the new recruits to her Guards corps, but Tatiana was becoming jealous. 'I would like so much to go to the review of the second division as I am also the second daughter and Olga was at the first so now it is my turn', she complained to Alexandra, adding that 'at the second division I will see whom I *must* see . . . you know whom . . . !!!!??!?!'[27] Tatiana too was confiding in her mother about her first teenage crushes. More military reviews followed in August, at the big parade ground at Krasnoe Selo, during which Olga and Tatiana, who were both accomplished horsewomen (having learnt to ride in 1903),[28] took great pride in riding out side saddle and in uniform to inspect the regiments of which their father had gifted them the honorary command on their 14th name days: the 3rd Elizavetgrad Hussars for Olga and the 8th Voznesensk Uhlans for Tatiana. Maria would have her own regiment too – the 9th Kazan Dragoons in 1913 – but a glum-faced Anastasia was still not old enough. The *Shtandart* officers had teased her that in view of her lively personality she should be made commander of the St Petersburg fire brigade.[29]

During the military reviews that spring the girls had enjoyed a visit from an English cousin, Prince Arthur of Connaught (son of Alexandra's uncle the Duke of Connaught), a captain in the Royal Scots Greys who had come as an observer. However, the unmarried twenty-seven-year-old prince had, as British ambassador's daughter Meriel Buchanan noted, other preoccupations: 'Prince Arthur is coming out next week for the manoeuvres and also (secretly) to look at the Emperor's daughter.'[30] This covert inspection of Olga is no surprise, although we know nothing of her impression of Arthur or his of her.* As the eldest Romanov daughter, she was approaching her sixteenth birthday, a marriageable age, and interest in her in the royal marriage market had long been gathering.* Aware of the need for her two eldest daughters to take their position in society, Alexandra was already planning their official appearance at two family weddings of the children of Grand Duke Konstantin, the first, of his oldest son, Ioannchik, to Princess Helena of Serbia at Peterhof on 21 August.

'They have all grown a lot,' Alexandra told Onor as she prepared for this, 'Tatiana is already taller than Olga, whose dresses almost reach the floor now. – Skirt hemlines drop and hair goes up when they reach the age of 16 – how time flies.' As for herself, she was likely to be absent: 'I will barely put in an appearance; will have to see how strong I am, and that won't be much.'[31] In the event, Alexandra was not well enough to attend Ioannchik's wedding but her five good-looking children made an impression, Alexey 'charming in the uniform of the Imperial family Riflemen' and the grand duchesses wearing Russian court dresses, 'white with pink flowers

---

* Prince Arthur finally found himself a bride in 1913 when he married Princess Alexandra, Duchess of Fife.

but no trains and pink *kokoshniki*'. The groom's brother thought they 'looked lovely'.[32] No doubt Ioannchik did too, for he had been carrying a torch for Olga since seeing her in 1904 at Alexey's christening. Even in November of 1909 he had still been holding out hope, for despite his having had a succession of short-lived romantic attachments in his search for a bride, Olga had left 'an indelible mark on him'. Ioannchik had travelled to the Crimea the previous autumn 'only out of hunger to see Olga', but having openly admitted his feelings to the tsar and tsaritsa there, had finally given up hope. 'They won't let me marry Olga Nikolaevna', he had told his father disconsolately.[33] But now, at last, the awkward, gangly Ioannchik, who was extremely unprepossessing as suitors go, had found a suitable royal bride, a fact which alarmed the intensely naïve Tatiana, 'How funny if they might have children, can they be kissing . . . ? What foul, fie! [sic]'[34]

Just three days later Grand Duke Konstantin's eldest daughter Tatiana was married to Prince Bagration-Mukhransky in a small family ceremony at Pavlovsk, attended by the imperial family. The weddings were closely followed at the end of the month by an important official visit to Kiev. The girls were increasingly deputizing for their mother during her bouts of illness and this trip marked their first major public role in this regard. They were in the Ukrainian city for the inauguration of a new statue to Alexander II, to mark the fiftieth anniversary of his liberation of the serfs in 1861, as well as to visit the famous Pechersky Monastery and attend two large military reviews on 1 and 2 September. Although Alexandra attended the unveiling of the statue and managed a long day of official duties on the 1st, she then retreated, exhausted. That evening Olga and Tatiana accompanied Nicholas to the Kiev Municipal Theatre for a performance of Rimsky-Korsakov's opera *The Tale of Tsar Saltan*. Here numerous local dignitaries and politicians, including Prime Minister Stolypin, joined them.

During the second interval Stolypin had been standing in the aisle, at the balustrade very near to the imperial box, when a young man rushed towards him with a gun and shot at him twice. 'Fortunately,' as Alexandra was relieved to tell Onor in a letter soon afterwards, 'N., O. and T. were in the foyer when it happened.'[35]

Sofya Tyutcheva who was there as chaperone remembered Olga suggesting they went outside to get some tea, Nicholas having complained of feeling so hot in their box.[36] Out in the foyer they 'heard two noises, like the sound of an object falling', Nicholas later wrote to his mother. He thought 'a pair of binoculars must have fallen on somebody's head from above', and ran back into the box to look:

> To the right I saw a group of officers and others dragging someone, a few ladies were screaming, and there right opposite me stood Stolypin. He turned slowly to face me, and made the sign of the cross in the air with his left hand.[37]

Olga and Tatiana had tried to restrain their father but as Nicholas instinctively reached towards Stolypin, he noticed that the prime minister had been hit. Stolypin slowly sank into his seat and everyone rushed to his aid, including Dr Botkin. Stolypin muttered a message for the tsar, which the Minister of the Imperial Court, Count Freedericksz, brought to him: 'Your Majesty, Petr Arkadevich has asked me to tell you that he is happy to die for you.' 'I hope there is no reason to talk of death', the tsar replied. 'I fear there is', replied Freedericksz – for one of the bullets had entered Stolypin's liver.[38]

Despite his wounds, Stolypin heroically managed, with assistance, to walk out of the theatre and into an ambulance, which rushed him to 'a first class private clinic' where he 'took Holy Communion' and 'spoke very lucidly'.[39] Meanwhile, his attacker, Dmitri Bogrov, a young lawyer from a prosperous Jewish family in the city (who had been both a revolutionary activist and an informer for the Okhrana), was set upon by members of the audience who would have lynched him if they could. After Bogrov was bundled off by the police the cast of the opera came onto the stage and joined the audience in singing the National Anthem, Nicholas at the front of his box 'obviously distressed but showing no fear'.[40] 'I left with the girls at eleven', he later wrote to Maria Feodorovna. 'You can imagine with what emotions.' 'Tatiana came home very tearful and is still a little shaken,' Alexandra told Onor the following day, 'whereas Olga put on a brave face throughout.'[41] The following morning Sofya Tyutcheva, who had not slept all night from the shock of what she had seen, was surprised to find the girls calmer than she expected after their experience. Noticing how disconcerted she was by this, their nurse Mariya Vishnyakova came up to her and whispered: 'He's already there', meaning Rasputin, who had happened to be in Kiev at the time. 'Then it all became clear to me', Tyutcheva later wrote.[42]

Hopes remained high that Stolypin would recover from his wounds and the bulletins seemed favourable. 'They think he is out of danger', Alexandra told Onor. 'His liver seems to be only slightly affected. The bullet hit his Vladimir Cross and then bounced off in another direction.'[43] Nicholas meanwhile was obliged to continue with his engagements in Kiev and on the 4th attended a major review of troops with the children, followed by visits to museums and to the first school to be founded in Kiev, now celebrating its hundredth anniversary.

The Russian writer Nadezhda Mandelshtam was an eleven-year-old pupil at that time. She remembered the day vividly and how moved she had been by the sight of 'the very handsome boy and four sad girls', one of whom, Maria, was the same age as herself. It prompted her to ponder the difficult lives they led:

> I suddenly understood that I was much happier than these unfor-
> tunate girls; after all, I could run around with the dogs on the
> street, make friends with the boys, not learn my lessons, make
> mischief, go to bed late, read all kinds of junk and fight with my
> brothers and anybody else. I and my governesses had a very
> simple arrangement: we'd leave that house together, purposefully,
> and then go our separate ways – they to their rendezvous and
> I to my boys – I didn't make friends with girls – you can only
> really fight with boys. But these poor princesses were bound in
> everything: they were polite, affectionate, friendly, attentive . . .
> they weren't even allowed to fight . . . poor girls.[44]

The tsar twice went to visit Stolypin again, but on both occasions Stolypin's wife Olga, blaming him for the attack, refused to allow Nicholas to see him.[45] On 5 September Stolypin died of sepsis and Olga Stolypina declined to accept the tsar's condolences. With martial law declared in Kiev and 30,000 troops on alert, fears spread of an anti-Jewish pogrom in retaliation, prompting many of the Jewish residents to flee the city. The imperial family meanwhile boarded their train and headed for the Black Sea coast and the *Shtandart*, Nicholas 'giving very strict instructions to the governor General Feodor Trepov', as he left, 'that he would not allow a pogrom against the Jews on any pretext whatsoever'.[46]

Bogrov was tried by military court and hanged ten days later in Kiev, despite a plea for clemency from Stolypin's widow. Having long anticipated his own violent death Stolypin had asked to be buried near the place of his murder and was interred at the Pechersky Monastery in Kiev. Alexandra might have mourned the manner of Stolypin's death but she did not mourn his loss, for he had always been implacably opposed to Rasputin. When the imperial party later arrived at Sevastopol en route to Livadia, bands and illuminations greeted them on the seafront. One of the ladies-in-waiting thought this inappropriate – as they all did, so soon after Stolypin's assassination – and said as much to Alexandra, who snapped: 'He was only a minister, but this is the Russian emperor.' Sofya Tyutcheva couldn't fathom her response: she had seen how distraught Alexandra had been and how she had comforted Stolypin's widow. What had provoked this sudden change of mood? 'There was only one thing I could put it down to,' she later concluded, convinced that the entire family was in absolute thrall to Rasputin. 'It was that same baleful influence which in the end destroyed the unfortunate Alexandra Feodorovna and all her family.'[47]

*

After the horror of Stolypin's murder the family was very glad to escape to the Crimea, where their newly constructed palace was ready for occupation. The Crimea had always been 'the loveliest gem in the crown of the czar', a territorial trophy annexed by Catherine the Great in 1783 at the end of numerous wars with the Ottoman Empire.[48] Gleaming white in the brilliant sunshine atop the rugged southern coast, the palace was surrounded by gardens of vibrant-coloured and sweet-smelling bougainvillea and oleander, trailing vines of glycinia, and all around 'a veritable riot of roses of every colour and shape'.*[49] There was plenty of shade too from

---

* During the Crimean War of 1854–6 British soldiers had written home describing

exotic palms, olive trees, and pines and cypresses, and below the palace, the family had its own private rocky beach and a sea to bathe in as blue as the Aegean. No wonder Livadia was named after the Greek word for a beautiful meadow or lawn. It literally was a heaven on earth for the Romanov children and they spoke of it always as 'their real home'. As one of the Romanov sisters later put it: 'In St Petersburg we work; but at Livadia we live.'[50] Livadia was also an important refuge for an increasingly world-weary Nicholas and his invalid wife. For those with money and social status the Crimea was the Russian equivalent of the French Riviera, with Yalta, 2 miles (3 km) from the palace, its most fashionable resort, and the Russian social set all arrived here for the balmy autumn months before the onset of the winter season in St Petersburg. Here, more than anywhere else in Russia, they were most likely to catch a glimpse of their elusive imperial family, for in Livadia the Romanovs were far more relaxed and informal than at Tsarskoe Selo.

The Livadia Palace was two-storeyed and Italian Renaissance in style, with large windows that let in the light, and faced in local white Inkerman limestone – prompting its popular name as the 'White Palace'. It had been completed inside sixteen months, including a second house for the imperial entourage, and had all the modern conveniences of central heating, lifts and telephones. Having taken possession on 20 September Nicholas wrote to his mother: 'We cannot find the words to express our joy and the pleasure of having such a house, built exactly as we wished . . . The views in all directions are so beautiful, especially of Yalta and the sea. There is so much light in the rooms and you remember how dark it was in the old house.'[51] Inside all was simplicity, much in the *style moderne* that Alexandra favoured. The private apartments on the second floor had the preferred white furniture and chintz fabrics, and as usual there were flowers everywhere.[52] The windows and balconies at the back of the palace gave out over the sea: Olga and Tatiana delighted in taking their morning French lessons with Pierre Gilliard out on the balcony. On the northern side of the

---

the exquisite flowers growing wild all over the peninsula. Many of them dug up Crimean crocus and snowdrop bulbs to take back to England with them.

palace facing inland, the palace looked out onto the rugged Crimean mountains in the distance. A cool and shady inner courtyard featured Italianate marble colonnades and a fountain surrounded by a pretty knot garden. It was a favourite place for the entourage to escape the heat of the day and sit and chat after luncheon.

An idyllic late summer and autumn at Livadia followed for the Romanov children. There were wonderful days of hiking in the hills with their father, taking drives along the coast to a favourite picnic spot – such as St George's Monastery perched high on the cliffs at Cape Fiolent – or journeys into the Crimean heartland, past trees heavy with succulent fruit, to the tsar's own vineyard at Massandra, which produced the finest wines in the Crimea. Day after sunny day was spent riding and playing tennis with Grand Duchess Xenia's children and other relatives who visited. Swimming was also a great favourite, though after Anastasia nearly drowned one day when an unexpectedly large wave hit them and Nicholas had to rescue her, he had had a swimming pool made of canvas sails attached to wooden posts erected down at the beach for the children's safety, where they could swim under the watchful eye of Andrey Derevenko.[53]

With her pathological dislike of studying and of any kind of constraints on her physical freedom, Anastasia was in clover, as she told their tutor PVP, who was staying in Yalta with Pierre Gilliard:

> Our rooms here are very large and clean and white and we have real fruit and grapes growing here . . . I am so happy that we don't have these horrid lessons. In the evening we all sit together, four of us, the gramophone plays, we listen to it and play together . . . I don't miss Tsarskoe Selo at all, because I can't even tell you how bored I am there.[54]

Everything about the palace filled the girls with energy and delight. They enjoyed nothing better than going up and running out along the galvanized roof and delighting in the noise their footsteps made. And the nights there were so full of light. Anastasia was entranced by the sky and loved going out on the roof to 'study the formations of the stars', for in the Crimea they seemed to shine extra-bright.[55]

During their stays at Livadia, as at home in Tsarskoe Selo, the family enjoyed regular film shows on Saturdays in the covered riding school. This was such an important event in their lives that the children would spend the following week talking about it.[56] Elizaveta Naryshkina was charged with vetting the films, requiring court photographer Alexander Yagelsky (who had also been designated to shoot official footage of the imperial family at all their public appearances) to edit out any parts she objected to.*[57] What the children saw for the most part were newsreels or travelogues from Yagelsky's own *Tsarist Chronicles* of the family, or films of educational merit. But they also saw dramas such as *The Defence of Sevastopol* – about the siege of the naval base during the Crimean War – which, at 100 minutes long, was the first major historical feature film to be made in Russia and which was premiered especially for the imperial family at the Livadia Palace on 26 October 1911.[58]

Nicholas also relished the informality of life at Livadia and the family gatherings they had there, for several of their Romanov relatives had summer homes in the vicinity. Grand Duchess George (Nicholas's cousin, a daughter of the King of Greece) was nearby at Harax; his sister Xenia and her husband Sandro and their seven children were at Ai-Todor; the Montenegrin sisters Militza and Stana had estates at Dulber and Chair, although they now had little contact with Nicholas and Alexandra. Other influential families spent the spring and autumn in the Crimea: the Vorontsovs at Alupka, the Golitsyns at Novyi Svet and the Yusupovs, who had two beautiful homes: one the Moorish palace of Kokoz inland on the road to Sevastopol, and the other at Koreiz on the coast of the Black Sea.

During the long summer evenings when the Romanovs visited Harax, Grand Duchess George's lady-in-waiting Agnes de Stoeckl would often find herself looking at the four lovely sisters and wondering 'what their future might be'. Twenty-three-year-old Prince Christopher of Greece, who had been visiting his sister Grand Duchess George that summer, confessed to Agnes that he 'greatly admired the Grand Duchess Olga . . . and he asked me if I thought he had any chance'. They talked it over with his sister and, after giving Christopher 'a stiff whisky and soda', Grand Duchess George dispatched him to the Livadia Palace to try his

---

* Yagelsky worked for the firm of K. E. von Gann, based at Tsarskoe Selo.

luck. He came back with his tail between his legs; Nicholas had been kind but firm: 'Olga is too young to think of such a thing as marriage yet', he had told him.[59]

That might be so, but Olga and Tatiana were growing up fast, and Sofya Tyutcheva had already noticed with some alarm their coquettish behaviour with some of the officers in the *Shtandart*.[60] Several of these men joined the family at Livadia for games of tennis, which were Nicholas's principal distraction from his heavy workload. Tennis matches were a golden opportunity for the eldest girls to see much more of their favourites: Nikolay Sablin, Pavel Voronov and Nikolay Rodionov.[61] Like Sofya Tyutcheva, General Mosolov noticed the older girls' growing interest in the opposite sex and how the sometimes childish games they played with officers 'changed into a series of flirtations all very innocent'. 'I do not, of course, use the word "flirtation" quite in the ordinary sense of the term', he pointed out, for 'the young officers could better be compared with the pages or squires of dames of the Middle Ages'. They were all intensely loyal to the tsar and his daughters and thus were 'polished to perfection by one of their superiors, who was regarded as the Empress's squire of dames'. What disturbed Mosolov, however, was the sisters' astonishing unworldliness: 'even when the two eldest had grown up into real young women one might hear them talking like little girls of ten or twelve'.[62]

Nevertheless, the physical transformation in Olga between her fifteenth and sixteenth birthdays had been considerable. Many remarked how the rather plain and serious grand duchess had now blossomed into an elegant beauty. Her tutor Pierre Gilliard had been taken aback, on returning to Russia from a visit to his family in Switzerland, by how Olga had become so slender and graceful. She was now 'a tall girl (as tall as me) who blushes violently as she looks at me, seeming as uncomfortable with her new self as she is in her longer skirts'.[63]

On her sixteenth birthday on 3 November 1911 Olga awoke to gifts from her parents of two necklaces, one of diamonds, one of pearls, and a ring. Alexandra, with typical frugality, had wanted one large pearl to be bought for each of her daughters every time she had a birthday so that by the time they all reached sixteen they would have enough for a necklace; a fact which the head of her private office Prince Obolensky considered a false economy. Alexandra was eventually persuaded, with the tsar's backing, to buy a five-string necklace that could be broken up into individual pearls, so that the pearls in the necklaces when complete would at least match.[64]

That evening, Olga appeared wearing a full-length, high-necked, tulle dress with a lace bodice and a deep sash round her waist pinned with roses, her cheeks flushed with excitement and her shining fair hair dressed on top of her head – an important signifier of her transition from girl to young woman. 'She was as excited over her debut as any other young girl', recalled Anna Vyrubova. But the girls were still thought of as two pairs: Tatiana was dressed similarly to Olga with her hair up, while Maria and Anastasia wore shorter matching dresses with their hair loose.[65]

The ball was the social event of the Crimean season, and Olga was thrilled to have her favourite officer Nikolay Sablin as her escort for the evening; while Tatiana was partnered by Nikolay Rodionov.[66] At a quarter to seven, 140 carefully selected guests assembled in the large upstairs state dining room for dinner. Agnes de Stoeckl recalled how

> Innumerable servants in their gold and scarlet liveries were standing behind each chair – those special ones called 'l'homme à la plume' with plumes in their hats. The ladies were in rich coloured gowns, the young girls mostly in white tulle, and the gorgeous uniforms seemed to belong to a feast from the eastern hemisphere.[67]

After a candlelit dinner, the dancing began to music from the regimental orchestra, as officers of the *Shtandart* (which was at anchor nearby at Sevastopol) and the Alexandrovsk cavalry division invited the ladies to dance. Nicholas proudly conducted his eldest daughter onto the dance floor for her first waltz, as a gaggle of admiring young officers gathered round to watch. It was a magical evening, with a full moon in a cloudless sky. The exotic Crimean location made it even more special, wrote Anna Vyrubova:

the glass doors to the courtyard thrown open, the music of the unseen orchestra floating in from the rose garden like a breath of its own wondrous fragrance. It was a perfect night, clear and warm, and the gowns and jewels of the women and the brilliant uniforms of the men made a striking spectacle under the blaze of the electric lights.[68]

Flushed with the thrill of dancing the mazurka, waltz, contre-danse, danse hongroise and cotillion, and heady with the Crimean champagne they had been allowed to drink for the first time, Olga and Tatiana spent the whole evening in high spirits, 'fluttering round like butterflies' as General Spiridovich recalled, and savouring every moment.[69] Never one to say much in her diaries, which she had first attempted keeping in 1906 at the age of eleven, Olga made little of the occasion:

> Today for the first time I put on a long white dress. At 9 p.m. was my first ball. Knyazhevich (Major-General of the Suite) and I opened it. I danced the whole time, right up till 1 a.m. and was very happy. There were many officers and ladies. Everyone was having a terribly good time. I am 16 years old.[70]

Rather as anticipated, the empress had made her excuses about attending the dinner but had come down afterwards to greet her guests, looking quite beautiful in a gold brocade gown and wearing vivid jewels in her hair and her corsage. By her side was Alexey, 'his lovely little face flushed with the excitement of the evening'. Alexandra sat down in a large armchair to watch the dancing (looking, as one lady recalled, 'like an Eastern potentate'). During the cotillion she went down onto the dance floor to place garlands of artificial flowers on the ladies' heads that she had made herself.[71] She tried several times to send Alexey off to bed, where he stubbornly refused to go. Eventually she left the room, upon which Alexey jumped up into her chair. 'Slowly his little head dropped and he slept', recalled Agnes de Stoeckl, upon which Nicholas, who had been sitting at a table playing bridge for most of the evening, went over and 'gently woke him up saying: "You must not sit in mama's chair" and led him quietly away to bed'.[72]

Other smaller family dances were enjoyed by the sisters that autumn at Harax and Ai-Todor but General Mosolov later recalled that 'the children long regarded [Olga's] ball as one of the greatest events in their lives'.[73] For on this one, special night in the Crimea the Romanov sisters had shown that despite the limitations of their till now sheltered lives, 'they were simple, happy, normal young girls, loving dancing and all the frivolities which make youth bright and memorable'.[74] Elizaveta Naryshkina could not help wishing that the girls would now be able to take their proper place in Russian aristocratic society. 'In this, however, I was to be disappointed.'[75] For although, when the family returned to Tsarskoe Selo, Olga and Tatiana were allowed to attend three more balls given by the Romanov grand dukes in the run-up to Christmas, their mother maintained a stern attitude about how 'harmful' she thought aristocratic society to be.[76]

But Olga, of all the girls the most deep-feeling and sensitive, was now struggling with her emotions, full of longing for something more from life. At sixteen she was already well aware of widespread discussion about her future marriage, only too painfully conscious that the men she most admired and felt comfortable with – the officers of the *Shtandart* and her father's Cossack Escort – would never, ever, be acceptable candidates.

Chapter Ten

CUPID BY THE THRONES

✣

In January 1912, on a week's visit to Russia as one of a delegation of British officials, Sir Valentine Chirol of *The Times* remembered with particular pleasure a lunch with the imperial family at Tsarskoe Selo. 'I happened to sit next to the little Grand Duchess Tatiana, a very attractive girl of fifteen', he recalled. She talked with ease in English and told him how she was 'longing to have another holiday in England'.

> When I asked her what she liked best there she whispered quickly, almost in my ear, 'Oh, it feels so free there,' and when I remarked that she surely enjoyed a great deal of freedom at home she pursed up her lips into a little pout and with a toss of the head pointed towards an elderly lady sitting at another small table close to ours who was her gouvernante.[1]

Rasputin's two daughters Maria and Varvara, who had been brought to St Petersburg by their father to be educated, also noticed how extremely curious the Romanov sisters were when they met them at Anna Vyrubova's. They plied the Rasputin sisters with questions: 'the life of a girl of fourteen living in the town, who went to school with other children, and once a week went to the cinema, sometimes to the circus, seemed to them the rarest and most enviable of wonders', recalled Maria.[2] In the years just before the war, she and her sister represented a rare female link of their own age with the outside world. The Romanov girls were especially anxious to know all about the dances Maria Rasputin attended, 'they would question her at length about her clothes and who was there and what dances she danced', recalled Sydney Gibbes.[3] Two other young visitors to Trina Schneider at her apartments in the Alexander Palace found themselves bombarded with similar questions. Maria and Anastasia often joined them at Trina's apartments after lunch and engaged the girls, Natalya and Fofa, in exuberant, mischievous games that were almost too much for Trina to cope with. In quieter moments Anastasia and Maria were endlessly inquisitive about their everyday lives. 'They asked us about school, our friends, our teachers and wanted to know how we spent our time off, which theatres we went to, what books we read, and so on.'[4]

For now, however, the world of the Romanov sisters was strictly controlled by their governess Sofya Tyutcheva, who was still holding fast to her continuing campaign against the corrupting influence of Rasputin and the world outside. According to Anna Vyrubova, Tyutcheva had been encouraged in her ongoing vilification of Rasputin by 'certain bigoted priests', one of whom was Tyutcheva's own cousin, Bishop Vladimir Putiyata.[5] By the end of 1911 things had reached crisis point, at a time when Alexandra was also coming into conflict with the dowager and her sister-in-law over her continuing patronage of Grigory. 'My poor daughter-in-law does not perceive that she is ruining the dynasty and herself', Maria Feodorovna had prophetically remarked to the murdered Stolypin's successor, Vladimir Kokovtsov. 'She sincerely believes in the holiness of an adventurer, and we are powerless to ward off the misfortune, which is sure to come.'[6] The situation had been greatly exacerbated by circulation in St Petersburg in December 1911 of the letters written in all innocence to Father Grigory two years previously by the four sisters and the tsaritsa, and which he had given to an associate and defrocked monk named Iliodor.* Iliodor had since fallen out with Rasputin and, out of spite, had entrusted the letters to a Duma deputy who had had them copied and circulated among his political colleagues. When they were brought to Kokovtsov's attention, he went straight to Nicholas. The tsar turned pale at the sight of the letters, but confirmed their authenticity before shutting them

---

*   Rasputin later claimed that Iliodor had stolen the letters from him.

in a drawer.[7] When she heard what had happened, Alexandra sent a furious telegram to Grigory, who was effectively banished back to Pokrovskoe and away from the family.

During the frantic damage limitation that followed, Sofya Tyutcheva was the first of Grigory's detractors to be targeted, accused of spreading malicious gossip about him and also of taking too stubbornly independent a line in her management of the girls.[8] Early in 1912 she was summoned to Nicholas's study, where he asked her, 'What is going on in the nursery?' – or, as Anna Vyrubova would have it, 'rebuked her severely'.[9] When Tyutcheva explained her position, voicing her objections to Rasputin's familiarity with the children and her own strongly held opinions on how the girls should be brought up, the tsar responded:

> 'So you do not believe in the sanctity of Grigory?' . . . I answered negatively and the Emperor said 'And what if I told you that all these difficult years I have survived only because of his prayers?' 'You have survived them because of the prayers of the whole of Russia, Your Majesty,' I replied. The Emperor started to say that he was convinced it was all a lie, that he did not believe these stories about R., that the pure always attracts everything dirty.[10]

Tyutcheva remained in her post for a while after this dressing-down, Nicholas and Alexandra always reluctant to dismiss anyone because of the attendant gossip, but finally, in March 1912 and still unrepentant, she was sent back to her home in Moscow, 'for talking too much and lying', as Alexandra told Xenia.[11] Iza Buxhoeveden was sorry to see how 'deeply distressed' Tyutcheva was to have to leave the girls, for she loved them dearly. But it was, sadly, her own fault: 'What she said carelessly was twisted and turned into marvellous stories, which did the Empress a great deal of harm.'[12] But she continued to write regularly and before too long was allowed to make occasional visits to see her former charges. Anastasia in particular remained strongly attached to her friend Savanna, and exchanged letters with her until 1916.[13]

Tyutcheva was not the only member of the imperial household to be caught up in the controversy. Mariya (Mary) Vishnyakova, who after seeing the girls through their early years had become nursemaid to Alexey in 1909, had at first been an ardent admirer of Grigory. But she had of late been suffering from the strain of her difficult job. When, in the spring of 1910, Alexandra recommended she go for a visit to Grigory at Pokrovskoe in the company of three other women, Vishnyakova had returned, accusing him of having sexually assaulted her and begging the empress to protect her children from his 'diabolical' influence.[14] There appears to be no foundation in the disturbed Vishnyakova's accusation. Anna Vyrubova and others described her as 'over-emotional'; indeed, according to Grand Duchess Olga Alexandrovna, during a subsequent investigation of Vishnyakova's allegations, the hapless nurse-maid was caught in bed with a Cossack from the imperial guard.[15] Nicholas and Alexandra were as reluctant to dismiss her as they had been Tyutcheva; she had served the family loyally for fifteen years and was greatly loved by the children. She was therefore sent to the Caucasus for a rest cure, and the following June, 1913, was quietly retired rather than dismissed from service, with a comfortable pension and her own three-bedroom flat in the commandant's quarters at the Winter Palace. Right up to the revolution, Nicholas and Alexandra continued to pay for Mary to have annual rest cures in the Crimea.[16] There would be no replacement for her though; her role would increasingly be taken by Alexey's *dyadka* Derevenko, nor would there be any new governess for his sisters. The imperial family closed ranks, trusting to just a few loyal retainers. Trina Schneider* would act as chaperone for Maria and Anastasia, while the older sisters would be accompanied on outings by one or other of Alexandra's ladies-in-waiting. Iza Buxhoeveden was finally taken on formally as a lady-in-waiting in 1914, after which she and Nastenka Hendrikova took over escorting Olga and Tatiana into town. But over and above them all and keeping an eagle eye on the girls' moral welfare was 'the old hen', mistress of the robes Elizaveta Naryshkina.[17]

The loss of Sofya Tyutcheva left a still sick Alexandra with a lot to prepare for the spring and summer seasons; for she had to 'select

---

* According to Dr Botkin's son Gleb, Schneider was 'extremely priggish', so much so that she 'forbade the Grand Duchesses to stage a play because the dialogue contained the highly improper word "stockings"'. Botkin, *Real Romanovs*, p. 79.

and organize the dresses, hats, coats for 4 girls' to see them through first a trip south to Livadia, then on to a series of formal engagements in Moscow in May for which the girls needed 'to be dressed very elegantly', and back to Moscow later in the year for the celebrations for the anniversary of the defeat of Napoleon in 1812. A selection of tea dresses and semi-formal dresses would be required, at considerable expense.[18]

Surviving accounts for Maria's wardrobe allowance during 1909–10 provide a fascinating insight into the kind of money being spent on each daughter on a wide range of items. All of Maria's accounts for that year are meticulously itemized, expenditure on wardrobe alone amounting to 6,307 roubles (something like £14,500 today). Everything is accounted for: from ribbons, pins, lace, combs, handkerchiefs; to perfume and soap sent from Harrods to the St Petersburg *parfumier* Brocard & Co; to her manicurist Madame Kühne; to Alice Guisser for repairs and cleaning of her lace; to her mother's *coiffeur* Henri-Joseph Delacroix; as well as payments for visits to the American dentist Dr Henry Wallison, who had premises on the upmarket Moika Embankment.[19] A considerable variety of footwear was purchased for Maria at Henry Weiss on 66 Nevsky Prospekt, whose shoes all bore the legend 'Fournisseur de S. M. L'Impératrice de Russie': thirty-two different pairs ranging from soft glacé leather pumps of various colours, to demi and high button boots, sandals, felt boots and fur-lined overshoes. The smart firm of Maison Anglaise on the Nevsky supplied silk and Lisle thread stockings; swimming costumes and bathing caps came from Dahlberg, and Robert Heath, 'Hatter to HM the Queen and all the Courts of Europe', sent out hats from his fashionable London store at Hyde Park Corner. The French couturier Auguste Brisac (next door to Weiss in a prime spot at 68 Nevsky Prospekt), worked exclusively for ladies of the imperial family and members of the court, his sixty staff creating the very latest Parisian gowns for special occasions. But for more simple, day-to-day clothing, Alexandra had garments made for her daughters by the Russian dressmaker Kitaev, and, true to her frugal nature, got him to alter hand-me-downs from the older girls to fit Maria, or enlarge clothes that she was growing out of. In one year alone Kitaev supplied:

a grey suit with a silk lining of a foreign fabric – 115 roubles, a blue sheet-wadded silk-lined suit – 125 roubles, a blue cheviot suit with a downy silk-lined collar and cuffs of dark mink – 245 roubles, a suit in the English style with a silk lining and a pleated skirt –135 roubles. He also altered a suit – made a new fur, a new lining and made the slip longer – 40 roubles. He also altered Olga Nikolaevna's old suit for her – 35 roubles; made a long overcoat of hand-made linen – 35 roubles; made two skirts longer and bought some more fabric for that; made 3 skirts longer and broader and made new linings for them – 40 roubles; made 4 jackets broader and their sleeves longer – 40 roubles; made new belts for two skirts and made them broader – 15 roubles; altered the eldest sister's riding suit – the jacket, the skirt and the riding breeches – 50 roubles; mended a jacket – 7 roubles.[20]

*

In the last week of Lent 1912, the family headed south to Livadia for their first Easter at the White Palace. They arrived in a still cold and snowy Crimea, at a time of religious contemplation and sobriety, with long hours spent standing in church and endless prayers before candle-lit icons. The children's time was occupied in the days before Easter in painting and decorating dozens of hard-boiled eggs that were traditionally exchanged to celebrate Christ's resurrection. On Great Saturday – a day when the bells rang out across Russia and the faithful filled the churches to bursting – the girls wore mourning, as was the tradition, during the final great service leading up to midnight, the sadness finally broken by the joyful announcement *Khristos voskres!* – 'Christ is Risen!' Although it was now the early hours of the morning, the entire household broke the long Lenten fast together, enjoying a great feast in the White Hall. Its centrepiece was the two sweet cakes so looked forward to after the long period of abstention: the *kulich*, a rich iced Easter cake made with almonds, candied orange peel and raisins; and *pashka*, a gloriously sweet blending of everything that the pious had not eaten for weeks: sugar, butter, eggs and cream cheese.

In private, as he had done every Easter since they were married (except during the Russo-Japanese War of 1904–5), Nicholas presented his wife with an exquisite Fabergé jewelled Easter egg to add to her collection, a tradition begun by his father in 1885, when Maria Feodorovna had received her own first Fabergé egg. This particular Easter, Fabergé's son Eugene delivered Alexandra's gift in person at the Livadia Palace.[21] It would become known as the Tsarevich Egg, for inside the outer shell of dark blue lapis lazuli mounted with a gold cagework of flowers, cupids and imperial eagles was a miniature portrait of Alexey encrusted with diamonds. On Easter Monday the family gathered in the Italian Courtyard for the ceremony of greeting the troops – in Livadia this being the crew of the *Shtandart* and officers of the Tsar's Escort. As Nicholas exchanged the traditional three kisses and greetings Tatiana and Olga helped hand out the painted porcelain Easter eggs that the imperial couple distributed every Easter.[22]

Whenever she was in the Crimea Alexandra always tried to visit the TB sanatoria in the region of which she was patron, two of which – the military and naval hospitals on the imperial estate at Massandra – she had had built and paid for out of her own fortune. There was also the Alexander III Sanatorium in Yalta, catering to 460 patients, which she had opened in 1901. The care of the sick had always been one of the few socially acceptable pursuits that royal princesses could engage in, and Alexandra was determined that her daughters should continue this family tradition. Elizaveta Naryshkina was somewhat concerned about the children being brought into contact with highly infectious TB patients: 'Is it safe, Madame,' she had asked the empress, 'for the young Grand Duchesses to have people in the last stage of consumption kiss their hands?' Alexandra's response was unequivocal: 'I don't think it will hurt the children, but I am sure it would hurt the sick if they thought that my daughters were afraid of infection.' The children might love Livadia but she wanted to ensure that they also learnt to 'realize the sadness underneath all this beauty'.[23]

In hospital visiting as in everything, the girls performed their duty without complaint and with a smile. All five children took part in White Flower Day, a major charitable event for the Anti-Tuberculosis League and the Yalta sanatoria, celebrated on St George's Day, 23 April. The idea had originated with Margareta,

Crown Princess of Sweden, and Alexandra had adopted it in Russia. The day got its name from the white daisies, or marguerites, that were carried wreathed round long wooden staffs. Holding their staffs of flowers and dressed in white, the Romanov children walked round the streets of Yalta taking donations in return for the gift of a flower, each of them proudly raising between 100 and 140 roubles that year.[24]

One of the big social events of the Crimean season was another charitable venture of the empress's: the Grand Charity Bazaar in aid of the sanatoria. Every year Alexandra enlisted the girls in busily knitting, embroidering and sewing, as well as painting water-colours and making other hand-made items for sale, straining her own eyes in the process. The bazaar had been held for the first time the previous year, on the pier at Yalta, where the stall under its white awning that she staffed with the girls had been besieged by the fashionable ladies of Yalta eager to buy something made by their own fair hands. There was barely room to move, with 'people pressing forward almost frenziedly to touch the empress's hand or her sleeve'.[25] This in itself created great anxiety for the officers of the Okhrana and *Shtandart*, on the lookout always for any attack on the family. Their guard had been raised that year when a mild-looking old man in an old-fashioned frockcoat had approached the empress and stretched out his hand offering her an orange, which she had politely accepted. 'It was the most ordinary looking fruit,' recalled Nikolay Vasilievich Sablin, 'but as we later said amongst ourselves, a terrible thought had flashed by, "That so-called Macedonian orange might have been a bomb!"'[26] The bazaar was a great success and raised thousands of roubles for Alexandra's good causes. It also provided an opportunity for people to see the elusive tsarevich. Anna Vyrubova remembered how on these occasions, 'smiling with pleasure, the Empress would lift him to the table, where the child would bow shyly but sweetly, stretching out his hands in friendly greeting to the worshipping crowds'. [27]

*

During the imperial family's time in Livadia many of their favourite officers from the *Shtandart* were in evidence and as usual the four sisters were 'allowed to have a little preference for this or that hand-some young officer with whom they danced, played tennis, walked, or rode' – though always in the presence of a chaperone.[28] That year Tatiana seemed to be taking a particular shine to Count Alexander Vorontsov-Dashkov – a hussar in the Life Guards from a distinguished Russian family, who was one of Nicholas's ADCs and a favourite tennis partner. Although Tatiana was not yet sixteen, the matchmakers would soon be busy pairing of her off. Indeed, they were already busily predicting future possible dynastic unions for all four girls. So anxious was the tsar to keep the Balkan states faithful to Russia, it was asserted, that he intended 'to utilize his four daughters, who are not to marry four Russian Grand Dukes, nor even four unorthodox Princes of Europe'. No, the four grand duchesses of Russia, so the rumour went, were to become 'Queens of the Balkans', with Olga a bride for Prince George of Serbia; Tatiana for Prince George of Greece; Maria for Prince Carol of Romania and Anastasia set for Prince Boris of Bulgaria – although other press reports had gone so far as to claim that Boris was in fact about to be betrothed to Olga.[29]

When Olga had celebrated her name day the previous July on board the *Shtandart*, among the gifts and bouquets of flowers presented to her by the officers had been a home-made card, the suggestiveness of which was obvious. 'What do you think it was?' Tatiana wrote to Aunt Olga. 'There was a cardboard frame with a portrait of David cut out from a newspaper.' Olga had 'laughed at it long and hard', but her less worldly sister Tatiana had been offended: 'Not one of the officers wishes to confess that he had done it. Such swine, aren't they?'[30] It can be no coincidence that eleven days prior to Tatiana's writing this letter, the formal investi-ture ceremony for their cousin David, as Prince of Wales, had taken place.

There is no doubt that ever since the coronation of the new king, George V, in June 1911, talk had been brewing in Britain that 'the next greatest event to which the people may look forward will be the marriage of Prince Edward of Wales [David], heir apparent to the throne'.[31] He was only seventeen but already the royal marriage brokers had drawn up a list of the seven most eligible princesses, with the names of both Olga and Tatiana at the top. The *Washington Post* was sceptical: 'A marriage with any Russian princess would certainly not be popular in England', it averred, citing the example of Maria Alexandrovna, Alexander II's daughter, who had married the Duke of Edinburgh and was now the Duchess of Saxe-Coburg, and who 'never in the least identified herself with English affairs or ways, but remained always a stranger'. The paper was certain that 'the same fate would probably attend a Russian queen'.[32]

All this foreign press speculation was of course entirely without foundation; for in Russia in 1912 it was assumed that Olga Nikolaevna's affections were for someone much closer to home. Of all the highborn dukes and princes whose names were being bandied about as possible husbands for the tsar's eldest daughter, his first cousin, twenty-year-old Grand Duke Dmitri, seemed to be the perfect candidate. Tall and slim – 'as elegant as a Fabergé statuette', in the words of his uncle Grand Duke Sergey – Dmitri was naturally sociable and witty; and, most important of all, he was a Russian.[33] His debonair manner was extremely disarming and he already had a well-known way with women. 'Nobody had an easier, a more brilliant debut in life than he', as his sister Maria recalled:

> He had a large fortune with very few responsibilities attached to it, unusually good looks coupled with charm, and he also had been the recognized favourite of the Tsar. Even before he had finished his studies and joined the Horse Guards, there was no young prince in Europe more socially conspicuous than he was both in his own country and abroad. He walked a golden path, petted and fêted by everyone.[34]

Dmitri and Maria were the children of Grand Duke Pavel Alexandrovich, who was in turn the youngest of the six sons of Tsar Alexander II. Their mother had died as the result of a boating accident that had triggered Dmitri's premature birth, and when in 1902 the widowed Pavel provoked scandal by marrying again, to a commoner, Nicholas, who was anxious to stem the incidence of morganatic marriages in the Romanov family, sent him into exile. With Pavel living in the south of France, his brother Grand Duke Sergey and his wife Ella, who had no children of their own, became Dmitri and Maria's guardians. After Sergey was assassinated in 1905 (his large estate eventually passed on to Dmitri by Ella), Nicholas and Alexandra effectively took over responsibility for his and Maria's upbringing. In May 1908 the widowed Ella had encouraged eighteen-year-old Maria into a dynastic marriage with Prince Wilhelm of Sweden. With the loss of his only and adored sibling Dmitri gravitated ever more towards the imperial family as surrogates and was now on such intimate terms with Nicholas and Alexandra that he often addressed them as Papa and Mama (even though Nicholas had eventually allowed Dmitri's own father to return to Russia). In 1909 Dmitri had entered the Officers' Cavalry School in St Petersburg, the traditional finishing establishment for young men of the Romanov aristocracy, at the end of which he was commissioned as a cornet in the Horse Guards. During those three years he often spent his free time out at Tsarskoe Selo and regularly joined the tsar in military manoeuvres at nearby Krasnoe Selo, often acting as Nicholas's aide-de-camp; in the spring of 1912 he had joined the family in Livadia for three weeks.

At some point during 1912, and in the light of the tsarevich's precarious health, Nicholas and Alexandra must have considered the possibility that, should Alexey die, Dmitri would be the ideal match for Olga as potential heir. Nicholas was intent anyway in creating her co-regent with her mother, should he die before Alexey reached the age of twenty-one.[35] Indeed, there was a great deal of logic in such a marriage; it would have been immensely popular in Russia, for Dmitri was one of their own; even better, from Nicholas and Alexandra's point of view, it would have spared Olga the agony, which she dreaded, of a marriage that might force to her leave Russia. A marriage to Dmitri Pavlovich would give him the title of joint heir presumptive, should Nicholas go even further and change the succession laws in Olga's favour after Alexey. Becoming tsar was a role that Dmitri coveted; at present he was sixth in line to the throne, but if he married Olga, that might all change.

Despite the twenty-three-year age difference, Dmitri and Nicholas greatly enjoyed each other's company; they loved playing billiards together in Nicholas's study and developed a father–son relationship so close that Dmitri always spoke extremely frankly – if not with a degree of bawdy, even homosexual innuendo – to him, in the manner

of fellow officers in the barracks, such as signing off this letter from
St Petersburg of October 1911:

> This capital of yours, or, to speak with perfect clarity, MY capital,
> does not favour us with good weather. It's so shitty that it's just
> frightful – dirty and cold . . . Well, and now I wrap my illegiti-
> mate mother in a firm embrace (the fault is mine – I am an
> illegitimate son, not she an illegitimate mother). I give the chil-
> dren a big, wet kiss, [and] you I clasp in my arms (but not without
> the proper respect). I am devoted to you with my whole heart,
> soul, and body (except, of course my arse hole).[36]

Dmitri's lewd and ambiguous manner often blurred the divide
between familial jesting and the dangerously erotic. While this might
be par for the course with his cousin the tsar, even a diluted form
of it might have been rather too near the knuckle for his unworldly
female cousins. As late as 1911 Dmitri still referred to the girls
collectively as children, at a time when rumours were gathering in
the foreign press of an imminent engagement between himself and
Olga. But there is no solid evidence to support any interest in Dmitri
on Olga's part; in fact rather the opposite, she appears to have found
his blokeish behaviour with her father – the badinage and endless
billiard playing – rather immature. And for someone as sexually
experienced as Dmitri, who already was demonstrating an interest
in strong-minded, older and often married women, Olga Nikolaevna
would have seemed a total innocent, if not, as has been suggested,
'a wet blanket'.[37]

In 1908 Nicholas had banned Dmitri, so Dmitri told his sister
Maria, from going out riding alone with Olga 'because of what had
happened the first time', probably an allusion to his mischievous
behaviour and penchant for telling dirty jokes.[38] Yet to all intents
and purposes it seemed by 1911 that he was being groomed as a
prospective husband for her. Certainly the signs were sufficient for
the foreign press to pick up on the gossip in St Petersburg and run
away with it. But in fact the possibility of an engagement was already
being anticipated much closer to home – within the imperial household itself – as General Spiridovich confirmed in his memoirs.
Everyone enjoyed Dmitri's presence, for he livened up the rather
dull atmosphere at court. 'The grand duke came often without

ceremony, after merely announcing his arrival over the phone to the emperor. Such was the emperor's affection for him that all the entourage already saw in him the future fiancé of one of the grand duchesses.'[39]

Although he had not excelled as officer material, at cavalry school Dmitri had proved himself to be an excellent horseman and in early June 1912 he returned to St Petersburg to take up serious training for the Russian equestrian team at the Stockholm Olympics to be held in July. At this point serious rumours began circulating of an engagement, for in her diary for 7 June, General Bogdanov's wife Alexandra – who held a monarchist political salon in St Petersburg – noted that 'Yesterday Grand Duchess Olga Nikolaevna was betrothed to Grand Duke Dmitri Pavlovich'.[40] The foreign press pounced on the rumours: the Dmitri–Olga 'romance' was repeated in the *Washington Post* in July, under the fanciful headline 'Cupid by the Thrones', where it was asserted that Olga had turned down an approach from Prince Adalbert, third son of the Kaiser, because 'she had given her heart to her cousin Grand Duke Dmitri Paulovitch [*sic*]'. What is more, the paper said, she and Dmitri had 'spoken of their affection' and Olga 'wore hidden a diamond pendant as a remembrance of these words'.[41]

The absence of any official announcement and the lack of clarity even among those in the imperial entourage were compounded by a sphinx-like remark from British ambassador's daughter Meriel Buchanan, a great friend of Dmitri Pavlovich, in her diary in August, which appears to be a response to the betrothal rumour:

I heard a rumour yesterday that a certain person is going to marry the Emperor's eldest daughter. I can't quite believe it considering all the high and mighty people who are panting to marry her. Of course she may have a coup de foudre for him and insist on having her own way.[42]

Whether or not the rumours were true, a possible marriage between Grand Duke Dmitri and Olga soon became problematic. By the autumn of 1912 he had fallen increasingly under the influence of a boyhood friend, Prince Felix Yusupov, and had rapidly been sucked into the racy lifestyle of the St Petersburg fast set that Yusupov patronized. The two men were now spending a riotous time in town, wining and dining, consorting with ballerinas and gypsy girls and driving fast cars. Like any bright young thing in the dying days before the First World War with too much money and not enough to occupy his time, Dmitri was also developing a dangerous gambling habit. He had his own palace by the Anichkov Bridge on St Petersburg's Nevsky Prospekt – gifted to him by Ella when she retreated to her convent – and conveniently located in sight of all the fashionable clubs. Dmitri began to haunt the Imperial Yacht Club next door to his favourite restaurant at the Astoria Hotel; when he was not running through his fortune playing poker and baccarat there, he would be doing so in Paris, at the Travellers Club on the Champs-Elysées.[43]

Sooner or later word of Dmitri's playboy lifestyle must have got back to Nicholas and Alexandra and also to Olga. It was already rapidly eroding his good looks, the boyish charm mutating into a dark-eyed, saturnine appearance, made worse by the onset of health problems. Olga might have been young but she was strong-willed, deeply religious and principled. By January 1913 she was noting a degree of disdain for Dmitri's habit of 'messing about with papa' that does not square with any romantic interest, although it could perhaps have been a case of teenage sour grapes. That same month Meriel Buchanan was more overt in her own opinion of the situation: 'He absolutely refuses to look at Olga I believe.'[44]

*

On 6 August, with the roses of Livadia still filling the gardens with their lovely perfume, the family sadly left the Crimea and returned to Peterhof for army manoeuvres at Krasnoe Selo, followed, on 20 August, by the consecration at Tsarskoe Selo of the family's newly built church, the Feodorovsky Sobor. This had been built a short walk from the palace and was also for the specific use of Cossacks serving with the Tsar's Escort. It would become the family's favourite place of worship and a significant feature in their spiritual lives, Alexandra in particular creating her own private retreat in a side chapel. Soon afterwards the family left Tsarskoe Selo by special train to Moscow to celebrate the centenary of Russia's defeat of Napoleon in 1812.

The focal point of the ceremonies was the battlefield of Borodino, 115 miles (185 km) west of Moscow, where, on 7 September 1812, 58,000 Russians had been killed or wounded in what had been a pyrrhic victory for the French. Within two months the exhausted and depleted Grande Armée withdrew from Moscow and into the catastrophe of the long winter retreat from Russia. On 25 August at Borodino Nicholas and Alexey reviewed units whose predecessors had fought in the original battle and were joined by the whole family at a religious ceremony held at Alexander I's campaign chapel nearby.[45] On the following day came more parades on Borodino Field, everyone walking solemnly behind the sacred Smolensk Mother of God icon with which Russian troops had been blessed before the battle, followed by prayers at the Spaso-Borodinsky Monastery and the Borodino monument. The whole family found it an intensely moving experience: 'A common feeling of deep reverence for our forebears seized *us all* there,' Nicholas told his mother, 'these were moments of such emotional grandeur as can rarely be surpassed in our days!'[46] On both occasions, with the emphasis on the tsar and his heir in their military uniforms, the girls looked the epitome of imperial grace in the now iconic ensemble of long white lace dresses and hats draped with large white ostrich feathers – 'four young girls, whose beauty and charm will gradually be revealed to a respectfully-admiring world, like the blooming of rare and lovely flowers in our hothouses'.[47] They were charming, enchanting even; but to ordinary Russians the four Romanov sisters remained as beautiful and inaccessible as storybook princesses.

After Borodino, the imperial party travelled on to Moscow and further celebrations of the 1812 anniversary at the Kremlin and elsewhere, culminating in a mass at the exquisite fifteenth-century Uspensky Sobor. On the last day of an exhausting programme of religious and public celebration, where the citizens of Moscow took full advantage of a rare glimpse of the entire imperial family together, a huge prayer service was held on Red Square in memory of Alexander I, the conquering tsar who had driven the French from

Russia. It was a highly emotive conclusion to the anniversary, the square echoing to the voices of a 3,000-strong choir, the booming of cannon firing the salute and the unforgettable sound of church bells ringing out across the heart of old Moscow.[48]

Chapter Eleven

THE LITTLE ONE WILL NOT DIE

❧

The festivities for Borodino had the inevitable impact on the tsaritsa and in early September 1912, the family headed off for one of Nicholas's favourite hunting venues, the Białowieża Forest, an imperial estate in eastern Poland (now in Belarus). The territory was part of the Russian Empire at the time, but before it was ceded to Russia during the partitions of the eighteenth century, it had long been the ancient hunting preserve of the kings of Poland. Here, across 30,000 acres (404,686 ha) of dense, virgin forest the tsar could take his pick, hunting for deer, wild boar, moose, wolves – and even the rare European bison, which thrived there. The four sisters, who were all now accomplished horsewomen, went for exhilarating morning rides with their father, leaving a frustrated Alexey, who was not allowed such dangerous pursuits, to be taken by car in search of the wildlife. Alexandra, meanwhile, stayed at home, 'lying here all on my own, writing letters and resting my weary heart'.[1]

It was hard for Alexey always to be excluded from vigorous family activities, although nothing could restrain him, given half a chance, from indulging in the kind of physical games with other children that so easily could cause him harm. Dr Botkin's children noticed his penchant for slapstick of the 'pie-throwing type' and his inability to 'stay in any place or at any game for any length of time'.[2] There was something always so restless about him. Agnes de Stoeckl recalled with horror seeing how that summer in Livadia he had joined his sisters in whirling round a very high maypole that Grand Duchess George had erected for her children at Harax, 'insist[ing] on running

holding the rope until the impetus lifted him gently into the air'.[3]
Everyone dreaded the repercussions if he hurt himself, but it had
long since proved impossible to contain Alexey's natural energies
and Nicholas had ordered that Alexey be allowed 'to do everything
that other children of his age were wont to do, and not to restrain
him unless it was absolutely necessary'. Court paediatrician Dr
Sergey Ostrogorsky had told Grand Duke Dmitri that Alexey did
not have 'the full-blown disease', 'but it will develop forcefully if
it's allowed to, which is exactly what's happening'. This was because
the empress was too indulgent with him and did not heed his,
Ostrogorsky's, advice, such as recently when

> Alexey was still suffering a great deal, Ostrogorsky ordered him
> to lie quietly and avoid all movement since [it] would inevitably
> bring much harm. So what do you think Alix did, the fool? When
> Ostrogorsky returned a week later, he found Alexey leaping and
> running with his sisters. The Empress, responding to the doctor's
> look of utter horror, said 'I wanted to surprise you!' But
> Ostrogorsky admitted that, after such surprises, one simply gives
> up.[4]

'Was that not truly idiotic of Alexandra?' Dmitri asked his sister;
but more to the point, it poses the question of whether Alexandra
had been sticking to Grigory's advice to ignore what the doctors
said and trust only in him and God for Alexey's well-being. The
fact was that Alexey had not benefited from the discipline of
governesses as his sisters had, and was extremely capricious. His
mother clearly could not control him, often rebuking Olga for not
minding her brother's manners. But poor Olga could not manage
Alexey and his 'peevish temper' any more than her mother could.[5]
The only authority he respected was his father's: 'one word was
always enough to exact implicit obedience from him', Sydney
Gibbes noted.[6]

There is no doubt that Alexey was often extremely difficult to
handle, yet the lovable and compassionate side of his personality
always in the end won through, for 'it was often only by the glint
of his eyes that one could realize the tumult that was passing in his
little soul'.[7] When he was well he was full of life: bright, intelligent
and brave, and everyone in the entourage was happy seeing it. Yet

there was always something intensely plaintive about this handsome little boy with the soulful eyes. He seemed so alone, aside from his devoted *dyadka* Derevenko. The company of other children – mainly Derevenko's own or Dr Botkin's – or occasional visits from royal cousins (with whom he did not always get along) were rare. In the main Alexey had only his sisters and his tutors for company.

Until the appointment of Pierre Gilliard and Sydney Gibbes, Alexey's carers had all been Russians, which in itself had isolated him, and as a result his English was much poorer than that of his sisters. However, thanks to Gilliard, who became an important figure in his life, Alexey did end up speaking better French than the girls.* But having so little contact with the outside world, he was often fearful when encountering strangers. Gerald Hamilton, a traveller to Russia that spring, and whose German aunts had known Alexandra in Hesse, had the good fortune to be invited to meet the imperial family at Tsarskoe Selo. As he sat taking tea with the tsaritsa, who talked animatedly of her Darmstadt schooldays, the tsarevich suddenly 'romped into the room' but immediately shrank back when he saw Hamilton's unfamiliar face. He seemed so nervous and timid, thought Hamilton, with the 'most extraordinarily gentle, almost beseeching eyes'.[8]

For now at least Alexey was in good health and he had for a while been accident-free, so much so that Alexandra had begun to hope that the doctors might be wrong in thinking his condition incurable. Earlier that year, in an attempt to make her sister-in-law Olga understand the extent to which she relied on Grigory, she had finally admitted 'that the poor little one has that terrible illness'. Olga could see that Alexandra had 'become ill because of it and w[ould] never fully recover'.[9] Her sister-in-law was adamant about how indispensable Grigory was, insisting to Olga Alexandrovna that 'the boy feels better the moment he is near him, or prays for him'. He had helped him yet again during their recent stay at Livadia when Alexey had had a 'haemorrhage in the kidneys', noted Olga's

---

* Tatiana once declared to Anna Vyrubova 'that she never would be able to carry on a conversation in French'; but all of the children spoke English fluently, 'from their cradles'. Dorr, *Inside the Russian Revolution*, p. 123.

sister Xenia, who also was now privy to the truth. Grigory, who had followed the imperial family to the Crimea, had been sent for and 'Everything stopped when he arrived!'[10]

During the long and exhausting celebrations at Borodino Alexey had been greeted by wildly enthusiastic crowds, ecstatic at seeing their tsarevich close to them. Alexandra had been proud of him for coming through the physical strain of it all so well. But then disaster had once more struck; while out on the river one day not long after their arrival at Białowieża – and ignoring the warnings of Derevenko – Alexey banged the inside of his thigh against one of the oarlocks when hastily jumping into a rowing boat.[11] A swelling developed in his left groin soon after, accompanied by pain and raised temperature. But after a week or so it appeared to ease and he seemed fit enough for the family to travel on to their smaller hunting lodge deep in the forest at Spala, though Alexey still had difficulty walking and had to be carried by Derevenko. He remained pale and frail for days but Alexandra refused to call in any additional doctors, entrusting Alexey's care to Dr Botkin only. He was not allowed to join the girls on mushroom-foraging expeditions in the forest and became restless and disgruntled; to pacify him, on 2 October Alexandra took him out for a carriage drive. The sandy road was very bumpy and uneven and before long Alexey was complaining of a sharp pain in his thigh. Alexandra ordered the driver to turn back, but by the time they reached the lodge he was screaming in agony and was carried into his bedroom in a state of semi-consciousness.[12] The juddering of the carriage had caused the still healing haematoma in his upper thigh to rupture and start bleeding again.

Dr Ostrogorsky was immediately sent for from St Petersburg, closely followed by Alexey's paediatrician Dr Feodorov. But nothing could calm him or alleviate the unremitting agony caused by the swelling, which was now spreading across his groin to his abdomen. On 6 October his fever rose to 102 degrees F (38.9 degrees C) and his heartbeat became irregular; the last strength in Alexey's body was being drained away by the pain and all the child could do was fretfully draw his left leg up tightly in an attempt to ease it. Dr Feodorov feared that an abscess would develop and blood poisoning might set in, leading to peritonitis. For the next four nights, Alexandra barely left Alexey's bedside – with Olga and Tatiana both taking turns to sit with him – refusing to rest or eat, forced to listen to him crossing himself and crying out over and over again with each contracting pain '*Gospodi pomilui*' – 'O Lord have mercy upon me!' – as the intensity of his screams faded into a hoarse cry and he slipped in and out of delirium.[13] 'Mama,' he called out in one of his lucid moments, 'don't forget to put a little monument on my tomb when I am dead.'[14]

In the midst of this crisis Pierre Gilliard watched in horrified fascination as Nicholas, Alexandra and the girls made heroic attempts to act as though nothing was seriously wrong, for they were surrounded by visitors: 'one shooting party succeeded another, and the guests were more numerous than ever'.[15] On one particular evening Maria and Anastasia performed a couple of scenes from Molière's *Le Bourgeois Gentilhomme* for a party of visiting Polish nobles. During the performance Alexandra had sat there, smiling and chatting with steely determination, as though nothing was amiss, but the minute the performance ended she rushed upstairs, as Gilliard recalled, with 'a distracted and terror-stricken look in her face'.[16] With guests to entertain out shooting, at luncheon and at dinner she and Nicholas struggled to maintain their composure, while upstairs, out of sight, their son's cries of pain echoed along the corridors – all, as Gilliard observed, in a last-ditch attempt to maintain the secret of his condition.

By 8 October and unable to do anything at all to help the stricken child, the doctors had given up hope. Feodorov had considered and quickly abandoned the idea of 'drastic measures' – surgical intervention to cut open the swelling, drain it and release the agonizing pressure in Alexey's abdomen – for even the incision would have been enough for him to bleed to death.[17] 'I do not have the strength to convey to you what I am experiencing', Dr Botkin wrote to his children that day. 'I am in no condition to do anything but walk around him . . . in no condition to think about anything except him and his parents . . . Pray, my children, pray daily and fervently for our precious heir.'[18]

The tsarevich was dying and the Russian people had to be prepared. Until now Alexandra had been adamant about any bulletins being issued but she finally relented. On the evening of the 9th, Feoderov and Dr Karl Rauchfuss, another leading paediatrician and head of a children's hospital in the capital who had arrived with him, composed a brief announcement to be published in the St Petersburg evening papers.[19] The children's religious instructor, Father Vasiliev, administered the last rites. Faced with the imminent death of her only son, Alexandra had no options left: she must appeal to Grigory for help. On her instructions, Anna Vyrubova sent a telegram to Rasputin in Pokrovskoe. His daughter Maria remembered it arriving the following morning, upon which Rasputin had prayed for some time in front of an icon of the Virgin of Kazan. Then he had gone to the telegraph office and sent word back to Alexandra: 'The Little One will not die. Do not allow the doctors to bother him too much.'[20] Later a second telegram arrived telling her, 'God has seen your tears and heard your prayers'; Alexey, Grigory again assured her, would recover.[21] A strange calm came over the tsaritsa from that moment; perhaps this transmitted itself to the stricken child and in turn calmed him, for his temperature dropped and he began to settle. At last reassured, Alexandra went down to dinner for the first time since the crisis had begun; 'she was radiant in her relief from anxiety', as General Mosolov recalled. The doctors, in contrast, 'seemed in utter consternation' at this dramatic turn-around.[22]

On the 10th Alexey was given Communion again: 'the poor thin little face with its big suffering eyes, lit up with blessed happiness as the Priest approached him with the Holy Sacrament. It was such a comfort to us all and we too had the same joy', Alexandra later told Boyd Carpenter. For her, Alexey's miraculous recovery was down to 'trust and faith implicite [sic] in God Almighty'.[23] He had not deserted her. And now, across the churches of Russia, the people too were praying for the heir's recovery.

On the afternoon of the 10th Nicholas noted in his diary that Alexey had at last slept soundly. The following day the doctors issued a press bulletin saying that the crisis was over. Dr Botkin was relieved to write and tell his children that 'our priceless patient' was 'undoubtedly significantly better . . . God heard our fervent prayers.' But the anguish for everyone had been terrible; it would be a long time before Alexey would be fully well again, and yet even now Botkin found himself wondering 'how many more occasions like this might there be along the way'.[24] In the interim, Dr Feodorov had summoned from St Petersburg his young assistant Dr Vladimir Derevenko, who would now become a permanent fixture in Alexey's care.

On 20 October Nicholas was able at last to write to his mother 'with my heart filled with gratitude to the Lord for His Mercy in granting us the beginning of dear Alexei's recovery'.[25] In a bulletin issued by the Minister of the Imperial Court, Count Freedericksz, on the 21st a detailed description was finally given to the Russian public of the 'abdominal haemorrhage and swelling' that had occurred, the raised temperature and the 'subsequent exhaustion and severe anaemia' which would need 'considerable time to cure completely' as would the free use of the tsarevich's left leg as a result of the 'bent hip muscle'. Signed by doctors Rauchfuss, Feoderov, Ostrogorsky and Botkin, the bulletin made no mention of haemophilia. For the Russian people, the cause of the illness would remain shrouded in mystery. The international press was, however, thick with speculation. 'Probably the illness of no child in the world is fraught with so much political significance as is that of the eight-year-old czarevitch,' wrote the *Daily News*, 'his death eventually might lead to an upheaval in Russia that would shake the Romanoff dynasty from its throne.'[26]

But what was *really* wrong with the tsarevich, everyone asked? Tuberculosis of the bone, a tumour, an abscess, kidney trouble, a fall from his pony, were all mentioned, with the American press even circulating an absurd story that 'during an unguarded moment' Alexey had been attacked and stabbed in the grounds of Spala by a 'nihilist'.[27] The St Petersburg correspondent of the London *Daily Telegraph* reported that the exact nature of the illness was 'for unexplained reasons into which one is reluctant to pry, kept dark, not merely from the general public, but from the highest state dignitaries, who are reduced to inference and conjecture'. The 'incomprehensible silence of the Court bulletins' was causing considerable anxiety among the Russian public, giving, as *The Times* observed, 'free scope to the sensation-mongers'.[28] On 4 November (22 October OS) it ran a headline, 'Cause of the Tsarevitch's illness', beneath which its St Petersburg correspondent wrote, 'In medical circles the illness of the Tsarevitch is attributed to a congenital condition of the blood, rendering reabsorption difficult in the case of rupture of the slightest vessel'.[29] This in itself was a tacit admission of haemophilia to anyone in the medical profession, and it was the London press that finally broke the story. On 9 November (27 October OS), the British medical journal *Hospital* announced that the tsarevich had haemophilia, a fact picked up the following day in the *New York Times* with its headline 'Czar's Heir Has Bleeding Disease', adding that this was 'long a characteristic of European Royal Families and Still Persists'.[30]

*

When Alexey was finally fit to travel, the most careful preparations were made for his return home to Russia. The sandy road from the hunting lodge at Spala to the railway station was carefully smoothed over, so that there 'should not be the slightest jolting' and the imperial train was driven no faster than 15 mph (24 kmh) so that the brakes need not be suddenly applied.[31] It was not until 24 November (OS) that Alexey finally was able to take his first bath 'in more than two months', Alexandra told Onor. During the daytime he was being 'wheeled around the upstairs rooms in my bath-chair' and only later did they finally begin carrying him down to her mauve boudoir.[32] Alexey would be lame for a year, during the course of which he was submitted to endless, rigorous treatment: 'electricity, massage, mud compresses, blue light bath with electric current on arm, & leg bath'; Alexandra hoped he might be able to stand on his leg again by Christmas.[33] Professor Roman Wreden, a pioneering orthopaedic surgeon, came from St Petersburg and fitted Alexey with a corrective iron leg caliper. The tsarevich found it extremely uncomfortable and complained to his mother, but Wreden was firm; Alexey must endure the discomfort if he was to be a future emperor. It was a candid remark that hit home, for word was already out that the Russian people had a cripple for an heir. Alexandra did not like having to face this unpalatable truth. And so Nicholas thanked the good professor, made him an honorary court physician, and never called on his services again.[34]

Alexey's recovery went hand in hand with his mother's. Alexandra did not make her first public appearance until 1 December, having been 'too utterly exhausted' for the last three months. But she took comfort in her son's compassion: 'Sweet angel wants to have my pains,' she wrote, 'says I can take his which are much less.'[35] But it was clear that this latest crisis had taken an irreversible toll on her: 'for seven years,' she told Boyd Carpenter, 'I suffer from the heart and lead the life of an invalid most of the time.'[36]

Her precious boy had, however, recovered from almost certain death, a fact that a still baffled Dr Feodorov confirmed was 'wholly inexplicable, from a medical point of view'.[37] But the tsarevich's survival had come at a high price – the emotional enslavement of his mother to Grigory Rasputin as the only person on God's earth who could keep her son alive. For after his return to St Petersburg that winter, Grigory had assured her that her son would be safe – all the time that he, Grigory, was alive.

Now more than ever Alexandra's daughters performed an essential role in the day-to-day care of their mother and brother, in a family life that was increasingly lived in the shadow of the sickroom. 'They are all 5 touching in their care for me', Alexandra told Boyd Carpenter; 'my family life is one blessed ray of sunshine excepting the anxiety for our Boy.'[38] But the psychological effect of Alexandra's chronic sickness was taking its toll: in their crucial formative years the four sisters, now more than ever, needed a mother's time and attention. But instead of living the carefree life of teenagers exploring the world around them, meeting new people and discovering new places, sickness and suffering had come to dominate their everyday lives, which they were learning to endure with extraordinary stoicism. 'My Mama darling,' wrote Maria, herself in bed suffering with a sore throat, on 14 December 1912:

> I thank you so *very* much for your dear letter. I am so sorry that your heart is still No. 2.* I hope your cold is better. My temperature now is 37.1 [99 degrees F] and my throat acks less than

---

* Alexandra created her own private code for the levels of intensity of her heart pain, ranging from 1 to 3, used in notes to her daughters.

yesterday. Am so sorry not to see you today, but sertenly its better for you to rest. 1000 kisses from your own loving Maria.[39]

For the four sisters, especially Olga and Tatiana, there was also a major public role to perform in the coming year – 1913 – of the Romanov Tercentary in promoting the popular image of the imperial family in their mother's frequent absences and in acting, too, as 'the faithful companions of their beloved father'. 'It was as if the young, beautiful princesses should protect the ever-threatened czar,' observed Baroness Souiny, 'and they did protect him.'[40]

*

Brilliant sunshine in a cloudless sky greeted a St Petersburg in the grip of the winter thaw, when on Thursday 21 February 1913 the streets were set ablaze with the most splendid decorations in red, white and blue in celebration of the Tercentary of the ascent of the Romanov dynasty to the throne of Russia.[41] At 8 a.m. that morning a twenty-one-gun salute from the Peter and Paul Fortress had announced the start of the celebrations. Every shopfront and lamp-post along the Nevsky Prospekt was festooned with the tsarist double-headed eagle and portraits of all the Romanov tsars, since Tsar Mikhail Feodorovich had accepted the nomination back in February 1613. Shops were full of commemorative items, special stamps bearing the tsar's head for the first time (it had previously been considered an insult to depict it), medals and coins were issued and a manifesto by Nicholas published in which he proclaimed his 'steadfast desire, in unalterable agreement with our beloved people, to continue to lead the Empire along the path of peaceful development of the national life'.[42]

Over the last few years Russia, which occupied one-sixth of the world's surface, had been enjoying a remarkable period of growth that had seen St Petersburg become one of the six largest cities in Europe. The economy was still an agricultural-based one, the cornerstone of its enormous wealth being cereal production, but this now outstripped that of the USA and Canada combined. The territories of the Russian Empire contained a burgeoning iron and steel industry; and yet to be exploited natural reserves in Central Asia and Siberia that were being opened up by a vast new Trans-Siberian

Railway network that was also linked to the valuable oilfields at Baku in Azerbaijan and Batumi in Georgia. In the City of London and on Wall Street, Russia, for so long viewed as Asiatic and backward, was now at last seen as a 'profitable field for investment'. As the *Illustrated London News* told its readers, 'the general public are beginning to awaken to the great riches and the greater potential riches – agricultural, mineral, and industrial – of the Empire of the Great White Tsar'.[43] There was much talk abroad too about the growing military and political might of imperial Russia – having as it did a potential war strength of 4 million men – a fact that had recently been confirmed by the establishment of the *entente cordiale* with Britain and France.

But it was not just in industrial and military strength that Russia was carving out a higher international profile for itself: the country was enjoying an extraordinary and unprecedented burst of artistic creativity – with the music of Stravinsky and Rachmaninov; the avant-garde paintings of Malevich, Kandinsky and Chagall; Diaghilev's Ballets Russes, featuring outlandish set and costume designs, by Léon Bakst; a musical stage graced by the legendary dancers Pavlova and Nijinsky and the opera singer Chaliapin; the innovative direction of Stanislavsky and Meyerhold in the theatre; and a vibrant 'Silver Age' of poetry dominated by Alexander Blok, Andrey Bely and Anna Akhmatova.

In tones of the highest optimism *The Times* in early 1913 was therefore predicting a rosy future for Russia: 'The House of Romanoff has done more than create a mighty Empire. It has flung wide the gates of knowledge to a great people, and has launched them upon all her boundless ways.'[44] But in order to ensure further economic development it still lacked one crucial element: a stable political system and a proper, constitutional government. Since 1906 the Duma had juddered from one crisis to the next in an increasingly emasculated form, three times being dissolved and then reinstated by Nicholas. The Fourth Duma of 1912, created in the wake of Stolypin's assassination, had been the most dysfunctional yet and the political mood that year of 1913 was 'antagonistic' in continuing response to the repressive measures instituted after the 1905 revolution.[45] Many Russians felt there was little to celebrate.

The Tercentary had brought a raft of concessions including amnesties and reductions in sentences for many prisoners – but not for those imprisoned for their opposition to tsarism.

In February Nicholas and Alexandra installed themselves and the children in the Winter Palace for the three days of official celebrations – their first real time in St Petersburg since 1905 – the focus of which was entirely religious. Thursday the 21st was a day of pious observance, with twenty-five different religious processions winding their way across the capital, singing hymns and bursts of the national anthem. From the Winter Palace, the imperial family led the procession of carriages, Nicholas and Alexey in uniform at its head in an open victoria, followed by closed state coaches containing Alexandra, Maria Feodorovna and the girls. It processed down the Nevsky Prospekt the short distance to the Kazan Cathedral for a very long *Te Deum* conducted by the Patriarch of Antioch, who had travelled from Greece specially, and attended by over 4,000 of the Russian nobility, and by foreign diplomats and dignitaries, as well as by representatives of the peasantry and from the duchy of Finland. 'It was all brilliance,' *Novoe Vremya* reported, 'the brilliance of the ladies' diamonds, the brilliance of the medals and the stars, the brilliance of the gold and silver of the uniforms.'[46] But it was not the spectacular beauty of the assembled costumes, the icons, lighted tapers and incense, that had moved everyone; it was the 'inexpressibly sad' sight of the tsarevich, who was still too lame to walk, being carried into the service by a Cossack, his 'white, pinched small face . . . gazing anxiously round him at all the sea of human beings before him'.[47]

Although the Okhrana had been prepared for trouble, on the streets of St Petersburg ordinary citizens, huddled in their quilted coats and felt boots, demonstrated a marked indifference towards much of the ceremonial. Prince Gavriil Konstantinovich later wrote that he had the 'distinct impression that there was no special enthusiasm in the capital for the Romanov Dynasty Jubilee'. Meriel Buchanan noticed it too: the crowds were 'strangely silent', she recalled, 'breaking into cheers only when they caught sight of the young Grand Duchesses smiling under their big flower-trimmed hats'.[48]

The ceremony at the Kazan Cathedral would be the first of many collective public professions of faith led by the imperial family that year, accompanied by much genuflection, crossing, and kissing of miracle-working icons, all intended to 'arouse a general upsurge of patriotic sentiment in the people' at a time of continuing political discontent.[49] Meriel Buchanan had, like many, hoped that the festivities 'would force the Imperial Family to come out of their seclusion, and that the Emperor, when he attended the Duma, would make some public announcement that would relieve the internal situation'.[50] But she was disappointed; it soon became apparent that the primary objective of the Tercentary was to reinforce the image of a national life driven by religious faith, harking back to the ancient mystical union of tsar and people, rather than one where democracy and the work of the Duma held any true significance. Indeed, many members of the Fourth Duma were squeezed out at the celebrations, the limited number of places being given to members of the aristocracy and monarchist organizations.[51]

Later that day Nicholas and Alexandra received a great procession of 1,500 dignitaries in the Nicholas Hall at the Winter Palace in order to accept their congratulations. It was a milestone for Olga and Tatiana to be present, wearing matching formal Russian court dresses. These were made in the workshop of Olga Bulbenkova, who specialized in ceremonial clothes for the court, and were full-length, off-the-shoulder style in white satin with long, pointed, open sleeves, a front panel of pink velvet and a detachable train decorated with garlands of artificial roses.[52] Across their chests both girls wore their orders of St Catherine on scarlet sashes, and on their heads *kokoshniki* of pink velvet encrusted with pearls and decorated with bows. It must have been a moment of great pride for them, for they had not worn full-length formal dresses before and it signalled their final arrival in the adult world of the court. The two sisters were never more beautiful, as official photographs taken of them by the family's favourite studio, Boissonnas & Eggler, testified. The reception itself was something new for both of them, 'a rare chance of seeing Petersburg society, and from their attentive, animated faces it was clear that they were trying to take everything in and remember all the faces'.[53]

That evening the still-crowded streets of St Petersburg were lit up with celebratory illuminations; it reminded Nicholas of his coronation, but the happiness of the occasion was marred by the news the following morning that Tatiana – who had not been feeling well for a day or so – was in bed with a fever. Alexandra had been too exhausted to take part in any of the public receptions during the day, where Maria Feodorovna had enjoyed the limelight in her stead. But the tsaritsa did steel herself to attend a gala performance of Glinka's opera, *A Life for the Tsar*, starring Chaliapin that evening at the Mariinsky Theatre. She and Nicholas received a standing ovation from the audience as they entered the imperial box with Olga. But Anna Vyrubova detected a false note: 'there was in the brilliant audience little real enthusiasm, little real loyalty'.[54] Alexandra looked extremely pale and sombre, thought Meriel Buchanan, 'her eyes, enigmatical in their dark gravity, seeming fixed on some secret inward thought that was certainly far removed from the crowded theatre and the people who acclaimed her'.[55] Flushed and uncomfortable at all eyes being directed on her, the tsaritsa sank gratefully into her chair but she 'looked listless, as though she were in pain', thought Agnes de Stoeckl and indeed such was her extreme discomfort and her anxious laboured breathing, that she left after the first act. 'A little wave of resentment rippled over the theatre', noted Meriel Buchanan. 'Was it not always the same story?' with the empress yet again making no effort to disguise her distaste for St Petersburg society.[56] For that is how her retreat that evening was perceived. Only her daughter Olga and her husband knew the terrible toll Alexey's recent near-fatal illness had taken on her. It was the 'sad knowledge' of her son's life-threatening condition that made the tsaritsa 'so extraordinary in her ways', thought Princess Radziwill. It explained why 'she hates so much to see anyone, or to take part in any festivity, even for the sake of her daughters'. For their part, as always, the Romanov sisters had made the best of things. 'The whole city was celebrating, a lot of people', Olga recalled of the day in her diary, but, sensing as she did an atmosphere of change in Russia, it had not passed without some apprehension on her part: 'Thank you God that everything is OK.'[57]

Chapter Twelve

LORD SEND HAPPINESS TO HIM,
MY BELOVED ONE

❧

The 23rd of February 1913 was a very special day for eighteen-year-old Grand Duchess Olga Nikolaevna, when, accompanied by her father, her mother and her aunt Olga, she attended her first major public ball in St Petersburg, at the Assembly of Nobles. The tsar and tsaritsa had not attended a ball in the city since the grand costume ball of 1903, and Alexandra was determined to be there for her daughter even though she had spent most of the day lying down; but once again she had been obliged to leave early.[1] Tatiana should have shared the occasion with her sister but she was ill in bed at the Winter Palace; a couple of days later the doctors confirmed that she had typhoid fever.*[2]

Olga had been determined not to let these disappointments spoil her evening. She looked lovely, 'dressed in a simple pale-pink chiffon frock'. Much as at her sixteenth birthday ball in Livadia, 'she danced every dance, enjoying herself as simply and wholeheartedly as any girl at her first ball'.[3] Her own record of the evening was rather

---

* In her letters Alexandra described it as 'typhus', much as she had Nicholas's attack in 1900 and Olga's in 1901, the names for the two quite different diseases often being used interchangeably at the time. Typhus is, however, lice-borne and caught in dirty, overcrowded conditions, which is clearly unlikely in either daughter's case. Tatiana is thought to have contracted typhoid fever from an infected drink of lemonade taken at the Winter Palace.

more prosaic: 'I danced a lot – it was so much fun. A ton of people
. . . it was so beautiful.'⁴ She enjoyed the quadrille and the mazurka
with many of her favourite officers and was happy to have her dear
friend Nikolay Sablin from the *Shtandart* in attendance. Meriel
Buchanan was captivated by the sight of the eldest grand duchess
that evening, dressed with 'classical simplicity', her only necklace a
simple string of pearls, but yet so irresistible with her 'tip-tilted
nose'. She 'had a charm, a freshness, an enchanting exuberance that
made her irresistible'.⁵ Meriel Buchanan remembered seeing her
'standing on the steps leading down from the gallery to the floor
of the ball-room, trying gaily to settle a dispute between three young
Grand Dukes who all protested that they had been promised the
next dance'. It prompted a pause for thought: 'watching her I
wondered what the future was going to hold for her, and which of
the many possible suitors who had been mentioned from time to
time she would eventually marry.'⁶

The issue of Olga's future marriage had, inevitably, gained in
importance during the Tercentary year. Until now the imperial sisters
had been a taboo subject in the Russian press, but here they were
for the first time being officially presented to the nation. Discussion
of Olga's role as eldest child had once more been raised behind the
scenes, when a crisis in the Russian succession broke during the
winter of 1912–13. When Alexey had been lying at death's door at
Spala, Nicholas's younger brother Mikhail had secretly gone off
to Vienna to marry his mistress, Natalya Wulfert – a divorcee and
a commoner – knowing that if Alexey died and he became heir
presumptive again Nicholas would forbid this morganatic marriage.
Mikhail hoped that if he married behind his brother's back it would
be accepted as a fait accompli, but Nicholas was furious. And his
response was draconian: he demanded Mikhail renounce his right
to the throne or immediately divorce Natalya in order to prevent
a scandal. When Mikhail refused to do so, Nicholas froze Mikhail's
assets and banished him from Russia. At the end of 1912 a manifesto
was published in the Russian papers removing Mikhail from the
regency, his military command and imperial honours. According to
the laws of succession, Grand Duchess Vladimir's eldest son Kirill

would become regent if Nicholas should die before Alexey was twenty-one, but he and his two brothers who followed in the pecking order were deeply unpopular in Russia. Instead Nicholas overruled existing law and ordered Count Freedericksz to draft a manifesto nominating Olga as regent with Alexandra as guardian during Alexey's minority. It was published early in 1913 without Nicholas seeking, as he should have done, the Duma's approval. It inevitably provoked a furious objection from Grand Duchess Vladimir.

From her well-connected position at the British Embassy, Meriel Buchanan could see that the imperial family was in a very bad way that year:

> The marriage of the Grand Duke Michael has caused a tremendous upheaval and they say dear Emp.[eror] is heartbroken. Nobody quite knows what is the matter with the little boy and if the worst should happen the question of succession becomes a serious one. Kyrill is of course the nearest but there is some doubt as to whether any of the Vladimir lot will be allowed to succeed as their mother was not an Orthodox when they were born. It would then come to Dimitri and he would have to marry one of the Emperor's daughters.[7]

Rumours were clearly still circulating about a match between Olga and Dmitri. The waspish Meriel found the thought rather amusing; she had seen much of Dmitri of late on the Petersburg social scene, where everyone had been learning the latest dance crazes. 'I had a very ardous [sic] lesson from Dimitri the other day', she wrote to her cousin. 'It would be rather "chic" if Dimitri were one day Emperor of all the Russias to be able to say that he taught me the Bunnyhug wouldn't it?'[8] All talk of the match soon, however, evaporated when Dmitri proposed to his cousin, Irina, Grand Duchess Xenia's only daughter, only to be spurned in favour of his friend Felix Yusupov. A distancing between Nicholas and Dmitri followed as the year wore on, even though Dmitri continued to serve as an ADC.

As for Olga, her romantic teenage thoughts were now firmly directed much lower down the ranks, towards a favourite officer, Alexander Konstantinovich Shvedov, a captain in the Tsar's Escort.

In her diary she referred to him by the acronym of AKSH and his presence at afternoon tea parties at Aunt Olga's was the focal point of her very limited social life for much of the first half of that year. These occasions were little more than get-togethers for high jinks with a group of favourite hand-picked officers; of dancing to the phonograph and playing childish games of cat-and-mouse, slap-on-hands, hide-and-seek and tag. They were nominally supervised by Olga Alexandrovna but regularly degenerated into a lot of giggling and boisterous play that brought the four sisters into close physical proximity with men with whom they otherwise could never have had such intimacy. It was the strangest and most perverse kind of interplay – but one in which both their mother and their aunt saw no harm. Here were Russian imperial grand duchesses on the brink of womanhood indulging in infantile behaviour, the end result of which was to leave the impressionable Olga swooning about a young man who in every other way was totally off limits. 'Sat with AKSH the whole time and strongly fell in love with him', she confided to her diary on 10 February, 'Lord, save us. Saw him all day long – at liturgy and in the evening. It was very nice and fun. He is so sweet.'⁹ For weeks afterwards the pattern of her life beyond lessons, walks with Papa, sitting with Mama and listening to Alexey say his prayers at bedtime was the occasional day release to Auntie Olga's in St Petersburg to play silly games and gaze longingly at the handsome mustachioed AKSH in his dashing Cossack *cherkeska*.*

Tatiana was distraught at having to miss out on many of the celebrations for the Tercentary in St Petersburg, not to mention the trips to Aunt Olga's, where she too had looked forward to seeing her favourite officers. Because of her illness (which Dr Botkin and Trina Schneider also soon contracted), the family was obliged to leave the Winter Palace on 26 February and return to Tsarskoe Selo; but before doing so Tatiana asked her nurse Shura Tegleva to telephone Nikolay Rodionov and tell him that she would love it if some of her officers would come and walk past her window at the Winter Palace so she could at least see them. Rodionov and Nikolay Vasilevich Sablin were only too happy to oblige and remembered

---

* A long Circassian collarless coat.

seeing the poor sick girl, wrapped in a blanket, bowing to them at the window.[10]

Upon her return to the Alexander Palace Tatiana was immediately quarantined from her sisters and was very ill for more than a month; on 5 March her beautiful long, chestnut hair had to be cropped short, though a wig was made of it for her to wear until her hair grew back sufficiently (which it had done by the end of December).[11] Confined at home with her invalid mother, each looking after the other, it wasn't until early April that Tatiana finally ventured outside onto Alexandra's balcony, but it was still too cold and snowy to stay for long. When she did at last go outside she was deeply self-conscious about the wig. One day, when she was playing a skipping game in the park with Maria Rasputin and some young officers from the Corps de Pages, Alexey's dog had run up to her barking; Tatiana got her foot caught in the rope, tripped and as she fell 'her hair suddenly tumbled down and, to our amazement, we saw a wig drop off', Maria recalled. Poor Tatiana 'revealed to our eyes and those of the two embarrassed officers, the top of her head where a few short, sparse hairs were just beginning to grow'. She was absolutely mortified, and 'with one bound she was on her feet, had picked up her wig and dashed towards the nearest clump of trees. We saw only her blushes and vexation and she did not appear again that day.'[12]

During the winter months of 1913 at the Alexander Palace, Nicholas's diary is a testament to his hands-on parenting of his four daughters in lieu of his perpetually sick wife. No matter the amount of paperwork on his desk, the number of meetings with ministers, public audiences and military reviews that filled his day, at this time of year when they were home at Tsarskoe Selo he always found time for his children. History may have condemned him many times over for being a weak and reactionary tsar, but he was, without doubt, the most exemplary of royal fathers. The months of January and February were a special time for him and his daughters, during which he treated them all to trips to see the ballets *The Little Humpbacked Horse*, *Don Quixote* and *The Pharoah's Daughter* – in which last they were thrilled to see Pavlova dance. As the eldest, Olga (and Tatiana, until illness prevented her) enjoyed the added bonus of seeing the operas *Madame Butterfly*, *The Legend of the Invisible City of Kitezh* and Wagner's *Lohengrin*, which latter Olga found particularly beautiful and moving.[13] But in the main, time with Papa was spent out in the park, whatever the weather, sharing invigorating walks, riding bicycles, helping him break the ice on the canals, skiing, sliding down the ice hill, and joined – when he was well enough – by Alexey wearing his specially made boot with a caliper. The girls so enjoyed having their father to themselves; he was a fast, unrelenting walker and they had all learned to keep up or be left behind, Olga in particular always walking closest to him on one side, Tatiana on the other, with Maria and Anastasia running back and forth in front of them, sliding on the ice and throwing snowballs. It was clear to anyone who encountered the tsar and his daughters in the Alexander Park how much pride he had in his girls. 'He was happy that people admired them. It was as though his kind blue eyes were saying to them: "Look what wonderful daughters I have."'[14]

*

On the evening of 15 May the family boarded the imperial train for Moscow and began a two-week trip in the steamship *Mezhen* up the Volga from Moscow in celebration of the Tercentary. It was an arduous tour during which they stopped off at the major religious sites of the Golden Ring, a route taken by the first Romanov tsar from his birthplace to Moscow in 1613.[15] It had been a major pilgrimage route for centuries and was one that Alexandra had long expressed a wish to see; Nicholas himself had not visited the area since 1881. From a succession of holy sites at Vladimir, Bogolyubovo and Suzdal the family travelled to Nizhniy Novgorod for a service at its beautiful Cathedral of the Transfiguration; then back along the Volga by steamer, arriving at Kostroma on 19 May. At each stop there was a traditional welcome of bread and salt from local dignitaries and clergy. Church bells rang out and military bands played, as huge crowds of peasants gathered along the river banks – some wading deep into the water – to catch a glimpse of the imperial family as they arrived (a fact which alarmed Alexandra who feared a catastrophe like the stampede at Khodynka Fields). But she enjoyed meeting the devoted old peasant *babushki* and would stop and talk to them on the river bank, giving them money and religious images.[16] Kostroma was the most important stop on their itinerary for it was here, at the Ipatiev Monastery,* that the sixteen-year-old Mikhail Romanov had taken refuge during a time of political upheaval in Russia, and where he was invited by a delegation of boyars from Moscow to take the throne. The monastery had its own Romanov Museum that the family visited after attending services in the cathedral, before going on to unveil a monument marking the Tercentary. This was undoubtedly the highlight of the trip with huge crowds voicing their enthusiasm for the imperial family as they processed through streets decorated with flags and Romanov insignia, the peasantry demonstrating their traditional loyalty to the 'little father' by falling on their knees when the national anthem was played.[17] Such devotion served to stiffen Alexandra's conviction that the ordinary people loved them: 'What cowards those State Ministers are', she told Elizaveta Naryshkina. 'They are constantly frightening the Emperor with threats and forebodings of a revolution, and here you see it yourself – we only need to show ourselves, and at once their hearts are ours.'[18]

Olga was thrilled when they arrived at Yaroslavl to see her dear AKSH in the honour guard that greeted them. After yet another crowded reception and a visit to an orphanage built to commemorate the Tercentary, the girls and Nicholas left Alexandra behind and headed for an exhibition of local manufacturing, a prayer service followed by dinner and musical entertainment, before they all finally boarded the train at midnight for Rostov. 'A ton of presents, got very tired, very long and boring, also very hot', Olga noted in her diary of that day. But 'nice, sweet AKSH was there. I was *terribly* happy to see him.' 'Poor Mama' was, however, very tired. 'Heart no. 3, hurts. Lord save her.'[19] The whole of the following day Alexandra remained in bed. During their time on the Volga Nikolay

---

* The house in which the Romanovs were held captive in 1918 in Ekaterinburg ironically had the same name, the Ipatiev House, after its owner, an engineer on the Trans-Siberian Railway named Nikolai Ipatiev.

Vasilievich Sablin saw the strain Nicholas was under coping with the demands of the schedule and a tetchy wife constantly prostrated by fatigue and eating virtually nothing; he noticed that she often went all day on just a couple of boiled eggs.[20]

*

The family arrived back in Moscow on 24 May for the climax of their tour; 'dear AKSH was once more smiling from across the crowd' among officers of the Tsar's Escort standing guard when they stepped from the carriages.[21] If the celebrations in St Petersburg had been muted, officialdom had ensured that those in the heart of ancient Muscovy were triumphal, mimicking the entry into Moscow of Tsar Alexander I in the early days of the 1812 war with France. However, Prince Wilhelm of Sweden, who was there for the celebrations, thought the crowds seemed subdued:

> The Emperor made restrained greetings to the right and the left without changing expression; it was impossible to detect any enthusiasm from either side. The *muzhiks* mostly stood there staring, a few made the sign of the cross or fell to their knees for the head of the church. It was more awe and curiosity than spontaneous warmth, more dutiful obedience than trust. Subjects kept down rather than free citizens. It was unpleasant, remote and as unlike how things are at home [in Sweden] as possible. The unbridgeable gap between the ruler and the people was more notable than ever.[22]

The ceremonials once more revealed Alexey's frailty, particularly on 25 May during the procession made by the family down the famous Red Staircase in the Kremlin, when people were shocked to see the tsarevich carried by one of the Cossacks from the Tsar's Escort. 'How sad to see the heir to the Romanov throne so weak, sickly, and helpless', wrote Prime Minister Kokovtsov, who noted also the gasps of sympathy that this sight evoked in the crowd.[23] The empress's discomfort was also clearly visible, an ugly red flush appearing on her face during the ceremony. In contrast, the four Romanov daughters seemed relaxed if somewhat inattentive at the end of what had been a gruelling two weeks. At the Kremlin, one of the guards noticed how they 'looked around, they were bored, they ate grapes and sweets', though they always 'behaved in a very natural and unpretentious manner'.[24]

Just before their return to Tsarskoe Selo, Olga and Tatiana attended a ball at Moscow's Assembly of Nobles. Alexandra was unable to endure more than an hour, but the two sisters happily opened the ball and took centre stage, dancing with many of the officers from the Erevan Regiment. And Olga's head was once more turned during the quadrille by the sight of 'AKSH's *sweet* smiling face from afar'.[25] En route to the railway station the following morning she thought she caught sight of him 'in a red cap on one of the balconies far away' and she saw him again soon at Aunt Olga's on 2 and 6 June. As usual, after tea, dinner and a cosy chat on the sofa, the Romanov sisters indulged in a succession of noisy and childish catch-me-if-you-can games in the garden with their regular group of officers including AKSH and another great favourite, Viktor Zborovsky from the Tsar's Escort. On the 6th, however, it all got wildly out of hand during a game of hide-and-seek upstairs when they 'horsed around terribly, turned everything upside down, especially one big wardrobe. 10 people got inside it, and also on top of it, broke the doors, laughed and had a lot of fun.'[26] A necessary dissipation of pent-up energies perhaps, but – for the older two sisters at least – there must have been an underlying sexual tension. But then, inevitably, the motor car came for them at 7 p.m. and took them all back to Tsarskoe Selo. Olga went back with a heavy heart, sad to have learned that day that AKSH was 'leaving for [the] Caucasus on Saturday. God save him.'

*

Throughout the 1913 Tercentary the tsarist publicity machine had promoted a paternalistic Romanov monarchy headed by a loving, devoted and virtuous family, an image perpetuated in the thousands of official photographs sold as postcards across Russia that year. But many of the Russian peasantry were bewildered by the official images, for they did not project an authoritarian all-powerful tsar, remote on his throne, as many of them certainly perceived him, but instead an ordinary, bourgeois man at the heart of a domestic unit dominated by women that called into question his manliness and with it his ability to rule.[27] The role of the four Romanov sisters as an adjunct to their brother meanwhile underlined their widespread depiction as uncontroversial, dutiful daughters, nowhere more so than in an official hagiography, made available in English translation as *The Tsar and His People*. Written for the Tercentary by a member of the imperial entourage, Major-General Andrey Elchaninov, it found time briefly to summarize the sisters as

> brought up in the rules of the Holy Orthodox Church and trained to be good and careful housewives . . . [They] are remarkable for their power of observation, kindness, and sympathy, and their manners are simple and gracious. They are very active in helping the poor, especially poor children, their presents taking the form not of money, but of useful objects which they have made or knitted themselves.[28]

Such a description set in stone the representation of the four girls as interchangeable and unremarkable, and it was one that they themselves compounded by often referring to themselves collectively as OTMA. The official view continued to be entirely bland with an emphasis on domestic pleasures over and above worldly ones: 'They seldom visit the theatre except during their holidays. Only at Christmas or on other feast-days are they taken to the opera by their parents.' Ironically, this was true enough; with hindsight one might say that in being denied contact with young men and women of their own social standing and the life experiences that went with it, the sisters were trapped in a stultifying, artificial world in which they were perpetually infantilized. 'Why were they never seen,' asked Meriel Buchanan, 'except at Te Deums, or Reviews, or on some State occasion?'[29] The one breath of fresh air in their lives remained their beloved Aunt Olga, but tea parties with her in St Petersburg were curtailed when, after returning from Moscow, the family headed straight off to Finland for four weeks' holiday in the *Shtandart*.[30]

They were all very tired after their Volga tour and the holiday was a rather subdued one for most of the family. But for Olga it was full of new interest for, in the absence of AKSH, she turned her attention to another handsome moustachioed officer on the

Shtandart, who in her diary she referred to as 'Pav. Al.'. The newly promoted Lieutenant Pavel Alexeevich Voronov was twenty-seven and had joined the *Shtandart* in April. From the moment she stepped on board on 10 June, Olga rapidly developed an attachment to him. Sometimes she sat with him in the front control room when he was on duty, or came there to dictate the day's log to him. Soon they had a favourite trysting place, between the telegraph room and one of the ship's funnels, where they often sat chatting with Tatiana and her favourite, Nikolay Rodionov. During the day Pavel sometimes joined the girls and their father on land, playing hot and vigorous games of tennis (he was Nicholas's favourite partner at the game) or going for walks or swimming. Back on board they watched film shows and played card games together. It all seemed so innocent and above-board, but under the surface Olga's emotions were in turmoil.

Everyone liked the easy-going Pavel Voronov, especially Alexey, whom Voronov often carried when he was unwell. By the end of June Olga was writing that 'he is so *affectionate*', and was snatching what small moments of intimacy she could, often simply sitting gazing at him as he kept watch on the bridge.[31] Any activity from which Pavel was absent or excluded was 'boring'; when he was there 'it was cosy and insanely nice to be with him'. By 6 July her feelings had deepened: 'I dictated the log journal to him. After that we sat on the couch until after 5.00. I love him, dear, *so much*.'[32] On 12 July on their last day in the *Shtandart* en route back to Peterhof she sat with Pavel in the control room all the way. 'It was awfully sad. The whole time while the gangway was extended, I stood with him. Left the yacht around 4.00. So *terribly* hard to part with the beloved *Shtandart*, officers and sweetie pie . . . Lord save him.'[33]

In the intervening weeks at Peterhof she received occasional telephone calls from Pavel and also the dependable Nikolay Sablin whom she so looked up to. It helped temper the sad litany of her mother's almost daily indispositions. Mama's heart hurt, her face hurt, her legs hurt; she was tired; she had a bad headache. Alexey was unwell too, his arm sore 'from waving his arms about too much when playing', so much so that in mid-July Grigory was called in to see him. He came at seven one evening, sat with Alexandra and

Alexey and then talked for a short while with Nicholas and the girls, before leaving. 'Soon after his departure,' Nicholas noted in his diary, 'the pain in Alexey's arm began to go, he calmed down and began to fall asleep.[34] Olga sat with her brother and her mother often when they were unwell, offering comfort – as too did Tatiana – in between the occasional horse ride or game of tennis. Her former crush, AKSH, reappeared from time to time in the Escort and she was happy to see him but her thoughts remained primarily with the *Shtandart* which was now sailing to the Mediterranean.

At the beginning of August the two older sisters began preparing in earnest for their first official appearance at army manoeuvres, to be held on the 5th at Krasnoe Selo. They practised their riding for several days beforehand for the auspicious day when they would review their regiments in uniform on horseback for the first time – Olga in the blue and red with gold trim of the 3rd Elizavetgrad Hussars on her horse Regent and Tatiana in the navy and blue of the 8th Voznesensk Uhlans on Robino. They were now the youngest female colonels in the world – and on the day proved how accomplished they were. 'Both Grand Duchesses led a pass in front of the Emperor at a gallop', escorted by Grand Duke Nikolay, Commander-in-Chief of the army.[35] 'It was a hot day and they were very nervous, but they were delightful and did their utmost. I believe the Emperor was very proud as he watched his daughters for the first – and alas! – for the last time in a military line-up', recalled Prince Gavriil Konstantinovich. But it was yet another milestone in their lives that their mother had been too ill to witness, shut away in her boudoir suffering from another bout of neuralgia.

Two days later, the family headed south to Livadia in the 40-degree C (104-degree F) heat of high summer. Alexey was still unwell, and grumbled about the mud-bath treatments he had to endure twice a week, which he hated. But he now had his own, official governor. Nicholas and Alexandra had originally considered appointing someone from their military or naval entourage, but eventually decided to offer the post to Pierre Gilliard. Not everyone approved; Gilliard was an impeccable pedagogue, very proper and punctilious but very un-Russian, as Nikolay Vasilievich Sablin noted.[36] Some said appointing a republican Swiss to look after the tsarevich was inappropriate. Gilliard accepted the appointment with considerable apprehension at what it entailed, having only just been privately informed by Dr Derevenko that Alexey had haemophilia. 'Will I ever get used to the terrible responsibility that I am taking on?' he asked his brother Frederick in a letter home.[37] He found Alexey very undisciplined; in his view the boy's nervousness and restless behaviour was exacerbated by the constant supervision of Derevenko. At the end of November his charge had yet another accident, falling off a chair he had climbed up on in the schoolroom and banging his leg. The subsequent swelling quickly spread from below the knee to his ankle. Another sailor from the *Shtandart*, Klimenty Nagorny, had recently been charged with sharing the task of looking after Alexey with Derevenko and proved to be 'touchingly kind', sitting up at night with him during this latest attack, while his sisters opened the door every now and then and tiptoed in to kiss him.[38] Yet again, the prayers of Grigory, who was in Yalta at the time, seemed to be the only thing that saved him; but, with the same alarming regularity, as after every injury, the frail tsarevich needed months of convalescence.

*

On 9 August when she had boarded the *Shtandart* in Sevastopol for the journey to Livadia, and saw Pavel Voronov once more, Olga began referring to him in her diary as 'S'. This was an abbreviation for the Russian words *sokrovishche* – treasure, *solntse* – sunshine and *schaste* – happiness, which were her frequently used epithets for those she cared about most. Her whole world for the rest of that year was bound up in Pavel Voronov. Day after day she refers to him: 'it's so boring without my S, ghastly'; 'it's empty without him'; 'didn't see S and was miserable'.[39] Pavel was perfection: sweet, kind, gentle, precious. At all times, no matter how briefly, she was always 'so happy, so terribly happy' to see him. Indeed, Olga was desolate when even a day passed without her spending time with the object of her affection and she snatched at the slightest sight or word of him like the lovesick teenager that she was. This experience went beyond the usual light flirting and coquetry that she and Tatiana had been indulging in for the last couple of years with the officers in the entourage. It was first love and it was painful. But it also had no future whatsoever. None of the well-drilled officers in the *Shtandart* ever breached the strict, unwritten code of honour that they adhered to in their relations with the daughters of the tsar. Voronov was clearly attracted to Olga, touched by her attention and certainly flattered; when the family left the ship for the White Palace, his fellow officers noticed how he often pointed his binoculars in its direction in hopes of catching a glimpse of her white dress on the balcony. Olga did likewise from her own vantage point – perhaps they had a private agreement to do so?[40]

Whatever Pavel Voronov might have felt in his heart, his tentative relationship with the tsar's eldest daughter was love held firmly at bay: furtive, affectionate and confidential glances, occasional chats over tea on deck, games of tennis, sticking photographs in albums together. There was even the occasional chance to partner her at small informal dances on the deck of the *Shtandart*, such as that held to celebrate Olga's eighteenth birthday, during which, as everyone noticed, she danced a great deal with Voronov. By December 1913, having spent the best part of five months in his company, Olga's feelings had inevitably intensified and she began confiding them in a special code – something her mother had done during her own youth – using symbols similar to Georgian cursive. Pavel was now 'her tender darling', suggesting a degree of reciprocal feeling on his part, and she was happier than she had ever been.[41] And then, in September, a worrying note entered her diary entries. Pavel was less in evidence. Olga would go several days without seeing him: 'It's so abominable without my S., *awful*'; even seeing her dear friend AKSH, who was on duty in the Escort at Livadia, didn't cheer her up.[42] Life returned to the same predictable routine of lessons in the morning, sitting with either her sick mama or brother, playing tennis and going on occasional walks or horse rides. From disappointment, to boredom, to petulance and finally pretending she really didn't care, Olga Nikolaevna ran the gamut of feelings of any teenager in love. Her attention wandered in the days without S and with typical, hormonal fickleness, she turned her thoughts back to AKSH, using a new nickname for him – Shurik – and reminding herself 'what a sweetheart' he was and how nice he looked in uniform wearing 'my favourite dark jacket'.[43]

It turned out that during his time off, Pavel had been making visits to the Kleinmikhels, close friends of the Romanov family who had an estate at Koreiz. One day Countess Kleinmikhel was invited to the White Palace to lunch. She arrived, bringing her young niece Olga with her. Suddenly it all became clear; Pavel Voronov and Olga Kleinmikhel were being steered in each other's direction. When Olga Nikolaevna saw him at a charity ball shortly after in October she already sensed a distancing between them: 'I saw my S once, during the quadrille, our encounter was strange somehow, a bit sad, I don't know.'[44] Soon after, with characteristic teenage sangfroid she announced: 'I am used to S. not being here by now', but oh how it hurt when on 6 November, at a small dance at the White Palace, she noticed that he 'danced the entire time with Kleinmikhels [sic]'.[45] She was miffed and several days later tried to shrug it off: 'It's good to see him and not good at the same time. Did not say a word to him and don't want to.'[46] There were always games of hide-and-seek in the palace with Shurik and Rodionov, during which she 'horsed around a lot', and a trip to see a film in Yalta. But when she returned home it was the same depressing scenario: Alexey was crying because his leg hurt; Mama was tired, and lying down and her heart was no. 2.[47]

By December Olga had become scared of her feelings for S and how they still dominated her thoughts and so it was as well that on the 17th the family left Livadia, although this year, in particular, it was a wrench to go. 'We all were left with such a longing for the Crimea', wrote Nicholas in his diary.[48] For Olga it was 'boring without all the friends, the yacht, and S., of course'. And then, on 21 December, she heard the news: 'I learned that S is to marry Olga Kleinmichael [sic].' Olga's response was brief but dignified: 'May the Lord grant happiness to him, my beloved.'[49]

Is it possible that Nicholas and Alexandra had deliberately contrived the engagement of Pavel Voronov to Olga Kleinmikhel, with a view to sparing Olga any further heartache in pursuing a hopeless love match? It was patently clear to everyone – and must have been to them – that she had fallen in love with him, though Pavel's true feelings for her are unknown. Perhaps he had sensed that his close friendship with the grand duchess was beginning to overstep the permitted mark and that he should therefore fall on his sword and remove himself from the frame. Nicholas and Alexandra were certainly more than happy to give their warm approval of his engagement to Olga Kleinmikhel, but for Olga Nikolaevna it was hard and her response was to suppress the pain she was feeling, even in her diary. Dealing with a broken heart was one thing, but having to continue seeing Pavel with his fiancée was quite another, as too was having to listen to her sisters excitedly discussing their wedding to come at Tsarskoe Selo.

In January Aunt Ella arrived at Tsarskoe Selo with Countess Kleinmikhel and Olga and 'S'; only now S – Olga's treasure, her happiness – was the other Olga's, 'not mine!' as she exclaimed in her diary. 'My heart aches, it's painful, I don't feel well and only slept for an hour and a half.'[50] That year Christmas was a sad one for her. After visiting her grandmother at the Anichkov Palace and presenting gifts to the officers of the Escort it was back to the same quiet routine, as the winter weather closed in on a bitter cold New Year's Eve at Tsarskoe Selo: 'At 11 p.m. had tea with Papa and Mama, and welcomed the New Year in the regimental church. I thank God for everything. Snow blizzard. –9 degrees.'[51]

All of the Romanov family found Pavel Voronov's wedding service on 7 February 1914, at the regimental church at Tsarskoe Selo, deeply moving. Olga kept her feelings to herself and did not even unburden them in her diary:

> At about 2:30, the three of us set out with Papa and Mama. We drove to the regimental church for the wedding of P. A. Woronoff and O. K. Kleinmichael at the regimental church. May the Lord grant them happiness. They were both nervous. We made the acquaintance of S's parents and 2 sisters, sweet girls. We drove to the Kleinmichael's. There were many people at the reception at the house.[52]

Immediately afterwards Pavel Voronov went on leave for two months with his bride, after which he was transferred to the post of commander of the watch on the imperial yacht *Aleksandriya*. Olga would still see Pavel from time to time at Tsarskoe Selo, and continued to refer to him as 'S' in her diary, but her brief experience of real love was over. His wife later recalled that 'of his four years' service in the proximity of the imperial family Paul kept a sacred memory'. But Pavel Voronov remained the soul of discretion about his relationship with Grand Duchess Olga Nikolaevna; it was a memory that he kept to himself until the day he died.[53]

Chapter Thirteen

GOD SAVE THE TSAR!

❧❧❧

The last great winter season of 1913–14 in St Petersburg was a glittering one in the opinion of many who witnessed it – 'even the dowagers' could not remember another like it.[1] Coming at the end of a successful Tercentary year, the succession of parties laid on by the greatest of Russia's noble houses would mark the 'sunset of the dynasty', as Edith Almedingen recalled – 'a sunset splendid enough to win a lodgment in the memory'.[2] Such unbridled splendour was of course confined to the playgrounds of the super-rich, who spent the season dissipating their crippling ennui in a 'vortex of worldly gaiety' during which they 'scarcely saw the daylight for weeks at a time during the six hours of the winter's sunshine'.[3] Behind the facades of their overheated, luxurious palaces and browsing in the high-class shops along the Nevsky Prospekt filled with Western luxury goods, the Russian aristocracy remained stubbornly oblivious to the visible unrest gathering across the city, fuelled by poverty, deprivation and continuing political oppression.[4]

There was a mass of high-society parties, amateur theatricals and masked balls to choose from that year, for those with an 'in' to the clique-ridden social scene, all described in detail and lavishly photographed on the pages of the high-society magazine *Stolitsa i usadba* [Capital and Country Estate], its title reflecting the charmed lives of those privileged to have homes in both locations. After Grand Duchess Vladimir's four-day Grand Christmas Bazaar had opened the season at the Assembly of Nobles, the hot tickets were for Princess Obolenskaya's Greek Mythology Ball at her big white palace on the Moika; Countess Kleinmikhel's fancy-dress ball with costumes designed by Bakst; and two more opulent balls – one in black-and-white and the other featuring wigs and multicoloured turbans – held by the fabulously wealthy Princess Betsy Shuvalova at her palace on the Fontanka. In addition there were endless, rather more sedate *bals blancs* for debutantes in white watched over by their chaperones, *bals roses* for young married women and dances at the various embassies, the two at the British Embassy on the English Embankment being the most sought after. At the Imperial Ballet at the Mariinsky Theatre society ladies flocked to see its star performers Mathilde Kschessinska and Anna Pavlova, while gentlemen could indulge in extravagant private dinners and gaming at Grand Duke Dmitri's favourite haunt, the Imperial Yacht Club.[5]

The tsaritsa of course would not dream of allowing her daughters to attend any of these functions; it was their grandmother who gave a special ball – at the Anichkov Palace on 13 February 1914 – to mark Olga's and Tatiana's official debut in society and which was the highlight of the social season. Guests were greeted by 'masters of ceremony in gold-embroidered court dress, black silk breeches and stockings, and buckled, patent leather shoes', holding 'thin ivory canes which made them look like rococo shepherds'.[6] From here they were herded past 'two tall black Ethiopian footmen in Oriental costume and high turbans' into the ballroom, where they awaited the entrance of the emperor and empress, followed by Tatiana and Olga, 'tall, slim lovely creatures' who looked at those assembled 'with a sort of amused curiosity'.[7] After the tsar had opened the ball with a ceremonial polonaise, there was a moment of confused embarrassment. 'Not a single young man made a move to ask the two grand duchesses to dance', noticed debutante Helene Iswolsky. 'Were they all too shy to make the plunge? Or was it the sudden realization that the two girls were strangers?'[8] After an embarrassing pause a few officers from the Tsar's Escort who had danced with them before were 'jockeyed into position', but it was clear that these young men 'did not belong to the smart set'; they were 'completely unknown, rather uncouth, common looking'.[9]

Alexandra managed to tolerate the ball for an hour and a half, leaving Nicholas with the girls until a wearying 4.30 in the morning, his daughters having 'refused to be torn away any earlier'.[10] But he had spent the whole evening looking timid and feeling uncomfortable: '*Je ne connais personne ici*', he confided to one dancing partner.[11] Such was the isolation in which he and his family had been living for the last eight years that they were completely out of touch with who was who in fashionable society. This fact did not go unnoticed by Nicholas's aunt, the forthright Duchess of Saxe-Coburg, who was in St Petersburg for the wedding of Grand Duchess Xenia's daughter Irina to Prince Felix Yusupov. She did not mince her words when describing the evening in a letter to her daughter Marie, the Crown Princess of Romania. The duchess had very decided views on the high-born company young women such as her great-nieces should keep. But instead,

> they were surrounded by a Chinese wall of Cossack and other third class officers who would not let any of the real good society ones come near them. As the girls know nobody in society, they simply hopped about like provincial demoiselles without anybody being presented to them and they were never made to talk with any of the ladies young or old.[12]

The duchess was appalled: 'Now fancy Grand Duchesses who perhaps will soon marry and perhaps leave the country not being properly introduced into the Petersburg society!'

> If I only think of my young days when before going out I knew all the ladies and the young gentlemen who were presented during a ball. As Alix has allowed her daughters to be engaged by their dancers instead of sending for them like we did (and liked it much better as we got all those we really wanted and not the bores, so that the young ladies even envied us) the whole of the old and good etiquette has been abandoned. The result is that only certain officers danced with them.[13]

This mattered not a jot to Olga and Tatiana, who continued to make the most of what precious few social engagements came their way that winter before the austerity of Lent was upon them. A few days later Alexandra allowed Anastasia and Maria to join them for a small *thé-dansant* at Grand Duchess Vladimir's palace, given 'almost in defiance of the cloistered tsarina' and in which the grand duchess

'made a great display of luxury and decoration', as though emphasizing to the sisters the lifestyle they were being deprived of by
their anti-social mother. Here Olga and Tatiana 'danced every dance
with wholehearted and intense enjoyment' and Meriel Buchanan
took pleasure in watching them 'whispering in a corner, fair head
and dark head close together, blue eyes and amber eyes alight with
merriment'.[14] But again, Nicholas, who accompanied them, looked
lost, not knowing any of the ladies and gentlemen present.[15]

The Duchess of Saxe-Coburg was totally exasperated with
Alexandra's endless retreats and non-appearances that season and
her daughters' total lack of social experience, but she had to admit
that she could not help admiring 'their great devotion to her'. 'How
trying it must be for young gay creatures to have an eternally ailing
mother', she told Marie.[16] Nevertheless, by 1914 the eldest two
Romanov daughters were finally coming into their own. St Petersburg
was full of rumours

> which coupled their names with those of one or two Foreign
> Princes, with that of a young Grand Duke very popular in Society
> [i.e. Dmitri Pavlovich]; the story of a too forward suitor who
> got his cheek severely slapped by the Grand Duchess Olga, the
> whisper of a romance with one of the officers attached to the
> Staff which was promptly squashed by those in authority.[17]

Was the latter, one wonders, an allusion to Voronov? Certainly,
all the royal princes of Europe were once more being thrown into
a mix that was being vigorously stirred by the 'matchmaking
busybodies' of the Continental press.[18] A 'sentimental crisis' was
now approaching in the careers of the tsar's two eldest daughters
according to *Current Opinion*, which depicted Olga as grave and
somewhat melancholy, a reminder of 'her august origin'. Yet even
so, who could miss the exquisiteness of her throat, her slender neck
and 'soft white arms dimpling at the elbow and the long tapering
fingers'? But it was Tatiana who intrigued. With her fascinating eyes
that 'alternated from deep grey to violet' she had 'all the seductive-
ness of a sprite'.[19] Both sisters were nevertheless noted for their
piety, their mother having admitted to a departing French ambassador: 'My ambition for my girls is that they may become Christian

ladies.'[20] Their modesty was also reflected in the continuing simplicity of their dress, a fact mourned by the French *modistes*: 'The Czarina will not allow her girls to don gold gauze or flaunt in the colours of the Avenue d'Alma.'[21] It was clear that the clothes of the young grand duchesses 'must still be made under the supervizion [*sic*] of their mother, as they were ten years ago'. Unsophisticated they might be but one thing impressed: the girls' military ranks were by no means a 'formality, a mere honour', for, gasped *Current Opinion*, 'the royal ladies can actually put their men through the drill', a fact which seemed to confirm that not only was Nicholas ensuring his daughters were privy to the mysteries of statecraft but that one or either might if necessary 'take their father's place on the throne with the same ease'.[22]

In all respects there were, by 1914, no two more wealthy, desirable and marriageable royal princesses than Olga and Tatiana Romanova. According to the Berlin *Tageblatt*, it was Tatiana who was now being paired off with the Prince of Wales, in anticipation of a projected visit he was to make to St Petersburg in the spring. The rumour soon received short shrift from George V's private secretary, Lord Stamfordham: 'There is not a vestige of truth in the statement . . . It is pure invention.'[23] Tatiana was also the object of an informal approach by Nikola Pašić, the Serbian prime minister, on behalf of the king, for his son Prince Alexander. The names of Boris of Bulgaria, Peter of Montenegro and Adalbert of Germany were all also once more raised and discussed. Meanwhile rumours persisted that 'Grand Duchess Olga is willing to become the consort of her second cousin, Grand Duke Demetrius Pavlovich, and that it is on his account that she has rejected the suggestion of other matrimonial alliances'.[24] The gossips would not let go of what they still perceived as the ideal match; but in fact Dmitri, whose disreputable reputation was growing, was suffering from tuberculosis of the throat and spending much of his time abroad for his health. Olga's diary for December 1913 had made quite clear the rather dim view that she took of him and his louche *badinage* during a visit to the family: 'Dmitri was talking nonsense.'[25]

Press speculation aside, by early 1914 Nicholas and Alexandra were clearly giving serious consideration to a new royal candidate for their eldest daughter: twenty-year-old Prince Carol of Romania, grandson of the Duchess of Saxe-Coburg. The initiative for the match seems to have been theirs, urged on by Foreign Minister Sergey Sazonov, who wished to ensure that the Romanian royal family, who were Hohenzollerns, were in the right political camp – Russia's and not Germany's – before the now inevitable war broke out. Such a dynastic union would certainly bring long-term political and economic benefits and Nicholas and Alexandra could see the logic in it.[26] Their sole reservation was 'that the grand duchess's marriage . . . should take place only as the result of a much closer acquaintance between the young people and on the absolute condition of their daughter's voluntary agreement to it'.[27] It was the *Washington Post* that on 1 February broke the story in the West of a possible engagement. 'Prince Charles [Carol] is a handsome, clever young man', it reported, and 'his bride-to-be has great musical talent and is a remarkably accomplished linguist. She is a general favourite in court circles.'[28] But in fact the couple had yet even to meet; Carol and his parents were due to visit St Petersburg in March, although everyone was already anticipating that an engagement would take place.

In the run-up to the Romanian visit and still in St Petersburg, the busybodying Duchess of Saxe-Coburg was doing her best to lay the ground for a favourable outcome, writing to Marie quashing the persisting rumours about Olga and her cousin: 'the imperial girls don't care at all for Dmitri', she insisted.[29] But how she pitied them:

> shut up at Zarskoe, never even allowed to come to the theatre, not one single amusement the whole winter. Of course Alix would not allow them to come to Aunt Miechen's [Grand Duchess Vladimir's] ball, they are only granted a Sunday afternoon at Olga's where they play *des petits jeux* [little games] with officers: now why this is considered *convenable* [appropriate] is a real puzzle to us all as Olga is a tomboy without any manners and her surroundings always second rate. She never sees the real society because it bores her to put on better manners.[30]

Indeed the duchess talked of how offended Maria Feodorovna was that her granddaughters spent so little time with her when in St Petersburg, preferring to pass their Sundays 'under the sole chaperonage of that madcap [aunt] Olga . . . for dinner and romps with the officers'. How ironic that a mother so scrupulous about her daughters' sense of propriety should allow them the 'greatest intimacy' with these young men, unsupervised, and 'in perfect independence without a lady to look after them'.[31] The duchess was anxious to prepare her daughter for what she considered a degree of difficulty when the Romanians arrived: 'People who think they know all have decided that Carol intends marrying Tatiana, not Olga, as the eldest could not be missed by her parents, being a great help to them and would remain in Russia.'[32]

The Crimea would have seemed the far more logical location for a first meeting, being only a short journey across the Black Sea from Romania, but the duchess assured Marie that the Romanovs would not invite them there. In Livadia 'the acquaintance would have been hopeless as the naval favourites would laugh into ridicule every prince that would come with matrimonial intentions'. The duchess was deeply disapproving of the girls' familiarity with the officers of the *Shtandart*, which she considered totally *infra dig*: 'Each girl, the big ones like the small ones, have their favourites, *qui leur font la cour* [who pay court to them] and Alix not only allows it but finds it natural and amusing.'[33] This particularly troubled the duchess's rigid sense of *comme il faut*. Despite the fact that 'Olga and Tatiana are very well educated', as well as being 'gay, natural and amiable', she felt they were entirely lacking in the sophisticated social skills of the kind needed by any young woman marrying into a royal court. 'You must put away all *our* ideas of imperial young ladies', she told her daughter. 'As they have now no governess, no lady, they cannot be taught any manners, they have *never* paid me a visit and I really don't know them at all.' Even their aunts Xenia and Olga had at least been 'allowed to go out and never had any intimacy with officers'.[34]

There was one other important topic that did not pass without comment – haemophilia. The duchess had clearly been checking the lie of the land in this regard ahead of her daughter's visit: 'What can I find out about inheriting that sad illness? We all know that it can be propagated, but the children can also escape. I can only quote Uncle Leopold's two children who never had it but Alice's boys inherited it."* It was, as the duchess concluded, 'a mere chance, but one is never sure. The risk is there always.'[35] Such comments beg the question of whether other royal houses had by now considered and rejected the Romanov daughters as prospective brides, for fear of haemophilia being brought into their families. And then there was the prospect of union with a country as politically unstable as Russia. The duchess's letters to her daughter that January and February are full of foreboding about the future of the country, with a tsar too timid to spend time with anyone beyond his family circle and a tsaritsa stubbornly isolated from society through a combination of perverted choice and physical incapacity, hiding herself away with her only two friends – her 'false prophet' and Anna Vyrubova. The duchess sensed a 'despair and hopelessness' in St Petersburg so great that 'people are panting with fear and anxiety of it all'. She was longing to get away – 'the heavy moral atmosphere simply kills me'.[36] Nevertheless she had tried to have a private word with Nicholas and Alexandra about the possible engagement. 'What shall I say? Do I think it very hopeful? They seem to wish it but Alix is so strange and I have not the slightest idea what she wishes about her daughters.' The duchess had long since given up on her, and now thought the tsaritsa 'absolutely mad'.[37]

On 15 March 1914 Crown Prince Ferdinand of Romania, his wife Marie and their son Carol arrived in St Petersburg and were installed in the west wing of the Alexander Palace. That same day, Grand Duchess Olga Nikolaevna officially completed her ten-year period of studies. Her final exams had covered the history of the Orthodox Church; Russian language (dictation, composition and answers on the history of Russian words); general and Russian history; geography and three foreign languages – English, French and German, with dictation and composition in each. (All these subjects had been taught at home; for physics lessons she and her

---

* Queen Victoria's son Leopold, Duke of Albany, who died after an attack of haemophilia brought on by a fall at the age of thirty-one, had a son and a daughter: his son Charles was not a haemophiliac but his daughter Alice was a carrier and passed it on to her sons, Maurice who died in infancy and Rupert who died of haemorrhaging after an accident when he was twenty.

sisters had gone to the Nicholas II Practical Institute in Tsarskoe Selo.)[38] In all of them Olga had received top marks, although she had struggled with English composition and German dictation. 'An average of 5 [out of marks 1 to 5],' she noted in her diary. 'Mama was pleased.'[39]

During the week of the Romanian visit she acted as escort to her second cousin Karlusha – as she referred to him (a somewhat belittling, Russian diminutive form of Carol's name). She seemed unimpressed with his shock of blond hair, sticky-out ears and bulbous blue eyes – the latter an unmistakable Hanoverian trait inherited from his English grandfather Alfred. Nevertheless Olga dutifully went everywhere with him: to church, for walks round the park, dinner with Grandmama at the Anichkov and a ball at the exclusive Smolny Girls Institute. She smiled and chatted and went through the motions (in so doing giving the lie to the Duchess of Saxe-Coburg's insistence that she had no social graces) but revealed nothing. A young secretary at the Romanian legation noted during the first day of the visit: 'The Imperial Family retired rather early to their chambers, with the daughters casting short and anxious glances at Carol. I found out later that they had not liked him.'[40] The gossips still insisted that Olga was not the object of Carol's interests. An American diplomat heard tell that he was actually 'trying to get Tatiana, but Olga must go first'.[41] In the event the two sets of parents were disappointed at the negative outcome but were not quite ready to give up. They agreed that the Russians would reciprocate with a visit to Constanza in June to enable the young couple to take a second look at each other. The Russian press made no comment on a possible marriage, but in London *The Times* put it eloquently into perspective: 'The view propounded in official quarters is that Russia would like to see Rumania as free to choose her friendships as Prince Carol and the Grand Duchess Olga are to follow the inclinations of their hearts.'[42]

Three days later, with a sigh of relief, the Romanovs boarded the imperial train for the south and Easter in Livadia. On board the *Shtandart* that year (and contrary to what the Duchess of Saxe-Coburg had heard) there had been a distinct shift in the attitude of the crew to the now teenage Romanov sisters. Nikolay Vasilievich Sablin noted in particular how Olga had 'turned into a real lady'.

On the *Shtandart*, like everywhere else, the officers had begun discussing the future marriages of the sisters and had come to 'a kind of unspoken agreement . . . to conduct themselves with these charming Grand Duchesses no longer as juveniles or little girls'.[43] Sablin was fully aware that the older two sisters 'preferred the company of certain officers to that of others' – no doubt an allusion to the favouritism for Rodionov and the now departed Voronov. But the former relationship the men had had with the sisters was now 'inadmissable': 'We had to remember they were the daughters of the tsar.' These were not the same little girls they had first encountered seven years previously, and they must all ensure that they behaved punctiliously, as officers and gentlemen. They did, however, gently tease the sisters, telling them 'that they would soon be brides and leave us'. In response the girls had laughed and promised that they would 'never marry foreigners and leave their beloved homeland'.[44] Sablin thought this was wishful thinking; for since when, he asked, had royal brides ever had freedom of choice? In this respect, however, he was most certainly wrong.

The men in the *Shtandart* were not the only ones to notice how the Romanov sisters were all becoming beautiful young women that last hot summer before the war. Visiting Count Nostitz's estate near Yalta one day, they were taken by the countess to feed the black swans on the lake: 'I thought how lovely they looked as they flitted in and out among the flower-beds in their light summer dresses, like so many flowers themselves', she recalled.[45] At a ball at the White Palace shortly afterwards the sisters enjoyed another magical Crimean evening, when 'a great golden moon hung low over the dark ruffled waters of the Black Sea, gilding the silhouettes of the tall cypress trees'.

> From the ball-room behind us came the dreamy lilt of a Viennese waltz, the light laughter of the Grand Duchesses Olga and Tatiana, their merry eyes sparkling with pleasure, as they drifted past the open windows, dancing with Jean Woroniecki and Jack de Lalaing.*[46]

---

* Foreign Office official Prince Jean Woroniecki, and Comte Jacques de Lalaing,

It was a perfect picture-book image; but it would be the girls' last ball in their beloved Crimea.

With the visit to Constanza imminent, Nicholas walked over to visit Grand Duchess George at Harax one last time before leaving, 'escaping from the horde of detectives and his bodyguard by taking the mountain paths'. As the duchess's lady-in-waiting Agnes de Stoeckl stood with him looking out over the sea in the still of the Crimean evening, he turned to her: 'We are in June now,' he said, 'we have had two very happy months, we must repeat them . . . Let us make a pact we all meet here again on 1 October.'[47] And then after a pause he added, 'more slowly, rather seriously' – 'After all, in this life we do not know what lies before us.'[48]

Alexandra too was privately expressing her apprehensions about what might be to come. During a discussion she had with Sergey Sazonov on the balcony of the White Palace before they left for Constanza, she spoke of the possible political repercussions of high-profile dynastic matches and the responsibilities her girls would have to take on. 'I think with terror . . . that the time draws near when I shall have to part with my daughters', she told him.

> I could desire nothing better than they should remain in Russia after their marriage. But I have four daughters, and it is, of course, impossible. You know how difficult marriages are in reigning families. I know it by experience, although I was never in the position my daughters occupy . . . The Emperor will have to decide whether he considers this or that marriage suitable for his daughters, but parental authority must not extend beyond that.[49]

Privately, although Sazonov had been bullish about the desirability of the Romanian match, saying that 'It's not every day that an Orthodox Hohenzollern comes along', Olga was already very clear in her mind, even before they had set sail. 'I will never leave Russia', she told her friends in the *Shtandart*, and she said as much to Pierre Gilliard too.[50] She was adamant that she did not want to

---

a secretary at the Belgian legation, were house guests of the Nostitz family at their estate at Yalta.

be a queen or princess in some foreign court. 'I'm a Russian, and mean to remain a Russian!'

*

On 1 June the Romanovs sailed from Yalta across the Black Sea to Romania. It was a glorious sunny day, 'smiling, windless and yet not too hot, a day of rare beauty', when the *Shtandart* steamed into view at Constanza escorted by the *Polyarnaya Zvezda*, like 'two marvelous Chinese toys of laquer, black and gold'.[51] Waiting on the quayside, the Romanian royal family caught sight of Nicholas on deck, 'a little white figure' and his wife 'very tall and dominat[ing] her family as a solitary poplar dominates the garden'. As for the girls, it was the same bland, collective view: 'four light dresses, four gay summer hats'.[52]

As they disembarked, the Romanovs were greeted by a fanfare of guns, flags, hurrahs, military bands and a warm welcome from King Carol and Queen Elizabeth, their son Crown Prince Ferdinand, his wife Marie and their children. Crown Princess Marie later wrote to her mother about their 'great Russian day', which had been an intensive fourteen hours of church service at the cathedral, family luncheon in a pavilion, high tea in the *Shtandart*, a military review, a gala banquet and speeches in the evening. 'From the first we all had a pleasant surprise, and that was Alix', Marie told her mother. 'She took part in everything except the parade and tried to smile and was anyhow very amiable.'[53]

Marthe Bibesco, a close friend of the Romanian royal family, saw it rather differently: the empress's eyes, she recalled, 'looked as if they had seen all the sorrow of the world and when she smiled . . . her smile had been one of ineffable sadness, like those smiles which play on the faces of the sick and the dying'.[54] As for the four sisters, they were 'sweet', and sat patiently through it all, Olga answering all Carol's questions as politely as she could. But her sisters, as Pierre Gilliard noticed, had 'found it none too easy to conceal their boredom' and 'lost no chances of leaning towards me and indicating their sister with a sly wink'.[55]

There was one thing, however, about the tsar's otherwise charming daughters that alarmed the Romanian party. Having come straight from endless sunny days in Livadia 'they were baked brown as nuts by the sun and were not looking their best'.[56] Sad to say, as Crown Princess Marie told her mother, they 'were not found very pretty'.[57] Marthe Bibesco went so far as to say that their unfashionably sunburnt faces made them as 'ugly as those of peasant women'.[58] The consensus was that the Romanov sisters were 'much less pretty than their photographs had led us to suppose'.[59] Olga's face 'was too broad, her cheek-bones too high', thought Marie, though she liked her 'open, somewhat brusque way'. Tatiana she found handsome but reserved; Maria was pleasant but plump though with 'very fine eyes'; and Anastasia's looks did not register with her at all, though she noticed how 'watchful' she was.[60] The girls seemed doomed to be unremarkable in the eyes of the Romanian court, although they could not be faulted for their solicitous care of their bored and rather petulant brother, with his face marked by 'a precocious gravity'. In taking the strain off their mother by entertaining and amusing Alexey throughout the day, the four sisters had remained 'a clan apart' from their Romanian cousins, and the presence of Alexey's shadow Derevenko reminded everyone 'of the horrible truth about this child'.[61]

Although Olga had, for obvious reasons, been 'the centre of all eyes', Carol had seemed to his mother to be 'not particularly attentive' to any of the girls; later it was said that he was 'not enamoured of Olga's broad, plain face and brusque manner'.[62] Certainly, neither he nor Olga showed any desire whatsoever in 'becoming more closely acquainted'.[63] Indeed, all four girls had shown far more interest in Carol's six-month-old baby brother Mircea, whom Olga had dandled on her knee in official photographs taken that day. In the end, the lasting impression left by the imperial family's visit to Constanza had been not of the girls, but the extraordinary proficiency with which the mischievous tsarevich had, at lunch, sat teaching two of the Romanian children, Prince Nicolas and Princess Ileana, how to spit grape pips into a lemonade bowl in the middle of the dining table.[64]

During the Romanians' earlier visit to St Petersburg Marie and Alexandra had already had a private word and had agreed then that 'neither of us could make any promises in the name of our children, that they must decide for themselves'.[65] Faced with an inconclusive outcome to this second meeting, they parted with a smile; they had done their duty, but the rest 'was in the hands of Fate'. The two families took a final drive through the streets of Constanza to displays of fireworks and a torchlight procession, but as they waved goodbye at midnight it seemed highly unlikely that the 'spark of love [would] be lighted between these two'.*[66]

It was only after the imperial family had left Constanza that Marthe Bibesco heard that the girls had, all along, had a secret plan to subvert the entire exercise. They had 'decided . . . to make themselves as ugly as they could' by soaking up the sun, hatless, on the journey from Livadia, 'so that Carol should not fall in love with any of them'.[67]

*

The Romanov family arrived back at Tsarskoe Selo on 5 June, in time for Anastasia's thirteenth birthday; it was followed by a visit from the First British Battle-Cruiser Squadron commanded by Sir David Beatty, an important mission intended to further bolster the *entente cordiale*. The squadron arrived at Kronstadt Island on Monday 9 June to a gun salute from Russian destroyers, thousands of pleasure boats with flags flying, and crowds of cheering Russians thronging the quayside opposite. For the British diplomatic community in St Petersburg 'a week of feverish gaiety' followed, during which Meriel Buchanan admitted to never getting to bed before 3 a.m.[68] The tsar entertained Admiral Beatty and his officers to lunch at Peterhof, and at a garden party at the summer villa of Grand Duke Boris Vladimirovich at Tsarskoe Selo the girls all plied the British officers with questions. The inquisitive Anastasia was the most demanding; 'her childish voice rang out above the hum of conversation', recalled

---

* Evidence suggests that after the failure of the Olga–Carol match, and in the light of his brother Mikhail's morganatic marriage in 1912, Nicholas began to seriously consider lifting the restrictions on marriages in the imperial family, having been forewarned of the problems that might be faced when and if the tsarevich came of age that 'there would not be a single suitable [royal] bride in the world'. See *Royalty Digest* 15, no. 7, January 2005, p. 220.

Meriel. 'You will take me up into your conning tower,' she implored, and added mischievously, 'Couldn't you let off one of the guns and just pretend it was a mistake?'[69]

Among the young officers on board one of the British ships, the *New Zealand*, was young Prince George of Battenberg, Alexandra's nephew, whose brother Dickie had taken a shine to Maria during the family's visit to Nauheim in 1910. Georgie came to stay with his cousins at Tsarskoe Selo during which time the officers of the *Shtandart* thought he paid a lot of attention to Tatiana, with whom he agreed to exchange letters.[70] On the last day of the squadron's official visit, 14 June, a morning of brilliant sunshine and cloudless skies, the imperial family returned the admiral's visit, dining on board HMS *Lion*, after which the girls were shown round 'every corner' of the ship by four eager young midshipmen who had been specially chosen by him. One of them, Harold Tennyson, remembered the thrill and honour: 'I showed round Princess Olga, who is extraordinarily pretty and most amusing.' She and her sisters were 'the most cheery and pretty quartette I have met for some time, and roared with laughter and made jokes the whole time'. 'If only they were not Princesses,' he confided rather ruefully in a letter home, 'I should not mind getting off with one!'*[71]

By the end of the afternoon the crew of the *Lion* were totally captivated by the Romanov sisters: they 'could talk of nothing but the Emperor's daughters, their beauty, their charm, their gaiety, the unaffected simplicity and ease of their manners'.[72] A farewell ball for 700 guests was to be held later that evening on board the *Lion* and *New Zealand* specially roped together for the purpose, but much to the visitors' dismay Alexandra refused to allow her daughters to attend. Meriel Buchanan noticed a look of 'wistful regret' on the faces of the British officers as they said goodbye to the four Romanov sisters. The girls, as always, accepted their mother's decision 'without demur or argument', though they had looked a little 'crestfallen' and when Olga boarded the imperial launch taking them back to Peterhof 'she looked back at the big grey ship, and waved her hand

---

*   Harold Tennyson was a grandson of the British poet laureate. He was drowned in January 1916 when his ship HMS *Viking* hit a mine in the English Channel.

to the officers standing to attention on deck'. She smiled, but there were tears in her eyes.[73] It was a moment that, decades later, Meriel Buchanan would recall with an intense regret tinged by hindsight: 'Happy voices, smiling faces, golden memories of a summer afternoon, of a world that could still laugh and talk of war as something far away.'[74]

*

On 15 June (28 NS), news came of the assassination at Sarajevo of Archduke Franz Ferdinand, heir to the Austro-Hungarian throne, by a Serbian nationalist. Nicholas made no mention of it in his diary: political assassination of this kind was a fact of everyday life in Russia and the potential significance of the act was made little of at first. Far more important was the family's imminent holiday among the Finnish skerries in the *Shtandart*. But it was rather subdued, Alexey having hurt his leg jumping on board and being once more laid up. At the end of the trip Alexandra told Anna Vyrubova that she sensed that the family's wonderful days in Finland were over and that they 'would never again be together on the *Shtandart*', though they hoped to be back on board in the autumn when they planned to visit Livadia, the doctors having recommended that Alexey and his mother both needed 'sunshine and a dry climate'.[75]

The family was back at the Lower Dacha at Peterhof on 7 July in time to greet the French president Raymond Poincaré on a four-day visit. The highlight was a review of the Guards at Krasnoe Selo, led by Nicholas on his favourite white horse, accompanied by all the Russian grand dukes, and with Alexandra and the children in open carriages also drawn by white horses. It would prove to be the last great parade of Russian imperial military glory: two days after the French president left, Austria-Hungary delivered an ultimatum to Serbia and on 15 July (28 NS) it declared war. Historically Russia had a duty to defend the Serbs as fellow Slavs and war now seemed inevitable. In between urgent meetings with ministers Nicholas, who remembered the debacle of the war with Japan and dreaded the prospect of hostilities, exchanged urgent messages with his German cousin Willy. 'With the aid of God it must be possible for our long-tried friendship to prevent the shedding of blood', he telegraphed.[76]

Meanwhile he reluctantly capitulated to his General Staff and sanctioned general mobilization, bringing a 600,000-strong Russian army onto a war footing. This provoked an aggressive response from Germany, now rallying to the support of Austria-Hungary. Final, frantic attempts at diplomatic mediation were made in this 'time of great anguish', during which Alexandra sent a desolate telegram to Ernie in Hesse: 'God help us all and prevent bloodshed.' She had, of course, also sought Grigory's wise counsel. He had been horrified at the prospect of war and had repeatedly begged her and Nicholas: 'the war must be stopped – war must *not* be declared; it will be the finish of all things.'[77]

On the evening of 19 July (1 August NS in Europe) Nicholas, Alexandra, Aunt Olga and the children went to church to pray. They had not long returned and were sitting down to dinner when Count Freedericksz arrived with formal notice, handed to him by the German ambassador in St Petersburg: Germany was at war with Russia. 'On learning the news the Tsarina began to weep,' recalled Pierre Gilliard, 'and the Grand Duchesses likewise dissolved into tears on seeing their mother's distress.'[78] '*Skoty!* [Swine!]' wrote Tatiana of the Germans in her diary that evening.[79] The following day, 20 July (2 August NS), was scorching hot. In anticipation of the imminent Russian declaration of war, people crowded the streets of St Petersburg as they had in 1904, parading with icons and singing the national anthem. The news spread like wildfire: 'women threw jewels into a collection made for Reservists' families', reported the correspondent of *The Times*.[80] At 11.30 a.m. about 50,000 people surrounded the British Embassy singing 'God Save the King' and 'Rule Britannia'.[81] Church bells rang out constantly, all day long. The whole city was one huge traffic jam of motor cars and droshkies and full of people shouting and singing and waving 'cheaply printed portraits of the beloved "Little Father"'.[82] The shop windows too were full of Nicholas's portrait 'and the veneration was so deep that men lifted their hats and women – even well-dressed elegant ladies – made the sign of the cross as they passed it'.[83] In the afternoon, Nicholas wearing field marshal's uniform, and Alexandra and the girls all in white, arrived in the capital in the *Aleksandriya*. Alexey, who was still recovering from his latest accident, had had to be left behind. From the royal landing stage at the Palace Bridge, the imperial family walked the short distance to the Winter Palace through crowds of people who fell onto their knees shouting hurrahs, singing hymns and calling out blessings to Nicholas.[84] 'Kostroma last year is nothing to this,' said one eyewitness, 'they'll lay down their lives for him.'[85]

At 3 p.m., after a gun salute had thundered out across the city, some 5,000 court officials, military and members of the aristocracy gathered in the Nicholas Hall of the Winter Palace for a solemn and intensely moving *Te Deum*, sung in front of the talismanic icon of the Virgin of Kazan. This was the same icon Field Marshal Mikhail Kutuzov had prayed to in August 1812 before leaving for Smolensk to take on Napoleon, who had just invaded Russia. During the service Nicholas 'prayed with a holy fervor which gave his pale face a movingly mystical expression', noted the French ambassador Maurice Paléologue, while Alexandra stood, characteristically tight-lipped, by his side.[86] The assembled crowd 'all looked tremendously tense and alive, as if gathering up their strength to offer it collectively to their ruler'.[87] 'Faces were strained and grave', recalled Maria Pavlovna. 'Hands in long white gloves nervously crumpled hand-kerchiefs and under the large hats fashionable at the time many eyes were red with crying'. After the service, the court chaplain read out the manifesto declaring that Russia was at war with Germany, after which Nicholas raised his right hand in front of the gospel and announced: 'We will not make peace until the last man and the last horse of the enemy shall have left our soil.'[88] Immediately afterwards, 'quite spontaneously, from some 5,000 throats broke forth the national anthem, which was not less beautiful because the voices choked with emotion. Then cheer upon cheer came, until the walls rang with their echo!'[89]

The tsar and tsaritsa then processed out. Nicholas's face was a blank; Alexandra more than ever looked like 'a Madonna of Sorrows, with tears on her cheeks' and stooped to console people as she passed; others fell on their knees or tried to grasp at Nicholas and kiss his hand. When he emerged on the balcony overlooking Palace Square, a vast crowd of around 250,000 people who had been patiently waiting 'quiet, with faces grave and rapt' knelt down 'as one' 'in mute adoration'.[90] Nicholas made the sign of the cross and brought Alexandra forward to greet them, after which he and she retreated inside. But the crowd did not want to let them go: 'Each time that the sovereigns left the balcony the people clamoured for their reappearance with loud hurrahs and sang *God Save the Tsar.*'[91]

The day had been 'absolutely wonderful', Tatiana later wrote in her diary, but that evening for once there were no games of dominoes for Nicholas, and no reading aloud to his family.[92] Returning to Peterhof at 7.15, they all spent it 'quietly'.[93] The next morning, central St Petersburg seemed like a ghost town. The magnet of everyone's attention was now the railway stations as column after column of troops marched in great lines towards them singing popular Russian folk songs, waving their khaki caps and leaving behind a trail of sobbing women and children.[94] On 22 July (4 August NS) Russia's ally Great Britain declared war on Germany, upon which Nicky received a telegram from the king, his cousin Georgie. They both were fighting 'for justice and right', he said, and he hoped 'this horrible war will soon be over'. In the meantime, 'God bless and protect you my dear Nicky . . . Ever your very devoted cousin and friend.'[95]

In those first heady days of July–August 1914 Russia was gripped by a consuming, almost feudal sense of nationhood that harked back to the old Mother Russia of legend. 'It seemed as if the Tsar and his people embraced each other strongly, and in this embrace stood before the great Russian land', declared *Novoe vremya* in suitably jingoistic terms.[96] The declaration of war was a fitting coda to all the ceremonial of the previous year's Tercentary. 'We believe unshakeably that all our faithful subjects will rise with unanimity and devotion for the defence of Russian soil', Nicholas had declared in his manifesto, adding the hope that 'internal discord will be forgotten in this threatening hour, that the unity of the Tsar with his people will become still more close'.[97]

The capital might have been gripped by intensely felt patriotism of a kind that every Russian knew from Tolstoy's *War and Peace*, but in the countryside most of the peasants were resigned rather than enthusiastic, knowing full well that the burden of the war effort would fall on them, as it had always done. Rasputin was in despair that his warning had gone unheeded and that he had not had the opportunity to persuade Nicholas, in person, against going to war.* The words of a telegram he had sent in the final days before war was declared have, ever since, been seen as prophetic:

> There is a terrible storm cloud over Russia: calamity, much grief, no ray of light, an incalculable ocean of tears, and as for blood – what can I say? There are no words, just an indescribable horror. I know they all want war from you, even those who are loyal, but without knowing that the price is destruction . . . Everything will be drowned in much blood.[98]

*

There remained one final grandiose public act of ceremonial for the Romanov family to perform – in Russia's historic capital, Moscow, on 5 August. The imperial court and the diplomatic community took the 444-mile (714.5-km) train journey south for what seemed to British ambassador Sir George Buchanan an occasion where 'the heart of Russia voiced the feelings of the whole nation'.[99] At the Kremlin on their way to the *Te Deum* at the Uspensky Cathedral, the tsar and tsaritsa walked in procession, followed by their daughters. Meriel Buchanan thought they seemed 'a little subdued and grave, their faces pale'; Olga in particular had had 'a rapt expression on her face'; Maria had been in tears and Meriel noticed how 'Anastasia turned to her now and then with a little admonishing word'.[100] Much to his parents' despair, Alexey had once more had to be carried. Now, more than ever, the heir to the Russian throne needed to be perceived as fit and well.

In a speech he made that day, Nicholas emphasized that the conflict embraced all Slavic peoples of the Russian Empire: this war would be nothing less than a defence of Slavdom against the Teutons. Sir George Buchanan was impressed by the power of the religious ceremony inside the Uspensky, which was 'beautiful and impressive beyond description':

---

* Rasputin was in hospital in Tyumen, western Siberia, recovering from a knife attack made on him by a mentally unstable woman that summer.

The long line of archbishops and bishops, in their vestments of gold brocade, their mitres sparkling with precious stones; the frescoes on the walls, with their golden background; the jewelled icons – all lent colour and brilliancy to the picture presented by the glorious old cathedral.

As soon as we had taken our places behind the imperial family the deep bass voice of a priest was heard chanting the opening passages of the liturgy, and then the choir, joining in, flooded the church with harmony as it intoned the psalms and hymns of the Orthodox ritual. As the service was nearing its close the Emperor and Empress, followed by the Grand Duchesses, went the round of the church, kneeling in deep devotion before each of its shrines or kissing some specially sacred icon presented them by the Metropolitan.

As he drove away with Maurice Paléologue, Buchanan 'could not help wondering how long this national enthusiasm would last, and what would be the feeling of the people for their "Little Father" were the war to be unduly prolonged'.[101] A long and costly war of attrition against Germany and Austria-Hungary, as Nicholas well knew, would fan the flames of social unrest in Russia yet more, as it had done during the war with Japan. For Alexandra, distraught and desperately worried for her brother Ernie and his family trapped in a Germany she no longer loved or recognized, the outbreak of war 'was the end of everything'.[102] All that was left now was to beg Grigory to pray with them for peace.

War of course put paid, at a stroke, to all talk of marriage for the two eldest Romanov sisters. Nor would there be any more cruises round the Finnish skerries or holidays in the Crimean sunshine; no more idling away the long sunny days of summer chatting and laughing with their favourite officers from the *Shtandart*; and no more Sunday afternoon teas with Aunt Olga, for she had volunteered as a nurse and had already headed off on a hospital train to the Russian front at Kiev.

On 1 August Tatiana recorded her aunt's departure and the usual mundane routine:

The five of us had lunch with Papa and Mama. In the afternoon we went for a walk like yesterday. Went on the swing and got caught in the rain. Had tea with Papa and Mama. We spoke on the phone to N. P. [Nikolay Sablin] and N. N. [Nikolay Rodionov] – to whom I sent my little icon to wear round his neck via N. P. The two of us had supper with Papa and Mama and Grandmother. Xenia and Sandro were there too. Then Kostya [Grand Duke Konstantin Konstaninovich] came to say goodbye as he's leaving for the war tomorrow with the Izmailovsk Regiment. We came back at 10.30. Papa read.[103]

The safe, unchallenging, insular world that the Romanov sisters had known until now was about to change dramatically.

Chapter Fourteen

SISTERS OF MERCY

꧁꧂

When Russia went to war in the summer of 1914, it was faced with a desperate shortage of nurses. With massive losses of almost 70,000 killed or wounded in the first five days of fighting, the Russian government predicted that at least 10,000 nurses would be needed. Stirred by patriotic duty, legions of the fashionable and aristocratic ladies of St Petersburg – or rather Petrograd, as the city was quickly renamed – as well as the wives and daughters of government officials, and professional women such as teachers and academics, rushed to do medical training and embrace the war effort. By September, with the need for nurses increasingly acute, the Russian Red Cross had reduced the usual year-long training to two months. Many women did not make the grade and with it the right to be called *sestry miloserdiya* – sisters of mercy – as nurses were termed in Russia.

From the day war broke out the tsaritsa was determined that she and her two eldest daughters should play their part; in early September they began their Red Cross training, taking on the self-effacing titles of Sister Romanova, numbers 1, 2 and 3.[1] Although Maria and Anastasia were too young to train they also were to play an active role, as hospital visitors. No one represented the female war effort in Russia more emotively than did the tsaritsa and her daughters through the two and a half long and dispiriting years of war that preceded the revolution of 1917. Everywhere – in newspapers, magazines and shop fronts – one prevailing, iconic image dominated – of the three imperial sisters of mercy soberly dressed in their Red Cross uniforms. *Stolitsa i usadba* featured them in uniform regularly on its pages, a fact that inspired many other Russian women to follow their example.² Edith Almedingen remembered a city full of young women burning with 'war-work fever' and wearing the 'short white veil and the scarlet pectoral cross on their white aprons'.³

War galvanized the ailing tsaritsa: 'Looking after the wounded is my consolation', she asserted.'⁴ Within three days of hostilities beginning Alexandra had taken command of the vast national war relief effort, re-establishing the huge supply depots that she had set up in the Winter Palace and elsewhere during the war with Japan. Aside from producing surgical bandages and other essential medical dressings, the depots also gathered and distributed pharmaceutical supplies, 'non-perishable foodstuffs, sweets, cigarettes, clothing, blankets, boots, miscellaneous gifts and religious items such as tracts, postcards, and icons', and sent them out to the wounded.⁵ Soon they were filled with well-heeled society ladies in their plain overalls learning to work sewing machines under the supervision of seamstresses to produce bed linen for the wounded, or sitting for hours on end packing gauze and rolling surgical bandages.⁶ All the major rooms of the Winter Palace – the concert hall and various other large reception rooms, as well as the imperial theatre and even the throne room – were converted into hospital wards for the wounded, their beautiful parquet floors covered with linoleum to protect them and filled with row upon row of iron beds. Soon, without fuss or fanfare, the tsaritsa and her two eldest daughters were seen not just in Petrograd and Tsarskoe Selo but as far as Moscow, Vitebsk, Novgorod, Odessa, Vinnitsa and elsewhere in the western and southern provinces of the empire, inspecting hospital trains and visiting many of the string of hospitals and depots set up by Alexandra; often they were joined by Maria and Anastasia, and Alexey too, when well. Elsewhere in Petrograd, the sizeable expatriate British community also rallied to the cause, led by ambassador's wife Georgina, Lady Buchanan who ran the British Colony Hospital for Wounded Russian Soldiers* that opened on 14 September in a wing

---

* Edith Almedingen acted as Lady Buchanan's Russian interpreter. The British

of the large Pokrovsky Hospital on Vasilevsky Island. Lady Georgina's daughter Meriel was soon working there as a volunteer nurse.[7]

As the last days of summer faded into autumn, the streets of Petrograd were transformed, with many buildings now serving as hospitals and flying the flag of the Red Cross alongside the Russian tricolour. Far fewer fine carriages and fashionable motor cars were to be seen processing up and down the Nevsky; instead the wide boulevard was witness to a never-ending cavalcade of ambulances ferrying the wounded to one or other hospital and a crush of wagons bearing supplies. Tsarskoe Selo too became a town of hospitals, its quiet leafy streets the thoroughfare now – morning, noon and night – for slow-moving Red Cross ambulances carrying the pale-faced wounded, as well as numerous private vehicles, many of them made available for this purpose from the imperial fleet of motor cars. Here as in Petrograd every available large building was commandeered for the care of the wounded. The great gilded reception rooms of the Catherine Palace were converted into hospital wards and depots and more than thirty of the private summer villas of the rich were given over for use as wartime hospitals. Such was the desperate need for beds as the wounded poured in, that soon much smaller private homes would be taking them in as well; in September Dr Botkin set up an improvised ward at his own home for seven patients.

All of the military hospitals at Tsarskoe Selo came under the supervision of Dr Vera Gedroits, a Lithuanian aristocrat who was the senior physician at the Court Hospital, and one of the first women to qualify as a doctor in Russia.[8] The Court Hospital was located in an extended and revamped 1850s mansion on Gospitalnaya ulitsa, and throughout the war it continued to serve the needs of the local community, with an upper floor of the main building set aside for an operating theatre for the war wounded and a ward for 200 lower ranks.[9] A single-storey annexe built shortly before the war in the courtyard garden of the hospital for the isolation of infectious patients was converted into a fully functioning hospital in its own right, with an operating theatre and six small wards accommodating a total of thirty beds. One of the wards was for all

---

Colony Hospital was also known as the King George V Hospital.

ranks brought down from the Catherine Palace Hospital for operations conducted by Gedroits; the remainder was for wounded
officers. The annexe – or 'the little house' or 'the barrack' as the
girls sometimes referred to it – became the hub of Olga and Tatiana's
daily lives as Red Cross nurses.*

During their training at the annexe under the exacting standards
set by Dr Gedroits, Olga and Tatiana came under the watchful care
of Valentina Chebotareva, the daughter of a military doctor, who
had been a nurse during the Russo-Japanese War. 'How distant they
were at first', she recalled of the tsaritsa and her daughters' first
days at the annexe. 'We kissed their hand, exchanged greetings . . .
and that's as far as it went.'[10] But Alexandra soon told the staff that
they were not to pay them any special attention and things quickly
changed. During their training the three women were to observe
Gedroits in the operating theatre and then graduate on to assisting
during operations, but their primary duty in the first days at the
annexe was to learn how to dress wounds. The days were particularly
long for Tatiana, as she was still completing her education and often
had an early morning lesson. Immediately afterwards, and before
they started work at the annexe, the tsaritsa and the girls would stop
to pray before the miracle-working icon of the Mother of God at
the little Znamenie Church located near the Catherine Palace, before
arriving at the annexe at around 10 a.m. to change into their uniforms
and begin work.

Every morning Olga and Tatiana were tasked with changing the
dressings of three or four patients each (though this increased as
the war went on and the numbers of wounded went up) as well as
undertaking the many menial tasks required of them – rolling bandages, preparing swabs, boiling the silk thread for stitching, and
machining bed linen. At one o'clock they would return home for
lunch and in the afternoon if the weather was fine they would
sometimes go out for a brief walk, a bike ride, or a drive with their
mother, but most often they returned to the hospital to spend time

---

* In order to avoid confusion with the Court Hospital and the Catherine Palace
Hospital, it was formally named Their Imperial Highnesses' No. 3 Hospital. For
clarity, it will be referred to hereafter as 'the annexe'.

with the wounded, chatting, playing board games or ping-pong with them and in the summer months croquet in the garden with those who could walk. Often they simply sat knitting or sewing items for refugees and war orphans while the soldiers chatted to them; sometimes they went off and sneaked a cigarette in their rest room. Always, inevitably, the cameras would be taken out at every opportunity and photographs taken of themselves with their wounded officers and friends. Some of these were later reproduced as postcards sold to raise funds for war relief. Others the girls carefully pasted into albums and shared with the wounded later.[11]

It took a while for Tatiana and Olga to get used to being around strangers and Tatiana in particular, just like her mother, suffered from a sometimes crippling reserve. Valentina Chebotareva recalled how, one day when they went upstairs in the Court Hospital together, they had had to walk past a group of sisters. Tatiana grabbed her hand: 'It's awful how self-conscious and scared I feel . . . I don't know who to say hello to and who not.'[12] This lack of social experience tipped over into simple things like going into shops. Once while waiting for the motor car to pick them up and take them back to the palace, Olga and Tatiana decided to pop into the Gostinny dvor – a parade of shops near the hospital. They were not in uniform so no one recognized them but they soon realized that they had no money on them, nor did they know how to go about buying anything.[13]

Until they completed their training at the end of October the girls and their mother also had a lesson in medical theory with Dr Gedroits at home every evening at 6 p.m., after which Olga and Tatiana would often go back to the hospital to help sterilize and prepare the instruments for the next day's operations with another nurse Bibi (Varvara Vilchkovskaya), with whom they became close friends. Whenever the girls took a break in the corridor outside the wards those patients able to walk would venture out to sit and chat with them and tell them stories. The girls would always have sweets in their pockets to share and often brought fruit and bunches of flowers from the Alexander Palace greenhouses. In the evenings some of the men gathered round the piano in the common room and sang – which Olga and Tatiana particularly enjoyed – but the

best days were festivals or holidays, when they would be joined by
Maria and Anastasia, and sometimes even Alexey. On evenings
when they went back home earlier the girls would often end up
telephoning the hospital for one last chat with their favourites.[14]

*

The Romanov sisters and their mother were not spared any of the
shock of their first confrontation with the suffering of the wounded
and the terrible damage done to their bodies by bombs, sabres and
bullets. Joined by Anna Vyrubova in their training, they were thrown
in at the deep end, dealing with men who arrived 'dirty, bloodstained
and suffering', as Anna recalled. 'Our hands scrubbed in antiseptic
solutions we began the work of washing, cleaning, and bandaging
maimed bodies, mangled faces, blinded eyes, all the indescribable
mutilations of what is called civilized warfare.'[15] Sometimes Anastasia
and Maria were allowed to come and watch them dressing the
wounds, and from 16 August the older girls began observing operations, at first civilian ones for appendixes and hernias, and the
lancing of swellings. But soon they were watching bullets being
taken out and on 8 September a trepanning for removal of shrapnel;
five days later they witnessed their first leg amputation.[16] Once
qualified they would be assisting – Alexandra usually handing the
surgical instruments to Gedroits and taking away amputated limbs,
the girls threading surgical needles and passing cotton-wool swabs.
On 25 November they saw their first wounded man die on the
operating table; Alexandra told Nicholas that their 'girlies' had been
very brave.[17]

In addition to their nursing training Olga and Tatiana were
assigned important public roles in the war effort by their mother,
although being among strangers in the capital chairing committees
was something they both dreaded and never enjoyed. On 11 August
an imperial *ukaz* was issued, establishing the Supreme Council for
the Care of Soldiers' Families and of Families of the Wounded and
Dead. It was headed by Alexandra, who nominated Olga as vice-
president with responsibility for its Special Petrograd Committee
– one of numerous subsidiary committees set up in cities across
Russia to raise funds for the central Supreme Council.[18] A month

later, Tatiana was given a similar role with the establishment of Her Imperial Highness Grand Duchess Tatiana Nikolaevna's Committee for the Temporary Relief of Those Suffering Deprivation in War-time. Under its chief administrator, Alexey Neidgardt, the Tatiana Committee, as everyone came to call it, dealt specifically with the growing refugee problem in Russia's western provinces – where civilian Poles, Jews, Lithuanians, Letts and Ruthenians had now become caught up in the fighting.

From its inception the Tatiana Committee proved to be a great success, in no small part thanks to Tatiana's high public profile as an imperial daughter and her active involvement with its work in setting up shelters, soup kitchens, maternity homes and refuges for orphaned children. The tedious bureaucracy of her Wednesday afternoon meetings in Petrograd was, however, a different matter, and she found Neidgardt a pompous bore. She also disliked the formalities, as one official recalled when he addressed her at a committee: 'If you should so please your imperial highness . . .' Tatiana was visibly embarrassed: 'she looked at me in astonishment and when I sat down next to her again, she gave me a sharp nudge under the table and whispered: "Are you off your head or what, to address me in that way?"'[19] She and Olga both hated such formali-ties. 'It's only at our hospital that we feel comfortable and at ease', admitted Olga to one of her patients.[20] Nevertheless, they both got on with their public duties conscientiously and without complaint, Tatiana often having to tackle committee paperwork after long days in the hospital. Alexandra helped her with this, for the welfare of refugees became an increasingly urgent issue as the war went on. The committee's budget was huge and rose to several million roubles – so much so that private donation soon was not enough to sustain it and the government had to step in.[21]

With Nicholas away for much of the time at Stavka – army HQ located at a railway junction near Baranovichi (in today's Belorussia) – Alexandra sent him regular updates on their daughters' progress. On 20 September she told him what a comfort it was 'to see the girls working alone & that they will be known more and learn to be useful'.[22] They seemed to adapt quickly to the new demands made on them, and, as Pierre Gilliard observed, 'with their usual natural simplicity and good humour . . . accepted the increasing austerity of life at Court'. Gilliard was especially impressed with their thoughtful attitude to their work and the fact that they had no problem with covering their beautiful hair in the nunlike nurse's wimple and spending most of their time in uniform. They weren't playing at being nurses – which from time to time Gilliard observed in other aristocratic ladies – but were true sisters of mercy.[23] Wartime volunteer Svetlana Ofrosimova who had lived at Tsarskoe Selo for several years noticed it too. 'I was struck by the change in them. Most of all I was moved by the deep expression of concentration on their faces, which were thinner and paler. There was a new kind of expression in their eyes.'[24] Maria Rasputin concurred: 'I found them grown taller, more serious, conscious of the responsibilities of the imperial family, bent on doing their duty with all their strength.'[25] This applied equally to the younger sisters; although their days were still taken up mainly with lessons they had to adjust to the long absences of their older siblings and all of them, with their father now away for much of the time, had to share the burden of their brother's and mother's frequent bouts of sickness.[26]

Until the war, with so much talk about Olga's marriage prospects, as well as her possible future role as heir to the throne after Alexey, much of the attention had inevitably been centred on her. She had always been the most outgoing and talkative of the two older sisters but during the war years it was Tatiana who would shine through. Prior to the war she had seemed to have all the makings of a coquette for, unlike Olga, she was very self-conscious about her appearance, had the figure of a mannequin and longed to have the fine clothes and beautiful jewels of fashionable St Petersburg ladies. 'Any frock, no matter how old, looked well on her', recalled Iza Buxhoeveden: 'She knew how to put on her clothes, was admired and liked admiration.'[27] 'She was a Grand Duchess from head to toe, so aristocratic and regal was she', recalled Svetlana Ofrosimova.[28] From the first, as a trainee nurse, there was something special about Tatiana that was quite different from heart-on-sleeve Olga, and that set her apart from her sisters. It was as though she had inside her her own completely private, distinctive world.[29] But it was one that Tatiana never allowed to intrude on her practical skills as a nurse and her devotion to duty.

ABOVE: Engagement photograph of the Tsarevich Nicholas and Princess Alix of Hesse, taken at Coburg, 1894.

ABOVE RIGHT: The tsaritsa, now styled Alexandra Feodorovna, with three-year-old Grand Duchess Olga and her new-born sister Maria, 1899.

The tsarevich Alexey, aged about three, with a Box Brownie.

Guérin-Boutron chocolate company trade cards, 1906,
featuring the Grand Duchesses Olga, Tatiana, Maria and Anastasia.

ABOVE: The Imperial Family
on duty at the Catherine
Palace, Tsarskoe Selo c. 1911.

RIGHT: A popular
mass-produced image of
the Imperial Family, from a
Russian calendar c. 1908.

LEFT: The tsaritsa in her lilac boudoir
with Anastasia next to her and Tatiana
seated (left) and Maria (right).

ABOVE: The Tsar allowing Anastasia a taste of his cigarette, Livadia 1912.

BELOW: The four Romanov sisters running a stall at their mother's annual charity bazaar on the quayside at Yalta, 1914.

ABOVE: Anastasia with members of the Imperial Entourage
on board the launch of the *Shtandart*.

BELOW: Olga and Tatiana visiting East Cowes, August 1909,
chaperoned by Dr Evgeny Botkin and Sofya Tyutcheva.

ABOVE: Olga at her lessons with French teacher, Pierre Gilliard.

BELOW: Anastasia in the schoolroom with her English teacher, Sydney Gibbes.

ABOVE: The four grand duchesses with their father.
Left to right: Anastasia, Maria, Tatiana and Olga.

BELOW: On board the *Shtandart*: Olga sitting next to Pavel Voronov,
with whom she fell in love. Far right is Tatiana's favourite tennis partner,
Nikolay Rodionov, with Anastasia standing next to him.

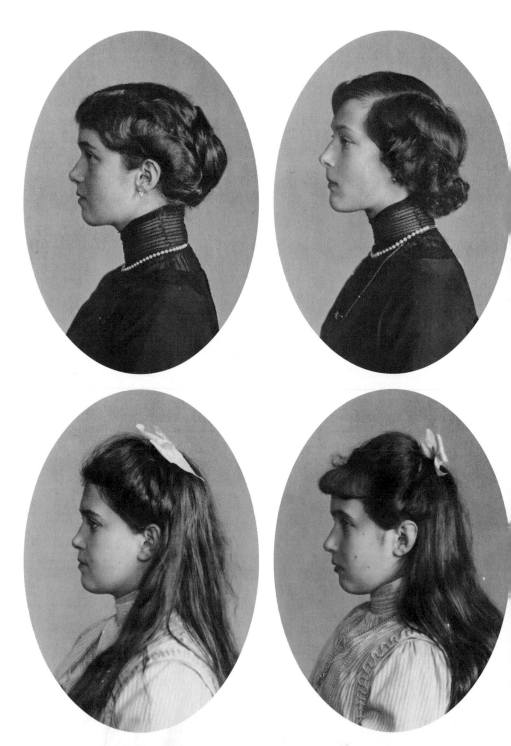

Profile portraits of the four grand duchesses, taken in 1914 as reference for a cameo made of them for a Fabergé Easter egg given by Nicholas to Alexandra that year. Clockwise from top left: Olga, Tatiana, Anastasia, Maria.

ABOVE: Olga and Tatiana wearing formal court dress for official photographs taken for the Romanov Tercentenary, 1913.

ABOVE RIGHT: The two older sisters wearing their regimental uniforms, Tatiana's of the Voznesensk Uhlans and Olga's of the Elizavetgrad Hussars.

RIGHT: Grand Duke Dmitri Pavlovich. As Nicholas II's cousin he was, for a brief time in 1912, considered the ideal dynastic match for Grand Duchess Olga by her parents.

ABOVE: Maria, Anastasia and Olga at one of their regular afternoon teas with officers from the Tsar's Escort. Far right Anastasia's favourite Viktor Zborovsky and seated next to him Olga's Aksh – Alexander Shvedov.

BELOW: Tatiana (left) and Olga (right) picking grapes with their father and Anna Vyrubova, probably in Nicholas's vineyard at Massandra in the Crimea.

Tatiana (top left), Olga (top right), Maria (bottom left) and Anastasia (bottom right) in fancy dress, 1916.

ABOVE: Olga and Tatiana receiving donations for the
Russian war effort, St Petersburg.

BELOW: Anastasia and Maria visiting wounded soldiers
at their hospital at Feodorovsky Gorodok.

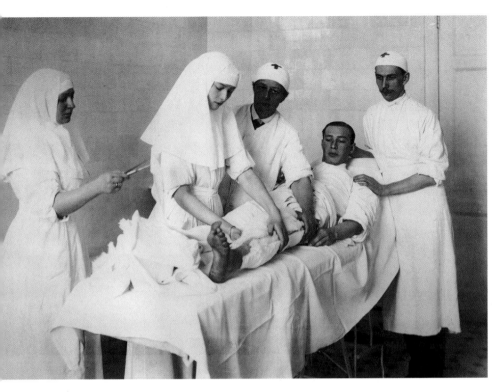

ABOVE: Tatiana bandaging a wounded officer – thought to be
Dmitri Malama – supervised by Dr Vera Gedroits on her left
and Valentina Chebotareva on her right.

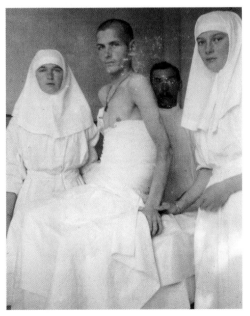

Tatiana with Vladimir Kiknadze, who
created quite an impression on her.

Olga and Tatiana changing dressings
on a wounded soldier.

ABOVE LEFT: A very rare formal photograph of Maria and Olga, 1916.

ABOVE: Tatiana recuperating from typhoid fever, Livadia 1913.

LEFT: Anastasia with shaven head, after her bout of measles. Taken in captivity, in the grounds of the Alexander Palace, June 1917.

ABOVE: The last photograph taken of Nicholas and Alexandra,
in captivity at the Governor's House, Tobolsk, late summer 1917.

BELOW: Olga pulling Alexey on his sledge, Tobolsk, winter 1917–18.

Father Ivan Storozhev
with his dog Daisy.
Storozhev was one of
the last people from the
outside world to see the
Romanov family before
they were murdered.

Father Storozhev's
missal, in which he
recorded conducting
a final *obednitsa* for
the Romanov family
at the Ipatiev House,
Ekaterinburg,
14 July 1918.

Precise and even bossy at times, Tatiana could, for some, seem too serious and – unlike Olga – lacking in spontaneity. But she was always ready to help others and her ability to apply herself in tandem with her altruistic personality made her admirably suited for nursing work. Whenever Alexey had been ill she had helped nurse him and followed the doctors' instructions with regard to medicines, as well as sitting with him. She was also unquestioningly tolerant of the demands of her mother; she 'knew how to surround her with un-wearying attentions and she never gave way to her own capricious impulses', as Gilliard recalled, which was something that Olga was increasingly becoming prey to.[30] Indeed, in everything she did Tatiana Nikolaevna would soon prove that she had perseverance of the kind her more emotionally volatile older sister lacked. Many of the nurses and doctors who observed her – as well as the patients themselves – later spoke of her as being born to nurse.

The outbreak of war so soon after the celebrations of the Tercentary had inevitably brought a complete turn-around in the popular perception of the Romanov sisters as lofty princesses. With their mother calling a wartime moratorium on the purchase of any new clothes for the family, official photographs of the svelte young women in court dress were replaced by images of the older sisters in uniform and of their younger siblings in rather plain, ordinary clothes that belied their imperial status. Alexandra felt that the sight of herself and her daughters in uniform helped to bridge the gap between them and the population at large in time of war. Some saw this as a terrible miscalculation: the vast majority of ordinary Russians, especially the peasantry, still looked upon the imperial family as almost divine beings and expected their public image to project that. As Countess Kleinmikhel observed, 'When a soldier saw his Empress dressed in a nurse's uniform, just like any other nurse, he was disappointed. Looking at the Tsarina, whom he had pictured as a princess in a fairy tale, he thought: "And that is a Tsarina? But there is no difference between us."'[31]

Similar expressions of distaste circulated among the society ladies of Petrograd who noted with a sneer how 'common' the grand duchesses' clothes were, 'which even a provincial girl would not dare to wear'.[32] They disliked this demystification of imperial women

– and worse, their association with unclean wounds, mutilation and men's bodies. They were horrified to learn that the empress even cut patients' fingernails for them. Alexandra's neglect of protocol – her acting as a common nurse – was seen as a *'beau geste'*, 'a cheap method of seeking popularity'.[33] Even ordinary soldiers were disappointed to see the tsaritsa and her daughters performing the same duties as other nurses or sitting on the beds of the wounded, rather than maintaining their exalted difference. 'The intimacy which sprang up between the Empress, her young daughters and the wounded officers destroyed their prestige,' said Countess Kleinmikhel, 'for it has been truly said: *"Il n'y a pas de grand homme pour son valet de chambre".*'*[34]

Be that as it may, many wounded soldiers came to be grateful for the care they received from Alexandra and her daughters during the war. In August 1914 Ivan Stepanov, a nineteen-year-old wounded soldier of the Semenovsk Regiment, arrived at the annexe at Tsarskoe Selo with his dressings unchanged for over a week. Conscious of his dirty appearance he felt discomforted at the prospect of being helped by the nurses who surrounded him in the treatment room – one of them, a tall gracious sister who smiled kindly as she bent over him, and opposite her two younger nurses who watched with interest as his filthy bandages were unwrapped. They seemed familiar, where had he seen these faces? Then suddenly he realized. 'Really, was it them . . . the empress and her two daughters?'[35] The tsaritsa seemed a different woman – smiling, younger-looking than her years. During his time in the hospital Stepanov witnessed many such instances of her spontaneous warmth and kindness, and that of her daughters.

Maria and Anastasia inevitably envied their older sisters' new and challenging role. But they soon had a small hospital of their own in which to do their bit for the war effort. On 28 August the Hospital for Wounded Soldiers No. 17 of Their Imperial Highnesses, the Grand Duchesses Maria Nikolaevna and Anastasia Nikolaevna was

---

* Kleinmikhel is quoting the famous aphorism by Madame Cornuel: 'No man is a hero to his valet' – although the original French was *'Il n'y avoit point de héros pour son valet de chambre'*.

opened just a stone's throw from the Alexander Palace in what was known as the Feodorovsky Gorodok (village).[36] Built between 1913 and 1917 as an adjunct to the Feodorovsky Sobor nearby and in the same ancient Russian Novgorod style, it was comprised of five buildings contained within a small Kremlin-like fortress wall with towers.* Two of the buildings were designated as a hospital for lower ranks and another one for officers was added in 1916. The two younger sisters would visit daily after lessons to sit and chat with the wounded, play board games, and even help the semi-literate patients to read and write letters. On a more serious note, they were already becoming used to sitting by the bedsides of wounded men, and sometimes had to deal with the trauma of their subsequent deaths. Like Olga and Tatiana they took endless photographs of themselves with their patients, nor did their visiting activities stop here. They supported fund-raising charity concerts for their hospital and often went to the bigger Catherine Palace Hospital and even some of those in Petrograd with their mother, as well as inspecting the hospital trains named after various members of the family. They might be too young to nurse but they were far from immune to the sufferings of the wounded, as Anastasia wrote and told Nicholas on 21 September:

> My precious Papa! I congratulate you on the victory. Yesterday we visited Alexey's hospital train. We saw many wounded. Three died on the journey – two of them officers . . . Pretty serious wounds, so much so that within the next two days one soldier may die; they were groaning. Then we went to the big Court Hospital: Mama and our sisters were dressing wounds, and Maria and I went round all the wounded, chatted to them all, one of them showed me a very big piece of shrapnel that they had taken out of his leg along with a large piece [of flesh]. They all said that they want to go back and get their revenge on the enemy.[37]

The girls wrote many loving letters to their father at army HQ, filling them with kisses and drawing signs of the cross to protect

---

* Badly damaged in the Second World War, it is now being restored for use by the patriarch of the Russian Orthodox Church.

him. With all four of them and their mother writing with devoted regularity, Nicholas was receiving several letters a day. Much of what the girls said only reiterated in rather laconic form what Alexandra herself told her husband in her own long, rambling missives. But the girls clearly missed their father terribly: 'You absolutely must take me with you next time,' Maria told him on 21 September, 'or I'll jump onto the train myself, because I miss you.' 'I don't want to go to bed, bah! I want to be there with you, wherever you are, as I don't know where it is', added Anastasia two days later.[38] Olga and Tatiana's letters suffered as a result of their heavy workload and were often quite cursory; but the quirky individuality of Anastasia's usually made up for it. Her breezy personality, signing off letters as 'your devoted slave, the 13-year-old Nastasya (Shvybzig)', constantly flitted from one point of interest to the next and must have been welcome entertainment for Nicholas during the long weeks away from his family. Anastasia took great delight in her letters of making fun of Maria's developing affection for Nikolay (Kolya) Demenkov, an officer in the Guards Equipage, and teased her about his chubbiness, calling him 'fat Demenkov'. Maria herself happily confided her affection for 'my dear Demenkov' to her father, for Kolya was already a firm favourite with the family.[39]

Alexandra had once observed in conversation with Anna Vyrubova that 'Most Russian girls seem to have nothing in their heads but thoughts of officers', but she appears not to have taken seriously what was now going on right under her very nose.[40] In 1914 she was still infantilizing her daughters as 'my little girlies' in letters to her husband, when they were all fast growing into young women with an interest in the opposite sex. What she saw as harmless affection was, for her oldest daughters, developing into afternoon trysts, sitting chatting on the beds of *nashikh* ('ours'). Olga's first favourites were Nikolay Karangozov, an Armenian cornet in the Cuirassier Life Guards, and the 'terribly dishy, dark' David Iedigarov, a Muslim from Tiflis and captain in the 17th Nizhegorod Dragoons who arrived in mid-October and created a strong impression on her (he was, however, married).[41] Iedigarov and Karangozov were the first of several swarthy, swashbuckling officers from the Caucasus – many of whom sported splendid moustaches – to arrive at the annexe during the war.

Tatiana meanwhile had fallen for the boyish charm of the clean-shaven Staff Captain Dmitri Malama, a Kuban Cossack from her own regiment of Uhlans who already was something of a legend for his gallantry in rescuing a fellow officer under fire. All of the sisters liked Malama and found him incredibly sweet and good-natured. Fellow patient Ivan Stepanov vividly remembered the 'fair haired and ruddy cheeked' young officer, so modest and with such dedication to his regiment, who was tormented by the fact that he was lying in hospital 'enjoying his life' while others were out there fighting.[42] Tatiana first dressed his wounds on 26 September; she was incredibly proud of her Uhlans and within days was sitting on Malama's bed at every opportunity, chatting and looking at photograph albums, much as her sister was doing with Karangozov, for the two men shared the same ward. Often in the evenings they would sing, with Olga playing the piano for them, making their ward, according to Stepanov, the noisiest and liveliest at the annexe.[43] Such evenings became the highlight of Olga and Tatiana's day, but like Maria and Anastasia they were always delighted to catch up with other old army friends who arrived on tours of duty. Men such as Olga's old favourite AKSH, now posted with the 1st squadron of the Tsar's Escort, who seemed as 'sweet' as ever, and his fellow officer, Staff Captain Viktor Zborovsky, the tsar's favourite tennis partner, for whom Anastasia was showing clear signs of devoted puppy love.

With their daily routine becoming increasingly mundane and largely restricted to Tsarskoe Selo, bad news from the front made all the girls, particularly Olga, fearful for their father, but they always felt themselves to be in safe hands with the officers of the Escort. In Aunt Olga's absence nursing in Rovno, Anna Vyrubova had taken to inviting the four sisters to tea with these officers at her house near the Alexander Palace. 'At 4 we had tea at Anna's with Zborovsky and Sh[vedov] – the darling', noted Olga on 12 October. 'So glad at last to see each other and chatted happily.' Tatiana was particularly pleased that same day to be able to talk on the phone to Dmitri Malama, who had enlisted Anna to buy Tatiana a special gift from him – 'a little French bulldog . . . it's unbelievably sweet. I'm so happy.'[44] She named the dog Ortipo – after Malama's cavalry horse.[45]

In advance of Ortipo's arrival, she wrote one of her typical apologetic notes to her mother:

> Mama darling mine,
>
> Forgive me about the little dog. To say the truth, when he asked should I like to have it if he gave it me, I at once said yes. You remember, I always wanted to have one, and only afterwards when we came home I thought that suddenly you might not like me having one . . . Please, darling angel, forgive me . . . 1000 kisses from your devoted daughter . . . Say, darling, you are not angry.

Ortipo was soon running riot at the palace; she was mischievous and disruptive (and before long pregnant), but she arrived at a fortuitous time, for Alexey's own dog Shot died not long after and she was a companion for Anastasia's dog Shvybzik. Ortipo's puppies, however, proved to be 'small and ugly' and the family did not keep them.[46] Sadly for Tatiana, Dmitri Malama recovered all too quickly from his wounds. He was discharged from the annexe on 23 October; 'Poor me, it's so awful', was as much as she could bring herself to write in her diary.[47]

On 4 November the Sisters Romanova took their final exams in surgery and two days later, along with forty-two other sisters, were issued with their nursing certificates at Red Cross headquarters in Tsarskoe Selo. By this time Alexandra had already set up around seventy hospitals across the town and its environs.[48] Work in the military hospitals had, by the beginning of 1915, recalled Sydney Gibbes, 'become the centre of their life and their engrossing occupation', for all four Romanov sisters. To some extent, as was inevitable, the education of the younger two suffered 'but the experience was so vitalizing that the sacrifice was certainly worth the making'.[49] As Anastasia wrote with enthusiasm to her teacher PVP at the time: 'This afternoon we all went for a ride, went to church and to the hospital, and that's it! And now we have to go eat dinner and then to the hospital again, and this is our life, yes!'[50] War had, ironically, opened up new horizons for all of them.

Chapter Fifteen

WE CANNOT DROP OUR WORK IN
THE HOSPITALS

In January 1915 an additional burden of concern was placed on the shoulders of the Romanov sisters when Anna Vyrubova was very seriously injured in a railway accident on the line between Petrograd and Tsarskoe Selo. She was brought to the annexe in a desperate state with a dislocated shoulder, double fracture of her left leg, lacerations to the right one and head and spine injuries. She was not expected to live. Her elderly parents arrived; Tatiana met them in tears, and gently escorted them down the corridor. Valentina Chebotareva remembered that night vividly:

> They sent for Grigory. I thought this was terrible, but I could not sit in judgment on another. The woman is dying, she believes in Grigory, in his saintliness, in [his] prayers. He arrived in a state of fright, his dishevelled beard shaking, his mouselike eyes flitting back and forth. He grasped Vera Ignateva [Dr Gedroits] by the hand: 'She'll live, she'll live'. But as she herself later told me: 'I decided to play the priest at his own game, thought for a moment and then said solemnly: 'Thank you, but I will save her.'

Gedroits's response did not go unnoticed by Nicholas who was home from Stavka at the time: 'Each to his own', he said, giving Gedroits a wry smile.[1] He spoke with the doctor for some time that evening, as Valentina recalled. It seemed clear to both women that the tsar 'without doubt did not believe in either Grigory's saintliness or his powers, but put up with him, like a sick person when exhausted by suffering clutches at straws'. But Grigory himself had been visibly drained by the experience of willing Anna's recovery. He always later claimed that he had 'raised Annushka from the dead', for against the odds she did indeed recover.[2]

After six weeks' dedicated care Anna was able to return home but her recuperation was a long one and she was disabled by her injuries for the rest of her life. Meanwhile, early that year, having driven herself relentlessly since day one of the war in the face of her already unstable health, Alexandra broke down completely. Dr Botkin ordered her to bed for six weeks. 'The nursing in the hospital and assisting at operations, tending and binding up the most hideous wounds,' Alexandra explained to a friend, 'is all less tiring than for hours visiting hospitals and talking with the poor wounded.' She struggled to carry on with some of her work at the annexe, 'Coming as privately and unexpectedly as possible, but it does not often succeed . . . One's greatest comfort is being with the dear wounded and I miss my hospitals awfully.'[3] When her energies failed her, Alexandra read and composed reports from her sickbed, meanwhile taking 'lots of iron and arsenic and heartdrops.'[4]

For the next few weeks, in addition to their nursing duties at the hospital, Olga and Tatiana would spend their days visiting Anna and often sitting with their mother or Alexey, who was suffering recurring pain in his arms from overdoing it when playing. Moments of private pleasure were increasingly rare, but when she could Tatiana would escape in the afternoons on her own to go riding. In the evenings, while her other sisters often sat playing board games or the gramophone, or Anastasia fussed round the two dogs – clearing up after their numerous accidents – Tatiana would sit quietly and read poetry. She found her mother's latest indisposition hard to take and constantly tormented herself that she was not doing enough to support her: 'Mama, sweet, I am so awfully sad. I see so little of you . . . It doesn't matter if sisters go earlier to bed – I'll remain. For me it is better to sleep less and see more of you, my beloved one.' 'In such moments,' she told Alexandra, 'I am sorry I'm not a man.'[5] She was now having to draw on all her strength of character to deal with the many duties required of her, as she told Nicholas in May:

Today I was in the hospital dressing the wounds of this poor unfortunate soldier with amputations of his tongue and ears. He's young and has a lovely face, from the Orenburg district and cannot speak at all, so wrote down how it all had happened to him, which Mama asked me to send on to you . . . and he was very happy. Princess Gedroits hopes that he will in time be able to speak, as only half his tongue had to be amputated. He is in a lot of pain. He has lost the top of his right ear, and the bottom of his left one. I am so sorry for the poor man. After lunch Mama and I went into Petrograd to the Supreme Council. We sat for an hour and a half – it was dreadfully boring . . . then Mama and I went all round the supply depot. And we've only just got back now at 5.30.[6]

Alexandra was convinced that their committee work was 'so good for the girls'; it would teach them to become independent and would 'develop them much more having to think and speak for themselves without my constant aid'.[7] It seems strange that, believing this, she had not allowed her daughters a greater role in society sooner; had she done so they would not still be grappling with the intense self-consciousness they suffered chairing committee meetings. Tatiana said these meetings made her want 'to dive under the table from fright'. As for Olga, in addition to her mother's interminable meetings at the Supreme Council, she had to sit and take donations every week, which Alexandra thought equally good for her: 'she will get accustomed to see people and hear what is going [on]', she told Nicholas, though she sometimes despaired of her: 'She is a clever child but does not use her brains enough.'[8]

With the arrival of spring in 1915, the family could not but ruefully cast their minds back on how life had been before the war. It was still snowing at Tsarskoe Selo in mid-April but one of their friends in Livadia had sent them gifts of Crimean flowers – glycinia, golden rain, purple irises, anemones and peonies. 'To see them in one's vases makes me quite melancholy', Alix told Nicky, 'Does it not seem strange, hatred and bloodshed and all the horrors of war – and there simply Paradise, sunshine and flowers and peace . . . Dear me, how much has happened since the peaceful, homely life in the fjords!'[9] They all longed for their usual visit to the Crimea.

But duty was paramount, as Tatiana told Pavel Voronov's wife Olga in June: 'It's the first summer that we are not going to live in Peterhof. We cannot drop our work in the hospitals. It would be distressing to live there and to think that there will be no yacht and no skerries. It's a pity there is no sea here.'[10]

The girls had from time to time still seen Pavel and Olga when they had visited Tsarskoe Selo, but the sad summer of 1913 and all the heartache attached to it had now faded for Olga, whose thoughts since the end of May had been increasingly revolving around a new arrival at the annexe: Dmitri Shakh-Bagov, a Georgian adjutant in the Life Grenadiers of the Erevan Regiment. This was one of the oldest and most prestigious regiments in the Russian army and the dearest to the imperial family after the Escort. But Dmitri's stay was short: 'After supper spoke on the phone to Shakh-Bagov and said goodbye as he is going back to his regiment tomorrow', Olga wrote in her diary on 22 June. 'I'm so sorry for him the darling, it's terrible, he is so sweet.'[11] Tatiana also had a favourite patient from the same regiment – an ensign from Azerbaijan called Sergey Melik-Adamov. He had the archetypal swarthy looks and large moustache of his predecessors, but his fellow patients found his pockmarked face unattractive and his loud jokes something of an embarrassment.[12]

Dmitri Shakh-Bagov's departure had a marked and immediate effect: 'Dear Olga Nikolaevna became sad,' recalled another patient, Ivan Belyaev, 'her cheeks lost their usual ruddiness, and her eyes darkened with tears.'[13] Soon afterwards, Dmitri's commanding officer Konstantin Popov was brought in wounded and joined Melik-Adamov in the 'Erevan' Ward. 'The Grand Duchesses greeted me like an old friend', he recalled, and began asking questions about how the regiment was, about the officers they knew and so on.

> What sweet simple people, I instinctively thought, and with every day I became more and more convinced of this. I was a witness of their daily work and was struck by their patience, persistence, their great skill for difficult work and their tenderness and kindness to everyone around them.[14]

Barely five weeks later, much to Olga's joy, and despite the unfortunate circumstances, Dmitri Shakh-Bagov was brought back to the hospital, having been seriously wounded on a reconnaissance mission near Zagrody in eastern Poland. He arrived on 2 August on a stretcher with a shattered leg and a hand wound, much thinner and looking very pale, and was immediately taken back to his former bed in the Erevan Ward.[15] He was operated on and his leg put in plaster but although he was supposed to be confined to bed he was soon up and hobbling round after Olga like a devoted puppy. 'It soon became noticeable how her previous mood returned . . . and her sweet eyes shone once more', noted Ivan Belyaev.[16] Olga's Dmitri now began appearing regularly in her diary in the affectionate form of Mitya. She spent every precious moment she could in his company – sitting with him in the corridor, on the balcony and in the ward, as well as during the evenings when she sterilized the instruments and made up the cotton-wool swabs. She had every reason to feel deeply for him, for everyone loved Mitya. Konstantin Popov was fulsome in his praise of him as 'a distinguished and brave officer, a rare friend and wonderfully good-natured person. If one were to add to this his handsome appearance and his great ability to wear his uniform and deport himself with distinction then you would have an example of the young Erevan officer in whom in truth our regiment prides itself.'[17] Mitya was 'very sweet and shy, like a girl', remembered Ivan Belyaev, and what is more, 'it was evident that he was completely in love with his nursing sister. His cheeks became brightly flushed whenever he looked at Olga Nikolaevna.'[18]

While Olga's head might have been turned, there was no diminution in the compassion and care that she, like Tatiana, continued to offer to all their patients. Valentina Chebotareva remembered a particularly traumatic operation at which both sisters had assisted and how bitterly they had wept when the patient had died. 'How poetic Tatiana Nikolaevna's caresses are! How warmly she speaks when she calls on the telephone and reads the telegrams about her wounded', Valentina wrote in her diary. 'What a good, pure and deep feeling girl she is.'[19] That summer, the highly reserved Tatiana, who had until now only shown passing interest in Dmitri Malama, appeared to have fallen for Vladimir Kiknadze – or Volodya as she was soon calling him – another Georgian and a 2nd lieutenant in the 3rd Guards Rifles Regiment. The two sisters began enjoying trysts as a foursome in the garden playing croquet with Kiknadze and Shakh-Bagov, and falling into a routine of shared smiles and confidences, sitting on their beds and looking at albums and taking each other's photograph. The war, for a while, did not seem quite so grim.

*

Throughout 1915 Nicholas had managed to make regular trips back home to Tsarskoe Selo but in August he made a momentous decision that would take him away from the family for even longer periods. A succession of Russian defeats on the Eastern Front, resulting in a massive retreat from Galicia, had already seen 1.4 million Russians killed and wounded and 1 million captured. Morale in a poorly equipped imperial army was haemorrhaging away. In response he dismissed his uncle Grand Duke Nikolay as Commander-in-Chief of the army and took over command himself, moving Stavka to Mogilev, 490 miles (790 km) due south of Petrograd. This decision, like every other the tsar made during the war, was guided by his deeply held belief that the people trusted in him as their spiritual leader and that the fate of himself, his family and Russia lay in God's hands. At 10 p.m. on 22 August the children went to the station with him. 'My precious papa!' Olga wrote as soon as he had left. 'How sad it is that you are leaving but this time it is with a special feeling of joy that we see you off, because we all fervently believe that your arrival there will more than ever raise the strong spirit of our mighty, national Army.' 'Here I am with this *new* heavy responsibility on my shoulders!' Nicholas told Alexandra upon his arrival. 'But God's will be fulfilled – I feel so calm.'[20] Two months later he made another important decision: at the end of a visit home he took Alexey back with him to Stavka, partly for company, as he missed the family so terribly, but also because he and Alexandra both believed that the tsarevich's presence would be a huge boost to army morale. Alexey, now aged eleven, was ecstatic; much as he loved his mother he was desperate to escape her suffocating presence and no doubt also the over-protectiveness of his sisters. As he would later complain: 'I hate going back to Tsarskoe to be the only man amongst all those women.'[21]

Since the outbreak of war Alexey had been playing soldiers at home, proudly strutting around in his soldier's greatcoat – 'quite like a little military man', as Alix told Nicky – standing guard, digging trenches and fortifications in the palace gardens with his *dyadki* and in the process sometimes provoking attacks of pain in his arms.[22] But aside from this he was in better health than he had been for years, and for some time now had had no serious attacks. It was hard for Alexandra to let her boy go, but she agreed on condition that Alexey's studies should not be interrupted. He was by now, however, woefully behind in his lessons and although he was followed to Stavka by both PVP and Pierre Gilliard, he rarely knuckled down to a full day's lessons, preferring the distractions of board games, playing his balalaika and enjoying the company of his new dog, a cocker spaniel named Joy.[23] At Stavka Alexey was in his element, sharing the same Spartan living conditions with his father, sleeping on campbeds, going on trips to army camps, inspecting the troops with him and enjoying the camaraderie of the soldiers, and taking particular pleasure in swimming with his father in the River Dnieper. Back at Tsarskoe everyone in the entourage felt the absence of father and son: 'life at the Imperial Palace became, if possible, even quieter', recalled Iza Buxhoeveden. 'The whole place seemed dead. There was no movement in the great courtyard. We ladies-in-waiting went to the Empress through a series of empty halls.'[24] Whenever Nicholas and Alexey returned on visits, 'the palace sprang to life'.

At Stavka the young heir made a strong impression on all who met him. True, he could still be brattish – particularly at table, where he had a penchant for throwing pellets of bread at his father's ADCs.[25] But his extraordinary energy lit up a room. 'It was the first time I had seen the Tsarevich when the door of our box flung open and he came like a gale of wind,' recalled US naval attaché Newton McCully:

> Full of life, healthy looking, and one of the handsomest young-sters I have ever seen, I was particularly glad to see him so closely because I had heard so many rumors about his being paralyzed – maimed for life – and so on. One could not wish to see a handsomer child. Undoubtedly he has been ill, but there are no signs of illness about him now – if anything perhaps a too exuberant vitality, perhaps an organism over-nervous.[26]

In mid-October, Alexandra, Anna Vyrubova and the girls visited Mogilev, in time to see Alexey awarded the Medal of St George 4th class. They were all delighted to see the continuing improvement in his health and strength. 'He was developing marvelously through the summer both in bodily vigor and gaiety of spirits', recalled Anna Vyrubova. 'With his tutors, M. Gilliard and Petrov, he romped and played as though illness were a thing to him unknown.'[27] The visit was a welcome break for the girls from their virtually monastic life at Tsarskoe. At Stavka they had more freedom to move around; they spent time playing with the children of railway workers and local peasants (whom Tatiana photographed for her album, scrupulously noting down all their names), though once more there were whisperings that the imperial sisters should not stoop so low in their friendships and that they looked scruffy and 'unroyal'.[28]

The Governor's House at Mogilev that served as HQ was too cramped to accommodate all the family, so Alexandra and the girls stayed on the imperial train, where Nicholas and Alexey dined with them in the evenings. The train was parked in the midst of wooded countryside and the girls were able to go walking unobserved and often unrecognized. Out in the woods they made bonfires and roasted potatoes with members of the Tsar's Escort, much as they had done on their Finnish holidays; they slept in the sunshine on the new-mown hay and even enjoyed the occasional cigarette given to them by Nicholas. For the rest of the time it was boat rides on the River Dnieper and games of hide-and-seek on the imperial train, and even occasional visits to the local cinematograph in Mogilev.[29] But in many of the photographs taken that October, Olga looked withdrawn and pensive, often sitting apart from the others. She came back from Stavka with a bad cough and Valentina Chebotareva immediately became concerned, not just about her melancholy frame of mind, but also her visibly declining health:

> Her nerves are completely shot to pieces, she's got thinner and paler. She hasn't been able to do the bandaging lately, can't bear to look at wounds and in the operating theatre is distressed, becomes irritable, tries to do things and can't control herself – feels dizzy. It's awful to see the child, how sad and overwrought she is. They say it's exhaustion.[30]

In her later memoirs Anna Vyrubova claimed that although Tatiana from the outset demonstrated 'extraordinary ability' as a nurse, 'Olga within two months [of her training] was almost too exhausted and too unnerved to continue'.[31] It was clear that the long hours were taking their toll on her, that she was less resilient emotionally and physically than Tatiana, and also far less focused. She could not cope with the trauma of some of the operations she witnessed, nor could she knuckle down to regular routine as easily as her sister. And now she was distracted yet again by her feelings – this time for Mitya Shakh-Bagov. The exhaustion she was suffering was compounded by severe anaemia and, like her mother, she was put on a course of daily arsenic injections. 'Olga's condition still not famous', Alexandra telegraphed Nicholas on 31 October, adding in a letter that their daughter had 'only got up for a drive & now after tea she remains on the sopha and we shall dine upstairs – this is my treatment – she must lie more, as goes about so pale and wearily – the Arsenic injections will act quicker like that, you see'.*[32]

A few days later they were all celebrating Olga's twentieth birthday, but of late she had hardly been to the annexe and when she did go, as she told her father, she 'didn't do anything, just sat with them. But they still make me lie down a lot.' She didn't like the daily arsenic injections from Dr Botkin: 'I reek of garlic a bit, which is not nice.'†[33] Whatever her private thoughts might have been at this time, Olga, like her sisters, retained a stoical acceptance of her lot. Fellow nurse Bibi happened to be visiting at the palace one evening when Olga and Tatiana were getting changed for dinner and choosing jewellery. 'The only shame is that no one can enjoy seeing me like this,' quipped Olga, 'only papa!' The remark was made, as Bibi told Valentina, totally without affectation. 'One, two and her hair's done (though no hairdo as such), and she didn't even

---

* Arsenic was a popular remedy for such ailments at the time. For example, diplomat's wife Dorothy Bosanquet spent time in Tsarskoe Selo in April 1916 when recovering from pleurisy, where she went every afternoon to the Palace Hospital to have an arsenic injection at 50 kopeks a time.

† If heated, arsenic oxidizes and produces arsenic trioxide, the smell of which resembles garlic. Plain arsenic also smells like garlic when it evaporates.

glance in the mirror.' It was typical of Olga to take little interest in her looks or bother about how she appeared to others. During her hours lying at home feeling unwell the chambermaid Nyuta had brought Olga a gramophone record – 'Goodbye Lou-Lou'. 'Echoes, no doubt, of things seen in the hospital', wrote Valentina in her diary, perhaps alluding to songs sung by Olga's officer friends there. 'It's sad for the poor children to have to live in this gilded cage.'[34]

When she was finally able, Olga returned to the annexe, but on a much reduced workload, mainly taking temperatures, writing prescriptions and machining bed linen. The lion's share of changing the dressings every morning was now done by Tatiana, who also did the injections and assisted Gedroits in surgery. Valentina and Tatiana had recently had to deal with a particularly unpleasant gangrenous wound that had required an urgent amputation. While Valentina rushed to prepare the Novocain, Tatiana, without need for instruction, had gathered together all the instruments, prepared the operating table and the linen. During the operation a good deal of hideous pus was drained away from the wound, and for once even Valentina had felt nauseous. 'But Tatiana Nikolaevna wasn't affected by it, only twitched at the groans and moans of the patient, and blushed scarlet.' She returned to the hospital at nine that evening to sterilize the instruments with Olga and went in to see the patient at ten, just before leaving. Sadly he took a turn for the worse in the night and died.[35]

It was this kind of traumatic situation with which Olga was no longer able to cope, although she visited for a short while most days, especially while Mitya was still there. And now Tatiana was cheered by the return of Volodya Kiknadze, who had been wounded again. The cosy foursomes they had enjoyed earlier in the summer were once more resumed as the girls spun out the evenings sterilizing instruments and preparing swabs. 'Who's to know the drama Olga Nikolaevna has been living through', wrote Valentina. 'Why is she wasting away, become so thin, so pale: is she in love with Shakh-Bagov?' Valentina was concerned at the amount of time the sisters were spending with their two favourites: 'As soon as she finishes the dressings, Tatiana Nikolaevna goes to do the injections, and then she sits down in a twosome with K[iknadze] . . . he sits down at the piano, playing something with one finger, and chats animatedly with our dear girl for a long time.' Bibi worried too; what if Elizaveta Naryshkina were to walk in on 'this little scene'? She would die of shock.

> Shakh Bagov has a fever and is in bed. Olga Nikolaevna spends the whole time sitting by his bed. The other pair joined them there yesterday and sat side by side on the bed looking through the album. K[iknadze] cosies up to her. Tatiana Nikolaevna's sweet childlike face can't hide a thing and is flushed and animated. But isn't all this close proximity, all this touching dangerous? I've become anxious about it. The others are getting jealous, and annoyed and I imagine they gossip and spread it around in town, and maybe even beyond.[36]

Dr Gedroits shared Valentina's concern; they both felt that Volodya Kiknadze was a ladykiller and was leading the impressionable Tatiana astray. Gedroits decided to send him away to the Crimea for recuperation, or rather – as she and Valentina both saw it – 'out of harm's way'. Even Mitya, Olga's 'precious one', was not beyond reproach; Gedroits had discovered that once, when drunk, he had shown private letters Olga had written to him to another patient. 'That is positively the last straw! The poor children!'[37]

*

Over at Stavka on 3 December 1915, Nicholas noted in his diary that 'Alexey started developing a cold yesterday'; he began sneezing and a nosebleed ensued.[38] Unable to stem the bleeding, Dr Feodorov advised that Alexey be taken back to Tsarskoe Selo. When they arrived on the 6th, Anna Vyrubova was shocked at

> the waxen, grave-like pallor of the little pointed face as the boy with infinite care was borne into the palace and laid on his little white bed. Above the blood-soaked bandages his large blue eyes gazed at us with pathos unspeakable, and it seemed to all around the bed that the last hour of the unhappy child was at hand.

Grigory had, of course, been sent for and arrived soon after. Much as before, he stood for a while by Alexey's bed and made the sign of the cross over him. Then he turned to Alexandra and said,

'Don't be alarmed. Nothing will happen'; then he left.[39] She never-theless sat up with her son all night and did not go to bed until 8 a.m. the following morning; 'half an hour later she got up and went to church', Tatiana told Valentina.[40] The following day a specialist named Dr Polyakov was called in and managed to cauterize the bleeding. Alexey remained in bed until 18 December but was still very frail. A disconsolate Nicholas had returned to Stavka alone on the 12th.

As Christmas 1915 approached Olga and Tatiana were feeling gloomy: Mitya and Volodya were soon to be discharged from the hospital. The girls begged their mother to intercede so they could at least stay for the holiday. On the 26th the girls 'arranged to come just for an hour to do the dressings' at the annexe, although not without 'secret thoughts' of chatting with Mitya and Volodya, as Valentina well knew. She was anxious to see the back of Kiknadze, whom she heard had been bragging of his conquest. 'People are gossiping, they see how he is constantly taking her to one side in the ward, away from the others . . . always whispering things quietly, secretively in a low voice.' Dr Gedroits was 'in a rage' about his inappropriate behaviour.[41]

On 30 December 1915 Olga noted wistfully in her diary that 'Mitya was at the commission, then came back and we sat nearly the whole time together, playing at draughts and it was so simple. He is good, God knows.' In the evening she spoke to him on the phone and heard the news she had dreaded: 'He has suddenly received orders from his regiment to go to the Caucasus in two days' time.'[42]

Chapter Sixteen

THE OUTSIDE LIFE

꙳

By the spring of 1916 the refugee crisis in the Russian Empire had become enormous, with something like 3.3 million people, many of them Jews displaced from the Pale of Settlement, by fighting on the Eastern Front.[1] With the urgent need for more refuges, orphanages and soup kitchens, Grand Duchess Tatiana Nikolaevna published a heartfelt appeal in aid of her committee in the Russian press. 'The war has ruined and scattered millions of our peaceful citizens', she wrote:

> Homeless and breadless, the unfortunate refugees are seeking shelter throughout the land . . . I appeal to you, all you kind-hearted people, to help the refugee physically and morally. At the very least give him the comfort of knowing that you understand and feel for him in his boundless misery. Remember the words of our Lord: 'I was an hungred, and ye gave me meat; I was thirsty, and ye gave me drink; I was a stranger, and ye took me in.' [Matthew, xxv: 35][2]

The Tatiana Committee not only sought to provide for refugees but also to register them and reunite families separated by the fighting. In particular it worked to ensure the welfare of children – many arriving from the war zone in a pitiful state, weak from hunger and lice-ridden – by setting up orphanages and schools for them. Early in 1916 a seventh home for refugee children and their mothers was opened in Petrograd under the auspices of the committee. It was funded by Americans in the city, led by the ambassador's wife, Mrs George Marye; later that year the Americans donated fifteen field ambulances.[3] The British also collaborated, sending out a team of female nurses and doctors to staff the British Women's Maternity Hospital in Petrograd which the Tatiana Committee was supporting to the tune of 1,000 roubles a month.[4]

After more than a year of war, word had spread into the foreign press of the exemplary work of the empress and her two eldest daughters. Olga and Tatiana were projected as virtuous heroines, 'The Beautiful "White Sisters" of the War', heading an army of 'ministering women carrying the snow-white sign of peace and the red cross of redemption'.[5] British journalist John Foster Fraser recalled how a '3-day Flag Day for collection for the refugees was begun with a big service in front of Kazan Cathedral':

> The idea of helping the distant war-sufferers came from the Grand Duchess Tatiana, aged seventeen . . . She is tall and dark and beautiful and mischievous, and the Russians adore her . . . When she started her fund to find bread and clothing for the people of Poland it was like the waving of a fairy wand . . . The appeal by their pretty princess was irresistible . . . It would have been difficult to find a shop window in Petrograd where there was not a large photograph of the young lady, with a softly twinkling side-glance as much as to inquire: 'well, how much have you given?'[6]

Alexandra was delighted to tell Nicholas on 13 January that Tatiana's name day 'was celebrated in town with great fanfare. There was a concert and presentations in the theatre . . . Tatiana's portrait with autograph was sold along with the programme.'[7] Money raised from the sale of postcards and portraits of Tatiana was going into the fund for her committee. 'I've seen elderly gentlemen sauntering along the Nevski with as long a row of little photographs of the princess across their rotund chests as the stretch of medals worn by a Petrograd policeman,' reported John Foster Fraser, 'and that is wonderful.'[8] For others, however, the imperial family was 'surrounded by wall after wall of isolation from the people', wrote American Richard Washburn Child, 'the Czarina and the four daughters, Olga, Tatiana, Marie and Anastasia, take some interest in charities, but otherwise are real to the Russian people only through their photographs'.[9]

Tatiana's public profile nevertheless had been considerably raised by the crucial work of her committee, in comparison to Olga's less visible role on the Supreme Council, although this undoubtedly had much to do with Olga's continuing ill health. Their mother too had been absent from meetings in Petrograd as well as the annexe hospital since before Christmas. She spent most of January and February suffering from a recurrence of excruciating neuralgia and toothache, as well as problems with her 'enlarged' heart, which left her 'constantly in tears' from the pain.[10] Dr Botkin gave her electrotherapy treatment for the neuralgia and her dentist visited numerous times, while Alexandra continued to dose herself on a wide range of proprietary medicines, including opium and 'Adonis and other drops to quieten the heartbeating'.[11] Anastasia had bronchitis and Alexey was also unwell, with pain in his arms from going out sledging. 'Both arms are bandaged & the right ached rather yesterday', Alexandra told Nicholas. Grigory had, since Anna's accident the previous year, been constantly on hand to pray and offer sage advice and told her Alexey's pain would 'pass in two days'.[12] Rasputin's increased influence over the empress in her husband's absence, and his now constant whisperings on matters military and political in Alexandra's ear, had been fanning the flames of gossip even more of late. 'The hatred grows not by the day but by the hour,' recorded an anxious Valentina Chebotareva, 'and transmits itself to our poor unfortunate girls. People think them of the same mind as their mother.'[13]

For Tatiana and Olga, life continued on its narrow, repetitive course. The foreign press might be reminding their readers that behind the wartime nurse's wimple, they were still considered 'the most beautiful children of royalty in Europe' as it speculated yet again on marital alliances with the Balkan states, but for Olga thoughts of love were still very firmly rooted in her own backyard.[14] Mitya Shakh-Bagov had recovered and was to leave the hospital in early January and she was taking the prospect of his second departure very hard. 'Olga has a tragic look once more', Valentina was sad to record. Part of it, she felt, was in response to the gossip about her mother and Rasputin. There was about her such 'terrible suppressed suffering':

Perhaps the imminent departure of Shakh-Bagov is adding to it – her trusty knight is leaving. He really is a fine fellow. He venerates her, like a sacred object. 'Olga Nikolaevna only need tell me that she finds Grigory disgusting, and he'd be dead the next day – I'd kill him'.[15]

Valentina felt that Mitya's instincts were 'primitive', but he was an 'honest man'. Tatiana meanwhile remained hard-working, self-effacing and 'touchingly gentle'. 'Everything is the same as ever here,' she told her father in February, 'nothing new.'[16] When she came to the hospital one evening to help sterilize the instruments and boil the silk thread she 'sat on her own in fumes of carbolic', recalled Valentina. When, on another occasion, Valentina had tried to relieve her of this task in advance, 'She caught me out. "Tell me please, what's the hurry! . . . If you can breathe in the carbolic, why can't I?"[17] Such were her proven capabilities as a nurse that by the autumn Tatiana was being allowed to administer the chloroform in operations. But while she remained steadfast, her still frail and increasingly melancholic sister was sinking into a depression. 'Olga assures [me] that she thinks she will remain a spinster', Valentina noted, even though she and Shakh-Bagov 'had been reading each other's palms and he had prophesied she would have twelve children'. Tatiana's hand was 'interesting': 'the line of fate is suddenly interrupted and makes a sharp turn sideways. They assure her that she will do something unusual.'[18] For the time being, however, Tatiana's day was filled with responsibility – at home and at the hospital – allowing her little or no time to herself. On 16 January she recorded a typical day:

> German lesson in the morning. At 10 o'clock went to the hospital. Dressed the wounds of Rogal of 149th Chernomorsk regiment, wound in skull, Gaiduk of 7th Samogitsk Grenadiers regiment, wound in left thigh, Martynov of the 74th Stavropol regiment, wound in left thigh, Shchetinin of the 31st Tomsk regiment, wound in left thigh, Melnik of the 17th Arkhangelsk regiment, wound in the right forearm, wound in right lower ribcage, Arkhipov of the 149th Chernomorsk regiment, wound in right hand with the loss of the fourth and fifth fingers, wound in right thigh. Then Bleish, Sergeyev, Chaikovsky, Ksifilinov, Martynov, Emelyanov – only

superficial wounds. Then at 12 went upstairs with Valentina
Ivanovna to the soldiers' ward to change Popov's dressings. Under
anaesthetic. His kidney was removed. Then went back and went
to see Tuznikov. Had lunch and drank tea with mama. Then had
a history lesson. The four of us went for a troika ride with Iza.
Then we were at the Big Palace for a concert. Then to vespers.
Had supper with mama and Anna. Then Nikolay Pavlovich [Sablin]
arrived. We said farewell to him as tomorrow he is going to join
his battalion, in the army.[19]

With their mother out of action it devolved to Olga and Tatiana
on 19 January to attend an important function on her behalf in
town, along with their grandmother as surrogate – the official
opening ceremony of the Anglo-Russian Hospital. This had been
set up in Dmitri Pavlovich's palace on the corner of the Fontanka
by the Anichkov Bridge – he having given it over to use as a wartime
hospital – and provided 188 beds and had its own operating theatre,
bandaging room, lab and X-ray facilities. Supplies were sent out from
England by Queen Mary's Needlework Guild and the War Hospital
Supply Depot, and its eight doctors and thirty nurses were British
and Canadian volunteers. One of them, Enid Stoker (a niece of the
novelist Bram Stoker), recalled their preparations for the opening:

> the hospital was cleaned and polished to the last degree and
> looked *lovely* with big pots of flowers and palms and all its own
> beautiful carving and marble . . . by 2.30 we were all standing
> in there dressed up to the nines in starched everythings . . . Then
> we heard a crowd moving slowly up the stairs, and a small dowdy
> woman in black, like a plain edition of Alexandra – (the Empress
> sister of our own queen) but with a very sweet expression – came
> in. The two little princesses, Olga and Tatiana, looked charming
> and so pretty in little ermine hats with white ospreys in them
> and little low-necked rose-coloured frocks and ermine furs and
> muffs.[20]

Everyone at the hospital remarked on how attractive the Romanov
girls were. Olga put on a good show of being cheerful and friendly.
Enid thought her 'the prettiest and really lovely', adding that the
sisters had been 'so jolly-looking and natural'. Other members of

the family would visit the hospital later, Enid Stoker remembering the arrival of Anastasia 'with her hair down her back and an Alice in Wonderland comb', and one 'unforgettable' day when the 'little Czarevitch' came – 'one of the most beautiful children I ever saw'.[21] Meriel Buchanan noted a similar response when Olga and Tatiana visited the English Colony Hospital run by her mother, where they toured the wards and talked to the patients, 'Olga often making them laugh with her whimsical merriment, her sister talking to them gently, but with a greater reserve. How kind they were, the soldiers told me afterwards, how lovely they looked.'[22] An appearance in civilian clothes was a rarity these days for the older Romanov sisters and for their mother too, so much so that people were taken aback when they saw them out of nurses' uniform. One Sunday morning on the way to church they 'went for half an hour to bid all good morning in the hospital', Alexandra told Nicholas and 'Like Babies they all stared at us in "dresses and hats" and looked at our rings and bracelets (the ladies too) and we felt shy and [like] "guests"'.[23]

*

A French journalist who had been granted the rare privilege of meeting Alexandra and the girls at their hospital remarked in 1916 that there was 'something of the serenity of the mystic about Olga Nikolaevna'.[24] It was a trait that perhaps more than anything defined her Russianness and one that became more pronounced as the war went on. Olga seemed more and more lost in her own private thoughts about the kind of life, and love, that she longed for. One day at the hospital, she had confided to Valentina her personal 'dreams of happiness': 'To get married, live always in the countryside winter and summer, always mix with good people, and no officialdom whatsoever.'[25] She would no doubt therefore have been horrified to know that Grand Duchess Vladimir had recently approached her mother suggesting that Olga should marry her thirty-eight-year-old son Boris. It hadn't surprised Alexandra, for the grand duchess's 'ambition to get [Boris] nearest to the throne is well known'.[26] 'The idea of Boris is too unsympathetic & the child would, I feel convinced, never agree to marry him and I should perfectly well understand her', she wrote to Nicholas at Stavka, intimating that 'other thoughts have filled the child's head and heart' – a possible allusion to her daughter's feelings for Mitya Shakh-Bagov of which she must, surely, have been aware. 'Those are a young girl's holy secrets wh[ich] others must not know of', she insisted. 'It would terribly hurt Olga, who is so susceptible.'[27]

As for Boris: to 'give over a well used half worn out, blasé young man to a pure, fresh girl, 18 years his junior, & to live in a house in which many a woman has "shared" his life . . . An inexperienced girl would suffer terribly, to have her husband 4th, 5th hand or more.'[28] The suggestion of Boris as a husband had been an all too painful reminder of the bad company Dmitri Pavlovich – the husband they had once hoped for for Olga – had slipped into of late. As far as Alexandra was concerned, Dmitri was now well and truly out of the frame: 'he is a boy without any caracter [*sic*] and can be lead by anybody.'[29] He was currently back in Petrograd pleading poor health, but 'doing no work and drinking constantly'. Alexandra wanted Nicholas to order him back to his regiment. 'Town and women are poison for him.'

One who might well have fitted the bill for Tatiana, had he been higher-born, was 'my little Malama', as Alexandra described him, for he was back in town. Many of the Russian cavalry regiments such as Dmitri's had been decimated in eastern Prussia; left with no regiment to transfer to, he had been appointed an equerry at Tsarskoe Selo. Alexandra, who seemed to have a special affection for him, invited him to tea. 'We had not seen him for 1½ years', she told Nicky. 'Looks flourishing more of a man now, an adorable boy still. I must say, a perfect son in law he w[ou]ld have been.' Ah, there was the rub. 'Why are foreign P[rin]ces not as nice!' she added. As circumspect as ever, Tatiana did not confide her thoughts on Dmitri Malama's return to either her diary or any letters.*[30] Her sister by contrast made her own feelings all too clear, when, out of the blue, a letter arrived from Mitya: 'Olga Nikolaevna in ecstasy, threw all

---

* Had circumstances been different one wonders whether at war's end Nicholas and Alexandra would have conceded that the only way to see their daughters happily married, in Russia, would have been to allow morganatic marriages for them to high-ranking officers.

her things around', recalled Valentina: 'She was on fire and jumping up and down: "Is it possible to have a heart attack at 20? I think I might just have one."'[31] The massages Olga was having in the mornings to help her mood swings did not seem to be having much effect. They were as pronounced as ever: Olga was 'grumpy, sleepy, angry' all the time, Alexandra complained to Nicholas in April, and 'makes everything more difficult by her [ill] humour'.[32]

*

While their older sisters were preoccupied at the annexe, Maria and Anastasia continued to watch over their own wounded at Fedorovsky Gorodok. Anastasia was now the proud honorary Commander-in-Chief of her own regiment, the 148th Caspian Infantry, gifted to her by her father just before her 14th birthday. Soon she was proudly writing to Nicholas at Stavka, signing herself 'Nastaska the Caspian'.[33] Sadly, she and Maria found themselves increasingly visiting the graves of those who had died; 'we are constantly having offices for the dead nowadays', Maria told Nicholas in August. Back in March, in a long and delightfully animated letter, she had described her own attempts, in deep snow and treacherous conditions, to find a couple of graves in the military cemetery of men from the lower ranks:

> It took an incredibly long time to get there because the roads were extremely bad . . . The snow was piled up very high on the side of the road, so that it was a job getting through it on my knees and from there jumping down. The snow there turned out to be above my knees, and although I had big boots on, I was already wet, but I decided all the same to go further. And not much further on I found a grave with the name Mishchenko, one of our wounded. I laid some flowers on it and went further and suddenly I saw the same name again. I looked at the marker to see what regiment he was and it turned out that this one was our wounded man and not the other. Well I laid flowers there too and had just managed to move forward when I fell on my back, and lay there spread-eagled and almost for a minute couldn't get up as there was so much snow that I couldn't put my hand down on the ground in order to brace myself.[34]

Anastasia and Tatiana meanwhile had gone off to another part of the cemetery to visit the grave of Alexandra's lady-in-waiting Sonia Orbeliani, who had died the previous December, leaving Maria with the cemetery caretaker to find the other grave she was searching for, which turned out to be near to the cemetery fence. To get there

we'd have to climb across a ditch. He stood in the ditch and said to me: 'I will lift you over'. I said: 'No'. He said: 'Let's try'. He did not of course manage to lift me to the other side, but dropped me right in the middle of the ditch. So there we both stood in the ditch, up to our tummies in snow and dying from laughter. It was very difficult for him to crawl out because the ditch was deep, and the same for me. But somehow or other he got out and then gave me his hand. I of course slipped down on my tummy back into the ditch about three more times, but at last I got myself out. And we did all this holding flowers in our hands. After that there was no way we could manage to crawl between the crosses as we both had overcoats on. But all the same, I did find the grave and at last we made it out of the cemetery.[35]

*

By March 1916 Alexandra was becoming increasingly distressed that she remained too unwell to do her war work. The strain of managing the five children on her own was also beginning to tell on her. 'Our train is just being emptied out & Marie's comes later in the day with very heavy wounded', she told Nicholas on 13 March, and there she was, 'despairing not to be able to go and meet them and work in the hospital – every hand is needed at such a time'.[36] She missed her husband so terribly: 'such utter loneliness . . . the children with all their love still have quite other ideas & rarely understand my way of looking at things, the smallest even – they are always right and when I say how I was brought up and how one must be, they can't understand, find it dull.' Dependable Tatiana, in her view, seemed to be the only one of the five with a level head on her shoulders – 'she grasps it'. Even the compliant Maria had become moody of late – particularly when she had her period – 'grumbles all the time and bellows at one'. Olga continued to be a problem, being 'always most unamiable about every proposition'.[37]

The war clearly was getting to all of them, and so in early May the five Romanov siblings were delighted to be taken on a trip on the imperial train, back at long last to their beloved Crimea. After visiting Alexandra's huge, forty-ward hospital for 1,000 wounded at Vinnitsa and its supply depots they travelled on to Odessa. After the obligatory church service, troop inspections and tree-planting they sailed to Sevastopol where Nicholas reviewed the Black Sea Fleet. 'I was so terribly glad to see the sea', Tatiana wrote in her diary.[38] It was their first visit to the Crimea since 1913 but sadly they did not go back to the Livadia Palace, even though the doctors said it would be good for Alexandra's health. 'It was, she said, "too great a treat to indulge in during the war".'[39] The sisters made the most of being able to lie in the warm sunshine, but when the time came, 'It was dreadfully sad to set off from the Crimea and leave the sea, the sailors and the ships', sighed Tatiana.[40] At the end of their trip, with Alexey well once more, Nicholas announced that he was taking him back to Stavka again. In August Sydney Gibbes was asked by Alexandra to join them there in order to continue with Alexey's English lessons. Nicholas had now promoted Alexey to corporal; he was finally settling down and at last seemed to be losing his shyness with strangers.

*

In mid-May both David Iedigarov and Nikolay Karangozov were back at the annexe hospital, wounded again; and then, almost a year to the day since his first admittance, Mitya Shakh-Bagov returned to Tsarskoe on a visit with a fellow officer, Boris Ravtopulo.[41] Olga's spirits immediately lifted: she started coming back to the annexe in the evenings to help sterilize the instruments and sew compresses and once more played the piano for the wounded and sat talking to them in the garden on warm summer days. The sad, dejected girl of a few weeks earlier was now doing her utmost to stay as late as possible at the hospital, chatting to Mitya who often came to visit the wounded.[42] Her health improved, as too did Alexandra's. The tsaritsa resumed her work at the annexe, though she was rarely able to stand to do the bandaging or assist in operations. Instead she spent her time sitting by patients' bedsides doing the fine embroidery at which she was so talented, and chatting to them.[43] The annexe had effectively become home for all five women in the absence of Nicholas and Alexey. They missed their menfolk; it was hard to 'be upstairs without Alexey', Tatiana told her father. 'Every time I pass through the dining-room at 6 p.m., I am surprised not to see the table laid for his dinner. And in general there's very little noise now.'[44] The annexe was such a huge comfort to them. 'Yesterday we spent the evening cosily in the hospital', Alexandra told Nicholas on 22 May. 'The big girls cleaned instruments with the help of Shah B. and Raftopolo [*sic*], the little ones chattered till 10 – I sat working and later made puzzles – altogether forgot the time and sat till 12, the Pss G [Dr Gedroits] also busy with puzzle!'[45]

The wounded – many very serious – were now coming thick and fast to both of the sisters' hospitals. But sadly for Olga, Mitya Shakh-Bagov left Tsarskoe Selo on 6 June. He departed for the Caucasus with an icon she had given him.[46] Valentina sympathized with the pain Olga was going through. Her attachment to Mitya was 'so pure, naïve and without hope', which made it so much harder to take. She found her a 'strange, distinctive girl' and saw how hard she was trying to bottle up her feelings: 'When [Mitya] left the poor thing sat on her own for more than an hour, her nose buried in her sewing machine, furiously sewing away with great concentration.' Then she suddenly became fixated on finding 'the little penknife that Bagov had sharpened on the evening before his departure'. She searched all morning and, as Valentina recalled, 'was beyond joy when she found it'. Everything connected with Mitya Shakh-Bagov was precious: after he left, Olga recorded every anniversary attached to his time at the hospital in her diary: when he had been wounded, when discharged, when returned, and, as Valentina noted, 'She also treasures a page from the calendar for the 6th June – the day he left'.[47]

Reverting to her former morose state of mind, Olga went through the motions of fulfilling her duties at the annexe – measuring and handing out the medicines, sorting the bed linen, arranging flowers and phlegmatically noting in her brief diary entries: 'Did the same as always. It's boring without Mitya.'[48] Day after day was much like any other, and she 'didn't do anything special': maybe a walk or drive in the afternoon, sewing pillowcases at the hospital in the evening, or board games with the wounded, playing the piano and then home to bed. But as Olga wilted like a fading flower Tatiana had lost none of her vigour nor her application to duty. Nicholas, who often referred to her as his secretary, was now entrusting her, rather than Olga, with regular requests to send items such as writing paper or cigarettes out to him at Stavka. On Tatiana's nineteenth birthday he had telegraphed Alexandra congratulating her: 'God bless dear Tatiana and may she always remain the good, loving and patient girl she is now and a consolation in our old days.'[49] Alexandra agreed; by September and once again full of aches and pains, she openly admitted to her husband 'I do so want to get quicker well again, have more work to do and all lies upon Tatiana's shoulders.'[50]

*

Whenever any of their favourite officers were wounded the family made special efforts to take care of their welfare. A case in point was Lieutenant Viktor Zborovsky, their old friend from the Tsar's Escort, who was seriously wounded at the end of May 1916. Nicholas himself sent special instructions from Stavka for Zborovsky to be brought back from Novoselitsky in the Caucasus to Tsarskoe Selo. Much to Anastasia's great joy, Vitya, as she affectionately called him, was brought to the officers' ward of the Feodorovsky Gorodok. His arrival raised everyone's spirits – despite the severity of his wounds. He looked 'brown and all right,' Alexandra told Nicky, 'pretends he has no pains, but one sees his face twitch. He is wounded through the chest, but feels the arm.'[51]

His Majesty's Own Cossack Escort, to give it its full title, was comprised of four squadrons, two of Kuban Cossacks and two of Tereks, who were distinguished wherever they went by their red Cossack parade uniforms and black Persian lamb hats. Under the command of Count Grabbe since January 1914, the Escort largely performed a ceremonial role, but for the Romanov family it was the heart and soul of the Russian army.* In July, when the four sisters

---

* The Escort had been formed in 1811 as a special security guard for Alexander I

visited Nicholas and Alexey at Stavka with their mother, they made a surprise visit to the Escort's summer camp. The soldiers sang old Cossack songs for them and performed their traditional dance – the *lezginka*. Tatiana recalled one particular thrilling exploit of theirs in a letter to Rita Khitrovo, a friend and fellow nurse at the annexe:

> Yesterday we went up on the banks of the Dnieper again. The squadron of our Escort came along singing, hurrying to catch up with us. They sang songs, and played games and we just lay on the grass and enjoyed it. When they left, Papa said to them that they should go along the same bank of the river, and that we'd stay here for a bit longer, then drive in a fast moving car lower down along the river. We caught up with the squadron which had been going at a march playing the *zurna** and singing. When we came alongside they put their horses into a full gallop behind us and flew along. Further on there was a steep ravine and a bend in the river. They had to cross it in a single stride as the earth was soft. They had already fallen behind us, but as soon as they came out of this ravine, then they began to catch us at a full gallop. It was terribly exciting. They were like real Caucasian horsemen at that pace. You can't imagine just how marvellous it was. They rode with a whoop and a shout. If they go into an attack like that, especially whole regiments of them, I think the Germans will run away out of fear and wonder at what's coming at them.[52]

Having such affection for the Escort, it is not surprising that Maria and Anastasia delighted in having Viktor Zborovsky as a patient at Feodorovsky Gorodok when the new officers' ward was opened there in June; they reported on his progress regularly in their letters to Nicholas. They were now visiting daily, although evenings were still mainly spent at the annexe hospital with Olga

---

during the Napoleonic Wars, although the job of protecting the imperial family's security had long since been taken over by the Okhrana and Spiridovich's men. During the war, one squadron remained at Tsarskoe Selo with the empress, another served at Stavka with Nicholas, a third was based in Petrograd and a fourth, in rotation with the other three, was fighting at the front.

* An Azeri or Turkish wind instrument popular in the Caucasus.

and Tatiana. At their own hospital the warm presence of the two younger sisters greatly enhanced the sense of homeliness that the place already exuded. In the autumn of 1916, Felix Dassel, an officer from Maria's regiment, the 5th Kazan Dragoons, was brought in, severely wounded in the leg. He found the hospital cosy and welcoming with a wood fire crackling in the grate – 'nothing like how you would imagine a military hospital to be'. His small ward was calm and intimate, the bed made up with snow-white linen. Shortly after he arrived the grand duchesses came for their regular visit and he remembered them vividly: 'Maria, my patron, stocky, with a round open face, good clear eyes, somewhat timid', stopped to ask whether he was in very much pain. 'Anastasia, the smaller of the two, with elfish, lusty eyes', greeted him in the same concerned, though rather inattentive, way, 'leaning on the end of the bed, observing me sharply, examining me, swinging a foot, rolling her handkerchief'.[53]

Not long afterwards Dassel fell into a delirium and was operated on; he woke up to find roses on the table by his bed from the grand duchesses, who had telephoned regularly to enquire on his progress. During his time at the hospital the girls visited Dassel once or twice a week; Maria always remaining 'a little self-conscious', while the forthright Anastasia was 'freer, impish, with a very dry humour', and, as he noticed, adept too at cheating at board games with her sister. She also liked to 'tease in a childish way' which brought reproachful, warning glances from Maria.[54] (The two sisters certainly still squabbled, as Tatiana told Valentina Chebotareva: they often had cat fights when 'Nastasya gets mad and pulls [Maria's] hair and tears out clumps of it'.)[55] Once Dassel started feeling better the girls celebrated his recovery by posing for photographs with him. He noticed how 'terribly proud of her hospital' Anastasia was: 'she feels like she's half grown up, on an equal footing with her older sisters'. Maria too talked with concern about the war, about the hunger in the towns and of people not knowing if their fathers or brothers at the front were still alive.[56]

Captain Mikhail Geraschinevsky of the Keksholm Imperial Guard had similar warm memories of Feodorovsky Gorodok where he was a patient for thirteen months. He noticed that 'the girls came every day except when they did not behave'; this, it would seem, was their mother's most effective punishment.[57] He remembered their care over one wounded soldier in particular who had a bullet lodged in his skull and had lost his memory, and how they had patiently sat with him, asking him questions in an attempt to help bring back his memory.[58] When he was home from Stavka on visits, Alexey sometimes visited too – he chatted and played dice with the soldiers, demanding they tell him all about the war. Like the patients at the annexe, the wounded here all loved the imperial children for their open and friendly manner: 'we could not tell them apart from ordinary children', recalled Geraschinevsky. He noticed how Alexey and his sisters always talked very fast with them in Russian, thinking that perhaps this was because 'they were so rarely in contact with strangers that they were always in a hurry to tell them all they knew before they would be called away'.[59] Whenever Anastasia and Maria sat at soldiers' bedsides, playing board and card games with them, there was always one thing in particular they wanted to know. 'They would ask us to tell them stories of the people from outside life. They would call "outside life" anything that was not in the castle [sic] and would listen intently not to miss one word.'[60]

While the Romanov sisters might still have little experience of 'outside life' – the world outside definitely wanted to see more of them. On 11 August Alexandra informed Nicholas that their daughters had spent all day posing for a new set of official photographs 'for giving away to their committees'.[61] As it turned out these would be the last official pictures ever taken of the four sisters – by photographer Alexander Funk.[62] Released from their usual all-purpose plain skirts and blouses the girls dressed in their best satin tea dresses with embroidered panels of roses, wearing their pearl necklaces and gold bracelets. Anastasia not having passed the socially liberating age of sixteen still had her long hair loose, but her three older sisters all had theirs specially marcel-waved and dressed in chignons, most probably by Alexandra's hairdresser Delacroix. The girls and their brother were now also being regularly captured on newsreel footage, most of it during official appearances, which was released for public consumption. Watching such films was one of the few forms of entertainment they enjoyed during the war years, although they were occasionally allowed the comic antics of Max Linder and André Deed, and morale-raisers such as *Vasilii Ryabov*, a documentary film about a war hero shot by the Japanese in 1904. John Foster Fraser recalled how when he was in Petrograd in the summer of 1916, Nicholas had had a cinematograph operator put together some film of the imperial family 'in unimperial circumstances'.[63] Fraser had applied for a copy of the film to use in lectures when he went back to the UK and had had it run for him by Pathé Frères in their dark room in Moscow:

> There was the Emperor on a see-saw with his son, the Czarevitch. There was a tug-of-war between the daughters, the grand duchesses, and their imperial father; the emperor lost, and was hilariously dragged along the ground. There was a snow-fight in which the Emperor was routed by his girls. There were picnic scenes. There was dancing on the royal yacht Standart.[64]

In all, 3,000 feet (914 m) of film showed the Romanovs at their most happy and informal. Nicholas had no objection to Fraser using the film but Alexandra, conscious of public image-making and in particular the future dynastic role of the heir, most certainly did and insisted that those parts 'which were not imperial' should be cut before the film could be shown in London.

*

With Olga continuing to pine for the absent Mitya, Tatiana resisted the temptation of being sucked into the same kind of visible emotional turmoil when Volodya Kiknadze was wounded again – this time in the spine – and returned to the annexe in September 1916. In fact Tatiana only recorded his departure for recuperation in the Crimea a month later; she was sad but said nothing more. Olga, however, seemed happy to grasp at any small reminders of her precious Mitya, whose mother she met in September, a fact that made her feel 'terribly happy to have a little piece of him'.[65] She saw Mitya again briefly in October when he was passing through and appeared unexpectedly at the hospital. He looked well and suntanned and she was pleased to note that he had changed his hair parting, but she was reticent about saying more, even in her diary.

'We stood in the corridor and then sat. Darned socks.'[66] The strain of having to internalize so many of her feelings left her frustrated, which she dissipated back at home by indulging in childish play with her younger sisters, chasing them round indoors on bicycles, while her more composed sister sat reading a book quietly in a corner. Olga was approaching her twenty-first birthday, but life and love had, it seemed, passed her by. It was 'Quite a venerable age!' as Alexandra observed in a letter to Nicholas, but if only their girls might one day find 'the intense love and happiness you, my Angel, have given me these 22 years. It's such a rare thing nowadays, alas!'[67]

Perhaps Olga was able to take some consolation in a gift from Alexey at Stavka – a cat that he had taken pity on, notorious as he was for rescuing stray cats and dogs there.[68] He seemed to be doing famously over at Mogilev with Nicholas, proud to inform his mother that he had recently been given an award by the Serbs of 'a gold medal with the inscription "For Bravery"'. 'I deserved it in my battles with the tutors', he told her.[69] He found himself obliged to write to Alexandra in November to remind her that his pocket money was overdue:

> My darling dear, sweet beloved mummy. It's warm. Tomorrow
> I shall be up. The salary! I beg you!!!!! Nothing to stuff myself
> with!!! In 'Nain Jaune'* also bad luck! Let it be! Soon I shall be
> selling my dress, books, and, at last, shall die of starvation.[70]

After the final words Alexey added a drawing of a coffin. His cry of anguish must have crossed with a letter from his mother in which she enclosed ten roubles and wrote apologetically, 'To my dear Alexei. To my dear corporal. I am sending you your salary. I am sorry I forgot to enclose it. . . . Kiss you fondly your own Mama. Alexey was ecstatic – 'Rich!! Drink barley coffee.'[71]

*

---

* This was a favourite board game with Alexey and his sisters. The board has five sections, each representing a playing card, and the game is played with dice, chips and slips of paper. The objective is to dispose of the cards in your hand, playing them in simple numerical sequence from 1 (Ace) to King, picking up bonuses along the way.

During these last two years of war and her husband's frequent absences at Stavka, Alexandra had seen her daughters grow up considerably. It pleased her to tell Nicholas that Grigory approved:

Our Friend is so contented with our girlies, says they have gone through heavy 'courses' for their age and their souls have much developed – they are really great dears . . . They have shared all our emotions and it has taught them to see people with open eyes, so that it will be a great help to them later in life.[72]

The experience of war had, in Alexandra's view, 'ripened' their girls, though 'They are happily at times great babies – but have the insight and feelings of the soul of much wiser beings'.[73] With this in mind, on 11 December 1916, she took all four daughters south on the imperial train to visit the ancient Russian city of Novgorod, for centuries a focal point of Orthodoxy and Russian spirituality. Upon arriving they attended a two-hour mass at the Cathedral of St Sophia, then visited a nearby hospital, a museum of church treasures, and in the afternoon a provincial hospital and a shelter for refugee children. The final stop on their brief visit was the Desyatinny Convent – where Alexandra particularly wished to meet a renowned and much venerated seer, the *staritsa* Mariya Mikhailovna. Olga later described to Nicholas how they entered the old nun's cell:

it was very narrow and dark and only one small candle was burning, which immediately went out, so they lit some kind of kerosene lamp without a shade and a nun, her eyes watering, held it. The old woman was lying behind a kind of piece of patchwork that was full of holes on a wooden bed. She had huge iron fetters on her and her hands were so thin and dark, just like religious relics. It seems she is 107 years old. Hair very very thin, dishevelled and her face covered in wrinkles. Eyes bright and clear. She gave each of us a little icon and some communion bread and blessed us. She said something to mama, that it would all soon be over and everything would be all right.[74]

Alexandra too was very taken by the sweetness of the old woman: 'always works, goes about, sews for the convicts and soldiers without spectacles – never washes. And of course no smell, or feeling of dirt.' More importantly, the *staritsa* had addressed her personally, telling her – exactly as Olga recalled – that the war would be over soon: 'And you beautiful one, she had said several times, "don't fear the heavy cross"' – as though in prophecy of a personal test of faith to come.[75] Others later told a different tale: Anna Vyrubova was sure that 'as the tsarina approached, the old woman cried out: "Behold, the martyred Empress Alexandra Feodorovna!"' Iza Buxhoeveden remembered much the same, adding that 'Her Majesty seemed not to hear'.[76] After receiving the *staritsa*'s blessing and the gift of an apple for Nicholas and Alexey (which they later dutifully ate, on Alexandra's instructions, at Stavka) the tsaritsa left Novgorod feeling 'cheered and comforted', telling Nicholas that the visit to Novgorod had reinforced her faith in the simple people of Russia. 'Such love and warmth everywhere, feeling of God and your people, unity and purity of feelings – did me no end of good.'[77] Those in the entourage who had accompanied her returned with very different feelings. Having heard what the *staritsa* had said they 'came back depressed and apprehensive for they felt the reception was an omen'.[78]

Alexandra's devoutly Orthodox belief and the continuing wise counsel and prayers of Grigory undoubtedly sustained her at a time when her perilous state of health would have felled a far stronger woman. 'She believes in Rasputin; she regards him as a just man, a saint, persecuted by the calumnies of the Pharisees, like the victim of Calvary', observed the French ambassador Maurice Paléologue: 'she has made him her spiritual guide and refuge; her mediator with Christ, her witness and intercessor before God.'[79] But when the tsaritsa returned to Tsarskoe Selo in December 1916 it was in a state of total denial about the rapidly changing atmosphere in the capital 19 miles (30.5 km) away. Edith Almedingen recalled 'the feverish texture of the last weeks of 1916', of a city 'brooding over a darkly uncertain future'. With prophecies of disaster for Nicholas's command as the army continued to suffer catastrophic casualties, another harsh winter approached, 'under the most sinister auspices'.[80] Cold, war weariness, hunger, the grim reality of food shortages leading to profiteering and rumour of famine, were all fermenting discontent, soon made manifest in strikes and food riots. 'The streets were just queues full of ceaseless whimpering chatter', wrote Almedingen.[81]

But the loudest chatter of all around the city came in public discussion of the empress's continuing close relationship with Rasputin. At the annexe Valentina Chebotareva worried about how the unrelenting vilification of the tsaritsa was impacting on her daughters and possibly imperilling them. 'Olga is holding out with difficulty,' she wrote, '[she] is either more light hearted or has better control over herself. How difficult it is to see them after all I've heard. Is it really true that they are threatened by imminent danger?' Valentina had heard that 'the young people, the social revolutionaries are resolved to remove them all – and her!'[82] 'If the Emperor appeared on Red Square today,' predicted Ambassador Paléologue in his diary on 16 December 1916, 'he would be booed. The Empress would be torn to pieces.'[83] Elizaveta Naryshkina agreed with him: 'What a multitude of things are coming to an end, Ambassador! And such a bad end.'[84] To the superstitious Russian people the imperial family seemed increasingly shackled to the mystical chains of fate. It was a uniquely Russian view and one that had long dictated that everything about to be unleashed in Russia was a manifestation of God's inexorable will.

Chapter Seventeen

TERRIBLE THINGS ARE GOING ON
IN ST PETERSBURG

❦

'Father Grigory went missing last night. They are looking for him everywhere – it's absolutely dreadful.' Such was the state of foreboding at the Alexander Palace on 17 December 1916 that even Anastasia noted Rasputin's disappearance. The girls and their mother had sat up until midnight, 'all the time waiting for a telephone call'; it never came. So anxious were they that in the end 'the four of us slept together. God help us.'[1] The following day there was still no news, but word was already out, as Maria wrote in her diary, that 'they suspect Dmitri and Felix'.[2] 'We are sitting together – can imagine our feelings – thoughts', Alexandra wrote to Nicholas in her characteristic staccato style, adding that they knew this much: Grigory had been invited to Felix Yusupov's palace on the evening of the 16th. 'There had been a 'big scandal . . . big meeting, Dmitri, Purishkevitch* etc. all drunk. Police heard shots, Purishkevitch ran out screaming to the Police that our Friend was killed.' The police were out searching for Grigory now but Alexandra was already utterly distraught: 'I cannot and won't believe that he has been killed. God have mercy.'[3]

If the story was true, then all the tsaritsa's hopes for the family's

---

* Duma member Vladimir Purishkevich was a reactionary and monarchist, a member of an extremist group known as the Black Hundreds that sought to save the autocracy from ruination, as they saw it, by Rasputin.

continuing protection from harm were shipwrecked. Only a month previously she had written to Nicholas reiterating her absolute faith in Grigory's help and guidance during these difficult years:

> Remember that for your reign, Baby, and us you *need* the strength prayers and advice of our Friend . . . Ah Lovy, I pray so hard to God to make you feel and realize, that He is our caring, were He not here, I don't know what might not have happened. He saves us by His prayers and wise counsils [*sic*] and is our rock of faith and help.[4]

Final confirmation of Rasputin's death, when it came, could not have been altogether unexpected, even for Alexandra, for gossip in the capital about his rise from messianic faith healer to meddler in affairs of state, and now a morose drunk, had long since reached boiling point. Demoralized by Nicholas's decision to enter the war, which he had predicted would be disastrous for Russia, Rasputin had allowed his life to fall into disarray. He saw nothing but doom hanging over Russia as the war dragged on and sought refuge in an almost permanent state of alcoholic oblivion.[5] Stories of his debauched late-night drinking sessions at Donon's Restaurant and a string of fashionable hotels – the Astoria, the Rossiya and the Europe – or hanging out with the Massalsky's Gypsy Chorus at the Samarkand, were legion.[6] In his cups, Rasputin had loudly boasted of his influence over the tsaritsa: 'I can make her do anything', he was said to have bragged earlier that year. In response Nicholas had summoned Rasputin to Tsarskoe Selo and reprimanded him. Rasputin admitted that he had indeed been 'sinful', but it was clear that he was now out of control. The gossip of 'magic cures and gay carousals' that had first greeted his arrival in St Petersburg had now turned into a 'conflagration of rumour' in which he and the empress were seen as representing 'Dark Forces' that were threatening to engulf Russia.[7] Alexandra was talked of as being 'a go-between in traitorous intrigues with the Germans' and Rasputin accused of being a German spy 'who had wormed his way into the confidence of the Tsarina for the purpose of obtaining military secrets'.[8] Such was the level of seething resentment levelled at the empress by the end of 1916 that members of the imperial family were openly suggesting she be sent to a remote convent for the sake of the country – and her own sanity. But first and foremost Rasputin had to be got rid of.

As they waited for news at the Alexander Palace, the girls and Alexandra's two closest friends – Anna Vyrubova and Lili Dehn – gathered round the despairing empress. The following night Tatiana and Olga slept in their mother's room. And then, on the 19th, they had 'confirmation that Father Grigory has been murdered, most probably by Dmitri, and thrown from the Krestovsky bridge', as Olga wrote in her diary. 'They found him in the water. So awful and can't bear to write about it. We sat drinking tea with Lili and Anna and the whole time felt Father Grigory among us.'[9]

One of the ADCs on duty at the time recalled the impact of the news on the grand duchesses:

> There, upstairs, in one of their modest bedrooms, the four of them sat on the sofa, huddled up closely together. They were cold and visibly terribly upset, but for the whole of that long evening, the name of Rasputin was never uttered in front of me . . .
> They were in pain, because the man was no longer among the living, but also because they sensed that, with his murder, something terrible and undeserved had started for their mother, their father and themselves, and that it was moving relentlessly towards them.[10]

At 6 p.m. on the evening of the 19th Nicholas arrived in haste from Stavka with Alexey, prompted by an urgent telegram he had received from his wife telling him that 'There is danger that these two boys are organizing something still worse' – a *coup d'état*, with the connivance of others in the Romanov family and in tandem with right-wing monarchists in the Duma.[11] Rumour had been abroad for some time that Dmitri Pavlovich and his clubbing crony Felix Yusupov were involved. English nurse Dorothy Seymour, at the Anglo-Russian Hospital, had met Dmitri several times socially and remembered him as 'beautiful to behold, vastly conceited, but superb in glorious youth and dash'. On the evening of 13 December, Dmitri had talked to Dorothy over dinner 'of many intrigues' and she had gathered that 'something was afoot'.[*12]

Details soon emerged that Dmitri, Yusupov and fellow conspirator Purishkevich had lured Rasputin to Felix's palace on the Moika at around midnight on the evening of Friday 16 December. Yusupov had picked Rasputin up from his flat on Gorokhovaya ulitsa and driven him there. In a basement dining room, he had plied Rasputin with booze and cream cakes sprinkled with cyanide. Incredulous that the poison failed to do its work and increasingly frantic that their assassination plot would fail, Yusupov had then shot Rasputin in the back with Dmitri Pavlovich's Browning revolver. But Rasputin still refused to die; it took two more bullets from Purishkevich (the first missed, the second hit Rasputin in the torso) before a fourth and fatal shot to the forehead finished him off.[13] Rasputin's body was then bundled into a piece of cloth, tied up with rope and taken in Dmitri Pavlovich's car to Petrovsky Island, where it was consigned to the Malaya Nevka through a gap in the ice.[14] At 6 that morning Dorothy Seymour recalled that Dmitri Pavlovich 'in mad spirits' had rushed into the Anglo-Russian Hospital with Yusupov to have a wound dressed in Yusupov's neck.[15]

After the frozen, mangled body was hauled out of the river and an autopsy performed it was reclaimed by the Romanovs. It was taken for burial in secret in the Alexander Park, close by the partially constructed northern wall of the new Church of St Serafim, which Anna Vyrubova was funding with the compensation monies from her accident. When Nicholas, Alexandra and their daughters arrived for the funeral at 9 a.m. on the morning of 21 December, Rasputin's zinc coffin had already been closed and lowered into the grave.[†16] After joining the officiating priest in prayers, each of them dropped white flowers on the coffin and then silently departed.[17] In Petrograd

---

* The French ambassador Maurice Paléologue noted at the time that several of the grand dukes, including Grand Duchess Vladimir's three sons and Grand Duke Nikolay (whom Nicholas had deposed as Commander-in-Chief) were 'talking of nothing less than saving tsarism by a change of sovereign'. The plan as he heard it was that Nicholas would be forced to abdicate in favour of Alexey with Nikolay Nikolaevich as regent. And Alexandra would be 'shut up in a nunnery'.

† Alexey was confined to bed at the time with stomach pains and did not attend.

meanwhile people were rejoicing on the streets. 'A dog's death for a dog', they shouted and – hailing Dmitri Pavlovich as a national hero – lit candles before the icons of St Dimitri in all the churches to give thanks for his gallant act of patriotism. Before Nicholas had even arrived back from Stavka, Alexandra had had Dmitri illegally placed under house arrest; her husband maintained this tough line, rejecting pleas of leniency from his royal relatives. 'No one has the right to murder', he responded fiercely to their plea for leniency. 'I know that many will have this on their conscience, as Dmitri Pavlovich is not the only one involved. I am astonished at your appeal to me.'[18] He immediately ordered Dmitri back to the army – at Qazvin on the Persian front.[19] Felix Yusupov was exiled to his estate 800 miles (1,300 km) south in the province of Kursk.

Alexandra's response to the savage murder of her wise counsellor was plain for all to see. 'Her agonized features betrayed, in spite of all her efforts, how terribly she was suffering', remembered Pierre Gilliard. 'Her grief was inconsolable. Her idol had been shattered. He who alone could save her son had been slain. Now that he was gone, any misfortune, any catastrophe was possible.'[20] Anna Vyrubova later described the empress's state of mind at that time as 'nearer the insanity they accused her of than she had ever been before'.[21] 'My heart is broken', Alexandra told Lili Dehn. 'Veronal* is keeping me up. I'm literally saturated with it.'[22]

Rasputin's death cast its terrible pall over the whole family. Olga was profoundly disturbed by it, as she told Valentina Chebotareva not long afterwards: 'Maybe it was necessary to kill him, but not in such a terrible way', a remark that suggests she had by now realized the full extent of his baleful influence over their mother. Olga was appalled that two members of her own close family were involved: 'one is ashamed to admit they are relatives', she said. Dmitri's role must have been particularly wounding for all of them.[23] General Spiridovich later claimed that Olga had always 'instinctively sensed there was something bad in Rasputin'.[24] But what troubled her even more was this: 'why has the feeling in the country changed against my father?' No one could give her an adequate explanation and she continued to appear 'filled with a growing anxiety'.[25]

---

* A popular and widely available barbiturate, used for insomnia.

Tatiana also took Rasputin's death very hard but kept her feelings to herself, treasuring the notebook in which she had written down extracts from his letters and telegrams as well as his pronouncements on various religious topics.[26] Her mother meanwhile clung to the bloodstained blue satin tunic that her beloved Grigory had been wearing on the night of his 'martyrdom', 'preserving it piously as a relic, a *palladium** on which the fate of her dynasty hangs'.[27] It was left to Dr Botkin to voice what many privately were thinking: 'Rasputin dead will be worse than Rasputin alive', he told his children; adding prophetically that what Dmitri Pavlovich and Yusupov had done was 'to fire the first shot of the revolution'.[28] 'Lord have mercy and save us this New Year 1917', was all Olga could think of as that difficult year came to an end.[29]

*

January opened on a sombre note for the Romanov family and their entourage. They attended a prayer service together at midnight and exchanged New Year greetings but Pierre Gilliard had no doubt that they had all entered a period of 'dreadful waiting for the disaster which there was no escaping'.[30] A last gasp of imperial ceremonial came during an official visit by Prince Carol of Romania and his parents, their country having finally entered the war on the side of Russia and its allies.[31] Alexandra decided to take advantage of a rare state dinner – held in Carol's honour on the 9th – to present Maria officially to the court. She and Nicholas still viewed their third daughter, albeit affectionately, as chubby and gawky; the previous evening the girls had all been trying on dresses and according to Tatiana, 'Maria had got so fat that she couldn't get into any of them'.[32] She had long taken her family's teasing with good heart and this occasion was no exception. 'She looked extremely pretty in her pale blue dress, wearing the diamonds that her parents gave to each of their daughters on her sixteenth birthday', recalled Iza Buxhoeveden, but unfortunately, 'Poor Maria slipped in her new high heels and fell when entering the dining hall on the arm of a tall Grand Duke'. 'On hearing the noise, the Emperor remarked

---

* A source of protection.

jokingly, "Of course, fat Marie."' After her sister had 'fallen over with a thud with all her might', as Tatiana recalled, she had sat there on the floor laughing 'to the point of embarrassment'. Indeed the whole occasion turned out to be quite amusing: 'After dinner papa slipped on the parquet floor, [and] one of the Romanians knocked over a cup of coffee.'[33] But it had all washed over Olga, who, still thinking of Mitya, had noted her former patient's twenty-fourth birthday in her diary. Valentina Chebotareva thought she had seemed particularly sad of late. 'Is that the fault of your guests?' Chebotareva had asked her. 'Oh, there's no threat of that now, while there's a war', Olga had added, alluding to the unspoken suggestion of a marriage.[34] Elizaveta Naryshkina had rather hoped that an engagement between Olga and Carol still might take place, for she found him 'charming'. But Anna Vyrubova had noticed that Prince Carol's 'young man's fancy [had] rested on Marie' at that dinner, despite her clumsy behaviour. Before he left for Moscow on 26th January, Carol made a formal proposal for her hand. Nicholas had 'good-naturedly laughed the Prince's proposal aside', saying that his seventeen-year-old daughter 'was nothing more than a schoolgirl'.[35] At Carol's final lunch with the family Elizaveta Naryshkina noticed how markedly the four sisters kept their distance from him and only Nicholas made any effort at conversation.[36] Behind the scenes, however, Carol's mother, Marie – now Queen of Romania – had had her hopes renewed the day of their departure from Russia, when she and her husband King Ferdinand had received 'ciphered telegrams from Russia'. 'It seems they still think about a marriage for Carol with one of Nicky's daughters,' she confided to her diary. She was surprised and gratified; 'one would have thought about it now when our poor little Country hardly exists, now when we have not even a house of our own left.* But on the whole it is flattering and might be taken as a good sign!' The only problem was Carol himself: 'I do not at all know if he wants to marry.'[37]

Two of the last private visitors to the Alexander Palace were the head of the Anglo-Russian Hospital, Lady Sybil Grey, and Dorothy Seymour. Having been in Petrograd since September 1916, Dorothy

---

* The Romanian royal family had been forced by the German invasion to leave the capital, Bucharest, in December 1916 for Iasi in the north-east.

had been excited to be sent an official invitation to meet the tsaritsa, telling her mother that 'It will be too annoying if they start a revolution before I have time to get down to see her'.[38] When she and Lady Sybil took the train out to Tsarskoe Selo, Dorothy found the whole experience, despite the difficult times, an 'amazing fairytale'.[39] They were met at the station 'by gorgeous officials, footmen, horses all white and prancing – Great State – At the palace door two glorious footmen with huge orange and red ostrich plumes on their heads.'[40] After being entertained to lunch by Iza Buxhoeveden and Nastenka Hendrikova the two women were taken 'through miles of palace and a huge banqueting room' to a door that was opened 'by a huge negro' and ushered in to meet Alexandra and Olga. The empress, wearing purple velvet and 'huge amethysts', seemed to Dorothy 'quite lovely' and 'wonderfully graceful'. But there was something haunted about her 'desperately sad eyes'. Olga, in her nurse's uniform, seemed very plain in comparison. 'Pretty eyes. Nice little thing, very pleasant and informal', recalled Dorothy. They sat and talked for almost two hours, at the end of which she came away impressed by Olga's spirituality and sensitivity. She was 'evidently a pacifist, and the war and its horrors [were] on her nerves'. Dorothy left with a sense of sadness and the overwhelming feeling that the room they had sat in – and the palace itself – were already 'heavy with tragedy'.[41]

*

The spectre of illness continued to dog the imperial family that winter; Alexandra was still suffering with her heart and legs and Alexey had recurring pain in his arm, and then swollen glands. Shortly after Dorothy Seymour's visit the still sickly Olga had gone down with a painful ear infection. The two invalids had been sharing the same room when, on 11 February, a couple of young cadets whom Alexey had befriended at Stavka had been brought in to play with him. Olga had remained in the room with them, and Alexandra had noticed that one of the boys was coughing; the following day he went down with measles.[42] By 21 February, Olga and Alexey both seemed unwell, but the doctors assured Nicholas that it was not measles, and he began packing for a return to Stavka. He had not wanted to leave Tsarskoe at this time, mindful of the gathering danger since Rasputin's murder of a possible coup against him. The warnings had been coming thick and fast from his own relatives, including his brother-in-law Sandro, who visited and begged Nicholas to concede to a proper, democratically elected Duma free of imperial interference; 'with a few words and a stroke of the pen, you could calm everything and give the country what it yearns for', he urged. To Sandro it was clear that Alexandra's constant meddling in affairs of state was 'dragging her husband into an abyss'. Even now she bridled at any talk of capitulation: 'Nicky is an autocrat. How could he share his divine right with a parliament?'[43] And now Nicholas's brother Grand Duke Mikhail was warning of imminent mutiny in the army if the tsar did not immediately return to Stavka. Nicholas listened to Sandro passively, as he always did, lighting one cigarette after another. He had no stomach for a fight, either with his relatives, his wife, or his government. His life was in the hands of God and he had long since abandoned all responsibility for it. Reluctant to leave the family, he nevertheless prepared to go. A highly strained atmosphere prevailed over lunch the day he left. Everyone seemed anxious and 'wanted to think more than talk'.[44]

No sooner had a drawn and hollow-cheeked Nicholas said farewell than it became clear not only that Olga and Alexey were coming down with measles, but that Anna Vyrubova too had been infected – and seriously so. On 24 February Tatiana joined them in the darkened sickroom, where their devoted mother wearing her Red Cross uniform nursed her three children.[45] All had terrible coughs and were suffering from headaches and earache as their temperatures rocketed.[46] Despite the seriousness of their condition Nicholas was already discussing the children's recuperation with Dr Feoderov at Stavka. He wrote and told Alexandra that the doctor considered it 'absolutely necessary for the children and Aleksei especially [to have] a change of climate after their complete recovery'. Perhaps, soon after Easter, he told Alexandra, they could take them to the Crimea? 'We will think it over quietly when I come back. . . . I won't be long away – only to put all things as much as possible to rights here and then my duty will be done.'[47]

*

In the grip of deep snow and remorseless sub-zero temperatures, Petrograd that winter of 1916–17 was a desperate place. The transport system was in disarray due to fuel shortages; a lack of labour, horses and implements was further affecting the production and transportation of food. There was no flour, and long queues could be seen everywhere for what little bread was baked; virtually no meat was to be had and sugar and butter could only be got on the black market. There was no wood for fuel and the streets were piled high with garbage. Talk of revolution was on everyone's lips. Petrograd was doomed, a *Chertograd* – 'Devil's town', as poet Zinaida Gippius wrote in her diary:

> The most frightening and crude rumours are disturbing the masses. It is a charged, neurotic atmosphere. You can almost hear the laments of the refugees in the air. Each day is drenched in catastrophes. What is going to happen? It is intolerable. 'Things cannot go on like this' an old cab-driver says.[48]

The 'first claps of thunder' were heard with riots and protests in the workers' districts of the Vyborg Side and Vasilievsky Island.[49] Soon hungry crowds were marching along the Nevsky prospekt as bakeries and food shops came under attack. By 25 February, and with a lift in the temperature, street disturbances were becoming widespread and violent, with acts of arson, looting and the lynching of policemen. The capital was seething with strikers. At the Alexandra Palace the tsaritsa remained convinced that none of this posed a serious threat. Bread rationing was all that was needed to bring the situation under control. 'It's a hooligan movement,' she wrote to Nicholas, 'young boys and girls running about and screaming that they have no bread; only to excite . . . if it were very cold they would probably stay indoors. But this will all pass and quieten down, if the Duma would only behave itself.'[50] Meanwhile she was proud to tell him that his two youngest daughters 'call themselves the sick-nurses – *sidelki* – chatter without end and telephone right and left. They are most useful.' The lift at the palace had stopped working and Alexandra was increasingly relying on Maria to do the running around that she could not manage, affectionately calling her 'my legs'.[51] But she was expecting both her younger daughters inevitably to succumb to the measles. Alexey was now covered in one great ugly rash, 'like a leopard – Olga has flat spots, Ania too all over, all their eyes and [their] throats ache'.[52]

By the 27th, a day of 'street brawls, bombs, shootings and numerous wounded and dead', shouts of 'Bread, victory!' and 'Down with the War!' could be heard everywhere on the streets of Petrograd.[53] Nicholas could not leave Stavka and meanwhile his children's temperatures had reached 39 degrees C (over 102 degrees F) or more.[54] With measles spreading at the Alexander Palace and unrest raging in the city, Alexandra struggled to maintain her equilibrium, still convinced that the disturbances, like the sickness, would pass; but the strain of it was ageing her and her hair was turning grey. 'Terrible things are going on in St Petersburg', she confided in her diary, shocked to hear that regiments she had always thought loyal to the throne – the Preobrazhensk and the Pavlovsk Guards – were even now mutinying.[55] She was therefore greatly cheered by the arrival of Lili Dehn, who had bravely come out to Tsarskoe Selo to offer moral support, leaving her son behind in the city with her maid. But by 10 p.m. that evening a message came from Duma chairman Mikhail Rodzianko advising that Alexandra and the children be evacuated from the Alexander Palace immediately. 'When the house is burning,' he had told Count Benkendorf, Minister of the Court, 'you take the children to safety, even if they are ill.'[56] Benkendorf immediately telephoned Mogilev and informed Nicholas. But the tsar was adamant: his family should stay put and wait until he could get back, which he hoped would be on the morning of 1 March.[57]

*

Many years later, Meriel Buchanan recalled the 'deathlike stillness of Petrograd' on the eve of revolution. 'There were the same wide streets we knew so well, the same palaces, the same golden spires and domes rising out of the pearl-coloured mists, and yet they all seemed unreal and strange as if I had never seen them before. And everywhere emptiness: no long lines of carts, no crowded trams, no *izvostchiks*,* no private

---

* An *izvozchik* is a driver of a horse-drawn cab, familiar all over Russian cities at the time.

carriages, no policemen.'[58] The following morning, 28 February, as rioting continued across the city, out at an Alexander Park deep in snow and in temperatures of -37.2 C (-35 F) the sound of intermittent firing and shouting could be heard, coming from the Tsarskoe Selo barracks. What had started as a group of renegade drunken soldiers firing in the air soon developed into a mutiny by most of the garrison and reserve battalions. Soon rifle fire was joined by the sound of military bands playing the *Marseillaise* to cheers of 'Hurrah!' The imperial family meanwhile had little protection beyond a few remaining loyal troops camped outside in the park in the bitter cold.

Seeing how desperate the situation was becoming, Lili offered to stay with Alexandra, having asked Nikolay Sablin and his wife, who lived in the same block of flats in the city, to take care of her son.[59] The sick children 'looked almost like corpses', she recalled. From their beds they could clearly hear the firing in town and asked her what the shooting was about. Lili pretended not to know; such noises always sound louder in the frost, she told them. 'But are you sure that's what it is?' Olga asked. 'You can see how even Mama is nervous, we are so worried about her sick heart. She is overtaxing herself too much. You absolutely must tell her to rest.'[60] It was hard maintaining an air of calm but Alexandra was adamant that she did not want the children to know anything until it was 'impossible to keep the truth from them'. That day she telephoned Bibi at the annexe, warning her of the dangerous situation now prevailing: 'It's all finished, everyone has gone over to their [the revolutionaries'] side. Pray for us, we need nothing more. As a last resort we are prepared to take the children away, even the sick ones . . . All three are in the same room in complete darkness, they are suffering greatly, only the little ones know everything.' Hearing this from Bibi, Valentina Chebotareva discussed the situation with her wounded patients. They all believed that Nicholas would 'uphold Rodzianko's government' when he returned. 'Salvation is possible,' Valentina wrote in her diary that night, 'but I am full of doubt.'[61]

At 10 p.m. on the evening of the 28th, anxious to thank the loyal troops still guarding them in the bitter cold outside, Alexandra emerged from the Alexander Palace holding Maria's hand and walked out to speak to them, the only light coming from the glow of fire on the horizon. Lili Dehn watched Alexandra from a window, 'wrapped in furs, walking from one man to another, utterly fearless of her safety'.[62] All was strangely silent in the park except for gunfire in the distance and the sound of boots crunching on snow as she and Maria 'passed like dark shadows from line to line', acknowledging the soldiers with a smile.[63] Many called out greetings and Alexandra stopped to talk to them, particularly the officers of the Tsar's Escort, who formed a protective circle round her as she returned to the palace. 'For God's sake,' she said before leaving them, insisting that they go inside and warm themselves, 'I ask all of you not to let any blood be shed on our account!'[64]

That night, Alexandra decided that Maria should sleep in her bed. In fact, one of the girls had slept in her room with her ever since Nicholas had left for Stavka, as they were all fearful of leaving their mother alone.[65] A bed was made up for Lili on the sofa in the girls' drawing room which connected directly into their bedrooms, where she also could be on hand if needed. Anastasia got the room ready, thoughtfully putting a nightgown for Lili on the bed, setting an icon on the bedside table and even a photo of Lili's son Titi from their own collection.[66] 'Don't take off your corset', Alexandra said, instructing both Lili and Iza Buxhoeveden to be ready to leave at a moment's notice. 'You don't know what might happen. The emperor will arrive tomorrow between 5 and 7 and we must be ready to meet him.'[67] That night, Lili and Anastasia found it hard to sleep; they got up to look out of the window and saw that a large gun had been positioned in the courtyard. 'How astonished Papa will be!' Anastasia had remarked, open-mouthed.[68]

Many of the palace servants fled that night, but in Petrograd, Duma chairman Mikhail Rodzianko was still managing to maintain order and the situation in the city seemed to have eased. 'They say that they've gone to Tsarskoe Selo to inform the empress of a change of government', wrote Elizaveta Naryshkina, who was currently trapped in the city. 'Full revolution has taken place peacefully.'[69] But this was not entirely so: revolutionary groups even now were heading for the Alexander Palace, intent on seizing Alexandra. Count Benkendorf surveyed the remaining troops he could count on: one battalion of the Guards Equipage, two battalions of the Combined

Regiment of Imperial Guards; two squadrons of the Tsar's Escort, one company of the Railway Regiment and one battery of field artillery brought over from Pavlovsk.[70]

Early in the morning of 1 March everyone was awake and anxiously expecting the tsar's arrival at any moment. But he didn't come. At Malaya-Vishera, a hundred miles (160 km) south in Novgorod province, insurgents on the line had turned his train back; the route to Petrograd and Tsarskoe Selo beyond was closed. The imperial train was instead diverted to Pskov. Here, unexpectedly, Nicholas was met by a deputation from the Duma who had come out by special train with one thought in mind: to force him to abdicate.

At Tsarskoe Selo a frantic Alexandra was firing off letters and telegrams to no avail; no reply came. And now Anastasia had gone down with measles too. Alexandra was intensely grateful for the support of Lili Dehn – 'an angel', who was 'inseparable' from her. Lili did her best to comfort Anastasia, who 'could not reconcile herself to the idea of being ill and kept crying and saying "Please don't keep me in bed"'.[71] 'God for sure sent it, for the good somehow,' Alix wrote to Nicky of their children's suffering. Later that same day she scrawled another letter: 'Your little family is worthy of you, so brave and quiet.'[72]

For seventy-two hours the household at Tsarskoe Selo waited. 'No news of the Emperor; we don't know where he is', wrote Elizaveta Naryshkina.[73] Meanwhile, over in a railway siding at Pskov, 183 miles (294.5 km) to the south-west, Nicholas had on 2 March abdicated the throne, not just for himself but his son also. His decision, it later emerged, was based on a candid conversation he had had with Alexey's paediatrician Dr Feodorov, about the nature of his son's condition. Feodorov had told him that although Alexey might live for some time, his condition was incurable. Nicholas knew that if his son became tsar under the required regency of his brother Grand Duke Mikhail, he and Alexandra, as former monarchs, would not be allowed to remain in Russia and would be sent into exile. Neither of them could contemplate separation from their son and so he abdicated for both of them.* But he also did so in the

---

*   As next in line Mikhail was offered the throne the following day but he declined to take it.

genuine hope that his abdication was the best thing both for Russia and the honour of the army – and that it might defuse the volatile political situation.[74] At Mogilev Nicholas had been joined by his mother Maria Feodorovna, who had travelled up from Kiev where she was now living. With the millstone of duty lifted from him, Nicholas sat quietly and dined with his mama, went for a walk, packed his things and after dinner played a game of bezique with her. He signed the declaration of abdication at 3 o'clock that afternoon and finally left Pskov at 1 a.m. 'with the heavy sense of what I had lived through', heading back to Mogilev to bid farewell to his military staff. All around him he saw nothing but 'betrayal, cowardice and deception'; there was only one place he wanted to be and that was with his family.[75] 'Now that I am about to be freed of my responsibilities to the nation,' Nicholas had remarked to the commander of the Tsar's Escort, Count Grabbe, 'perhaps I can fulfill my life's desire – to have a farm, somewhere in England.'[76]

Back at the Alexander Palace the tsaritsa was still fervently praying for news of her husband. Meanwhile the first rumours began to reach the capital that Nicholas had abdicated. Shortly afterwards, the Guards Equipage, on the orders of their commander Grand Duke Kirill, were ordered to leave the palace, for Kirill had thrown in his lot with the new provisional government. The tsaritsa watched as the naval colours – so familiar from the family's many trips on the *Shtandart* – were marched away. But as the Guards left, others such as Rita Khitrovo, one of Olga and Tatiana's fellow nurses from the annexe, were arriving to offer help. Even some servants who had been stranded in the city had managed to make their way back to Tsarskoe Selo on foot. Outside their windows the children were greatly comforted to see their 'dear Cossacks . . . with their horses, standing around their officers and singing their songs in low voices', as Maria told her father.[77] But it was a terrible time for her and her mother as they watched over the sickroom: Olga and Tatiana were very much worse, with abscesses in their ears. Tatiana had gone temporarily deaf, and her head was swathed in bandages. Olga had been coughing so much that she had completely lost her voice.[78]

Prime Minister Rodzianko continued to urge that the children be got away to safety but Alexandra was adamant: 'We're not going anywhere. Let them do what they will, but I won't leave and will not destroy the children [by doing so].'[79] Instead, she asked Father Belyaev of the Feodorovsky Sobor to bring the icon of Our Lady of the Sign from the Znamenie Church and hold prayers upstairs for the children: 'We put the Icon on the table that had been prepared for it. The room was so dark that I could hardly see those present in it. The empress, dressed as a nurse was standing beside the bed of the heir . . . a few thin candles were lit before the icon', the priest recalled.[80] In the afternoon, Ioannchik's wife, Princess Helena, bravely made her way over to see Alexandra. She was shocked at how the last two weeks had dramatically aged her. There was no doubting her courage and she found her 'extremely dignified':

> Even though she had gloomy forebodings about the fate of her imperial spouse and fear for her children, the empress impressed us with her sangfroid. This composure may have been a characteristic of the English blood that flowed in her veins. During these tragic hours she did not once show any sign of weakness, and like any wife and mother she lived through those minutes as a mother and woman would.[81]

'Oh my, our 4 invalids go on suffering,' Alexandra wrote to Nicholas that day, not knowing if her letter would reach him, 'only Marie is up and about – calm and my helper growing thin as [she] shows nothing of how she feels.' There is no doubt, however, that recent events had finally cowed Alexandra's combativeness. A new note of meekness was to be discerned, as she assured Nicholas that 'Sunny blesses, prays, bears up by faith and her martyr's [Grigory's] sake . . . she assists into *nothing* . . . She is now only a mother with ill children.'[82]

On the afternoon of 3 March it was Grand Duke Pavel (still resident at his home at Tsarskoe Selo) who arrived finally bringing news of Nicholas. 'I heard that N[icky] has abdicated, and also for Baby', Alexandra noted curtly in her diary.[83] She was shocked but remained outwardly calm; in private she wept bitterly. Sitting with the grand duke over supper, she talked of a new and different future. 'I may no longer be Empress, but I still remain a Sister of Mercy', she told him. 'I shall look after the children, the hospital, and we will go to the Crimea.'[84] In the midst of this crushing news Maria remained the only one of the five children still not affected by sickness, but even she was convinced, as she told Iza Buxhoeveden, that she was 'in for it'.[85] It was hard for her to keep her mother going on her own and protect her from harm, as all four sisters had done so conscientiously all their adult lives.

That afternoon Alexandra received Viktor Zborovsky, one of the most trusted officers of the Escort guarding the palace. She thanked him for his continuing loyalty and reiterated that no blood should be shed in protecting the family. As Zborovsky was leaving Maria stopped him and they ended up chatting for an hour. He was deeply moved by the great change in her during recent days. 'Nothing remained of the former young girl', he told his colleagues later; in front of him stood 'a serious sensible woman, who was responding in a deep and thoughtful way to what was going on.'[86] But the strain of it all was telling on her. That evening Lili heard the sound of weeping and went to look: 'In one corner of the room crouched the Grand Duchess Marie. She was as pale as her mother. She *knew* all! . . . She was so young, so helpless, so hurt.'[87] 'Mama cried terribly', Maria told Anna Vyrubova, when she visited her sickbed to talk about her father's abdication. 'I cried too, but not more than I could help, for poor Mama's sake'; but Maria was terrified that they would come and take her mother away.[88] Such 'proud fortitude' was but one instance of what Anna later recalled was 'shown all through those days of wreck and disaster by the Empress and her children'.[89]

Cornet S. V. Markov was another loyal officer allowed in to see Alexandra that day. He entered via the basement, which he remembered was full of soldiers of the Combined Regiments taking a break from the cold, and was taken upstairs through many rooms still full of the lingering fragrance of flowers. In the children's apartments he came to a door on which was fixed a piece of paper on which was written 'No entry without the permission of Olga and Tatiana'.[90] A big table in the middle of the room was covered with French and English magazines, scissors and water-colours, where Alexey had been cutting out and pasting pictures before his illness. Alexandra came in and surprised him by saying, 'Hello dear little Markov.' She was dressed in her nurse's white, 'her sunken eyes very tired from sleepless nights and fear, expressive of unbearable suffering'. During their conversation she asked Markov to remove his imperial insignia – rather than have some drunken soldier on the street tear them from his jacket – and to tell his fellow officers to do likewise. She thanked them all for their loyalty and made the sign of the cross over him as he left.[91]

Alexandra was right to be fearful for the loyal troops still guarding her since they did so at increasing risk to themselves. They all took the news of the emperor's abdication very hard. None more so than Viktor Zborovsky: 'Something incomprehensible, savage, unreal had happened that was impossible to take in', he wrote in his diary on 4 March. 'The ground fell away from under one's feet . . . It had happened . . . and there was nothing! Empty, dark . . . It was as though the soul had taken flight from a still living body.'[92] For the last couple of days, in an attempt to demoralize those out at Tsarskoe Selo, a false rumour had been put about in Petrograd that the men of the Escort had defected. But this was far from the truth. When Alexandra at last made contact with Nicholas on the 4th one of the first to hear the news from her was Viktor Zborovsky. She wanted to reassure him that despite the pernicious rumours, she was in no doubt of the Escort's loyalty and that she and Nicholas 'were right to look upon the Cossacks as our true friends'. She also asked him, as she had Markov, to tell the officers of the Escort to remove their imperial insignia. 'Do this for me,' she urged, 'or I will once more be blamed for everything, and the children might suffer as a result.'[93] The men of the Escort took this instruction hard when Zborovsky brought it: for them it was a deeply dishonourable act and some of them wept and refused to comply: 'What kind of Russia is it without the tsar?' they asked.[94] Honour, for the Escort, died hard and they were prepared to defend theirs to the death.

On 5 March Princess Helena tried to telephone Alexandra at the palace, only to find that the lines had been cut. With no telephones, no trains to Tsarskoe Selo, palace supplies of food and wood dwindling, no electricity or running water, domestic staff defecting and a crowd of curious and increasingly belligerent onlookers gathering outside the palace gates, the situation was becoming very dangerous for Alexandra and the children: 'A curtain of bayonets separated the Imperial Family from the living world.'[95] Lili Dehn noticed that Alexandra was now sometimes smoking cigarettes to ease her stress. It wasn't until 5 March that Valentina Chebotareva at the annexe finally saw news of the abdication in the papers. 'At the hospital it is as silent as the grave', she noted. 'Everyone is shaken, downcast. Vera Ignatievna [Gedroits] was sobbing like a helpless child. We really were waiting for a constitutional monarchy and suddenly the throne has been handed to the people. In the future – a republic.'[96]

Alexandra was now urging all of her entourage that they had the right to leave if they so wished. But even Lili Dehn refused to desert her, insisting she would stay 'no matter what'.[97] She feared she would never see Titi again, nor her husband, who was away on a military mission to England, but she was determined not to desert her empress. Iza Buxhoeveden, Nastenka Hendrikova and Trina Schneider – as well as the ever-present Dr Botkin and Count and Countess Benkendorf – all rallied round as well. Anna Vyrubova was still lying ill in the other wing of the palace, but her moral support at this time was crucial, as too was that of Elizaveta Naryshkina, who had at last managed to get back to Tsarskoe Selo from Petrograd. 'Oh such emotional turmoil!' she wrote of their reunion:

> I was with the empress: calm, very sweet, much largesse of spirit. It strikes me that she has not quite grasped that what has happened cannot be put right. She told me: 'God is stronger than people.' They have all endured extreme danger and now it is as though order has been reestablished. She does not understand that there are consequences to all mistakes, and especially her own . . . the condition of the sick children is still serious.[98]

It was around 7 March that Alexandra regretfully decided, on the urging of Lili Dehn, to begin the systematic destruction of all her letters and diaries.[99] Lili was worried that if they fell into the wrong hands they might easily be misinterpreted, or worse be deemed treasonous and used against her and Nicholas. And so, over the course of the following week, the two women sat together day after day in the girls' sitting room, taking great piles of letters from a huge oak chest in which Alexandra had stored them and burning them in the fireplace. All of Alexandra's most treasured letters from her grandmother Queen Victoria, her brother Ernie and many other relatives were ruthlessly consigned to the flames, but the hardest of all to part with were undoubtedly the hundreds of letters she had received from Nicky since the day of their engagement in 1894. Occasionally she stopped to read parts of them and weep before tossing them into the flames. And then too there were her many diaries, satin-covered ones dating from her childhood and the later leather-bound ones, which even now she was still keeping.* Everything remorselessly was turned to ash – with one exception: Nicky's letters to her from Stavka during the war years, which Alexandra was determined to preserve as proof, should it be needed, of their undying loyalty to Russia.[100] But on Thursday the 9th one of Alexandra's maids came in and 'begged us to discontinue' as Lili recalled. The half-charred papers were being carried up the chimney and settling on the ground outside where some of the men were picking them up and reading them.[101]

In the sickroom, signs of recovery among the children were slow to come. Although Alexey was improving and his temperature dropping, Olga now was suffering from one of the complications of measles, encephalitis – inflammation of the brain – and Anastasia's temperature was worryingly high. And then on the evening of the 7th the inevitable happened: Maria began to feel unwell and soon was running a temperature of 39 degrees C (over 102 degrees F). '"Oh I did so want to be up when Papa comes," she kept on repeating, until high fever set in and she lost consciousness.'[102]

On Wednesday 8 March Alexandra finally received news of Nicholas from Count Benkendorf – that he was safe and back at Mogilev, and would be returning to the Alexander Palace the following morning. At midday, General Lavr Kornilov, Commander-in-Chief of the Petrograd military district, arrived in the company of Colonel Evgeny Kobylinsky, newly appointed head of the military garrison at Tsarskoe Selo. 'Kornilov announced that we are shut up

---

* Alexandra took her current diary with her to Tobolsk and continued writing it until the night before her death in July 1918. These diaries were recovered after the family were murdered and are now in the Russian State Archives, GARF.

. . . From now [we] are considered pris[oners] . . . may see nobody fr[om] outside', Alexandra noted dispassionately.[103] As Benkendorf understood it at the time, the imperial couple would only be under arrest until the children had recovered, after which 'the Emperor's family would be sent to Murmansk [an ice-free port on Russia's extreme north-west border] where a British cruiser would await them and take them to England'.[104] This was the hoped-for swift resolution to the problem of what to do with the former tsar, announced by the new Minister of Justice, Alexander Kerensky, in Moscow the previous day, and in response to an initial offer of help from King George V. 'I will never be the Marat of the Russian Revolution', Kerensky had grandly declared, but the hopes of a speedy and safe evacuation of the imperial family would soon prove to be a pipe dream.[105]

That morning Elizaveta Naryshkina had gone to church, during which the congregation had hissed when prayers were said for the tsar. When she got back to the palace Benkendorf told her:

> We are arrested. We do not have the right either to go out of the palace, or telephone; we are only allowed to write via the Central Committee. We are waiting for the Emperor. The Empress asked to have prayers said for the Emperor's return trip. Refused![106]

Those in the entourage who wanted to leave, Kornilov told Alexandra that morning, had only forty-eight hours to do so; after that they too would be under house arrest. Many left hurriedly soon after in a 'veritable orgy of cowardice and stupidity, and a sickening display of shabby, contemptible disloyalty', recalled Dr Botkin's son Gleb.[107] Dr Ostrogorsky, the children's paediatrician, sent word that he 'found the roads too dirty' to get out to Tsarskoe Selo any more.[108] Much to his dismay Sydney Gibbes, who had been in Petrograd for the day on the 10th – his day off – was not allowed back into the palace. Even worse, however, was the news that the men of the Escort and Combined Regiments were to be sent away and replaced by 300 troops of the 1st Rifles, sent by the provisional government.

Although Maria already knew the truth, it was no longer possible for Alexandra to keep the news of their father's abdication from the other children. They took it calmly, although Anastasia resented the fact that her mother and Lili had not told them, but 'as Papa is coming, nothing else matters'.[109] Tatiana was still so deaf from the otitis brought on by her measles that Iza Buxhoeveden noticed that 'she could not follow her mother's rapid words, her voice rendered husky with emotion. Her sisters had to write down the details before she could understand.'[110] It was a bewildered and downcast Alexey, now on the mend, who was full of questions. 'Shall I never go to G.H.Q. again with Papa?' he asked his mother. 'Shan't I see my regiments and my soldiers? . . . And the yacht, and all my friends on board – shall we never go yachting any more?' 'No,' she replied. 'We shall never see the "Shtandart" . . . It doesn't belong to us now.'[111] The boy was concerned too about the future of the autocracy. 'But who's going to be tsar, then?' he quizzed Pierre Gilliard. When his tutor responded that probably no one would be, it was only logical that he should then ask: 'But if there isn't a Tsar, who's going to govern Russia?'[112]

Wednesday 8 March was an intensely melancholy day for Alexandra, for the men of the Escort were to leave that afternoon. They had all spent a sleepless night pondering their enforced departure and were intensely gloomy, unable to 'understand or believe that the situation was hopeless'.[113] Shortly before they left, the Escort asked Viktor Zborovsky to pass on their loyal sentiments to the empress. It was with profound regret, Viktor told her, that they had no option but to obey the order to leave. Alexandra asked him to thank all the men on behalf of herself and the children for their loyal service. 'I ask you all to refrain from any kind of independent action that might only delay the emperor's arrival and affect the fate of the children', she said, adding, 'Starting with myself, we must all submit to fate.'[114]

Zborovsky had found it hard to speak when Alexandra handed him some small icons – her farewell gift to the Escort. She then took him through to Olga and Tatiana's room where both were still ill in bed. It took all Zborovsky's powers of self-control not to break down in front of the children. Silently, he bowed low to them, and then to Alexandra and kissed her hand. 'I can't remember how I left', he wrote in his diary later, 'I went without turning round. In my hand I clutched the little icons, my chest felt tight, something heavy was gathering in my throat that was about to break out into a groan.'[115]

After the Escort rode away, all the entrances to the palace were locked and sealed except for a single exit via the kitchen and the main entrance for official visitors. 'We were prisoners', Pierre Gilliard recorded starkly in his diary.[116] Lili Dehn remembered a very bright moon that night: 'the snow lay like a pall on the frost-bound Park. The cold was intense. The silence of the great Palace was occasionally broken by snatches of drunken songs and the coarse laughter of the soldiers' (of the new palace guard). In the distance, they could all hear the intermittent firing of guns.[117]

A hundred or more miles (160 km) away to the south, as the frost of another perishing winter night descended and the wind gathered, the imperial train carrying Nicholas II, last tsar of Russia and now plain Colonel Romanov, was heading back towards Tsarskoe Selo.

Chapter Eighteen

GOODBYE. DON'T FORGET ME

❧

Nicholas II's return to Tsarskoe Selo on 9 March 1917 was the most painful of rude awakenings: 'sentries on the street and surrounding the palace and inside the park, and inside the front entrance some kind of officers'.[1] Upstairs he found his wife sitting in a darkened room with all their children; they were all in good spirits, though Maria was very ill. Hugely relieved to be back home he soon discovered that even his most innocuous daily habits were to be severely restricted. That afternoon he was refused permission to go for his usual long walk in the Alexander Park; his domain now comprised a small recreation-area-cum-garden at the immediate rear entrance of the palace. Here he took up a spade and cleared the footpath with his aide Prince Vasili Dolgorukov – the only officer allowed to return with him from Stavka – their guards looking on with amusement.[2]

Lili Dehn was shocked when she saw Nicholas. He was 'deathly pale, his face covered with innumerable wrinkles, his hair was quite grey at the temples, and blue shadows encircled his eyes. He looked like an old man.'[3] To Elizaveta Naryshkina he seemed calm on the surface; she admired his astonishing self-control and his apparent indifference to being addressed not as tsar but as an army officer, which effectively was all he now was.[4] Although the palace commandant, Pavel Kotzebue, referred to him politely as 'the ex-Emperor' most of Nicholas's captors called him Nikolay Romanov or even 'little Nikolay'.[5] He tried hard not to react to the petty humiliations from some of the more truculent guards: 'They blew tobacco smoke in his face . . . A soldier grabbed him by the arm and pulled one way, while others clutched him on the other side and pulled him in an opposite direction. They jeered at him and laughed at his anger and pain', Anna Vyrubova later recalled.[6] But Nicholas did not react: 'Despite the circumstances in which we now find ourselves,' he wrote in his diary on the 10th, 'the thought that we are all together cheers and comforts us.'[7] Maria's condition, however, was becoming a serious cause for concern; her temperature was running at over 40 degrees C (104 degrees F). Alexandra and Lili moved her from her small nickel campbed to a proper double bed, the better to nurse her. With the exhausted girl drifting in and out of delirium they spent their time constantly sponging her down, brushing her now horribly tangled hair and changing her sweat-drenched nightdress and bedding. To make matters worse, she had developed pneumonia as well.[8]

*

Shortly after Nicholas's return, during the days of uncertainty about where the family might eventually be allowed to live, Elizaveta Naryshkina had suggested that Nicholas and Alexandra accept any offer to leave the country; she and Count Benkendorf would look after the children until they were well enough and then bring them to them later.[9] Thoughts of evacuating the children ahead of Nicholas's return had indeed been in Alexandra's mind, even after they fell sick, and she had discussed various options with her entourage.[10] Perhaps she could get them north into Finland; she asked Dr Botkin if he thought 'in their present physical condition' they could cope with the journey. Botkin's response was unequivocal: 'at the moment I would be less afraid of measles than of the revolutionaries.'[11] However, any thoughts Alexandra might have had were abandoned when Nicholas countermanded her suggestion and insisted they wait for his projected return on 1 March. Had he arrived home then, the family might all have been speedily evacuated, but once he was trapped at Stavka and Alexandra placed under house arrest the whole situation dramatically changed. The British ambassador, Sir George Buchanan, had been in an agony of frustration since the beginning of the year: 'I shall not be happy till they are safely out of Russia', he had said, but tentative negotiations with the British government for a possible refuge in England had quickly stalled.[12] The offer from George V, made on 9 March (22nd NS) in response to a request from Russia's Foreign Minister Pavel Milyukov, had spoken only of asylum for the duration of the war. Other options were quickly discussed and dropped: Denmark was too close to Germany; France would not entertain the idea. Alexandra had at one point said that she would prefer to go to Norway where she felt the climate would suit Alexey, although she would certainly be glad to see England again, should it come to it.[13] But wherever the family went, she and Nicholas both thought in terms only of a temporary refuge until the situation eased and they could hopefully be allowed to return and live quietly in Russia – preferably the Crimea.[14]

The British government continued to discuss the issue throughout March, while Alexander Kerensky pondered the family's evacuation, perhaps to Port Romanov (Murmansk), from where a British cruiser could take them through German-patrolled waters to England under a white flag. But then George V had had a change of heart. The king was uneasy that the former tsar's arrival in England would create problems for his government – which had already acknowledged the revolution – and in so doing threaten the safety of his own throne. The most important thing was to keep the new revolutionary Russia on side and in the war, and this transcended any familial loyalty to Nicholas. By the time George's Foreign Secretary Arthur Balfour was instructed on 24 March (6 April NS) to suggest that the Russian government 'make some other plan for the future residence of their imperial majesties', far too much precious time had been lost.[15] A powerful, grassroots opposition to any evacuation had escalated, particularly among the pro-Bolshevik executive committees of the Petrograd and Moscow soviets.[16] Any attempt to get the family out by train would have been blocked by the heavily politicized railwaymen of Petrograd, who, according to *Izvestiya* (the new organ of the Petrograd soviet), had already 'wired along all railway lines that every railway organization, each station-master, every group of railway-workmen, is bound to detain Nicholas II's train whenever and wherever it may appear'.[17]

Izvestiya reflected the ugly mood building in the capital. An evacuation of the family could not be permitted, the paper railed, for the ex-tsar was privy to all state secrets relating to the war and was 'possessed of colossal wealth' that he would be able to access in the comfort of exile.[18] Nicholas must be held under the strictest isolation pending the meting out of a new, Soviet form of justice. Yet amid so many accusations levelled against them Nicholas and Alexandra had in fact remained intensely loyal to Russia and all talk of any political betrayal on their part was entirely unfounded; indeed, Nicholas had already been worrying that his abdication might damage the allied offensive. As far as exile was concerned, neither he nor Alexandra had any desire for the sybaritic expatriate lifestyle of 'wandering about the Continent, and living at Swiss hotels as ex-Royalties, snapshotted and paragraphed by representatives of the picture papers'. They shrank from such 'cheap publicity', asserted Lili Dehn, and considered it their duty to stand by Russia whatever the cost.[19]

Arriving in Russia just after Nicholas's return, the Anglo-Irish journalist Robert Crozier Long was immediately struck by the 'unexampled reversal of ranks and conditions which . . . the Revolution had brought about in the most despotic and class-crystallized country of Europe'. He travelled out to Tsarskoe Selo to report on the tsar's incarceration and encountered an unnerving atmosphere. The town was 'a microcosm of the Revolution'; at the Alexandrovsky Station he was greeted by 'crowds of untidy revolutionary soldiers, all with red badges', the stationmaster was an army corporal and 'portraits of Nicholas II and his father Alexander III lay in tatters in a rubbish heap'. The authorities were finding it hard to keep the lid on renegade elements in the town that resented any form of indulgence shown to the prisoners and were keen to exert their own form of rough justice on the tsar and tsaritsa. The railings of the Alexander Park had now become a public sideshow where people gathered in order to catch a glimpse of the former tsar and his family whenever they emerged in the garden.[20]

The family's daily routine, having always been mundane, now became even more predictable. They all got up early except Alexandra and by 8 a.m. Nicholas was often seen walking outside with Dolgorukov, or undertaking some kind of physical work – breaking the ice on the waterways and clearing the snow. It was all too painful for Elizaveta Naryshkina to watch: 'How far has he sunk who once owned the riches of the earth and a devoted people! How splendid his reign could have been, if he had only understood the needs of the era!'[21] After a plain lunch at 1 p.m., and as the weather improved and the girls recovered, the family worked outside digging up the turf and preparing the ground for a vegetable garden to be planted in the spring. When it was warm enough Alexandra would join them in her wheelchair, where she sat embroidering or tatting. In the afternoon the younger children had their lessons, and later, if the weather continued fine, they returned to the garden until the light began to fade. Much to their surprise, the guards found themselves watching over a family that was 'quiet, unprovocative, unfailingly polite to one another and to them, and whose occasional sadness bore the stamp of a dignity their jailers could never emulate and were reluctantly compelled to admire'.[22] Some of the sentries exploited public curiosity by taking money from people wanting a closer look at the tsar and his children. The family moved out of sight as best they could when this happened, but even so they were not immune to insult not just from onlookers but also from their own guards. 'When the young Grand Duchesses or the Empress appeared at a window, the sentries made obscene gestures which were greeted with shouts of laughter from their comrades.'[23] A few of the soldiers guarding them persisted in referring to Nicholas as the tsar or ex-tsar, and one officer, it was said, was dismissed 'after being caught kissing the hand of the Grand Duchess Tatiana', but these were exceptions. Other cruel gestures served only to hurt: the children's rowing boat was soiled with excrement and graffiti, and out in the park Alexey's pet goat was shot and the pet deer and swans too – probably for food.[24]

Many found Nicholas's extraordinary passivity in the face of insult disturbing: 'The Tsar felt nothing; he was neither kind nor cruel; merry nor morose; he had no more sensibility than some of the lowest forms of life. "A human oyster" is how the later commandant, Evgeny Kobylinsky, would describe him.'[25] As for Alexandra, Elizaveta Naryshkina found her conversation increasingly disjointed and incomprehensible. No doubt the constant headaches and dizzy spells as ever impinged on it, but Elizaveta had by now come to the conclusion that Alexandra's unbalanced mental state had become 'pathological'. 'It should serve to acquit her' should it come to the worst, she hoped, 'and perhaps will be her only salvation.' Dr Botkin agreed with her: 'He now feels as I do when seeing the state the empress is in and berates himself for not having realized it sooner.'[26]

Inside the palace much had changed. 'Along the wide corridors covered with thick soft carpets, where formerly efficient, silent servants glided noiselessly, throngs of soldiers now reeled, with coats unbuttoned, in muddy shoes, caps on the side of their heads, unshaved, often drunk, and always noisy.'[27] Visitors to the family were strictly forbidden (although members of the entourage were occasionally allowed to see their relatives). Use of the telephone or telegraph was forbidden and the family was ordered to speak Russian at all times. Correspondence was vetted by Kotzebue, who having served with Alexandra's Uhlans was sympathetic and often allowed letters through without the formal checks being made. But he was soon replaced, and letters were later even tested for invisible ink.[28] The family was still allowed to celebrate religious services on Sundays and high holidays, led by Father Belyaev from the Feodorovsky Sobor, who held them in a field chapel erected behind a screen in the corner of an upstairs room.[29]

Although it was mid-March Maria was still very sick and Anastasia had developed such acute earache that her eardrums had had to be pierced to relieve the pressure in them.[30] And then on the 15th Anastasia developed a secondary infection – pleurisy – on a day when Maria's temperature hit 40.6 degrees C (over 105 degrees F). Both children were prostrated by fits of terrible coughing.[31] In a letter to Rita Khitrovo, Tatiana wrote that Anastasia wasn't able to eat either, 'because it all comes back again'. Both her sisters, she said, were 'very patient and lie quietly. Anastasia is still deaf and you have to shout so that she can hear what you're saying to her.' Her own hearing was much better, although she was still having problems with her right ear. She couldn't say much more: 'Remember that they are reading your and my letters.'[32]

By the 18th Maria was so ill that Alexandra sent Anna Vyrubova an anxious note, fearful that she was dying. Anastasia too was 'in a critical condition, lungs and ears being in a sad state of inflammation'. 'Oxygen alone was keeping the children alive', administered by a doctor who had come out voluntarily from Petrograd to attend them.[33] It was not until 20 March that Anastasia and Maria's temperatures finally began to drop. They were at last over the worst, much to their parents' relief, though were still very weak and sleeping a lot.[34] Alexey was recovering too and Tatiana, the most robust of all the children, was much better. But Olga still seemed very under par.

There was now a new palace commandant – Pavel Korovichenko – who was introduced to the family on 21 March by Kerensky when he arrived on an inspection. Before leaving that day, Kerensky announced that Anna Vyrubova was to be removed. The stigma of her previous close association with Rasputin was still bringing with it accusations of her being involved in 'political plots' against the new regime.[35] Her presence at the palace, it was felt, served only to inflame revolutionary hatred of the imperial family. To lose Anna was a disaster for an emotionally drained Alexandra, but even worse was Kerensky's decision to take her other close friend Lili Dehn away too. Before Lili left Alexandra hung a small icon round her neck as a blessing and Tatiana rushed in with a small leather photograph case containing photos of her parents – taken from her own bedside table. 'If Kerensky *is* going to take you away from us, you shall at least have Papa and Mama to console you', she said, and then she turned to Anna and begged for 'a last memory' of her as a keepsake. Anna gave her the only thing she had – her wedding ring.[36]

Lili was still wearing her nurse's uniform when she and Anna were taken out to the waiting cars. Alexandra and Olga seemed calm and impassive as they left, but Tatiana was openly sobbing – 'this the girl whom history had since described as "proud and reserved"', but on this occasion, as Lili remembered, 'ma[king] no secret of her grief'. Both women were heartbroken to be so unjustly and forcibly removed after so many years of loyal service to the family; Anna, still weak both from the measles and the injuries sustained in her accident, could barely walk, even with the help of crutches. As their car drove away in the rain, Anna could just make out 'a group of white-clad figures crowded close to the nursery windows' watching them go. From Tsarskoe Selo the two women were taken to the Palace of Justice in Petrograd; after being held for two days in a freezing cold room with little food Lili was allowed to go home to her sick son Titi.[37] But Anna was transferred to the notorious Trubetskoy Bastion of the Peter and Paul Fortress where she was held for interrogation and not released until July.

With all the children recovered, the family still nursed the hope that it would be allowed to go into temporary exile and on 23 March Nicholas noted that he had been going through his books and papers, packing up everything he might wish to take with him 'if we should leave for England'.[38] But Lent came and there was still no news. Father Belyaev was allowed to come and stay at the Alexander Palace to conduct services, albeit closely observed at all times by the highly suspicious members of the guard. On Saturday 25 March Anastasia got up for the first time and joined the family for lunch. The following morning, Palm Sunday, she sat down and wrote what was probably her first letter since her illness; and she wrote it to the person closest to her favourite officer – Viktor Zborovsky's sister, Katya.

Like her sisters Rimma and Xenia, Katya had been serving as a nurse during the war, at Feodorovsky Gorodok.[39] Three years older than Anastasia, she had sometimes been brought out from St Petersburg to play with her when they were younger and had become a close friend, thanks to their common bond with her brother Viktor. During the war, all four Romanov sisters often sent gifts to their Escort favourites – especially hand-knitted items of warm clothing to take to the front. They also treasured their photographs of Vitya (Viktor), Shurik (Alexander Shvedov) and Skvorchik (Mikhail Skvortsov) taken at tea parties at Anna Vyrubova's. After they were shut up in the Alexander Palace the girls were desperate to stay in touch with the Escort and Katya became the conduit, allowed a pass into the palace to come and deliver and fetch letters.[40]

Until now Anastasia had been something of a sluggish letter writer compared to her sisters, but with little to do she began writing regularly to Katya in order to have news of Viktor. 'Tatiana asks me to send this blanket for Makyukho [one of the officers] for his young son', she wrote on the 26 March:

> He apparently is her godson. What is his name? Give the remaining socks and shirts to your brother and he can hand them out to his colleagues. We are sorry there aren't enough for everyone, but we are sending all we have left. At the bottom of these two boxes is written which item is to be given to our former wounded. Maria is still ill, but I got up yesterday, and am very glad about that, as I had been confined to bed for about four weeks, though I am still weak in the legs.
>
> Please ask your brother again to return the group [photographs] that we sent you last time. We think of you all often and send huge greetings. Write and tell us sometimes, dear Katya how everyone is and so on, we are always so happy to have news. Jim [her dog] is well and happy.* Send my best to Sidorov. Warmest greetings to your mother and brother. All the best! I kiss you warmly, Your Anastasia. These little icons are from mother for all the officers.[41]

At a time when such simple acts of friendship and remembrance preoccupied the four sisters, a positive 'outpouring of venom' against the imperial family was filling the Petrograd press. Some of it took the form of lurid cartoons of the former tsar and tsaritsa – of Alexandra reclining in a bath full of blood, or Nicholas watching mass hangings – or featured descriptions of elaborate, bloated meals of caviar, lobster and sturgeon gorged on by the imperial family while Petrograd starved.

> There was a cartoon of the Emperor lighting a cigarette with a hundred-rouble note. There was a nauseating story about 'the proof' that Grand-Duke Alexis was the son of [Monsieur] Philippe. There were sketches of the young grand-duchesses' 'private' lives written by their 'lovers'.[42]

---

* The dog has often been named elsewhere as Jem or Jemmy but the Katya letters confirm its name as above. There has also been discussion – based perhaps on the faulty recall of Anna Vyrubova – that Jim belonged to Tatiana, but again Anastasia's letters to Katya make abundantly clear that the dog was hers.

'The joint excesses of Nero, Caligula, the Sforzas and the Borgias would have suggested a mild nursery-story' in comparison with the lurid press accounts that Edith Almedingen remembered reading that spring. Yet still the accusations against Nicholas and Alexandra escalated, so much so that on 27 March, during the judicial investigation into Anna Vyrubova, Kerensky ordered that the couple should be separated in order to prevent collusion between them, should any trial ensue. For the next three weeks they were allowed to meet only twice daily at meals, Nicholas appearing almost glad to escape his wife's draining presence for a while.[43] They adhered strictly to the new rules imposed on them, fearing that if they did not one or both of them might be taken away, like Anna, to the Peter and Paul Fortress.* Kerensky had actually wanted to separate Alexandra from the children, confining them with their father, but Elizaveta Naryshkina had appealed saying this was too cruel: 'It would mean death to her. Her children are her life.'[44] It was as well that Kerensky relented, for on 27 March Olga was back in bed again with swollen glands and a sore throat; once more her temperature climbed to nearly 40 degrees C (104 degrees F).[45] On 4 April Alexandra noted that her daughter was now suffering from 'inflammation around the heart'.[46]

Over Easter weekend the entire household, including the remaining servants, were grateful to be allowed to pray together, though at one stage Belyaev had had to contend with a noisy funeral service being held in the park outside for supposed 'victims of the Revolution'– in fact, those killed during wine-shop rioting and pillaging in the town a few days previously.[47] All five children had made confession to him on Good Friday, Olga in bed and Maria in a wheelchair, and he was impressed by their 'mildness, restraint [and] obedience to their parents' wishes'. They seemed to him so innocent, so 'ignorant of worldly filth'.[48] The late-night communion service for *Velikaya Subbota* (Great Saturday) on 1 April was especially poignant for everyone (though Olga and Maria were too sick to attend). Afterwards eighteen sat down at table to break the fast.

---

* On 12 April this ruling was overturned and they were allowed to share a bedroom again.

There was a huge Easter *kulich*, decorated eggs, ham and veal, sausage and vegetables, but for Iza Buxhoeveden it was 'a dismal repast, like a meal in a house of mourning', during which Nicholas and Alexandra were obliged to sit apart, the tsaritsa hardly speaking. She ate nothing and drank only a cup of coffee, saying she was 'always on a diet'.[49]

Beautiful spring weather greeted Easter Sunday, 'a day of great joy despite the human suffering', recalled Elizaveta Naryshkina. Nicholas presented her with a porcelain egg with his insignia. 'I shall treasure it as a good memory', she wrote in her diary. 'How few loyal people they have left . . . One cannot be certain of the future: everything depends on whether the Provisional Government can hold on or whether the anarchists will win – the danger is unavoidable. How I wish that they could leave as soon as possible, seeing that they are now all well.'[50] It being a Sunday and a public holiday, crowds gathered outside the railings to gawp at the tsar when he came out to work in the garden, surrounded by guards with fixed bayonets. 'We look like convicts with their warders', Pierre Gilliard remarked ruefully.[51] People were now taking day trips out from the capital to stand and stare and there were as many again on Easter Monday, gathered to watch Nicholas shovelling the snow away from the canal. They stood there in silence, 'like watching a wild animal in a cage', recalled Valentina Chebotareva. 'Why do they have to do this?'[52] The family had at least been consoled by another wonderful service that day but afterwards, when Elizaveta Naryshkina went to see the grand duchesses in their sickroom, she had been alarmed to see how much thinner Maria was, though 'very much prettier; the expression on her face sad and gentle. You can see that she has suffered a lot and that what she has been through has left a deep mark on her.'[53]

At the annexe hospital, Valentina Chebotareva was continually saddened and frustrated by the lack of contact, particularly with her beloved Tatianochka. 'We know little about the prisoners, although letters regularly arrive', but these were extremely circumspect. She was worried about writing too often, which might be seen as a provocation by those who did not understand her close friendship with the grand duchesses. Any letters sent in signed with pet names and not in full immediately fell under suspicion as being some kind of coded message – there had already been problems with the authorities taking exception to letters sent by 'Lili' and 'Titi' or sometimes even 'Tili' – a combination of the two.[54] Knowing that they could now never return to the annexe, Tatiana had asked Bibi and Valentina to send back the things they had left there. Valentina worried that this too might be looked upon suspiciously, but nevertheless she packed up their nurses' smocks, photo albums and other mementoes, together with a last photograph of them taken with their wounded in the dining room.[55] Tatiana in return sent gifts of shirts, pillows and books for the patients from herself and Olga. 'Tell darling Bibi that we love her and kiss her fondly', she wrote, adding plaintively, 'What are Mitya and Volodya doing?'[56] The girls sent Easter greetings on the Sunday but Valentina was worried to read how ill Olga was and that 'Alexey Nikolaevich is in bed having hurt his arm – another haemorrhage'. She had heard that when Kerensky had recently visited, he had asked Alexey, 'Do you have everything you need?' to which the child had responded:

'Yes, only I'm bored and I love the soldiers so much.'
'But there are so many all around and in the garden.'
'No, not that kind, they aren't going to the front – it's those that I love.'[57]

There were indeed plenty of soldiers all around, so much so that Tsarskoe Selo was now being called *Soldatskoe Selo* [Soldiers' Village] for, as a British businessman in Petrograd remarked, 'The Tsarskoe Selo municipal authorities are as ultra-Red as Versailles in 1789.'[58]

It was now April and the days were beginning to drag – 'one and the same, in a state of spiritual anguish', as Elizaveta Naryshkina noted.[59] While Tatiana was often out in the garden with Nicholas helping to break the ice around the bridges, Alexandra remained preoccupied with Olga and Maria, who were still confined to their rooms. 'Olga is still very weak poor thing,' wrote a despondent Elizaveta Naryshkina on 9 April, 'her heart has been strained by unremitting illness over the last two months . . . She is very sweet; and Maria is enchanting even though still in bed with the last vestiges of pleurisy.'[60] Tatiana meanwhile was pining for the annexe: 'It's sad that now we are better we can't come and work in the hospital again. It's so strange to be at home in the morning and not to be doing the dressings.' Who was doing them, she asked Valentina.[61] 'What will happen to our old hospital now?' 'Forgive me for so many questions dear Valentina Ivanovna, but it's so interesting to know what is happening with you. We constantly remember how good it was to work at the hospital and how we all got along together.'[62]

Korovichenko had been doing his best to defend the right of the girls to send and receive so many letters. 'They had been hard workers, worked like real sisters of mercy', he told Valentina. 'Why should they be deprived in Easter Week of the joy of exchanging greetings with their former wounded and their work colleagues?' He vetted all their letters and their content was 'absolutely innocent'. 'Often Sister Khitrovo and other nurses [send letters] which I have handed on.' He had, however, 'a whole box full of letters to the Romanov family' that he had chosen not to allow through.[63] Among the letters being allowed out by Korovichenko were those from Anastasia to Katya Zborovskaya. 'Truly He is Risen!' Anastasia exclaimed at the opening of an Eastertide letter, in which she enclosed one of the first snowdrops of spring from the garden and told Katya that she and Tatiana were now going out for walks and helping to break the ice. But, worryingly, Anastasia also confided that 'After Olga had a sore throat, something happened to her heart, and she has rheumatism now' – suggesting that Olga's 'inflammation of the heart' was in fact the far more serious post-measles complication of rheumatic fever.[64]

By mid-April, with the younger children back at their desks, a new modified timetable of lessons was set up for them and shared among the remaining members of the entourage. Nicholas began teaching Alexey geography and history; Alexandra took on religious doctrine and catechism, as well as giving Tatiana tuition in German; Olga, when recovered, helped teach her siblings English and history. Iza Buxhoeveden gave Alexey and his younger sisters piano lessons, and also taught them all English. Trina Schneider tutored them in maths and Russian grammar; Nastenka Hendrikova taught Anastasia history and gave her art lessons with Tatiana; Dr Botkin took on

Russian literature with Alexey and Dr Derevenko volunteered to give him science lessons. Pierre Gilliard continued his French lessons with all five children. Everyone pulled together to try and create as normal an environment as possible in such abnormal circumstances.[65] The family appeared to be quietly adjusting to its new, highly circumscribed life; one of the young subaltern guards told Elizaveta Naryshkina how impressed he was: 'having come down from his pedestal' even the emperor seemed contented, so long as his routine was not disturbed and he could have 'his walks and tea at five o'clock'.[66]

Increasingly absorbed in thoughts of God, Alexandra seemed to draw especial comfort from her Bible lessons with the children. The girls made a point, as they always did, of remembering her name day on 23 April when all the *arestovanniye* – 'those under arrest' as Nicholas called them – gave her little home-made gifts.[67] Olga composed a poem specially:

> You are filled with anguish
> For the suffering of others.
> And no one's grief
> Has ever passed you by.
> You are relentless
> Only toward yourself,
> Forever cold and pitiless.
> But if only you could look upon
> Your own sadness from a distance,
> Just once with a loving soul –
> Oh, how you would pity yourself.
> How sadly you would weep.[68]

On 30 April, Anastasia was delighted to tell Katya, in a letter enclosing several postcards for Viktor and the other officers, that now that the ground had at last begun to thaw 'we all together started to dig our own kitchen garden . . . The weather is wonderful today, and it is very warm, so we have worked for a long time.' The sisters had rearranged their rooms upstairs as they adapted to their changed circumstances: 'We are all now sitting together and writing in the same Red Room, where we still live, as we do not want to move to our bedroom.' They had attached a swing to the gymnastic rings in the doorway, where 'we swing so nicely that the screws probably won't last long'.[69]

May came but the cold weather still lingered. There was snow and a cold wind the day Nicholas turned forty-nine; Alexey was suffering from pains in his arms yet again and was back in bed, and the ever loyal Elizaveta Naryshkina had bronchitis, brought on by the perishing cold in the unheated rooms. Thoughtful as always, Nicholas came and sat with her and Alexandra sent a posy of anemones picked from the garden, but on the 12th Elizaveta had to be sent away to the Catherine Palace Hospital to be nursed. As she said goodbye to Nicholas 'both of us had a premonition that we would never be together again. We embraced repeatedly, and he kissed my hands incessantly.'[70]

Work in the garden remained the only outlet for pent-up energies and May was spent by everyone busily weeding carrots, radishes, onions and lettuce, watering them and watching with pride as the 500 cabbages they had planted began to swell in their neatly ordered rows. When Nicholas, still wearing his khaki soldier's tunic, had exhausted all possible work in the vegetable garden he began a vigorous and systematic felling of dead trees, sawing them up ready for winter. It was now warm enough to take Alexey out in the rowing boat on the pond near the Children's Island, or ride bicycles with his daughters. And they had the dogs – Alexey's Joy, Tatiana's Ortipo and Anastasia's Jimmy, as well as two kittens produced by the cat from Stavka that Alexey had given Olga.[71]

Nicholas seemed perfectly contented to work up a sweat doing physical labour: 'Congenial work in the vegetable garden,' he noted on 6 May, 'we began to dig beds. After tea vespers, supper, and evening reading – [I am] much more with my sweet family than in normal years.'[72] It was hard to 'be without news of dear Mama,' he admitted, 'but I am indifferent toward everything else'.[73]

As the Maytime lilac blossom came into full bloom, 'the aroma of the garden was wonderful when you sat by the window', observed Nicholas; the girls revelled in it too.[74] Anastasia was bright and chirpy in her letters to Katya, telling her on the 20th how much they enjoyed their work in the garden:

We have already planted a lot; the total number of beds is sixty so far, but we are going to plant more. As now we do not have to work that much, we often just lie and warm ourselves in the sun. We have taken a lot of pictures, and we even processed the film ourselves.

But it was hard to have to tell Katya, who had now left Tsarskoe Selo with her family and gone south, that their hospitals were to be closed soon 'and everybody will go away, to my great sorrow'.

We are thinking of everybody a lot; now while I am writing this letter, my sisters are sitting next to me in the room and are drinking tea, and Maria is sitting on the window sill and writing letters; they all talk a lot, and make writing letters difficult. They kiss you many times. Are you still roller-skating? Do you feel cosy living with your mother in a new place? I'm sending you a sprig of lilac from our garden; let it remind you of northern spring . . . Well Katya, sweetheart, I have to finish . . . Huge regards to everybody from us! May the Lord be with you. I kiss you as deeply as I love you. Your A.[75]

For all the sisters, thoughts were increasingly turning to the things they missed so much. 'Today, quite softly, I could hear the sound of the Catherine Palace bells', Olga told her friend Zinaida Tolstaya. 'I wish so much that I could sometimes go to Znamenie.'[76] Anastasia felt the same: 'We often hear the bells of the good cathedral and feel so sad,' she told Katya on 4 July, 'but it is always nice to remember the good times, right?' She wondered all the time about Viktor and the other officers and how they were all doing.[77] 'This time last year we were in Mogilev', she recalled wistfully on the 12th. 'It was so nice there, as well as the last time we were there in November! We constantly think and talk about you all.' There were, she said, one or two amusing or interesting things she would have liked to tell Katya, but she could not write about it in her letters: 'you surely understand this, don't you?' By now, as Count Benkendorf recalled, even the accommodating Korovichenko had begun to complain about the 'enormous correspondence of the young Grand Duchesses, which took up a great deal of his time and prevented him from delivering us our correspondence as quickly as he might'.[78]

One of the highlights of family life, aside from receiving letters, was occasional showings of Alexey's collection of cinematographs, thanks to the gift of a projector and a large number of films made to him by Pathé during the war. Otherwise, evening entertainment was confined to Nicholas reading aloud. During the five months of their incarceration at the Alexander Palace, he got through a considerable number of popular French and English novels: Alexander Dumas's *Comte de Monte-Cristo* and Alphonse Daudet's adventure stories *Tartarin de Tarascon* and *Tartarin sur les Alpes*; Gaston Leroux's popular *Le mystère de la chambre jaune* was a great favourite, but undoubtedly the most popular were Conan Doyle's stories – *The Poison Belt*, *The Hound of the Baskervilles*, *A Study in Scarlet* and *The Valley of Fear*.

Such diversions into adventure and fantasy served only to distract the family for a short while from the realities of their imprisonment. As the stifling heat of summer gathered – a time when they would have been enjoying the sea breezes at Peterhof or the Crimea – 'Tsarskoe was a *dead* place. Its windows were almost hidden by the straggling branches of the unclipped trees,' recalled Lili Dehn, 'grass grew between the stones of its silent courtyard.' Shortly before leaving Petrograd, she had managed to get out there to try and catch sight of the family: 'I walked to and fro gazing up at the windows, but those within the Palace gave no sign of life. I wanted to call aloud that I was there, but I dared not imperil their safety or my own'.[79] Valentina Chebotareva too was complaining of the inertia of the town; it had entirely changed in character and lost all its pride and vigour. Now all you could see were soldiers wandering around aimlessly, chewing sunflower seeds, lounging on the grass. They had taken the fish from the ponds and trampled all the flowerbeds in the public gardens. 'We hear little of the children now', she wrote sadly. 'Over there they live a monotonous life. The children amuse each other, Olga and Maria with history . . . They dig in the garden, have planted carrots themselves.' 'Yesterday,' as they told her, 'we went a little way on our bicycles. In the evenings we gather together and Papa reads aloud. Alexey walks with Papa a lot more' – that was the sum total of their lives. As for their mother – she was 'think[ing] only of the past'.[80] The increasingly religiose tone of Alexandra's letters was evidence of her determined withdrawal from the real world into a mystical contemplation of death and redemption. The Bible and the scriptures, she said, provided her with the answers to all of life's questions and she was proud of her children's responsiveness: 'they understand many deep things – their souls are growing through suffering.'[81] Suffering had become the family's *métier*; God, she knew, would crown them for it.

On her sixteenth birthday on 5 June Anastasia received 'a pair of earrings, and my ears were pierced', she told Katya, though 'this is, so to say, small news'.[82] But this was soon spoiled by the loss of all her hair. Ever since their attack of measles, all the girls had found their hair was falling out in great hanks – Maria's especially – and early in July they had to have their heads shaved. A day later Alexey did likewise, in sympathy. Pierre Gilliard captured their stoical response in his diary and on camera:

> When they go out in the park they wear scarves arranged so as to conceal the fact. Just as I was going to take their photographs, at a sign from Olga Nicolaievna [*sic*] they all suddenly removed their headdress. I protested, but they insisted, much amused at the idea of seeing themselves photographed like this, and looking forward to seeing the indignant surprise of their parents.

Gilliard was comforted to see that 'their good spirits reappear from time to time in spite of everything'. He put it down to the girls' 'exuberant youth'. But although they took the loss of their beautiful long hair in good heart their morbidly introspective mother saw it quite differently; Pierre's photograph, she said, made them look like the condemned.[83]

'Poor Mama is terribly bored; can't at all get used to the new life and the circumstances here,' Olga told her aunt Olga on 21 June, 'although on the whole we can all be grateful that we will be together and in the Crimea.'[84] With a flare-up of conflict in Petrograd, discussion of the family's evacuation had once again resumed. On 4 July Elizaveta Naryshkina had heard rumours that a 'group of young monarchists have got up an insane project: to take them away by car at night to one of the ports where an English steamer would be waiting'. But she was fearful 'of a repetition of

Varennes' – the attempted flight in 1791 of the deposed Louis XVI, his wife and his family that had resulted in the king and queen's arrest and execution.[85]

Faced with a possible Bolshevik coup against the provisional government that summer, and worried about plots to spirit the Romanovs away, Kerensky, (who had now taken over as prime minister), came to the Alexander Palace to see Nicholas. Radical elements in the Petrograd soviet might try to storm the palace and he told him that the family 'would likely go south, given the proximity of Tsarskoe Selo to the uneasy capital'.[86] As Count Benkendorf understood it, Kerensky thought 'it would be more prudent for His Majesty and his family to . . . settle in the interior of the country, far from factories and garrisons, in the country house of some landed proprietor'.[87] The possibility of Grand Duke Mikhail's estate at Brasovo, near Orel 660 miles (1060 km) to the south, was discussed; but it was soon discovered that local peasants would be hostile.[88] There had even been talk of sending the family to the Ipatiev Monastery at Kostroma. Nicholas and Alexandra still clung to hopes of the Crimea, for his mother and sisters and their families were now living there, but this was out of the question as far as Kerensky was concerned; travelling all that way by train, through the heavily politicized industrial cities of central Russia, would be impossible.[89]

'We all thought and talked about our forthcoming journey', Nicholas wrote on 12 July. 'Strange to think of leaving here after 4 months in seclusion.'[90] The following day he began 'surreptitiously, to gather together my things and books', still nursing hopes of the Crimea where he 'could live like a civilized man'.[91] It appeared that Kerensky intended moving them some time after Alexey's birthday, but by now, although the Romanovs did not yet know it, he was considering other, very different options.[92]

Out in the palace garden and oblivious to this, the children were able to savour their first home-grown vegetables and were learning to cut hay. It was extremely hot and Alexey had been amusing himself squirting water over the girls from the water pump. They didn't mind: 'It's so good out in the garden', Tatiana told her friend Zinaida Tolstaya:

but even better when you go deep into the wood, where it is quite wild and you can go along the little paths and so on . . . Oh how envious I was to read that you saw the dreadnoughts *Alexander III* and the *Prut.* This is what we miss so much – no sea, no boats! We had grown so used to spending practically the whole summer on the water, at the skerries; in my opinion there is nothing better; it was the best and happiest of times – after all, we went sailing for nine years in a row and even before, when we were quite small; and now it's so strange to have been here for three years without the water, there's no other such feeling in the summer for me as we only used to live at Tsarskoe Selo in the winter and sometimes in the spring, till we went to the Crimea. Right now the lime trees are in full bloom and it smells so divine.[93]

By the middle of the month the family was packing in earnest for the hoped-for journey south. And then, on Friday 28 July, Nicholas noted with dismay:

After breakfast we found out from Count Benkendorf that they are sending us, not to the Crimea, but to one of the distant provincial towns three or four days' journey to the east! But where exactly they don't say – even the commandant doesn't know. And there we were still counting on a long stay in Livadia![94]

For the next two days as everyone hurried to sort out the items they most wished to take with them, there was still no clear indication of where exactly they were going. Hopes were finally dashed when, on the 29th, they were told 'that we must provide ourselves with warm clothing.' Pierre Gilliard was dismayed: 'So we are not to be taken south. A great disappointment.' They had been told to expect a five-day journey; Nicholas soon worked it out. Five days on a train meant they were going to Siberia.[95]

*

With the family's departure fixed for 31 July, the members of the entourage had to decide whether they would be prepared to travel with them into a decidedly uncertain future. Pierre Gilliard had no doubts about where his duty lay, as he explained in a letter to his family in Switzerland on the 30th: 'I have thought about all the possible eventualities and am not frightened by what awaits me. I feel I must go to the very end . . . with God's grace. Having benefited from happy days, should I not share with them the bad days?'[96] Ladies-in-waiting Trina Schneider and Nastenka Hendrikova also prepared to go with the family, but Iza Buxhoeveden was about to undergo an operation and would have to join them later; Sydney Gibbes, still stuck in Petrograd, hoped to do likewise.[97]

On 30 July everyone did their best to celebrate Alexey's thirteenth birthday. Alexandra asked that the icon of Our Lady of the Sign should be brought from the Znamenie Church for a special *Te Deum* led by Father Belyaev. It was a very emotional experience and everyone was in tears: 'Somehow it was especially comforting to pray to her holy image together with all our people', wrote Nicholas, in the knowledge that it would probably be for the last time.[98] Later, the household went outside in the garden to take farewell photographs of each other and out of habit Nicholas sawed some wood, telling Benkendorf (who, too old and with an ailing wife, was remaining at Tsarskoe) to distribute the vegetables and wood among those servants who had remained loyal during their captivity. Valentina Chebotareva had sent Tatiana a note that day congratulating them on Alexey's birthday: 'As for you, my dear child, allow this old V[alentina] I[vanovna] who loves you so much to mentally make the sign of the cross over you and kiss you warmly.'[99]

Instructed to be ready to leave at midnight on Monday 31 July, the family assembled in the semicircular hall, downstairs by the rear entrance. The elegant marble reception room looked like 'a customs hall', as chambermaid Anna Demidova noted. She was horrified at the mountains of luggage that two hours later had yet to be carried out to the waiting trucks; by 3 o'clock the men loading it all had hardly made a dent in the pile and everyone was getting anxious about the delay to their departure, which had been scheduled for 1 a.m.[100] Finally everything was loaded, but now rumours were flying that their train had not even left Petrograd.[101] They all sat there, dog tired, and waited with sinking hearts as the night wore on. The girls wept a great deal and Alexandra was extremely agitated.

Dr Botkin spent the night going from one to the next with valerian drops to calm them down. Alexey kept trying to lie down and sleep but in the end gave up. Wan with fatigue, he sat 'perched on a box, and holding his favourite spaniel "Joy" by a leash' as his father paced up and down, endlessly lighting cigarettes.[102] They were all grateful for the offer of tea when it finally came at 5 a.m.

Behind the scenes, Kerensky's evacuation plans had been on the brink of failure. During the night, workers at Petrograd's Nikolaevsky Station, who had been preparing the train had begun to hesitate about whether they would allow it to leave. 'All night long there had been difficulties, doubts and vacillations. The railwaymen delayed the shunting and coupling, put through mysterious phone calls, made inquiries somewhere.'[103] Dawn was already breaking when the train – comprised of *wagons-lits* and a restaurant car of the Chinese Eastern Railway – finally arrived at Tsarskoe Selo's Alexandrovsky Station more than five hours late and was parked down the tracks, away from the main entrance.[104] The station itself 'was surrounded by soldiers, and troops with loaded rifles' who had 'marched out and lined both sides of the road from the palace to the station, each soldier carrying in his belt sixty rounds of ammunition'.[105]

Word by now had got out in Tsarskoe Selo that something was afoot and as the sun rose on 1 August a triple cordon of guards in front of the palace was having to hold back an 'immense crowd of people hooting and shouting menacingly', keen to get one last look at *Nikolashka-durachok** as he was taken away.[106] At about 5.15, four motor cars finally arrived. It was clearly going to be impossible to take the family out past the crowds at the main gate; they would have to cross the Alexander Park to reach the station at its western end. The entourage tried to steel themselves and remain cheerful during this final farewell, refusing to say the usual *Do svidaniya* but repeating the more emphatic *Do skorogo svidaniya*, 'till we see each other soon'.[107] Much to her despair the tsaritsa had not been allowed to say farewell to all of her most faithful retainers, particularly her elderly mistress of the robes, Elizaveta Naryshkina, who had served

---

* 'Little Nicholas the fool'.

three tsaritsas. But she sent her a note: 'Farewell, darling motherly friend, my heart is too full to write any more.'[108] It was only now, as Alexandra left the palace, that Kerensky, who on their previous encounters had found her 'proud and unbending, fully conscious of her right to rule' saw for the first time 'the former Empress simply as a mother, anxious and weeping'.[109]

When the family arrived at the station – their cars surrounded by a mounted escort of Dragoons – they had to walk down the heavy moist sand of the railway embankment to get to their train, which had been mocked up with flags and placards proclaiming it was part of a 'Red Cross Mission'.*[110] Alexandra could barely manage the walk, nor could she climb up onto the footboard and had to be 'pulled up with great difficulty and at once fell forward on her hands and knees'. A military escort, headed by Evgeny Kobylinsky, was to travel with them and their immediate entourage on this train; a second train was waiting nearby for the remainder of the servants and the guards.[111]

When everyone in the Romanov entourage had taken their places, Kerensky ran up and shouted, 'They can go!' and 'The whole train immediately shuddered off in the direction of the imperial branch line'. As it did so the quiet and watchful crowd that had gathered as one 'suddenly stirred themselves, and waved their hands, their scarves and caps', in an eerily silent farewell.[112] The sunrise was beautiful, noted Nicholas, as the train headed north in the direction of Petrograd before swinging south-east in the direction of the Urals; his attitude to departure as an ordinary civilian from his home of twenty-two years was as phlegmatic as it had been to his abdication.

'I will describe to you how we travelled', Anastasia later wrote of their journey, in an essay for Sydney Gibbes, in which as usual she struggled with her English spelling:

---

* Sources vary on precisely which national flag the train was travelling under. Some say Japanese, others, including Anna Demidova in her diary, say American. She clearly talks of Chinese cooks working in the restaurant car and a railway worker eyewitness confirms that the cars were provided by the Chinese-Eastern Railway – a line that operated effectively as an extension of the Trans-Siberian Railway into Manchuria, via Harbin, and out to the Pacific coast at Vladivostok.

We started in the morning and when we got into the train I went to sleap, so did all of us. We were very tierd because we did not sleap the whole night. The first day was hot and very dusty. At the stations we had to shut our window curtanse that nobody should see us. Once in the evening I was looking out we stoped near a little house, but there was no station so we could look out. A little boy came to my window and asked: 'Uncle, please give me, if you have got, a newspaper.' I said: 'I am not an uncle but an aunty and have no newspaper.' At the first moment I could not understand why did he call me 'Uncle' but then I remembered that my hear is cut and I and the soldiers (which were standing next to me) laugh very much. On the way many funy things had hapend, and if I shall have time I shall write to you our travel farther on. Goodbye. Don't forget me. Many kisses from us all to you my darling. Your A.[113]

It was only now, on the train, that the family was finally informed of their destination.[114] 'And so ended this act of the tragedy, the final episode of the Tsarskoe Selo period', wrote Valentina Chebotareva in her diary after they had gone. 'What', she wondered, 'awaits them in Tobolsk?'[115]

Chapter Nineteen

ON FREEDOM STREET

❧

'Why are there so many soldiers on this train?' asked one of the grand duchesses, as it pulled out of the Alexandrovsky Station. They were all of course used to being escorted by the military, 'but the great number on this occasion excited her surprise'.[1] In all, 330 men and 6 officers of the 1st, 2nd and 4th Rifles accompanied the Romanovs on their journey to Siberia, the 1st occupying the compartments on either side of the family. Whenever the train passed through a station the blinds were kept tightly drawn and the doors locked and it stopped only in sidings at rural halts where there were few, if any, of the curious to ask questions.

Back in Petrograd, when the news got out that the imperial family had been sent away, there was considerable confusion about where it was heading for. Talk of the Crimea abounded; others heard that the train was going west to Mogilev, and out of Russia. 'This caused a panic in the Narva suburb of Petrograd', recalled Robert Crozier Long:

> A crowd of Bolshevik working-men proclaimed that the counter-revolutionary Government of Kerensky had treacherously sent the Tsar for safety to Germany, and that the result would be an immediate invasion with the aim of Restoration.[2]

Elsewhere rumour was rife that the train was heading all the way out to Harbin in Manchuria – a destination already becoming a refuge for White Russians fleeing the revolution.[3] Perhaps Kerensky had this in mind as an ultimate destination, but for now the objective was to get the Romanovs beyond the tentacles of Petrograd's militants.*

Despite the close proximity of so many guards, chambermaid Anna Demidova did not find the journey unpleasant. That first day on the train, as she noted in her diary, it was unbearably hot, but their compartments were very clean and comfortable and the food laid on in the restaurant car was surprisingly good, prepared by Chinese and Armenian cooks of the railway line.[4] Alexey and his mother, who were both exhausted, did not join them, but dined together in her compartment. Finally at 7.30 in the evening, the heat still oppressive, they were all allowed off the train to stretch their legs and Anna and the girls even stopped to pick bilberries and cowberries. But they were all apprehensive about where they were headed:

> It's hard thinking about where they are taking us. While you're on the way there you think less of what lies ahead, but your heart is heavy when you start to think about how far you are from your family and if and when you might see them again. I haven't seen my sister once in five months.[5]

But she slept well that night, relieved after two weeks of terrible uncertainty and very little sleep that she now at least knew their destination, although the thought of Tobolsk made her heart sink. Later that day when the train pulled up at a rural halt, she heard questions being asked of one of the guards by a railway official:

> 'Who's on the train?
> 'An American Red Cross Mission.'
> 'Then why does no one show themselves and come out of the wagons?'
> 'It's because they are all very sick, barely alive.'[6]

Resting in her compartment, Alexandra sat scrupulously noting down the stations as they passed: Tikhvin – Cherepovets – Shavra

---

* It has been suggested that Kerensky had considered Tobolsk as a stopgap and that from there he did indeed hope to evacuate the family out to the safety of Japan on the Trans-Siberian Railway via Manchuria.

– Katen – Chaikovsky – Perm – Kamyshevo – Poklevskaya: aside from Perm, all obscure way stations in a vast empire that she and Nicholas had never got to know and from which they were now to be for ever separated.

Later on, near the River Slyva at Kama, they were allowed off the train once more for an hour's walk; they stopped to admire the view of the beautiful valley of Kungur and the girls picked flowers. Now more at ease, that evening Anna Demidova played whist with Dr Botkin, Ilya Tatishchev and Vasili Dolgorukov.[7] Another long hot day followed as they crossed the endless Russian steppe with its vast fields of ripening grain stretching far into the distance. The train finally crossed the Urals into western Siberia on the 4th and rattled on through the big railway junction at Ekaterinburg. Nicholas noticed a distinct chill in the air by the time they pulled up in sight of the landing stage at Tyumen at 11.15 that evening.[8]

There was no railway line to Tobolsk and it was accessible by boat only for the brief four months of summer, so the family now boarded the American-built steamer the *Rus* for the remainder of their journey. They were given no special privileges on board, just plain hard beds like everyone else; much to the disgust of Anna Demidova there were no carafes of water in any of the cabins, and the most primitive washing facilities. She came to the conclusion that the boat was designed for people who didn't wash very much. It took all night to load all the baggage and the escort onto two additional steamers, the *Kormilets* and the *Tyumen*, and it was not till 6 a.m. on 5 August that the *Rus* finally set off on the 189-mile (304-km) river journey to Tobolsk.[9]

The low-lying river banks on either side were thinly populated and had little to distinguish them. Dr Botkin's son Gleb later recalled 'the same brown fields, the same groves of sickly looking birches. Not a hill, not the slightest elevation of any sort to break the monotony of the landscape.'[10] Thirty-six hours later and now on the wider waters of the Tobol River, the boat entered the Irtysh – 'a little sluggish stream that drains, or partially drains one of the great marshes of eastern Siberia' – which brought them into Tobolsk.[11] Having heard of the former tsar's imminent arrival, many gathered to catch sight of him. 'Literally the entire town, I am not exaggerating, spilled out on to the shore', recalled Commissar Makarov of the guard.[12] The church bells were ringing for the Feast of the Transfiguration and as the *Rus* drew up at the landing stage at 6.30 on the evening of 6 August, Nicholas recalled that the family's first sight was 'the view of the cathedral and the houses on the hill'.[13] Below, on the banks of the Irtysh, Tobolsk itself was a jumble of low wooden houses and dirt roads built on treeless marshland. It was significant for two things: as a former place of exile – Feodor Dostoevsky had spent ten days in a cell here in transit to Omsk in 1850 – and as the haunt of mosquitoes 'said to be of a size and a ferocity unequalled elsewhere'.[14] Malaria haunted the miasmas of the marshy forests that stretched for miles around the town.

A small, eighteenth-century kremlin of white stone – the only one of its kind in Siberia – dominated the view from the top of a steep bluff inland, and was pretty much all that Tobolsk had to offer the adventurous tourist. Its major attraction was the former bishop's palace – now a courthouse – the St Sophia Cathedral, and a museum containing 'large collections of old instruments of torture: branding tools, used to stamp the foreheads and cheeks of prisoners, instruments for pulling out the center bone of the nose [a favourite of torturers during the reign of Boris Godunov], painful shackles, and other horrible devices'.[15] Churches dominated the town: twenty had been built to serve a population of around 23,000 people. Kerensky knew Tobolsk, having visited it in 1910, and had chosen it for the Romanovs, not as a lesson in the iniquities of tsarism, but because it had no industrial proletariat, no railway depots or factories seething with political activists, and because for eight months of the year it was 'shut off from the world . . . as remote from human association as the moon'.[16] The Siberian winter was a better policeman than any prison; as Olga was soon to discover: 'Tobolsk is a forgotten corner when the river freezes.'[17]

While the family waited on board the *Rus*, Kobylinsky, Dolgorukov, Tatishchev and Makarov went ahead to inspect the family's accommodation. The former Governor's House – hastily rechristened Freedom House – was located on the also appropriately revolutionary Freedom Street. It was one of the two best buildings that the town had to offer, and had the advantage of surrounding boardwalks to spare the pedestrian from the quagmire of the intractable autumn mud. But two hours later the three men came back with grim faces: the 'dirty, boarded-up, smelly house' had 'terrible bathrooms and toilets' and in its present state, was totally uninhabitable.[18] Until three days previously it had been used as a barracks by deputies of the local Workers' and Soldiers' Soviet, who had left it filthy and practically stripped of furniture. There were no chairs, tables, wash-stands, or even carpets. The double winter windows were grimy and had not been removed and there was rubbish everywhere. Forced to remain on board the *Rus* and in order to pass the time while waiting for the house to be got ready, the Romanov family took some excursions on the river and made the most of any opportunity to get off and walk.

Anna Demidova had meanwhile gone on ahead to help prepare the house and had been deeply depressed at the sight of its derelict interior. Soon she was trudging round town with Nastenka Hendrikova and Vasili Dolgorukov in search of household supplies: jugs and ewers for the washstands, buckets, tins of paint, flat-irons, inkpots, candles, writing paper, wool and thread for darning, as well as a much needed laundress to handle all the family's washing. She stopped to admire the fur coats and warm *valenki* on sale in the market – all at horribly inflated prices, deliberately raised in the knowledge of the imperial entourage's arrival in town. But otherwise 'everything here is very primitive' she noted in her diary.[19] Makarov meanwhile had been hunting for a piano for Alexandra and the grand duchesses as well as additional furniture, while a team of upholsterers, carpenters, painters and electricians was gathered together – some of them German prisoners of war – to refurbish the house at speed.[20] Most urgent were repairs to the inadequate plumbing, but there was also considerable concern about where exactly the authorities would put all the staff who could not be accommodated in the Governor's House.

'The family is bearing everything with great sangfroid and courage', wrote Dolgorukov. 'They apparently adapt to circum-stances easily, or at least pretend to, and do not complain after all their previous luxury.'[21] Finally, on Sunday 13 August the house was ready. Only one carriage was laid on to take Alexandra from the ship to the house, accompanied by Tatiana; the rest of the family, servants and entourage walked the mile (1½ km) into town. When they entered, the whole of the ground floor was a mass of luggage and packing cases; nevertheless they were allowed an impromptu Sunday service conducted by the local priest, who went round blessing the rooms with holy water.[22]

Although their packing had been hurried, Alexandra had ensured that they had brought with them not just their personal clothing and possessions but also many of their favourite pictures, silver tableware, monogrammed china, table linen, a phonograph and records, their cameras and photographic equipment, favourite books, a trunkful of photograph albums, and another containing all Nicholas's letters and diaries (which he had not destroyed). The girls had left behind all their beautiful court dresses and their large picture hats, bringing only simple linen suits, white summer dresses, skirts, blouses, sunhats and, as instructed, plenty of warm cardigans, scarves and hats, fur jackets and thick felt coats.

The family was accommodated on the first floor of the two-storey house, with the girls sharing a corner bedroom facing the street. Alexey had another with his *dyadka* Nagorny in a small room next to it.*[23] There was a bedroom for Nicholas and Alexandra, as well as a study for him and a private drawing room for her, a bathroom and toilet. A large upstairs ballroom opposite Nicholas's study would be used for church services, furnished with the field chapel that the family had brought with them from Tsarskoe Selo and with Alexandra's lace bedspread serving as an altar cloth. Services would be conducted by the priest and deacon from the nearby Blagoveshchensky Church, assisted by four nuns from the Ivanovsky Convent outside town, who came to sing the liturgy (and also brought welcome gifts of eggs and milk).[24]

With a typical lack of complaint the four sisters immediately set about making the most of their new surroundings by ensuring that

---

* Alexey's other *dyadka*, Derevenko, did not travel with them to Tobolsk; his behaviour towards the boy had changed since the revolution. He had become harsh and churlish in his manner towards Alexey and was no longer perceived as the kind and trustworthy carer he had once been.

the room they shared was as congenial as possible. It had a traditional, tall white-tiled stove in the corner, a small sofa scattered with
cushions, a table which was soon stacked with books, pens and
writing paper. Simple white bentwood chairs stood at the foot of
each of the girls' four modest campbeds, brought from the Alexander
Palace and surrounded with screens covered with colourful throws
and shawls, which the girls also draped on the bare and draughty
white walls to create a sense of warmth and intimacy. On their tiny
bedside tables the sisters crammed their favourite knick-knacks, icons
and photographs. Each girl also fixed many pictures on the wall
above her own bedhead: the younger two opting for fond reminders
of the Tsar's Escort in their Cossack uniforms at Mogilev and other
friends, relatives, pets and much-loved wounded officers, while their
older sisters' more sober tastes focused on religious images and a
large photograph of their parents on board the *Shtandart*.[25]

The dining room was located downstairs, as was a room occupied
by Pierre Gilliard where he also gave the children lessons. Later
on, shared rooms downstairs were allocated to the maids Alexandra
Tegleva and Elizaveta Ersberg who looked after the children,
Mariya Tutelberg who attended Alexandra, and other staff including Nicholas's valet Terenty Chemodurov. For now the rest of the
entourage and servants were housed in the even more ill-prepared
and uncongenial Kornilov House opposite: Nastenka Hendrikova
and her maid Paulina Mezhants, Dr Botkin (who in mid-September
was joined by his two children, Gleb and Tatiana), Dr Derevenko
and his family, Tatishchev and Dolgorukov. Here, occupying crudely
partitioned cubicles in a large draughty hall, and with very little
concession to privacy, the women were later joined by Trina
Schneider and her two maids Katya and Masha and another tutor,
Klavdiya Bitner.[26] Although the family remained under house arrest
with only the yard outside to move about in and occasional excursions to the nearby church, the entourage and servants were, for
the time being, allowed to go about freely in town.

*

The weather remained hot and sunny in Tobolsk well into September,
but the family had been deeply disconsolate to see that the 'so-called

garden' was a 'nasty little vegetable patch' that would only grow a few cabbages and swedes at best.[27] In addition, at the back of the house were a lean-to greenhouse, woodshed and barn, and a few spindly birch trees. There were no flowers or shrubs at all. The only concession for the children was a couple of swings. Nicholas was bitterly disappointed that the garden offered no scope for the physical labour and recreation that he craved, though within days he had chopped down a dry pine tree and was allowed to put up his horizontal bar on which he did his daily chin-ups. To the side of the house the authorities had hastily created a square dusty courtyard for recreation – twice a day, between 11 and 12 and after lunch until dusk – in a fenced-off part of the unpaved road.

The uncertainties of the family's new environment were very quickly compounded by the increasingly erratic arrival of letters. 'My dear Katya,' Anastasia wrote within days of their arrival, 'I am writing this letter to you being certain that you will never get it . . . It is so sad to be unable to hear from you. We often, often think and talk of you . . . Have you received my letter of 31 July and the card that I wrote long ago?' She was now numbering her letters in hopes of keeping track of them. But her thoughts were already turning to happier times: 'Ask Victor whether he still remembers last autumn. I am now remembering a lot . . . everything good, of course!' Enclosing a red petal from a poppy in the garden she apologized for having so little to say: 'I cannot write anything interesting . . . we spend our time monotonously.'[28]

The monotony was, however, broken soon after by unexpected news: Olga's friend Rita Khitrovo had arrived in Tobolsk anxious to see the family and pass on to them some fifteen or so letters (which she had hidden in a travelling pillow), as well as gifts of chocolate, perfume, sweets and biscuits, and icons sent by various friends.[29] The highly-strung and excitable twenty-two-year-old, whose ingenuousness and devotion to Olga – to the point of hero-worship – were equalled only by her fearlessness, had taken it upon herself to make the journey without any thought of the possible repercussions. Refused admittance to the Governor's House, Rita went to the Kornilov House opposite to see Nastenka Hendrikova, from where she waved and blew kisses to the four sisters who had come out on the balcony to try and catch a glimpse of her.

But her arrival alarmed the authorities. During her journey she had sent postcards home that had been intercepted and interpreted as suspicious. It was thought she might be colluding with Anna Vyrubova and other monarchist friends in a conspiracy to rescue the family, rumours of a nebulous plot by 'Cossack officers' having already been circulating in Tobolsk. Soon afterwards, on the orders of Kerensky, men came to inspect all the things Rita had brought for the family. The letters were checked and deemed harmless, but she was put under arrest and sent back to Moscow for questioning. Hearing the story later, Valentina Chebotareva thought a 'mountain had been made out of a molehill', for Rita insisted that her journey had been undertaken entirely out of a personal desire to see the family. But she had, unwittingly, caused them harm: 'an obliging fool is more dangerous than an enemy', as Valentina observed.[30] Commissar Makarov was recalled by the Provisional Government and replaced by a new man, Vasily Pankratov.

Pankratov was an archetypal, old-school revolutionary. The son of peasants, he had been active in the extremist *Narodnaya Volya* [People's Will] movement of the 1880s and in 1884 had been sentenced to death for killing a gendarme in Kiev. It was only his youth that had saved him from the gallows; instead he served four-teen years incarcerated in the notorious Shlisselburg Fortress and from there was sent into exile in Yakutiya before being freed in the political amnesty of 1905. His revolutionary career might have been a textbook one but to Nicholas, Pankratov would be 'the little man'.[31] But adjust to him he did, for Pankratov, who did his best by the family within the constraints placed upon him, would be their only link with the outside world. During the weeks that followed, the family and Pankratov would learn much about each other and develop a polite, respectful relationship.

The first thing that had struck the new commissar was seeing the family at prayer. He noted how devotedly Alexandra came and arranged the temporary altar, covered it with her embroidery, the candles and icons before the arrival of the priest and nuns for the service. There was a punctiliousness to every aspect of the family's religious observance: after the entire suite and servants had all assembled, in their designated places according to rank, the family entered through the side doors and everyone bowed to them. During the service Pankratov noticed how frequently – and fervently – the Romanovs crossed themselves. He could not but be impressed that 'the whole family of the former tsar had given themselves up to a truly religious state of mind and feeling' – even if it was one that was beyond his comprehension.[32]

With their lives so grounded in religious acceptance it took no time at all for the family to slip back into the same kind of quiet, uneventful routine that they had followed under house arrest at the Alexander Palace. Having always been so physically active, Nicholas was intensely frustrated by the lack of exercise and took to walking up and down the yard forty or fifty times in an hour, though soon he was able to busy himself sawing wood for the winter. Alexey's only outside interest, until the arrival of a playmate in the shape of Dr Derevenko's son Kolya later that month, was in the dogs. Much of the girls' time was spent, when not helping their father saw logs, in chasing Joy and Ortipo away from the refuse tip at the back of the yard, where they persisted in rootling around for food.[33] The heat was too much for Alexandra, who would sometimes sit on the balcony under a parasol sewing, before retiring indoors. She was rarely up and out of her room before lunchtime and often remained alone in the house when the others were outside – painting and sewing, or playing the piano. Much of her time was spent in religious contemplation and reading the gospels, her thoughts on which she continued to pour into long homiletic letters to her friends, particularly Anna Vyrubova.

The food at the Governor's House was surprisingly good and plentiful in comparison with the desperate shortages now being endured in Petrograd. Many of the locals looked favourably on the former tsar and his family, and gifts of food began to arrive. Some doffed their caps when passing by on the street; others occasionally even kneeled down and crossed themselves. Old habits died hard, even here, and Alexandra still wrote out menu cards for each day's modest meals. The atmosphere was less stressful too. Evenings were spent playing the usual games of bezique and dominoes, or bumble puppy and nain jaune, and Nicholas as always read aloud – his first choice on arrival in Tobolsk being *The Scarlet Pimpernel*. He then set about revisiting the classics of Russian literature. 'I have decided to re-read all our best writers from beginning to end (I'm reading English and French books too)', he told his mother.[34] Having just worked his way through Gogol, he moved on to Turgenev. But, as Pankratov noted with amusement, the members of the entourage often seemed to get bored with having to sit in silence as he read and would begin to whisper among themselves or even nodded off to the monotonous sound of his voice.[35] Nevertheless, reading was undoubtedly a boon for all the family. Sydney Gibbes soon arrived with more favourite books for the children: English adventure stories such as Alexey's great favourite *Cast Up by the Sea* by Sir Samuel Baker, the novels of Walter Scott (Tatiana and Anastasia loved *Ivanhoe*), Thackeray, Dickens and H. Rider Haggard. Such indeed was the hunger for reading material that Trina Schneider wrote to PVP in Petrograd asking him to send more books – the stories of Fonvizin, Derzhavin, Karamzin, which the children didn't have, as well as books on Russian grammar and literature.[36] Tatiana wrote too, asking him to send out her set of Alexey Tolstoy's novels that she had unfortunately not brought with her.

But even the best of books could not for long fend off the crippling boredom that was infecting the entire entourage and which was so clearly reflected in everyone's diaries and letters. Alexey's perfunctory diary contained nothing but repetitious complaints: 'Today passed just as yesterday . . . It is boring.'[37] Even Alexandra could write nothing but 'I spent the day, as usual' . . . 'Everything was the same as yesterday'. And Nicholas echoed her: 'The day passed as always' . . . 'The day passed as usual'.[38] By 25 August he was already noting that 'Walks in the garden are becoming incredibly tedious; here the sense of sitting locked up is much stronger than it ever was at Tsarskoe Selo.'[39] To keep himself occupied he dug out a pond in the garden, helped by Alexey, for the ducks and geese that had been brought in, and he also built a wooden platform on the roof of the greenhouse where he and the children could sit soaking up the sunshine and watch the world go by below. The locals were fascinated when they saw them there, or on the balcony, especially when they saw the girls: 'Their hair was shorn like little boys' . . . We thought that was the fashion in Petrograd,' recalled one local, 'later, people said they had been sick . . . still they were very pretty, very clean.'[40]

At midday on Friday 8 September – the Nativity of the Virgin – the family was allowed out for the first time to attend service at the nearby Blagoveshchensky Church. They went on foot, pushing Alexandra in her wheelchair through the public garden where there was no one around, but were greatly disconcerted to see a crowd waiting for them outside the church. 'The emperor was still the emperor in Tobolsk', it appeared.[41] 'It was very unpleasant', Alexandra wrote, but she was 'grateful that I had been in a real church for the first time in six months'.[42]

Pankratov noticed how much pleasure this small concession had evoked:

> As Nicholas II and the children walked through the public garden, they looked this way and that, talking in French* about the weather, the garden, as though they had never seen it before, although the gardens were located directly opposite their balcony, from where they could clearly see them every day. But it is one thing to see something from a distance, from behind bars as it were, and quite another to see it when almost at liberty. Every tree, every twig and bush and bench acquired its own unique charm . . . From the expression on their faces and the way they moved one could tell they had all undergone some particular personal trial.[43]

On their way through the gardens Anastasia fell over while craning her neck to look at things and her sisters and father laughed at her clumsiness. Alexandra did not react. 'She sat there majestically in her wheelchair and said nothing.' She hadn't been sleeping at night – tormented by another bout of neuralgia and toothache. Once again, what most evoked public curiosity as the family passed was the girls' heads: 'Why was their hair cut short like boys?' people asked.[44] By the end of September, however, their hair was getting quite long again, though Anastasia told Katya that it had been 'such a pleasure to have short hair'.[45]

---

* No doubt to prevent the guards understanding what they were talking about.

On 14 September when they attended church a second time the family went at 8 a.m. to avoid the crowds: 'You can just imagine how great our joy was,' Tatiana wrote to her aunt Xenia, 'as you will remember how inconvenient our field chapel at Tsarskoe Selo was.'[46] But a chill autumnal rain the previous day had brought a transformation in the surrounding streets, and they were now a sea of mud: 'If they hadn't laid wooden boards on the road it would be impossible to get through', said Anna Demidova.[47] Nicholas was now spending as much time as he could outside sawing wood. Pankratov was astonished at his prodigious energy. From time to time Alexey, Tatishchev, Dolgorukov, and even an uncomfortable-looking Pierre Gilliard (inappropriately dressed in trilby and wing collar) were enlisted to help, but Nicholas wore them all out. Pankratov sent word to the local authorities that the ex-tsar enjoyed sawing wood so much that in response they sent in great piles of birch trunks for him to cut up.[48] The whole family was counting its luck at the continuing fine weather. 'It's so good that we sit in the garden a lot or in the courtyard in front of the house', Tatiana told her aunt Xenia:

> It's terribly nice that we have a balcony, which the sun warms from morning to evening. It's good to sit there and watch people coming and going on the street. It is our only entertainment . . . We've managed to play skittles in front of the house and we play a kind of tennis, though of course without a net, for the sake of practice. Then we walk up and down, so we don't forget how to walk – 120 paces in all, which is considerably shorter than the deck [of the *Shtandart*].[49]

Tatiana calculated that you could walk round the entire kitchen garden in three minutes flat, but at least there was the livestock to look after, which now included five pigs housed in the former stables – all no doubt destined to provide food during the winter to come.[50]

The beginning of October brought the long-awaited arrival from Tsarskoe Selo of carpets, curtains and window blinds in time for the approaching winter, but the wine brought from the imperial cellars was confiscated by the guards and poured into the Irtysh.[51] Far more welcome, however, was Sydney Gibbes, who on 5 October arrived.

on the boat from Tyumen – one of the last before the ice made the river impassable – along with a new tutor for the children, Klavdiya Bitner. Gibbes brought cards and gifts from Anna Vyrubova, now out of prison, including her favourite perfume which Maria said reminded them all of her. How they missed her, she wrote to Anna: 'It's terribly sad that we don't see each other, but God grant that we shall meet again and what joy that will be.'[52]

It was not long before Sydney Gibbes found himself once more having to contend with Anastasia's quirky and inattentive behaviour in class. On one occasion, having lost his temper, he told her to 'shut up'; the next time she handed in her homework she had added a new nameplate to her exercise book – 'A. Romanova (Shut up!)'.[53] Klavdiya Bitner found Anastasia a trial too – lazy in lessons and often ill-mannered.[54] She had been a teacher at the Mariinsky girls' school at Tsarskoe Selo and during the war had volunteered as a nurse at one of the hospitals where she had looked after Kobylinsky who had been wounded at the front. A romance had developed between them and when he was sent with the family to Tobolsk, Kobylinsky had wangled a job for Klavdiya teaching Maria, Anastasia and Alexey Russian language, literature and maths. Both she and Pankratov remained distinctly unimpressed with the standard of the children's education, particularly Alexey's, unaware perhaps that it had been constantly interrupted through illness. Pankratov was shocked at how little they, and their father for that matter, knew of Siberia, its geography and peoples.[55] As winter set in, one of the grand duchesses had been amazed at the sight of people on the streets wearing 'strange white and grey costumes trimmed with fur'. Pankratov realized she was referring to the reindeer-skin traditional dress worn by Yakuts, Khanty and Samoyedic peoples living in the region. Had the sisters never seen pictures of these inhabitants of their father's vast Russian Empire in their geography books, he wondered? Such strangers from the 'outside life' were, for the girls, precisely the kind of people they had so longed to learn about, but had never had a chance to discover. Pankratov found them at times extremely naïve: you only had to talk to them about the most mundane things in the world outside and it was 'as if they had never seen anything, never read anything, never heard anything', a highly biased view but one that was clearly ignorant of the breadth of the education the girls had in fact been receiving until the revolution had disrupted it.[56]

Lessons, for all their limitations in such highly constrained circumstances, were, in Sydney Gibbes's estimation, an important distraction that helped the younger children get through the monotony of the day. Indeed, he felt that the only one of the grand duchesses who seemed 'dull' was Olga, who didn't have any formal lessons, although she did continue with her own independent study, wrote poetry and practised her French by reading stories to Alexandra. It seemed painfully clear to Gibbes, though, that the family's 'greatest hardship', especially Nicholas's, was the lack of free exercise, 'the yard being a poor substitute for their Alexander Park'.[57] On one occasion Maria had said to him that they were all, otherwise, quite contented and that she 'could live at Tobolsk for ever if only they would be able to walk out a little'.[58] But Nicholas's repeated requests to Pankratov to be allowed into town were refused. 'Are they really afraid that I might run off?' he asked. 'I will never leave my family.'[59] He seemed to have no comprehension of the security problems that this would pose. The local government of Tobolsk was still holding on but not far away, in Tomsk, the workers' soviet there was already demanding that the Romanovs be taken to prison.

'We keep doing the same things every day', became the regular complaint of all the family, as Anastasia told Katya on 8 October. One thing that lightened the girls' day was the visits of a cleaning woman who brought her little boy Tolya with her. The sisters loved playing with him for he reminded them of a little boy at Stavka called Lenka whom they had taken under their wing. 'Ask your brother; he met him', Anastasia told Katya. Mention of Lenka once again prompted the remembrance of happier times with the Tsar's Escort at Mogilev: 'What are you doing? I want to see you all *awfully badly*! . . . When I look at the street through the window, I see everything covered with snow and feel so sad, because it is winter already, and I love summer and warmth.'[60] 'Till now we've had no reason to complain about the weather, as it's been warm,' Olga told Xenia that same day, 'but now we are freezing.' She envied her living in the Crimea with her mother and sister. 'No doubt it's wonderful where you are. The sea so bluish-green . . . We are all well and our life is the same, so there is nothing interesting that I can write about.'[61]

For ten days in the second half of October came a less than pleasant change to the daily routine when the former imperial dentist, Sergey Kostritsky, travelled all the way from the Crimea to check the family's teeth and perform some urgent dental work on Nicholas and Alexandra, who both suffered endless problems. Kostritsky arrived with letters and gifts from Maria Feodorovna, Xenia and Olga and was accommodated in Pankratov's lodgings. Inevitably, the two men discussed the family and agreed that even here in Tobolsk, they were still 'suffocating in the same stilted formal atmosphere' that had prevailed at court. It had created a real 'spiritual hunger' in them and a 'thirst to meet with people from a different milieu'. Hidebound tradition 'dragged them down like a dead weight and made them the slaves of etiquette'.[62] Pankratov might have wished more time had been given to the girls' broader education, instead of to the niceties of 'how to stand, how to sit and what to say, and so on', but despite that he was impressed with how willingly they chopped wood and cleared the snow – 'their simple life gave them much pleasure'.[63] With most of the winter wood now cut the girls were helping their father to pile it up in the wood store and clear the snow in the yard, as well as from the steps and roofs of the outbuildings. Pankratov caught Maria one day struggling to do this with a broken spade. Why hadn't she asked for a replacement, he enquired, adding that he had not thought she would wish to do such things. 'But I love this kind of work', she had replied.[64] So long as the weather was fine and they could work outside in the fresh air the girls were happy. 'Bright sun . . . makes my mood immediately better', Olga wrote to PVP, with the weather continuing 'divine' well into November. 'So don't think that it is always bad. Not at all. As you know, we don't get dejected easily.'[65]

But dejection must have descended at the end of the month when the family heard of the October Revolution in Petrograd. 'A second revolution', Alexandra wrote in her diary on the 28th, when the news finally reached Tobolsk. 'Provisional government replaced. The Bolsheviks led by Lenin and Trotsky have occupied the Smolny.

Winter Palace badly damaged.'[66] Only the day before Nicholas had written a cheerful letter to his mother: 'I'm chopping a lot of wood, usually with Tatishchev . . . The food here is excellent and plenty of it, a big difference with Tsarskoe Selo, so that we have all settled down well in Tobolsk and have put on 8–10 pounds [3.5–4.5 kg] in weight.'[67] Petrograd and their former lives were now so much past history for Nicholas that the Bolshevik coup did not particularly register with him and he didn't even mention it in his diary; the weather was excellent, he had walked a lot and chopped wood, that was the sum total of his world now.[68] For a long time he made no comment about the October Revolution: 'Nicholas II suffered silently and never talked to me about it', Pankratov recalled. Eventually he merely expressed outrage at the sacking of the Winter Palace. It was mid-November before Nicholas finally received the newspaper accounts and deemed this second revolution 'Far worse and more shameful than the events of the Time of Troubles'. The turbulent years of the interregnum in the sixteenth century seemed to have far more resonance for him now than the recent past.[69]

Chapter Twenty

THANK GOD WE ARE STILL IN
RUSSIA AND ALL TOGETHER

༺❦༻

A heavy fall of snow greeted Olga's birthday on 3 November, for which she received modest presents of three pots of cyclamen and some strong-smelling geraniums. 'Dear Olga has turned 22,' Nicholas wrote in his diary, 'it's a pity that the poor thing has to spend her birthday in this present environment.'[1] For a mournful and introspective Alexandra, Olga's birthday was, this sad difficult year of 1917, a talismanic day – a day of remembrance rather than celebration. Thirty-nine years previously to the day, her little sister May had died of diphtheria; and on this same day fourteen years ago Ernie's daughter Elisabeth had died suddenly when staying with them at Skierniewice. Against this comment in her diary Alexandra added the left-facing *sauwastika* symbol of which she was so fond, her use of it denoting the cycle of life and death.

For Olga herself – twenty-two, unmarried, and a prisoner in snowbound Siberia – it must have been a particularly bleak birthday. She had remained very thin since her illness and had become increasingly withdrawn and anxious, so much so that Sydney Gibbes had found her rather short-tempered at times. But her innate love and kindness still illuminated her letters to friends and family. On 9 November she wrote with affection to her aunt Xenia saying they were all well and cheerful. She had rescued a half-dead potted lemon tree from the conservatory and brought it back to life with careful watering. She was sorry that she had nothing interesting to tell her and that Xenia could not come and visit them, 'as we've arranged things very nicely and feel completely at home here'.[2]

'We live here as though on a ship at sea, and the days all resemble one another', Nicholas wrote to Xenia with the same sense of quiet resignation.[3] But the lack of news depressed him: 'No papers at all, or even telegrams, have come from Petrograd for a long while. This is awful in such trying times.'[4] When newspapers finally did arrive they said little. Denied access to *The Times*, 'we were reduced to a nasty local rag printed on packing paper,' recalled Pierre Gilliard, 'which only gave telegrams several days old and generally distorted and cut down'.[5] Nevertheless Nicholas was grateful for any news; Sydney Gibbes noticed how he 'would read through a newspaper from beginning to end, and when he had finished, would start again'.[6] He was rereading his old diaries too, which he found 'a pleasant occupation' and a distraction from his interminable routine.[7]

'We have not had any significant changes in our life so far', Anastasia told Katya on 14 November. Apart from propelling themselves back and forth on the swing outside and from there dropping down into a heap of snow, or pulling Alexey around on his sledge, there was only the endless piling up of logs. 'This work kept us busy. That is the way we live here, not very exciting, is it?' Anastasia found herself endlessly apologizing to Katya: 'I am terribly sorry that my letter turned out to be so stupid and boring, but nothing interesting happens here.'[8] Her sense of frustration and irritation grew in her next letter: 'I am starting to write this letter to you for the third time, because it either turns out messy, or very stupid! . . . Of course we have not played tennis for a long time. We swing, walk, and saw logs. Inside the house we read and study.'[9]

'The children are getting very bored without their walks', Anna Demidova wrote to a friend at the end of the month. Indeed,

> there is a terrible boredom among the entourage. Frost, thaw, sunshine – darkness. The days fly by. Reading out loud in the evenings, needlework or bezique. We're making Christmas presents. On the 21st they suddenly once more would not allow us out to church and wouldn't even let us have a service at home – everything hangs on the whim of others. And it is at such difficult times that we particularly long for church . . . It's hard

to write letters when others read them, but I'm grateful all the same to have them.[10]

The unreliability of the postal system was a major frustration for everyone. All of the girls' and Alexandra's correspondence testifies to many letters and parcels never reaching them in Tobolsk, or the people they sent them to. 'Every time I went over to the house,' recalled Pankratov, 'one or other of the Grand Duchesses would meet me with the question – are there any letters?'[11] Their own were full of endless questions about old friends, former patients, where they were and what they were doing – though hopes of their ever knowing the answer were rapidly receding. 'Forgive me for so many questions,' Maria apologized to her friend Vera Kapralova, 'but I so want to know what you are doing and how everyone is.'[12] 'Do you have news of any of ours?' echoed her sister Olga. 'As always, my postcards are uninteresting and full of questions.'[13] And again, the same day, to Valentina Chebotareva: 'Did you receive my letter of 12/10? I'm very sad not to have had news of you for such a long time.'[14] Tatiana, more restrained, seemed for her part almost to enjoy the isolation: 'everything is quiet in our distant little town. It's good to be so far from the railway and large towns, where there are no cars and only horses.'[15] But she admitted to Valentina Chebotareva, 'we feel as though we are living on some kind of faraway island where we receive news from another world . . . I play the piano a lot. The time goes quickly and the days pass completely unnoticed.'[16]

By early December the temperature was dropping well below zero; on the 7th and 8th it hit –23 degrees C (–9.4 degrees F). 'We shiver in the rooms,' Alexandra told Anna Vyrubova, 'and there is always a strong draught from the windows.'[17] It was so cold indoors that even the hardy Nicholas sat in his Cossack *cherkeska*. The girls huddled together to try and keep warm; 'the dogs are running around and begging to get in our laps', Tatiana told Zinaida Tolstaya, all of them glad of the warmth of a friendly animal. 'We do not have enough space for everybody,' Anastasia wrote to Katya, 'so one of us is writing while sitting on the sofa and holding the paper on her lap. It is pretty chilly in the room, so our hands do not write properly.'[18] Spirits were beginning to sag until Sydney Gibbes came up with a new way of passing the cold, dark winter days. He suggested that the children perform some one-act plays; he had brought a selection with him. They started rehearsing after their afternoon recreation, and created an improvised theatre in the ballroom upstairs. On the evening of 6 December Maria, Alexey and Gilliard performed a twenty-minute playlet, *Le fluide de John* by Maurice Hennequin.[19]

At last, on 10 December, the family was allowed out to mass again. 'We are always so happy when they let us go to church', Tatiana wrote to her aunt Xenia:

> although you can't compare this church with our cathedral,* but all the same it's better than indoors . . . I often remember Tsarskoe Selo and the lovely concerts we had at the hospital; do you remember how amusing it was when our wounded did the *lezginka* dance; I also remember our walks at Pavlovsk and your little carriage, and the morning jaunts past your house. How long ago that all seems, doesn't it? Well, I must stop now.[20]

Although they were all getting chilblains from the intense cold, the girls had at last had things to do in the run-up to Christmas, helping their mother make presents for the entourage and even the guards as well. Alexandra knitted woollen waistcoats and painted cards and bookmarks. She and the girls were using up every last precious scrap of material and knitting wool to ensure that everyone had something to open on Christmas Eve. 'They were all expert needlewomen', remembered Iza Buxhoeveden, 'and managed to make the prettiest things out of the coarse, hand woven, country linen, on which they drew their own designs.'[21] 'I am knitting stockings for the small one', Alexandra told Anna on the 15th.

> He asked for a pair as all his are in holes. Mine are warm and thick like the ones I gave the wounded, do you remember? I make everything now. Father's trousers are torn and darned, the girls' under-linen in rags. Dreadful, is it not? I have grown quite gray. Anastasia is now very fat, as Marie was, round and fat to the waist, with short legs. I do hope she will grow. Olga and Tatiana are both thin, but their hair grows beautifully so that they can go without scarves.[22]

---

* The Feodorovsky Sobor at Tsarskoe Selo.

With food supplies considerably better in Tobolsk than Petrograd, she had sent Anna precious gifts of flour, sugar, macaroni and sausage, as well as a hand-knitted scarf and stockings. In return Anna had sent a parcel with perfume, a blue silk jacket for Alexandra and pastilles for the children.[23] Alexandra regretted that unlike her husband she had no old diaries and letters to read through. 'I have not a line of yours', she told Anna. She had 'burnt everything':

> All the past is a dream. One keeps only tears and grateful memories. One by one all earthly things slip away, houses and possessions ruined, friends vanished. One lives from day to day. But God is in all and nature never changes. I can see all around me churches (long to go to them) and hills, the lovely world.[24]

Her heart lifted when, on 19 December, Iza Buxhoeveden finally arrived in Tobolsk, with her Scottish travelling companion Miss Mather. Disappointingly, however, militants in the 2nd Regiment of the guard refused to allow her into the Governor's House and she had to put up at the Kornilov House and content herself with catching only glimpses of the family.[25] When the girls first saw her 'they began to gesticulate wildly . . . in a moment all four Grand Duchesses were at the window waving their hands, while the youngest jumped up and down in her excitement'.[26] They were all terribly disappointed that Iza was not allowed to join them, even for Christmas; three weeks later she was told to move into lodgings in town.

'Christmas is coming,' Trina Schneider wrote to her colleague PVP in Petrograd, 'but this year it will be an especially sad one – far from our friends and families.' Olga too, in response to a comment from her aunt Xenia about recent misfortunes, was trying hard not to feel melancholy:

> They always say that nothing good or happy endures for long, or rather doesn't last; but I also think that even awful things must come to an end some time. Isn't that so? Things are as quiet with us as they can be, thank God. We are all well and cheerful and are not losing heart.
>
> I dreamed about grandmother today. I've just put on an orange scarf and for some reason it reminded me of your sitting room

in Petrograd. My thoughts are jumping from one thing to another, which is why this letter seems so incoherent, for which I ask your forgiveness. Well, what else is there to write?[27]

Having made their many Christmas gifts the girls did their best to decorate the tree. 'We have a Christmas tree standing in the corner and it gives off such a wonderful smell, not at all like the ones at Tsarskoe', Olga told Rita Khitrovo.

It's a special kind and is called a 'balsamic fir'. It smells strongly of orange and mandarin, and resin trickles down its trunk all the time. We don't have any decorations; only some silver rain and wax candles, church ones of course, as there aren't any other kind here.[28]

The tree 'smelled divine', Tatiana wrote to PVP, 'I don't remember such a strong scent anywhere else.'[29] Its presence inevitably inspired thoughts of absent friends: 'At Christmas we will be especially thinking of the past', Anastasia wrote to Katya. 'How much fun we had . . . I would like to write and tell you a lot, but it is so sad that everything is being read!'[30]

At midday on Christmas Eve everyone gathered for liturgy in the upstairs hall and after lunch they arranged the tree and presents. The family also decorated a tree for the twenty men of the guard, and at half past four took them their gifts, as well as special things to eat. Alexandra presented each soldier with a gospel and a hand-painted bookmark. Nor did she forget Iza, sending gifts to the Kornilov House of 'a tiny Christmas tree and some tablecloths and pillows embroidered by herself and her daughters, to which the Emperor added a little vase with his cipher on it'.[31]

'After supper on Christmas Eve,' Olga wrote to Rita,

we handed out the presents to everyone, the majority being various items of our own needlework. As we were sorting them out and deciding who to give what to, it reminded us so much of our charity bazaars at Yalta. You remember how much there always was to get ready? We had vespers at around 10 last night and the tree was lit. It was lovely and cosy. The choir was large and sang well, only too much like a concert, which I don't like.[32]

Surrounded by those who had remained faithful to them through these last difficult nine months, the Romanov family sang with great heart – and hope. Pierre Gilliard felt a special sense of 'peaceful intimacy' that Christmas, as though they all, truly, were like 'one big family'.[33]

Early on Christmas Day the family walked to church in the snow for the early morning service, conducted in front of the icon of the Mother of God brought specially from the Abalatsky Monastery 17 miles (27 km) from Tobolsk. During the service, when Father Alexey Vasiliev intoned the *mnogoletie* – the prayer for the long life of the family – he failed to omit their imperial titles. Militants in the guard who heard this loudly complained to Pankratov. The result was a total ban on the family's attending any more services in church.[34] It was a disheartening end to Christmas, and to the year. After a glass of tea in the early evening of 31 December, 'we went our separate ways – without waiting for the New Year', Nicholas noted in his diary. His final thoughts that year's end were elsewhere: 'Lord God, save Russia.'[35]

Alexandra's were more explicit: 'Thanks be to God that all seven of us are alive and well and together,' she wrote in her diary that same night, 'and that he has kept us safe all this year as well as all those who are dear to us.' But a similar message she sent to Iza was far more emphatic: 'Thank God we are still in Russia and all together.'[36]

*

The Siberian winter, in all its merciless fury, finally arrived in Tobolsk in January 1918. Until then the single-digit sub-zero temperature had been generally tolerable and the Romanov family had begun to wonder whether the savage winter foretold them was a myth. But as January passed Alexandra recorded the plummeting temperature. It was –15 degrees C (5 degrees F) on the 17th; five days later it was down to –29 degrees C (–20 degrees F) and with a searing cold wind to boot. In the depths of winter Tobolsk became a 'city of the dead', 'a living tomb', a 'listless, lifeless place, whose mournful appearance sinks into the soul'.[37] All the children had been ill again – this time with German measles, brought into the house by Alexey's playmate Kolya Derevenko, but luckily their symptoms lasted only a few days.[38]

The severe cold lingered throughout February; it was mid-March before the thermometer struggled above freezing. Even indoors with the tiled stoves stoked with logs it was 'mortally cold'.[39] 'The logs were damp, so they could not warm up the house at all; they just smoked', Anastasia told Katya.[40] The windows were thick with ice and the wind rattled at the frames and penetrated every aperture. 'The Grand Duchesses' bedroom is a real ice-house', Pierre Gilliard noted in his diary; their fingers were so stiff with cold that they could barely write or sew.[41] Being on the corner their room caught the worst of the winter wind and recently the temperature in there had been as low as –44 C (–47.2 F). They wrapped themselves in their thickest long knitted cardigans and even wore their felt boots indoors, but they could still feel the wind whistling down the chimney.[42] In desperation, they took to sitting in the corridors, or went and huddled in the kitchen, though that, alas, was full of cockroaches.[43]

'Lost in the immensity of distant Siberia', the long dark days of winter passed, for everyone, in a continuing atmosphere of quiet acceptance and 'family peace', as both Pierre Gilliard and Sydney Gibbes recalled.[44] The children remained patient and uncomplaining, always kind-hearted and willing to help and support the others, although it was clear to Gibbes that the elder two sisters 'realized how serious things were becoming'. Even before leaving Tsarskoe Selo, Olga had told Iza Buxhoeveden that she and her sisters 'put on brave faces for their parents' sake'.[45] Everyone who spent those last months with the family noticed their quiet fortitude in the face of so much desperate uncertainty. 'My respect for the Grand Duchesses only grew the longer our exile lasted', recalled Gleb Botkin.

> The courage and unselfishness they displayed were indeed remarkable. My father marveled at the exhibition of cheerfulness – so often an assumed one – by which they strove to help and cheer their parents.
>
> 'Every time the Emperor enters the dining room with a sad expression on his face,' my father told me, 'the Grand Duchesses push each other with their elbows and whisper: "Papa is sad today. We must cheer him up." And so they proceed to do. They begin to laugh, to tell funny stories, and, in a few minutes, His Majesty begins to smile.'[46]

The girls' engaging warmth extended to their friendly relations with the soldiers of the guard, particularly those of the 1st and 4th regiments. 'The Grand-Duchesses, with that simplicity which was their charm, loved to talk to these men', observed Gilliard. It was easy to understand why; the soldiers seemed, to the sisters, 'to be linked with the past in the same way as themselves. They questioned them about their families, their villages, or the battles in which they had taken part in the Great War.'[47] Nicholas and Alexey meanwhile had grown so close to the men of the 4th that they often went to the guardhouse in the evening to sit and talk with them and play draughts.

Klavdiya Bitner, the most recent addition to the entourage, soon came to her own very clear perception of the five children during the last months of their lives. She had no doubt that it was the brisk and efficient Tatiana who was the absolute linchpin at the Governor's House: 'if the family had lost Alexandra Feodorovna, then its protector would have been Tatiana Nikolaevna'.

> She had inherited her mother's nature. She had many of her mother's features: strength of character, a tendency to keeping life in order, and an awareness of her duty. She took charge of organizing things in the house. She watched over Alexey Nikolaevich. She always walked with the emperor in the yard. She was the closest person to the empress. They were two friends . . . She loved running the household. Loved doing embroidery and ironing the linen.[48]

But there was also a trait in Tatiana's personality that she shared with her father – and that was her absolute, crippling reticence. Her ability to keep her feelings bottled up and privy to no one became even more marked during the final months of captivity. Nobody ever penetrated that intense reserve; 'It was impossible to guess her thoughts,' recalled Sydney Gibbes, 'even if she was more decided in her opinions than her sisters.'[49]

Klavdiya Bitner found the gentle and soft-hearted Olga, who in so many ways was Tatiana's opposite, so much easier to love, for she had inherited her father's warm, disarming charm. Unlike Tatiana, Olga hated being organized and loathed housework. With her love of books and her preference for solitude, it seemed to Klavdiya that 'she understood the situation considerably more than the rest of the family and was aware of how dangerous it was'. There was an air of sadness about Olga that suggested to Klavdiya – much as it had done for Valentina Chebotareva – some kind of hidden unhappiness or disappointment. 'There were times when she smiled when you would sense that the smile was all on the surface, and that deep down inside her soul, she was not smiling, but sad.'[50] Olga's finely tuned nature clearly predisposed her to a sense of impending tragedy, accentuated by her love of poetry and her increasing concentration, in her reading, on religious texts. She withdrew ever more into herself, listening to the many church bells ring across Tobolsk and writing to friends about the beauty of the extraordinarily clear night skies and the astonishing brilliance of the moon and stars.[51]

Some time that winter Olga wrote to a family friend, Sergey Bekhteev (the brother of Zinaida Tolstaya), who was himself a budding poet and had published his first collection in 1916. Bekhteev had sent some of his verse to the family in captivity and in response Nicholas had asked Olga to write and thank him. This surviving fragment, more than anything else that has come down to us, sums up both Olga's mood and that of her father in those final months:

> Father asks me to tell all who have remained loyal to him and those over whom they might have an influence, that they should not avenge him, for he has forgiven everyone and prays for them all; that they should not themselves seek revenge; that they should remember that the evil there now is in the world will become yet more powerful, and that it is not evil that will conquer evil – only love.*[52]

Bekhteev later took this letter as the inspiration for a composition of his own that echoes these sentiments and which begins,

---

* There is an echo in Olga's words of Romans xii: 19 and 21: 'Beloved, never avenge yourselves, but leave it to the wrath of God; for it is written, "Vengeance is mine, I will repay," says the Lord.' . . . 'Do not be overcome by evil, but overcome evil with good.'

'Father asks us to tell everyone, there is no need to weep and murmur / The days of sufferings are sent us all / For our great general sin'.[53]

Of all the Romanov sisters, sweet, accommodating Maria remained the most self-effacing, her consistently loving and stoical personality inviting the least amount of comment or criticism. Everyone, including the guards and even Commissar Pankratov, adored her. For Klavdiya Bitner, Maria was the archetypal, wholesome Russian girl: 'kind hearted, cheerful, with an even temper, and friendly'.[54] In contrast, Anastasia, whom she found 'uncouth', never seduced Klavdiya. The constant playfulness and challenge to authority in the classroom soon began to grate: 'She wasn't serious about anything.' But worse, in Klavdiya's opinion, was the way that Anastasia 'always took advantage of Maria'.[55] 'They were both behind in their lessons', she recalled, an opinion that reinforced Pankratov's view. 'Neither of them could write essays and [they] had not been trained how to express their thoughts.' Anastasia was 'still an absolute child and you had to treat her as you would a child'. Sydney Gibbes tended to agree; the youngest Romanov sister's social development, in his opinion, had been arrested and he thought her the 'only ungraceful member of the family'.[56]

Others of course saw Anastasia's irrepressible personality quite differently; she was the family's 'cheer-leader' who kept everyone's spirits up with her high energy and mimicry.[57] She certainly could be very juvenile at times and Dr Botkin had been shocked at her sexually precocious 'shady anecdotes' and wondered where she had collected them.[58] She had a penchant too for drawing 'dirty' pictures and making the occasional outrageous comment. But all in all, at Tobolsk, her 'gay and boisterous temperament proved of immeasurable value to the rest of the family', for when she chose to, 'Anastasia could dispel anybody's gloom'.[59] But now, even she was often overcome with an intense sadness, thinking about their hospital and those who had died: 'I suppose there's no one now to visit the graves of our wounded,' she wrote to Katya, 'they've all left Tsarskoe Selo'; but she kept a postcard of Feodorovsky Gorodok on the writing table because 'the time we spent at the hospital was so terribly good'. She was pining for news of Katya and her brother Viktor. 'I have not received letters nos. 21, 23, 24, 26, 28, 29 – all these letters that you wrote to this address', she complained plaintively, suggesting Katya address them to Anna Demidova instead as 'letters to her are of less interest to these people'. 'It's awful to think of how long we have not seen you . . . If God allows, we will see each other some time, and it will be possible to tell you a lot of things, both sad and funny, and in general, how we live.' But, she added, 'I will not write about it of course.'[60]

Perhaps Anastasia's madcap behaviour was in fact indicative of a 'heroic effort', as Gleb Botkin saw it, a way of helping the family 'stay cheerful and keep their spirits up', her relentless offensive being, in its own way, a form of self-protection.[61] She was without doubt the star of the show in a series of playlets, in French and English, staged by Gibbes and Gilliard during the final three weeks of January and last two of February. The biggest hit was *Packing Up* – 'a very vulgar but also very funny farce by Harry Grattan' in which Anastasia played the male lead, Mr Chugwater, and Maria his wife.[62] During her energetic performance on 4 February the dressing gown Anastasia was wearing flew up, exposing her sturdy legs encased in her father's Jaeger long johns. Everyone 'collapsed in uncontrolled laughter' – even Alexandra, who rarely laughed out loud. It was, remembered Gibbes, 'the last heartily unrestrained laughter the Empress ever enjoyed'. The play had been so 'awfully amusing & really well and funnily given' in Alexandra's estimation, that a repeat performance was demanded.[63]

Despite Anastasia's attention-grabbing performances, it was Alexey who won Klavdiya Bitner's heart at Tobolsk. 'I loved him more than the others,' she later admitted, though he seemed to her subdued and terribly bored. Although he was very behind in his education and read badly, she found him 'a good, kind boy . . . intelligent, observant, receptive, very gentle, cheerful, ebullient'. Like Anastasia, he was by nature 'very capable but a little lazy'. But he was an extremely quick learner, hated lies and had inherited his father's simplicity. Klavdiya admired the patience with which Alexey endured his condition. 'He wanted to be well and hoped this would be so', and he often asked her, 'Do you think this will go?'[64] At Tobolsk he continued to defy the limitations placed on him and threw himself enthusiastically into vigorous games with Kolya

Derevenko using home-made wooden daggers and guns. In early January the boys helped Nicholas and the other men build a snow mountain out in the courtyard. Once the snow was piled up Gilliard and Dolgorukov began carting out bucket after bucket of water to pour over it and make it icily smooth. 'The children are sledging their hearts out on a snow mountain and taking the most amazing falls', Alexandra wrote to a friend. 'It's a wonder they haven't broken their necks. They're all covered with bruises, but even so, this is the only distraction they have, either that or sit at the window.'[65] Alexey inevitably banged himself but it was, ironically, Pierre Gilliard who was the snow mountain's first real casualty; he twisted his ankle badly and was laid up for several days.[66] Shortly afterwards Maria, too, took a tumble and ended up with a black eye.

While most of the entourage tried hard to enjoy the distractions of the snow mountain, and sneak a look over the fence from its summit, anxieties about the deteriorating situation in the country at large frequently bubbled to the surface. 'Everything they are doing to our poor country is so painful and sad,' Tatiana wrote to Rita Khitrovo, 'but there is one hope – that God will not abandon it and will teach these madmen a lesson.'[67] Trina Schneider was profoundly depressed. Whenever she received news from outside, she admitted that it reduced her to a state of despair. 'I don't read the papers any more, even if they manage to get here,' she told PVP, 'it's become so awful. What kind of times are these – everyone does what they want . . . If you only knew my frame of mind. No hopes at all – none . . . I don't believe in a better future, because I won't live to see it – it's too far off.'[68] Meanwhile, the only aspiration that Alexandra clung to, as she told a friend, was 'to achieve the possibility of living tranquilly, like an ordinary family, outside politics, struggle and intrigue'.[69]

On 14 February – the first official day of the changeover to the New Style, Gregorian calendar* – Alexandra noted despondently

---

* On 31 January the Bolshevik government switched to the Gregorian calendar, immediately jumping forward fourteen days to 14 February. Nicholas however persisted in writing his diary with old style dates, while Alexandra noted both. The girls dated their letters variously OS and NS, often making it difficult to

how 'many of the nicest soldiers left'.[70] Their favourite guards in the Special Detachment, the 4th Rifles – good troop soldiers, many of whom had been conscripted at the outbreak of war – were sent away and replaced by the new breed of revolutionary Red Guards; Pankratov too was removed from his post as commissar responsible for the imperial family. On the 24th, the family clambered onto the top of the snow mountain to get the best view, as three more large groups of the Rifles marched away. Of the 350 men who had accompanied them from Tsarskoe Selo, only around 150 remained.[71] The new revolutionary guards were far more threatening: 'One can never predict how they are going to behave', remarked Tatiana. These guards had been incensed when the family climbed up and made themselves visible above the level of the fence, in so doing exposing themselves to possible pot shots, for which the guards might be held responsible.[72] They promptly voted to remove the snow mountain (by hacking a trench through the middle), though some who took part in its destruction did so, as Gilliard noticed, 'with a hang-dog look (for they felt it was a mean task)'. The children were, inevitably, utterly 'disconsolate'.[73]

Soon the new guards held another meeting and another vote – that none of them should wear epaulettes, thereby putting everyone on the new, socialist, level playing field. For Nicholas the soldier this was the ultimate dishonour; he refused to comply, opting instead to wear a coat to conceal his own when among the guards outside. But the change in regime brought further unwelcome news. Kobylinsky, who remained in nominal charge of the Governor's House, received a telegram informing him that Lenin's new government was no longer prepared to pay the family's living expenses beyond 600 roubles a month per person, in other words a total for the seven members of the family of 4,200 roubles a month.[74] Alexandra spent several days going through all the household accounts with Gilliard. They had for some time been running up considerable credit with the shopkeepers of Tobolsk and could no longer sustain such a large household. There was nothing for it

---

distinguish which they were using. For the sake of clarity, all dates from 14 February 1918 are New Style.

– they would have to let ten servants go. This caused the family considerable distress, as many of those servants had brought their families to join them and, as Gilliard rightly noted, their devotion to the imperial family in following them to Tobolsk would 'reduce them to beggary'.[75] In the end, several insisted on staying, for no pay.

From 1 March, in addition to the tightening of the budget, everyone was put on rations, just like the rest of the country. Nicholas Romanov, 'ex-emperor', of Freedom Street, with six dependants, was issued with ration card no. 54 for flour, butter and sugar.[76] Coffee (which Alexandra depended upon) was now virtually unobtainable. But once again, gifts of food began to arrive 'from various kind people who have heard about our need to economize on our outgoings for food', wrote Nicholas; he found the generosity of the donors 'so touching!'[77] In response Alexandra painted little icons on paper to send as gifts of thanks. A few days later one of Nicholas's old staff members at Mogilev arrived in Tobolsk with a gift of 25,000 roubles from monarchist friends in Petrograd, as well as books and tea.[78] But it was not just food rationing that hit everyone hard; they could not replace their increasingly threadbare clothes. By March Alexandra was grateful for any parcels of clothing from Anna Vyrubova that reached them: warm jumpers and jackets for the last of the chill weather, blouses and hats for the spring, and a military suit, vest and trousers for Alexey. From Odessa Zinaida Tolstaya sent a wonderful parcel of perfume, sweets, crayons, albums, icons and books, although several others she sent never arrived.[79]

Everyone drew further in on themselves as the strictures of Lent approached. Alexandra and the girls were practising their singing of the Orthodox liturgy, for they could not afford to pay the choristers any more. It was hard listening to the sound, outside on the street, of the festivities for *Maslenitsa* – Butter Week – one of the most joyful festivals in the Russian Orthodox calendar. 'Everyone is merry. The sledges pass to and fro under our windows; sound of bells, mouth-organs, and singing', wrote Gilliard. Alexey proudly noted in his diary on the 16th that he had eaten sixteen *bliny* at lunch before the onset of Lent, when everyone fasted for the first week. They were all looking forward to the church services to come.

'We hope to do our devotions next week if we are allowed to do so', Alexandra told Lili Dehn:

I am already looking forward to those beautiful services – such a longing to pray in church . . . Nature is beautiful, everything is shining and brilliantly lighted up . . . We cannot complain, we have got everything, we live well, thanks to the touching kindness of the people, who in secret send us bread, fish, pies, etc. . . . We too have to understand through it all that God is greater than everything and that He wants to draw us, through our sufferings, closer to Him . . . But my country – my God – how I love it, with all the power of my being, and her sufferings give me actual physical pain.[80]

On 20, 22 and 23 March the household were allowed to attend church for the first time in two months, at which they were able to hear the choir sing 'our favourite, familiar hymns'.[81] It was 'such a joy and a consolation', wrote Alexandra. 'Praying at home is not the same thing at all.'[82] But Lent was also, inevitably, a time of sad reflection. Nicholas's mind went back to his abdication the previous year; his last farewell to his mother at Mogilev; the day he arrived back at Tsarksoe Selo. 'One remembers this past difficult year unwillingly! But what yet awaits us all? It's all in God's hands. All our hopes are in him alone.'[83] Having powered his way through most of Leskov, Tolstoy and Lermontov, he was now rereading the Bible from start to finish. Day after day he blanked out his thoughts chopping wood and loading it into the woodshed, the children helping him and revelling in being out in the glorious spring sunshine. But in truth life within the Governor's House had become deadening beyond belief. The children found captivity 'irksome', noted Gilliard. 'They walk round the courtyard, fenced in by its high paling through which they can see nothing.'[84] Lack of exercise was worrying Anastasia: 'I haven't quite turned into an elephant yet,' she told her aunt Xenia, 'but may do so in the near future. I really don't know why it's suddenly happened; maybe it's from too little exercise, I don't know.'[85]

The children were still bitterly disappointed by the 'stupid' action of the guards in wrecking the snow mountain, but tried their best to find consolation in the most prosaic of outdoor tasks. 'We have found new things to do: we saw, chop and split wood – it's useful and very jolly work . . . we're helping a lot . . . clearing the paths and the entrance.' Anastasia was proud of their physical labours: 'we have turned into real yardmen'; events of the last traumatic year had taught her and her sisters to take pleasure in the smallest of practical achievements.

Chapter Twenty-one

THEY KNEW IT WAS THE END
WHEN I WAS WITH THEM

After the arrival of the new guards, and with it a distinct hardening in attitude towards the imperial family, everyone in the entourage had become increasingly fearful for their safety. Rowdy and undisciplined elements were making their presence felt in town too. Russia was descending into civil war and the breakdown in law and order had finally reached Tobolsk. 'How much longer will our unfortunate motherland be tormented and torn apart by internal and external enemies?' Nicholas wondered in his diary. His despondency increased with news that Lenin's government had signed the Brest–Litovsk Treaty with Germany; his abdication, for the sake of Russia, had, he felt, been in vain. 'It sometimes seems as though there's no strength left to endure, that you don't even know what to hope for, what to wish for', he confided in his diary.[1]

By mid-March 'all kinds of rumours and fears' were stirred up at the Governor's House by the arrival in Tobolsk from Omsk of a detachment of Bolshevik Red Guards, who promptly began imposing their demands on the local government. They were closely followed by even more militant groups from Tyumen and Ekaterinburg, who roamed the town, terrorizing the inhabitants with threats of hostage-taking (a favourite occupation of Bolshevik hardliners) and agitating to take control of the Romanovs and remove them from Tobolsk.[2] In response, Kobylinsky doubled the guard at the Governor's House and increased the patrols round it. But nothing could dispel the palpable sense of danger, which fed into an already fatalistic attitude among many in the entourage. 'I have come here knowing quite well that I shall not escape with my life', Tatishchev told Gleb Botkin. 'All I ask is to be permitted to die with my Emperor.'[3] Nastenka Hendrikova was equally gloomy and had said openly to Iza Buxhoeveden that 'she had a premonition that all our days were numbered'.[4]

For a while, earlier in the year and before the changeover in the guard, escape had seemed a very real possibility to Pierre Gilliard – given the obvious sympathies of Kobylinsky and the more relaxed attitude then of most of his men. Gilliard felt that a rescue could have been effected, with the help of a group of dedicated monarchist officers. But Nicholas and Alexandra had both been adamant that they would not contemplate any 'rescue' that involved the family being separated 'or leaving Russian territory'.[5] To do so, as Alexandra explained, would be for them to break their 'last link with the past, which would then be dead for ever'. 'The atmosphere around us is fairly electrified. We feel that a storm is approaching,' she told Anna Vyrubova at the end of March, 'but we know that God is merciful, and will take care of us.' She did, however, admit that 'things are growing very anguishing'.[6]

At the end of March the greater part of everyone's anguish was once more focused on Alexey, who had been confined to bed with a bad cough. The strain of his violent coughing had provoked a haemorrhage in his groin, which soon brought excruciating pain of the kind he had not experienced since 1912. Over at the Kornilov House, Iza Buxhoeveden encountered a deeply despondent Dr Derevenko just back from visiting the boy. 'He looked very gloomy and said that [Alexey's] kidneys were affected by the haemorrhage, and in that God-forsaken town none of the remedies he needed could be got. "I fear he will not pull through," he said, shaking his head, his eyes full of anxiety.' The terrible shadow of Spala haunted the Governor's House for many days, as Alexey's temperature rose and bouts of agonizing pain led him to confess to his mother at one point: 'I would like to die, Mama; I'm not afraid of death.' Death itself had no hold over him for his fears were elsewhere. 'I'm so afraid of what they may do to us here.'[7]

Alexandra hovered at her son's bed, as she had always done, trying to soothe him, watching him become 'thin and yellow' and 'with enormous eyes' – just as at Spala.[8] Their footman Alexey Volkov felt that this attack was, if anything, worse than the earlier incident, for this time both Alexey's legs were affected. 'He suffered terribly, wept and cried out, calling for his mother all the time.' Alexandra's anguish at his suffering and her own impotence was terrible. 'She grieved . . . like she had never grieved before . . . she just could not cope and she wept as she had never wept before.'[9] Hour after hour she sat 'holding his aching legs' because Alexey could lie only on his back, while Tatiana and Gilliard took it in turns to massage them with the Fohn apparatus they often used to keep his blood circulating.[10] But Alexey's nights were extremely restless, interrupted by bouts of severe pain. It was not until 19 April that Dr Derevenko noted hopeful signs that the 'resorption' (of the blood from the swelling into his body) was 'going well', although Alexey was still very frail and in a great deal of discomfort.[11]

*

During Alexey's latest crisis an order had come on 12 April that, for security reasons, all those at the Kornilov House – except for the two doctors, Botkin and Derevenko and their families – must move into the Governor's House. The house was already overcrowded, but by partitioning off some of the rooms with screens and doubling up, everyone managed, without too much grumbling, to squeeze into the ground floor, in order to 'avoid intruding upon the privacy of the Imperial Family' upstairs.[12] The exception was Sydney Gibbes, who refused point-blank to share with Gilliard, with whom he did not get on. Together with his toothless old maid Anfisa, Gibbes was allowed to lodge in a hastily converted stone outbuilding near the kitchen – in smelling distance of the pig-swill.[13] From now on, only the doctors were free to move back and forth; the rest of the entourage were no longer allowed into town and were, effectively, under house arrest.

Two weeks later news came that a high-ranking political commissar from Moscow, Vasily Yakovlev, had arrived in Tobolsk to take charge of the family. 'Everyone is restless and distraught', wrote Gilliard.

'The commissar's arrival is felt to be an evil portent, vague but real.'[14] Anticipating an inspection and search of their things, Alexandra immediately set about burning her recent letters, as did the girls; Maria and Anastasia even burned their diaries.[15] Yakovlev, it soon turned out, had arrived with 150 new Red Guards and instructions to remove the family to an unspecified location. But when he and his deputy Avdeev arrived at the house it was clear that 'the yellow-complexioned, haggard boy seemed to be passing away'.[16] Alexey was far too unwell to be moved, Kobylinsky argued in alarm; Yakovlev agreed to defer the family's departure, only to be countermanded by Lenin's Central Committee, which ordered him to remove the former tsar without delay. Nicholas refused point-blank to travel alone to an undisclosed destination. When Yakovlev conceded that he could bring a travelling companion – either that or be taken by force – Alexandra was faced with the most agonizing of decisions. Aghast at the thought of what might happen to her husband if taken to Moscow (visions of a trial by a French-Revolutionary-style tribunal), she went through hours of mental torment, trying to decide what to do for the best. Her maid Mariya Tutelberg tried to comfort her but Alexandra said:

> Don't make my pain worse, Tudels. This is a most difficult moment for me. You know what my son means to me. And I now have to choose between son and husband. But I have made my decision and I have to be strong. I must leave my boy and share my life – or my death – with my husband.[17]

It was clear to the four sisters that their mother could not travel without one of them to support her. Olga's health was still poor and she was needed to help nurse Alexey. Tatiana must take over the running of the household; even Gibbes asserted that she was 'now looked upon as the head of the Family in the place of the Grand Duchess Olga'.[18] After discussing it among themselves, the girls agreed that Maria should accompany their mother and father, leaving court jester Anastasia to 'cheer all up'.[19] The hope was that in about three weeks' time, when Alexey was stronger, they would be able to join their parents.

Nicholas and Alexandra spent most of that afternoon sitting by

Alexey's bed while the most essential items for their journey were packed. Tatiana asked Yakovlev where they would be taken – was her father to be put on trial in Moscow? Yakovlev dismissed the idea, insisting that from Moscow her parents 'would be taken to Petrograd, and from there out through Finland to Sweden and then Norway'.[20] That last evening everyone sat down to dinner, at a properly laid table complete with menu cards, just as they had always done. 'We spent the evening in grief', Nicholas confided to his diary, Alexandra and the girls frequently weeping. Alexandra's stoicism completely gave way as she faced the prospect of leaving the son she had watched over so obsessively for the last thirteen years. Later, when everyone sat down together to take tea before bed, she appeared composed. They all 'did their best to hide [their] grief and to maintain outward calm', wrote Gilliard. 'We felt that for one to give way would cause all to break down.' 'It was the most mournful and depressing party I ever attended,' recalled Sydney Gibbes, 'there was not much talking and no pretence at gaiety. It was solemn and tragic, a fit prelude to an inescapable tragedy.'[21] Many years later he insisted, 'They knew it was the end when I was with them'; that evening, though the words remained resolutely unspoken, everyone had a clear sense of what might lie ahead.[22]

Nicholas retained his outward steely calm to the very end, but 'to leave the rest of the children and Alexey – sick as he was and in such circumstances – was more than difficult', he admitted in his diary and 'of course, no one slept that night'.[23] At 4 a.m. the following morning, 26 April, Nicholas 'had a handshake and a word for everyone and we all kissed the Empress's hand', recalled Gibbes, before, wrapped in long Persian lamb coats, Alexandra and Maria accompanied him out to the waiting tarantasses.*[24]

'When they left it was still dark,' recalled Gibbes, but he ran for his camera, and 'by a lengthy exposure I succeeded in getting a picture of the Empress' tarantas – though it was impossible to take

---

* Alexandra and Maria were allowed the luxury of a hooded tarantas, but Nicholas and the others travelled in a local Siberian form of transport, a *kosheva* – a low-slung wheel-less carriage suspended on long poles – the interiors without seats spread with straw.

one of the departure.'[25] The sisters sobbed as they kissed goodbye; but it was the timorous maid Anna Demidova who was travelling with the tsaritsa (along with Dr Botkin, Dolgorukov and servants Terenty Chemodurov and Ivan Sednev), who had been the one finally to voice everyone's innermost anxiety. 'I am so frightened of the Bolsheviks, Mr Gibbes. I don't know what they will do to us.' Her fright as the mournful row of carriages and their escort of mounted Red Army guards drove away into the cold grey dawn was 'pitiable to see'.[26]

From her window at the Kornilov House, Tatiana Botkina watched them go:

> The carriages passed the house at breakneck speed, swerved round the corner, and disappeared. I cast a glance at the Governor's residence. Three figures in grey stood on the steps for a long time yet, watching the distant ribbon of the road; then they turned and slowly walked back into the house.[27]

*

After the departure – destination unknown – of Nicholas, Alexandra and Maria 'a sadness like death invaded the house', as the valet Volkov remembered. 'Before, there had always been a certain liveliness, but after the departure of the imperial couple, silence and desolation overwhelmed us.'[28] 'The feeling was noticed even in the soldiers', Kobylinsky noted.[29] Olga 'wept terribly' when her mother and father left but she and her sisters kept themselves busy and their minds distracted fulfilling an urgent task entrusted them by Alexandra.[30] Although many of Alexandra's large pieces of jewellery had already been smuggled out for safe-keeping at the Abalaksky or Ivanovsky monasteries, from where they were to be used by monarchist sympathizers to raise funds for a possible escape (the money never arrived), the girls had recently been helping Anna Demidova and the maids Mariya Tutelberg and Elizaveta Ersberg 'dispose of the medicines as agreed'.[31] This was Alexandra's code for the concealment of pearls, diamonds, brooches and necklaces in the family's clothes, undergarments and hats, with larger stones being disguised under cloth buttons. With their departure perhaps only three weeks away the women frantically worked to complete the task in time, supervised by Tatiana, who despite advice to leave the jewels in safe-keeping in Tobolsk had insisted on following her mother's instructions to the letter.[32] With Alexey still sick there was no thought of lessons. Everyone was too preoccupied with keeping him amused and raising his morale, as he 'toss[ed] and moan[ed] on his bed of pain, always sighing for his mother, who couldn't come'.[33]

Although word that the family was safe came from one of the drivers who had taken them as far as Tyumen, it was several days before any letters arrived. Because the rivers were still ice-bound the party was having to travel overland and the roads were terrible – 'horses up to their chests in water crossing rivers. Wheels broken several times', as Maria later reported.[34] On the 29th the first letter arrived, written at their first overnight stopover at Ievlevo. 'Mother's heart is hurting very much as a consequence of the awful road to Tyumen – they had to travel over 200 versts [140 miles/225 km] by horses along a horrible road', Tatiana wrote to a friend.[35] The journey improved thereafter, and Alexandra sent a telegram: 'Travelling in comfort. How is the boy? God be with you.'[36] They were now on a train but still did not know where they were headed. 'Darling, you must know how dreadful it all is', Olga wrote to Anna Vyrubova as they waited for news.[37] But it was not till 3 May – a week since their parents' departure – that the children finally learned, by telegram, that Nicholas, Alexandra and Maria were now not in Moscow – as they had all imagined – but in Ekaterinburg, a town in the Western Urals, 354 miles (570 km) south-west of Tobolsk. The three girls and their brother now could do nothing but wait out the long anxious days till they could join them there.

The girls kept themselves busy, taking it in turns to read and play games with Alexey, who was making a very slow recovery. If the weather was fine they took him outside in the wheelchair. In the evenings Olga sat with him when he said his prayers; afterwards the girls joined Nastenka in her room rather than sit upstairs on their own, and then went to bed early. 'Mama, dear soul, how we miss you! In every, every way. It is so empty', Olga wrote to Alexandra in a long letter spread over several days. 'Every now and then I go into your room and then I feel as though you are there and that is so comforting.' Easter was approaching and they were doing their best to prepare for it, though this was the first time, as a family, that they had ever been separated during this the most important festival in the Russian Orthodox calendar. 'Today, there was an enormous religious procession with banners, icons, numbers of clergy and a crowd of faithful. It was so beautiful with the glorious sunshine and all the church bells ringing.'[38] Zinaida Tolstaya had sent painted Easter eggs, a cake and some jam, and an embroidered napkin for Alexandra. But Good Friday brought wind and rain and a temperature barely above zero. 'It is terrible not to be together and not to know how you really are, for we are told so many different things', wrote Olga.[39] But together the girls had decorated their field chapel, arranging branches of velvety, scented pine on either side of the iconostasis – its smell reminding them of Christmas – and bringing pots of flowers and plants from the greenhouse (though they were struggling to keep the three dogs out in case of their trying to 'water' the pots). 'We would so like to know how you have celebrated this Feast of Light and what you are doing,' Olga continued on Easter Sunday, 'the Midnight Liturgy and Vigil went very well. It was beautiful and intimate. All the side lamps were lit, but not the chandelier, it was light enough.' That morning they had greeted the staff and handed out Easter eggs and little icons, just as their mother had always done; and they had eaten the traditional *kulich* and *pashka*.[40]

When a letter finally came from Maria, briefly describing their new environment at the Ipatiev House in Ekaterinburg, it was deeply disconcerting: 'We miss our quiet and peaceful life in Tobolsk', she wrote. 'Here there are unpleasant surprises every day.'[41] Their own Easter had been extremely modest: food was brought from the communal canteen in town and many of their belongings were in a terrible state, dusty and dirty from the bumpy journey. There was a poignant postscript for Anastasia from Nicholas: 'I am lonesome without you, my dear. I miss you pulling funny faces at the table.'[42]

The three sisters were intensely relieved when the letters from Ekaterinburg finally began to arrive. Alexandra and Maria wrote daily but many of the twenty-two or so letters that they sent never reached Tobolsk. 'It was truly dreadful to be without news all that time', Tatiana wrote on 7 May:

> We see from the window that the Irtych [sic] is calm here. Tomorrow we expect the first steamer from Tioumen [sic]. Our pigs have been sold, but there is still the sow which had six piglets . . . Yesterday we ate our poor turkey, so now there is only his wife . . . It is deadly boring in the garden. No sooner are we out there than we are looking at our watches to see when we can go back inside . . . We suffer a great deal in our souls for you, my darlings; our only hope is in God and our consolation in prayer.[43]

Even the resolute Tatiana was finding it hard to keep going: 'I am so afraid of losing courage,' she told her father, 'I pray a lot for you . . . May the Lord God guard you, save you, protect you from all evil. Your daughter Tatiana who loves you passionately for ever and ever.'[44]

With the ice melting, the Irtysh was in full flood and the boats began to sail to Tyumen once more. The girls could hear their sirens in the distance and hopes lifted that they would soon be able to travel.[45] At Ekaterinburg Maria was eagerly anticipating their arrival. 'Who knows, perhaps this letter will reach you just before you leave. God bless your journey and keep you safe from all harm . . . Tender thoughts and prayers surround you – all that matters is to be together again soon.'[46]

Being reunited was the one and only preoccupation of all the letters sent between Tobolsk and Ekaterinburg in those final, intervening days – along with messages of love. 'How are you surviving and what are you doing?' asked Olga, in what would be her last letter from Tobolsk. 'How I would love to be with you. We still do not know when we shall leave . . . May Our Lord protect you, my dear beloved Mama and all of you. I kiss Papa, you and M. many times over. I clasp you in my arms and love you. Your Olga.'[47]

'It is difficult to write anything pleasant,' Maria wrote in a letter to Alexey, 'for there is little of that kind here.' Her optimism, however, remained undimmed. 'But on the other hand God does not abandon us, the sun shines and the birds sing. This morning we heard the dawn chorus.'[48] The reality of their new surroundings was, however, grim. They no longer enjoyed any of the small privileges they had been granted at Tobolsk and were under constant, and close, surveillance. Letters now had to be addressed c/o The Chairman, The Regional Executive Committee, Ekaterinburg.[49]

Of the three sisters left behind at Tobolsk it was the sixteen-year-old Anastasia who through it all retained an undimmed sense of joy in the shrinking world around them. Writing to Maria about their mundane daily routine, she told her:

> We take turns having breakfast with Alexey and make him eat, although there are days when he eats without needing to be told. You are in our thoughts all the time, dear ones. It is terribly sad and empty; I really don't know what comes over me. We have the baptismal crosses of course and we received your news. So God helps and will help us. We arranged the iconostasis beautifully for Easter, all with spruce, which is how they do it here, and flowers too. We took pictures, I hope they come out . . . We swung on the swing, and how I laughed when I fell off, what a landing, honestly! . . . I have a whole wagonload of things to tell you . . . We've had such weather! I could shout out loud at how good it is. Strange to say, I've got more sunburned than the others, a real Arrrab [*sic*]! . . .
>
> We're sitting together right now, as always, but we miss your presence in the room . . . I'm sorry this is such a jumbled letter, but you know how my thoughts fly around and I can't write it all down, so throw in whatever comes into my head. I want to see you so much, it's terribly sad. I go out and walk, and then come back. It's boring inside or out. I swung; the sun came out but it was cold, and my hand can hardly write.[50]

She and her sisters had done their best to sing the liturgy during the Easter service, Anastasia told Maria, but 'whenever we sing together it doesn't come out right because we need that fourth voice. But you're not here and so we make a joke about it . . . We constantly think and pray for everyone: Lord help us! Christ be with you, precious ones. I kiss you, my good, fat Mashka. Your Shvybz.'[51]

*

On 17 May the most intimidating band of Red Guards yet arrived at the Governor's House, this time from Ekaterinburg, led by a man named Rodionov. They were 'the most frightful-looking, dirty, ragged, drunken cut-throats' Gleb Botkin had ever seen. Rodionov was in fact a Latvian named Yan Svikke and from the first nobody liked him. Kobylinsky thought him cruel, 'a low bully'.[52] Cold and suspicious by nature, Rodionov was constantly on the watch for conspiracy: he ordered a humiliating daily roll-call and the girls had to ask his permission to come downstairs from their room and go out into the yard. They were ordered not to shut the door to their room at night and when the priest and nuns came on 18 May to conduct vespers Rodionov had them searched and posted a sentry right by the altar to watch them during the ceremony.[53] Kobylinsky was appalled: 'This so oppressed everyone, had such an effect on them that Olga Nikolaevna wept and said that if she had known that this would happen she would never have asked for a service.'[54]

Alexey was still extremely frail and barely able to sit up for more than an hour or so at a time. Nevertheless, within three days of arriving, Rodionov decided the boy was well enough to travel. For several days now the staff had been preparing for their departure. 'The rooms are empty, little by little everything's being packed away. The walls look bare without the pictures', Alexey wrote to his mother.[55] Anything not to be taken was to be 'disposed of' in town – if it wasn't looted by the guards first. Most of the entourage prepared to leave with the children. Dr Botkin's daughter Tatiana begged for her and her brother to be allowed to go with the sisters but was refused. 'Why should such a handsome girl as you are want to rot all her life in prison, or even be shot?' Rodionov sneered. 'In all probability they will be shot.' He was equally callous when he told Alexandra Tegleva about what was in store: 'Life down there is very different.'[56] The day before the children left, Gleb Botkin went up to the Governor's House to try and catch a last glimpse of them. He saw Anastasia at a window; she waved and smiled, upon which Rodionov came rushing out telling him no one was permitted to look at the windows and that the guards would shoot to kill if anyone tried.[57]

On their last day in Tobolsk the household gathered together for farewell meals of *borshch* and hazel hen with rice for lunch and veal with garnish and macaroni for dinner, washed down with the last two bottles of wine that they had managed to keep hidden from the guards.[58] At 11.30 the following morning, 20 May 1918, the children were taken to the landing stage and once more boarded the *Rus*, where, to their great joy, they were greeted by Iza Buxhoeveden. Olga told her that they were 'lucky to be still alive and able to see their parents once more, whatever the future might bring'.[59] But Iza was shocked by the change in her, and in Alexey too – both of whom she had not seen close-to since the previous August:

> He was terribly thin and could not walk, as his knee had got quite stiff from lying with it bent for so long. He was very pale and his large dark eyes seemed still larger in the small narrow face. Olga Nicolaevna had also greatly changed. The suspense and anxiety of her parents' absence . . . had changed the lovely, bright girl of twenty-two into a faded and sad middle-aged woman.[60]

The children seemed to think that Iza's being allowed to rejoin them 'heralded further small concessions' from their Bolshevik captors.[61] But this was far from the case. Constant intimidation and humiliation followed on the two-day river journey to Tyumen. The guards were rude and boorish and they frightened everyone. Rodionov's behaviour was callous; he locked Alexey and Nagorny in their cabin at night, despite Nagorny remonstrating that the sick boy needed access to the toilet. Rodionov also insisted that the three sisters and their female companions keep their cabin doors open at all times, even with the guards standing immediately outside. None of the women undressed at night, during which they had to endure the noise of the rowdy guards drinking and making obscene comments outside their open doors.[62]

On arrival at Tyumen the children were transferred to a dirty, third-class carriage on a nearby waiting train, where, much to their distress, they were separated from Gilliard, Gibbes, Buxhoeveden and the others, who were put into a goods wagon with crude wooden benches. Some time after midnight on 23 May, the train finally drew to a halt at a suburban freight station on the outskirts of Ekaterinburg. It was cold and frosty and they were all left there to shiver, chilled to the marrow, till morning. Eventually Rodionov and a couple of commissars came for the children.[63] But neither Gibbes, nor Gilliard, nor Iza Buxhoeveden was allowed to go any further. Tatishchev, Nastenka and Trina were also refused, as too were all the other staff except for Nagorny. 'Tatiana Nicolaevna tried to take the matter lightly', as Iza kissed her goodbye. 'What is the use of all these leave-takings?' she asked. 'We shall all rejoice in each other's company in half an hour's time!', Tatiana had said reassuringly. But, as Iza later recalled, one of the guards came up to her just then and, with an ominous voice, said, 'Better say "Good-bye", citizenness', and 'in his sinister face I read that this was a real parting'.[64]

Pierre Gilliard watched from the train as the four children were brought out: 'Nagorny the sailor . . . passed my window carrying the sick boy in his arms; behind him came the Grand Duchesses, loaded with valises and small personal belongings.' They were surrounded by an escort of commissars in leather jackets and armed militiamen. He tried to get out of the train to say goodbye, but 'was roughly pushed back into the carriage by the sentry'. He watched in dismay as Tatiana trailed along last in the freezing rain, struggling to carry her heavy suitcase while holding her dog Ortipo under her other arm, as her shoes sank into the mud. Nagorny, who had meanwhile lifted Alexey into one of the waiting one-horse droshkies, turned to offer assistance but the guards pushed him away.[65]

A local Ekaterinburg engineer who was at the station that morning, having been tipped off that the children were due to arrive, had stood there in the downpour hoping to see them. Suddenly he caught sight of 'three young women, dressed in pretty, dark suits with large fabric buttons'.

> They walked unsteadily, or rather unevenly. I decided that this was because each one was carrying a very heavy suitcase and also because the surface of the road had become squelchy from the incessant spring rain. Having to walk, for the first time in their lives, with such heavy luggage was beyond their physical strength . . . They passed by very close and very slowly. I stared at their

lively, young, expressive faces somewhat indiscreetly – and during those two or three minutes I learned something that I will not forget till my dying day. It felt that my eyes met those of the three unfortunate young women just for a moment and that when they did I reached into the depths of their martyred souls, as it were, and I was overwhelmed by pity for them – me, a confirmed revolutionary. Without expecting it, I sensed that we Russian intellectuals, we who claim to be the precursors and the voice of conscience, were responsible for the undignified ridicule to which the Grand Duchesses were subjected . . . We do not have the right to forget, nor to forgive ourselves for our passivity and failure to do something for them.[66]

As the three young women passed him, the engineer was struck by how

everything was painted on those young, nervous faces: the joy of seeing their parents again, the pride of oppressed young women forced to hide their mental anguish from hostile strangers, and, finally, perhaps, a premonition of imminent death . . . Olga, with the eyes of a gazelle, reminded me of a sad young girl from a Turgenev novel. Tatiana gave the impression of a haughty patri- cian with an air of pride in the way she looked at you. Anastasia seemed like a frightened, terrified child, who could, in different circumstances, be charming, light-hearted and affectionate.[67]

That engineer was, forever after, haunted by those faces. He felt – indeed he hoped – 'that the three young girls, momentarily at least, sensed that what was imprinted on my face wasn't simply a cold curiosity and indifference towards them'. His natural human instincts had made him want to reach out and acknowledge them, but 'to my great shame, I held back out of weakness of character, thinking of my position, of my family'.[68]

From the window of their train Pierre Gilliard and Sydney Gibbes had craned their necks to catch a last sight of the girls as they got into the waiting droshkies. 'As soon as they were all in, an order was given, and the horses moved off at a trot with their escort.'[69]

It was the last any of those who had loved, served and lived with the four Romanov sisters since their childhood ever saw of them.

Chapter Twenty-two

PRISONERS OF THE URAL
REGIONAL SOVIET

There was still snow on the ground in Ekaterinburg that morning in late May when the children arrived at the Ipatiev House from Tobolsk. Nicholas and Alexandra had only had a few hours' warning of their arrival and despite their joy at being reunited with them, had only to look at their faces to know that 'the poor things had had to endure a great deal of moral anguish during their three-day journey'.[1]

After four weeks of painful and uncertain separation the four Romanov sisters were intensely happy to be together again. Their campbeds were yet to be sent on from Tobolsk, but they happily slept together on the floor in their new room on an accumulation of cloaks and cushions until the beds arrived.[2] But the reunion was soon marred when, when, much to his parents' intense frustration, Alexey managed to slip and bang his knee. Nicholas and Alexandra put him to bed in their room, where he lay for several days in agony; it was 5 June before he was able to join the others outside in the garden.

Two huge wooden palisades surrounded the Ipatiev House, ominously designated 'the house of special purpose' by their Bolshevik captors. They were so high that, from inside the house, the Romanovs could not even see the tops of the trees.[3] What little was visible of the blue sky above had been obliterated in mid-May when the windows in all the family's rooms were painted with whitewash, creating what seemed like a blanket of fog outside.[4]

It was dreadfully cramped and stuffy inside the first-floor rooms that served as the Romanovs' new accommodation. For this was in no way a home – but a prison – and it was abundantly clear to everyone that they would have to endure a rigorous regime here quite different from those at Tobolsk or the Alexander Palace.[5] There were armed guards everywhere: on the street, inside and outside the palisades surrounding the house, on the roof, in the garden. Guards also manned machine-gun nests in the basement, the mansard, the garden and even the belfry of the Voznesensky Sobor across the road. An announcement in the *Uralskaya zhizn* by Bolshevik War Commissar Filipp Goloshchekin, in overall charge of the family's incarceration in the city, had made the hardening of the official attitude towards the former imperial family all too plain:

> All those under arrest will be held as hostages, and the slightest attempt at counterrevolutionary action in the town will result in the summary execution of the hostages.[6]

The days had been monotonous enough in Tobolsk but at Ekaterinburg the pace of life was slowed to an intolerable tedium. No papers were delivered and no letters. One solitary parcel, of a few eggs, coffee and chocolate, had been received from Grand Duchess Ella on 16 May; but she too was now a prisoner, at Alapaevsk 95 miles (153 km) away to the north.[7] With no letters allowed in or out the girls were deprived of the one thing that had kept them going all this time – contact with their friends. Visitors, of course, were forbidden. The imperial family was cast adrift; they had 'no news of anybody', as Alexandra noted in her diary.[8]

Outdoor recreation at Ekaterinburg was restricted to a mournful little garden with a few stubby trees that was even smaller than the one at Tobolsk. But as always Nicholas and the girls made the most of every opportunity to get outside during their two brief daily exercise periods, and the girls sometimes swung in a couple of hammocks put up between the trees for them by the guards. Alexey, when he was well enough, was carried down, often by Maria, and sat in their mother's wheelchair. But during recreation periods one of the sisters always remained indoors with Mama, who with the temperature rising into the mid 20s C (high 70s F) rarely ventured out. Yet even these brief snatches of summer were enough, as Nicholas noted, for them to catch the wonderful scent of flowers 'from all the gardens in the town' that was heavy on the air, even if they could not see them beyond the palisade.[9] The unsealing of one small window in their rooms on 10 June to allow in a refreshing breeze was a major concession in the otherwise dreary regularity of their highly constrained lives. It was punctuated by regular acts of humiliation from the guards, such as searches of their belongings, confiscation of their money and attempts to remove even Alexandra's and the girls' gold bracelets from their wrists. Tatiana and Maria's request that their confiscated cameras be returned to them so that they could at least amuse themselves with photography was also refused.[10]

The month of June brought several family birthdays beginning with Alexandra's 46th on the 6th; it passed unnoticed, Nicholas in bed with painful haemorrhoids and Alexey also indoors for most of the day, despite the beautiful weather.[11] Tatiana's 21st followed on 11 June but was a very modest day for such an auspicious stage in her life, the highlight being the surprise treat of fruit compote at lunch prepared by Kharitonov. There were of course no presents; Tatiana spent the day reading to her mother: extracts from Alexandra's favourite book, the *Complete Yearly Cycle of Brief Homilies for Each Day of the Year* by an Orthodox priest, Grigory Dyachenko.[12] Later she played cards with Alexey and read to him and before bed enjoyed the prosaic novelty of helping her sisters wash everyone's pocket-handkerchiefs.[13] Poor Anna Demidova had been struggling single-handedly with all the family's personal washing (the bed linen still being sent out to a laundry) and the sisters had happily volunteered to help, as they did with darning everyone's worn-out socks, stockings and underwear.[14]

Anastasia's seventeenth birthday – 18 June – was a very hot day when again there were no celebrations and the girls spent the time learning another new practical skill – how to knead, roll and bake bread with Kharitonov.[15] Soon they were helping him more and more in the kitchen in an effort to dissipate their crushing sense of boredom. But it was unbearably airless indoors and even Alexandra preferred to be outside when her health allowed. Evenings now were one interminable game of bezique after another and rereading the few books left to them. Tatiana seemed always to be doing the lion's share of looking after her mother and Alexey; her nursing skills were also called on when Dr Botkin suffered a severe attack of kidney pain and she gave him an injection from the family's precious supply of morphine.[16] Olga was now terribly thin and pale, and at Ekaterinburg had become ever more withdrawn and morose. One of the guards, Alexey Kabanov, remembered her visible unhappiness, how she hardly talked and was 'uncommunicative with the other members of her family apart from her father' – with whom she always walked arm in arm during recreation in the garden.[17] But she did not spend as much time there as her three other sisters, who all seemed to him far more cheerful and animated, often breaking into folk songs when they walked round with the dogs. Maria, so strong and stoical, seemed still the most rounded and unaffected, 'the incarnation of "modesty elevated by suffering"', as one guard recalled, remembering a poem by Tyutchev.[18] At first – much as at Tobolsk – the younger sisters had been keen to engage with their captors, asked them about their lives and their families and showed them their photograph albums. They were dreadfully bored, they told them: 'We were so much happier in Tobolsk.'[19] But the arrival of a new and exacting commandant, Yakov Yurovsky, put paid to any more such fraternization.

The weather was positively 'tropical' according to Nicholas on Maria's 19th birthday on 27 June.[20] Four days previously the family had been comforted by 'the great blessing of a real *Obednitsa* and vespers' – when a priest and deacon had been allowed in to conduct the first service for the family in three months.[21] But they were two of only a handful of people to see them in these new and very straitened circumstances. Those on the outside trying to look in could only guess at what Russia's former imperial family was having to endure at the hands of its intimidating Bolshevik captors.

*

During the final eight weeks of the Romanov family's captivity many people – the curious, the covert, the foolhardy – and even royal relatives such as the intrepid Princess Helena – made their way up Voznesensky Prospekt to the Ipatiev House, to try and catch a glimpse of them. But none was admitted, bar Dr Derevenko, who was staying in town and had been allowed in to treat Alexey and put his swollen knee in plaster.

Local children were rather more adventurous. They often came near and tried to peep through the palisades surrounding the house. One sunny day soon after the family's arrival, nine-year-old Anatole Portnoff came out of the Voznesensky Sobor opposite after morning service and ran across the road to take a look. He found a gap in the paling and peeped through and there, standing directly in front of him, so he later claimed, he saw Tsar Nicholas 'taking a walk about the grounds'. But a sentry soon came rushing up, 'unceremoniously grabbed him by his coat and told him to be on his way'.[22]

Vladimir and Dimitri Storozhev, sons of a priest at the Ekaterininsky Sobor, were more persistent, for their home was next door to the Ipatiev House and they managed to communicate 'by gestures and talking over the fence with the girls of the imperial family'.[23] Eleven-year-old Vladimir loved flying his kite from their roof, from which vantage point he could often 'see the tsar's children playing in Upatiev's [sic] yard, and the tsar himself would come out once a day and split wood for an hour or so'.[24] But the Storozhev family was fearful of the intimidating Red Guards who watched over the Romanovs and who often went out summarily searching nearby houses and arresting people at will. Their father had made the family all sleep in one room, by the door, 'so if someone comes in and starts shooting, we will all be together'.[25]

It was Father Ivan Storozhev who was one of the last people from the outside to see the imperial family alive, at a service he conducted in the house at 10.30 a.m. on Sunday 14 July. Guards from the Ipatiev House had banged on his door early that morning. Father Storozhev thought they had come for him, but no, they wanted him to go next door to conduct a service for the family. 'Just stick strictly to what the service is all about', they warned. 'We don't believe in God now, but we remember what the service, the funeral service, is all about. So, nothing but the service. Don't try to communicate or anything or else we'll shoot.'[26]

Having climbed the stairs past young guards bristling with weapons, Storozhev found the family gathered in their sitting room, a table for the service specially prepared by Alexandra featuring their favourite icon of the Most Holy Mother of God. The girls were simply dressed in black skirts and white blouses; their hair, he noticed, had grown quite a lot since his previous visit on 2 June, and was now down to their shoulders.

During the service, the whole family had seemed to Storozhev to be greatly oppressed in spirit – there was a terrible weariness about them, quite markedly different from his previous visit, when they had all been animated and had prayed fervently.[27] He came away shaken to the core by what he had seen. The Romanovs had, uncharacteristically, all fallen to their knees when his deacon, Buimirov, had sung rather than recited 'At Rest with the Saints' – the Russian Orthodox prayer for the departed.* It seemed to give them great spiritual comfort, he noted, though for once they had not joined in the responses to the liturgy, something they would normally have done.[28] At the end of the service they had all come forward to kiss the cross and Nicholas and Alexandra had taken the sacrament. Covertly, as Storozhev passed them to leave, the girls softly whispered a thank-you. 'I knew, from the way they conducted themselves,' Father Storozhev later recalled, 'that something fearful and menacing was almost upon the Imperial Family.'[29]

The following morning the family appeared to have regained their equilibrium when four women, sent by the officious-sounding Union of Professional Housemaids, came to wash the floors. Perhaps the women's presence alone – as ordinary people from the world outside – brightened their mood. The Romanovs seemed relaxed, gathered together in the sitting room, and smiled when the women entered. They were strictly forbidden to speak to them, but by an exchange of looks and smiles it was clear that the four sisters were only too happy to help the women move the beds in their room; they would have helped them wash the floors too if they could. One of the women, Evdokiya Semenova, remembered their sweet, friendly

---

* This prayer is normally only sung (rather than recited) at Russian Orthodox funerals.

manner and how 'every gentle look was a gift'.[30] Although Yurovsky had ordered that the door to their room be kept open the girls managed to chat, *sotto voce*, with the women as they worked, and when his back was turned, Anastasia with typical irreverence cocked a snook at him. They told the women how much they missed having any physical work, although Olga was suffering with her health and could not do much. But Maria in particular was as vigorous as ever. 'We would do the most arduous work with the greatest pleasure; washing dishes is not enough for us', they said.[31] The women were greatly moved by the girls' quiet acceptance of their situation and told them that they hoped they would not have to endure such suffering for much longer. They thanked the women. Yes, they still had hope, they said; there was still a sparkle in their kind eyes.

After the women left at lunchtime the family settled back into their quiet routine, reading, playing cards, walking the same small, dusty circuit in the garden. But in the early hours of the morning of Wednesday 17 July, they were unexpectedly awoken by their captors and ordered to dress. Told that they were being moved downstairs for their safety from unrest and artillery fire in the city, they complied without question. In an orderly line Nicholas, Alexandra and their five children, Dr Botkin and their three loyal servants Demidova, Trupp and Kharitonov, walked quietly down the wooden stairs from their apartments, across the courtyard and into a dingy basement room. As they went, there were 'no tears, no sobs and no questions'.[32]

Later that morning, young Vladimir Storozhev recalled, 'I was on the roof flying my kite, when Father called me down and told me they had been shot. It was July seventeenth, I remember, and very hot.'[33]

Many weeks later, on 16 August, one of the last affectionate postcards, sent during the first week of Lent by Olga to a friend in Kiev, like so many others written by the four sisters that were never delivered, finally arrived back in Petrograd bearing an official stamp: 'Returned due to military circumstances.'[34]

Epilogue

VICTIMS OF REPRESSIONS

On the day of their arrival in Ekaterinburg, the seventeen remaining members of the entourage who had accompanied the children were left to sit for several hours on their train while it was shunted back and forth before finally coming to a halt. Later, Gibbes and Gilliard saw the footman Volkov, Kharitonov the cook, Trupp the valet and the kitchen boy Leonid Sednev taken off and put in droshkies which took them to join the family at the Ipatiev House. Ilya Tatishchev, Nastenka Hendrikova and Trina Schneider were taken away next; Tatishchev to the Ipatiev House, but Trina and Nastenka were transported to Perm with the footman Volkov. Here they languished in prison until, on 4 September, the Cheka came for them and they were taken out with a group of hostages, and shot. Their bodies, at least, were soon recovered, by the Whites, the following May.[1]

Ilya Tatishchev and Vasili Dolgorukov were removed from the Ipatiev House not long after their arrival there and taken to prison where they too were shot, on 10 July 1918; their bodies were never found. En route to a similar death in Perm in September Volkov, by a miracle, managed to escape being shot with Trina and Nastenka; he survived to tell his story and died in exile in Estonia in 1929.[2] Before leaving the Alexander Palace, Anna Demidova had sent her things home to Cherepovets in anticipation of returning there after seeing the imperial family safely off to exile somewhere. During the Stalinist years, her family was forced, out of fear, to destroy most of the valuable photographs and documents she entrusted to them. But her diary, discovered in the Ipatiev House, survives in GARF, the State Archives in Moscow.[3] The rest of the servants who had loyally volunteered to go with the family to the Ipatiev House, like Anna, shared their violent fate, their bodies dumped in the same mass grave in the Koptyaki Forest outside Ekaterinburg. The little kitchen boy Leonid Sednev escaped the carnage, having been taken from the house the day before. He was sent back to his family in Kaluga. But the tentacles of Stalinist repression finally caught up with him and he was arrested and shot by the NKVD in 1941 or 1942.

On 23 May Sydney Gibbes and Pierre Gilliard had been left sitting on the train at Ekaterinburg with Iza Buxhoeveden and Alexandra Tegleva and some of the other former servants in a state of growing apprehension until Rodionov finally reappeared at 5 p.m. and told them they were free. The train would, however, be their home for the best part of the next month, for they were obliged to live on it while waiting for permits to leave the city. During that time Gibbes and Gilliard walked past the Ipatiev House on numerous occasions and made repeated visits to the English consul Thomas Preston, who lived nearby, to find out what was being done to help the imperial family; but Preston's requests to be granted access to them were also consistently refused. On one occasion, when approaching the house, Gilliard and Gibbes happened to catch sight of the valet Ivan Sednev (Leonid's uncle) and Alexey's *dyadka* Nagorny being brought out of the front door. Soon afterwards, the Ekaterinburg Cheka shot both of them.

On 26 May the group on the train was finally ordered back to Tobolsk but en route was stranded at Tyumen – now under martial law and besieged by a huge wave of refugees fleeing the fighting along the Trans-Siberian Railway.[4] It was here, their money running out and short of food, that they finally had news in July of the murder of the tsar, though at the time nothing was said about the fate of Alexandra and the children. When Ekaterinburg fell to the Whites on 25 July, Gibbes and Gilliard returned to the city and made their way back to the Ipatiev House. The interior had been stripped of its furnishings, though a great deal of small personal belongings of the family had been left strewn around the rooms and Gibbes rescued a few things, including the Italian glass chandelier from the grand duchesses' bedroom. They saw the dim and grimy basement room where the family had been killed and found it 'sinister beyond expression'.[5]

Finally, in February 1919, Gilliard, Gibbes, Tegleva and Buxhoeveden made their way east to Omsk, where Gilliard joined the French Military Mission. He, Tegleva and Gibbes subsequently gave evidence to the Sokolov Commission set up by Alexander Kolchak, leader of the White forces, at the end of July 1918 to investigate the murder of the family, as too did Klavdiya Bitner, Kobylinsky, Pankratov and many others. Gilliard and Tegleva eventually travelled on to Switzerland via Japan and the USA and were married in Geneva in 1922. Gilliard went back to teaching French, as a professor at Lausanne University. In 1923 he published an account of his time in Russia: *Thirteen Years at the Russian Court*. He died in 1962.

In Omsk in 1919 Sydney Gibbes joined the British Military Mission, and later left Russia for Harbin, where he worked for the Chinese Maritime Customs for many years. In April 1934, he converted to Russian Orthodoxy and was ordained as a priest. On his return to England in 1937 he settled in Oxford, where he founded his own religious community of St Nicholas the Wonderworker. After his death in 1963 the community went into decline, but it is now thriving, and has its own church in Headington, Oxford.

From Omsk, Iza Buxhoeveden travelled on the Trans-Siberian Railway to Manchuria and on to Vladivostok on the Pacific coast, from where she took a boat to the USA and eventually made her way to Europe. She lived for a while in Denmark and then in Germany before accepting a post in England as lady-in-waiting to Alexandra's sister Victoria, Marchioness of Milford Haven. She lived in a grace-and-favour apartment at Hampton Court till her death in 1956, and wrote three memoirs of her time with the Imperial Family.[6]

Elizaveta Naryshkina, who was seventy-nine when the Romanovs left Tsarskoe Selo, eventually told her story to the Austrian writer René Fülöp-Miller, in Moscow some time in the 1920s. Published in 1931, *Under Three Tsars* is, however, a heavily edited version of her wonderful and extremely valuable diaries for the last year at Tsarskoe Selo. These survive in GARF and are extensively quoted in Nicholas and Alexandra's diaries for 1917–18 that were published in Russia in 2008. Naryshkina eventually emigrated to Paris, dying in the Russian Emigrants' Home in Sainte Geneviève-des-Bois in 1928.

Klavdiya Bitner later married Evgeny Kobylinsky and they settled in Rybinsk in central Russia, where they had a son, Innokenty. Here in 1927 Kobylinsky was arrested for supposed 'counter-revolutionary activities'; he was held in the much-feared Butyrki Prison near Moscow, where he was probably tortured before being shot that December. Klavdiya did not escape; in September 1937 she too was arrested. Two weeks later she was taken to the Butovo Poligon, a favourite killing ground of the NKVD during the Great Terror, located in woodland 15 miles (24 km) outside Moscow. Here she was shot and her body thrown into a mass grave – just one of 21,000 victims of the purges who were dumped there during 1937–8. The Kobylinskys' orphaned son was abandoned; his fate is unknown.

During the terrible anarchy that raged in Ekaterinburg after the murder of the Romanovs, and under threat of being taken hostage by the Cheka, Father Ivan Storozhev fled the city. He and others dug a hole in the cellar of a convent and walled themselves in with a supply of food until the Czech Legion and the Whites liberated the city.[7] From there he joined the White Army as a chaplain and with his family fled to Harbin in China. Storozhev served as a respected priest at St Nicholas's Russian Orthodox Church in Harbin and taught religion in the town's commercial school, becoming a leading member of the émigré community by the time of his death in 1927.[8]

Of the Romanov sisters' closest friends from the hospitals at Tsarskoe Selo, Rita Khitrovo managed to get her precious papers, including her letters from Olga and Tatiana, to safe-keeping in Paris. She emigrated to Yugoslavia and then to the USA, dying in New York in 1952; her papers have recently been donated to GARF. Dr Vera Gedroits settled in Kiev where she continued to work and teach, becoming chair of the faculty of surgery at the Kiev Medical Institute. She died of cancer in 1932. After the annexe hospital was closed in late 1917, Valentina Chebotareva continued to work as a nurse in military hospitals. She died of typhus in Novocherkassk in south-western Russia on 6 May 1919. Her son Gregory emigrated to the USA, ensuring the survival of his mother's diary and letters, which form a key testimony of the Romanov sisters during the war years at Tsarskoe Selo.

After the revolution, Anastasia's friend and confidante Katya Zborovskaya had gone south, back to the family's original home in the Kuban, where she worked as a nurse in a TB hospital. Her brother Viktor fought on with former members of the Tsar's Escort on the side of the Whites in southern Russia, before he was wounded again in 1920. He was evacuated to Lemnos with his family and settled in Yugoslavia. Katya had been sick and unable to travel with the family at the time they left, but she had had the foresight to entrust to them her precious letters and postcards from Anastasia and other mementoes of the Romanovs, which the family took with them into exile. Viktor died in 1944, but his widow and her daughter eventually settled in California where they have since placed Anastasia's letters to Katya in safe-keeping with the Hoover Institution Archives.

As for Katya's fate, like that of her dear friend Anastasia, she would become a representative 'victim of repression' during the terrifying round-ups of perceived 'enemies' by the new Soviet state – and in particular those having any links to the imperial family. On 12 June 1927 she was arrested on a trumped-up charge of 'counter-revolutionary activities', under the notorious article 58 of the new Soviet Criminal Code. She was sentenced to three years' imprisonment, without trial, by a three-man kangaroo court – or *troika* – on 18 August 1927 and sent to the Gulag in Central Asia. A few letters found their way to her family but said very little; and then they suddenly stopped. Katya died in the Gulag, one of many millions who perished during the Stalin years. In 2001 she was rehabilitated in the mass pardoning of political prisoners who died or were murdered during Stalin's terror, instituted after the fall of communism.[9]

It was another six years, however – and only after considerable and protracted legal wrangling – before the Russian Prosecutor General's office finally saw fit to rehabilitate Olga, Tatiana, Maria and Anastasia Romanova, their parents and brother, as 'victims of political repressions'.[10]

Acknowledgements

No book is ever the work of a lone author beavering away in splendid isolation and in this, my eleventh, I have more than ever before drawn on the knowledge, expertise, generosity and goodwill of a considerable number of people both here in the UK, and around the world.

I first began thinking about a book on the four Romanov sisters when researching and writing my book *Ekaterinburg* in 2007. They were in my head and my heart then, as I walked round the city, musing on their lives and personalities, and their tragic fate, with constant echoes of Chekhov's *Three Sisters* in the background; the allusion to that great play is therefore deliberate. After *Ekaterinburg* was published in the UK in 2008 (in the USA as *The Last Days of the Romanovs*) I had the great good fortune to encounter the wonderful network of Romanov buffs on the Royalty Weekend circuit – a conference held annually in Ticehurst, East Sussex. From day one I met with nothing but kindness, interest and enthusiasm for my project and many offers to share material. The support for my book that began at Ticehurst continued as my own network of Romanov experts expanded, even during a hiatus when I feared the book might not, after all, be signed. What kept me going in my determination to write it was the friendship and stalwart support of two key people – Sue Woolmans and Ruth Abrahams – who believed in the book as passionately as I did and wanted to see me write it. My first and primary debt of gratitude therefore goes to them, not just for unstintingly sharing material, looking out for new information, sharing books, sending mountains of photocopies, photographs and emails full of nuggets of information, but also for never letting me think I could not do it.

During the research process many other people gave absolutely invaluable help: first and foremost Rudy de Casseres in Finland, who helped winkle out the most obscure references in rare and difficult-to-obtain Russian sources with great cheerfulness and persistence and who was a rigorous fact-checker in the final stages. Various people helped me with translations: Hannah Veale from German, Karen Roth from Danish, Trond Norén Isaksen from Swedish. Priscilla Sheringham kindly checked my French translations, and David Holohan and Natalya Kolosova my Russian. I emailed endless questions to many friends, historians and writers who all generously responded, sharing their thoughts and further information: Janet Ashton, Paul Gilbert of the Royal Russia web site, Coryne Hall, Griff Henniger, Michael Holman, Greg King, Ilana Miller, Geoffrey Munn at Wartski's, Neil Studge Rees, Ian Shapiro, Richard Thornton, Frances Welch, Marion Wynn and Charlotte Zeepvat. Special thanks must go to Will Lee for sharing his considerable research on Grand Duke Dmitri Pavlovich and translations of some of Dmitri's unpublished letters; to John Wimbles for passing on to me transcriptions of some of the wonderful letters of the Duchess of Saxe-Coburg – the product of his many years of diligent work in the Romanian Archives; to Sarah Miller for sharing hard to find sources and for much discussion of OTMA by email; to Mark Andersen at the Chicago Public Library for helping track down old US magazine articles; to Phil Tomaselli for checking the National Archives at Kew for any further light on the aborted British asylum offer of 1917, and for advice on British involvement in the murder of Rasputin in 1916.

Many of the illustrations in this book were generously shared with me by two dedicated private collectors, Ruth Abrahams and Roger Short. Without their wonderful generosity I would not have been able to afford the range of illustrations that this book enjoys. I am also profoundly grateful to two other private individuals for making available to me their precious family archives: John Storojev for material on his grandfather Father Ivan Storozhev, and Victor Buchli for granting me special access to the Katia Zborovskaia Letters held at the Hoover Institution in California, as well as sharing much other valuable information and photographic material with me.

In 2011 I had the pleasure of a wonderful research trip to St Petersburg with Sue Woolmans, Karen Roth and Maggie Field, who shared in my enjoyment of all the wonderful places connected with the Romanov story and endured with good humour my frequent need to divert for cups of coffee. I am grateful to the GB–Russia Society for generously providing me with a grant towards the cost of this trip, and special thanks to Dr David Holohan, their talks organizer, for arranging it. In St Petersburg we were very well looked after by Pavel Bovichev, Vasili Khokhlov and his brother Evgeniy who answered endless questions and drove us around well beyond the call of duty, always with a smile. Pavel has continued to track down books for me in Russia and take reference photographs of locations in St Petersburg, for which I am extremely grateful.

I am, as ever, indebted to Pamela Clark, Registrar of the Royal Archives at Windsor, who with kindness and efficiency provided me with family letters as well as material relating to the Romanov visits to Balmoral and Cowes, and I am grateful for the permission of Her Majesty Queen Elizabeth II to quote from them. Nottingham Archives allowed access to Meriel Buchanan's papers and the Imperial War Museum to those of Dorothy Seymour; the British Library for Alexandra's letters to Bishop Boyd Carpenter; the Bodleian Library Special Collections for the Sydney Gibbes Papers. My thanks also must go to Tessa Dunlop for alerting me to material in the Romanian State Archives; to Stanley Rabinowitz at the Amherst Center for Russian Culture for access to the Roman Gul' Archive; to Richard Davies at the Leeds Russian Archive for two happy days making a speculative search of much wonderful material held there; to Tanya Chebotarev for sending scans of the Mariia Vasil'evna Fedchenko Papers and the Mariia Aleksandrovna Vasil'chikova Memoirs from the Columbia University Archives; and most particularly to Carol Leadenham and Nicholas Siekierski at the Hoover Institution for helping me obtain access to the Katia Zborovskaia Papers. My wonderful researcher at Hoover, Ron Basich, did a most efficient job in checking and scanning a considerable amount of material on my behalf.

The text of *The Romanov Sisters* was read and commented upon at my request by Sue Woolmans, Ruth Abrahams, Rudy de Casseres and Chris Warwick: I am eternally grateful for their insightful comments, suggestions and corrections. Fellow writers and friends Christina Zaba and Fiona Mountain also read key sections and gave their views, and have offered their valuable positive support throughout the writing process.

I am deeply grateful to Charlie Viney for originally representing this book and his support in the research and writing process and to my agent Caroline Michel for her passion and commitment to the book's continuing journey through the production process to publication and beyond. My publishers have been totally supportive and enthusiastic and a joy to work with: I am most grateful to Georgina Morley at Pan Macmillan in the UK for her guidance, scrupulous editing and energy, and her sensitivity to the book's subject. I am particularly indebted to Editorial Manager Nicholas Blake for his patience and meticulous care in checking the text and seeing it safely through to press. Charlie Spicer at St Martin's Press in the USA has for several years now given his solid support for my work and I greatly value his continuing friendship. My family as always has proudly supported my work; my brother Peter continues to maintain my web site and keep it up to date, for which my eternal thanks.

Living with the four Romanov sisters has been a particularly intense, emotional experience but also a very gratifying one. They – and Russia, for which I have an enduring love – have inspired me as a writer and I sincerely hope that I have done them, and their all too short lives, justice. I would welcome any new information, photographs or insightful comments on them that readers might care to share with me, either via my web site www.helenrappaport. com/ or via my agent at www.petersfraserdunlop.com/.

Helen Rappaport,
West Dorset, January, 2014

Notes

Abbreviations

ASM	Zvereva, *Avgusteishie sestry miloserdiya*
BL	British Library
Correspondence	Kleinpenning, *Correspondence of the Empress Alexandra*
DN I	Mironenko, *Dnevniki Imperatora Nikolaya II*, vol. I
Dnevniki	Khrustalev, *Dnevniki Nikolaya . . . i . . . Aleksandry*, 2 vols
DON	*Diary of Grand Duchess Olga Nicolaievna, 1913*
EEZ	Ekaterina Erastovna Zborovskaia letters, Hoover Institution
Fall	Steinberg and Khrustalev, *Fall of the Romanovs*
LD	Kozlov and Khrustalev, *Last Diary of Tsaritsa Alexandra*
LP	Maylunas, *Lifelong Passion*
Nikolay	*Nikolay II Dnevnik* [1913–1918]
NZ	Chebotareva, *Novyi Zhurnal*
PVP	Petr Vasilievich Petrov
RA	Royal Archives
SA	Fomin, *Skorbnyi angel*
SL	Bing, *Secret Letters*
WC	Fuhrmann, *Wartime Correspondence*

Prologue – The Room of the First and Last Door

1 The cat Zubrovka was given to Alexey at Stavka – Army HQ – in 1916 by General Voiekov, one of the tsar's aides. See Bokhanov, *Aleksandra Feodorovna*, p. 286. There is, however, some confusion about its ownership. In her letters to Katya Zborovskaya, Anastasia refers to the cat as being Olga's; see e.g. letter 8–9 June: 'Olga's cat has two kittens pretty enough to eat; one of them is red and the

other is gray'; letter to Katya, 26 June: 'Olga's cat Zubrovka (the one from Mogilev, remember) . . . well she has two small kittens'. EEZ.
2 Natalya Soloveva, 'La Tristesse Impériale', p. 12.
3 See Long, *Russian Revolution Aspects*, p. 6; Kuchumov, *Recollections*, p. 19.
4 Guide to Tsarskoe Selo, 1934, @: http://www.alexanderpalace.org/palace/detskoye.html
5 See Zeepvat, *Romanov Autumn*, pp. 320–4.
6 Kelly, *Mirror to Russia*, p. 176.
7 Holmes, *Traveler's Russia*, p. 238; Griffith, *Seeing Soviet Russia*, p. 67.
8 Kelly, *Mirror to Russia*, p. 178; see chapter 10.
9 Delafield, *Straw without Bricks*, p. 105; Kelly, *Mirror to Russia*, p. 178.
10 Bartlett, *Riddle of Russia*, p. 241.
11 Cerutti, Elisabeta, *Ambassador's Wife* (London: Allen & Unwin, 1952), p. 99.
12 Bartlett, *Riddle of Russia*, p. 249.
13 Ibid.; Greenwall, *Mirrors of Moscow*, p. 182.
14 Marie Pavlovna, *Things I Remember*, p. 34.
15 Bartlett, *Riddle of Russia*, p. 248.
16 See Yakovlev, *Aleksandrovsky dvorets*, pp. 388–9, 393–5.
17 Greenwall, *Mirrors of Moscow*, p. 182.
18 Hapgood, 'Russia's Czarina', p. 108.
19 Kuchumov, *Recollections*, pp. 20–2; Suzanne Massie, *Pavlovsk: The Life of a Russian Palace* (London: Hodder & Stoughton, 1990), p. 178.
20 Bartlett, *Riddle of Russia*, p. 249.
21 Chebotareva, diary for 6 August, *SA*, pp. 587–8.
22 *Saturday Review* 159, 27 April 1935, p. 529.

One – Mother Love

1 Seawell, 'Annual Visit', p. 324; see also Miller, *Four Graces*, for the early life of these sisters.
2 *Evening Star*, 3 July 1862.
3 Karl Baedeker, *A Handbook for Travellers on the Rhine from Holland to Switzerland* (London: K. Baedeker, 1864), p. 171.
4 Seawell, 'Annual Visit', p. 323.
5 *Davenport Daily Leader*, 8 July 1894.
6 Helena and Sell, *Alice, Grand Duchess of Hesse*, p. 14.

7 Duff, *Hessian Tapestry*, p. 91.

8 Noel, *Princess Alice*, pp. 169, 177.

9 Fulford, *Darling Child*, p. 159.

10 'The Czarina', *Canadian Magazine*, p. 302.

11 Fulford, *Beloved Mama*, pp. 23, 24.

12 *Children's Friend* 36, 1896, p. 167.

13 Ibid.

14 Helena and Sell, *Alice, Grand Duchess of Hesse*, p. 270.

15 Noel, *Princess Alice*, p. 215.

16 Helena and Sell, *Alice, Grand Duchess of Hesse*, p. 304.

17 Ibid., p. 295.

18 Noel, *Princess Alice*, p. 230.

19 Letter of 13 December 1882, RA VIC/Z/87/121.

20 E.g. letter of 26 December 1891, RA VIC/MAIN/Z/90/82–3, letter 19.

21 Letter of 15 April 1871, in Bokhanov *et al.*, *Romanovs*, p. 49.

22 G. W. Weippiert, in *Davenport Daily Leader*, 8 July 1894.

23 Queen Victoria's journal for 27 April 1892, in Zeepvat, *Cradle to Crown*, p. 133.

24 Hough, *Advice to a Granddaughter*, p. 116.

25 15 February 1887 to Vicky, Bokhanov *et al.*, *Romanovs*, p. 53; Hough, *Advice to a Granddaughter*, p. 88.

26 Hibbert, *Queen Victoria*, pp. 318, 329.

27 Vacaresco, *Kings and Queens*, p. 161.

28 Vassili, *Behind the Veil*, p. 226.

29 26 December 1893, RA VIC/Z/90/66.

30 Poore, *Memoirs of Emily Loch*, p. 154.

31 21 October 1894, in Miller, *Four Graces*, p. 93.

32 Mandache, *Dearest Missy*, p. 172.

33 Poore, *Memoirs of Emily Loch*, p. 155.

34 *Westminster Budget*, 6 June 1894, p. 37.

35 Letters to Nicky: 22 April 1894, *LP*, p. 59; 25 May 1894, *LP*, p. 70.

36 *Westminster Budget*, 22 June 1894, p. 4.

37 Malcolm Neesom, *Bygone Harrogate* (Derby: Breedon Books, 1999), p. 9.

38 *LP*, p. 68.

39 'Concerning Her Grand Ducal Highness, Princess Alix of Hesse', *Armstrong's Harrogate Almanac* (Harrogate, Yks: J. L. Armstrong, 1895), p. 2.

40 Ibid.

41 Swezey, *Nicholas and Alexandra*, p. 58.
42 *Correspondence*, p. 157.
43 *LP*, p. 110.
44 *New Weekly Courant*, 1 December 1894.
45 Radziwill, *It Really Happened*, pp. 88–9.
46 26 November 1894 OS, *Correspondence*, p. 166.
47 20 November 1894 OS, *Correspondence*, pp. 163 and 164.
48 Queen Victoria to Victoria of Milford Haven, 31 March 1889 in Hough, *Louis and Victoria*, p. 149.
49 G. E. Buckle (ed.), *Letters of Queen Victoria . . . 1886 to 1901*, 3rd series (London: John Murray, 1931), vol. 2, p. 454.
50 *Guardian*, 7 November 1894.

Two – La Petite Duchesse

1 Buxhoeveden, *Before the Storm*, p. 148.
2 Vorres, *Last Grand Duchess*, p. 73.
3 *LP*, 11 December 1894, p. 117.
4 *Correspondence*, 20 February 1895, p. 180.
5 Ibid., 28 February 1895, p. 181.
6 Ibid.
7 Ibid., 7 January 1895, p. 171; see also p. 174.
8 Ibid., 5 March 1895, p. 183.
9 For a discussion of the Russian laws of succession, see Harris, 'Succession Prospects'.
10 *Correspondence*, 17 December 1894, p. 170.
11 W. T. Stead, 'Interview with Nicholas', in Joseph O. Baylen, *The Tsar's 'Lecturer-General': W. T. Stead and the Russian Revolution of 1905* (Atlanta: Georgia State College, 1969), p. 49.
12 Vay de Vaya and Luskod, *Empires*, p. 10.
13 *Correspondence*, 30 June 1895, p. 197.
14 Ibid., 5 July 1895, p. 203.
15 Swezey, *Nicholas and Alexandra*, pp. 2–3.
16 *Correspondence*, 15 September 1895, p. 222.
17 Evgeniya Konradovna Günst (a Russian of German extraction) was a much sought-after midwife to European royalty and delivered several of Nicholas and Alexandra's relatives' babies, including Marie of Romania's son Carol in 1893 and her daughter Elisabeta in 1894. After delivering Ernie and Ducky's baby Elisabeth in Darmstadt in February 1895, Günst returned to Russia for the

birth of Grand Duchess Xenia's first baby Irina in July. She was still in service to royal clients in 1915, when, in turn, she delivered Irina's first baby by her husband Prince Felix Yusupov. There are numerous references to her in this guise in Mandache, *Dearest Missy*.

18 *Correspondence*, 21 August 1895, p. 216.

19 RA VIC/MAIN/Z/90/81: 31 October (12 November NS) 1895.

20 *SL*, pp. 98–9.

21 Ibid., p. 100.

22 *Correspondence*, 9 October 1895, p. 225.

23 Reuters telegram, *North Eastern Daily Gazette*, 12 November (NS) 1895; *Aberdeen Weekly Journal*, 4 November 1895 (NS).

24 RA VIC/MAIN/Z/90/83: 4 November (17 November NS) 1895.

25 Collier, *Victorian Diarist*, p. 4.

26 *DN I*, p. 234.

27 RA VIC/MAIN/Z/90/83: 4 November (17 November NS) 1895.

28 *LP*, p. 144; *DN I*, pp. 234, 246. See also Ella's letter to Queen Victoria: RA VIC/MAIN/Z/90/83.

29 *DN I*, p. 235.

30 Queen Victoria's Journal, vol. 102, p. 116, accessible @: http://www.queenvictoriasjournals.org/home.do

31 RA VIC/Main/Z/90/82: 13 November (25 November NS) 1895.

32 Durland, *Royal Romances*, p. 134.

33 Collier, *Victorian Diarist*, p. 4.

34 *Woman's Life*, 27 March 1897.

35 Tillander-Godenhielm, 'Russian Imperial Award System', p. 357.

36 *LP*, p. 130.

37 Two Russian Girls, 'Nestful of Princesses', p. 937; Buxhoeveden, *Life and Tragedy*, p. 56; *LP*, p. 244. Accounts vary on the number of volleys but 101/301 appears to be correct. Under the rules laid down by Nicholas I in 1834, there would be 201 volleys for any other sons born after the male heir. See N. P. Slavnitsky, 'Sankt-Peterburgskaya Krepost i tseremonii, svyazannye s rossiiskim tsarstvuyushchim domom', in *Kultura i iskusstvo v epokhu Nikolaya I* [conference papers] (St Petersburg: Alina, 2008), pp. 143–4.

38 'Alleged Dynamite Conspiracy', *Daily News*, 15 September 1896.

39 *Pall Mall Gazette*, 16 November 1895 (NS).

40 *Woman's Life*, 27 March 1897 (NS), p. 81.

41 *Westminster Budget*, 17 January 1896 (NS), p. 14.

42 Collier, *Victorian Diarist*, p. 4; *Westminster Budget*, 29 November 1895 (NS).

43 *DN I*, p. 235; *LP*, letter to Queen Victoria, 12 November 1895, p. 131.

44 Collier, *Victorian Diarist*, p. 4. See also Eagar, *Five Years*, pp. 78–9 for a fuller description of the christening ceremony, as performed for the third daughter, Maria.

45 10 December 1895, Mandache, *Dearest Missy*, p. 245.

46 See Zeepvat, *Cradle to Crown*, p. 39; Buxhoeveden, *Life and Tragedy*, p. 99. Orchie later returned to England, where she died in 1906.

47 *Correspondence*, 12 December 1895, p. 227.

48 *DN I*, p. 242; *Correspondence*, p. 229.

49 Zeepvat, *Cradle to Crown*, p. 20; *LP*, p. 133.

50 *Birmingham Daily Post*, 27 November 1895.

51 *Correspondence*, 9 January 1896, pp. 229–30.

52 Ibid., 13 April 1896, p. 230; *DN I*, p. 269.

53 RA VIC/ADD1/166/27: 20 May 1896.

54 Ibid.

55 Lutyens, *Lady Lytton*, p. 79.

56 Welch, *Russian Court at Sea*, p. 56; *DN I*, p. 270.

57 *Correspondence*, 12 July 1896, p. 232.

58 'Alleged Dynamite Conspiracy': see extensive coverage of this in the British press July–September 1896, @: http://www.britishnewspaperarchive.co.uk/

59 RA VIC/MAIN/H/47/92.

60 *Leeds Mercury*, 26 September 1896.

61 *DN I*, p. 297.

62 Ramm, *Beloved and Darling Child*, p. 195.

63 Lutyens, *Lady Lytton*, p. 75.

64 *Huddersfield Daily Chronicle*, 1 October 1896.

65 *Yorkshire Herald*, 2 October 1896.

66 *DN I*, p. 297.

67 *Windsor Magazine* 41, no. 240, December 1914, pp. 4–5; *Hampshire Telegraph*, 23 January 1897.

68 Buxhoeveden, *Life and Tragedy*, p. 73.

69 *SL*, p. 114; 'Daughters of Royal Houses', *Woman's Life*, 27 March 1897, pp. 81–2. When, a few years later, sailors on the *Shtandart* jokingly referred to Olga as the *duchesse*, she indignantly retorted that she was no 'duchess' but a Russian princess. See Sablin, *Desyat' let*, p. 140.

70 See e.g. *Church Weekly*, 14 September 1900.

71 Zimin, *Tsarskie dengi*, p. 177. Two weeks before Olga's birth the

sum of 318,913 roubles as well as 60,000 French francs were put into a fund for the child and invested in stocks and shares. By 1908 the roubles had increased to 1,756,000.

72 'Daughters of Royal Houses', *Woman's Life*, 27 March 1897, p. 82.
73 Mandache, *Dearest Missy*, p. 281.
74 Almedingen, *Empress Alexandra*, p. 64.
75 Moe, *Prelude*, p. 100.
76 *Correspondence*, 26 March 1897, p. 239.
77 Ibid., p. 240.
78 Günst was awarded a pension for applying the forceps so skilfully during the birth of Tatiana. The pension was paid until 1917; she was also given regular free holidays in the Crimea. See Zimin, *Tsarskie dengi*, p. 19.
79 Marfa Mouchanow, *My Empress* (New York: John Long, 1918), p. 91.

Three – My God! What a Disappointment! . . . A Fourth Girl!

1 RA VIC/ADDU/127.
2 *DN I*, pp. 343–4; Swezey, *Nicholas and Alexandra*, p. 66.
3 *LP*, p. 163; ibid.
4 *Isle of Man Times*, 12 June 1897.
5 *Boston Daily Globe*, 14 June 1897.
6 For descriptions of Alexandra's mauve boudoir, see King, *Court of the Last Tsar*, p. 199; Marie Pavlovna, *Things I Remember*, pp. 34–5; Buxhoeveden, *Life and Tragedy*, pp. 51–2; 'Famous Opal-hued Boudoir of Alexandra', accessible @: http://www.alexanderpalace.org/palace/mauve.html
7 *Brisbane Courier*, 19 October 1897.
8 Vassili, *Behind the Veil*, pp. 291–2; *SL*, pp. 126–7.
9 Marie Pavlovna, *Things I Remember*, p. 34.
10 'Something About Dolls', *English Illustrated Magazine* 24, 1901, p. 246; *Danville Republican*, 30 December 1897.
11 *LP*, p. 166.
12 Bariatinsky, *My Russian Life*, p. 88.
13 *SL*, 21 November 1897, pp. 128–9.
14 If Alexandra miscarried this must have happened very early in the pregnancy. It has also been suggested that she may have suffered a miscarriage around the time of the coronation, in May 1896, but as she was seen riding soon afterwards, this seems unlikely. See

Hough, *Advice to a Granddaughter*, p. 13; King, *Court of the Last Tsar*, p. 123.

15 Poore, *Memoirs of Emily Loch*, p. 194.

16 Ibid., pp. 194–5; 'The Good Works of the Empress of Russia', *Review of Reviews* 26, no. 151, July 1902, p. 58.

17 Poore, *Memoirs of Emily Loch*, pp. 199–200.

18 Ibid., p. 224.

19 Almedingen, *Empress Alexandra*, p. 76.

20 *Correspondence*, 2 April 1898, p. 244.

21 Mandache, *Dearest Missy*, p. 349.

22 *LP*, 20 September 1898, p. 174.

23 *SL*, 30 October 1898, pp. 130–1.

24 King, *Court of the Last Tsar*, p. 124.

25 Zeepvat, introduction to Eagar, *Six Years*, pp. 7–8, 14.

26 Eagar, *Six Years*, p. 49.

27 Ibid., p. 52; Marie Pavlovna, *Things I Remember*, p. 34; for Vishnyakova, see Zimin, *Detskiy mir*, pp. 73–4.

28 Marie Pavlovna, *Things I Remember*, pp. 34–5, 51.

29 See *LP*, pp. 184–5; *DN I*, pp. 470–1; *LP*, p. 183.

30 Buxhoeveden, *Life and Tragedy*, p. 92; *DN I*, p. 476.

31 *LP*, p. 185.

32 Ibid., p. 186.

33 Mandache, *Dearest Missy*, p. 383.

34 *Lloyds Weekly Newspaper*, 2 July 1899 (NS).

35 *Weekly Standard and Express*, 29 July 1899 (NS).

36 *Lloyds Weekly Newspaper*, 2 July 1899 (NS).

37 Eagar, *Six Years*, pp. 78–9.

38 *LP*, p. 188.

39 *Lloyds Weekly Newspaper*, 6 August 1899; *Fort Wayne Sentinel*, 5 August 1899; *Cedar Rapids Evening Gazette*, 5 August 1899.

40 Eagar, *Six Years*, p. 52.

41 Ibid., pp. 70–1.

42 'The Czarina of Russia', *Otago Witness*, 4 January 1900. Eagar, 'Russian Court in Summer'.

43 Vyrubova, *Memories*, p. 3; Bariatinsky, *My Russian Life*, pp. 66, 87.

44 Buxhoeveden, *Life of Alexandra*, pp. 78–9; Almedingen, *Empress Alexandra*, pp. 70–1.

45 Mee, 'Empress of a Hundred Millions', p. 6.

46 Zimin, *Detskiy mir*, pp. 15–16.

47 *Daily News*, 15 December 1900; *Sunday Gazette*, 11 December 1898.

48 Zimin, *Detskiy mir*, pp. 17–18; W. F. Ryan, *The Bathhouse at Midnight: Magic in Russia* (Stroud, Glos: Sutton, 1999), p. 112; Boris Yeltsin, *Against the Grain* (London: Simon & Schuster, 1990), pp. 79–80.

49 *SL*, pp. 138–9.

50 See e.g. *Standard*, 30 November 1900.

51 Considerable rumour had been in circulation since 1897 that the after-effects of a head wound, inflicted on Nicholas by an attacker during a tour to Japan in 1891, had led to pressure on his brain caused by coagulated blood gathering at the site of the injury. It was further reported that he had had his skull trepanned by a German surgeon, Dr Bergman, to relieve it during his 1899 visit to Darmstadt; this claim was refuted but the rumours persisted. See *Middlesborough Daily Gazette*, 18 January 1897; *Dundee Courier*, 27 January 1897; *Westminster Budget*, 29 January 1897; *Daily News*, 24 November and 15 December 1900.

52 'The Truth about the Czar', *Daily News*, 15 December 1900.

53 *DN I*, p. 564.

54 See Harris, 'Succession Prospects', pp. 65–6.

55 Harcave, *Memoirs of Count Witte*, p. 194; Crawford, *Michael and Natasha*, pp. 25–6.

56 Harcave, *Memoirs of Count Witte*, p. 297; Bogdanovich, *Tri poslednykh samoderzhtsa*, p. 269.

57 'The Truth about the Czar', *Daily News*, 15 December 1900. In 1917 Ernest Rumley Dawson openly cited the tsaritsa's case history in his *The Causation of Sex in Man* (London: H. K. Lewis), p. 218, in which he argued that 'to secure a different sex child to the child last born, we must first find the ovulation month of the last child – i.e. the month during which the ovum shed was fertilised', and from there 'find the months which correspond in sex to the one which provided the last ovum'. Dawson's simple conclusion was that 'during these months, therefore, no intercourse must take place'. He went on to claim that his method had worked for several of his clients in the nobility and aristocracy and then took a look at the case of the tsaritsa, claiming that she had had four daughters consecutively, and at last a son, 'because on four occasions a female ovulation was unfortunately fertilised'. 'The long-wished-for heir, the Cesarewitch, was born in August 1904. Tracing back, we find that the ovulation month must have been November 1903. If, therefore, September 1900 was a female ovulation period, and produced the Princess Anastasia, we know

that September 1901 would be a male, September 1902 a female, and September 1903 a male ovulation period; therefore October 1903 would be a female ovulation, and November 1903 was a male ovulation, which being fertilised, the long-looked-for son and heir was duly born in August 1904, his birth being by this plan correctly foretold by me.' There is no evidence to show whether or not Nicholas and Alexandra did indeed consult directly with Dawson or follow his theories in attempting to conceive a son. Professor Schenk had died in 1902.

58 'Four Little Maids', *Delphos Daily Herald*, 16 July 1901.
59 Ibid.
60 *SL*, p. 139.
61 *DN I*, p. 577.
62 *LP*, p. 204; in von Spreti, *Alix an Gretchen*, p. 117, the illness is described as typhus.
63 Letter to Toni Becker, 19 May 1901, in Kuhnt, *Briefe der Zarin*, p. 123; Eagar, *Six Years*, pp. 131–2.
64 Zimin, *Detskiy mir*, p. 16.
65 *DN I*, p. 599.
66 Eagar, *Six Years*, p. 132.
67 Anon. [Casper], *Intimacies of Court and Society*, p. 137.
68 *LP*, p. 206.
69 *Daily Mail*, 19 June 1901.
70 Paléologue, *Alexandra-Féodorowna*, p. 16.
71 Anon. [Casper], *Intimacies of Court and Society*, p. 137.
72 Paoli, *My Royal Clients*, p. 124.
73 Cassini, *Never a Dull Moment*, p. 150.
74 Holmes, *Travelogues*, p. 50.
75 Philippe stayed at Znamenka 9–21 July. See *DN I*, pp. 605–7.

Four – The Hope of Russia

1 Mintslov, *Peterburg*, pp. 37–8; Hapgood, *Russian Rambles*, p. 50.
2 Durland, *Royal Romances*, p. 135.
3 The spelling and the ordering of Philippe's names vary widely but Nizier Anthelme Philippe is the name recorded on his tombstone. See Robert D. Warth, 'Before Rasputin: Piety and the Occult at the Court of NII', *Historian* XLVII, May 1985, pp. 323–6 (p. 327, n. 16). Warth is the most reliable source for Philippe; see also Spiridovich, *Les Dernières années*, vol. 1 , pp. 80–4.

4 Paléologue, *Ambassador's Memoirs*, pp. 185–6.

5 Hall, *Little Mother of Russia*, pp. 190–1.

6 Zimin, *Detskiy mir*, p. 19.

7 *DN I*, p. 588.

8 See *LP*, p. 219; Shemansky and Geichenko, *Poslednye Romanovy v Petergofe*, p. 90.

9 See Nicholas's diary for July, *DN I*, pp. 605–6 and also pp. 629, 642.

10 Paléologue, *Ambassador's Diary*, p. 188; see also Zimin, *Detskiy mir*, pp. 25–6.

11 Shemansky and Geichenko, *Poslednye Romanovy v Petergofe*, p. 52.

12 *LP*, p. 214.

13 *DN I*, p. 654.

14 Naryshkin-Kurakin, *Under Three Tsars*, p. 171.

15 *Pravitelstvennyi vestnik*, no. 183, 21 August 1902.

16 The condition Alexandra had been suffering from is nowadays called a molar pregnancy. Hydatidiform moles form in the uterus when a non-viable egg – usually one where two sperm have entered at the moment of fertilization – implants itself in the lining of the womb and begins to grow. Instead of multiplying in the normal way, the cells mutate, and in some cases can become cancerous, and the placenta develops into a cyst. In Alexandra's case, her body had ultimately rejected this mass of cells growing in the lining of her womb, but the condition would have raised her hormone levels, resulting in nausea and tiredness which were common symptoms in all her pregnancies, thus reassuring her that the pregnancy was progressing normally. Russian historian Igor Zimin rediscovered the private report in the Russian archives in 2010. See Zimin, *Detskiy mir*, pp. 22–5.

17 Ibid., pp. 21–2.

18 'The Tsar: A Character Sketch', *Fortnightly Review* 75, no. 467, 1 March 1904, p. 364.

19 *Anglo-Russian* VI, no. 5, November 1902, p. 653.

20 Ibid., p. 654.

21 Moe, *Prelude*, p. 104, n. 114.

22 Zimin, *Detskiy mir*, p. 27; Fuhrmann, *Rasputin*, p. 36.

23 *Post-Standard*, Syracuse, 21 September 1902; *Boston Sunday Globe*, 16 November 1902; *Post-Standard*, Syracuse, 17 November 1902.

24 *Pittsburgh Chronicle-Telegraph*, as quoted in the *Kalona News*, Iowa, 8 November 1901.

25 Anon. [Casper], *Intimacies of Court and Society*, p. 133.

26 *The Times*, 11 July 1903.
27 Naryshkin-Kurakin, *Under Three Tsars*, p. 175.
28 See Paléologue, *Ambassador's Memoirs*, pp. 190–1; *DN I*, pp. 740–1. For a fuller description of the visit to Sarov, see Rounding, *Alix and Nicky*, pp. 44–7; Moe, *Prelude*, pp. 54–7. For the fate of Seraphim's remains, which were vandalized under the Soviets, see John and Carol Garrard, *Russian Orthodoxy Resurgent: Faith and Power in the New Russia* (Princeton, NJ: Princeton University Press, 2008), ch. 2.
29 Eagar, *Six Years*, pp. 159–60.
30 *DN I*, p. 764; Eagar, *Six Years*, pp. 164–5.
31 Durland, *Royal Romances*, pp. 165–6; *Daily Mirror*, 29 December 1903; Eagar, *Six Years*, p. 169.
32 *DN I*, p. 765.
33 Eagar, 'Christmas at the Court of the Tsar', p. 30.
34 Ibid.
35 *LP*, p. 240.
36 Durland, *Royal Romances*, pp. 185–6; Eagar, *Six Years*, p. 172.
37 Eagar, 'Further Glimpses', p. 366; Eagar, *Six Years*, p. 177.
38 Quoted in the *Brisbane Courier*, 1 October 1904.
39 Letter to Boyd Carpenter, 29 December 1902 (OS), BL Add. 46721 f. 238; Bokhanov, *Aleksandra Feodorovna*, p. 147, quoting the American author George Miller.
40 Almedingen, *Empress Alexandra*, p. 68.
41 See Zimin, *Detskiy mir*, pp. 28–9.
42 'New Czarevitch', *Daily Express*, 13 August 1904.
43 Buxhoeveden, *Before the Storm*, pp. 237–8.
44 *DN I*, p. 817; *LP*, p. 244.
45 Zimin, *Tsarskie dengi*, p. 28.
46 *Unitarian Register* 83, 1904, p. 901.
47 For fuller details, see 'The Cesarevitch', *The Times*, 25 August 1904.
48 *LP*, p. 244.
49 Ulla Tillander-Godenhielm, 'The Russian Imperial Award System during the Reign of Nicholas II 1894–1917', *Journal of the Finnish Antiquarian Society* 113, 2005, p. 358.
50 Fedchenko Papers, 'Vospominaniya o Marii Fedorovne Geringere', ff. 27–8.
51 Buxhoeveden, *Before the Storm*, pp. 240–1. It is unclear whether all four sisters attended the actual ceremony as reports vary considerably. Olga and Tatiana were certainly in the procession going to the church but *The Times* reported that the four girls did

not attend the actual ceremony but watched 'from an alcove' – see *The Times*, 25 August 1904.

52 Ioann Konstantinovich, letter from Livadia to his family, 9–17 September 1904, in *Rossiiskii Arkhiv* XV, 2007, p. 426.

53 Eagar, *Six Years*, p. 223; Buxhoeveden, *Before the Storm*, p. 241.

54 Durland, *Royal Romances*, p. 135; Almedingen, *Empress Alexandra*, p. 106.

55 'Passing Events', *Broad Views*, 12 September 1904, p. 266.

56 Howe, *George von Lengerke Meyer*, p. 100.

57 'Passing Events', *Broad Views*, 12 September 1904, p. 266.

58 Thomas Bentley Mott, *Twenty Years as a Military Attaché* (London: Oxford University Press, 1937), p. 131.

59 Zimin, *Detskiy mir*, p. 31.

60 *LP*, p. 245.

61 Roman Romanoff, *Det var et rigt hus . . . Erindringer af Roman Romanoff prins af rusland, 1896–1919*, Copenhagen: Gyldendal, 1991, pp. 58–9. I am grateful to Karen Roth for this translation from the Danish.

62 Fedchenko, 'Vospominaniya', f. 15.

63 Marie Pavlovna, *Things I Remember*, p. 61.

64 Zimin, *Tsarskie dengi*, pp. 30–1.

65 'The Hope of Russia – The Infant Tsarevich', *Illustrated London News*, front cover, 31 March 1906.

66 *LP*, p. 240; Wilton and Telberg, *Last Days of the Romanovs*, p. 33.

67 This remained the predicted life expectancy until the 1960s when the first really effective treatment – Factor VIII plasma, a blood-clotting protein – was introduced.

Five – The Big Pair and the Little Pair

1 See Frederick Doloman, 'How the Russian Censor Works', *Strand Magazine* 29, no. 170, February 1905, p. 213.

2 *LP*, p. 251.

3 Elton, *One Year*, p. 110. See also *SL*, pp. 247–8; 'Cannon Fired at the Czar', *The Call*, San Francisco, 20 January 1905.

4 The following year Nicholas's security forces insisted that the ceremony take place out of town, at the lake in front of the Catherine Palace at Tsarskoe Selo.

5 Min's assassin, Zinaida Konoplyannikova, was hanged soon afterwards at the Shlisselburg Fortress – the first female

revolutionary to be executed since Sofya Perovskaya, one of the assassins of Alexander II, in 1881. The American ambassador to St Petersburg, George von Lengerke Meyer, made a report to US Senator Lodge summarizing the number of attacks and assassinations carried out in Russia between 1900 and 1906: 'killed or injured by bombs, revolvers, assaults: 1,937 officials and important persons, 1 grand duke, 67 governors, general governors and town prefects; 985 police officers and policemen; 500 army officers and soldiers; 214 civil functionaries, 117 manufacturers, 53 clergymen.' See Howe, *George von Lengerke Meyer*, p. 329.

6   Marie Pavlovna, *Things I Remember*, p. 76.

7   'Home Life of the Czar', *London Journal*, 14 February 1903, p. 150.

8   Ibid.

9   See Spiridovich, *Last Years*, pp.12–17.

10   Mossolov, *At the Court*, p. 36.

11   See 'Terrible Bomb Outrage', *Advertiser*, Adelaide, 2 October 1906.

12   'Children Without a Smile', *Washington Post*, 28 May 1905.

13   Andrei Almarik, *Rasputin: dokumentalnaya povest*, ch. IX, accessible @: http://www.erlib.com/Андрей_Амальрик/Распутин/9/

14   Ibid.; Kokovtsov, *Iz moego proshlago* 2, p. 348; Wyrubova, *Muistelmia Venäjän*, p. 105.

15   Ibid. See also Wheeler and Rives, *Dome*, pp. 348–9. A monument to the victims of the attack on Stolypin's villa was erected on the site in 1908, and surprisingly survived the Soviet era.

16   For a more balanced view of Rasputin by a close member of the family who witnessed him first hand, see Olga Alexandrovna's memoirs in Vorres, *Last Grand Duchess*, ch. 7, pp. 133–46. An interesting and objective contemporary view that does much to demystify him can also be found in Shelley, *Blue Steppes*, ch. V, 'The Era of Rasputin'.

17   Spiridovich, *Last Years*, p. 109; see Nicholas's diary entries for 1 November 1905, 18 July, 12 October, 9 December 1906, accessible @: http://lib.ec/b/384140/read#t22

18   Gilliard, *Thirteen Years*, p. 26.

19   Poore, *Memoirs of Emily Loch*, p. 301.

20   'The Tsar's Children', *Daily Mirror*, 29 December 1903.

21   'Tottering House of the Romanoffs'.

22   Marina de Heyden, *Les Rubis portent malheur* (Monte Carlo: Editions Regain, 1967), p. 27.

23   Bonetsakaya, *Tsarskie deti*, p. 332.

24   Spiridovich, *Last Years*, p. 26.

25 Girardin, *Précepteur des Romanov*, p. 45.

26 Ibid. In 1906 Stana would divorce the duke and marry her sister's brother-in-law Grand Duke Nikolay, effecting, for a while, an even closer rapport with Nicholas and Alexandra, until Stana and Nikolay became alienated from the imperial couple in the wake of Rasputin's increasing influence.

27 For the daily routine of family life at Tsarskoe Selo, see e.g. Alexey Volkov's *Memories*, ch. 10, accessible @: http://www.alexanderpalace. org/volkov/8.html

28 *LP*, letter from Alexandra when in Pskov, 4 August 1905, p. 278.

29 Bokanov, *Love, Power and Tragedy*, p. 112.

30 'Tottering House of the Romanoffs'.

31 Buxhoeveden, *Before the Storm*, p. 258.

32 'The Tsar's Children', *Daily Mirror*, 29 December 1903.

33 Ibid.

34 Wortman, *Scenarios of Power*, p. 331; Letter to Boyd Carpenter, 29 December 1902 (11 January 1903 NS), BL Add 46721 f. 238.

35 *LP*, p. 256.

36 Durland, *Royal Romances*, p. 187; Eagar, *Six Years*, p. 163.

37 Eagar, 'Christmas at the Court of the Tsar', p. 27.

38 Eagar, *Six Years*, p. 214.

39 *LP*, p. 221.

40 Eagar, *Six Years*, p. 169.

41 *Daily Mirror*, 29 December 1903.

42 Durland, *Royal Romances*, p. 197.

43 Virubova, *Keisarinnan Hovineiti*, p. 230.

44 Minzlov [Mintslov], 'Home Life of the Romanoffs', p. 163; Eagar, 'Further Glimpses', p. 367; Durland, *Royal Romances*, p. 188.

45 Eagar, *Six Years*, p. 71.

46 Minzlov, 'Home Life of the Romanoffs', p. 162. For perhaps the best portrait of the much-written-about Anastasia, see her aunt Olga's account in Vorres, *Last Grand Duchess*, pp. 108–13. Note these very detailed and personal memories were the basis for Olga Alexandrovna's emphatic rejection of false claimant Anna Anderson.

47 Minzlov, 'Home Life of the Romanoffs', p. 162.

48 Eagar, 'Russian Court in Summer', p. 390.

49 Durland, *Royal Romances*, pp. 202–3.

50 Eagar, 'Further Glimpses', pp. 366–7.

51 King and Wilson, *Resurrection of the Romanovs*, p. 24.

52 Buxhoeveden, *Before the Storm*, p. 245.

Six – The *Shtandart*

1 See Zimin, *Tsarskaya rabota*, pp. 262–4.
2 See *SL*, pp. 216–18; Hall, 'No Bombs, No Bandits'.
3 Grabbe and Grabbe, *Private World*, p. 91.
4 For a detailed description of the interior of the *Shtandart* and life on board the yacht in 1906, see Nikolay Sablin, *Desyat let*, pp. 18–39. See also King, *Court of the Last Tsar*, pp. 274–85 and Tuomi-Nikula, *Imperatory*.
5 Sablin, *Desyat let*, p. 234.
6 The sick Orbeliani was given her own suite of rooms at the Alexander Palace where Alexandra paid for her care and nursed her as her health declined. Sonya died in her arms in December 1915 – see Vyrubova, *Memoirs*, p. 371. Alexandra's care of and concern for Orbeliani is typical of how she always looked after those dear to her. See Zimin, *Detskiy mir*, pp. 365–6.
7 Dehn, *Real Tsaritsa*, p. 38; Vorres, *Last Grand Duchess*, p. 137. For an assessment of Vyrubova's character see Dehn, *Real Tsaritsa*, pp. 48–9.
8 Grabbe and Grabbe, *Private World*, p. 57.
9 21 September 1906, Nikolai, accessible @: http://lib.ec/b/384140/read#t22
10 See Linda Predovsky, 'The Playhouse on Children's Island', *Royalty Digest*, no. 119, May 2001, pp. 347–9.
11 'Take the "Bumps": Little Grand Duchesses Experiment with Toboggan in Czar's Park', *Washington Post*, 25 March 1907.
12 Kulikovsky, *25 Chapters*, p. 75.
13 Ibid.
14 Ibid., p. 74; Vorres, *Last Grand Duchess*, p. 111.
15 Ibid.
16 Kulikovsky, *25 Chapters*, p. 75.
17 Vorres, *Last Grand Duchess*, p. 112.
18 Ibid.; Kulikovsky, *25 Chapters*, p. 74.
19 Zeepvat, introduction to Eagar, *Six Years*, pp. 33, 34.
20 Bonetskaya, *Tsarskie deti*, p. 332. For more on Trina Schneider, a Baltic German, original name Schneiderlein, see Chernova, *Vernye*, pp. 169–75, 565.
21 The pet name Savanna was a contraction of the names Sofya Ivanovna. See Sof'ya Ivanovna Tyutcheva, 'Za neskolko let do katastrofy', Vospominaniya'.
22 According to an editorial note, these memoirs were dictated by

Tyutcheva to a niece in January 1945.

23 Dehn, *Real Tsaritsa*, p. 75.

24 'Children of the Czar', *Scrap-Book* V, 1908, p. 60.

25 Eagar, *Six Years*, p. 226.

26 John Epps was born in 1848 and went to Russia in 1880 at the age of thirty-one. When he died in Australia in 1935 he had in his possession numerous drawings and schoolbooks by the four Romanov sisters. These went missing for many years, then finally resurfaced in Australia in 2004, with a relative, Janet Epps. Sadly the author has not been able to trace either her or the current location of these precious memorabilia. See @: http://www.abc. net.au/worldtoday/content/2004/s1220082.htm

27 See Trewin, *Tutor to the Tsarevich*, p. 10 and Zeepvat, *Cradle to Crown*, p. 223.

28 Zimin, *Detskiy mir*, p. 163.

29 Nicholas [Gibbes], 'Ten Years', p. 9. C. S. Gibbes Papers, List 1 (76), Statement by Gibbes, 1 December 1928.

30 Welch, *Romanovs and Mr Gibbes*, p. 33.

31 For details of the girls' curriculum, see Girardin, *Précepteur*, p. 49, Zimin, *Detskiy mir*, pp. 162–4, Zimin, *Vzroslyi mir*, pp. 497–8, although there is some inconsistency in the timings of lessons.

32 The plotters – eleven men and seven women of the Socialist Revolutionary Party, among them 'the Madonna-like' Mariya Prokofieva and the equally attractive general's daughter 'Madame Fedosieff', both of whom the western press depicted as precursors of Mata Hari – went on trial in August behind closed doors and a total press blackout. Three of the male conspirators were sentenced to death and hanged and several of the women involved were jailed or, in Prokofieva's case sent into exile. See 'Beautiful Women Accused of Plotting against the Tsar', *Penny Illustrated Paper*, 31 August 1907; *SL*, p. 228.

33 Norregaard, 'The Czar at Home', *Daily Mail*, 10 June 1908.

34 Ibid.

35 Vyrubova, *Memories*, p. 33.

36 The strong and resourceful Dina, as Alexey called him, was increasingly relied on to protect the tsarevich against any harm and paid a generous salary in recognition of this. He would henceforth sleep in the room next to Alexey's in all the imperial residences. See Zimin, *Detskiy mir*, pp. 82–3.

37 Tuomi-Nikula, *Imperatory*, pp. 188–9. See also the account in Spiridovich, *Last Years*, pp. 174–5.

38 Sablin, 'S tsarskoy semei na "shtandarte"', f. 4. See also ch. 9 of Spiridovich, *Last Years* and Sablin's account in *Desyat let*, pp. 100–4.

39 See Tuomi-Nikula, *Imperatory*, pp. 188–90; Vyrubova, *Memories*, p. 34.

Seven – Our Friend

1 Dehn, *My Empress*, p. 81.
2 'The Three-year-old Heir to the Throne of the Czar', *Current Literature* 43, no. 1, July 1907, p. 38.
3 Botkin, *Real Romanovs*, p. 28; Spiridovich, *Last Years*, p. 179.
4 Durland, *Royal Romances*, p. 206; Bonetskaya, *Tsarskie deti*, p. 324.
5 Wheeler and Rives, *Dome*, p. 356.
6 Welch, *Romanovs and Mr Gibbes*, p. 37.
7 René Fulop-Miller, *Rasputin: The Holy Devil* (London: G. P. Putnam, 1927), p. 25.
8 Radziwill, *Taint*, p. 196. See also 'The Three-year-old Heir', pp. 36–8.
9 Vorres, *Last Grand Duchess*, p. 142. Olga Alexandrovna's is one of the very few reliable sources for Alexey's first serious haemophilia attacks. See also Zimin, *Detskiy mir*, p. 35.
10 Ibid.
11 Rasputin, *Rasputin*, p. 114.
12 For accounts of this 1907 accident, see Zimin, *Detskiy mir*, p. 35; Vorres, *Last Grand Duchess*, pp. 142–3; Spiridovich, *Raspoutine*, p. 71; Rasputin, *Rasputin*, p. 115.
13 De Jonge, *Life and Times of Rasputin*, p. 154.
14 Vorres, *Last Grand Duchess*, p. 142.
15 Buxhoeveden, *Before the Storm*, p. 119.
16 Dolgorouky, 'Gone For Ever', TS, Hoover Institution, p. 11.
17 Bokhanov, *Aleksandra Feodorovna*, p. 193; Dehn, *My Empress*, p. 103.
18 Fedchenko, 'Vospominaniya', f. 27. See also Almarik re the 'New One' coined by Alexey, @: http://www.erlib.com/Андрей_Амальрик/Распутин/9/
19 Vorres, *Last Grand Duchess*, p. 138.
20 C. E. Bechhofer, *A Wanderer's Log* (London: Mills & Boon, 1922), p. 149, and also ch. VII.
21 Ibid., p. 150.
22 Dehn, *My Empress*, p. 103.

23   Shelley, *Blue Steppes*, p. 85; see ch. VI, 'Days and Nights with Rasputin'.

24   For a summary, see Nelipa, *Murder of Rasputin*, pp. 26–9.

25   Sablin, 'S tsarskoy semei na "Shtandarte"', f. 9.

26   Ibid., f. 10.

27   Ibid.

28   Welch, *Romanovs and Mr Gibbes*, p. 43; Bowra, *Memories*, p. 65.

29   According to Almedingen, *Empress Alexandra*, p. 121, Alexandra sent two telegrams to Rasputin in Pokrovskoe and he assured her that 'her little son would never die of his illness'.

30   *SL*, p. 231; Zimin, *Detskiy mir*, p. 35; Massie, *Nicholas and Alexandra*, p. 143.

31   Almedingen, *Empress Alexandra*, p. 122.

32   Marie of Romania, *Story of My Life*, pp. 474–5.

33   Ular, *Russia from Within*, p. 41; Radziwill, *Taint*, p. 208.

34   Zimin, *Detskiy mir*, p. 36.

35   Almedingen, *Empress Alexandra*, p. 122.

36   *LP*, pp. 315–16.

37   *LP*, p. 320.

38   Bonetskaya, *Tsarskie deti*, p. 400.

39   *LP*, p. 318.

40   Ibid., p. 319.

41   Bonetskaya, *Tsarskie deti*, pp. 407–8.

42   Ibid., p. 409.

43   Ibid.

44   *LP*, p. 321; Bokhanov, *Aleksandra Feodorovna*, p. 195.

45   *LP*, p. 321.

46   Bokhanov, *Aleksandra Feodorovna*, p. 195.

47   Vorres, *Last Grand Duchess*, p. 141.

48   Prime Minister Stolypin had also commissioned a private investigation of Rasputin by the Okhrana. A damning report, like that on Philippe in 1902, it was shown to Nicholas and Alexandra but they chose to ignore it.

49   Naryshkin-Kurakin, *Under Three Tsars*, p. 196.

50   See @: http://traditio-ru.org/wiki/Письма_царских_дочерей_Григорию_Распутину The letters came into the possession of a monk and associate of Rasputin's named Iliodor (Sergey Trufanov), who claimed that when Rasputin had met him at Christmas 1909 in Pokrovskoe, he had shown Iliodor numerous letters sent to him by Alexandra and the girls, and had given him

seven of these letters as a 'souvenir'. The text of the letters appeared in a book on Rasputin by the Russian dissident writer Andrey Almarik that was published in French in 1982. The Russian text can be found online @: http://www.erlib.com/Андрей_Амальрик/Распутин/9/. Some of the letters were also published in S. P. Istratova, *Zhitie bludnogo startsa Grishki Rasputina* (Moscow: Vozrozhdenie, 1990), pp. 1015–16. Note that the letters appear to have been redacted at some point and are quoted in various forms in different sources. No single source has yet come to light that gives them in full.

51 See also Dehn, *Real Tsaritsa*, p. 105; Fuhrmann, *Rasputin*, pp. 94–5, quoting GARF F612, op1, d 42, 1.5. It is impossible to know for certain the identity of Nikolay; he could have been one of any number of officers in the imperial entourage whom Olga saw in church on Sundays. Bearing in mind the frequency with which she saw him and was photographed with him on board the *Shtandart*, it has been suggested that Olga had developed a crush on Nikolay Sablin. But at twenty-nine, a trusted member of her father's entourage, and almost twice Olga's age, Sablin seems an unlikely candidate for such a young teenage girl.

52 See @: http://traditio-ru.org/wiki/Письма_царских_дочерей_Григорию_Распутину /

Eight – Royal Cousins

1 Tyutcheva, 'Za neskolko let'.
2 Sablin, *Desyat let*, p. 145.
3 Zeepvat, 'One Summer', p. 12.
4 *Anglo-Russian* XII, 11 May 1909, p. 1265.
5 Keith Neilson and Thomas Otte, *The Permanent Under-Secretary for Foreign Affairs, 1854–1946* (Abingdon, Oxon: Routledge, 2009), p. 133.
6 See 'Petitions of protest against the visit to England of the Emperor of Russia', RA PPTO/QV/ADD/PP3/39. The original letters of protest can be seen at the National Archives at Kew.
7 'The Detective', *Nebraska State Journal*, 9 October 1910; 'Guarding the Tsar', *Daily Mirror*, 3 August 1909.
8 Lord Suffield, *My Memories, 1830–1913* (London: Herbert Jenkins, 1913), p. 303.

9 British press accounts were many and detailed; see e.g. *Daily Mirror*, 31 July to 5 August, which published numerous photographs. For a Russian view of the visit, see Spiridovich, *Last Years*, pp. 312–19 and Sablin, *Desyat let*, pp. 148–58.

10 Richard Hough, *Edward and Alexandra*, p. 236.

11 See: Sablin, *Desyat let*, p. 151; Alastair Forsyth, 'Sovereigns and Steam Yachts: The Tsar at Cowes', *Country Life*, 2 August 1984, pp. 310–12; 'Cowes Week', *The Times*, 7 August 1909.

12 'The Cowes Week', *Isle of Wight County Press*, 7 August 1909.

13 RA QM/PRIV/CC25/39: 6 August 1909.

14 When it was mooted that the Prince of Wales would attend Nicholas's coronation in Moscow in 1896 a Russian official was said to have remarked, 'We cannot very well manage to protect two Czars!' See 'Alien's Letter from England', *Otago Witness*, 29 September 1909.

15 Anne Edwards, *Matriarch: Queen Mary and the House of Windsor* (London: Hodder & Stoughton, 1984), p. 169.

16 Duke of Windsor, *A King's Story* (London: Prion Books, 1998), p. 129.

17 'Cowes Regatta Week', *Otago Witness*, 29 September 1909.

18 Hough, *Edward and Alexandra*, p. 381.

19 Sir Henry William Lucy, *Diary of a Journalist*, vol. 2, *1890–1914* (London: John Murray, 1921), p. 285.

20 *Correspondence*, p. 284.

21 Zimin, *Detskiy mir*, p. 381; see also Alexandra's letter to Tatiana, 30 December 1909, *LP*, p. 307.

22 Spirovich, *Last Years*, p. 322, though he refers to the doctor only as 'M.X.' [Monsieur X possibly]. See also Naryshkin-Kurakin, *Under Three Tsars*, pp. 192–3.

23 Confirmed in Mackenzie Wallace, letter to Knollys, RA W/55/53, 7 August 1909. See also Spiridovich, *Last Years*, pp. 321–3.

24 The suggestion is made by Zimin that many people suspected a lesbian undercurrent in Vyrubova's behaviour towards Alexandra. Dr Fischer had sensed this and as a result was forced out, to be replaced by the more accommodating Botkin. See Zimin, *Detskiy mir*, pp. 380–3 and Bogdanovich, *Tri poslednykh samoderzhtsa*, p. 483.

25 Almedingen, *Empress Alexandra*, p. 123.

26 *LP*, p. 320.

27 Spiridovich, *Last Years*, p. 347.

28 Ibid.

29 See Dorr, *Inside the Russian Revolution*, p. 113.
30 Spiridovich, *Last Years*, p. 347.
31 Almarik, @: http://www.erlib.com/Андрей_Амальрик/Распутин/9/
32 Gregor Alexinski, *Modern Russia* (London: Fisher Unwin, 1915), p. 90.
33 Spiridovich, *Last Years*, p. 409.
34 Wheeler and Rives, *Dome*, p. 347. The now forgotten account of Post Wheeler and his wife Hallie Rives is exceptionally vivid for the years 1906–11 in St Petersburg.
35 Ibid., pp. 342–3.
36 Fraser, *Red Russia*, pp. 18, 19.
37 Ibid., p. 20.
38 Wheeler and Rives, *Dome*, p. 411.
39 Ular, *Russia from Within*, pp. 71, 83. For a fascinating contemporary account of the grand dukes see pp. 71–100.
40 Wheeler and Rives, *Dome*, p. 347.
41 Considered highly erotic if not immoral, *Three Weeks*, published in 1907, was banned in many places. Some said it was loosely based on the Empress Alexandra but Glyn had certainly not had her in mind when writing it. See Joan Hardwick, *Addicted to Romance: Life and Adventures of Elinor Glyn*, London: André Deutsch, 1994, p. 155. The book sold 5 million copies and prompted the popular rhyme: 'Would you like to sin / With Elinor Glyn / On a tiger skin? / Or would you prefer / To err with her / On some other fur?'
42 Glyn, *Elinor Glyn*, p. 178.
43 Glyn, *Romantic Adventure*, p. 180.
44 Ibid., pp. 183, 182.
45 Ibid., p. 182.
46 Ibid., p. 184.
47 Ibid.
48 Ibid., p. 204.
49 Ibid., pp. 194, 204–5. Tragically, Glyn's original, and no doubt fascinating, diary of her time in Russia was destroyed in a house fire in 1956.
50 Glyn's novel *His Hour*, based on her Russian trip and published in October 1911, which she dedicated to Grand Duchess Vladimir, also reflected her own strong sense of impending disaster in Russia.
51 Ibid., p. 347.
52 Ibid., p. 354.

53 Ibid.
54 'A Former Lady in Waiting Tells of a Visit to Tsarskoe-Selo', *Washington Post*, 2 May 1909.
55 Wheeler and Rives, *Dome*, pp. 355–6.
56 'A Visit to the Czar', *Cornhill Magazine* 33, 1912, p. 747.
57 Minzlov, 'Home Life of the Romanoffs', p. 164; Ryabinin, 'Tsarskaya Semya v Krymu osen 1913 goda', p. 83.
58 *LP*, p. 330, letters of 7 and 11 March.
59 *LP*, p. 334, 17 May 1910.
60 Quoted in Titov, 'OTMA', p. 44. Anastasia destroyed all her diaries in 1917 but some notebooks survive in GARF, from which this quotation would appear to be taken.
61 Bogdanovich, *Tri poslednykh samoderzhtsa*, pp. 506–7.
62 See Sablin, *Desyat let*, pp. 215–16.
63 Vyrubova, *Memories*, p. 63.
64 *LP* p. 330; Bokhanov, *Aleksandra Feodorovna*, pp. 217–18.
65 *LP*, p. 331; Naryshkin, *Under Three Tsars*, p. 196.
66 *LP*, pp. 342–3.
67 Ktorova, *Minuvshee*, p. 88; Dehn, *Real Tsaritsa*, p. 102.
68 See Ktorova, *Minuvshee*, p. 87.
69 Almedingen, *Empress Alexandra*, p. 125.

Nine – In St Petersburg We Work, But at Livadia We Live

1 *SL*, p. 254; Vyrubova, *Memories*, p. 50.
2 King, 'Requiem', p. 106.
3 Hunt, *Flurried Years*, p. 133.
4 Ibid.
5 Ibid., pp. 133–4.
6 Baroness W. Knell, in *Gleaner*, 6 December 1910.
7 Hough, *Mountbatten*, pp. 22–3. John Terraine, *Life and Times of Lord Mountbatten* (London: Arrow Books, 1980), p. 25.
8 Poore, *Memoirs of Emily Loch*, p. 305. For Emily Loch's account of this visit see pp. 302–11. In February 1912 Alexandra allowed pocket money of 5 roubles a month to be paid to the younger two girls. Zimin, *Detskiy mir*.
9 Marie, Furstin zu Erbach-Schönberg, *Reminiscences* (London: Allen & Unwin, 1925), p. 358.
10 Ibid., p. 359.
11 Maria Vasil'chikova, Memoir, f. 14. See also Madeleine Zanotti,

quoted in Radziwill, *Nicholas II*, p. 195. For the Nauheim visit see King, 'Requiem'.

12 Hough, *Mountbatten*, p. 23.

13 Hough, *Louis and Victoria*, p. 262, letter, 29 December 1911.

14 *LP*, p. 335.

15 Ibid., pp. 335–6.

16 Buxhoeveden, *Before the Storm*, p. 288.

17 'Tragedy of a Throne: Czarina Slowly Dying of Terror', *Straits Times*, 6 January 1910.

18 *Advertiser*, Adelaide, 12 January 1910.

19 Wheeler and Rives, *Dome*, p. 405.

20 Ibid.

21 Ibid.

22 Ibid., p. 406.

23 Hall, *Little Mother*, p. 234.

24 Wheeler and Rives, *Dome*, p. 407.

25 *Correspondence*, 19 April, p. 290.

26 Korshunova *et al.*, *Pisma . . . Elizaveta Feodorovny*, p. 258.

27 *LP*, p. 342.

28 See letter of Prince Ioann Konstantinovich, 7 March 1903, *Rossiiskiy arkhiv* XV, p. 392.

29 Sablin, *Desyat let*, p. 241.

30 19 August 1911 entry, Meriel Buchanan diary, BuB 6, MB Archive, Nottingham University. See also *Correspondence*, Alexandra's letter to Onor, 13 August, p. 350.

31 Ibid.

32 Gavriil Konstantinovich, *Marble Palace*, p. 128.

33 Ioann Konstantinovich, letters to his father, 2 November 1909 and 3 December 1910, *Rossiskiy arhkiv*, pp. 415–19.

34 Bokhanov *et al.*, *Romanovs*, p. 127.

35 *Correspondence*, p. 351.

36 For Tyucheva's account of the assassination of Stolypin, see Tyutcheva, 'Za neskolko let'.

37 *LP*, p. 344.

38 Tyutcheva, 'Za neskolko let'.

39 *Correspondence*, p. 351.

40 Galina von Meck, 'The Death of Stolypin', in Michael Glenny and Norman Stone, *The Other Russia* (London: Faber & Faber, 1990).

41 *Correspondence*, p. 351.

42 Tyutcheva, 'Za neskolko let'.

43 *Correspondence*, p. 351.

44 'The Creation of Nadezhda Isakovlevna Mandel'shtam', in Helena Goscilo (ed.), *Fruits of Her Plume: Essays on Contemporary Women's Culture* (New York: M. E. Sharpe, 1993), p. 90.

45 Tyutcheva, 'Za neskolko let'.

46 Zeepvat, 'Valet's Story', p. 304.

47 Tyutcheva, 'Za neskolko let'.

48 William Eleroy Curtis, *Around the Black Sea* (London: Hodder & Stoughton, 1911), p. 265.

49 Buxhoeveden, *Before the Storm*, p. 294; Vyrubova, *Memories*, p. 37.

50 Sergey Sazonov, introduction to *Per Zhilyar, Imperator Nikolai II i ego semya* (Vienna: Rus, 1921), p. vi. It is unclear whether this was said by Olga or Tatiana. See also Grabbe and Grabbe; Grabbe, *Private World*, p. 75.

51 Kalinin and Zemlyanichenko, *Romanovy i Krym*, p. 80.

52 See Vyrubova, *Romanov Family Album*, pp. 84–7.

53 Vorres, *Last Grand Duchess*, p. 110; Vyrubova, *Romanov Family Album*, p. 103; Zimin, *Vzroslyi mir*, p. 323.

54 Brewster, *Anastasia's Album*, p. 30.

55 Kalinin and Zemlyanichenko, 'Taina Velikoi Knyazhny', p. 243; Mikhail Korshunov, *Taina tain moskovskikh* (Moscow: Slovo, 1995), p. 266.

56 Mossolov, *At the Court*, p. 61.

57 See Victor Belyakov, 'Russia's Last Star: Nicholas II and Cinema', *Historical Journal of Film, Radio and Television* 15, no. 4, October 1995, pp. 517–24.

58 Zemlyanichenko, *Romanovy i Krym*, p. 83.

59 De Stoeckl, *My Dear Marquis*, p. 127. It has been suggested that this proposal was made later, but in the context of de Stoeckl's memoir it is clearly 1911.

60 See Sablin, *Desyat let*, p. 234.

61 See Spiridovich, *Les Dernières années*, vol. 2, pp. 142–3.

62 Mossolov, *At the Court*, p. 247.

63 Girardin, *Précepteur*, p. 51.

64 See Zimin, *Tsarskie dengi*; Mossolov, *At the Court*, p. 41.

65 Spiridovich, *Les Dernières années*, vol. 2, p. 151.

66 Vyrubova, *Romanov Family Album*, p. 86; see also Spiridovich, *Les Dernières années*, vol. 2, pp. 148–9.

67 De Stoeckl, *Not All Vanity*, p. 119.

68 Vyrubova, *Romanov Family Album*, p. 86.

69 Spiridovich, *Les Dernières années*, vol. 2, p. 151.

70 Titov, 'OTMA', p. 33. There are 12 volumes of Olga's diaries in

GARF dating from 1905 to 1917, but many of them are incomplete or with brief entries and 1910 is missing. Only the first few pages of her 1917 diary survive.

71 For an account of the ball, see Kamarovskaya, *Vospominaniya*, pp. 173–6; Spiridovich, *Les Dernières années*, vol. 2, pp. 150, 151.

72 De Stoeckl, *Not All Vanity*, p. 120; Kamarovskaya, *Vospominaniya*, pp. 173–6.

73 Mossolov, *At the Court*, p. 61.

74 Vyrubova, *Romanov Family Album*, p. 86.

75 Naryshkin-Kurakin, *Under Three Tsars*, p. 201.

76 Vyrubova, *Memories*, p. 44.

Ten – Cupid by the Thrones

1 Sir Valentine Chirol, 'In Many Lands. III: Glimpse of Russia before the War', *Manchester Guardian*, 15 August 1928.

2 Rasputin, *Rasputin My Father*, pp. 75–6.

3 Bowra, *Memories*, pp. 65–6.

4 Natalya Soboleva, 'La Tristesse Impériale'.

5 Vyrubova, *Memories*, p. 64.

6 Hall, *Little Mother*, p. 238.

7 It has been argued that the letters were faked but both Anna Vyrubova and Vladimir Kokovtsov saw them and had no doubt of their authenticity. See Kokovtsov, *Iz moego proshlogo*, vol. 2, pp. 20, 27, 42–4; Moe, *Prelude*, pp. 204–7; Vyrubova, *Memories*, p. 65.

8 For Tyutcheva's independent line see Bogdanovich, *Tri poslednykh samoderzhtsa*, p. 511. See also Bokhanov, *Aleksandra Feodorovna*, pp. 217–19 for a very damning, and perhaps biased, take on Tyutcheva.

9 Vyrubova, *Memories*, p. 65.

10 *LP*, pp. 331–2.

11 Ibid., p. 351; Buxhoeveden, *Life and Tragedy*, p. 152.

12 Ibid., pp. 152–3.

13 GARF in Moscow holds 616 folios of letters written by Tyutcheva to Anastasia during 1911–16.

14 Zimin, *Detskiy mir*, p. 75; *LP*, p. 331.

15 Vyrubova, *Memories*, p. 81; Vorres, *Last Grand Duchess*, p. 141; Bokhanov, *Aleksandra Feodorovna*, p. 220.

16 See *Correspondence*, letter to Ernie, 29 July 1912, p. 312; Zimin, *Detskiy mir*, p. 75.

17 *Correspondence*, p. 317.

18 Ibid., pp. 354–5.

19 For Wallinson, see the front-page story, 'Kings and Emperors Like Their American Dentists', *The Call*, San Francisco, 15 November 1903.

20 This expenditure covered May 1909 to May 1910 but is representative of the kind of money spent on the sisters' wardrobes. Quotation courtesy of Bob Atchison, @: http://www.alexanderpalace. org/palace/mexpenses.html

21 King, 'Livadia', p. 23.

22 Ibid., p. 21.

23 Buxhoeveden, *Before the Storm*, p. 296; Buxhoeveden, *Life and Tragedy*, p. 180.

24 For Alexandra's and the children's charitable work in Livadia see King, 'Livadia', p. 25; King, *Court of the Last Tsar*, p. 450; Zimin, *Detskiy mir*, p. 322; Vyrubova, *Memories*, pp. 34–7, 46; Spiridovich, *Les Dernières années*, pp. 145–6; Buxhoeveden, *Before the Storm*, pp. 293–6.

25 Sablin, *Desyat let*, p. 257.

26 Ibid.

27 Vyrubova, *Memories*, p. 46.

28 Ibid., p. 80.

29 *Hackney Express*, 19 September 1903; *The Times*, 18 September 1911.

30 Bokhanov *et al.*, *Romanovs*, p. 124.

31 *Washington Post*, 25 June 1911.

32 'Won't Wed Czar's Daughter', *Washington Post*, 30 November 1913.

33 Radzinsky, *Last Tsar*, p. 106.

34 Marie, Grand Duchess of Russia, *Princess in Exile* (London: Cassell, 1932), p. 71.

35 See Harris, 'Succession Prospects', pp. 75–6.

36 Letter to Nicholas, 16 October 1911 (translation courtesy of Will Lee); V. I. Nevsky ed., *Nikolai II i velikie knyazya*, Leningrad: Gosudarstvennoe izdatelstvo, 1925, p. 46.

37 Lisa Davidson, profile of Dmitri Pavlovich @: http://www. alexanderpalace.org/palace/Dmitri.html

38 TS letter to Marie Pavlovna, 4 May 1908 (translation courtesy of Will Lee).

39 Spiridovich, *Les Dernières années*, vol. 2, p. 186.

40 Bogdanovich, *Tri poslednykh samoderzhtsa*, p. 510.

41 'Cupid by the Thrones', *Washington Post*, 21 July 1912.

42 Meriel Buchanan journal, August 1912, f. 33.
43 For the Dmitri/Yusupov relationship, see Moe, *Prelude*, pp. 238–9 (information on Dmitri Pavlovich's gambling from Will Lee).
44 DON, p. 9; Meriel Buchanan journal, f. 42.
45 See Rounding, *Alix and Nicky*, p. 190; Wortman, *Scenarios*, pp. 380–2.
46 *SL*, pp. 270–1.
47 Nekliudoff, *Diplomatic Reminiscences* (London: John Murray, 1920), p. 73.
48 See Wortman, *Scenarios*, pp. 381–2; Bokhanov, *Aleksandra Feodorovna*, pp. 217–18.

Eleven – The Little One Will Not Die

1 *Correspondence*, 15 September 1912, p. 360.
2 Botkin, *Real Romanovs*, pp. 73–4.
3 De Stoeckl, *My Dear Marquis*, p. 125.
4 TS Letter, 7 February 1910, from Tsarskoe Selo to his sister Marie Pavlovna (translation courtesy of Will Lee). It is interesting to note that in their book about their battle with their own son's severe haemophilia, authors Robert K. Massie and Suzanne Massie also asserted that 'relatively speaking, Alexis was a mild haemophiliac . . . The difference was that once the Tsarevich began to bleed, nothing could stop the hemorrhage' – in other words his form of the condition would not be life-threatening today; it was the inability of medical science at the time to treat it that was the problem; Robert Massie and Suzanne Massie, *Journey* (New York: Knopf, 1975), p. 114.
5 Radziwill, *Taint*, p. 397.
6 Untitled TS memoirs, List 1 (82) Sydney Gibbes Papers, Bodleian Library, fo 4.
7 Ibid.
8 Gerald Hamilton, *The Way It Was With Me* (London: Leslie Frewin, 1969), p. 29.
9 *LP*, p. 351.
10 Ibid.
11 Official statement of 3 November 1912, reported in *The Times*, 4 November. Some sources state, as per Spiridovich in *Les Dernières années*, vol. 2, pp. 284–5, that the bleeding was caused by Alexey hitting himself when jumping from the side of the large majolica

bathtub. The boating accident is given as the cause by Nicholas himself in a letter to his mother, *SL*, p. 275 and also by Mossolov, *Court*, pp. 150–1, Vyrubova, *Memories*, p. 90, Vorres, *Last Grand Duchess*, p. 143 and Gilliard, *Thirteen Years*, p. 32.

12 See Vyrubova, *Memories*, p. 92.
13 *SL*, p. 276.
14 Spiridovich, *Les Dernières années*, vol. 2, p. 93; Vyrubova, *Memories*, p. 93.
15 Gilliard, *Thirteen Years*, p. 29.
16 Ibid., p. 27.
17 Mossolov, *Court*, p. 151.
18 Melnik-Botkina, *Vospominaniya*, p. 124.
19 *LP*, p. 357.
20 Vyrubova, *Memories*, p. 94; Rasputin, *Rasputin*, p. 177; Rasputin, *Rasputin My Father*, p. 72. Mossolov, *Court*, p. 151, has it differently, saying that Rasputin's message told the tsaritsa that the tsarevich must not be 'allowed to be martyred by the doctors'. Many sources seem to have conflated the contents of the two telegrams.
21 Rasputin, *Rasputin*, p. 177.
22 Mossolov, *Court*, p. 152.
23 Alexandra Feodorovna, letter to Boyd Carpenter, 24 January 1913, ff. 241–2.
24 Melnik-Botkina, *Vospominaniya*, p. 125.
25 *SL*, p. 275.
26 *Daily News*, Maryland, 23 October 1912.
27 Ibid. See also 'Tragedy of the Czarevitch', 12 December 1912, which repeats the rumour about Dmitri Pavlovich marrying Olga and becoming heir-designate.
28 *The Times*, 4 November 1912.
29 Ibid.
30 *New York Times*, 10 November 1912.
31 Mossolov, *Court*, p. 152; see also de Jonge, *Life and Times of Rasputin*, pp. 213–14.
32 *Correspondence*, p. 361.
33 Letter to General Alexander Pfuhlstein, 20 December 1912, in von Spreti, *Alix an Gretchen*, pp. 187–8.
34 Spiridovich, *Les Dernières années*, vol. 2, pp. 293–4.
35 Letter to General Alexander Pfuhlstein, 20 December 1912, in von Spreti, *Alix an Gretchen*, p. 188.
36 Alexandra Feodorovna, letters to Boyd Carpenter, BL Add 46721, vol. 5, 24 January/7 February, ff. 240–1.

37 Vorres, *Last Grand Duchess*, p. 143.
38 Alexandra Feodorovna, letters to Boyd Carpenter, BL Add 46721, vol. 5, 24 January/7 February, f. 243.
39 *LP*, p. 364.
40 Baroness Souiny, *Russia of Yesterday and Tomorrow* (New York: Century, 1917), p. 119.
41 For useful overviews of the Tercentary see King, *Court of the Last Tsar*, ch. 23; Wortman, *Scenarios of Power*, pp. 383–96.
42 *The Times*, 7 March 1913.
43 'Imperial Russia', *Illustrated London News*, Supplement, July 1913, pp. xviii, xxi; Radzinsky, *Last Tsar*, pp. xxi, 109.
44 'The Romanoff Celebrations', *The Times*, 6 March 1913.
45 Wortman, *Scenarios of Power*, p. 383.
46 Quoted in ibid., p. 386; see also *The Times*, 7 March 1913.
47 Vassili, *Taint*, p. 404.
48 Gavriil Konstantinovich, *Marble Palace*, p. 165; Buchanan, *Dissolution of an Empire*, p. 35.
49 Wortman, *Scenarios of Power*, p. 384.
50 Buchanan, *Dissolution of an Empire*, pp. 34–5.
51 See Wortman, *Scenarios of Power*, p. 388.
52 For the dresses, see @: http://www.nicholasandalexandra.com/dresso&t.html
53 Lidiya Leonidovna Vasilchikova, *Ischeznuvshaya Rossiya: Vospominaniya . . . 1886–1919* (St Petersburg: Peterburgskie sezony, 1995), p. 267.
54 Vyrubova, *Memories*, p. 99.
55 Buchanan, *Dissolution of an Empire*, p. 36.
56 Ibid., pp. 36–7; see also Hall, *Little Mother*, pp. 244–5.
57 *DON*, p. 23.

Twelve – Lord Send Happiness to Him, My Beloved One

1 Buxhoeveden, *Life and Tragedy*, p. 175.
2 See Buchanan, *Dissolution of an Empire*, pp. 36–7; Gavriil Konstantinovich, *Marble Palace*, p. 165.
3 Buchanan, *Dissolution of an Empire*, p. 37.
4 *DON*, p. 24.
5 Buchanan, *Queen Victoria's Relations*, p. 211.
6 See Harris, 'Succession Prospects', pp. 74–5; Crawford, *Michael and Natasha*, p. 134.

7   Meriel Buchanan diary, January 1913, BuB 6, MB Archive, Nottingham University, f. 41.
8   Ibid., 19 February 1913, f. 45.
9   *DON*, p. 19.
10 Sablin, *Desyat let*, p. 286. Nicholas was clearly aware of Tatiana's fondness for Nikolay Rodionov, but chose not to harm his career by transferring him from the *Shtandart*. See Vyrubova, *Keisarinnan Hovineiti*, p. 226, and web site accessible @: http://forum.alexanderpalace.org/index.php?topic=7272.0
11 *Correspondence*, p. 362, 18 March 1913: 'Tatiana is still in bed, but she will move to a sofa tomorrow. She is always cheerful and looks well with her short hair'; and 27 December 1913, p. 367, 'Tatiana's hair has grown nice and thick, which means she no longer needs to wear a wig'.
12 Rasputin, *Real Rasputin*, pp. 100–1.
13 See *DON*, pp. 8, 9, 11, 12, 16, 18 and 21.
14 Ofrosimova, 'Tsarskaya semya', p. 138.
15 See Spiridovich, *Les Dernières années*, pp. 234–5; 'Imperial Russia: Her Power and Progress', Supplement to the *Illustrated London News*, 19 July 1913.
16 Sablin, *Desyat let*, pp. 297–8.
17 For the ceremonies at Kostroma, see Wortman, *Scenarios of Power*, pp. 391–3.
18 Naryshkin-Kurakin, *Under Three Tsars*, p. 206.
19 *DON*, p. 61.
20 Sablin, *Desyat let*, pp. 296–7.
21 *DON*, p. 63.
22 Prince Wilhelm, *Episoder* (Stockholm: P. A. Norstedt & Söners Förlag, 1951), pp. 144–5 (translation courtesy of Trond Norén Isaksen).
23 Heresch, *Blood on the Snow*, p. 41.
24 Sergeant Alexander Bulgakov, quoted in ibid., p. 42.
25 *DON*, p. 64.
26 Ibid., p. 70.
27 See Rowley, 'Monarchy and the Mundane', pp. 138–9.
28 Elchaninov, *Tsar*, pp. 58–9. For a discussion of the Romanov public image during the Tercentary, see Slater, *Many Deaths*, ch. 7, 'Family Portraits'. A two-shilling English paperback edition of the book was also published.
29 Buchanan, *Queen Victoria's Relations*, p. 212; Elchaninov, *Tsar*, p. 60.

30 For this holiday see Nicholas's diary for 10 June to 11 July, in *Nikolay*, pp. 48–58.

31 See e.g. *DON*, pp. 81, 82, 87.

32 Ibid., pp. 87–8.

33 Ibid., p. 91.

34 *Nikolay*, 17 July 1913, p. 59.

35 Gavriil Konstantinovich, *Marble Palace*, p. 177.

36 Sablin, *Desyat let*, pp. 324–5.

37 Girardin, *Précepteur*, p. 60.

38 *Correspondence*, p. 317; Gilliard, *Thirteen Years*, p. 43.

39 Kalinin and Zemlyachenko, 'Taina Velikoi Knyazhny', pp. 245–6. This excellent chapter presents an enlightening overview of the Olga–Voronov story.

40 Cherkashin, 'Knyazhna i Michman'.

41 Barkovets, 'Grand Duchess Olga Nikolaevna', in Swezey, *Nicholas and Alexandra*, p. 78.

42 *DON*, p. 126.

43 Ibid., p. 141.

44 Barkovets, 'Grand Duchess', in Swezey, *Nicholas and Alexandra*, p. 76.

45 *DON*, p. 148.

46 Kalinin and Zemlyachenko, 'Taina Velikoi Knyazhny', p. 257; *DON*, pp. 143, 148, 154.

47 Ibid., p. 156.

48 *Nikolay*, p. 100.

49 Barkovets, 'Grand Duchess', in Swezey, *Nicholas and Alexandra*, p. 79.

50 Ibid.

51 *DON*, p. 172.

52 Swezey, *Nicholas and Alexandra*, p. 79.

53 When war broke out in 1914, Pavel Voronov fought in the 2nd Guards battalion and served in the Tsar's Escort. But he fell ill with a heart complaint and was sent on leave during February–March 1917 when the Revolution broke. In April 1917 he was transferred to the Crimean Fleet; then into the reserve in August, after which he went into hiding from Bolshevik commissars. During the winter of 1920, Pavel and Olga escaped Russia in the British steamer *Hanover* and settled in the USA, where Pavel died in 1964. He never wrote any memoirs of his time with the imperial family, perhaps out of an enduring respect for the feelings he knew Olga Nikolaevna had held for him. In her own memoirs his wife Olga makes no mention of their romance either.

Thirteen – God Save the Tsar!

1 W. B., *Russian Court Memoirs*, p. 64.
2 Almedingen, *Empress Alexandra*, p. 131.
3 W. B., *Russian Court Memoirs*, p. 64; Anon. [Casper], *Intimacies of Court and Society*, p. 138.
4 Some of the most vivid accounts of that last social season are given in the various memoirs of ambassador's daughter Meriel Buchanan; see e.g. *Diplomacy and Foreign Courts*, *Dissolution of an Empire* and *Ambassador's Daughter*. See also: Kochan, *Last Days of Imperial Russia*, ch. 2, 'Haute Société in St Petersburg' and King, *Court of the Last Tsar*, ch. 27, 'The Last Season'.
5 Buchanan, *Diplomacy and Foreign Courts*, pp. 147–8, 155; Buchanan, *Ambassador's Daughter*, p. 116.
6 Iswolsky, *No Time to Grieve*, p. 83.
7 Ibid.
8 Ibid.
9 Ibid., p. 85.
10 Buxhoeveden, *Life and Tragedy*, p. 181.
11 Iswolsky, *No Time to Grieve*, p. 85.
12 Duchess of Saxe-Coburg to Crown Princess Marie of Romania, 17–19 February 1914, TS (courtesy of John Wimbles).
13 Ibid.
14 Buchanan, *Diplomacy and Foreign Courts*, p. 160.
15 Iswolsky, *No Time to Grieve*, p. 85.
16 Duchess of Saxe-Coburg to Crown Princess Marie of Romania, 17–19 February 1914, TS (courtesy of John Wimbles).
17 Buchanan, *Diplomacy and Foreign Courts*, p. 160.
18 *Lloyds Weekly Newspaper*, 2 November 1913.
19 'Sentimental Crisis', p. 323.
20 Ibid., p. 323.
21 Ibid., p. 324. Even Sydney Gibbes remarked on the girls' lack of style: 'every so often their "toilets" looked dreadfully out of place, simple as they usually were'; and the men in the *Shtandart* noticed too that 'the way they dressed, truth to tell, was not always fashionable and was even old-fashioned'. Gibbes, TS Memoirs, List 1 (82), f. 7; Sablin, *Desyat let*, pp. 317–18.
22 Ibid.
23 *Lloyds Weekly Newspaper*, 2 November 1913.
24 Biddle, 'The Czar and His Family', p. 6.
25 *DON*, p. 162.

26 For the political ramifications of the match see Gelardi, 'Carol & Olga'.

27 Kalinin and Zemlyachenko, *Romanovy i Krym*, p. 260; Sazonov, *Fateful Years*, p. 109.

28 'May Wed Czar's Daughter', *Washington Post*, 1 February 1914; Biddle, 'The Czar and His Family', p. 6.

29 Letter to Crown Princess Marie of Romania, 27 January 1914, TS (courtesy of John Wimbles).

30 Ibid.

31 Duchess of Saxe-Coburg to Crown Princess Marie of Romania, 7 February 1914, TS (courtesy of John Wimbles).

32 Duchess of Saxe-Coburg to Crown Princess Marie of Romania, 17–19 February 1914 (courtesy of John Wimbles).

33 Duchess of Saxe-Coburg to Crown Princess Marie of Romania, 7 February 1914 (courtesy of John Wimbles).

34 Ibid.

35 Ibid.

36 Ibid.

37 Ibid.

38 Titov, 'OTMA', p. 29.

39 Ibid., p. 334.

40 'Romanians in 1910s Russia', accessible @: http://www.rri.ro/arh-art.shtml?lang=1&sec=9&art=28280

41 James Lawrence Houghteling, *A Diary of the Russian Revolution*, New York: Dodd, Mead & Company, 1918, p. 10; Virubova, *Keisarinnan Hovineiti*, p. 230.

42 *The Times*, 31 March 1914.

43 Sablin, *Desyat let*, pp. 316, 318.

44 Ibid., p. 318.

45 Azabal, *Countess from Iowa*, p. 144; Azabal, *Romance and Revolutions*, pp. 140–1.

46 Azabal, *Romance and Revolutions*, p. 141.

47 De Stoeckl, *Not All Vanity*, pp. 137–8.

48 Ibid., p. 138.

49 Sazonov, *Fateful Years*, p. 110.

50 Elsberry, *Marie of Romania*, p. 101; Spiridovich, *Les Dernières années*, vol. 2, p. 455; Gilliard, *Thirteen Years*, p. 94.

51 Bibesco, *Royal Portraits*, p. 92.

52 Ibid., p. 93.

53 Crown Princess Marie of Romania to the Duchess of Saxe-Coburg, 18 June 1914.
54 Bibesco, *Royal Portraits*, p. 94.
55 Gilliard, *Thirteen Years*, p. 95.
56 Crown Princess Marie of Romania to the Duchess of Saxe-Coburg, 1 June 1914.
57 Ibid.
58 Bibesco, *Royal Portraits*, p. 94.
59 Ibid., p. 95.
60 Marie of Romania, *Story of My Life*, p. 329.
61 Bibesco, *Royal Portraits*, p. 96.
62 Crown Princess Marie of Romania to Duchess of Saxe-Coburg, 18 June 1914; Elsberry, *Marie of Romania*, pp. 100–1.
63 Marie of Romania, *Story of My Life*, p. 575.
64 Buxhoeveden, *Life and Tragedy*, p. 182; Bibesco, *Royal Portraits*, p. 99; Elsberry, *Marie of Romania*, p. 102.
65 Marie of Romania, *Story of My Life*, p. 330.
66 Crown Princess Marie of Romania to Duchess of Saxe-Coburg 18 June 1914.
67 Bibesco, *Royal Portraits*, p. 99.
68 Buchanan, *Dissolution of an Empire*, p. 73.
69 Buchanan, *Ambassador's Daughter*, p. 118.
70 Sablin, *Desyat let*, p. 343.
71 *Harold Tennyson RN*, p. 198.
72 Buchanan, *Queen Victoria's Relations*, p. 216.
73 Ibid., p. 217.
74 Buchanan, *Diplomacy and Foreign Courts*, p. 164.
75 Vyrubova, *Memories*, p. 103; *Correspondence*, p. 368.
76 Buchanan, *My Mission to Russia*, vol. 1, p. 204.
77 Dehn, *Real Tsaritsa*, p. 106.
78 Gilliard, *Thirteen Years*, p. 106.
79 *ASM*, p. 13.
80 *The Times*, 3 August 1914 (NS).
81 Ibid.
82 Merry, *Two Months in Russia*, p. 83.
83 W. B., *Russian Court Memoirs*, p. 73.
84 *ASM*, p. 13.
85 Almedingen, *Empress Alexandra*, p. 134.
86 Paléologue, *Ambassador's Memoirs*, p. 41.
87 Marie Pavlovna, *Things I Remember*, p. 162.

88 Azabal, *Romance and Revolutions*, p. 153.
89 Cantacuzène, *Revolutionary Days*, p. 162.
90 Azabal, *Romance and Revolutions*, p. 153; Marie Pavlovna, *Things I Remember*, p. 163.
91 Ibid.
92 *ASM*, p. 13.
93 *Nikolay*, p. 157.
94 Arbenina, *Through Terror to Freedom*, pp. 20–1.
95 *LP*, p. 398.
96 Wortman, *Scenarios of Power*, p. 401.
97 *The Times*, 4 August 1914 (NS).
98 A. Varlamov, *Grigoriy Rasputin-Novyi* (Moscow: Molodaya Gvardiya, 2007), p. 424.
99 Buchanan, *My Mission to Russia*, vol. 1, p. 214.
100 Florence Farmborough, *Nurse at the Russian Front* (London: Constable, 1974), p. 21; Buchanan, *Queen Victoria's Relations*, p. 217; Buchanan, *Dissolution of an Empire*, p. 102.
101 Buchanan, *My Mission to Russia*, vol. 1, pp. 214–15.
102 Vyrubova, *Memories*, p. 105.
103 *ASM*, p. 14.

Fourteen – Sisters of Mercy

1 Dehn, *Real Tsaritsa*, p. 69.
2 See e.g. issue no. 25 for 5 January 1915, p. 21. Several other female members of the Russian imperial family became wartime nurses – notably Grand Duchess Olga Alexandrovna and Grand Duchess Marie Pavlovna – and were featured on the magazine's pages.
3 Almedingen, *Tomorrow Will Come*, p. 84.
4 *WC*, p. 15.
5 Henniger, 'To Lessen Their Suffering', p. 5.
6 Gromov, *Moi vospominaniya za 50 let*, p. 30.
7 For the work of the British Colony Hospital, see Buchanan, *Dissolution of an Empire*, ch. XI.
8 Like many Russian women of her generation refused permission to study medicine in Russia, Gedroits had travelled to Switzerland to study and qualified in Lausanne in 1898, returning to Russia in 1900 to work as a doctor. An accomplished abdominal surgeon, she had served on the front line during the Russo-Japanese War.

See J. D. Bennett, 'Princess Vera Gedroits: Military Surgeon, Poet and Author', *British Medical Journal*, 19 December 1992, pp. 1532–4.

9 See *SA*, pp. 234, 250–2; *ASM*, pp. 5–7.

10 *NZ* 181, p. 178. Note that many of the excerpts from Chebotareva's diary cited in *SA* have been heavily redacted by the editor Fomin, who has removed any negative comments about the girls and about Alexey's bad behaviour. In particular Chebotareva's criticism of the empress's relationship with Anna Vyrubova and Rasputin is totally excised. See e.g. ch. 15, n. 1, below. All entries in this regard are therefore taken from the uncut *NZ* version.

11 Details of Olga and Tatiana's daily routine at the annexe hospital can be found in their letters and diary entries for 1914–16, in *ASM*. See also articles by Stepanov and Belyaev and Valentina Chebotareva's diary in *SA* as well as the fuller version of the diary in *NZ* and Popov, *Vospominaniya*, pp. 131–2.

12 *SA*, p. 337.

13 Tschebotarioff, *Russia My Native Land*, p. 60.

14 See note 12 above.

15 Vurubova, *Memories*, p. 109.

16 See *ASM*, pp. 18, 19; *SA*, p. 234.

17 *WC*, p. 53.

18 Paul P. Gronsky and Nicholas J. Astrov, *The War and the Russian Government* (New York: Howard Fertig, 1973), pp. 30–1. For photographs of Olga and Tatiana taking donations at their Petrograd committees, see *Stolitsa i usadba* no. 23, 1 December 1914, pp. 20–1.

19 Tyan'-Shansky, 'Tsarstvenniya deti', p. 55.

20 Pavlov in *SA*, p. 413.

21 W. B., *Russian Court Memoirs*, p. 159; Vyrubova, *Romanov Family Album*, p. 117; Melnik-Botkina, *Vospominaniya*, pp. 17–18; Ofrosimova, 'Tsarskaya semya', pp. 144–5.

22 *WC*, p. 16.

23 *SA*, pp. 235, 249.

24 Ofrosimova, 'Tsarskaya semya', p. 144.

25 Gilliard, *Thirteen Years*, p. 129.

26 Rasputin, *Real Rasputin*, p. 103.

27 Buxhoeveden, *Life and Tragedy*, p. 155; W. B., *Russian Court Memoirs*, p. 159.

28 Ofrosimova, 'Tsarskaya semya', p. 146.

29 Ibid.

30 Gilliard, *Thirteen Years*, p. 75.
31 Kleinmikhel, *Shipwrecked World*, pp. 216–17, 327; Buchanan, *Dissolution of an Empire*, p. 125. See also Rowley, 'Monarchy and the Mundane'.
32 Kleinmikhel, *Shipwrecked World*, p. 217.
33 Bokhanov, *Aleksandra Feodorovna*, p. 275.
34 Kleinmikhel, *Shipwrecked World*, p. 217.
35 *SA*, p. 251.
36 See *SA*, pp. 812–13.
37 *ASM*, p. 22.
38 Ibid., p. 23.
39 See *ASM*, Anastasia's letter to Nicholas, 26 August 1916, p. 124. For Maria see e.g. *ASM*, pp. 44, 49. Alexandra, who seemed to condone her daughter's crush on Demenkov, called him 'Marie's fat fellow'; see *WC*, p. 335.
40 Vyrubova, *Memories*, p. 4; *LP*, p. 407.
41 *ASM*, p. 34.
42 *SA*, p. 271.
43 See de Malama, 'The Romanovs'.
44 *ASM*, p. 32.
45 Ibid., p. 33; de Malama, 'The Romanovs', p. 185.
46 *LP*, p. 404; *ASM*, p. 136.
47 Ibid., p. 41.
48 Ibid., p. 5; Vyrubova, however, talks of '85 hospitals' at Tsarskoe Selo, *Memories*, p. 108.
49 Gibbes, untitled TS memoir, Gibbes Papers, Bodleian, f. 9.
50 Brewster, *Anastasia's Album*, p. 46.

Fifteen – We Cannot Drop Our Work in the Hospitals

1 *NZ* 181, pp. 180–1. Note that the bulk of this entry referring to Rasputin has been redacted in the version of Chebotareva's diary in *SA*, p. 295.
2 De Jonge, *Life and Times of Rasputin*, p. 248.
3 Letter to Evelyn Moore, 26 December 1914 (8 January 1915), in E. Marjorie Moore (ed.), *Adventure in the Royal Navy 1847–1934: Life and Letters of Admiral Sir Arthur William Moore* (Liverpool: privately printed, 1964), pp. 121–2. The admiral's sister Evelyn Moore was a lady-in-waiting to Queen Victoria, whom Alexandra had known before her marriage.

4   *WC*, p. 112. See footnote p. 251.
5   *LP*, pp. 431–2.
6   *ASM*, pp. 99–100.
7   *WC*, p. 28.
8   *WC*, pp. 237–8.
9   *WC*, pp. 122, 130.
10 Letter to Olga Voronova, 2 June 1915, accessible @: http://www.alexanderpalace.org/palace/tdiaries.html
11 *ASM*, p. 111.
12 *SA*, p. 311.
13 Ibid., p. 315.
14 Popov, *Vospominaniya*, p. 131.
15 *SA*, p. 315.
16 Ibid.; Popov, *Vospominaniya*, 133.
17 Quote accessible @: http://saltkrakan.livejournal.com/658.html. See also Popov, *Vospominaniya*, p. 133.
18 *SA*, p. 311.
19 Ibid., pp. 298, 300.
20 *ASM*, p. 122; *WC*, p. 181.
21 Anon. [Stopford], *Russian Diary*, p. 37.
22 *WC*, p. 261.
23 Anon. [Stopford], *Russian Diary*, p. 37.
24 See Shavelsky, *Vospominaniya poslednego protopresverita russkoi armii i flota*, vol. I, pp. 360–2.
25 Buxhoeveden, *Life and Tragedy*, pp. 210, 212.
26 Newton A. McCully, *An American Naval Diplomat in Revolutionary Russia* (Annapolis, MD: Naval Institute Press, 1993), p. 98.
27 Vyrubova, *Memories*, p. 143.
28 See Galushkin, *Sobstvennyi ego . . . konvoy*, pp. 199–202 for an account of OTMA at Stavka.
29 See e.g. the photographs in Michael of Greece and Maylunas, *Nicholas and Alexandra*, pp. 215–21 and Grabbe and Grabbe, *Private World*, pp. 152–8. *SA*, p. 302; see also *WC*, p. 279.
30 *SA*, p. 302; see also *WC*, p. 279.
31 Vyrubova, *Memories*, p. 109.
32 *WC*, p. 279.
33 *ASM*, p. 145.
34 *NZ* 181, pp. 206–7.
35 *SA*, p. 305.
36 *NZ* 181, p. 206.
37 *Nikolay*, p. 285.

38 Ibid.
39 Vyrubova, *Memories*, p. 170.
40 *NZ*, p. 207.
41 Ibid., p. 208.
42 *ASM*, p. 151.

Sixteen – The Outside Life

1 Stanislav Kon, *The Cost of the War to Russia* (London: Humphrey Milford, 1932), p. 33.
2 Reproduced in *Argus*, Melbourne, 23 February 1916.
3 *Logansport Journal-Tribune*, 2 January 1916; *New York Times*, 25 September 1916.
4 For the work of the Tatiana Committee, see Peter Gatrell, *A Whole Empire Walking: Refugees in Russia during World War I* (Bloomington: Indiana University Press, 1999), pp. 44–7 and Violetta Thurstan, *The People Who Run: Being the Tragedy of the Refugees in Russia* (London: Putnam, 1916), which has much information on the Petrograd maternity hospital.
5 *Atlanta Constitution*, Magazine Section, 14 November 1915.
6 Fraser, *Russia of To-Day*, pp. 24–5.
7 *WC*, p. 366.
8 Fraser, *Russia of To-Day*, p. 26.
9 Richard Washburn Child, *Potential Russia* (London: T. Fisher Unwin, 1916), p. 76.
10 *SA*, p. 337.
11 *WC*, p. 361; see also *WC*, p. 366 re her taking opium.
12 Ibid., p. 381.
13 *SA*, p. 336.
14 *Daily Gleaner*, 4 August 1915.
15 *NZ* 181, pp. 210–11.
16 *ASM*, p. 157.
17 *SA*, p. 338.
18 *NZ* 181, p. 211.
19 *ASM*, p. 156.
20 Farson, 'Aux Pieds', p. 16. Harmer, *Forgotten Hospital*, pp. 73–5; diary of L. C . Pocock 19 January/1 February 1916, in G. M. and L. C. Pocock Papers, IWM. For photographs see *Stolitsa i usadba*, no. 54, 15 March 1916, p. 9; also *Ogonek*, no. 3, 31 January 1916.
21 Farson, 'Au Pieds', p. 17.

22 Buchanan, *Queen Victoria's Relations*, p. 218.

23 *WC*, p. 486.

24 Markylie, 'L'Impératrice en voile blanc', p. 17.

25 *SA*, p. 337.

26 *WC*, p. 404.

27 *WC*, pp. 369–70; note that this quotation has been wrongly identified by Furhmann as alluding to Olga Alexandrovna, Nicholas's sister, but that attribution is clearly erroneous, given the context.

28 *WC*, p. 388.

29 Ibid., p. 356.

30 *WC*, p. 421. Although he is not mentioned again by Alexandra in *WC* after March 1916, Malama apparently remained at Tsarskoe Selo till the Revolution, after which he returned to southern Russia. In August 1919 he was in command of a unit of White Army troops fighting the Bolsheviks in the Ukraine when he was captured, and executed soon after by firing squad. Although some sources claim he was killed in battle, according to Peter de Malama, Mitya's body was recovered and buried with full military honours at Krasnodar. See de Malama, 'The Romanovs'.

31 *SA*, p. 339.

32 *WC*, p. 450.

33 *Nikolay*, p. 239; *ASM*, p. 107 and see note on p. 439.

34 *ASM*, pp. 162–3.

35 Ibid., p. 163.

36 *WC*, p. 412.

37 Ibid., pp. 432, 413.

38 *ASM*, p. 178.

39 Buxhoeveden, *Life and Tragedy*, p. 238.

40 *ASM*, p. 179.

41 Boris Ravtopulo had developed a strong admiration for Tatiana since first seeing her photographs. As a young officer, taking part in the Tercentary celebrations in St Petersburg in 1913, he was at the ball attended by the two sisters before Tatiana fell ill with typhoid and he had breached etiquette and asked her to dance. He took the liberty of asking her a second time, at the risk of being rejected. Afterwards, he took her back to her seat, kissed her hand, and promised, so he later claimed, that he would 'never again dance a single dance with anyone else from here to the grave'. He kept his promise for sixteen years, before finally marrying in 1929. See web site accessible @: http://saltkrakan.livejournal.com/2520.html

42 See *ASM*, pp. 179, 181, 182, 186.

43 *SA*, p. 412.

44 *ASM*, p. 180.

45 *WC*, p. 472.

46 See *ASM*, pp. 185–6.

47 *NZ* 181, p. 231.

48 *ASM*, p. 186.

49 *WC*, p. 482.

50 Ibid., p. 590.

51 Ibid., p. 500.

52 Letter to Rita Khitrovo from Stavka, July 1916; Hoover Tarsaidze Papers, Box 16, Folder 5. This original transcript has some gaps. The quotation can be found in full in Galushkin, *Sobstvennyi ego . . . konvoy*, pp. 241–2.

53 Dassel, *Grossfürstin Anastasia Lebt*, p. 16. Felix Dassel later became embroiled in the fraudulent claim of Anna Anderson aka Franziska Szankowska that she was Grand Duchess Anastasia, miraculously escaped from death at the Ipatiev House. Dassel published his memories of the hospital at Feodorovsky Gorodok five months before he met Anna Anderson in 1927; see King and Wilson, *Resurrection*, pp. 166–7, 303.

54 Ibid., pp. 19, 22.

55 *NZ* 181, p. 223.

56 Dassel, *Grossfürstin Anastasia Lebt*, pp. 20, 25.

57 Geraschinevsky, 'Ill-Fated Children of the Czar', p. 159.

58 Ibid., p. 171.

59 Ibid., p. 160.

60 Ibid.

61 *WC*, p. 556.

62 See ibid. Prior to the war Alexander Funk had worked with the St Petersburg photographer Karl Bulla, but at the time of this photographic session appears to have moved mainly into war photography.

63 Foster Fraser, 'Side Shows in Armageddon', pp. 268–9; see also Paléologue, *Ambassador's Memoirs*, p. 507.

64 Foster Fraser, 'Side Shows in Armageddon', pp. 268–9.

65 *ASM*, p. 217.

66 Ibid., p. 220. Some weeks later she received a telegram from him, from Mozdoka in northern Ossetiya in the Caucasus. She saw him briefly on 22 December 1916 (see *ASM*, p. 237), but did not mention him again, except for noting his birthday on 9 February 1917. A fellow officer at the annexe heard he was later made

commander of a hospital train (see *SA*, p. 220). Nothing more is known of Dmitri Shakh-Bagov, other than a possible sighting in the autumn of 1920 when the Red Army was on the brink of victory in Zakavkaz, when one of the Ezid resistance groups based in Echmiadzin was commanded by an officer named Shakh-Bagov. This may well have been Dmitri, who, like David Iedigarov, may have been a Georgian Muslim. For photographs and a résumé of what is known of Olga's Mitya, see web site @: http://saltkrakan.livejournal.com/658.html

67 *WC*, p. 636.
68 Galushkin, *Sobstvennyi ego . . . konvoy*, p. 197.
69 Bokhanov *et al.*, *Romanovs*, p. 268.
70 Ibid., p. 228.
71 Ibid., p. 233.
72 *WC*, p. 660.
73 Ibid., p. 681.
74 *ASM*, p. 233; see also *WC*, p. 670. Staritsa Mariya died in January 1917, and was later canonized.
75 *WC*, p. 670.
76 Vyrubova, *Memories*, p. 148; Buxhoeveden, *Life and Tragedy*, p. 223.
77 *WC*, p. 670.
78 Buxhoeveden, *Life and Tragedy*, p. 223.
79 Paléologue, *Ambassador's Memoirs*, pp. 541, 677.
80 Ibid., p. 676.
81 Almedingen, *Empress Alexandra*, p. 92.
82 *SA*, p. 349.
83 Paléologue, *Ambassador's Memoirs*, p. 731.
84 Ibid., p. 680.

Seventeen – Terrible Things Are Going on in St Petersburg

1 *ASM*, p. 236. Although Anastasia later destroyed her diaries this appears to be a rare survival, perhaps in a notebook.
2 Ibid.
3 *WC*, p. 684.
4 Ibid., p. 651.
5 Fuhrmann, *Rasputin*, ch. 11, p. 112.
6 Ibid., p. 140.
7 Ibid., p. 228. 'Dark Forces' became the code name for Rasputin used by British agents.

8   Eugene de Savitsch, *In Search of Complications: An Autobiography* (New York: Simon & Schuster, 1940), pp. 15 and 16.

9   *ASM*, p. 236.

10 A. A. Mordvinov, quoted in *LP*, p. 507.

11 *WC*, p. 68; Paléologue, *Ambassador's Memoirs*, p. 740.

12 Dorothy Seymour, MS diary, 26 December (NS) 1916; Paléologue, *Ambassador's Memoirs*, p. 74. Dorothy Nina Seymour was the well-connected daughter of a lord and granddaughter of an admiral of the fleet. Prior to volunteering as a VAD, she had been a woman of the bedchamber to Queen Victoria's daughter, Helena – Princess Christian of Schleswig-Holstein – herself a great patron of women's wartime nursing. Dorothy left Petrograd on 24 March (NS) 1917 and in December that year married General Sir Henry Cholmondely Jackson. She died in 1953. Her vivid and engaging diary from November 1914 to May 1919 is in the IWM, as are 49 letters written during the same period – though few of these are from Petrograd because of the difficulties in sending mail from Russia during the war and revolution.

13 It is still unclear who fired the fourth bullet into Rasputin's skull. Recent studies have claimed that Oswald Rayner and Stephen Alley – agents of the British Special Intelligence Mission in Petrograd – played a role in the murder. It has also now been suggested that wounds on Rasputin's corpse indicate that he was tortured before being killed, in an attempt to ascertain whether he had indeed been a German spy – an act in which the British agents might well have participated. The Special Intelligence Mission was certainly privy to the plot and its members had their own good reasons to back any conspiracy to kill Rasputin or at least remove him from his position of influence over the empress.

14 There is an enormous amount of literature on Rasputin and the circumstances of his murder, much of it contradictory, some of it contentious. The most recent books include: Fuhrman, *Rasputin* (2012); Moe, *Prelude* (2011), see ch. IX, 'Death in a Cellar'; and Margarita Nelipa's extensive study *The Murder of Grigorii Rasputin* (2010), which contains detailed police and forensic evidence. For British involvement see Richard Cullen, *Rasputin: The Role of the British Secret Service in his Torture and Murder* (London: Dialogue, 2010) and Andrew Cook, *To Kill Rasputin* (Stroud, Glos: History Press, 2006).

15 Dorothy Seymour, MS diary, 30 December 1916.

16 *ASM*, p. 237.

17 Vyrubova, *Memories*, pp. 182–3; Dehn, *Real Tsaritsa*, pp. 122–3. Rasputin did not rest in peace for long. Shortly after the revolution his corpse was dug up and taken into Petrograd and burnt. Recent evidence suggests that it was cremated in the boiler room of the Polytechnic Institute in the northern suburbs of Petrograd and the ashes scattered by the roadside. See Nelipa, *Murder of Rasputin*, pp. 459–60.

18 Oleg Platonov, *Rasputin i 'deti dyavola'* (Moscow: Algoritm, 2005), p. 351.

19 Paléologue, *Ambassador's Memoirs*, p. 735; NZ 181, p. 208. Dorothy Seymour, MS diary, 6 January NS/24 December OS, IWM.

20 Gilliard, *Thirteen Years*, p. 183.

21 Dorr, *Inside the Russian Revolution*, p. 121.

22 Dehn, *Real Tsaritsa*, pp. 137–8.

23 NZ 182, p. 207.

24 Spiridovich, *Les Dernières années*, vol. 2, p. 453.

25 Ibid., p. 452; Buchanan, *Queen Victoria's Relations*, p. 220.

26 This 158-page notebook kept between 1905 and 1916 survives in the Russian State Archives, GARF 651 1 110.

27 Paléologue, *Ambassador's Memoirs*, p. 739.

28 Botkin, *Real Romanovs*, p. 127.

29 *ASM*, p. 239

30 Gilliard, *Thirteen Years*, p. 183.

31 In their later memoirs both Iza Buxhoeveden and Anna Vyrubova said that this visit took place in the autumn of 1916, but it was recorded in Alexandra and Nicholas's diaries and comments relating to Maria's mishap clearly date it to 8 January 1917. See *Dnevniki* I, p. 46.

32 NZ 182, p. 204.

33 Buxhoeveden, *Life and Tragedy*, p. 235; NZ 181, p. 204.

34 NZ 182, p. 205.

35 Naryshkina diary, quoted in *Dnevniki* I, p. 50; Vyrubova, *Memories*, p. 86. Note that the manuscript of the Naryshkina diary, an extremely valuable eyewitness account of the imperial family's last months at Tsarskoe Selo, is held in the state archives in Moscow, at GARF f. 6501.op.1.D.595.

36 Naryshkina diary, quoted in *Dnevniki* I p. 96.

37 Queen Marie of Romania diary, 12/26 January 1917. Romanian State Archives. My thanks to Tessa Dunlop for alerting me to this.

38 Letter to her mother and sister, 1 December 1916, IWM.

39 17 December (4 December OS), letter to mother and sister.

40 Dorothy Seymour, MS diary, 4 February (NS) 1917, IWM.
41 Ibid.
42 See *Dnevniki* I, pp. 134, 139; Savchenko, *Russkaya devushka*, p. 43.
43 Alexander, *Once a Grand Duke*, pp. 282–3.
44 *Dnevniki* I, p. 166.
45 Ibid., p. 171; *ASM*, p. 241.
46 See web site @: http://www.alexanderpalace.org/palace/mdiaries.html
47 *WC*, p. 691.
48 Zinaida Gippius, *Sinyaya kniga: Peterburgskiy dnevnik 1914–1918* (Belgrade: Radenkovicha, 1929), p. 39.
49 Almedingen, *Empress Alexandra*, p. 190.
50 *WC*, p. 692; see also Dorr, *Inside the Russian Revolution*, pp. 129–30.
51 Buxhoeveden, *Life and Tragedy*, p. 251.
52 *WC*, pp. 694, 695.
53 Naryshkina, *Under Three Tsars*, pp. 217, 212.
54 *NZ* 182, p. 211; see also pp. 210–12, *Dnevniki* I, p. 193.
55 *Dnevniki* I, p. 200; Buxhoeveden, *Life and Tragedy*, p. 267.
56 Zeepvat, 'Valet's Story', p. 329.
57 *Dnevniki* I, p. 206
58 Buchanan, *Ambassador's Daughter*, p. 146.
59 Dehn, *Real Tsaritsa*, p. 155.
60 Ibid., p. 152; see also Buxhoeveden, *Life and Tragedy*, p. 254, re the night of 28 February.
61 *NZ* 182, p. 213.
62 Dehn, *Real Tsaritsa*, p. 156.
63 Buxhoeveden, *Life and Tragedy*, p. 255. See also *Dnevniki* I, p. 223; Galushkin, *Sobstevennyi ego . . . konvoy*, p. 262.
64 Ibid., p. 265. For a valuable account of the Tsar's Escort at the Alexander Palace during the early days of the revolution and the key role of Viktor Zborovsky at that time, see ibid., pp. 262–80.
65 Dehn, *Real Tsaritsa*, p. 184.
66 Ibid., pp. 151–2.
67 Ibid., pp. 157–8.
68 Ibid., p. 158.
69 Naryshkina diary, quoted in *Dnevniki* I, p. 232.
70 Buxhoeveden, *Life and Tragedy*, p. 254; Benkendorf, *Last Days*, pp. 6–7.
71 Dehn, *Real Tsaritsa*, p. 160; *WC*, p. 698.
72 *WC*, p. 700.

73 Naryshkina diary, quoted in *Dnevniki* I, p. 253.

74 *Dnevniki* I, p. 253.

75 Ibid., pp. 254, 266.

76 Paul Grabbe, *Windows on the River Neva* (New York: Pomerica Press, 1977), p. 123.

77 Letter to Nicholas, 3 March, accessible @: http://www.alexanderpalace.org/palace/mdiaries.html

78 Ibid.; Dehn, *Real Tsaritsa*, p. 164; Buxhoeveden, *Life and Tragedy*, p. 251.

79 *Dnevniki* I, p. 258.

80 *Fall*, p. 138.

81 *Dnevniki* I, p. 259; P. Savchenko, *Gosudarynya imperatritsa Aleksandra Feodorovna* (Belgrade: Nobel Press, 1939), p. 91.

82 *WC*, p. 701.

83 *Dnevniki* I, p. 290.

84 Ibid., p. 293.

85 Buxhoeveden, *Life and Tragedy*, p. 262.

86 Galushkin, *Sobstvennyi ego . . . konvoy*, p. 274.

87 Dehn, *Real Tsaritsa*, p. 166.

88 Vyrubova, *Memories*, p. 338.

89 Ibid.

90 Markov, quoted in *Dnevniki* I, p. 309.

91 Markov, *Pokinutaya Tsarskaya Semya*, pp. 93, 95–7; see also Dehn, *Real Tsaritsa*, p. 170; *Dnevniki* I, pp. 309–10.

92 Galushkin, *Sobstvennyi ego . . . konvoy*, p. 276.

93 Ibid.

94 Ibid.

95 Penny Wilson, 'The Memoirs of Princess Helena of Serbia', *Atlantis Magazine* 1. no. 3, 1999, p. 84.

96 *NZ* 182, p. 215.

97 Ktorova, *Minuvshee*, p. 96. Lili's husband Charles, a lieutenant in the Guards Equipage, was on a military mission to England when the revolution broke out.

98 Naryshkina diary, quoted in *Dnevniki* I, p. 333.

99 Dehn, *Real Tsaritsa*, p. 174. Alexandra mentions the destruction of her papers in her diary entries from 8 March, although Lili recalled the process beginning on 7 March. See *Dnevniki* I, pp. 340, 366, 378, 382, etc.

100 Dehn, *Real Tsaritsa*, pp. 173–4, 176. Some 1,700 letters and telegrams between Nicholas and Alexandra during the war years therefore survived and are preserved in GARF, Moscow. See

Fuhrmann's introduction to *WC*, pp. 8–11.

101 Dehn, *Real Tsaristsa*, p. 178.
102 Ibid., pp. 174, 184.
103 *Fall*, p. 42.
104 Benkendorf, *Last Days*, p. 8; *Fall*, p. 114.
105 *Fall*, p. 114.
106 Naryshkina diary, quoted in *Dnevniki* I, p. 352.
107 Botkin, *Real Romanovs*, pp. 141, 142. One of those who appeared to desert the family at this time was their former close friend Nikolay Sablin, who spent much of his life in exile in the USA trying to justify why he did not go with the family to Tobolsk. In conversation with Roman Gul in Paris shortly before his death in 1937, Sablin insisted several times that 'the emperor, through [Admiral] Nilov, had sent word that I had acted correctly in not going with them'. Nevertheless, Sablin appeared to be haunted by the fact, as Gul noticed, and was chastised by many in émigré monarchist circles who told him that 'your place was with the imperial family to the very end'. General Count Ilya Tatishchev, who voluntarily went to Tobolsk in Sablin's stead, was murdered with the imperial family in Ekaterinburg in 1918. See Roman Gul, 'S Tsarskoy semi na "Shtandarte"', TS, Amherst Center for Russian Culture. See also Radzinsky, *Last Tsar*, p. 189.
108 Ibid.
109 Dehn, *Real Tsaritsa*, p. 183.
110 Buxhoeveden, *Life and Tragedy*, p. 270.
111 Dehn, *Real Tsaritsa*, p. 183.
112 Gilliard, *Thirteen Years*, p. 215.
113 Galushkin, *Sobstvennyi ego . . . konvoy*, pp. 279, 280.
114 Ibid., p. 279.
115 Ibid., p. 280.
116 Benkendorf, *Last Days*, p. 17; Gilliard, *Thirteen Years*, p. 165.
117 Dehn, *Real Tsaritsa*, p. 185.

Eighteen – Goodbye. Don't Forget Me

1 *Dnevniki* I, p. 367.
2 Botkina, *Vospominaniya*, p. 63; *Dnevniki* I, p. 370.
3 Dehn, *Real Tsaritsa*, p. 189.
4 Naryshkin-Kurakin, *Under Three Tsars*, p. 220.

5 Long, *Russian Revolution Aspects*, p. 13.

6 Dorr, *Inside the Russian Revolution*, p. 132.

7 *Dnevniki* I, p. 378; see also *The Times*, 22 March 1917 (NS).

8 Dehn, *Real Tsaritsa*, p. 1297; Buxhoeveden, *Life and Tragedy*, pp. 262–3.

9 Buxhoeveden, *Life and Tragedy*, p. 274.

10 A tantalizing story survives which suggests that thoughts of getting her children to safety had occurred to Alexandra even before then, perhaps at the end of 1916. A letter in the archives of the Royal Navy Submarine Museum in Gosport describes how an English businessman, Frank Best, who had a large timber company in the Baltic at Riga and Libau and who exported wood via Archangel during the First World War, was called to a secret meeting at the British Embassy some time late in 1916. Here he was met by the tsaritsa and others who discussed the possibility of his making his sawmill available to house the Romanov children in secret until they could be collected by a ship of the Royal Navy and taken to England. Best willingly agreed and as a symbol of her gratitude the tsaritsa gave him an icon of St Nicholas, the patron saint of children. Sadly no written evidence has been found to support this story other than a letter written retrospectively in 1978 describing the plan in brief. The icon, however, does survive; it was donated by Best's widow to the chapel of HMS *Dolphin* in 1962. See letter of Rev. G. V. Vaughan-James, 13 March 1978, Royal Navy Submarine Museum, A 1917/16/002.

11 Botkin, *Real Romanovs*, p. 140.

12 Buchanan, *Dissolution of an Empire*, p. 195.

13 Buxhoeveden, *Life and Tragedy*, p. 276.

14 Almedingen, *Empress Alexandra*, p. 211.

15 *LP*, p. 567.

16 See Pipes, *Russian Revolution*, p. 332.

17 Quoted in Ariadna Tyrkova-Williams, *From Liberty to Brest-Litovsk* (London: Macmillan, 1919), p. 60.

18 Quoted in *Dnevniki* I, pp. 384–5.

19 Dehn, *Real Tsaritsa*, p. 198. Many years of debate and recrimination followed with regard to the failure to evacuate the family in time, with accusations variously made – against Kerensky and his government, the British ambassador Buchanan, the prime minister Lloyd George and George V himself. Buchanan's daughter Meriel later concluded that Lloyd George had advised against it because of fear of losing British public support for Russia as a wartime ally. But

historian Bernard Pares, a great authority on Russia at the time, thought that the Romanov asylum 'could have made no possible difference to the Russian Army, already then in the process of disintegration' and that Kerensky had done 'everything he could to save the Imperial Family'. Appraising the situation with hindsight, a hundred years on, and taking into account the extremely volatile situation in revolutionary Petrograd in the spring of 1917, it seems clear that the logistical problems of getting the family out of such a huge country, by the only viable means – rail – to Murmansk or any other exit point by sea from Russia were well nigh impossible. In the end the failure to do so was the result of circumstance rather than an absence of will. Later, before the renewed upheavals of the July days, it became possible once more to evacuate the family, and the subject would once more be discussed. For a fuller discussion of the Romanov asylum issue see Rappaport, *Ekaterinburg: Last Days of the Romanovs*, ch. 11.

20 Long, *Russian Revolution Aspects*, pp. 5, 7.
21 Naryshkin-Kurakin, *Under Three Tsars*, p. 222.
22 Almedingen, *Empress Alexandra*, p. 211.
23 Kleinmikhel, *Shipwrecked World*, p. 245.
24 Ibid., p. 246; Dehn, *Real Tsaritsa*, p. 183; Buxhoeveden, *Life and Tragedy*, p. 284.
25 Long, *Russian Revolution Aspects*, p. 14.
26 Naryshkina diary, quoted in *Dnevniki* I, pp. 434, 436, 438, 439.
27 Marie Pavlovna, *Things I Remember*, p. 305.
28 Long, *Russian Revolution Aspects*, p. 13.
29 *Dnevniki* I, p. 383.
30 Buxhoeveden, *Life and Tragedy*, p. 262.
31 See *Dnevniki I*, pp. 398, 399; Naryshkin, *Under Three Tsars*, p. 221.
32 Quoted in *Dnevniki* I, pp. 400–1.
33 Vyrubova, *Memories*, p. 221; Anon. [Stopford], *Russian Diary*, p. 144. Buxhoeveden, *Life and Tragedy*, pp. 266–7.
34 *Dnevniki* I, p. 405.
35 Dehn, *Real Tsaritsa*, p. 211; Benkendorf, *Last Days*, p. 29.
36 Dehn, *Real Tsaritsa*, pp. 213–14; Vyrubova, *Memories*, p. 225.
37 Ibid. Lili was later given permission to travel south and left Russia with Titi via Odessa. She managed to get her letters and papers to England, where she was reunited with her husband. They had two more daughters and lived in England for seven years. Widowed in 1932, she inherited an estate in Poland but in 1939 was forced to flee again. In 1947 she emigrated to Venezuela with Titi, and

eventually joined her daughter Maria. She died in Rome in 1963. After her release from prison Anna Vyrubova was confined to house arrest at her aunt's house on Znamenskaya ulitsa in Petrograd. From there she was deported to Finland, where she died in 1964.

38 *Dnevniki* I, p. 424.
39 The Zborovsky family had a strong tradition of imperial service. Viktor's and Katya's father, Erast Grigorevich, had been a highly decorated long-serving officer under Alexander III and one-time deputy commander of the Escort. Alexander III stood as godfather to Xenia Zborovskaya.
40 Galushkin, *Sobstvennyi ego . . . konvoy*, p. 329: 'Two nurses from the Feodorovsky Hospital of the grand duchesses were given passes to see the empress. One of them was the sister of Sotnik Zborovsky. Every time she returned from the palace she brought greetings from the empress and the grand duchesses.'
41 Ibid., p. 362.
42 Almedingen, *Empress Alexandra*, pp. 209–10; see also Buxhoeveden, *Life and Tragedy*, p. 288.
43 Benkendorf, *Last Days*, pp. 65–6.
44 Ibid., p. 65; *Dnevniki* I, pp. 430, 433.
45 Ibid., pp. 429, 434.
46 Ibid., pp. 429, 452.
47 See Belyaev's description of the Easter services in *Fall*, pp. 140–6.
48 Bokhanov, *Aleksandra Feodorovna*, p. 145.
49 Belyaev, quoted in *Dnevniki* I, p. 447; Buxhoeveden, *Life and Tragedy*, p. 296.
50 *Dnevniki* I, p. 449.
51 Gilliard, *Thirteen Years*, p. 226.
52 *NZ* 182, p. 220.
53 *Dnevniki* I, p. 451.
54 *NZ* 182, p. 217; *Dnevniki* I, p. 473.
55 *NZ* 182, p. 218; *Dnevniki* I, p. 472.
56 *NZ* 182, p. 218.
57 Ibid.
58 Anon. [Stopford], *Russian Diary*, p. 145.
59 *Dnevniki* I, p. 460.
60 Ibid., p. 465.
61 *NZ* 182, p. 222.
62 *SA*, p. 584.
63 *NZ* 182, p. 224.

64 Letter to Katya, 12 April 1917, EEZ.
65 M. K. Diterikhs, 'V svoem krugu', in Bonetskaya, *Tsarskie deti*, p. 366; Melnik-Botkina, *Vospominaniya*, pp. 57–8. See also letter in *Dnevniki* I, p. 492.
66 *Dnevniki* I, p. 478.
67 Ibid., p. 484.
68 *Fall*, p. 148; original Russian in *Dnevniki* I, p. 486.
69 Letter to Katya, 30 April 1917, EEZ.
70 Naryshkin-Kurakin, *Under Three Tsars*, p. 227.
71 Maria to Katya, 8–9 June 1917, EEZ; See also Anastasia to Katya, 29 June 1917, EEZ.
72 *Dnevniki* I, p. 503.
73 Ibid., p. 548.
74 Ibid., p. 518. See also Anastasia to Katya, letter no. 4, 30 May, EEZ.
75 Anastasia to Katya, unnumbered letter, 20 May 1917, EEZ.
76 Quoted in *Dnevniki* I, p. 598.
77 Letter to Katya, no. 8, 4 July 1917, EEZ.
78 Letter to Katya, no. 11, 12 July 1917, EEZ; Benkendorf, *Last Days*, p. 97.
79 Dehn, *Real Tsaritsa*, p. 233.
80 *NZ* 182, p. 233.
81 Letter to Alexander Syroboyarsky, 28 May 1917, Bokhanov, *Aleksandra Feodorovna*, p. 277. This letter is a typical example of the heavily religious overtones of many of Alexandra's letters at this time.
82 Anastasia to Katya, letter, 11 June 1917, EEZ.
83 Gilliard, *Thirteen Years*, p. 232. See also *Dnevniki* I, pp. 576–7 and Tatiana's letter to Grand Duchess Xenia, 20 July, in ibid., p. 599.
84 *Fall*, p. 154.
85 Naryshkina diary, quoted in *Dnevniki* I, p. 578.
86 *Dnevniki* I, p. 587; Kerensky, *Catastrophe*, p. 271.
87 Benkendorf, *Last Days*, p. 49; *Dnevniki* I, pp. 588–9.
88 Ibid., p. 613; see also *Dnevniki* II, p. 11.
89 Bulygin, *Murder of the Romanovs*, pp. 119–20.
90 *Dnevniki* I, p. 591.
91 Ibid., pp. 592, 593; Long, *Russian Revolution Aspects*, p. 240.
92 Melnik-Botkina, *Vospominaniya*, pp. 62–3.
93 Letter of 17 July, quoted in *Dnevniki* I, pp. 596–7.
94 Ibid., p. 606.
95 Gilliard, *Thirteen Years*, p. 95; Naryshkin-Kurakin, *Under Three Tsars*, p. 228.

96 Girardin, *Précepteur*, p. 119.
97 Buxhoeveden, *Life and Tragedy*, p. 306.
98 *Dnevniki* I, p. 611.
99 *NZ* 182, p. 235.
100 'Iz Dnevnika A. S. Demidovoi', in Kovalevskaya, *S Tsarem*, p. 57, entry for 2 August.
101 Ibid.
102 Buxhoeveden, *Life and Tragedy*, pp. 305–6; *NZ* 182, p. 236.
103 Kerensky, *Catastrophe*, p. 275; Bulygin, *Murder of the Romanovs*, p. 129.
104 *Dnevniki* II, p. 8.
105 Dorr, *Inside the Russian Revolution*, p. 137.
106 *NZ* 182, p. 237.
107 'Vospominaniya o Marii Fedorovne Geringere', ff. 38, 39.
108 Galitzine, *Spirit to Survive*, p. 60.
109 Richard Abraham, *Alexander Kerensky* (London: Sidgwick & Jackson, 1987), p. 157; Kerensky, *Catastrophe*, p. 275.
110 'Iz Dnevnika A. S. Demidovoi' in Kovalevskaya *S Tsarem* p. 57, entry for 2 August.
111 Bykov, *Last Days of Tsardom*, p. 40; Naryshkin-Kurakin, *Under Three Tsars*, p. 229.
112 Melnik-Botkina, *Vospominaniya*, p. 63; *Dnevniki* II, p.80.
113 Trewin, *Tutor to the Tsarevich*, p. 75.
114 *Dnevniki* II, p. 8.
115 *NZ* 182, p. 237.

Nineteen – On Freedom Street

1 Dorr, *Inside the Russian Revolution*, p. 139.
2 Long, *Russian Revolution Aspects*, p. 241.
3 Archive documents show that there was concern even in August among the authorities in the Urals that the train was headed all the way to Harbin, the secret plan thought to be to evacuate the family to Japan. See TsAGOR CCCP f. 1235 (VTsIK op.53.D.19.L.91, quoted in Ioffe, *Revolyutsiya I semya Romanovykh*, p. 197.
4 'Iz Dnevnika A. S. Demidovoi', in Kovalevskaya, *S Tsarem*, p. 57, entry for 2 August.
5 Ibid., p. 58.
6 Ibid., p. 59.
7 Ibid.

8 *Dnevniki* II, p. 17.
9 'Iz Dnevnika A. S. Demidovoi', in Kovalevskaya, *S Tsarem*, p. 60, entry for 4 August.
10 Botkin, *Real Romanovs*, p. 155.
11 Dorr, *Inside the Russian Revolution*, p. 140.
12 Sergeant Major Petr Matveev, 'Notes and Reminiscences about Nicholas Romanov', in Sverdlovsk Archives; quoted in Radzinsky, *Last Tsar*, p. 192.
13 *Dnevniki* II, p. 21.
14 Durland, *Red Reign*, p. 373; De Windt, *Russia as I Know It*, p. 121.
15 Durland, *Red Reign*, pp. 373–4; De Windt, *Russia as I Know It*, pp. 121–2.
16 Dorr, *Inside the Russian Revolution*, p. 140. See also Kerensky, quoted in *Dnevniki* I, pp. 589–90.
17 Letter to Zinaida Tolstaya, Nepein, *Pered Rasstrelom*, p. 136.
18 Vasili Dolgorukov, letter to his brother, 14 August; quoted in *LP*, p. 583.
19 'Iz Dnevnika A. S. Demidovoi', in Kovalevskaya, *S Tsarem*, p. 65; Buxhoeveden, *Life and Tragedy*, pp. 310–11; 'Iz Dnevnika A. S. Demidovoi', in Kovalevskaya, *S Tsarem*, pp. 62–3.
20 Melnik-Botkina, *Vospominaniya*, p. 69.
21 *LP*, p. 583.
22 *Dnevniki* II, pp. 29–30.
23 The jury is still out on Derevenko's behaviour after the revolution. Having been extremely well paid and well treated by the Imperial Family, who extended their generosity to his children and even his sick relatives, Derevenko appears to have been sent away having been discovered pilfering from Alexey's belongings. From Petrograd he sent numerous requests to rejoin the family in Tobolsk (which suggests he still had a degree of loyalty to the family), but was never allowed to travel there, leading to accusations that he had betrayed them. He is thought to have died of typhus in Petrograd in 1921. See Zimin, *Detskii Mir*, pp. 86–8.
24 *Dnevniki* II, p. 50; see Maria's letter of 17 May, in Nepein, *Pered Rasstrelom*, p. 166.
25 This description has been drawn from photographs of the girls' room, of which three, taken from different angles, have survived. See e.g. Trewin, *Tutor to the Tsarevich*, pp. 84–5. A very damaged photograph sent to Katya Zborovskaya can be found at EEZ.
26 'Iz Dnevnika A. S. Demidovoi', in Kovalevskaya, *S Tsarem*, p. 68.
27 *Dnevniki* II, p. 30.

28 Anastasia, letter to Katya, no. 13, 15 August, EEZ.

29 Bulygin, *Murder of the Romanovs*, p. 195; Elizabeth Zinovieff, *A Princess Remembers* (New York: Galitzine, 1997), p. 119.

30 Chernova, *Vernye*, p. 449; *NZ* 2, pp. 246, 248. 'Iz Dnevnika A. S. Demidovoi', in Kovalevskaya, *S Tsarem*, p. 65; Wilton and Telberg, *Last Days of the Romanovs*, p. 183. Khitrovo later wrote her own account under her married name: M. Erdeli, 'Razyasnenie o moei poezdke v Tobolsk', *Dvuglavyi orel*, no. 30, 1922, pp. 6–11. For a detailed discussion of the incident see Ioffe, *Revolyutsiya i semya Romanovykh*, pp. 201–7 and Chernova, *Vernye*, pp 447–53. See also Buxhoeveden, *Life and Tragedy*, pp. 314–15.

31 Radzinsky, *Last Tsar*, p. 199.

32 *Dnevniki* II, p. 64.

33 See Olga's letter to PVP: 23 November, in *Dnevniki* II, p. 175.

34 Letter to Maria Feodorovna, 27 October, quoted in *Dnevniki* II, p. 138.

35 Pankratov memoirs, quoted in *Dnevniki* II, p. 75.

36 Schneider, letter to PVP, 9 October 1917, quoted in *Dnevniki* II, p. 114.

37 Brewster, *Anastasia's Album*, p. 53.

38 See e.g. *Dnevniki* II, pp. 45, 46, 52, 54, 55. For Nicholas see ibid., e.g. pp. 54–5.

39 Ibid., p. 47.

40 Radzinsky, *Last Tsar*, p. 195.

41 Buxhoeveden, *Life and Tragedy*, p. 313.

42 *Dnevniki* II, p. 72. See also Tatiana's description in a letter to Xenia, Nepein, *Pered Rasstrelom*, pp. 147–8.

43 Pankratov, quoted in *Dnevniki* II, p. 73.

44 Pankratov, quoted in *Fall*, p. 265.

45 Anastasia, letter to Katya, no. 14, 20 September, EEZ.

46 *Dnevniki* II, p. 80.

47 'Iz Dnevnika A. S. Demidovoi', in Kovalevskaya, *S Tsarem*, p. 670.

48 *Dnevniki* II, p. 87; *Fall*, pp. 265–6.

49 Quoted in *Dnevniki* II, p. 86.

50 Quoted in *Dnevniki* II, p. 106.

51 *Dnevniki* II, p. 88.

52 Vyrubova, *Memories*, p. 325.

53 Trewin, *Tutor to the Tsarevich*, p. 73.

54 Ross, *Gibel tsarskoy semi*, p. 424.

55 *Dnevniki* II, p. 148.

56 Pankratov, quoted in ibid., p. 142. For a translated extract of Pankratov's memoirs, see *Fall*, pp. 259–97, though this does not always match the original Russian extracts quoted in *Dnevniki*.
57 Gibbes, untitled TS memoir, Bodleian, f. 8.
58 Ibid., f. 12.
59 Pankratov, quoted in *Dnevniki* II, pp. 160–1.
60 Anastasia, letter to Katya, no. 16, 8 October, EEZ.
61 Quoted in *Dnevniki* II, p. 112.
62 Ibid., p. 128.
63 Ibid., p. 129.
64 Ibid., p. 148.
65 Quoted in *Fall*, pp. 199–200.
66 *Dnevniki* II, p. 139.
67 Quoted in ibid., p. 138.
68 Ibid., p. 139.
69 Ibid., pp. 163, 168.

Twenty – Thank God We Are Still in Russia and All Together

1 *Dnevniki* II, p. 150. See also Nicholas's letter to Xenia, 9 November, ibid., p. 159.
2 Trewin, *Tutor to the Tsarevich*, p. 72; *Dnevniki* II, p. 159.
3 *Fall*, p. 201.
4 *Dnevniki* II, p. 161.
5 Gilliard, *Thirteen Years*, p. 243.
6 Bowra, *Memories*, p. 66.
7 *Dnevniki* II, p. 164.
8 Anastasia, letter to Katya, 14 November, EEZ.
9 Ibid., 21 November, EEZ.
10 Quoted in *Dnevniki* II, p. 176.
11 Ibid., p. 85.
12 Nepein, *Pered Rasstrelom*, p. 163.
13 Ibid., p. 126.
14 Ibid., p. 158.
15 Quoted in *Dnevniki* II, p. 183.
16 Ibid., p. 197.
17 Vyrubova, *Memories*, p. 242.
18 Letter to Zinaida Tolstaya, 10 December, quoted in *Dnevniki* II, p. 199; Anastasia, letter to Katya, no. 22, 10 December, EEZ.

19 See *Dnevniki* II, p. 193–4. Other plays would follow in the New Year on 14, 21, 28 January, 4, 11, 18 and 25 February (OS). See Trewin, *Tutor to the Tsarevich*, pp. 78–83.
20 *Dnevniki* II, p. 199.
21 Buxhoeveden, *Left Behind*, p. 29.
22 Vyrubova, *Memories*, p. 249.
23 *Fall*, p. 211; Vyrubova, *Memories*, p. 318.
24 Ibid., p. 313; *Fall*, pp. 213–14.
25 See *Dnevniki* II, p. 216; Buxhoeveden, *Left Behind*, pp. 23–4.
26 *Dnevniki* II, p. 217.
27 Nepein, *Pered Rasstrelom*, p. 121.
28 *Dnevniki* II, p. 224.
29 Letter to PVP, 27 December, *Dnevniki* II, p. 218.
30 Anastasia, letter to Katya, 5 December, EEZ.
31 Buxhoeveden, *Left Behind*, p. 29.
32 Quoted in *Dnevniki* II, p. 224.
33 Gilliard, *Thirteen Years*, p. 128.
34 Botkin, *Real Romanovs*, pp. 178–9.
35 *Dnevniki* II, p. 230.
36 Ibid.; Buxhoeveden, *Life and Tragedy*, p. 313.
37 Harry de Windt, 'Ex Czar's Place of Exile: A Picture of Tobolsk', reproduced from *Manchester Guardian* in *Poverty Bay Herald*, 6 February 1918.
38 See Alexey diary, in Eugénie de Grèce, *Le Tsarévitch*, p. 207; Hendrikova diary quoted in Ross, *Gibel tsarskoy semi*, p. 226. Massie, *Last Diary*, p. 21, confirms that Anastasia did indeed contract measles, though some sources deny this. It is also confirmed in letter to Katya, no. 25, 19 January 1918, EEZ.
39 Alexandra, letter to Anna Vyrubova, *Memories*, p. 327.
40 Letter, 26 January 1918, EEZ.
41 Gilliard, *Thirteen Years*, p. 253.
42 For the cold that winter, see Anastasia to Anna Vyrubova, 23 January 1918 in Vyrubova, *Memories*, p. 327; Olga, letter to Rita Khitrovo, 21 January 1918 in Nepein, *Pered Rasstrelom*, p. 129; Nicholas, diary entries for 17–23 January, *Dnevniki* II, pp. 258–65.
43 See Anastasia to Katya, letter, 26 January, EEZ; Nepein, *Pered Rasstrelom*, p. 129.
44 Gilliard, *Thirteen Years*, p. 253. Nicholas [Gibbes], 'Ten Years', p. 12.
45 Ibid; Buxhoeveden, *Life and Tragedy*, p. 322.
46 Botkin, *Real Romanovs*, pp. 178–9.

47 Gilliard, *Thirteen Years*, p. 245.
48 Bitner in Ross, *Gibel tsarskoy semi*, pp. 422–3.
49 Trewin, *Tutor to the Tsarevich*, p. 73.
50 Bitner in Ross, *Gibel tsarskoy semi*, p. 423.
51 See e.g. letter to Zinaida Tolstaya, 14 January 1918, Coutau-Begari, p. 35 and to Valentina Chebotareva, 12 January 1918, in Alferev, *Pisma iz zatocheniya*, p. 200.
52 *Pravoslavnaya zhizn* July 1968, no. 7 pp. 3–4. The provenance of this extract is confirmed in Princess Barbara Dolgorouky's unpublished memoirs, 'Gone For Ever: Some Pages from My Life in Russia, 1885–1919', Hoover Institution Archives, TS fo. 82. Bekhteev went into exile in 1920 and settled first in Serbia and then in Nice, where the existence of this letter and the poem Bekhteev wrote based on it became well known in Russian émigré circles. See also Chernova, *Vernye*, pp. 476–7.
53 Quoted in Titov, 'OTMA', p. 36.
54 Bitner, quoted in Ross, *Gibel tsarskoy semi*, pp. 423–4.
55 Ibid.
56 Trewin, *Tutor to the Tsarevich*, p. 74.
57 Botkin, *Real Romanovs*, p. 179.
58 Ibid., p. 180.
59 Ibid., p. 179.
60 Letter no. 25 to Katya, 19 January; letter no. 24, 24 January, EEZ.
61 Botkin, *Real Romanovs*, pp. 179, 180.
62 List 1 (14) Tobolsk books, Sydney Gibbes Papers; Trewin, *Tutor to the Tsarevich*, pp. 82–3.
63 Ibid., p. 74; *LD*, p. 41.
64 Bitner testimony in Ross, *Gibel tsarskoy semi*, p. 424.
65 *LD*, p. 17.
66 For Alexey see Alexandra's diary for 26 and 30 January, in ibid., pp. 32, 36.
67 Quoted in *Dnevniki* II, p. 252.
68 Quoted in ibid., p. 267.
69 Ibid., p. 268.
70 *LD*, p. 38.
71 *Dnevniki* II, p. 292.
72 Letter to Zinaida Tolstoya, 6 January 1918, Coutau-Begari, p. 35.
73 Wilton and Telberg, *Last Days of the Romanovs*, p. 196; Gilliard, *Thirteen Years*, p. 255.
74 Kobylinsky statement in Wilton and Telberg, *Last Days of the Romanovs*, p. 197.

75 Gilliard, *Thirteen Years*, p. 255. For the household economies see *Dnevniki* II, pp. 296–8.

76 *LP*, p. 609.

77 *Dnevniki* II, p. 312.

78 Ibid., p. 332.

79 Vyrubova, *Memories*, p. 337; Coutau-Begari, p. 35.

80 Dehn, *Real Tsaritsa*, pp. 244, 246.

81 *Dnevniki* II, p. 325.

82 Quoted in *LD* p. 72.

83 *Dnevniki* II, p. 328.

84 Gilliard, *Thirteen Years*, p. 256.

85 *Dnevniki* II, pp. 327–8.

Twenty-one – They Knew It Was the End When I Was with Them

1 *Dnevniki* II, p. 316.

2 Ibid., p. 336.

3 Botkin, *Real Romanovs*, p. 192.

4 Buxhoeveden, *Left Behind*, pp. 68–9.

5 Gilliard, *Thirteen Years*, p. 256.

6 Vyrubova, *Memories*, p. 341.

7 Trewin, *Tutor to the Tsarevich*, p.95; Buxhoeveden, *Left Behind*, p. 49.

8 Vyrubova, *Memories*, p. 338.

9 Volkov statement, in Ross, *Gibel tsarskoy semi*, p. 450.

10 Vyrubova, *Memories*, p. 338.

11 *LD*, p. 102.

12 Wilton and Telberg, *Last Days of the Romanovs*, p. 200.

13 Melnik-Botkina, *Vospominaniya*, pp. 95–6.

14 Gilliard, *Thirteen Years*, p. 259.

15 *Dnevniki* II, p. 368.

16 *Fall*, p. 238.

17 Ross, *Gibel' tsarskoy semi*, p. 412.

18 Wilton and Telberg, *Last Days of the Romanovs*, p. 250.

19 *LD*, p. 108.

20 Melnik-Botkina, *Vospominaniya*, p. 106; Botkin, *Real Romanovs*, p. 194.

21 Gilliard, *Thirteen Years*, p. 262; Trewin, *Tutor to the Tsarevich*, p. 98.

22 'British Abbot who was Friend of Murdered Czar', *Singapore Free Press*, 20 March 1936. Now Father Nicholas, Gibbes was interviewed en route through Singapore to the Holy Land. Nicholas [Gibbes], 'Ten Years', pp. 13–14.

23 *Dnevniki* II, p. 374.
24 Trewin, *Tutor to the Tsarevich*, p. 98; Buxhoeveden, *Life and Tragedy*, p. 331.
25 Nicholas [Gibbes], 'Ten Years', p. 14; Bulygin, *Murder of the Romanovs*, p. 209; Kobylinsky statement in Ross, *Gibel tsarskoy semi*, p. 304.
26 Trewin, *Tutor to the Tsarevich*, p. 98.
27 Melnik-Botkina, *Vospominaniya*, p. 104.
28 Zeepvat, 'Valet's Story', p. 332.
29 Statement in Ross, *Gibel tsarskoy semi*, p. 304.
30 Bitner statement in ibid., p. 423.
31 Trewin, *Tutor to the Tsarevich*, p. 100.
32 Ibid., p. 130; Melnik-Botkina, *Vospominaniya*, p. 108.
33 Gibbes, TS memoirs, f. 12.
34 Gilliard, *Thirteen Years*, p. 263.
35 Tschebotarioff, *Russia My Native Land*, p. 197.
36 Gilliard, *Thirteen Years*, p. 263.
37 Vyrubova, *Memories*, p. 342.
38 Olga's letter, 28 April to 5 May 1918, Wilson, 'Separation and Uncertainty', no. 25, p. 4. The letters covering April–May 1918 translated into English in this series of articles (nos. 25–8) are taken from the French versions of the original Russian in the *Journal Intime de Nicolas II*, 1934, and Eugénie de Grèce, *Le Tsarévitch: enfant martyr.* The translations are therefore at third hand, as the original Russian MS sources, if they still survive, have not as yet been made available.
39 Ibid., p. 5.
40 Ibid.
41 See web site @: http://www.tzar-nikolai.orthodoxy.ru/n2/pism/12.htm#9
42 Wilson, 'Separation and Uncertainty', no. 26, p. 41.
43 Ibid., no. 27, p. 82.
44 Ibid., p. 83.
45 Ibid., p. 84.
46 Quoted in *Dnevniki* II, p. 417.
47 Wilson, 'Separation and Uncertainty', no. 28, p. 114.
48 Ibid., p. 115.
49 Maria, postcard to Ella, quoted in *Dnevniki* II, p. 430.
50 *Dnevniki* II, pp. 425–6. Note that transcriptions of this widely quoted letter vary and some translations based on them (e.g. *Fall*, pp. 301–2) contain possible errors.

51 Ibid., p. 426.
52 Bulygin, *Murder of the Romanovs*, p. 228.
53 Ibid., p. 229.
54 Wilton and Telberg, *Last Days of the Romanovs*, p. 213.
55 Wilson, 'Separation and Uncertainty', no. 28, p. 114.
56 Bulygin, *Murder of the Romanovs*, p. 230; Botkin, *Real Romanovs*, p. 207.
57 Ibid., p. 208.
58 Trewin, *Tutor to the Tsarevich*, pp. 101–2.
59 Buchanan, *Queen Victoria's Relations*, p. 231.
60 Buxhoeveden, *Left Behind*, pp. 68–9.
61 Ibid., p. 71.
62 Bulygin, *Murder of the Romanovs*, p. 230; Nicholas [Gibbes], 'Ten Years', p. 14.
63 Rodionov remained in Ekaterinburg to help organize the guard at the Ipatiev House. According to Plotnikov, *Gibel tsarskoy semi*, pp. 195, 475–6, most of the seventy-two-man escort to Ekaterinburg were Latvian chekists. Rodionov went on to work for the NKVD in the 1930s.
64 Buxhoeveden, *Left Behind*, p. 73.
65 Gilliard, *Thirteen Years*, p. 269.
66 Speranski, *'La Maison'*, pp. 158–9.
67 Ibid., pp. 159–60, 161.
68 Ibid., p. 161.
69 Trewin, *Tutor to the Tsarevich*, p. 104; Nicholas [Gibbes], 'Ten Years', p. 14.

Twenty-two – Prisoners of the Ural Regional Soviet

1 *Dnevniki* II, p. 438.
2 Ibid.
3 *LD*, p. 157.
4 *Dnevniki* II, p. 427.
5 Ibid., p. 458.
6 Quoted in ibid., p. 456.
7 *LD*, p. 137.
8 Ibid., p. 151.
9 *Dnevniki* II, p. 487.
10 *Dnevniki:*, p. 475.
11 *LD*, p. 159; *Dnevniki* II, p. 465.

12 *LD*, p. 194.

13 *Dnevniki*, p. 469; *LD*, p. 163.

14 See *LD*, 27 May, 10 June, pp. 148, 162.

15 Ibid., pp. 169, 170; *Dnevniki* II, p. 479.

16 Ibid., p. 490; *LD*, p. 175.

17 Testimony of Alexander Strekotin, in Zhuk, *Ispoved tsareubiits*, p. 450; Testimony of Alexey Kabanov, in ibid, p. 129; see also p. 144.

18 Speranski, '*La Maison*', p. 164.

19 Testimony of Alexander Strekotin in Zhuk, *Ispoved tsareubiits*, p. 446 and variant of this on p. 450.

20 *Dnevniki* II, p. 497.

21 *LD*, p. 175.

22 'The 90th Birthday of A. E. Portnoff', accessible @: http://www.holyres.org/en/?p=223

23 Peter Hudd (Hudiakovsky), taped reminiscences, University of Illinois at Springfield Archives, accessible @: http://www.uis.edu/archives/memoirs/HUDD.pdf

24 Shoumatoff, *Russian Blood*, p. 142.

25 Peter Hudd (Hudiakovsky), taped reminiscences, University of Illinois at Springfield Archives, accessible @: http://www.uis.edu/archives/memoirs/HUDD.pdf

26 Ibid.

27 Storozhev's testimony, in Ross, *Gibel tsarskoy semi*, p. 98.

28 Ibid., p. 100; Shoumatoff, *Russian Blood*, p. 142.

29 'Kak eto bylo', *Tientsin Evening Journal*, Russian edition, 17 July 1948, front page.

30 Speranski, '*La Maison*', p. 119. See also Starodumova statement in Ross, *Gibel tsarskoy semi*, pp. 81–2.

31 Speranksi, '*La Maison*', p. 120.

32 Statement of Pavel Medvedev, in Radzinsky, *Last Tsar*, p. 336.

33 Shoumatoff, *Russian Blood*, p. 142.

34 Christie's catalogue, 29 November 2012, lot 116. Card sent from Tobolsk, 29 March 1918.

Epilogue – Victims of Repressions

1 *Dnevniki* II, p. 572.

2 See Alexei Volkov, *Souvenirs d'Alexis Volkov* (Paris: Payot, 1928); translated extracts can be found in Zeepvat, 'Valet's Story'.

3 Demidova's diary can be found at: GARF f. 601. Op. 1. D. 211. It

was published in Munich in *Veche. Nezavisimyi ruskii almanakh*, 1989, no. 36, pp. 182–92. For the fate of her Romanov memorabilia, see http://www.ogoniok.com/archive/1916/4461/30-40-42.

4 For the experiences of Gibbes, Gilliard and Buxhoeveden after their separation from the Romanov family, see Trewin, *Tutor to the Tsarevich*, Gilliard, *Thirteen Years* and Buxhoeveden, *Left Behind*.

5 Gilliard, *Thirteen Years*, p. 274. Gibbes brought the glass chandelier back with him to England. It was for a while kept in his chapel in Oxford, and then was taken with the rest of the Gibbes collection of Romanov memorabilia to Luton Hoo, until this country house was sold off and developed into a hotel. Its present whereabouts is uncertain.

6 See Buxhoeveden, *Before the Storm, Life and Tragedy* and *Left Behind*.

7 Shoumatoff, *Russian Blood*, p. 142.

8 In emigration in Harbin, Anatole Portnoff (see note 22, chapter 22) sang in Father Storozhev's choir. Private information.

9 Private information.

10 See web site @: http://rt.com/news/members-of-russia-s-royal-family-rehabilitated/

Bibliography

ARCHIVES

Alexandra Feodorovna, memoir [in French], Mariia Aleksandrovna Vasil'chikova Papers, Bakhmeteff Archive, Columbia University.

Alexandra of Hesse, Princess, letters to Queen Victoria, Royal Archives.

Barbara Dolgorouky, Princess, Memoirs ('Gone For Ever: Some Pages from My Life in Russia, 1885–1919'), Hoover Institution Archives.

Bosanquet, Dorothy, letters from Tsarskoe Selo, Bosanquet Family Papers, Leeds University Library, GB 206 MS 1456/182–4.

Buchanan, Meriel, diaries 1910–17 and newspaper cuttings, Buchanan Collection, Bu B 6, Nottingham University Library.

Elizaveta Feodorovna, Grand Duchess, letters to Queen Victoria, Royal Archives.

Imperial family, papers relating to visit to Balmoral 1896 and Cowes 1909, Royal Archives.

Pocock, L. C., Petrograd Diary 1916–17, box ref.: 85/28/1, Imperial War Museum.

Ryabinin, A., 'Tsarskaya Semya v Krymu osen 1913 goda', 'Zhizn' i Tsarstvovanie Imperatora Nikolaya II: Sbornik', in Tarsaidze Papers, part 2, Hoover Institution Archives.

Sablin, Nikolay Pavlovich, 'S tsarskoy semei na "shtandarte"', TS, Roman Gul' Archive, Amherst Center for Russian Culture, Massachusetts.

Seymour, Dorothy, manuscript diary, Petrograd 1916–17, box ref. 95/28/1, catalogue no. 3210, Imperial War Museum.

Tyan-Shansky, N. D. Semonov, 'Tsarstvennyya Deti', in 'Zhizn' i Tsarstvovanie Imperatora Nikolaya II: Sbornik', part I, TS, Tarsaidze Papers, Hoover Institution Archives.

'Vospominaniya o Marii Fedorovne Geringere', MS in Mariia Vasil'evna Fedchenko, Papers, Bakhmeteff Archive, Columbia University.

Zborovskaia, Ekaterina Erastovna, letters, 1917–18, collection no. 2000C3, Hoover Institution Archives.

BIBLIOGRAPHY

Newspapers and Magazines

Anglo-Russian, The
Atlantis Magazine
Cassell's Magazine
Cosmopolitan
Current Literature
Current Opinion
European Royal History Journal
Daily Mirror
Girl's Own Paper
Girls' Realm
Harper's Weekly
Illustrated London News
Ladies' Home Journal
Letopis' voiny, 1913–18
Literary Digest
Littell's Living Age
McClure's Magazine
Munsey's Magazine
New York Times
Niva
Noviy Zhurnal
Novoe Vremya
Ogonek
Outlook
Pearson's Magazine
Penny Illustrated Paper
Quiver
Review of Reviews (UK edition)
Royalty Digest
Russkoe Slovo
Scribner's Magazine
Stolitsa i usad'ba, 1913–18
Strand Magazine
Washington Post
Westminster Review
World's Work
Young Woman
Youth's Companion

BIBLIOGRAPHY

Digital Newspaper and Historical Archives

Alexander Palace Time Machine
Newspaperarchive.com
19th-century UK Periodicals, British Library
19th-century Newspapers, British Library
New York Times Digital Archive
Papers Past, New Zealand
Proquest British Periodicals
Proquest Periodicals Archive
Proquest Periodicals Index
Royal Russia News Archive
The Times Digital Archive
Trove Digitised Newspapers
Washington Post Digital Archive

PRIMARY SOURCES

1. Romanov Family Letters and Diaries

In the continuing absence of any complete collected editions, letters and diaries by OTMA are scattered over a wide range of sources.

Alferev, E. E., *Pisma svyatykh tsarstvennykh muchenikov iz zatocheniya*, St Petersburg: Spaso-Preobrazhenskogo Valaamskogo monastyrya, 1998, 3rd edn, revised and enlarged.

Baker, Raegan, ed., *1913 Diary of Grand Duchess Olga Nikolaievna*, trans. Marina Petrov, Ontario: Gilbert's Royal Books, 2008.

Bing, Edward J., *The Secret Letters of the Last Tsar: Being the Confidential Correspondence between Tsar Nicholas II and the Dowager Empress Marie*, New York: Longmans, Green & Co., 1938.

Bokhanov, Alexander, *Aleksandra Feodorovna*, Moscow: Veche, 2008 [letters written March 1917 to April 1918, pp. 276–352].

Bokhanov, Alexander *et al.*, *The Romanovs: Love, Power and Tragedy*, London: Leppi Publications, 1993.

Bonetskaya, N. K., *Tsarskie deti*, Moscow: Izdatelstvo Sretenskogog Monastyrya, 2004.

Brewster, Hugh, *Anastasia's Album*, London: Little Brown, 1996.

Eugénie de Grèce, *Le Tsarévitch, enfant martyre*, Paris: Perrin, 1990 [Alexey's letters and diaries 1916–1918; OTMA's letters 1918].

Fjellman, Margit, *Louise Mountbatten, Queen of Sweden*, London: Allen & Unwin, 1968 [Appendix: Letters from the Russian Imperial Family, pp. 222–8].

Foman, S. V., *Skorbnyi angel; tsaritsa-muchenitsa Alexandra Feodorovna, novaya v pismakh, dnevnikakh i vospominaniyakh*, Moscow: S. F. Fomin, 2005.

Fuhrman, Joseph T., ed., *The Complete Wartime Correspondence of Tsar Nicholas II and the Empress Alexandra, April 1914–March 1917*, Westport, CT: Greenwood Press, 1999.

Galushkin, N. V., *Sobstvennyi ego imperatorskogo velichestva konvoy*, Moscow: Tsentrpoligraf, 2008.

Goncharenko, Oleg, *Pisma tsarskoy semi iz zatocheniya*, new edn, Moscow: Veche, 2013.

Ioann Konstantinovich, Grand Duke, letters to his family, in *Rossisskii arkhiv: Istoriya otechestva v svidetelstvakh i dokumentakh*, Moscow: Studiya TRITE, vol. XV, 2007, pp. 392, 419–20, 435–6.

Khrustalev, V. M., ed., *Dnevniki Nikolaya II i Imperatritsy Aleksandry Fedorovny, 1917–1918*, 2 vols, Moscow: Vagrius, 2008.

Kleinpenning, Petra H., ed., *The Correspondence of the Empress Alexandra of Russia with Ernst Ludwig and Eleonore, Grand Duke and Duchess of Hesse, 1878–1916*, Norderstedt: Herstellung und Verlag, 2010.

Korshunova, T. V., *et al.*, *Pisma prepodobnomuchenitsy velikoi knyagini Elizavety Feodorovny*, Moscow: Pravoslavnoe Sestrichestvo vo Imya Prepodobnomuchenitsy, 2011.

Kozlov, V. A. and Khrustalev, V. M., *The Last Diary of Tsaritsa Alexandra*, intro. Robert K. Massie, London: Yale University Press, 1997.

Kudrina, Yu V., *Imperatritsa Mariya Feodorovna: Dnevniki, pisma, vospominaniya*, Moscow: Olma-Press, 2001.

Kuhnt, Lotte Hoffmann, *Briefe der Zarin von Russland an ihre Jugendfreundin Toni Becker* (1887–94), Norderstedt: Herstellung und Verlag, 2009.

Kulikovsky, Paul *et al.*, *25 Chapters of My Life*, Forres: Librario Publishing, 2009.

Lichnevsky, M., *Lettres des Grands Ducs à Nicholas*, Paris: Payot, 1926.

McLees, Nectaria, *Divnyi svet*, Moscow: Palomnik, 1998.

Maliyutin, A. Yu., *Tsesarevich: dokumenty, vospominaniya, fotografii*, Moscow: Vagrius, 1998.

Mandache, Diana, *Dearest Missy*, Falkopin: Rosvall Royal Books, 2010.

Maylunas, Andrei and Sergei Mironenko, *A Lifelong Passion: Nicholas and Alexandra, Their Own Story*, New York: Doubleday, 1997.

Mironenko, S. V., ed., *Dnevniki imperatora Nikolaya II 1894–1918*, vol. 1, *1894–1904*, Moscow: ROSSPEN, 2011.

Olivier Coutau-Begari, sale catalogue [in French], 14 November 2007 [autograph letters by Alexandra, Olga, Maria and Tatiana sent from Tobolsk October 1917–May 1918], accessible @: http://tinyurl.com/culcvbq

Nepein, Igor, *Pered rasstrelom: Poslednie pisma tsarskoi semi . . . 1917–18*, Omsk: Knizhnoe Isdatelstvo, 1992.

Nicholas II, *Dnevnik Nikolaya Romanova* [1913–18], Moscow: Zakharov, 2007.

Spreti, Heinrich, Graf von, ed., *Alix an Gretchen, Breife der Zarin Alexandra Feodorovna an Freilin Margarethe v. Fabrice aus den Jahren 1891–1914*, Germany: privately printed, 2002.

Steinberg, Mark D. and Vladimir M. Khrustalev, *The Fall of the Romanovs*, London: Yale University Press, 1995.

Syroboyarsky, General A. V., *Skorbnaya pamyatka, 1918–17 July–1928*, New York: privately printed, 1928.

Tschebotarioff, Gregory P., *Russia My Native Land*, New York: McGraw Hill, 1964 [letters from Olga and Tatiana].

Wilson, Rev. Terence A. MacLean, 'Separation and Uncertainty' – translated extracts from the *Journal Intime de Nicolas*, 1934, vol. II, and letters of the imperial family in exile (from Princess George of Greece, *Le Tsaréevitch*), covering April–May 1918, in *Royalty Digest: A Journal of Record* 3, nos. 25, 26, 27, 28, June–October, 1993.

Zvereva, Nina, *Avgusteishie sestry miloserdiya*, Moscow: Veche, 2006.

2. Memoirs, Diaries, Letters and Biographies Relating to the British and Russian Courts

Alexander, Grand Duke, *Once a Grand Duke*, New York: Garden City Publishing, 1932.

Almedingen, E. M., *The Empress Alexandra 1872–1918*, London: Hutchinson, 1961.

Anon. [Albert Stopford], *The Russian Diary of an Englishman, Petrograd, 1915–1917*, London: Heinemann, 1919.

Anon. [Rebecca Insley Casper], *Intimacies of Court and Society: An Unconventional Narrative of Unofficial Days by the Widow of an American Diplomat*, New York: Dodd Mead, 1912.

Bariatinsky, Princess Anatole Marie, *My Russian Life*, London: Hutchinson, 1923.

Benkendorff, Pavel Konstantinovich, *Last Days at Tsarskoe Selo*, London: Heinemann, 1927.

Bogdanovich, A. V., *Tri poslednykh samoderzhtsa*, Moscow: Novosti, 1990.

Botkin, Gleb, *The Real Romanovs*, London: Putnam, 1932.

Buchanan, Sir George, *My Mission to Russia*, vol 1, London: Cassell, 1923.

Buchanan, Meriel, *Diplomacy and Foreign Courts*, London: Hutchinson, 1928.

—— *The Dissolution of an Empire*, London: John Murray, 1932.

—— 'The Grand Duchess Olga Nicholaievna', in *Queen Victoria's Relations*, London: Cassell, 1954.

—— *Ambassador's Daughter*, London: Cassell, 1958.

Bulygin, Captain Paul, *The Murder of the Romanovs*, London: Hutchinson, 1935.

Buxhoeveden, Baroness Sophie, *The Life and Tragedy of Alexandra Fyodorovna*, London: Longmans, Green, 1928.

—— *Left Behind: Fourteen Months in Russia During the Revolution*, London: Longmans, Green, 1929.

—— *Before the Storm*, London: Macmillan, 1938.

Chebotareva, Valentina, 'V dvortsovom lazarete v Tsarskom Sele: Dnevnik 14 Iyuliya 1915–5 Yanuarya 1918', in *Novyi Zhurnal* 181, 1990, pp. 173–243 and 182, 1990, pp. 202–72.

Collier, Mary, *A Victorian Diarist: Extracts from the Journals of Mary, Lady Monkswell*, London: John Murray, 1944.

Dehn, Lili, *The Real Tsaritsa*, London: Thornton Butterworth, 1922.

Demidova, Anna, 'Iz dnevnika A. S. Demidovoi', in O. T. Kovalevskaya, *S tsarem i za tsarya: Muchenicheskii venets tsarskikh slug*, Moscow: Russkii Khronograf, 2008, pp. 56–70.

Duff, David, *Hessian Tapestry*, London: David & Charles, 1979.

De Stoeckl, Agnes, *Not All Vanity*, London: John Murray, 1951.

—— *My Dear Marquis*, London: John Murray, 1952.

Durland, Kellogg, *Royal Romances of To-day*, New York: Duffield, 1911.

Eagar, Margaretta, *Six Years at the Russian Court*, Bowmanville, Ont.: Gilbert's Books, [1906], with an introduction by Charlotte Zeepvat, 2011.

Elton, Renee Maud, *One Year at the Russian Court 1904–1905*, London: John Lane, 1918.

Eulalia, Infanta of Spain, *Court Life from Within*, New York: Dodd, Mead, 1915.

Fabritsky, S. S., *Iz proshlogo: Vospminaniya fligel-adyutanta gosudarya imperatora Nikolai II*, Berlin: n.p., 1926.

Fulford, Roger, ed., *Darling Child: Private Correspondence of Queen Victoria and the German Crown Princess, 1871–1878*, London: Evans Brothers, 1976.

—— *Beloved Mama: Private Correspondence of Queen Victoria and the German Crown Princess, 1878–1885*, London: Evans Brothers, 1981.

Galitzine, Princess Nicholas, *Spirit to Survive: Memoirs of Princess Nicholas Galitzine*, London: William Kimber, 1976.

Gavriil Konstantinovich, Grand Duke, *Memories in the Marble Palace*, Bowmanville, Ont.: Gilbert's Books, 2009.

Gilliard, Pierre, *Thirteen Years at the Russian Court*, London: Hutchinson, 1921.

Girardin, Daniel, *Précepteur des Romanov*, Lausanne: Actes Sud, 2005.

Grabbe, Paul and Beatrice Grabbe, eds, *The Private World of the Last Tsar*, London: Collins, 1985.

Gromov, A. M., *My Recollections through Fifty Years: Recollections of an Artisan Worker of the Winter Palace . . . 1879–1929*, ed. and trans. Stephen R. de Angelis, Sunnyvale, CA: Bookemon, 2009.

Harcave, Sidney, ed., *The Memoirs of Count Witte*, New York: M. E. Sharpe, 1990.

Helena Augusta Victoria and Karl Sell, *Alice, Grand Duchess of Hesse*, London: G. P. Putnam's Sons, 1885.

Hibbert, Christopher, *Queen Victoria in Her Letters and Journals*, London: Viking, 1984.

Hough, Richard, *Louis and Victoria: The First Mountbattens*, London: Hutchinson, 1974.

— *Advice to a Granddaughter: Letters from Queen Victoria to Princess Victoria of Hesse*, London: Heinemann, 1975.

— *Mountbatten: Hero of Our Time*, London: Weidenfeld & Nicolson, 1985.

Iswolsky, Helene, *No Time to Grieve*, Philadelphia, PA: Winchell, 1985.

Kalinin, Nikolay and Marina Zemlyachenko, 'Taina Velikoi Knyazhny', ch. 8 of *Romanovy i Krym*, Simferopol: Biznes-Inform, pp. 237–64.

Kamarovskaya, E., *Vospominaniya*, Moscow: Zaharov, 2003.

Kleinmikhel, Countess, *Memories of a Shipwrecked World*, London: Brentano's, 1923.

Kokovtsov, Graf V. N., *Iz moego proshlago: Vospominaniya 1903–1919 gg.*, 2 vols, Paris: Mouton, 1933.

Kovalevskaya, O. T., *S tsarem i za tsarya: Muchenicheskii venets tsarskikh slug*, Moscow: Russkii Khronograf, 2008.

Lutyens, Mary, ed., *Lady Lytton's Court Diary*, London: Rupert Hart-Davis, 1961.

Marie, Queen of Romania, *The Story of My Life*, New York: Scribner's, 1934.

Marie Pavlovna, Grand Duchess, *Things I Remember*, London: Cassell, 1930.

Markov, Sergey, *Pokinutaya tsarskaya semya, 1917–18, Tsarskoe Selo–Tobolsk–Ekaterinburg*, Moscow: Palomnik, 2002.

Melnik-Botkina, Tatiana, *Vospominaniya o tsarskoi seme*, Moscow: Zakharov, 2009.

Mossolov, A. A., *At the Court of the Last Tsar*, London: Methuen, 1935.

Naryshkin-Kurakin, Elizaveta, *Under Three Tsars*, New York: E. P. Dutton, 1931.

Noel, Gerard, *Princess Alice: Queen Victoria's Forgotten Daughter*, London: Michael Russell, 1974.

Paléologue, Maurice, *An Ambassador's Memoirs 1914–1917*, London: Hutchinson, 1973.

Paoli, Xavier, *My Royal Clients*, London: Hodder & Stoughton, 1911.

Poore, Judith, *The Memoirs of Emily Loch, Discretion in Waiting*, Forres, Moray: Librario Publishing, 2007.

Popov, K., *Vospominaniya kavkazskogo grenadera, 1914–1920*, Belgrade: Russkaya Tipografiya, 1925.

Radziwill, Catherine, *The Taint of the Romanovs*, London: Cassell, 1931.

Ramm, Agatha, ed., *Beloved & Darling Child: Last Letters Between Queen Victoria & Her Eldest Daughter 1886–1901*, Stroud: Sutton Publishing, 1990.

Ross, Nikolay, *Gibel tsarskoy semi*, Frankfurt am Main: Posev, 1987.

Sablin, Nikolay, *Desyat let na imperatorskoi yakhte 'Shtandart'*, St Petersburg: Petronius, 2008.

Sazonov, Serge, *The Fateful Years 1906–1916*, London: Jonathan Cape, 1928.

Speranski, Valentin, *'La Maison à destination spéciale': La tragédie d'Ekaterinenbourg*, Paris: J. Ferenczi & Fils, 1929.

Spiridovich, Alexandre, *Les Dernières années de la court de Tsarskoe Selo*, 2 vols, Paris: Payot, 1928.

—— *Last Years of the Court at Tsarskoe Selo*, Bowmanville, Ont.: Gilbert's Books, 2010.

Trewin, J. C., *Tutor to the Tsarevich: Charles Sydney Gibbes*, London: Macmillan, 1975.

Tyutcheva, Sofya, 'Za neskolko let do katastrofy, Vospominaniya', @ http:// bib.rus.ec/b/327889/read

Vassili, Paul, *Behind the Veil at the Russian Court*, London: Cassell, 1913.

Virubova [Vyrubova], Anna, *Keisarinnan Hovineiti*, Helsinki: Otava, 1987.

Volkov, A. a., *Okolo tsarskoy semi*, Moscow: Chastnaya Firma 'Ankor', 1993.

Vorres, Ian, *The Last Grand Duchess*, London: Hutchinson, 1964.

Vyrubova, Anna, *Memories of the Russian Court*, New York: Macmillan, 1923.

—— *Romanov Family Album*, London: Allen Lane, 1982.

W. B. [a Russian], *Russian Court Memoirs, 1914–1916*, London: Herbert Jenkins, 1917.

Wheeler, Post and Hallie Erminie Rives, *Dome of Many Coloured Glass*, New York: Doubleday, 1955.

Woronoff, Olga, *Upheaval*, New York: G. P. Putnam's, 1932.

Zimin, Igor, *Detskiy mir imperatorskikh rezidentsii. Povsednevnaya zhizn rossiiskogo imperatorskogo dvora*, St Petersburg: Tsentropoligraf, 2010.

3. Newspaper and Magazine Articles

'Alien's Letter from England: Cowes Regatta Week', *Otago Witness*, 29 September 1909.

'Autocrat of the Nursery', 20 June 1912 and 'Forming the Tsarevitch's Character', 11 July 1912, *Youth's Companion* 86, 1912, pp. 330, 356.

Belloc, Marie, 'Her Imperial Majesty the Czarina of Russia', *Woman at Home*, February 1895, pp. 427–33.

Biddle, Winthrop, 'The Czar and His Family', *Munsey's Magazine* LI, February 1914, no. 1, pp. 3–5.

'Camera Bug to Czar Nicholas Photograph Album of G. N. Taube', *Life Magazine* 72, 9 June 1972, pp. 69–70.

Cherkashin, Nikolay, 'Knyazhna i michman: istoriya poslednei lyubvi docheri Nikolaya II', *Rossiiskaya gazeta*, no. 3336, 1 November 2003, @: http://www.rg.ru/2003/11/01/olga.html

Chernavin, T., 'The Home of the Last Tsar', *Slavonic and East European Review* 17, 1938–9, pp. 659–67.

'The Children of the Tsar', *The Scrap-Book* 5, part 1, January–June 1908, p. 60.

'Children Without a Smile', *Washington Post*, 28 May 1905.

'The Czar at Home', *Harper's Weekly* 48, 17 September 1904, pp. 143–5.

'The Czarina', *Canadian Magazine* 19, May–October 1902, pp. 301–4.

'Daughters of Royal Houses: The Grand-duchess Olga of Russia', *Woman's Life* 68 no. 6, 27 March 1897, pp. 81–2.

Demidova, Anna, 'Dnevnik 1917', *Veche: nezavisimyi russkii almanakh*, Munich, 1989, no. 36, pp. 182–92.

Dubensky, Major-General, 'With the Tsar and Tsarevitch at the Front', *20th Century Russia and Anglo-Russian Review*, October 1916, pp. 31–3.

Eagar, Margaretta, 'Christmas at the Court of the Tsar', *Quiver*, January 1906, pp. 26–30.

—— 'Further Glimpses of the Tsaritsa's Little Girls', *Girl's Own Paper and Woman's Magazine* vol. XXX, 1909, pp. 366–7.

—— 'More about the Little Grand Duchesses of Russia', *Girl's Own Paper and Woman's Magazine* vol. XXX, 1909, pp. 535–5.

[Eagar, Margaretta] 'The Russian Court in Summer', *The Star* [Christchurch, NZ], 30 September 1905, reprinted from *Woman at Home*.

Erdeli, Margarita [Rita Khitrovo], 'Razyasnenie o moei poezdke v Tobolsk', *Dvuglavyi orel* 30, no. 1, (14) May 1922, pp. 6–11.

Farson, Daniel, 'Au Pieds de l'Impératrice', *Wheeler's Review* 27, no. 3, 1983, pp. 14–18.

Foster Fraser, Sir John, 'Side Shows in Armageddon', *Harper's Monthly*, January 1919, pp. 264–9.

'Four Little Maids: Home Life of the Children in the Royal Family of Russia', *Delphos Daily Herald* (Ohio, USA), 16 July 1901.

Gelardi, Julia P., 'Carol & Olga: "They must decide for themselves"', *Royalty Digest* X, no. 2, August 2000, pp. 50–7.

Geraschinevsky, Michael Z., 'The Ill-Fated Children of the Tsar', *Scribner's Magazine* 65, no. 2, February 1919, pp 158–76.

Gibbes, 'Ten Years', see Nicholas, Very Revd Archimandrite, below.

Hall, Coryne, 'The Tsar's Visit to Cowes', *Royalty Digest* VI no. 2, August 1996, pp. 39–42.

—— '"No Bombs, No Bandits". Holidays in Finland', part 2, *Royalty Digest* 144, June 2003, pp. 360–5.

—— 'Why Can Other Boys Have Everything . . .?', *European Royal History Journal*, June 2004, pp. 3–7.

—— 'The Tsar's Floating Palace: *The Shtandart*', *European Royal History Journal* LXXXII, August 2011, pp. 23–30.

Hapgood, Isabel, 'Russia's Czarina', *Harper's Bazaar* 40, February 1906, pp. 103–9.

Harris, Carolyn, 'The Succession Prospects of Grand Duchess Olga Nikolaevna (1895–1918)', *Canadian Slavonic Papers* LIV, nos 1–2, March–June 2012, pp. 61–84.

Helena, Princess of Serbia, 'I Was at Ekaterinburg', *Atlantis Magazine: In the Court of Memory* 1, no. 3, 1999, pp. 78–92.

Henninger, Griffith, '"To Lessen Their Suffering": A Brief History of the Empress Alexandra's War Relief Organizations, July 23 1914–March 2 1919', unpublished paper, Southern Conference of Slavic Studies, Savannah, 30 March 2012.

Hodgetts, Bradley, 'The Czar of Russia at Home, Minute Picture of Court Life at St. Petersburg During the Last Century', *Cassell's Magazine* 30, September 1904, pp. 342–3.

'How the Czar's Five Children Live in the Shadow of Death', *Current Literature* 53, December 1912, pp. 642–6.

'How the Czarina's Superstitions Helped to Bring the Russian Revolution', *Current Opinion* 69, September 1920, pp. 358–60.

'How the Russian Censor Works', *Strand Magazine* 29, no. 170, 1905, pp. 206–16.

Hulme, John, 'The Homely Tsar', *Pearson's Magazine* 7–8, January 1902, pp. 34–41.

'Imperial Russia: Her Power and Progress', *Illustrated London News*, 31-page special supplement, July 1913.

Janin, Général M., 'Au G.Q.G. russe', *Le Monde Slave*, May 1916, pp. 1–24.

Khitrovo, Rita, see above, Erdeli, Margarita.

King, Greg, 'Livadia under Nicholas II', *Atlantis Magazine: In the Courts of*

Memory. Special double issue on the Romanovs and the Crimea, 3, no. 3 (no date) pp. 5–35.

—— 'Requiem: The Russian Imperial Family's Last Visit to Darmstadt, 1910', *Atlantis Magazine: In the Courts of Memory* 2, no. 2, (no date), pp. 104–14.

King, Greg and Penny Wilson, 'The Departure of the Imperial Family from Tsarskoe Selo', *Atlantis Magazine: In the Courts of Memory*, special *Fate of the Romanovs* edition, September 2003, pp. 12–31. Also available @: http://www.kingandwilson.com/fotrextras/

Malama, Peter de, 'The Romanovs – The Forgotten Romance', *Royalty Digest* 162, December 2004, pp. 184–5.

Markylie, M., 'L'Impératrice en voile blanc: Tsarskoié-Sélo et les Hopitaux de Sa Majesté Alexandra Féodorovna', *Revue des deux mondes*, 1 April 1916, pp. 566–83.

Mee, Arthur, 'Empress of a Hundred Millions', *The Young Woman* VIII, October 1899, pp. 1–6.

Minzlov, S. R. [Sergey Mintslov], 'Home Life of the Romanoffs, II', *Littell's Living Age* 322, 1924, pp. 161–6.

Morris, Fritz, 'The Czar's Simple Life', *Cosmopolitan* 33, 5 September 1902, pp. 483–90.

'The Most Beautiful Woman on any Throne', *Current Literature* XLI, no. 5, November 1906, pp. 514–16.

'A Nestful of Princesses: the Four Little Daughters of the Tsar', see below, Two Russian Girls.

Nicholas, Very Revd Archimandrite [Charles Sydney Gibbes], 'Ten Years with the Russian Imperial Family', *Russian American Monthly* VI, no. 87, December 1949, pp. 9–15.

Norregaard, B. W., 'The Czar at Home', *Daily Mail*, 10 June 1908.

Ofrosimova, Svetlana, 'Tsarskaya semya (iz detskikh vospominanii)', *Bezhin lug* 1, 1995, pp. 135–48.

'People of Note: The Home Life of the Czar', *The London Journal*, 14 February 1903, p. 150.

Rowley, Alison, 'Monarchy and the Mundane: Picture Postcards and Images of the Romanovs 1890–1917', *Revolutionary Russia* 22, no. 2, December 2009, pp. 125–52.

'Royal Mothers and Their Children', *Good Housekeeping* 54, no. 4, April 1912, p. 457.

Schwartz, Theodore, 'The Czarina and Her Daughters', *Munsey's Magazine* 39, 1908, pp. 771–8.

Seawell, Molly Elliot, 'The Annual Visit of the Czar and Czarina to Darmstadt', *Alaskan Magazine* 1, no. 7, October 1900, pp. 323–34.

'Sentimental Crisis in the Careers of the Czar's Eldest Daughters', *Current Opinion* 55, 1913, pp. 323–4.

Soloveva, Natalya, 'La Tristesse Impériale', *Rodnye dali* 202 (Los Angeles), 1971, pp. 12–15.

Svitkov, N., 'Olga Nikolaevna, Velikaya Knyazhina i Tsarevna-Muchenitsa (1895–1918), *Pravoslavnaya Zhizn* 7, 1951, pp. 8–13.

Titov, I. V., 'OTMA: O velikikh knyazhnyakh Olge, Tatyane, Marii i Anastasii Nikolaevnykh', *Dvoryanskoe sobranie* 4, 1996, pp. 28–45.

'The Tottering House of the Romanoffs', *Washington Post*, 26 November 1905.

'The Truth about the Tsar', *Daily News*, 15 December 1900.

'The Tsar's Children', *Daily Mirror*, 29 December 1903.

Two Russian Girls, 'A Nestful of Princesses: The Four Little Daughters of the Tsar', *Girls' Realm* 4, June 1901, pp. 937–41.

'A Visit to the Czar', *Cornhill Magazine* 33 [new series], December 1912, pp. 741–8.

Warth, R. D., 'Before Rasputin: Piety and Occult at the Court of Nicholas II', *Historian* 47, no. 3, 1985, pp. 323–37.

'Which Prince Shall She Wed', *The Woman's Magazine* 29–30, 1914, p. 7.

Wilson, Rev. Terence A. McLean, 'Granny is Marvellously Kind and Amiable to Us', *Royalty Digest* XXX, September 1996, pp. 66–70.

Wynn, Marion, 'Romanov Connections with the Anglo-Russian Hospital in Petrograd', *Royalty Digest*, XII no. 7, January 2003, pp. 214–19.

—— '"Princess Alix was Always Extremely Homely": Visit to Harrogate, 1894', *Royalty Digest*, XI, no. 1, pp. 51–4.

Zeepvat, Charlotte, '"This Garden of Eden", The Russian Imperial Family and the Crimea', *Royalty Digest* II, no. 1, July 1992, pp. 2–14.

—— 'The Lost Tsar', *Royalty Digest*, VIII no. 1, July 1998, pp. 2–6.

—— 'The Valet's Story' (Alexis Volkov), part 1, *Royalty Digest* 105, March 2000, pp. 258–63; part 2, 106, May 2000, pp. 302–7; part 3, 107, June 2000, pp. 329–34.

—— 'Two Olgas – and the Man They Loved', *Royalty Digest* 129, March 2002, pp. 258–63.

SECONDARY SOURCES

Alekseeva, Irina, *Miriel Byukenen: svidetelnitsa velikikh potryasenii*, St Petersburg: Liki Rossii, 1998.

Almedingen, Edith, *Tomorrow Will Come*, London: The Bodley Head, 1961.

Arbenina, Stella, *Through Terror to Freedom*, London: Hutchinson, 1929.

Ashton, Janet, *The German Woman*, Huddersfield, Yks: Belgarun, 2008.

Azabal, Lilie Bouton de Fernandez- (Countess Nostitz), *The Countess from Iowa*, New York: G. P. Putnam's Sons, 1936.

Azabal, Lilie de Fernandez, (Countess Nostitz), *Romance and Revolutions*, London: Hutchinson, 1937.

Barkovets, A. and V. Tenikhina, *Nicholas II: The Imperial Family*, St Petersburg: Arbris, 2002.

Bartlett, E. Ashmead, *The Riddle of Russia*, London: Cassell, 1929.

Bibesco, Marthe, *Royal Portraits*, New York: D. Appleton, 1928.

Bowra, Maurice, *Memories 1898–1939*, London: Weidenfeld & Nicolson, 1966.

Buchanan, Meriel, *Queen Victoria's Relations*, London: Cassell, 1954.

Cantacuzène, Julia, *Revolutionary Days*, Chicago, IL: Donnelley, 1999.

Cassini, Countess Marguerite, *Never a Dull Moment*, New York: Harper & Brothers, 1956.

Chernova, O. V., *Vernye: O tekh, kto ne predal Tsarstvennykh muchennikov*, Moscow: Russkii Khronograf, 2010.

Crawford, Rosemary and Donald Crawford, *Michael and Natasha: The Life and Loves of the Last Tsar of Russia*, London: Weidenfeld & Nicolson, 1997.

Dassel, Felix, *Grossfürstin Anastasia Lebt*, Berlin: Verlagshaus fur Volksliteratur und kunst, 1928.

De Jonge, Alex, *Life and Times of Grigory Rasputin*, London: Collins, 1982.

Delafield, E. M., *Straw without Bricks: I Visit Soviet Russia*, London: Macmillan, 1937.

De Windt, Harry, *Russia as I Know It*, London: J. B. Lippincott, 1917.

Dorr, Rheta Childe, *Inside the Russian Revolution*, New York: Macmillan, 1917.

Durland, Kellogg, *Red Reign: The True Story of an Adventurous Year in Russia*, New York: Century, 1908.

Elchaninov, Major-General Andrey, *The Tsar and His People*, London: Hodder & Stoughton, 1914.

Elsberry, Terence, *Marie of Romania*, London: Cassell, 1973.

Emery, Mabel S., *Russia through the Stereoscope: A Journey across the Land of the Czar from Finland to the Black Sea*, London: Underwood & Underwood, 1901.

Fraser, John Foster, *Red Russia*, London: Cassell, 1907.

—— *Russia of To-day*, London: Cassell, 1915.

Fuhrmann, Joseph T., *Rasputin: The Untold Story*, New York: John Wiley, 2012.

Ganz, Hugo, *Russia the Land of Riddles*, New York: Harper, 1904.

Glyn, Anthony, *Elinor Glyn: A Biography*, London: Hutchinson, 1968.

Glyn, Elinor, *Romantic Adventure*, New York: E. P. Dutton, 1937.

Greenwall, Harry James, *Mirrors of Moscow*, London: Harrap, 1929.

Griffith, Hubert Freeling, *Seeing Soviet Russia*, London: John Lane, 1932.

Hall, Coryne, *Little Mother of Russia*, Teaneck, NJ: Holmes & Meier, 2006.

Hapgood, Isabel, *Russian Rambles*, London: Longman, Green, 1895.

Harmer, Michael, *The Forgotten Hospital*, Chichester, Sx: Chichester Press, 1982.

Heresch, Elisabeth, *Blood on the Snow: Eyewitness Accounts of the Russian Revolution*, New York: Paragon House, 1990.

Holmes, Burton, *Burton Holmes Travelogues*, vol. 8, *St. Petersburg, Moscow, The Trans-Siberian Railway*, New York: The McClure Company, 1910.

—— *The Traveler's Russia*, New York: G. P. Putnam's Sons, 1934.

Hough, Richard, *Edward and Alexandra: their Private and Public Lives*, London: John Muray, 1921.

Howe, M. A. De Wolfe, *George von Lengerke Meyer: His Life and Public Services*, New York: Dodd Mead, 1918.

Hunt, Violet, *The Flurried Years*, London: Hurst & Blackett, 1926.

Ioffe, Genrikh, *Revolyutsiya i semya Romanovykh*, Moscow: Algoritm, 2012.

Kelly, Marie Noele, *Mirror to Russia*, London: Country Life, 1952.

Kerensky, Alexander, *The Catastrophe*, New York: Kraus Reprint, 1927.

King, Greg, *The Court of the Last Tsar*, New York: John Wiley, 2006.

—— *The Last Empress*, London: Aurum Press, 1995.

King, Greg and Penny Wilson, *Resurrection of the Romanovs*, New York: John Wiley, 2011.

Kochan, Miriam, *The Last Days of Imperial Russia 1910–1917*, London: Weidenfeld & Nicolson, 1976.

Ktorova, Alla, *Minuvshee: prashchury i pravnuki*, Moscow: Minuvshee, 2007.

Kuchumov, Mikhail A., *Recollections and Letters of Chief Curator Mikhail A. Kuchumov*, ed. and trans. Stephen R. Angelis, Sunnyvale, CA: Bookemon, 2011.

Long, Robert Crozier, *Russian Revolution Aspects*, New York: E. P. Dutton, 1919.

Malofeev, Gennadiy, 'Russkie knyazhny', in Vladimir Dolmatov (ed.), *Romanovy, podvig vo imya lyubvi*, Moscow: Dostoinstvo, 2010, pp. 63–84.

Massie, Robert K., *Nicholas and Alexandra*, New York: Atheneum, 1967.

Merry, W. Mansell, *Two Months in Russia July–September 1914*, Oxford: B. H. Blackwell, 1916.

Michael, Prince of Greece, and Andrei Maylunas, *Nicholas and Alexandra: The Family Albums*, London: Tauris, 1992.

Miller, Ilana, *The Four Graces: Queen Victoria's Hessian Granddaughters*, East Richmond Heights, CA: Kensington House Books, 2011.

Miller, Sarah, *The Lost Crown*, New York: Atheneum, 2011.

Mintslov, Sergey, *Peterburg v 1903–1910 gg.*, Riga: Izd. 'Kniga dlya vsekh', 1931.

Moe, Ronald C., *Prelude to the Russian Revolution: The Murder of Rasputin*, Chula Vista, CA: Aventine Press, 2011.

Nekliudoff, A., *Diplomatic Reminiscences*, London: John Murray, 1920.

Nelipa, Margarita, *The Murder of Grigorii Rasputin*, Bowmanville, Ont.: Gilbert's Books, 2010.

Paléologue, Maurice, *Alexandra-Féodorowna impératrice de Russie*, Paris: Librairie Plon, 1932.

Pipes, Richard, *The Russian Revolution*, London: Fontana Press, 1999.

Plotnikov, Ivan F., *Gibel Tsarskoi semi: Pravda istorii*, Ekaterinburg: Sverdlovskaya Regionalnaya Obshchestvennaya Organizatsiya 'Za dukhovnost I nravstvennost', 2003.

Radzinsky, Edvard, *The Last Tsar: The Life and Death of Nicholas II*, London: Hodder & Stoughton, 1992.

Radziwill, Catherine, *Nicholas II, the Last of the Tsars*, London: Cassell, 1931.

—— *It Really Happened: An Autobiography*, New York: Dial Press, 1932.

Rappaport, Helen, *Ekaterinburg: The Last Days of the Romanovs*, London: Hutchinson, 2008.

Rasputin, Maria, *The Real Rasputin*, London: John Long, 1929.

—— *Rasputin My Father*, London: Cassell, 1934.

—— *Rasputin: The Man Behind the Myth*, London: W. H. Allen, 1977.

Rounding, Virginia, *Alix and Nicky: The Passion of the Last Tsar and Tsarina*, New York: St Martin's Press, 2012.

Savchenko, P., *Russkaya devushka*, Moscow: Trifonov Pechensky Monastyr 'Kovcheg', 2001.

Shavelsky, Georgiy, *Vospominaniya poslednego protopresverita russkoi armii i flota*, 2 vols, New York: Izd. Im. Chekhova, 1954.

Shelley, Gerard, *The Blue Steppes: Adventures Among the Russians*, London: J. Hamilton, 1925.

—— *The Speckled Domes: Episodes in an Englishman's Life in Russia*, London: Duckworth, 1925.

Shemansky, A. and O. Geichenko, *Poslednye Romanovy v Petergofe: Putevoditel po Nizhnei Dache*, 2nd edn, Leningrad: Gosudarstvennyi Petergofskii Muzei, 1930.

Shoumatoff, Alex, *Russian Blood: A Family Chronicle*, New York: Vintage Books, 1990.

Slater, Wendy, *The Many Deaths of Tsar Nicholas II: Relics, Remains and the Romanovs*, London: Routledge, 2007.

Souny-Sedlitz, Baroness, *Russia of Yesterday and Today*, privately printed, 1917.

Spiridovich, A., *Raspoutine, d'apres les documents russes et les archives privés de l'auteur*, Paris: Payot, 1935.

—— *Velikaya voina i fevralsakya revolyutsiya 1914–1917 godov*, 3 vols, New York: Vseslavyanskoe Izdatelstvo, 1960–2.

Swezey, Marilyn Pfeifer (ed.), *Nicholas and Alexandra: At Home with the Last Tsar and His Family*, Washington, DC: American–Russian Cultural Cooperation Foundation, 2004.

Sydacoff, Bresnitz von, *Nicholas II: Behind the Scenes in the Country of the Tsar*, London: A. Siegle, 1905.

Tillander-Godenhielm, Ulla, 'The Russian Imperial Award System during the Reign of Nicholas II 1894–1917', *Journal of the Finnish Antiquarian Society (Helsinki)* 113, 2005, pp. 357–9.

Tuomi-Nikula, Jormaand Paivi, *Imperatory na otdykhe v Finlyandii*, St Petersburg: Izdatelstvo Dom "Kolo", 2003.

Ular, Alexander, *Russia from Within*, London: Heinemann, 1905.

Vacaresco, Hélène, *Kings and Queens I Have Known*, London: Harper & Brothers, 1904.

Vasyutinskaya, E. F., et al., *Na detskoi polovine: Detstvo v tsarskom dome OTMA i Alekseya*, Moscow: Pinakoteka, 2000.

Vay de Vaya and Luskod, Count Peter, *Empires and Emperors of Russia, China, Korea and Japan*, London: John Murray, 1906.

Vecchi, Joseph, *The Tavern in My Drum: My Autobiography*, London: Odhams Press, 1948.

Warwick, Christopher, *Ella, Princess, Saint and Martyr*, Hoboken, NJ: John Wiley, 2006.

Welch, Frances, *The Romanovs and Mr Gibbes*, London: Short Books, 2002.

—— *The Russian Court at Sea*, London: Short Books, 2011.

Wilton, Robert and George Gustav Telberg, *The Last Days of the Romanovs*, London: Thornton Butterworth, 1920.

Wortman, Richard, *Scenarios of Power: Myth and Ceremony in Russian Monarchy*, abridged edn, Princeton, NJ: Princeton University Press, 2006.

Wyrubowa, Anna, *Muistelmia Wenäjän howista ja wallankumouksesta*, Pori, Finland: Satakunnan Kirjateollisuus Oy, 1923.

Yakovlev, V. I., *Alekandrovsky Dvorets-muzei v Detskom Sele*, Leningrad: Izd. Upravlenie Destskoselskimi I Pavlovskimi Dvortsami-Muzeyami, 1927.

Zeepvat, Charlotte, *Romanov Autumn: Stories from the Last Century of Imperial Russia*, Stroud, Glos: Sutton, 2000.

—— *From Cradle to Crown: British Nannies and Governesses at the World's Royal Courts*, Stroud, Glos: Sutton, 2006.

Zimin, Igor, *Vzroslyi mir: Povsednevnaya zhizn rossiiskogo imperatorskogo dvora*, St Petersburg: Tsentrpoligraf, 2010.

—— *Tsarskie dengi: Dokhody i raskhody doma Romanovykh*, St Petersburg: Tsentropoligraf, 2011.

—— *Tsarskaya rabota, XIX – nachalo XX v. Povsednevnaya zhizn rossiiskogo imperatorskogo dvora*, Moscow: Tsentropoligraf, 2011.

Index